Expert Systems
and Applied Artificial Intelligence

Expert Systems and Applied Artificial Intelligence

EFRAIM TURBAN
California State University at Long Beach

In collaboration with
Louis E. Frenzel, Jr.

Macmillan Publishing Company
New York

Maxwell Macmillan Canada
Toronto

Maxwell Macmillan International
New York Oxford Singapore Sydney

Cover art: Steve Lyons
Editor: Ed Moura
Production Editor: Mary M. Irvin
Cover Designer: Thomas Mack
Production Buyer: Pamela D. Bennett

This book was set in Palatino by Monotype Composition, Inc. and was printed and bound by R.R. Donnelley/Virginia. The cover was printed by Lehigh Press.

Macmillan Publishing Company
866 Third Avenue
New York, New York 10022

Macmillan Publishing Company is part of the
Maxwell Communication Group of Companies.

Maxwell Macmillan Canada, Inc.
1200 Eglinton Avenue East, Suite 200
Don Mills, Ontario M3C 3N1

Library of Congress Cataloging-in-Publication Data
Turban, Efraim.
     Expert systems and applied artificial intelligence / Efraim
Turban, in collaboration with Louis E. Frenzel.
         p.   cm.
     Includes bibliographical references and index.
     ISBN 0-02-421665-8
     1. Artificial intelligence.   2. Expert systems (Computer science)
I. Frenzel, Louis E.   II. Title.
Q335.T85   1992   91-28413
006.3—dc20   CIP

Printing: 2 3 4 5 6 7 8 9   Year: 3 4 5

The Macmillan Series in Information Technology

Ramos/ Schroeder & Simpson	Data Communication and Networking with Novelle Netware, 0-02-407791-7, 1992
Regan & O'Connor	Automating the Office: Systems and End-User Computing, 0-02-399165-8, 1989
Roche	Managing Information Technology in Multinational Corporations, 0-02-402690-5, 1992
Rowe	Business Telecommunications, Second Edition, 0-02-404104-1, 1991
Sprankle	Problem Solving and Programming Concepts, Second Edition, 0-02-415340-0, 1992
Turban	Decision Support and Expert Systems: Management Support Systems, Second Edition, 0-02-421663-1, 1990
	Expert Systems and Applied Artificial Intelligence, 0-02-421665-8, 1992
Wenig	Introduction to C.A.S.E. Technology Using the Visible Analyst Workbench, 0- 675-21367-3, 1991

Dedicated to all my students,
whose natural intelligence far exceeds that of any machine

Preface

The 1990s were declared the decade of the brain by the U.S. Government. In this decade, researchers from many disciplines will concentrate on biological, biochemical, biotechnological, and many other related systems, including the area of artificial intelligence and its derivatives.

Expert Systems and Applied Artificial Intelligence is a comprehensive, mangerially oriented introductory book whose primary objective is to support college level courses on applied artificial intelligence technologies and particularly on expert systems in departments of accounting, computer sciences, decision sciences, industrial engineering, information technology, management engineering, management information systems, and public administration.

This book is also appropriate for management development programs and in-house seminars. Finally, this text should be useful as a reference book by any technology-oriented manager.

Unique Aspects of this Book

This book is devoted mainly to applied expert systems. It does cover, however, four additional applied AI topics: natural language processing, computer vision, speech understanding, and intelligent robotics. In addition to basic theory, the book presents examples of close to 80 applied AI systems in a variety of industries.

Each chapter of this book ends with:

□ Chapter highlights
□ Key terms
□ Questions for review
□ Questions for discussion
□ Exercises (in most chapters) including debate issues
□ Cases (in some chapters)
□ Extensive, up-to-date bibliography

A comprehensive glossary is provided at the end of the book.

Support for the Instructor

The following support items are available:

□ *Instructor's Manual.* The manual includes answers to all review questions, discussion questions, exercises, cases and *LISP and Prolog Supplements.* The supplements cover all the essentials of LISP and Prolog, including review questions and exercises.
□ *Test Bank.* A comprehensive multiple choice-type test bank supplements the text.
□ *Software Support* (Student Versions). Adopters of this book will receive:

1) A copy of *EXSYS EL* development tool. Instructions of how to use EXSYS EL are also provided.
2) A copy of *EXSYS Professional.*
3) A copy of *Level5 Object* is provided for those who like to build expert systems using frames. Again, detailed instructions are provided.
4) A run-time version of NeuroShell and a demo of NeuroWindows is available upon request.

All software is provided free of charge with permission to reproduce it for student's use without any fees.

Acknowledgements

First and foremost, we acknowledge the contribution of Louis E. Frenzel, Jr. Without his valuable collaboration, this book could not have been produced. While unable to co-author the text, Mr. Frenzel granted permission for the use of significant material from two of his books: *Crash Course in Artificial Intelligence and Expert Systems* and *Understanding Expert Systems*. Both books were published by Howard W. Sams & Co. of New York in 1987.

Second, the work of Mr. Frenzel was updated by Yuval Schahar of Stanford University. Specifically, he added information on some most interesting developments related to Chapters 8–11.

Third, Larry Medsker, of the American University, who is devoting much of his energy to studying the relationships between neural computing and artificial intelligence, was kind enough to write most of the material in Chapter 18.

Instructions on how to use Level5 Object were written by Don Barker of Gonzaga University. Instructions on how to use VP Expert were written by Glen Gray of California State University at Northridge.

Fourth, quality control and evaluation is essential to the success of any book. Merrill Warkentin, of George Mason University, volunteered to class test selected chapters of the early version of the book. The feedback provided by Merrill and by his students was invaluable.

Other reviewers who provided input are:
Terry A. Byrd, Florida State University; Michael Goul, Arizona State University; Henry C. Lucas, Jr., New York University; James M. Ragusa, University of Central Florida; John J. Sviokla, Harvard University; Bayard E. Wynne, Indiana University, who also tested the manuscript; and David C. Yen, Miami University.

Fifth, this kind of book needs software support. Contributions were made by EXSYS, Inc., Albuquerque, New Mexico (EXSYS EL, EXSYS Professional), Information Builders, Inc., New York (Level5 Object), Ward Systems Group, Inc., Frederick, Maryland (NeuroShell, NeuroWindows).

Putting together this kind of book required lots of tedious work of typing, editing, organizing, and reviewing. The majority of these tasks were conducted by Peggy Davis from Eastern Illinois University, assisted by Debbie Kallas, Jayan Kandathil, Judy Lang, Terri Reidy, and Rhonda Salesberry. Proofreading of such a long text is not an easy job. Here is where Gerry Bedore of the University of Phoenix made invaluable contribution. Also, my daughter Sharon contributed her proofreading skills. Copy editing of this type of text was not any easy task. Mary Konstant of MCK Communication Services, Inc., contributed all her talents to translate the AI jargon into an easy-to-read text.

Finally, the Macmillan Publishing Co. team needs to be commended. Charles Stewart started this project and guided me in its initial steps. Contribution by the following team members is also appreciated: Ed Moura, Mary Irvin, and Pam Bennett. Last, but not least, Vernon Anthony, a former Macmillan editor, provided continuous support and help.

To all the contributors, reviewers, editors, and assistants—many thanks to you for your help, without which this exciting book could not have been made.

Contents

xiii

Chapter 9   Speech (Voice) Recognition and Understanding   315

Chapter 10   Computer Vision   337

Chapter 11   Robotics and AI

Part 4 Building Knowledge-based Systems 399

Chapter 12 Building Expert Systems 401

Chapter 13 Tools for Expert Systems 453

Contents

Part 6   Advanced Topics and the Future   619

Chapter 18   Neural Computing and AI   621

Part 7 Applications and Cases

Chapter 20 Expert Systems: Illustrative Applications 699

Chapter 21   A Student Project and a Major Case Study   741

Chapter 22   Decision Automation: Mission-Critical Expert Systems   765

Part 1

Fundamentals

Artificial intelligence is a dynamic and varied field. Its applied technologies range from expert systems to computer vision. In Part I we present three topics. First, AI is defined, its major characteristics and benefits are described, and its major technologies are outlined (Chapter 1). Then we shift to generic problem-solving topics that are related to artificial intelligence. These topics are important because a major emphasis of this book is applying artificial intelligence in decision making and problem solving (Chapter 2). Such applications are done mainly by using the technology of expert systems, which is surveyed in Chapter 3. Expert systems—their operation, construction, and use—are the major focus of this book.

Chapter 1

Applied Artificial Intelligence: An Overview

Artificial intelligence (AI) is a subdivision of computer science devoted to creating computer software and hardware that attempt to produce results such as those produced by people. Computers already emulate some of the simpler activities of the human mind. They can perform mathematical calculations, manipulate numbers and letters, make simple decisions, and perform various storage and retrieval functions. In these applications, the computer is exceptional and usually exceeds humans in performance. Computers greatly speed up and simplify some aspects of the human thought process. AI technologies advance us one step further: they enable us to automate or enhance more complex tasks that were done manually. AI technologies are being integrated with other computer-based information systems so that the capabilities and applicability of computers are greatly increased.

The concept of artificial intelligence and the commercial applications that result from research in this area may change the way some organizations operate and are managed. This chapter introduces you to AI and its applications in the following sections:

1.1 Introduction

The past few years have witnessed an increased interest in applied AI. The topic is enjoying tremendous publicity. Many major periodicals have published cover stories on AI or have dedicated special issues to it. Dozens of books on AI have appeared on the market. Many AI newsletters are being published regularly, and conferences and conventions on this topic are being held worldwide. To a certain extent, AI has become a sensation. The number of AI vendors in the United States broke the 200 mark in March 1985 (see Dicken and Newquist [8]), and it approached 400 in 1991.

The commercial applications of AI are projected to reach several billion dollars annually. Major management consulting firms (e.g., Arthur D. Little, Inc. and Andersen Consulting) are deeply involved in applied AI. Many research institutions in the United States and all over the world are also heavily involved in AI research projects.

These developments may have a significant impact on many organizations, both private and public, and on the manner in which organizations are being managed. The fundamentals of AI and its major technologies are described in the remainder of this chapter.

1.2 Definitions

Artificial intelligence is a term that encompasses many definitions (see Appendix A at the end of this chapter). The various topics in the following sections define and explain the major areas that fall within applied AI. Most experts agree that AI is concerned with two basic ideas. First, it involves studying the thought processes of humans (to understand what intelligence is); second, it deals with representing those processes via machines (computers, robots, etc.).

One well-publicized definition of AI is as follows: Artificial intelligence is behavior by a machine that, if performed by a human being, would be called intelligent. A thought-provoking definition is provided by Rich [20]: "Artificial Intelligence is the study of how to make computers do things at which, at the moment, people are better." Mark Fox of Carnegie-Mellon University often says that AI is basically a theory of how the human mind works. Winston and Prendergast [27] list three objectives of artificial intelligence:

1. Make machines smarter (primary goal)
2. Understand what intelligence is (the Noble laureate purpose)
3. Make machines more useful (the entrepreneurial purpose)

Let us explore the meaning of the term *intelligent behavior*. Several abilities are considered signs of intelligence:

□ Learn or understand from experience
□ Make sense out of ambiguous or contradictory messages
□ Respond quickly and successfully to a new situation (different responses, flexibility)
□ Use reason in solving problems and directing conduct effectively
□ Deal with perplexing situations
□ Understand and infer in ordinary, rational ways
□ Apply knowledge to manipulate the environment
□ Acquire and apply knowledge
□ Think and reason
□ Recognize the relative importance of different elements in a situation

Although AI's ultimate goal is to build machines that will mimic human intelligence, the capabilities of current commercial AI products are far from exhibiting any significant success when compared with the abilities just listed. Nevertheless, AI programs are getting better all the time, and they are currently useful in conducting several tasks that require some human intelligence.

An interesting test designed to determine if a computer exhibits intelligent behavior was designed by Alan Turing and is called the **Turing Test.** According to this test, a computer could be considered to be smart only when a human interviewer, conversing with both an unseen human being and an unseen computer, could not determine which is which. The idea of the Turing Test has been challenged by John Searle; see Bourbaki [4] and exercise 4.

The definitions of AI presented to this point concentrated on the notion of intelligence. The following definitions and characteristics of AI focus on decision making and problem solving.

Symbolic Processing

When human experts solve problems, particularly the type that are considered appropriate for AI, they do not do it by solving sets of equations or performing other laborious mathematical computations. Instead, they choose symbols to represent the problem concepts and apply various strategies and rules to manipulate these concepts. According to Waterman [26], the AI approach represents knowledge as sets of symbols that stand for problem concepts. In

AI jargon a **symbol** is a string of characters that stands for some real-world concept. Here are some examples of symbols:

□ Product
□ Defendant
□ 0.8

These symbols can be combined to express meaningful relationships. When these relationships are represented in an AI program, they are called **symbol structures.** The following are examples of symbol structures:

□ (DEFECTIVE product)
□ (LEASED-BY product defendant)
□ (EQUAL (LIABILITY defendant) 0.8)

These structures can be interpreted to mean "the product is defective," "the product is leased by the defendant," and "the liability of the defendant is 0.8." They may, however, be interpreted differently. This is one of the problems we encounter in building AI systems.

To solve a problem, an AI program manipulates these symbols. The consequence of this approach is that knowledge representation—the choice, form, and interpretation of the symbols used—becomes very important.

Symbolic processing is an essential characteristic of artificial intelligence as reflected in the following definition: Artificial intelligence is that branch of computer science dealing with symbolic, nonalgorithmic methods of problem solving. This definition focuses on two characteristics of computer programs:

1. Numeric versus symbolic: Computers were originally designed specifically to process numbers (**numeric processing**). People, however, tend to think symbolically; our intelligence seems to be based, in part, on our mental ability to manipulate symbols rather than just numbers. Although symbolic processing is at the core of AI, this does not mean that AI does not involve math; rather, the emphasis in AI is on manipulation of symbols.

2. Algorithmic versus nonalgorithmic: An **algorithm** is a step-by-step procedure that has well-defined starting and ending points and that is guaranteed to reach a solution to a specific problem. Computer architecture readily lends itself to this step-by-step approach. Many human reasoning processes, however, tend to be nonalgorithmic; in other words, our mental activities consist of more than just following logical, step-by-step procedures.

Heuristics

Heuristics (rules of thumb) are included as a key element of AI in the following definition: "Artificial intelligence is the branch of computer science that deals with ways of representing knowledge using symbols rather than numbers and with rules-of-thumb, or heuristics, methods for processing information" (*Encyclopaedia Britannica*).

People frequently use heuristics, consciously or otherwise, to make decisions. By using heuristics one does not have to rethink completely what to do every time a similar problem is encountered. The topic of heuristics will be revisited in Chapter 2.

Inferencing

Artificial intelligence involves an attempt by machines to exhibit *reasoning* capabilities. The reasoning consists of **inferencing** from facts and rules using heuristics or other search approaches. Artificial intelligence is unique in that it makes inferences by employing the pattern-matching (or recognition) approach.

Pattern Matching

The following definition of AI focuses on pattern-matching techniques: Artificial intelligence works with pattern-matching methods which attempt to describe objects, events, or processes in terms of their qualitative features and logical and computational relationships.

1.3 Brief History of AI

The history of AI can be divided into a variety of ages. Winston and Prendergast [27] use the following classifications.

First are *prehistoric* times. Thousands of years ago people were irresistibly drawn to the idea of creating intelligence outside the human body. Several examples date back to Greek mythology (e.g., Daedalus, the creator of artificial winds, also attempted to create artificial people). Many other examples can be found in different cultures.

The first recognizable milestone for AI was the year 1884. At that time a scientist named Charles Babbage first experimented with machines that he hoped would exhibit some intelligence. Augusta Ada, Countess of Lovelace (for whom the Ada programming language was named), was Babbage's main sponsor. She was besieged by the press, who wondered if Babbage's machines would ever be as smart as people. At that time, she intelligently denied that it would ever be possible, because she knew this application would not occur in the near future and, therefore, should not be mentioned.

Toward the end of this period there were several attempts to associate computers and intelligence. In 1950 Claude Shannon suggested that computers would be able to play chess. The field of cybernetics (e.g., the work of Norbert Wiener) also pointed to the functional similarities between humans and machines.

The prehistoric times extended to about 1960, because people who wanted to work on the computational approach of understanding intelligence did not have sufficiently powerful computers.

The Dartmouth Conference—Beginning of the Dawn Age

The AI revolution started in 1956 at a conference conducted by Dartmouth College. At this conference the name "artificial intelligence" was suggested by John McCarthy, one of the organizers of the conference. The participants in this conference are considered the pioneers of AI. Among them were Marvin Minsky (founder of the AI lab at MIT), Claude Shannon (from Bell Labs), Nathaniel Rochester (of IBM), Allen Newell (first president of the American Association of Artificial Intelligence), and Herbert Simon (a Nobel Prize recipient from Carnegie-Mellon University). The conference generated much enthusiasm, and some participants predicted that in ten years computers would be as smart as people—a hopelessly romantic prediction.

The *dawn age* was sparked by certain successes. A program for solving geometric analogy problems like those that appear on intelligence tests was developed. Another development was a program that did symbolic integration, spawning MACSYMA[1] and other mathematical systems. These two examples, analogy and integration, are particularly important because they introduced ideas that have become extraordinarily popular in the creation of expert systems. Unfortunately, the success of the dawn age created unrealistic expectations about the ease with which creating intelligent computers might happen.

The next period can be described as the *dark age* (1965–1970) because little happened. A dry spell occurred because the tremendous enthusiasm generated by the dawn age led many people to believe that the enterprise of creating intelligent computers would be a simple task. Computer scientists searched for a kind of philosopher's stone, a mechanism that when placed in a computer would require only the addition of data to become truly intelligent. The dark age was largely fueled by overexpectations.

Next, a *renaissance* (1970–1975) took place. During this period, AI researchers began to make systems like MYCIN[2] that caught people's attention. Such systems are the foundations of today's excitement.

The renaissance was followed by the *age of partnerships* (1975–1980), a period when researchers in AI began to admit that there were other researchers, particularly linguists and psychologists, with whom people working in AI could form fruitful liaisons.

The present age can be described as the *age of entrepreneurs*, or the commercialization of AI. Currently, attempts are being made to take AI out of

---

[1]MACSYMA is an expert system that solves complex algebraic and calculus problems. Using symbolic processing, MACSYMA's solutions could otherwise only be approximated by numeric methods.

[2]MYCIN is a pioneering expert system in the field of medical diagnosis. Refer to Appendix C at the end of Chapter 3.

the lab and apply it in the real world. What is new is the commercial availability of hardware and software that make it possible to develop economically justifiable AI applications for a wide range of end-user organizations previously served only by more traditional data processing methods. The pivotal software tool for AI was LISP (list processing programming language), developed by John McCarthy in 1957. Unlike the programming languages with which we are most familiar—BASIC, FORTRAN, COBOL, Pascal, and APL, to mention a few—LISP deals with complex objects such as rules, sentences, and names, not just numbers. Therefore, LISP lends itself to the development of flexible systems that can accommodate ambiguities and complex interrelationships among data.

The pivotal hardware tool for users of LISP was the LISP machine, or symbolic processor: a computer system that had a logical architecture specifically designed to efficiently and effectively support AI program development and execution.

The emergence of AI as a viable commercial technology can also be attributed to the recent development of semiconductor devices, computer architectures, and other technological developments. Twenty years ago computer hardware was expensive in relation to humans doing similar tasks. Today, the opposite is true. In addition, AI takes up a lot of memory, but memory is now relatively inexpensive. Numeric processing techniques and software that can make the most efficient use of computer hardware have become the dominant technology.

1.4 Artificial Versus Natural Intelligence

The potential value of artificial intelligence can be better understood by contrasting it with natural, or human, intelligence. According to Kaplan [16], AI has several important commercial advantages:

- AI is more *permanent*. Natural intelligence is perishable from a commercial standpoint in that workers can change their place of employment or forget information. AI, however, is permanent as long as the computer systems and programs remain unchanged.
- AI offers *ease of duplication and dissemination*. Transferring a body of knowledge from one person to another usually requires a lengthy process of apprenticeship; even so, expertise can never be duplicated completely. However, when knowledge is embodied in a computer system, it can be copied from that computer and easily moved to another computer, sometimes across the globe.
- AI can be *less expensive* than natural intelligence. There are many circumstances in which buying computer services costs less than having corresponding human power carry out the same tasks (over the long run).
- AI, being a computer technology, is *consistent and thorough*. Natural intelligence is erratic because people are erratic; they do not perform consistently.

□ AI can be *documented*. Decisions made by a computer can be easily documented by tracing the activities of the system. Natural intelligence is difficult to reproduce; for example, a person may reach a conclusion but at some later date may be unable to re-create the reasoning process that led to that conclusion or to even recall the assumptions that were a part of the decision.

Natural intelligence does have several advantages over AI:

□ Natural intelligence is *creative*, whereas AI is rather uninspired. The ability to acquire knowledge is inherent in human beings, but with AI, tailored knowledge must be built into a carefully constructed system.
□ Natural intelligence enables people to benefit from and *use sensory experience* directly, whereas most AI systems must work with symbolic input.
□ Perhaps most important, human reasoning is able to make use at all times of a wide *context of experience* and bring that to bear on individual problems; in contrast, AI systems typically gain their power by having a very narrow focus.

The advantages of natural intelligence over AI result in the many limitations of expert systems, which are discussed in detail in Chapter 3.

Computers can be used to collect information about objects, events, or processes; and, of course, computers can process large amounts of information more efficiently than people can. People, however, instinctively do some things that have been very difficult to program into a computer: they recognize relationships between things; they sense qualities; and they spot patterns that explain how various items relate to each other.

Newspaper photographs are nothing more than collections of minute dots, yet without any conscious effort, people discover the patterns that reveal faces and other objects in those photos. Similarly, one of the ways that humans make sense of the world is by recognizing the relationships and patterns that help give meaning to the objects and events that they encounter.

If computers are to become more intelligent, they must be able to make the same kinds of associations among the qualities of objects, events, and processes that come so naturally to people.

1.5 Knowledge in AI

Definitions

In the field of information systems it is customary to distinguish between data, information, and knowledge.

Data. The term *data* refers to numeric (or alphanumeric) strings that by themselves do not have a meaning. They can be facts or figures to be processed.

Information. Information is data organized so that it is meaningful to the person receiving it.

Knowledge. **Knowledge** has several definitions. For example, according to the *Webster's New World Dictionary of the American Language,* knowledge is:

- a clear and certain perception of something.
- understanding.
- learning.
- all that has been perceived or grasped by the mind.
- practical experience, skill.
- acquaintance or familiarity.
- cognizance; recognition.
- organized information applicable to problem solving.

Data, information, and knowledge can be classified by their degree of abstraction and by their quantity (Figure 1.1). Knowledge is the most abstract and exists in the smallest quantity.

Another definition of knowledge is that given by Sowa [23]: "Knowledge encompasses the implicit and explicit restrictions placed upon objects (entities), operations, and relationships along with general and specific heuristics and inference procedures involved in the situation being modeled."

Uses

Although a computer cannot have (as yet) experiences or study and learn as the human mind can, it can use knowledge given to it by human experts. Such

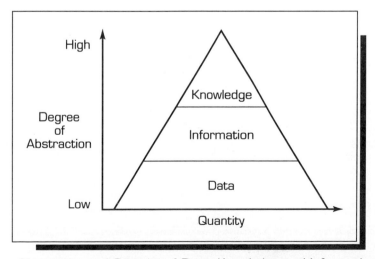

FIGURE 1.1 Abstraction and Quantity of Data, Knowledge, and Information

knowledge consists of facts, concepts, theories, heuristic methods, procedures, and relationships. Knowledge is also information that has been organized and analyzed to make it understandable and applicable to problem solving or decision making. The collection of knowledge related to a problem (or an opportunity) to be used in an AI system is called a **knowledge base.** Most knowledge bases are limited in that they typically focus on some specific subject area or domain.

Once a knowledge base is built, artificial intelligence techniques are used to give the computer inference capability. The computer will then be able to make inferences and judgments based on the facts and relationships contained in the knowledge base.

Knowledge Bases and Knowledge-based Organizations

With a knowledge base and the ability to draw inferences from it, the computer can now be put to some practical use as a problem solver and decision maker. Figure 1.2 illustrates the concept of a computer using AI in an application. By searching the knowledge base for relevant facts and relationships, the computer can reach one or more alternative solutions to the given problem. The computer's knowledge base and inferencing capability augment those of the user. This ability can be applied to different areas ranging from problem solving to the interpretation of languages and scenarios.

The importance of AI and knowledge bases is rapidly increasing. Therefore, many people believe that we are moving from the information age into the *knowledge age,* and some even talk about knowledge-based organizations and societies.

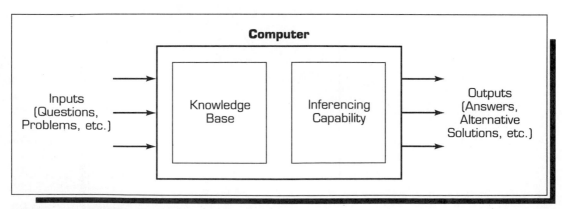

FIGURE 1.2 Applying AI Concepts with a Computer

1.6   How AI Differs from Conventional Computing

Artificial intelligence is software that permits a computer to duplicate some functions of the human brain *in a limited way*. Although special artificial intelligence hardware can be built, most AI is software that runs on mainframes, minicomputers, workstations, and even on personal computers.

AI programs can be written in virtually any computer language and have been written in assembly language, BASIC, Fortran, Pascal, C, and Forth. However, some **programming languages** have been developed especially for AI applications. The two most popular AI programming languages are LISP and PROLOG, both of which will be discussed later in this book.

Conventional Computing

In conventional computing we tell the computer how to solve the problem. The computer is given data and a step-by-step program that specifies how the data is to be used to reach an answer. In artificial intelligence, the computer is given knowledge about the subject area plus some inferencing capability. The AI program determines the specific procedure for arriving at a solution.

Conventional computer programs are based on an algorithm, which is a clearly defined, step-by-step procedure for solving a problem. It may be a mathematical formula or a sequential procedure that will lead to a solution. The algorithm is converted into a computer program (sequential list of instructions or commands) that tells the computer exactly what operations to carry out. The algorithm then uses data such as numbers, letters, or words to solve the problem (a typical example is the preparation of a payroll in an organization).

Table 1.1 summarizes some of the ways traditional computers process data. This process is limited to very structured applications. If we give the computer a knowledge base and inferencing capability, however, the computer can be used to support nonstructured applications that so far have been restricted to manual solutions. As a result, the computer may become a far more useful tool that supplements and enhances human capabilities.

AI Computing

AI software is based on symbolic representation and manipulation. In AI, a symbol is a letter, word, or number that is used to represent objects, processes, and their relationships. Objects can be people, things, ideas, concepts, events, or statements of fact. By using symbols, it is possible to create a knowledge base that states facts, concepts, and the relationships among them. Then various processes are used to manipulate the symbols to generate advice or a recommendation for solving problems. The process in AI is qualitative rather than quantitative as it is in algorithmic computing.

Virtually all digital computers are algorithmic in their operation, based on the von Neuman concept: instructions stored in memory are executed sequentially to

TABLE 1.1 How Computers
Process Data

Process	Manipulation
Calculate	Perform mathematical operations such as add, subtract, multiply, divide, find a square root, etc. Solve formulas
Perform logic	Perform logic operations such as "and," "or," "invert," etc.
Store	Remember facts and figures in files
Retrieve	Access data stored in files as required
Translate	Convert data from one form to another
Sort	Examine data and put it into some desired order or format
Edit	Make changes, additions, and deletions to data and change its sequence
Make decisions	Reach simple conclusions based on internal or external conditions
Monitor	Observe external or internal events and take action if certain conditions are met
Control	Take charge of or operate external devices

perform some desired operation. Algorithmic software can be written in such a way as to permit symbolic representation and manipulation.

Once a knowledge base is built, some means of using it to solve problems must be developed. How does the AI software reason or infer with this knowledge base? The basic techniques are **search** and **pattern matching.** Given some initial start-up information, the AI software searches the knowledge base looking for specific conditions or patterns. It looks for matchups that satisfy the criteria set up to solve the problem. The computer literally hunts around until it finds the best answer it can give based on the knowledge it has.

Even though AI problem solving does not take place directly by algorithmic processes, algorithms, of course, are used to implement the search process.

A word of caution! Some people believe that AI is magic. It is not. AI is basically a different approach to programming computers, and it should be treated as such. Therefore, although there are some profound differences between AI and conventional computing, there are also many similarities. For example, developing an AI system should be treated like the development of any other computer system. We use system analysis and design in AI in a manner very similar to the way we use it in other computer systems. We may use different terminology, but an AI system is a computer-based information system (CBIS), although it has some different characteristics (Table 1.2).

TABLE 1.2 Artificial Intelligence Versus Conventional Programming

Dimension	Artificial Intelligence	Conventional Programming
Processing	Mainly symbolic	Primarily computing
Nature of input	Can be incomplete	Must be complete
Search	Heuristic (mostly)	Algorithms
Explanation	Provided	Usually not provided
Major interest	Knowledge	Data, information
Structure	Separation of control from knowledge	Control integrated with information (data)
Nature of output	Can be incomplete	Must be correct
Maintenance and update	Relatively easy, due to modularity	Usually difficult
Hardware	Mainly workstations and personal computers	All types
Reasoning capability	Yes	No

1.7 Does a Computer Really Think?

Knowledge bases and search techniques certainly make computers more useful, but can they really make computers more intelligent? AI specialists, computer scientists, and others regularly debate this question. The fact that most AI programs are implemented by search and pattern-matching techniques leads to the conclusion that computers are not really intelligent. You can give the computer a lot of information and some guidelines about how to use this information. Using that information and those criteria, the computer can come up with a solution. All it does is test the various alternatives and attempt to find some combination that meets the designated criteria. When that is done, typically a solution is achieved. So the computer appears to be "thinking" and often gives a satisfactory solution. Obviously, there are degrees of intelligence as Figure 1.3 shows. The human mind occupies the high end on an intelligence spectrum and simple logic circuits the low end. AI lies somewhere in between.

Another way to look at this issue is to examine the Chinese room analogy. Assume that you speak only English, and you are isolated in a room with a set of rules and procedures for translating Chinese characters into other Chinese characters. You are then given Chinese characters to translate. Using your rule book, you create other characters, which you send out. The inputs may be questions, the outputs answers. Does a successful translation process mean you are intelligent? Or does the process of just following rules and procedures presuppose the lack of intelligence?

Even though you got the right answers, can you really say that you know and understand Chinese? No, yet you completed a useful task. All a computer

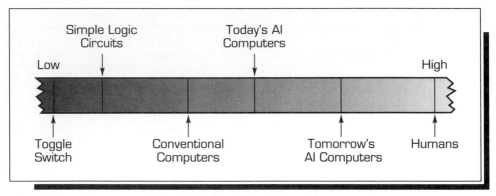

FIGURE 1.3 Spectrum of Intelligence or "Brain Power"

does in AI applications is translate input symbols to appropriate output symbols according to a set of rules given to it in a program. The computer does not understand the knowledge it contains.

Intelligence is difficult to identify. Any test for intelligence has only limited value and effectiveness; it may work for some cases and not for others. The problem is that intelligence is difficult to define and visualize because it encompasses so many things.

Let's face it. Although AI is making computers smarter and more powerful, the dream of building a machine that can fully duplicate the human brain will probably not be realized in our lifetime. Despite major advances in all areas of computer science, many question whether we will ever be able to create a computer that will accurately emulate the function of a human mind. Dreyfus and Dreyfus [9] feel that the public is being misled about AI—its usefulness is overblown and its goals are impossible. They say we will never be able to establish rules for all the ways we think. The human mind is just too complex to duplicate (see Box 1.1).

Of course, some think researchers are getting closer to a smart machine each year, but there are still many unanswered questions. For example, how do you represent skills, manual dexterity, learning ability, moods, imagination, emotions, creativity, and "gut feeling"? To answer such questions, researchers are turning to related fields such as philosophy, psychology, linguistics, and neuroscience, not just computer science. Thus, the interdisciplinary field of cognitive science has been born. Research in microbiology suggests that future computers will use molecular logic circuits rather than silicon electronic circuits, thereby greatly increasing circuit density and reducing size. Still, practical machines based on such techniques are many years away, if ever.

Nevertheless, despite criticisms, AI methods are valuable. They are showing us how we think and how to better apply our intelligence. AI techniques will make computers easier to use and make greater knowledge available to the

---

Box 1.1: Computers Can't Learn Common Sense Overnight

Giving common sense to computers seems a fruitful way to endow machines with more intelligence. The trouble? There's too much common sense out there.

Douglas Lenat, a research scientist at Microelectronics & Computer Technology Corp., Austin, Tex., is finding out just how much there is. Five years ago, he began work on a database that will contain all the common-sense knowledge needed to understand every entry in the *Encyclopaedia Britannica.* The project, dubbed "Cyc," is one of the most ambitious undertakings ever in the field of artificial intelligence. The goal: to produce a program that can understand texts, reason and perform routine tasks on behalf of a human master.

Lenat's view is that a computer can't act smart unless it possesses the basic ideas that people have about how the world works. Examples include the following sentences. No child can be older than his parents. On a cloudy day, it's a good idea to carry an umbrella. Shirts can be purchased in clothing stores.

It's easy to produce such sentences—too easy. "We originally thought there were about one million basic common-sense sentences," he said. "Now we think there are tens of millions."

Still, such common-sense statements are central to the human mind. By mapping them out—a job that will keep him and his colleagues busy for at least another five years—Lenat thinks he'll obtain the building blocks for a system that's superior to expert-system programs, which seek to mimic reasoning by applying rules consistently and handling only a bare minimum of facts about the world.

(*Source: The Wall Street Journal*, October 11, 1990. For further details see Guha and Lenat [13].)

---

masses. Perhaps it does not matter if we do not fully duplicate the human brain. Even when we simulate parts of it, the resulting software or hardware is very useful.

1.8   Advantages and Disadvantages of AI

AI is sure to be a big hit with computer users once it becomes more widely known and firmly established. But there is also a downside. Let's examine some of the pros and cons of AI software. Additional advantages and disadvantages of specific AI technologies are discussed later in appropriate chapters.

The Good News

For openers, AI software will make any computer, be it a $500 home computer, a powerful mini, or a multimillion dollar supercomputer, more user-friendly than any of these machines are now. Users will be able to communicate with the computer in their own natural language—English or any other language—rather than have to use the cryptic commands and syntax of operating systems, languages, and application programs. With AI, an untrained user will be able to approach the machine and accomplish useful work. Computers will be no more difficult to use than the telephone.

Special natural language interfaces will have to be written to achieve these ambitious results, and already many commercial natural language interfaces are available for popular computers and software packages. The database management system (DBMS) is one of the first types of conventional software to take advantage of natural language interfaces. These interfaces permit fast, easy access to data without tricky programming. Spreadsheets, word processing packages, operating systems, and other application programs are expected to eventually incorporate AI methods to improve user-friendliness and thus increase productivity.

Another major benefit is that computers will be far more useful. It has been said that computers are a solution looking for a problem. However, not all problems yield to an algorithmic or data processing solution, which are the core of the conventional CBIS. Not all problems require calculation or data storage and retrieval. There are many problems to be solved that do not fit the capabilities usually associated with a conventional computer.

Artificial intelligence can change all that. With AI techniques, a whole new realm of opportunities opens up. New kinds of problems can be solved. The same computers that do data processing can now address problems associated with acquiring and accessing knowledge, making decisions, and otherwise performing some functions heretofore reserved only for humans. AI is great for "messy" problems in which the data are unknown or incomplete or in which there are no known algorithms. Such capabilities, combined with users' expertise, can lead to improved performance and productivity. AI techniques as used in expert systems have the potential to make problem solving and decision making in specific domains faster and easier.

One area in which we are likely to see major improvements due to AI is the general handling of information. Most of us are voracious users, generators, and dispensors of information of all kinds. There is so much information that there is simply no way to track, catalog, or access it all. Industries have grown up in an attempt to tackle various aspects of information handling. Libraries have been established to help collect and dispense information.

But despite all these efforts, most of us are still in **information overload;** there is simply too much information to deal with. Furthermore, we do not always know that it exists or how to obtain it once we know that we need it.

And while the information glut is real, we need that information desperately. We need it to do our jobs competently, and we want information so that we can live an informed, intelligent life.

Computers can help immensely to conquer the information problem, even though most of us would agree that they are just as much a part of the problem as they are the solution. There is no way to stop or even slow down the generation of new information, and we probably would not want to even if we could. The secret is to find a way to use the computer to collect, catalog, and dispense the information in an organized way. Huge computer databases are being built to permit the convenient storage and retrieval of information. Information utilities are being formed to catalog and store information of all varieties so it may be accessed by anyone via a computer terminal over telephone lines.

Artificial intelligence will help relieve our information overload. It will provide new means of finding and accessing the information we need. In addition, natural language interfaces will make computer databases easier to tap.

But perhaps the most important aspect of AI is that it will force, or encourage, the conversion of information into knowledge. Typically, you have to analyze the information, organize it, sift through it, and extract from it what is important to you. At the point information becomes knowledge, it can be applied to solving a problem or making a decision.

The Bad News

Surely, as with everything, there must be a downside to AI. As far as applications go, AI offers only advantages or benefits, but not without a price. Overall, computers will become a more powerful and useful tool, but the increased cost might represent a disadvantage to some. Medium- or large-scale AI applications usually require very powerful computers with fast CPUs and lots of memory. Most AI research and many AI applications until 1990 were implemented on mainframes and big minicomputers such as Digital Equipment Corp.'s (DEC) VAX series.

On the other hand, microcomputers are getting faster and more powerful. Sixteen-bit and 32-bit machines are commonplace. Memory chips are getting denser and cheaper. The 386 chips are common and inexpensive. As a result, many AI applications can be readily implemented on workstations and on faster personal computers. Thus, the cost disadvantage is slowly going away.

Another disadvantage is the difficulty of AI software development. AI programs are incredibly complex. As a result, they take more time to develop and they are far more expensive. Software development tools such as improved AI programming languages and expert system shells help speed up and simplify AI software development, but they, too, are expensive and require some talent to use.

In addition, few programmers are capable of dealing with AI. As colleges graduate more AI computer scientists and the field grows, there will be more programmers to write the software, but now there is a severe shortage.

Finally, with the exception of expert systems, few practical AI products have reached the market. There are several natural language interfaces, a few voice recognition systems, and lots of languages and software development tools, but that's about it. One interesting application is the use of fuzzy logic (see Box 1.2 and Chapter 7). Of course, many products are expected in the future.

Box 1.2: Would You Buy a Fuzzy Product?

Korean home appliance makers are using a new technology to improve many of their products. With the technology, fuzzy theory, subjective human experiences can be quantified and programmed into appliances. The intelligent machines can then make fuzzy decisions such as increasing washing time in a fuzzy washing machine or controlling elevators.

Goldstar Co. offers a washing machine that can program itself by analyzing fabric content and volume of each load, then choosing optimum water temperature, water level and spin-drying time. The machine cost $4.3 million to develop.

"Goldstar *doubled* its usual monthly sales of washing machines in the first month after artificial intelligence machines were available," said Chun Seong-Ho, a Goldstar spokesman. Sales of the machines totaled 20,500 in the initial month ending October 26, 1990.

Chun forecast that 70 to 80 percent of all electronic home appliances will offer fuzzy logic or artificial intelligence by 1995.

"In Japan, electronics goods with fuzzy logic are already so popular that it seems to me that those that do not offer fuzzy applications within a few years will not be able to survive," he said.

Indeed, other Korean manufacturers, clearly not wanting to be washed up, have introduced their own fuzzy products. Daewoo Electronics and Samsung Electronics offer fuzzy washing machines; Samsung's can make appropriate choices for 584 sets of washing conditions, according to the company.

All of Korea's big three electronics firms—Goldstar, Samsung and Daewoo—will be providing additional products that feature fuzzy logic. For example, Chun noted that Goldstar will be exporting VCRs equipped with artificial intelligence to the United States and Europe sometime in 1991.

(*Source: Bangkok Post*, December 19, 1990.)

1.9 The AI Field

The development of machines that exhibit intelligent characteristics involves many different sciences and technologies, such as linguistics, psychology, philosophy, computer hardware and software, mechanics, hydraulics, and optics. The intersection between psychology and AI centers on the areas known as cognition and psycholinguistics. Philosophy and AI come together in the areas of logic, philosophy of language, and philosophy of mind. Intersections with linguistics include computational linguistics, psycholinguistics, and socio-linguistics. Mutual interactions between electrical engineering and AI include image processing, control theory, pattern recognition, and robotics.

Lately there have been contributions from management and organization theory (e.g., decision making, implementation), statistics, mathematics, management science (heuristic programming, cost-effectiveness), and management information systems (MIS).

The various disciplines that participate in the AI field overlap and interact. Thus, it is difficult to classify the AI field according to these disciplines. A much more practical classification scheme is achieved by considering the outputs, that is, the applied areas of *commercial applications*.

Artificial intelligence is not in itself a commercial field; it is a science and a technology. It is a collection of concepts and ideas that are appropriate for research but that cannot be marketed. However, AI provides the scientific foundation for several growing commercial technologies. (See Davis [6].) The major areas are expert systems, natural language processing, speech understanding, robotics and sensory systems, computer vision and scene recognition, and intelligent computer-aided instruction. These are illustrated in Figure 1.4 and are discussed next.

Expert Systems

Expert systems are computerized advisory programs that attempt to imitate the reasoning processes and knowledge of experts in solving specific types of problems. They are used more than any other applied AI technology. Expert systems are of great interest to organizations because of their potential to enhance productivity and to augment work forces in many specialty areas where human experts are becoming increasingly difficult to find and retain. Current applications are restricted to relatively limited and narrowly defined areas of expertise (called *domains*).

Human experts tend to specialize in relatively narrow problem-solving areas or tasks. Typically, human experts possess these characteristics: they solve problems quickly and fairly accurately, explain what (and sometimes how) they do, judge the reliability of their own conclusions, know when they are stumped, and communicate with other experts. They can also learn from experience, change their points of view to suit a problem, and transfer knowledge from one

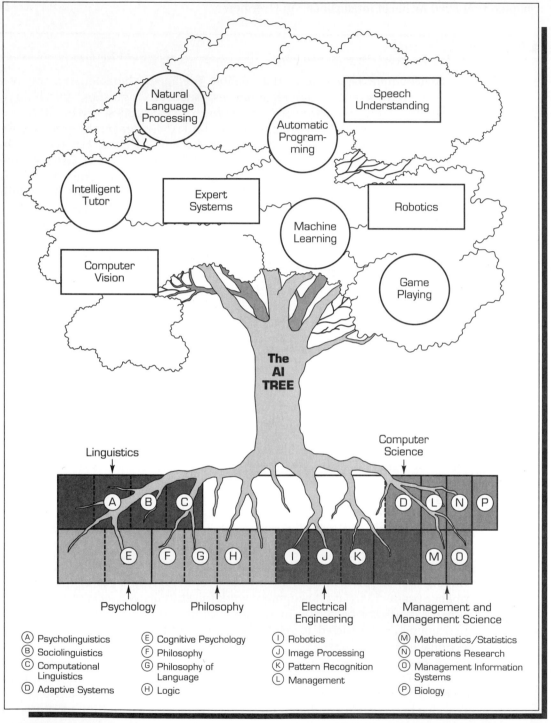

FIGURE 1.4 The Disciplines of AI (the Roots) and the Applications (*Source:* Adapted from N. Cercone and G. McCalba, "Artificial Intelligence: Underlying Assumptions and Basic Objectives," *Journal of the American Society for Information Science* [September 1984] and from G. S. Tuthill, *Knowledge Engineering* [Blue Ridge Summit, Pa.: TAB Books, 1990].)

Box 1.3: How Expert Systems Can Perform Useful Tasks

Suppose you manage an engineering firm that bids on many projects. Each project is, in a sense, unique. You can calculate your expected cost, but that's not sufficient to set up your bid. You have background information on your likely competitors and their bidding strategies. Something is known about the risks—possible technical problems, political delays, material shortages, or other sources of trouble. An experienced proposal manager can put all this together and, generally, arrive at a sound judgment concerning terms and bidding price. However, you do not have that many proposal managers who have the time to concentrate on preparing and negotiating major proposals. This is where expert systems become useful. An expert system can capture the lines of thinking the experienced proposal managers can follow. It can also catalog information gained on competitors, local risks, et cetera, and can incorporate your policies and strategies concerning risk, pricing, and terms. It can help your younger managers work through to an informed bid consistent with your policy.

Suppose you are a life insurance agent and you are a very good one; however, your market has changed. You are no longer competing only with other insurance agents. You are also competing with banks, brokers, money market fund managers, and the like. Your company is now pushing a whole array of products, from universal life insurance to venture capital funds. Your clients have the same problems as ever, but they are more inquisitive, more sophisticated, and more conscious of tax avoidance and similar considerations. How can you give them advice and put together a sensible package for them when you are more confused than they are?

Financial planning systems and estate planning guides have been part of the insurance industry's marketing kit for a long time. However, sensible financial planning takes more skill than the average insurance agent has or can afford to acquire. This is one reason why the fees of professional planners are as high as they are. A number of insurance companies are currently investing heavily in artificial intelligence techniques in the hope that these techniques can be used to build sophisticated, competitive, knowledge-based financial planning support systems to assist their agents in helping their clients.

(*Source:* Publicly disclosed project description of Arthur D. Little, Inc.)

domain to another. Finally, they use tools, such as rules of thumb, mathematical models, and detailed simulations to support their decisions.

Knowledge is a major resource, and it often lies with only a few experts. It is important to capture that knowledge so others can use it. Experts get sick or become unavailable and knowledge is thus not always available when needed. Books and manuals can capture some knowledge, but they leave the problem of a particular application up to the reader. Expert systems can provide a direct means of applying expertise. An expert system permits the knowledge and experience of one or more experts to be captured and stored in a computer. This knowledge can then be used by anyone who requires it. The purpose of an expert system is not to replace the experts, but simply to make their knowledge and experience more widely available. Typically, there are more problems to solve than there are experts available to handle them. An expert system permits others to increase their productivity, improve the quality of their decisions, and solve problems when an expert is not available.

Natural Language Processing

Natural language technology gives computer users the ability to communicate with the computer in their native language. This technology allows for a conversational type of interface, in contrast to one of computer jargon, syntax, and commands. Limited success in this area is typified by current systems that can recognize and interpret written sentences relating to very restricted topics. Although this ability can be used to great advantage with some applications, a general *natural language processing* (NLP) system is not yet possible.

The field of natural language processing is divided into two subfields:

☐ Natural language *understanding* investigates methods of allowing the computer to comprehend instructions given in ordinary English so that computers can understand people more easily.
☐ Natural language *generation* strives to have computers produce ordinary English language so that people can understand computers more easily.

Our interest in this book is mainly in the former.

Speech (Voice) Understanding

Speech understanding is the recognition and understanding by a computer of spoken language.

Speech understanding is a process that allows one to communicate with a computer by speaking to it. The term **speech recognition** is sometimes applied only to the first part of the process: recognizing the words that have been spoken without necessarily interpreting their meanings. The other part of the process, in which the meaning of the speech is ascertained, is called **speech understanding.** It may be possible to understand the meaning of a spoken sentence without actually recognizing every word.

Natural language processing is an attempt to allow computers to interpret normal statements expressed in a natural human language, such as English or Japanese. The process of speech understanding, in contrast, attempts to translate the human voice into individual words and sentences understandable by the computer. A combination of speech understanding and NLP will be required to realize the capability of the computer to converse in a manner normal to humans.

Robotics and Sensory Systems

Sensory systems, such as vision systems, tactile systems, and signal processing systems, when combined with AI define a broad category of systems generally referred to as *robotics*. A robot is an electromechanical device that can be programmed to perform manual tasks. The Robotic Institute of America formally defines a robot as "a reprogrammable multifunctional manipulator designed to move materials, parts, tools, or specialized devices through variable programmed motions for the performance of a variety of tasks."

Not all of robotics is considered to be part of AI. A robot that performs only the actions that it has been preprogrammed to perform is considered to be a "dumb" robot, possessing no more intelligence than, say, a dishwasher. An "intelligent" robot includes some kind of sensory apparatus, such as a camera, that collects information about the robot's operation and its environment. The intelligent part of the robot allows it to *respond* and adapt to changes in its environment, rather than just to follow instructions "mindlessly."

Robots combine sensory systems with mechanical motion to produce machines of widely varying intelligence and abilities. The research and application areas under the sensory systems umbrella include machines that sense, move, and manipulate their environment. Assembly line operations, particularly those that are highly repetitive or hazardous, are beginning to be performed by robots.

The difference between the automatic machine and an intelligent robot is that the robot senses its environment and modifies its behavior as a result of the information gained. The intelligent robot is thought to have humanlike capabilities and attributes. For example, some robots are distinguished from regular automation by their ability to deal with uncertainty.

Computer Vision and Scene Recognition

Visual recognition has been defined as the addition of some form of computer intelligence and decision making to digitized visual information received from a machine sensor. The combined information is then used to perform, or control, such operations as robotic movement, conveyor speeds, and production-line quality. The basic objective of computer vision is to interpret pictures rather than generate pictures (which preoccupies computer graphics). What "interpreting pictures" means differs depending on the application. For example, in interpreting pictures taken by satellite, it may be sufficient to roughly identify regions of crop damage. On the other hand, robot vision systems may find it necessary to precisely identify assembly components to correctly affix the components to the item being assembled.

Research in machine vision may enhance the abilities of automated systems to handle the manipulation of unlike objects in multiple orientations, such as forms lying on a table or parts moving on a conveyor belt. Optical recognition systems, for example, can retrieve handwritten or typed data from a form and reformat it for storage.

Intelligent Computer-aided Instruction

Intelligent computer-aided instruction (ICAI) refers to machines that can tutor humans. To a certain extent, such a machine can be viewed as an expert system. However, the major objective of an expert system is to render advice, whereas the purpose of ICAI is to teach.

Computer-assisted instruction, which has been in use for many years, brings the power of the computer to bear on the educational process. Now AI methods are being applied to the development of *intelligent* computer-assisted instruction systems in an attempt to create computerized "tutors" that shape their teaching techniques to fit the learning patterns of individual students.

ICAI applications are not limited to schools; as a matter of fact, they have found a sizable niche in the military and corporate sectors. ICAI systems are being used today for various tasks such as problem solving, simulation, discovery, learning, drill and practice, games, and testing. Such systems are also being used to support impaired people.

Even though ICAI programs are user interactive, use knowledge bases, and employ some AI technologies (like natural language interfaces), there is some debate about whether the programs themselves are really examples of AI. Often these programs are databases structured to respond to specific inputs with specific answers within a predetermined structure.

Other Applications

AI has been developed in several other commercial areas (see Winston and Prendergast [27]). Some interesting examples are discussed next.

Automatic Programming. In simple terms, programming is the process of telling the computer exactly what you want it to do. Developing a computer program frequently requires a great deal of time. A program or a system (a group of interrelated programs) must be designed, written, tested, debugged, and evaluated—all as part of an information system development process.

The goal of automatic programming is to create special programs that act as "intelligent" tools to assist programmers and expedite each phase of the programming process. The ultimate aim of automatic programming is a computer system that could develop programs by itself, in response to and in accordance with the specifications of a program developer.

Intelligent Workstations. Intelligent workstations increase the productivity of engineers and computer programmers by providing them with a computerized environment that helps them do their jobs faster. For example, Sun Microsystems Corp. produces workstations for electronic design. The stations allow an engineer to sit in front of a high-performance graphics terminal that "speaks" engineering language and utilizes special symbols. The station allows for simulated what-if experimentation with both the logic design and the layout design of electronic products. Other workstations are being used to support computer programmers by providing each programmer with an "electronic helper." Intelligent workstations for managers, which are now in a developmental stage, will support the various activities that managers perform.

Summarizing News. Some computer programs read stories in newspapers or other documents and make summaries in English or several other languages. This helps in handling the information overload problem.

Translation from One Language to Another. Computer programs are able to translate words and simple sentences from one language to another. For example, a package called LOGOS is used for translating from English to German (and German to English).

1.10   The Future of AI

So what does the future hold? Plenty. First, AI research and development will continue, and all of the various subfields will evolve and improve. New software techniques will be discovered. Improved software development tools will be created for easier development of expert systems and other AI applications.

Advances will also occur in hardware. In addition to the usual ongoing developments in semiconductor technology that will bring us larger and faster microprocessors and RAM chips, entirely new devices will be created. Special search, pattern-matching, and symbolic computing chips are being developed. The new parallel computing and especially neural computing architectures, with multiple CPUs operating simultaneously, will bring a whole new dimension to AI.

For the immediate future, you can expect to see AI added to existing software. Natural language interfaces will become a common feature on many applications programs, and intelligent databases are being developed. Internally, programs will use segments of AI to make some performance improvements. Expert systems that advise on many important topics will become widely available.

Generally speaking, however, there will be relatively few stand-alone AI application products. Expert systems are the exception. Predictions are that AI software will, in most applications, be combined with conventional algorithmic software; that is, AI subroutines, including expert systems, will be embedded in traditional software. AI will be virtually transparent to the user.

There is a great concern within the AI and software communities that too much will be expected of AI. AI researchers are particularly upset over the excessive amount of media hype that AI has been receiving during the past few years. They fear that the public's expectations will be far beyond what AI can

---

Box 1.4: The Fifth-Generation Project

Artificial intelligence is often referred to as the fifth generation of computer technology. The Japanese plan to create a fifth-generation computer to leapfrog the leaders in this field. If successful, it will represent a highly significant event in human history. The Japanese are determined to shed their imitator image and make a revolutionary push. They plan to create a computer that can talk, listen, learn, and make sophisticated decisions. That means an extensive utilization of AI techniques.

Some of the objectives of this fifth-generation computer are as follows:

- Provide a high intelligence level to cooperate with people
- Assist people to discover and develop unknown fields
- Offer vast knowledge bases
- Aid in management
- Solve social problems
- Acquire new perceptions by simulating unknown situations
- Offer significant software productivity improvement
- Reduce time and cost to develop computerized systems by a factor of ten

Ultimately, the computer is to have the capability to recognize continuous speech, possess super vision, make intelligent decisions, perform self-repair, and augment the decision maker in general.

For a detailed discussion of Japan's Fifth-generation Project, see Feigenbaum and McCorduck [11] and Chapter 17 in this text.

really deliver. That is certainly a legitimate concern, but such media buildups occur with many new high-tech methods and products.

So, although AI is an excellent technology, it is not the panacea we might like it to be. Look at it for what it really is: some special software techniques now developed to the point that they can be practical and useful. Where possible, consider AI another computer-based information system that can expand the applicability of computers and increase productivity and compatibility. Look for ways to use it, but do not expect miracles. On rare occasions, AI may give a miraclelike solution, but more likely it will not. It will deliver evolutionary rather than revolutionary improvements.

So far you have been introduced to the highlights of AI. In subsequent chapters, you will be exposed to a wide range of applications and techniques.

1.11 Plan of the Book

The book is divided into seven major parts (Figure 1.5). Part 1, Fundamentals, provides an overview of the AI field, a discussion of problem solving in AI (Chapter 2), and an overview of expert systems (Chapter 3).

The subject of Part 2 is knowledge engineering. All AI technologies process knowledge of some sort. Acquiring (Chapter 4), representing (Chapter 5), inferencing (Chapter 6), and dealing with uncertain knowledge (Chapter 7) constitute what is called knowledge engineering.

Part 3 presents AI technologies. In addition to expert systems, described in Chapter 3, there are four major technologies: natural language processing (Chapter 8), speech recognition and understanding (Chapter 9), computer vision (Chapter 10), and robotics (Chapter 11).

Part 4, Building Knowledge-based Systems, shows that the development process of expert systems can be very complex (in large systems) or fairly simple (in small systems). First, an overview of the process is provided (Chapter 12) and then the tools are described (Chapter 13). Finally, the design of the user-machine interface is discussed (Chapter 14).

Part 5 concerns implementation. Putting AI technologies to work may be a complex task. First, there is the issue of system integration (Chapter 15). Implementation plans and issues are also critical (Chapter 16), mainly because of the many potential impacts of AI (Chapter 17).

Advanced topics are introduced in Part 6. This part includes two chapters: one on neural computing (Chapter 18) and one about special topics and the future of AI (Chapter 19).

Applications and cases in Part 7 conclude the main text of the book. Several illustrative applications (Chapter 20) are followed by a project and a business case study (Chapter 21). Chapter 22 presents examples of mission-critical expert systems.

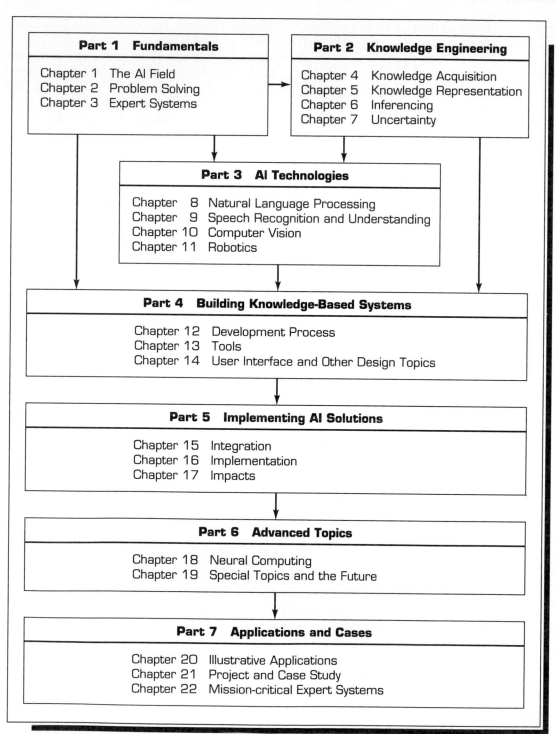

FIGURE 1.5 Plan of the Book

Chapter Highlights

- Artificial intelligence is an interdisciplinary field that can be defined many ways.
- The primary objective of AI is to build computers that will perform tasks that can be characterized as intelligent.
- The major characteristics of AI are symbolic processing, use of heuristics instead of algorithms, and application of inference techniques.
- AI is about thirty-five years old; yet its commercialization started to take off only in the 1980s.
- AI has several major advantages over people: it is permanent, it can be easily duplicated and disseminated, it can be less expensive than human intelligence, it is consistent and thorough, and it can be documented.
- Natural (human) intelligence has advantages over AI: it is creative, it uses sensory experiences directly, and it reasons from a wide context of experiences.
- Knowledge rather than data or information is the key concept of AI.
- A knowledge base is the collection of knowledge related to a specific issue (problem or opportunity).
- AI includes a mechanism that enables it to reason about certain problems based on the facts about the situation and the knowledge stored in the knowledge base.
- We are moving into an era of knowledge-based organizations.
- AI applications can be programmed in conventional computer languages as well as in special AI languages (e.g., LISP, PROLOG).
- In conventional computing we tell the computer how to solve the problem. In AI we tell the computer what the problem is and give it the knowledge needed to solve similar problems and the necessary procedures to use the knowledge.
- All digital computers are algorithmic in their operation, but they can be programmed for symbolic manipulation.
- The basic techniques of reasoning are search and pattern matching (recognition).
- Despite the fact that AI computers cannot think, they can be very valuable by increasing the ways computers can be used.
- The major application areas of AI are expert systems, natural language processing, speech understanding, intelligent robotics, computer vision, and intelligent computer-aided instruction.
- Expert systems, the most applied AI technology, attempt to imitate the work of experts. They apply expertise to problem solving.
- Natural language processing is an attempt to allow users to communicate with computers in a natural language. Currently, conversation is done via the keyboard; in the future, it will be carried out by voice.
- Speech understanding will enable people to communicate with the computer by voice.

□ An intelligent robot is one that can respond to changes in its environment. Most of today's robots are "dumb."

□ Sensory systems are essential for making robots intelligent, but they can also be used by themselves or with other computerized systems.

□ Computer vision allows the interpretation of pictures or other visible objects.

□ Computers can be used as tutors. If they are supported by AI, they can improve training and teaching.

□ Several other applications of AI are moving from the laboratories to the real world. They range from automatic computer programming to translation of human languages.

□ The various AI technologies can be integrated among themselves and with other computer-based technologies.

Key Terms

algorithm	natural language	speech recognition
artificial intelligence	natural language	speech understanding
expert system	processing	symbol
inferencing	numeric processing	symbol structure
information overload	pattern matching	symbolic processing
intelligent computer-	programming language	Turing Test
aided instruction	robotics	visual recognition
knowledge	search	
knowledge base	sensory system	

Questions for Review

1. Define artificial intelligence.
2. What is the Turing Test?
3. What do we mean by inferencing?
4. Describe the following periods in the history of AI: prehistoric, dawn, dark, renaissance, partnership, and enterpreneur.
5. List the major advantages artificial intelligence has over natural intelligence.
6. List the major disadvantages of artificial compared with natural intelligence.
7. Distinguish between data, information, and knowledge.
8. Define a knowledge base.
9. How does the computer use the knowledge base?
10. What are the major differences between traditional computing and AI?
11. Explain why AI is beneficial even though computers cannot really think.
12. List the major AI technologies.
13. Define expert system.
14. Distinguish between a natural language and a programming language.
15. Define natural language processing.
16. Define speech recognition and understanding.

17. What is a robot? How does it relate to AI?
18. What is the difference between an automatic machine and an intelligent robot?
19. Define visual recognition as it applies to computer technology.
20. List the major benefits of intelligent computer-aided instruction.

Questions for Discussion

1. Inflated expectations were a major problem with AI in the past. Why? Is this a problem today? Why or why not?
2. What are the major factors that can help push AI from the lab to the real world?
3. Compare and contrast numeric and symbolic processing techniques.
4. Compare and contrast conventional processing from artificial intelligence processing.
5. "Speech understanding or even recognition could increase the number of managers using the computer directly tenfold." Do you agree? Why or why not?
6. List and discuss the steps involved in processing of data by computers.

Exercises

1. Interview an information systems manager in a company. Determine the extent to which the company is using AI technology. Also, ask what the company plans for the next three to five years. Are there any problems? (List and discuss.) Prepare a two-page report on your visit.
2. Debate 1: Computers are programmed to play chess. They are getting better and better and soon may beat the world champion. Do such computers exhibit intelligence? Why or why not?
3. Debate 2: Prepare a table showing all the arrangements you can think of that justify the position that computers cannot think. Then prepare arguments that show the opposite.
4. Debate 3: Bourbaki (reference 4) describes Searle's argument against the use of Turing's Test. Summarize all the important issues in this debate.

References and Bibliography

1. Alexander, I., and P. Burnett. *Thinking Machines*. New York: A. Knopf, 1987.
2. Barr, A., and E.A. Feigenbaum. *The Handbook of Artificial Intelligence*. Vol. 1. Los Altos, Calif.: William Kaufmann, 1981.
3. Bloomfield, B.P., ed. *The Question of Artificial Intelligence: Philosophical and Sociological Perspectives*. London: Croom Helm, 1988.
4. Bourbaki, N. "Turing, Searle and Thought." *AI Expert* (July 1990).
5. Cohen, P.R., and E.A. Feigenbaum. *The Handbook of Artificial Intelligence*. Vol. 3. Los Altos, Calif.: William Kaufmann, 1982.

6. Davis, D.B. "Artificial Intelligence Goes to Work." *High Technology Business* (April 1987).

7. de Garis, H. "What If AI Succeeds? The Rise of the Twenty-First Century Artilect." *AI Magazine* 10 (Summer 1989):16–22.

8. Dicken, H.K., and H.P. Newquist, eds. *AI Trends '85.* Scottsdale, Ariz.: DM Data, 1985 (Annual report in the AI industry).

9. Dreyfus, H., and S. Dreyfus. *Mind Over Machine.* New York: Free Press, 1988.

10. *Environmental Scan Report on Artificial Intelligence.* Washington, D.C.: U.S. Dept. of the Treasury, IRS, December 1983.

11. Feigenbaum, E.A., and P. McCorduck. *The Fifth Generation Computer.* Reading, Mass.: Addison-Wesley, 1983.

12. Gill, K.S., ed. *Artificial Intelligence for Society.* New York: John Wiley & Sons, 1986.

13. Guha, R.V., and D.B. Lenat. "CYC A Midterm Report." *AI Magazine* (Fall 1990).

14. Hill, W.C. "The Mind at AI: Horseless Carriage to Clock." *AI Magazine* 10 (Summer 1989):29–41.

15. Johnson-Laird, P.N. *The Computer and the Mind.* Cambridge, Mass.: Harvard Univ. Press, 1988.

16. Kaplan, S.J. "The Industrialization of Artificial Intelligence: From By-Line to Bottom-Line." *AI Magazine* (Summer 1984).

17. Lugar, G.F. *Artificial Intelligence and the Design of Expert Systems.* Reading, Mass.: Addison-Wesley, 1989.

18. Mongar, R.F. "AI Applications: What's Their Competitive Potential?" *Journal of Information Systems Management* (Summer 1988).

19. Narasimhan, R. "Human Intelligence and AI: How Close Are We to Bridging the Gap?" *AI Expert* (April 1990).

20. Rich, E. *Artificial Intelligence.* New York: McGraw-Hill, 1983.

21. Rubinger, B. *Applied Artificial Intelligence in Japan.* New York: Hemisphere Publishing, 1989.

22. Shapiro, S.U., ed. *Encyclopedia of Artificial Intelligence.* New York: John Wiley & Sons, 1987.

23. Sowa, J.F. *Conceptual Structures.* Reading, Mass.: Addison-Wesley, 1984.

24. Stevens, L. *Artificial Intelligence: The Search for the Perfect Machine.* N.J.: Hayden Book Co., 1985.

25. Unger, J.M. *The Fifth Generation Fallacy: Why Japan Is Betting Its Future on Artificial Intelligence.* New York: Oxford Univ. Press, 1987.

26. Waterman, D. *A Guide to Expert Systems.* Reading, Mass.: Addison-Wesley, 1986.

27. Winston, P.H., and K.A. Prendergast, eds. *The AI Business.* Cambridge, Mass.: MIT Press, 1984.

Appendix A: Definitions of Artificial Intelligence

1. "The goal of work in artificial intelligence is to build machines that perform tasks normally requiring human intelligence."—Nils J. Nilsson, *Problem-Solving Methods in Artificial Intelligence*, p. vii.

2. "Research scientists in Artificial Intelligence try to get machines to exhibit behavior that we call intelligent behavior when we observe it in human beings."—James R. Slagle, *Artificial Intelligence: The Heuristic Programming Approach*, p. 1.

3. The goal of artificial intelligence research is "to construct computer programs which exhibit behavior that we call 'intelligent behavior' when we observe it in human beings."—Edward A. Feigenbaum & Julian Feldman, *Computers and Thought*, p. 3.

4. "Thinking is a continuum, an *n*-dimensional continuum . . . comparisons can be made between men and machines in the continuum of thinking . . . In this context then, the goal of research of artificial intelligence can be stated—it is simply an attempt to push machine behavior further out into this continuum."—Paul Armer, "Attitudes Towards Intelligent Machines" in Feigenbaum & Feldman, *Computers and Thought*, pp. 390–92.

5. "The field commonly called artificial intelligence may, perhaps, be described as the totality of attempts to make and understand machines that are able to perform tasks that, until recently, only human beings could perform and to perform them with effectiveness and speed comparable to a human."—Ranan B. Banerji, *Theory of Problem Solving: An Approach to Artificial Intelligence*, p. 1.

6. "Artificial Intelligence (is) defined generally as the attempt to construct mechanisms that perform tasks requiring intelligence when performed by humans."—George W. Ernst and Allen Newell, *GPS: A Case Study in Generality and Problem Solving*, p.1 .

7. "B. Raphael . . . has suggested that AI is a collective name for problems which we do not yet know how to solve properly by computer."—Donald Michie, "Formation and Execution of Plans by Machine" in Fendler & Meltzer, *Artificial Intelligence and Heuristic Programming*, p. 101.

8. "(1) Does the program utilize a model of its task environment? . . .
    (2) Does the program use its model to perform plans of action to be executed in the task environment?
    (3) Do these plans include directed sampling of the task environment so as to guide execution along conditional branches of the plan?
    (4) Can the program reformulate a plan when execution leads to states of the environment which were not predicted in the model?
    (5) Can the program utilize the record of failures and successes of past plans to revise and extend the model inductively?
   If the answers to all these questions are affirmative, then the program undoubtedly represents an exercise in artificial intelligence. If only some are affirmative, then it is a partial exercise in AI. If the answers are all

negative, then it is a partial exercise in AI. If the answers are all negative, then we are probably dealing with an exercise in conventional data-processing, industrial automation, numerical analysis, pattern recognition, or the like. Such programs may be *clever,* often to a superhuman degree, without prompting the word 'intelligent' as a description of their operations."—Donald Michie, "Formation and Execution of Plans by Machine" in Findler & Meltzer, *Artificial Intelligence and Heuristic Programming,* pp. 101, 2.

9. "Artificial Intelligence (is) the science of making machines do things that would require intelligence if done by men."—Marvin Minsky, *Semantic Information Processing,* p. v.

10. "The capability of a device to perform functions that are normally associated with human intelligence, such as reasoning, learning and self-improvement. Related to machine learning." *American National Standard Vocabulary for Information Processing.*

11. "The capability of a device to perform functions that are normally associated with human intelligence, such as reasoning, learning and self-improvement. It includes the study of computers and computer-related techniques to increase the intellectual capabilities of man. Just as tools and powered machinery extend the physical power of man, computers, data-processing machines, and other programmed equipment extend his mental powers. The field of artificial intelligence includes the study of techniques for making more effective use of digital computers and other forms of perception and identification; artificial learning; and the study of self-organizing, self-adapative, self-repairing, automatic fault detection, location, and correction techniques. In a general sense, artificial intelligence includes the study of the use of programmed machinery for the solution of problems involving logic or reasoning, with the additional requirement that performance improves with experience or operation, such as the ability to play a game, like chess or checkers, improves with each game played, as long as the machine is informed of the results of each game."—Martin H. Weik, *Standard Dictionary of Computers and Information Processing,* pp. 166, 7.

12. " 'Artificial Intelligence' is the ability of machines to do things that people would say require intelligence. Artificial Intelligence (AI) research is an attempt to discover and describe aspects of human intelligence that can be simulated by machines. Alternately, AI research may be viewed as an attempt to develop a mathematical theory to describe the abilities and actions of things (natural or man-made) exhibiting 'intelligent' behavior, and serve as a calculus for the design of intelligent machines."—Philip C. Jackson, Jr., *Introduction to Artificial Intelligence,* p. 1.

13. "Artificial Intelligence is the science of making computers smart. It is practiced both by those who want to make computers more useful and by those who want to understand the nature of intelligence . . . The idea (of the latter group) is not to make programs simulate intelligence but to make programs *be* intelligent."—Patrick H. Winston, brochure describing *Artificial*

Intelligence; a Self-Study Subject, Center for Advanced Engineering Study, MIT, p. 2.

14. "What is or should be (AI researchers') main scientific activity—*Studying the structure of information and the structure of problem-solving processes independently of applications and independently of its realization in animals or humans.*"—John McCarthy, Review of "Artificial Intelligence: A General Survey" by Prof. Sir James Lighthill, FRS. *Artificial Intelligence* 5(1974), 317–322, p. 317.

15. "By 'artificial intelligence' I therefore mean the use of computer programs and programming techniques to cast light on the principles of intelligence in general and human thought in particular."—Margaret Boden, *Artificial Intelligence and Natural Man,* p. 5.

16. Artificial Intelligence is the study of ideas which enable computers to do things that make people seem intelligent . . . The central goals of Artificial Intelligence are to make computers more useful and to understand the principles which make intelligence possible."—Patrick Winston, *Artificial Intelligence,* p. 1.

This list is reprinted from H. K. Dicken and H. P. Newquist, eds., *AI Trends '85* (Scottsdale, Ariz.: Relayer Group, 1985).

Chapter 2

Problem Representation and Problem-solving Strategies

One of the major objectives of AI is for machines to perform tasks—especially decision making—like humans. Decision making, or problem solving, is a difficult task, even for people. Using reasoning in problem solving is one of the major characteristics of intelligent behavior. To understand how AI and particularly expert systems operate, it is necessary to know the process of problem solving and the approaches used by AI. This chapter presents the fundamentals of these topics in the following sections:

2.1   Problem Solving and Decision Making

Problem solving is often associated with the performance output of thinking creatures. It is a mental activity of finding a solution to a problem. The term *problem*, however, is somewhat misleading. We usually infer that a problem means dealing with trouble or distress. Although this is true in some cases, it is not true in all situations. For example, analyzing a potential merger, which is an examination of *opportunity*, can be considered problem solving, and so is the discovery of a new technology. The term *problem solving* was introduced by mathematicians. In the world of business, the term **decision making** is routinely used as equivalent to problem solving. The AI community uses *problem solving* fairly commonly and therefore we will use it in this text.

Humans follow a fairly standard process when they solve problems. This process is described at the beginning of this chapter. To understand how machines are programmed to solve problems, we introduce the Newell-Simon model of information processing. Next, the issue of problem solving in AI is presented, starting with the necessary representation of problems and followed by some basic approaches to reasoning. Attention is then given to several search methods used in problem solving in general and in AI in particular. Overall, this chapter intends to provide the basic foundations necessary to understanding the use of applied AI technologies.

2.2   The Process of Problem Solving

The process of problem solving is viewed differently by researchers depending on their education and experience. For example, Bell et al. [1] describe several approaches to problem solving and decision making ranging from the purely quantitative to one that is based solely on intuition. Six major steps are generally observable in the process: problem identification and definition, identification of criteria for finding a solution, generation of alternatives, search for solution and evaluation, choice and recommendation, and implementation (Figure 2.1). Some scholars use different classifications. For example, Simon's classical approach identifies three phases: intelligence, design, and choice [16].

Although the process in Figure 2.1 is shown as being linear, it is rarely so. In reality steps may be combined, and based on work in a certain step, revisions may be made in earlier steps; that is, the process is iterative (cyclical). A brief definition of each of the steps follows:

  □ Step 1—Problem identification and definition: A problem (or opportunity) must first be recognized. Its magnitude and importance are determined and defined.

  □ Step 2—Identification of criteria: Solution to a problem depends on the criteria used to judge the possible alternatives. For example, finding a good investment depends on criteria (or objectives) such as safety,

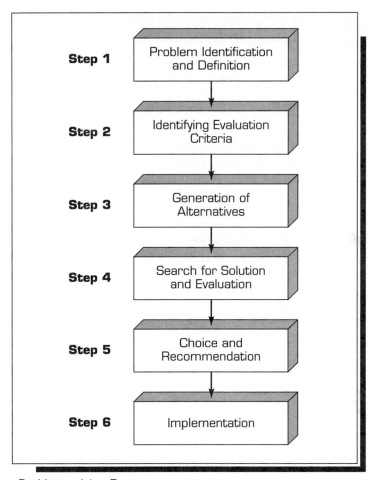

FIGURE 2.1 Problem-solving Process

liquidity, and rate of return. In this step we determine what the criteria are and their relative importance.

□ Step 3—Generation of alternatives: By definition, it is necessary to examine two or more courses of action (one of which can be doing nothing) to be in a decision situation. Generation of potential solutions requires creativity and ingenuity.

□ Step 4—Search for solution and evaluation: This step involves examination of the solution candidates in light of the criteria outlined earlier. It is basically a *search* process since we are looking for the best or "good enough" solutions. Several search, evaluation, and reasoning methodologies can be used in this step.

□ Step 5—Choice and recommendation: The product of a search is selecting a solution to recommend as a remedy for the problem.

□ Step 6—Implementation: To solve the problem, the recommended solution needs to be successfully implemented.

Actually, the process is more complex, because in each step there could be several subdecisions that need to be made, each of which follows a similar process.

Applied AI technologies can be used to support all of the six steps. However, most of the AI action takes place in support of steps 4 and 5. Specifically, expert systems are used to find a solution among alternatives, which are assumed to be given. Thus the role of AI is basically conducting a *search* and an *evaluation* using some inference capabilities. Despite the narrow role of AI today, it is hoped that with the passage of time, the technologies will play a much larger role in all steps of the process.

Nevertheless, AI technologies have another big advantage. Although AI can effectively handle only two steps in the problem-solving process, AI is used in many other tasks that are not classified as problem solving or decision making. For example, expert systems are useful in configuration of computer orders. They are also used to mimic human "help centers" (providing information that is available in catalogs or manuals), and they can be used in planning, complex scheduling, and interpretation of information.

2.3   Human Problem Solving—An Information Processing Approach

A major goal of AI is understanding human intelligence. By attempting to model human intelligence on the computer, we are forced to learn how we store knowledge and use it. We begin to understand our own thought patterns, reasoning techniques, and problem-solving approaches. We learn how we learn, and our strengths and weaknesses are revealed. The result is a better understanding of our minds, which can lead to improved ways of learning and applying our intelligence to real-world problems. The science devoted to such studies is called cognitive science, and one interesting area in it is the way humans and computers process information. In applying AI, we consider a special approach to problem solving and decision making. This approach is based on the belief that problem solving can be understood as information processing; it is based on a cognitive approach that uses a qualitative description of the ways in which people are similar and of the manner in which people think. Of special interest to AI is the Newell-Simon model of human information processing.

Newell-Simon Model

Allen Newell and Herbert A. Simon [10] proposed a model of human problem solving that makes use of the analogy between computer processing and human information processing. This model can help us understand how AI works and what its limitations are. The human information processing system consists of the following subsystems: a perceptual subsystem, a cognitive subsystem, a motor subsystem, and external memory. Figure 2.2 illustrates the memories and processors included in each subsystem.

Perceptual Subsystem. External stimuli are the input for the human information processing system. These stimuli enter through sensors like our eyes and ears. The **perceptual subsystem** consists of these sensors along with buffer memories that briefly store incoming information while it waits processing by the cognitive subsystem.

Cognitive Subsystem. Human senses are constantly placing a huge amount of information in the buffer memories. Whenever there is a need to make a decision, the **cognitive subsystem** selects the appropriate information. Like a central processing unit in a computer, the elementary processor obtains the information necessary to make this decision from the sensory buffers and transfers it to the **short-term memory.** The processor works in cycles, which are analogous to the "fetch-execute" cycles of the computer. During each cycle the processor obtains information from a memory, evaluates it, and then stores the information in another memory.

The cognitive system contains three parts: the elementary processor; the short-term memory; and the interpreter, which interprets part or all of the program of instructions for problem solving. This program will depend on a number of variables such as the task and the intelligence of the problem solver.

In the simplest tasks, the cognitive system merely serves as a point for transferring information from sensory inputs to motor outputs. Habitual tasks, such as reaching to turn off a light switch, are like that. The performer needs to coordinate the action, but there is little to no "deep thought" involved. In fact, the "thinking" that occurs during such behavior is impossible to recover.

More complex tasks involve more information. That, in turn, calls for more elaborate processing. To accomplish these tasks, the cognitive processor will draw on a second memory system: long-term memory.

Long-term memory consists of a large number of stored symbols with a complex indexing system. There are competing hypotheses about what the elementary symbols are and how they arrange themselves. In the simplest memory model, related symbols are associated with one another. In a more elaborate model, symbols are organized into temporal scripts. Another view is that memory consists of clusters of symbols called "chunks." A chunk is a unit of stored information—it can be a digit, a symbol, or a word associated with a set or pattern of stimuli. Chunks are hierarchically organized collections of still smaller chunks. In this conception, memory is a vast network of chunks. It requires only a few hundred milliseconds to read (recall) from long-term memory, but the write time (commitment to memory) is fairly long (say, $5N$ to $10N$ seconds, for N symbols, where N = number of symbols involved).

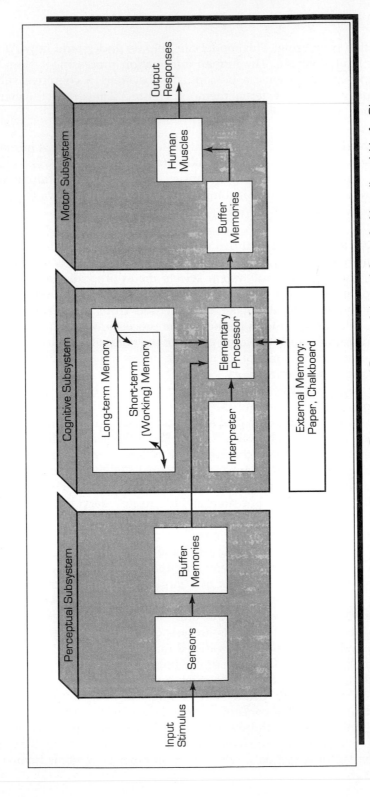

FIGURE 2.2 Newell-Simon Model of Human Information Processing. (*Source:* Adapted from A. Newell and H. A. Simon, *Human Problem Solving* [Englewood Cliffs, N.J.: Prentice-Hall, 1972].)

Human beings can support the decision-making process with another memory, the external one. The external memory consists of external media like a pad of paper or a chalkboard. The processing, retrieval, and storage of data by computers can be thousands and millions of times faster than that of humans. Humans are also limited in their ability to generate, integrate, and interpret probabilistic data.

The three memories are shown in Figure 2.2. The long-term memory has essentially unlimited capacity. The short-term memory is quite small. It holds only five to seven chunks. However, only about two chunks can be retained while another task is being performed. This suggests that part of the short-term memory is used for input and output processing. This is one of the major limitations of the human as compared with a computer. The limits of the short-term memory can be expanded, for example, through analogies, associations, or the use of graphics. A graph may provide, in a few chunks, the same information as a large number of data items would. And so graphics play an important role in the support of managerial decision making.

The human operates according to this model in serial rather than parallel fashion. This means that a human can perform only one information processing task at a time, whereas a computer may operate in either serial or parallel designs.

Motor Subsystem. After scanning and searching memories, the processor sends information to the **motor subsystem.** Motor processors initiate actions of muscles and other internal human systems. This, in turn, results in some observable activity, for example, talking.

2.4   Problem Solving in AI

Applied AI technologies are being associated primarily with the search and evaluation steps of the problem-solving process. The objective is to automate these steps as much as possible. First let us look at search strategies in general, and then identify those that are used in AI.

Search Approaches

Many approaches and strategies are used to search for an appropriate solution to problems. Some of these approaches are informal; they involve intuition, "gut feeling," or just acting on impulses. Formal approaches can be classified into three categories: optimization, blind search, and use of heuristics. Optimization involves numeric, quantitative analysis, whereas blind search and heuristics may involve either numeric or qualitative (symbolic) analysis.

The categories are shown in Figure 2.3 and are discussed briefly next.

Optimization. Optimization attempts to find the best possible solution by using mathematical formulas that model specific situations. The problem domain

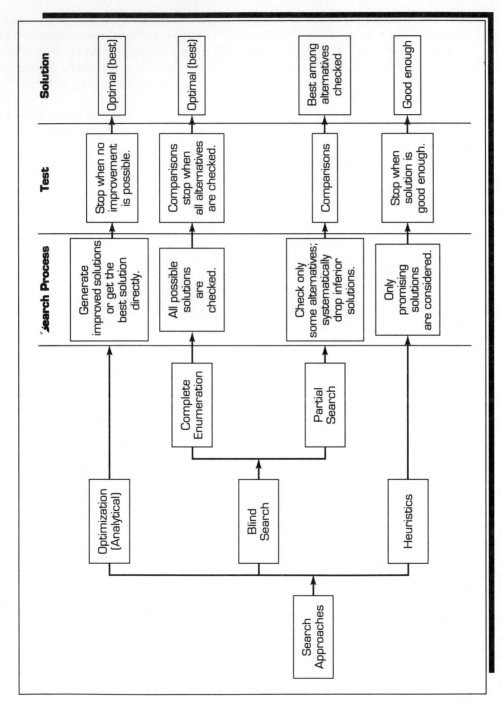

FIGURE 2.3 Formal Search Approaches

must be fairly structured, and the optimization is conducted by using either a one-step formula or an algorithm. Recall that an algorithm is a step-by-step search process in which solutions are generated and tested for possible improvements. An improvement is made whenever possible and the new solution is subjected to an improvement test. The process continues until no further improvement is possible.

Optimization is used extensively in non-AI technologies such as operations research (management science) and mathematics. The major differences between optimization and other analytical quantitative methods and heuristics are shown in Table 2.1. In AI, blind search and heuristic search are used extensively.

Blind Search. In conducting a search, a description of a desired solution is given. This is called a goal. For example, a goal can be to identify the best location for a plant or to approve or disapprove a request for a loan. The possible steps leading from initial conditions (e.g., information about the alternatives or existing symptoms) to the goal are viewed as the search steps. Problem solving is carried out by searching through the *space* of possible solutions.

Blind search techniques explore the alternatives and events of a decision situation, one at a time. Two types of blind search exist. In **complete** (exhaustive) **enumeration** all alternatives are considered; therefore, an optimal solution is discovered. In incomplete (partial) search, the search continues until a good

TABLE 2.1 Comparing Decision Approaches

Problem-solving Dimension	Heuristic	Optimization or Analytical
Approach to learning	Learns more by acting than by analyzing the situation and places more emphasis on feedback.	Employs a planned sequential approach to problem solving; learns more by analyzing the situation than by acting and places less emphasis on feedback.
Search	Uses trial and error and spontaneous action.	Uses formal rational analysis.
Approach to analysis	Uses common sense, intuition, and feelings.	Develops explicit, often quantitative models of the situation.
Scope of analysis	Views the totality of the situation as an organic whole rather than as a structure constructed from specific parts.	Reduces the problem situation to a set of underlying causal functions.
Basis for inferences	Looks for highly visible situational differences that vary with time.	Locates similarities or commonalities by comparing objects.

Source: G. B. Davis, *Management Information Systems: Conceptual Foundations, Structure, and Development* (New York: McGraw-Hill, 1974), p. 150.

enough solution is found. In blind situations the search path is arbitrary. No intelligent decision making is employed to direct the search.

There are practical limits on the amount of time and computer storage available for blind searches. Although in principle the blind search method can eventually find a solution to most search situations, the method is not practical for large problems because too many potential solutions must be visited before a good enough solution is found.

Also, in many situations, a **combinatorial explosion** is created. In conducting a blind search one may encounter a situation where the number of alternatives to be considered expands exponentially. Such problems are called combinatorial problems. A major characteristic of combinatorial problems is that the number of alternative solutions increases *much faster* than the size of the problem. For example, in a problem of matching candidates and jobs, by increasing the number of candidates and jobs from 10 to 11 (a 10 percent increase), the number of potential matchings increases by 1,100 percent to 39,916,800. An increase from 10 to 12 (20 percent increase) will cause the number of alternatives to increase to about 480,000,000, or about 13,200 percent.

As a result, a blind search may take years to accomplish, even with the aid of sophisticated computers (see exercise 3).

Heuristic Search. For many applications, it is possible to find specific information to guide the search process and thus reduce the amount of computation. This is called heuristic information, and the search procedures that use it are called **heuristic search** methods.

Webster's New World Dictionary defines *heuristic* as "helping to discover or learn." There are other definitions. As an adjective, heuristic means serving to discover. As a noun, a heuristic is an aid to discovery. A heuristic contributes to the reduction of search in a problem-solving activity.

Heuristics (derived from the Greek word for discovery) are decision rules regarding how a problem should be solved. Heuristics are developed on a basis of solid, rigorous analysis of the problem and sometimes involve designed experimentation. Some examples of heuristics are given in Table 2.2.

Heuristic problem solving is the implementation of heuristics in problem-solving or in decision-making situations. Problem solving based on heuristics

TABLE 2.2 Examples of Heuristics

Construction	It costs $2 million to build one mile of a highway.
Purchase stocks	Do not buy stocks whose price-to-earnings ratio is larger than 10.
Travel	Do not go on the freeway between 8 and 9 A.M.
Capital investment in high-tech projects	Consider only projects whose estimated payback period is less than two years.
Purchase of a house	Buy only in a good neighborhood, but buy there only at the lower price range.

is a very old practice in comparison to science based on reason. Several terms are used in practice to describe the use of heuristics: hints, intuition, judgment, rules of thumb, and inspiration.

Heuristic search is much *faster* and *cheaper* than a blind search. The results are considered good enough, and in the case of quantitative analysis they are very close to optimal solutions. The specific methods of heuristic search are described in section 2.7.

Search Directions

A search in AI can be goal directed, data directed, or a combination of both. These approaches will be discussed in more detail in Chapter 6.

Data-directed (Forward) Search. A **data-directed search** starts from available information (or facts) and tries to draw conclusions regarding the situation or the goal attainment. For example, if a company is losing sales volume, the search attempts to find out why (e.g., because of insufficient advertising).

Goal-directed (Backward) Search. A **goal-directed search** starts from expectations of what the goal is or what is to happen; then it seeks evidence that supports (or contradicts) those expectations (or hypotheses). For example, we expect that sales declined because we think our advertising budget is insufficient. The goal-directed search will confirm or deny our expectations.

Artificial intelligence—in contrast with conventional problem-solving techniques such as operations research, management science, or decision support systems—employs basically blind and heuristic approaches. Table 2.3 shows some of the differences between AI and non-AI tools. The application of these

TABLE 2.3 AI Versus Non-AI Tools: Search and Reasoning

AI (Expert Systems)	Operations Research or Decision Support Systems
Heuristic reasoning	Mechanistic/monotonic reasoning
Symbolic manipulation	Numeric and alphanumeric manipulation
Dynamic decision process	Static decision process
Remembers information	Doesn't remember information
Prediction and inference	What-if scenarios or IF-THEN scenarios (in DSS)
Data-pattern driven	Control driven
Multiple solutions	Single solution
Search intensive	Computation intensive
Recursive	Iterative
Certainty factors	Truth or falseness

Source: Modified from D. D. Wolfgram, et al., *Expert Systems for the Technical Professional* (New York: John Wiley & Sons, 1987), p. 10 (Table 1.1).

approaches enables AI to tackle problems that conventional programming cannot handle.

2.5   Problem Representation in AI

To understand how the blind and the heuristic searches work, it is necessary first to illustrate how problems are represented in AI.

State-Space Representation

The general process of solving any problem using AI involves three major elements: problem states, a goal, and operators. Problem states define the problem situation and existing conditions.

States are snapshots of varying conditions in the environment. For example, a state can be "you cannot start your car," or "there is an oil leak." States can also be potential alternative solutions to problems. All states are unique. The goal is the objective to be achieved, a final answer, or a solution; for example, your goal is finding what is wrong with your car. There may be more than one goal. **Operators** are procedures used for changing from one state to another. An operator describes a process whereby some action is taken to change the initial state into another state that more closely approaches the goal. Operators move the problem from one state to the next, following the guidance of a master control strategy, until a goal is reached. An operator could be an algorithmic subroutine.

Figure 2.4 shows the relationship between the initial state, procedures, and goal. The initial conditions provide the states that are manipulated by procedures to achieve the goal. A **control strategy** selects or guides the procedures.

It is important to point out that even though we may treat search as being separate from the knowledge representation scheme, the two are very much interrelated. The selection of a particular knowledge representation method will greatly affect the type of search and control strategy used.

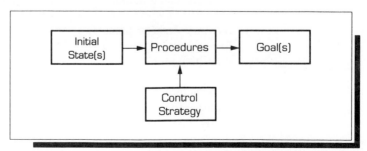

FIGURE 2.4   Relationship between Initial State(s), Procedures, and Goal(s) in the Search Process

A **state space** represents the set of all attainable states for a given problem. It is often useful to express the problem graphically because graphics illustrate not only the state space, but also the search process. The most common graphic presentations are described next.

Graphic Presentations

Directed State Graph. Figure 2.5 is a **state graph** for a simple problem: attempting to find the best path from one city, the source (S), to another city, the destination, or goal (G). This state graph is a map showing the various intermediate towns and cities that would be passed through in reaching the desired destination. In such a problem, there often will be several alternative routes. The problem is to reach the destination in the least amount of time, or using the shortest route.

The nodes in a state graph are interconnected by arcs, or links, which usually have arrows showing the direction from one state to the next. The arcs represent the application of an operator to a node. The numbers above the arcs represent the distance (or travel time) between nodes.

In practice, it is difficult to represent a state graph such as that in Figure 2.5 in a software form. For example, some of the paths through the state graph can be retraced repeatedly. The path "S to node B to node A back to node S" could be repeated over and over again. Such endless loops cannot be tolerated

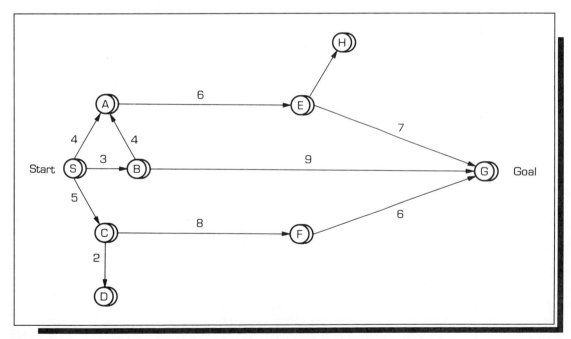

FIGURE 2.5 State Graph Showing Alternate Routes from the Start (S) to the Goal (G)

in a computer program and, therefore, some procedure must be followed to eliminate undesired cyclical conditions such as this. This is done by converting the state graph into a search tree.

Search Tree. A **search tree** based on the state graph in Figure 2.5 is illustrated in Figure 2.6. The new tree diagram states the same problem but in a slightly different format. The network thus formed is more like a hierarchy. Note that some of the nodes are repeated to eliminate the cyclical loop problem described earlier.

A special language has been developed to describe a search tree. For example, the initial state node is called the *root node*. It usually describes the object (or topic). Other nodes branch out from the root. These successor, or descendant, nodes are also sometimes referred to as children. They are intermediate nodes. Working backwards through the tree, nodes are said to have predecessors, ancestors, or parents. Nodes with no children or successors are called *leaf nodes*. They designate the end of the search, either by arriving at a goal or by being at a dead end. The interconnecting arcs are referred to as branches. Note in Figure 2.6 that a search tree is divided into various levels that are a function of the hierarchy. These levels describe the *depth* of the tree. The root node is usually designated level 0, and successively deeper levels are

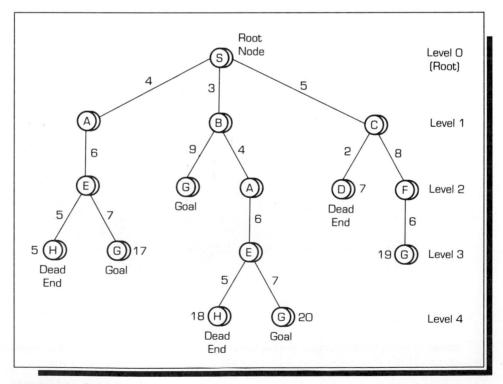

FIGURE 2.6 Search Tree

designated sequentially from numbers 1 through the highest level required to represent the state space.

AND/OR branches are another aspect of search trees. The branches from a node to its successors can represent two or more alternative paths to subgoals. One path or another could lead to the goal. We call these OR nodes because one branch, OR another, OR another could be the path to the goal.

In some problems, however, the successor nodes might represent problem states that must all be achieved or traversed before the goal is reached. These are referred to as AND nodes. One subgoal AND another subgoal (AND possibly others) must be achieved to solve the problem.

A search tree is also known as problem reduction representation because it can be used to divide a problem into subproblems in a clear way. Box 2.1 illustrates such a representation.

2.6 Blind Search Methods

A blind search is a collection of procedures used arbitrarily to search a state space. Blind search methods can be classified as exhaustive or partial (Figure 2.7), and the two partial methods are distinguished as breadth-first and depth-first methods.

Exhaustive Search

In an **exhaustive search** operators are used to generate successor states. Beginning at the root node, the search continues until a solution is found. The idea behind an exhaustive search is to examine the *entire* tree in an orderly manner, using all the operators and generating as many successor nodes as possible to find the desired solution.

Starting with the root node, several procedures are possible for proceeding through the tree; but the approaches are usually inefficient. In very large problems, a huge number of new states are generated and many alternatives are considered. As a result, it takes a considerable amount of time and effort to find the solution. Very-high-speed computers make blind search acceptable for some problems; however, others are too large for an exhaustive search.

Consider the possible number of moves in a chess game—estimated to be 10 to the 120th power. For such cases, a heuristic search is more appropriate. However, for many other cases the following two partial blind search methods can be effective.

Partial Search

Breadth-first Search. A **breadth-first search** examines all of the nodes (states) in a search tree, beginning with the root node. The nodes in each level are examined completely before moving on to the next level. A simple breadth-first search is illustrated in Figure 2.8. The numbers inside the node circles designate the sequence in which the nodes are examined. In this instance, the search (follow the broken line) would actually end at node 7, as that is the goal state.

A breadth-first search of the state space will usually find the shortest path between the initial state and the goal state, with the least number of steps.

Box 2.1: Buying a New Car

How should you buy a new car? Well, you can divide the problem into three subproblems—analysis, shopping, and financing—as shown in the illustration.

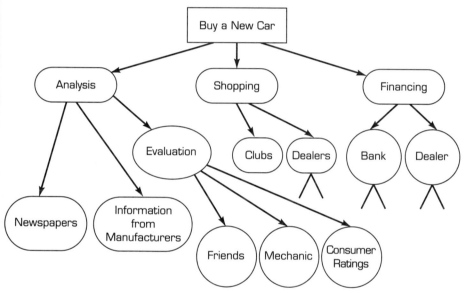

Problem Reduction Approach to Buying a New Car

Subproblem 1, analysis, can be divided further to reading newspapers and magazines, requesting information from manufacturers, and checking evaluations. The last subproblem can be divided into evaluation by friends, by consumer magazines, or by your friendly mechanic. Shopping and financing can be broken down to subproblems in a similar manner.

The problem is subdivided until no further subdivision is necessary. At this time a solution to the subproblem is available. (Perhaps your solution is a red Saab.)

The process requires operators to transform problems into subproblems and then to further subproblems. Also, the solutions to the subproblems (called primitive problem statements) must be related to the initial goal.

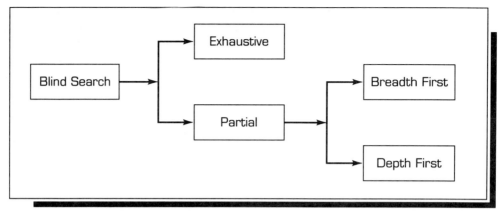

FIGURE 2.7   Blind Search Methods

The process usually starts at the initial state node and works *downward* in the tree from left to right. A terminal node is not necessarily a goal node; it can be a dead-end node. Breadth-first procedures are good when the number of paths emanating from each goal is relatively small and where the number of levels in each branch is of a different depth (number of levels).

Depth-first Search. A **depth-first search** begins at the root node and works downward to successively deeper levels. An operator is applied to the node to generate the next deeper node in sequence. This process continues until a solution is found or backtracking is forced by reaching a dead end.

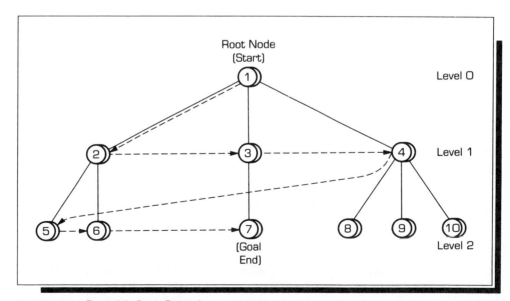

FIGURE 2.8   Breadth-first Search

A simple depth-first search is illustrated in Figure 2.9. Again, the numbers inside the nodes designate the sequence of nodes generated or searched. This process seeks the deepest possible nodes. If a goal state is not reached in this way, the search process *backtracks* to the next highest level node where additional paths are available to follow. This process continues downward and in a left-to-right direction until the state goal is discovered. Here, the search would actually end at node 13.

When a dead-end node is discovered, such as node 4 in Figure 2.9, the search process *backtracks* so that any additional branching alternative at the next higher node level is attempted. The search backs up to node 3. It has no alternate paths, so the search backtracks to node 2. Here, another path through node 5 is available. The path through node 6 is explored until its depth is exhausted. The backtracking continues until the goal is reached.

The depth-first search guarantees a solution, but the search may be a long one. Many different branches will have to be considered to a maximum depth before a solution is reached. (By setting a "depth bound," it is frequently possible to reduce the search.) The method is especially attractive in cases where short paths exist and where there are no lengthy sub-branches.

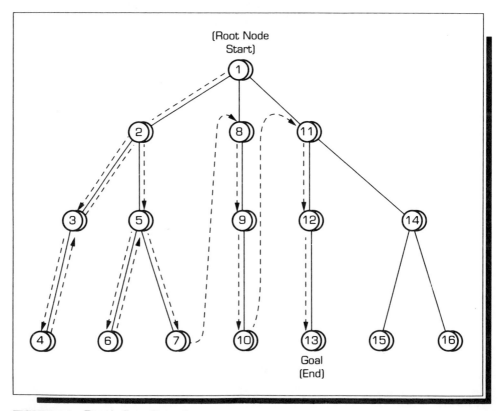

FIGURE 2.9 Depth-first Search

2.7   Heuristic Methods

Heuristic search methods are designed to reduce the amount of search for a solution (see Box 2.2). When a problem is presented as a search tree, the heuristic approach attempts to reduce the size of the tree by pruning nonvital or nonpromising nodes. For example, when the Coast Guard searches for a missing person at sea, they don't check the entire ocean. Currents, winds, and other factors are used to limit the search area. Although such an approach does not guarantee that the person will be found, it does work well in most cases, saving time and expediting the search. Such an approach is not optimal, so it is termed *good enough*. The question is to determine what to consider and what not to consider in the search. There are several methods, or approaches, to answer such a question. Some representative methods, which are sometimes used in conjunction with each other, are presented next. Heuristics do, however, have some limitations (see Box 2.3).

Representative Approaches

Generate and Test. The basic idea is to **generate** (via rules) possible candidate solutions and devise a **test** to determine if the solutions are indeed good. An example is opening a combination lock without knowing the combination. One way to execute this search is to follow a five-step procedure (suggested by Wolfgram et al. [21]):

Box 2.2: Major Benefits of Heuristics

Heuristic methods can be advantageous in the search process.

1. Heuristic approaches have an inherent flexibility, which allows them to be used on ill-structured and complex problems.
2. Although an exact (blind search) solution procedure may exist, it may be computationally prohibitive to use, or unrealistic in its data requirements. In such cases, heuristic methods are better.
3. The heuristic method, by design, may be simpler for the decision maker to understand, especially when it is composed of (or supported by) qualitative analysis. Hence, the chances of implementing the proposed solution are much higher.
4. A heuristic method may be used as part of an iterative procedure that guarantees the finding of an optimal solution.

(*Source*: Condensed from E. Turban and J. Meredith, *Fundamentals of Management Science*, 5th ed. [Homewood, Ill.: Richard D. Irwin, 1991].)

Box 2.3: Major Disadvantages and Limitations of Heuristics

Despite their potential advantages, heuristics should not be considered an easy way out. They do have several disadvantages and limitations.

1. The inherent flexibility of heuristic methods can lead to misleading or even fraudulent manipulations and solutions.
2. Certain heuristics may contradict others that are applied to the same problem, which generates confusion and lack of trust in heuristic methods.
3. Optimal solutions are not identified. *Local improvement* heuristics can short-circuit the best solution because they lack a global perspective. The gap between the optimal solution and the one generated by heuristics may be large; potential losses may exceed the benefits. Since an optimal solution is not generated, it is frequently difficult to evaluate the recommendations generated by heuristic problem solving.
4. Heuristics are not as general as algorithms; therefore, they can normally be used only for the specific situations intended. For this reason, special computer programs are necessary for each heuristic.
5. Enumeration heuristics that consider all possible combinations in practical problems can seldom be achieved.
6. Sequential decision choices can fail to anticipate future consequences of each choice.
7. Interdependencies in one part of the system can sometimes have a profound influence on the whole system.

(*Source:* Based in part on A.M. Geoffrion and T.J. van Roy, "Caution: Common Sense Planning Methods Can Be Hazardous to Your Corporate Health," *Sloan Management Review* [1979].)

1. Add a specification criterion (e.g., a known symptom, such as it is common to open a combination lock by turning it first to the left).
2. Try a path that satisfies the specification.
3. Determine whether the path is plausible; "prune" that path if it is not plausible.
4. Move to the next path.
5. Check to see if all specifications have been mentioned. If not, add the next specification criterion and reiterate the steps by returning to step 1. If all specifications have been resolved, the process is complete.

The generate and test method is effective only if pruning can be done early in the search so many paths can be eliminated.

Hill Climbing. The **hill-climbing** method is similar to a depth-first blind search. However, paths are not selected arbitrarily, but in relationship to their proximity to the desired goal. The search tree in Figure 2.10 illustrates the concept. Each production process I, II, and III can continue for several stages, in which several states (nodes) exist. The numbers above the nodes designate the potential number of defects in a specific product at a certain state in the process. The more stages we go through, the fewer defects we will find. The target is to find the method with the minimum number of defects.

A depth-first search goes to I, then to II, and then to III. If the desired number of defects is two, then the process is speedy. But, if the goal is one defect, then the entire tree will have to be visited. In the hill-climbing method, nodes B, C, and D are compared, and a search starts in branch I (the lowest number of defects—8). Since one defect was not discovered, backtracking is done to branch III. (III is done before II since there are fewer defects on D than on C.) The search goes to D and H; backtracking is then exercised and the D—G—J path leads to the desired solution. Path A—C—F was *not* visited. Thus, hill climbing is faster than a depth-first search.

Variations of this method exist, and the saving over a blind search can be substantial if large trees are involved.

Induction. **Induction** means to generalize from a smaller (or simpler) version of the same problem. Two features of induction are essential. First, in the problem statement the problem must be modeled in terms of the associated (or predicted) data. Second, the induced result must be tested against real examples to verify its reasonableness.

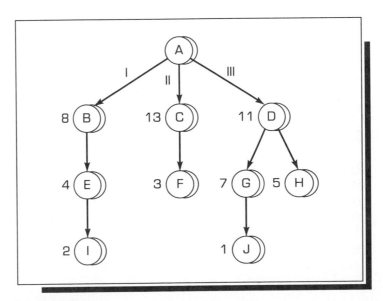

FIGURE 2.10 Hill Climbing

Construction. The input for methods based on the construction strategy is the data that defines a specific instance of the problem. A solution is built up one component at a time. A construction strategy begins by examining this data and attempting to identify an element that is likely to be a valuable part of a good final solution. Next, successive additional elements of a solution are added. Once the final solution has been built up, it may be obvious that *improvements* can be made. Therefore, the hill-climbing procedure is often applied to the output of the construction method.

Component Analysis Strategy. Some problems are so large or so complicated that the only practical approach is to break them into manageable portions. These portions are then dealt with independently by heuristics and/or algorithms. The solutions for the portions are then combined. Of course, it may be extremely difficult to piece the solutions to the different components into an acceptable plan. This approach is also called the *decomposition method.*

Best First. In the **best-first approach,** which is based on some heuristic evaluation function, you select the next move by searching for the *best* available solution that you can move to in one step, no matter where it is located on the tree. For example, you are about to cross a stream and there are many rocks on your way. First you go the most promising one, then you look around and make the best progress you can. If you evaluate only one jump at a time, you are using the best-first approach. This procedure is often labeled "greedy," since it is shortsighted. It searches only one step at a time instead of looking at the entire set of steps.

Exercise 9 illustrates the danger of following this approach. An implementation of the best-first approach is called the A* algorithm.

Other Approaches. Several other heuristic approaches can be useful, especially when numeric analysis is involved. For details and for a discussion on how to select an appropriate method see Newell and Simon [10], Foulds [3], and Silver et al. [15].

Example of a Heuristic Search:
Traveling Salesperson Problem (TSP)

The Problem. A traveling salesperson must visit N cities in a territory. The salesperson starts from a base, visits each city once, and returns to his or her home city at the end. The TSP attempts to find the best route (in terms of least cost, or least distance).

The Difficulty. The number of possible routes (R) (counting only one direction route) is $R = 0.5(N - 1)!$

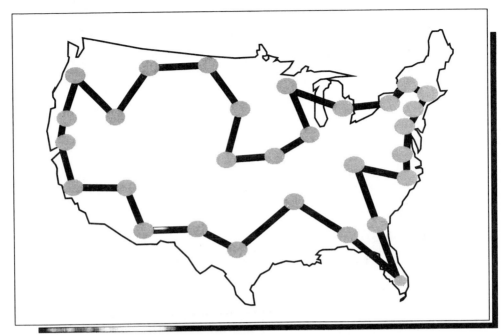

FIGURE 2.11 Heuristic Solution to the Traveling Salesperson Problem (*Source:* A. J. Rowe, "The Meta Logic of Cognitively Based Heuristics," special report, Univ. of Southern Southern California, Los Angeles, 1988.)

For ten cities there are 181,440 routes, for eleven cities there are about 2 million different routes, and for twenty cities there are approximately 6.1×10^{16} routes. This is a typical combinatorial problem. With the addition of just a few more cities, the problem grows to an astronomical number of alternatives.

The Solutions. Complete enumeration and algorithms are inefficient or ineffective. Heuristic solutions provide good enough solutions, sometimes very quickly.

Heuristic Solutions. A heuristic solution is shown in Figure 2.11. The solution has been derived in a single iteration. The heuristic is: "Start from any point, build up an *exterior* path, with no crossovers or backtracking, and return to the original city."

See exercise 4 at the end of the chapter for another heuristic problem.

2.8 Control Strategies

Once a search method is selected it needs to be activated. That is, it is necessary to decide which operators to apply and when to apply them. In a rule-based system, for example, we must decide which rule to check next. Four basic control strategies are common: forward chaining, backward chaining, means-end, and least commitment. A brief description of each is given in this section, while a detailed illustration will be provided in forthcoming chapters.

Forward Chaining

The **forward chaining** method emulates human deductive reasoning. It is a data-driven process that starts when certain information is provided by the user. Clues are collected as we move toward a conclusion. For example, review the search processes shown in Figures 2.8 and 2.9. See also Box 2.4.

Backward Chaining

Backward chaining is a goal-driven search strategy. It begins with the goal and works backward towards the initial conditions. The process starts with a hypothesis; a search is then launched to find and verify the necessary supporting facts. The process ends with the acceptance or rejection of the hypothesis. Details of this and the previous strategy, which form the backbone of rule-based inferencing, are given in Chapter 6.

Means-End Analysis

Means-end analysis is an iterative process of subdividing the difference between the current state and the goal state until the difference is eliminated. The solution shows the *means* by which to traverse the knowledge base. The method applies a set of operators that assist in moving us toward the goal. The method attempts to achieve the difference reduction in the most efficient manner; that is, by selecting the appropriate operators, in the proper sequence. For example, you live in a ranch near Austin, Tex., and you would like to see the Statue of Liberty in New York. You have a short vacation. The distance between Austin and New York is about 1,800 miles (the "difference"). The operator that is most effective in reducing this difference is to "fly." To activate this operator you need to reach an airport which is 23 miles away. Now you need a means to satisfy a subgoal of getting to the airport. For that you need another operator (e.g., drive or be driven in a cab). In either case, you have to get a car; similarly, several more operators will be needed to help reach your goal (see exercise 5).

Least Commitment

According to the **least commitment control strategy,** we assume that no decision should be made until there is enough information. To activate this approach,

Box 2.4: Brain Teaser—Red and Blue Exchange Problem

Suppose you have two red (R) tokens and two blue (B) ones. Currently they are organized on a five slot board as follows:

R	R		B	B

The middle slot is empty. Your objective (the goal) is to exchange places as shown here:

B	B		R	R

You would like to do it as fast as possible. There are three legal moves (operators):

1. Move a token one space at a time. Red moves to the right (only) and blue moves to the left (only).
2. You may jump over one occupied slot, adjacent to you. For example:

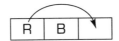

   Remember, red jumps to the right only and blue to the left only.

3. You cannot take a token off the board.

Question: What is the smallest number of moves that is necessary to complete the exchange? See exercise 16.

(*Source:* Adapted from P. Harmon and D. King, *Expert Systems* [New York: John Wiley & Sons, 1985].)

we need to know what is "enough information." Also, we need to know what to do when there is *not* enough information (e.g., how to get additional information, or when to make a guess). This control strategy could be combined with neural computing (Chapter 18) to increase the reliability of the "guesses."

Control strategies are implemented by a control program called the **inference engine.** The program determines how and in what sequence the state space, which is the **knowledge base,** is searched. The inference engine and the knowledge base are the two major components of the most widely used AI technology—expert systems.

2.9   A Search Example

To help you understand the concepts of search trees and techniques, let's consider an example. Refer to Figure 2.12. A computer-controlled robot arm is to be used to move the blocks on a table in a particular sequence from the initial state to the goal state. An AI search program will determine the sequence of movement of the arm.

The operator for this program is a command that says "move X to Y," or rather "put block X on top of another block, Y, or on the surface of the table." Here X and Y are general terms that refer to the individual blocks or the table surface. In Figure 2.12, X or Y may be A, B, C, or the table. A specific version of the operator might be "move C to A." Here, X = C and Y = A. The operator says to put block C on top of block A. To use the operator, there must be nothing else on top of X, the block that is to be moved. If Y is a block and not the table surface, there should be nothing on top of Y.

Using the operator repeatedly, we can generate the complete search tree for this problem. That is, we can determine all possible moves beginning with the initial state. Each time we use the operator we create a new node. The initial and goal nodes are indicated in Figure 2.13.

Once the search tree is drawn, we can answer these two questions: Which produces the lowest-cost search from initial state to goal, a depth-first or breadth-first search? Is the search forward or backward?

The search tree for this problem is illustrated in Figure 2.13. All possible moves are illustrated. For example, node 1 is obtained by moving block A from block B to the surface of the table with the operator command, "move A to table." Node 2 is obtained by moving A from B to C. Node 3 is obtained by moving C to A. The remaining nodes are generated in a similar manner.

The idea of the search is to get to the goal state as quickly as possible with the fewest moves. If we assume that the cost of any move from one node to another is one, then a depth-first search produces the "lowest-cost" solution. The cost is number of arcs traversed, including any in backtracking. The depth-first search has the following node sequence: 0—1—4—9—4—1—5—10. That is seven node transitions. The breadth-first search is 0—1—2—3—4—5—6—7—8—9—10, or ten node transitions. Thus the depth-first search is faster and has the lowest cost. Work through this yourself to be sure you understand it. Forward reasoning (chaining) is used as we move from the initial state to the goal state.

Chapter Highlights

- □ Problem solving is similar to decision making where both problems and opportunities are examined.
- □ Humans follow a fairly standard problem-solving process.

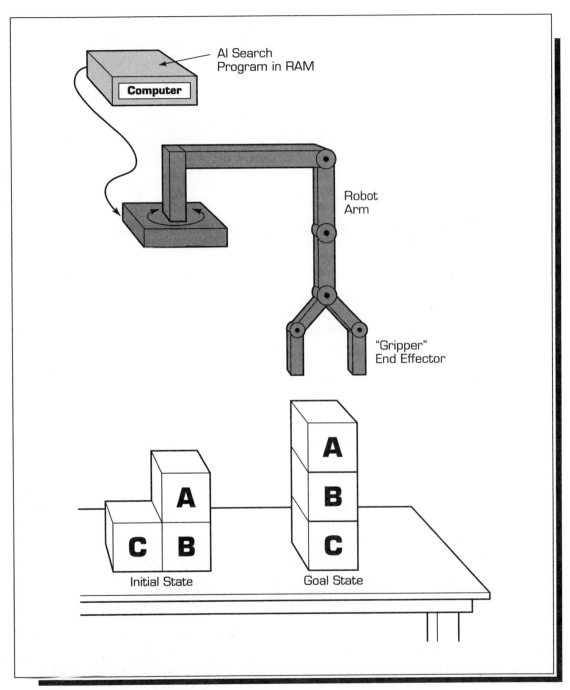

Computer

AI Search
Program in RAM

Robot
Arm

"Gripper"
End Effector

A
C B
Initial State

A
B
C
Goal State

FIGURE 2.12 Example of a Search

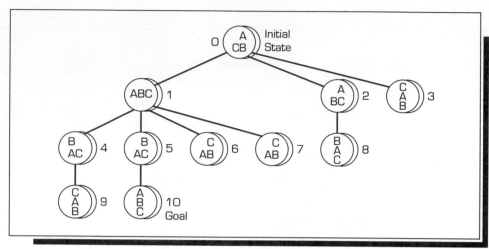

FIGURE 2.13 Search Tree for the Block Moving Problem

□ The process starts with problem definition and ends with implementation of the selected course of action.

□ The six steps in the problem-solving process are problem identification and definition, criteria identification, generation of alternative solutions, search for solution and evaluation, choice and recommendation, and implementation.

□ A model of human problem solving is composed of perceptual, cognitive, and motor subsystems and external memory. It explains how information is processed for problem solving.

□ Applied AI technology attempts to imitate the process that people follow. Commercial systems have been successful mainly in the search and choice steps.

□ Three basic search strategies exist: optimization, blind search, and heuristic search. The last two are used extensively in AI technologies.

□ Blind search is an arbitrary procedure; it can be either exhaustive, leading to a best solution, or incomplete, leading to a good enough solution.

□ Blind search can be a lengthy process, even when high-power computers are used.

□ Combinatorial explosion is the geometric multiplication of search state possibilities that often makes blind search impractical for real-world problems.

□ Heuristic search employs rules that can expedite the search. It is an application of judgment, intuition, and rules of thumb.

□ AI search techniques are either data driven (toward a goal), goal driven (starting from the goal), or a combination of both.

□ The search process begins with an initial state or known fact. A control strategy uses procedures to manipulate the initial state to reach a goal or conclusion. This repetitive process is called search.

□ Problem solving in AI is presented as a state-space arrangement. Procedures, which are called operators, are employed to move from an initial status to a target.

□ Problems to be solved can be represented as a state space made up of nodes connected by arcs to show the various problem states and how they are interrelated.

□ Most AI problems are represented in the form of a graph or network made up of nodes and arcs and called a search tree. The search tree has an initial or starting state, multiple intermediate problem states, and one or more goal states.

□ Blind search examines all possible states in the search tree looking for a solution. It is costly and time consuming but will always yield a conclusion.

□ The methods of partial blind search are breadth-first and depth-first.

□ A breadth-first search examines all states in a search tree one at a time from left to right and top to bottom one level at a time. Beginning with the initial state, a breadth-first search looks at all the states on each level before proceeding to the next lower level. The search stops when a goal state is found.

□ Depth-first search examines all problem states. It seeks successively deeper problem states rather than those on the same level, and then it backtracks, if required, until a goal state is found.

□ Several procedures employing heuristic search can reduce the time for search, but they yield only good enough solutions.

□ In rule-based systems control strategies called forward and backward chaining are used. Means-end and least commitment strategies can also be used.

□ A forward chaining search is one that begins at the initial state and continues to the goal state (a data-driven approach).

□ A backward chaining search begins with a potential goal state (goal-driven approach) and works backward through the search tree seeking proof, justification, or support.

Key Terms

AND/OR branch	exhaustive search	long-term memory
backward chaining	forward chaining	means-end analysis
best-first approach	generate and test	motor subsystem
blind search	goal-directed search	operator
breadth-first search	heuristics	optimization
cognitive subsystem	heuristic search	perceptual subsystem
combinatorial explosion	hill climbing	problem solving
complete enumeration	induction	search tree
control strategy	inference engine	short-term memory
data-directed search	knowledge base	state (of a problem)
decision making	least commitment	state graph
depth-first search	control strategy	state space

Questions for Review

1. Define problem solving and compare it with decision making.
2. List the various steps of the problem-solving process.
3. Discuss this statement: Criteria should be determined before alternatives are generated.
4. Which of the steps in the problem-solving process are particularly amenable for AI and why?
5. List the four types of memory of human information systems.
6. Describe the major components of the Newell-Simon model.
7. The Newell-Simon model is said to present problem solving as information processing. Explain why.
8. List and define the three major search strategies.
9. Optimization is not considered an AI approach. Why?
10. Why are heuristics more acceptable to managers than algorithms?
11. Define blind search. List two major advantages and two major disadvantages.
12. Give two definitions of heuristics. Why are there several definitions?
13. What are the major advantages of heuristic search? What are the major limitations?
14. Compare data-directed (forward) with goal-directed (backward) searches.
15. What is a state-space representation and search? What is its role in AI?
16. Define operators and describe their role in AI.
17. What is control strategy? What does it do? Give examples of control strategy.
18. What is the advantage of a state tree over a state graph?
19. What is the purpose of an AND/OR branch?
20. Explain the difference between breadth-first and depth-first searches.
21. Explain how a heuristic method can reduce the size of the search tree.
22. Explain the phrase generate and test.
23. Compare and contrast hill climbing and depth-first search.
24. The best-first method is described as "greedy." Explain why.
25. Compare and contrast the concepts of forward chaining and backward chaining. Explain which is data driven and which is goal driven.
26. Define means-end analysis and give an example (different from the one in the book).

Exercises

1. Study the search tree given here. The numbers above the nodes illustrate the profit associated with a project designated by the specific nodes. The goal is to find a project with a value of twenty or higher.
   a. Use a breadth-first approach to identify the node.
   b. Use a depth-first approach to identify the node.
   c. Use a hill-climbing approach to identify the node.
   d. Compare the efficiency of the search approaches in this case. (Count the number of paths checked and nodes visited.)

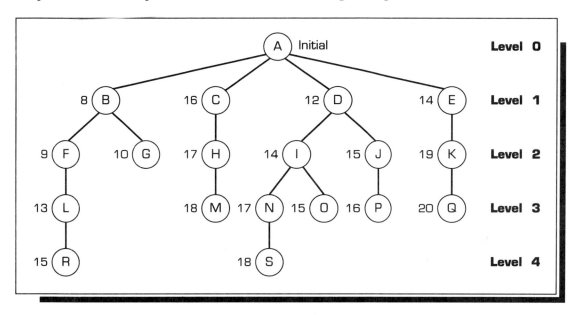

2. Use the best-first approach to solve the previous problem. You can go only within one level in each move.
3. In a typical chess game there are 10^{120} possible moves. You developed a computer that can examine 300 billion moves in one second! (It will take many years before we can have such a computer.) With this computer you are attempting to conduct a blind search, checking all moves. How long will it take to complete the search?
4. a. Apply the best-first approach to the traveling salesperson problem in the figure given here. The numbers are distances. Start from city 5.
   b. Change the data on arc 5 to 7, to 6 (from 4) and resolve.

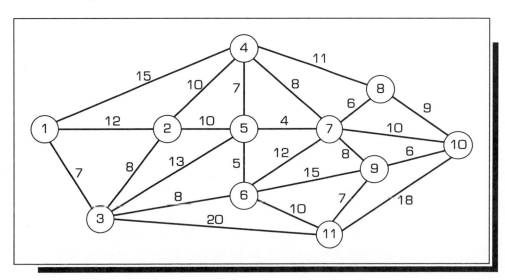

5. List all the "operators" to be used in getting from your ranch in Austin, Tex., to the Statue of Liberty in New York. You may use your car, which you will park in remote airport parking. Your target is located on an island reachable only by commercially operated boat.

6. Prepare a table that will compare information processing by a human (per Newell-Simon) and information processing by a regular computer. Highlight the similarities and the differences. What are the advantages of the human over the computer and vice versa?

7. Read the article "Caution: Common Sense Planning Models Can Be Hazardous to Your Health" (A. M. Geoffrion and T. J. van Roy, *Sloan Management Review*, 1979). Prepare a list of the major hazards and discuss them briefly.

8. Assume you plan to drive from New York to Los Angeles to arrive midafternoon for an appointment. To arrive fresh, you want to drive no more than two hours the day you arrive, but on other days, you're willing to drive eight to ten hours. One logical way to approach this problem is to start at Los Angeles, your goal, and work backward. You would first find a place about two hours from Los Angeles for your final stopover before arrival; then plan the rest of your trip by working backward on a map until your route is planned completely. You have a limited number of days to complete the trip.

   How would you analyze the problem starting from New York? What are the major differences? Which approach would you use? Why?

9. Your mission is to process three jobs on one machine (one after the other) with the least possible changeover time. The machine is currently empty. The table below shows you how long it takes, in minutes, to change from one job (or from "empty") to another. Use the best-first approach, starting from the empty position, to determine a proposed sequence. Then conduct a complete enumeration and compare the results.

From Job	To Job 1	2	3
empty	25	20	30
1	0	35	20
2	50	0	20
3	45	10	0

10. There are 150 million cars in the United States. Someone has suggested that a national license plate be used to register all cars. The plate will include four letters followed by three digits. Some people say that four letters and three digits will be sufficient for identifying all cars, but others say, "No way!" Who do you think is right and why? (Be specific.)

11. The table shows a doctor's patients, who are waiting for their appointments, and the corresponding projected treatment times. The doctor wishes to schedule the patients to minimize average waiting time. Formulate two

heuristic rules and compare them with taking the patients in the order given (A, B, . . . , F).

Patient	Treatment Time (hours)
A	1.0
B	.2
C	2.0
D	1.5
E	.1
F	.7

12. It is fairly hot outside and the water is not running in your house. Your mission is to find out why there is no water. Usually, it's because of frozen pipes or because the water department closed the main valve for repairs. You know that immediately after the main valve is turned off there is a banging noise in the pipes. Use a generate-and-test approach to solve this problem.

13. Many managers know that a small percent of the customers contribute to most of the sales. Similarly, most of the wealth in the world is concentrated in the hands of a few. This phenomenon is called the 20-80, the A-B-C, or the value-volume, and it is attributed to the famous economist, Pareto. How can this phenomenon be used in modeling? What kind of approach is it—optimization, blind search, or heuristic?

14. Assume that you know that there is one irregular coin (either lighter or heavier) among twelve. Using a two-pan scale you must find that coin (is it lighter or heavier?) in no more than three tests.
   a. Solve this problem and explain the weighing strategy that you use.
   b. What approach to problem solving did you use in this case?

15. Your mission is to invest in the stock market. To do so you need to select a broker, open an account, and then start to trade. Prepare a problem reduction tree that will describe how you invest in the market.

16. Solve the brain-teaser problem (Box 2.4) by complete enumeration. Show the entire search tree. Can it be solved by heuristics? (If yes, try some.) Can it be solved by any other approach?

References and Bibliography

1. Bell, D.E., et al. *Decision Making*. New York: Cambridge Univ. Press, 1988.
2. Findler, N., and B. Meltzer. *Artificial Intelligence and Heuristic Programming*. New York: Elsevier, 1971.
3. Foulds, L.R. "The Heuristic Problem-Solving Approach." *Journal of the Operational Research Society* (October 1983).

4. Geoffrion, A.M., and T.J. van Roy. "Caution: Common Sense Planning Methods Can Be Hazardous to Your Corporate Health." *Sloan Management Review* (1979).

5. Genesereth, M.R., and N.J. Nilssen. *Logical Foundations of Artificial Intelligence*, San Mateo, Calif.: Morgan Kaufman, 1987.

6. Golden, B.L., and A.A. Assad. "A Decision-Theoretic Framework for Comparing Heuristics." *European Journal of Operations Research* 18 (1984).

7. Harmon, P., and D. King. *Expert Systems*. New York: John Wiley & Sons, 1985.

8. Jeter, M.W. *Mathematical Programming—An Introduction to Optimization*. New York: Marcel Dekker, 1986.

9. Lugar, G.F., and W.A. Stubblefield. *Artificial Intelligence and the Origin of Expert Systems*. Redwood City, Calif.: Benjamin-Cummings, 1989.

10. Newell, A., and H.A. Simon. *Human Problem Solving*. Englewood Cliffs, N.J.: Prentice-Hall, 1972.

11. Patterson, D.W. *Introduction to Artificial Intelligence and Expert Systems*. Englewood Cliffs, N.J.: Prentice-Hall, 1990.

12. Pearl, J. *Heuristics: Intelligent Search Strategies for Computer Problem Solving*. Reading, Mass.: Addison-Wesley, 1984.

13. Ramsay, A. *Formal Methods in Artificial Intelligence*. Cambridge: Cambridge Univ. Press, 1988.

14. Rowe, A.J. "The Meta Logic of Cognitively Based Heuristics." Special Report. Los Angeles, Univ. of Southern California, 1988.

15. Silver, E.A., et al. "A Tutorial on Heuristic Methods." *European Journal of Operational Research* (no. 5, 1980).

16. Simon, H. *The New Science of Management Decisions*. rev. ed. Englewood Cliffs, N.J.: Prentice-Hall, 1977.

17. Stainton, R.S., and D.B. Papoulias. "Heuristics—The Rational Approach." *European Journal of Operational Research* 17 (1984).

18. Taylor, J., and W. Taylor. "Searching for Solutions." *PC Magazine* (September 15, 1987).

19. Turban, E., and J. Meredith. *Fundamentals of Management Science*. 5th ed. Homewood, Ill.: Richard D. Irwin, 1991.

20. Widman, L.E., et al. *Artificial Intelligence, Simulation and Modelling*. New York: John Wiley & Sons, 1989.

21. Wolfgram, D.D., et al. *Expert Systems for the Technical Professional*. New York: John Wiley & Sons, 1987.

22. Zanakis, S.H., et al., "Heuristic Methods and Applications: A Categorized Survey." *European Journal of Operational Research* (no. 43, 1989).

Chapter 3

Fundamentals of Expert Systems

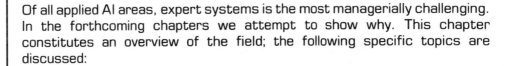

Of all applied AI areas, expert systems is the most managerially challenging. In the forthcoming chapters we attempt to show why. This chapter constitutes an overview of the field; the following specific topics are discussed:

3.1   Introduction

The name *expert systems* was derived from the term *knowledge-based expert systems*. An **expert system** is a system that employs human knowledge captured in a computer to solve problems that ordinarily require human expertise. Well-designed systems imitate the reasoning processes experts use to solve specific problems. Such systems can be used by nonexperts to improve their problem-solving capabilities. Expert systems (ES)[1] can also be used by experts as knowledgeable assistants. ES are used to propagate scarce knowledge resources for improved, consistent results. Ultimately, such systems could function better than any single human expert in making judgments in a specific, usually narrow, area of expertise (referred to as a **domain**). This possibility may have a significant impact both on advisory professionals (financial analysts, lawyers, tax advisors, etc.) and on organizations and their management.

The purpose of this chapter is to introduce the fundamentals of expert systems. A brief history is followed by an actual case. The case leads to a presentation of the basic ideas of ES as well as to its capabilities and structure. Finally, various types of ES, their benefits, and their limitations are discussed.

3.2   History of Expert Systems

Expert systems were developed by the AI community as early as the mid-1960s. This period of AI research was dominated by a belief that a few laws of reasoning coupled with powerful computers would produce expert or even superhuman performance. One attempt in this direction was the General-purpose Problem Solver.

General-purpose Problem Solver

The General-purpose Problem Solver (GPS), a procedure developed by Newell and Simon [11] from their Logic Theory Machine, was an attempt to create an "intelligent" computer. Thus, it can be viewed as a predecessor to ES. GPS tries to work out the steps needed to change a certain initial situation into a desired goal state (see Chapter 2). For each problem to be solved, GPS is given (1) a set of operators that can change a situation in various ways, (2) a statement of what preconditions each operator needs to be true before it can be applied, and (3) a list of postconditions that will be true after the operator has been used. It also has an optional set of heuristics for operators to try first. In ES terms, these form a rule base.

---

[1]ES is both a singular and plural abbreviation (expert system or expert systems).

GPS attempts to find operators that reduce the difference between a goal and current states. Sometimes the operators cannot operate on the current states (their preconditions are not suitable). In such cases, GPS sets itself a subgoal: to change the current state into one that is suitable for the operators. Many such subgoals may have to be set before GPS can solve a problem.

GPS, like several other similar programs, did not fulfill its inventors' dreams. Nevertheless, such programs did produce extremely important side benefits. For example, PROLOG is an AI computer language based on Robinson's work on automatic theorem proving [13]. LISP compilers and "garbage collectors" (which will be discussed later in this book) are also based on work in the area of general problem-solving methodology.

Early Expert Systems

The shift from general-purpose to special-purpose programs occurred in the mid-1960s with the development of DENDRAL[2] by E. Feigenbaum at Stanford University, followed up by the development of MYCIN (see Appendix C at the end of this chapter). At that time researchers also recognized that the problem-solving mechanism is only a small part of a complete, intelligent computer system.

The construction of DENDRAL (one of the first two expert systems ever built) led to the following conclusions:

- General problem solvers are too weak to be used as the basis for building high-performance ES.
- Human problem solvers are good only if they operate in a very narrow domain.
- Expert systems need to be constantly updated for new information. Such updating can be done efficiently with rule-based representation.
- The complexity of problems requires a considerable amount of knowledge about the problem area.

By the mid-1970s, several expert systems had begun to emerge. Recognizing the central role of knowledge in these systems, AI scientists worked to develop comprehensive knowledge representation theories and associated general-purpose decision-making procedures and inferences. Within a few years it became apparent that these efforts had limited success for reasons similar to those that doomed the first general problem solvers. "Knowledge," as a target of study, is too broad and diverse; efforts to solve knowledge-based problems in general were premature. On the other hand, several different approaches to knowledge representation proved sufficient for the expert systems that employed them. A key insight was learned at that time: *The power of an ES is derived from*

---

[2]Systems referred to in this chapter are described in Appendix A at the end of the chapter.

the specific knowledge it possesses, not from the particular formalisms and inference schemes it employs. In short, an expert's knowledge per se seems both necessary and nearly sufficient to develop an expert system.

Figure 3.1 displays some of the developmental directions within the ES field. The field spans more than two decades, and because most projects continue for many years, the temporal positions shown in the figure are only approximate.

By the beginning of the 1980s, ES technology, first limited to the academic scene, began to appear as commercial applications. Notable were XCON (see Appendix C) and XSEL (developed from R-1, at Digital Equipment Corp.) and CATS-1 (developed at General Electric).

In addition to building ES, a substantial effort was made to develop tools for speeding up the construction of ES. These tools included programming tools like EMYCIN (see Chapter 13) and AGE, knowledge acquisition tools like EXPERT and KAS, and tools for learning from experience such as META-DENDRAL and EURISKO.

Such tools became commercially available starting in 1983. Most of the early development tools required special hardware (e.g., LISP machines), but since the late 1980s, development software can run on regular computers including microcomputers.

The following list indicates the latest developments in the expert system area:

- Availability of many tools (Chapter 13) that are designed to expedite the construction of ES at a reduced cost
- Dissemination of ES in thousands of organizations, some of which use hundreds or even thousands of specific systems
- Extensive integration of ES with other computer-based information systems, especially, integration with databases and decision support systems
- Increased use of expert systems in many tasks, ranging from help desks to complex military and space shuttle applications
- Use of ES technology as a methodology for expediting the construction of regular information systems
- Increased use of the object-oriented programming approach in knowledge representation
- Development of complex systems with multiple sources of knowledge, multiple lines of reasoning, and fuzzy information
- Use of multiple knowledge bases

3.3   The Case of CATS-1 (DELTA)

Problem

General Electric's (GE) top locomotive field service engineer, David I. Smith, had been with the company for more than forty years. He was the top expert

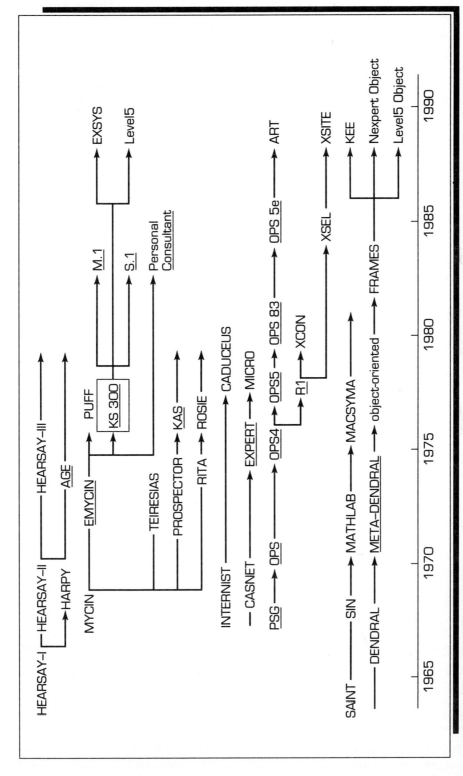

FIGURE 3.1 Evolution of Selected Expert Systems and Expert System Development Tools; Underlining Indicates Development Languages (*Source:* Modified from F. Hayes-Roth, et al., *Building Expert Systems* [Reading, Mass.: Addison-Wesley, 1983].)

in troubleshooting diesel electric locomotive engines. Smith was traveling throughout the country to places where locomotives were in need of repair to determine what was wrong and to advise young engineers about what to do. The company was very dependent on Smith. The problem was that he was nearing retirement.

Traditional Solution

GE's traditional approach to such a situation was to create teams that paired senior and junior engineers. The pairs worked together for several months or years, and by the time the older engineers finally did retire, the younger engineers had absorbed enough of their seniors' expertise to carry on troubleshooting or other tasks. This practice proved to be a good short-term solution, but GE still wanted a more effective and dependable way of disseminating expertise among its engineers, and preventing valuable knowledge from retiring with David Smith. Furthermore, having railroad service shops throughout the country requires extensive travel by an expert or moving the locomotives to an expert, because it is not economically feasible to have an expert in each shop.

Expert System

In 1980, GE decided to build an ES by modeling the way a human troubleshooter works. The system builders spent several months interviewing Smith and transferring his knowledge to a computer. The computer programming was prototyped over a three-year period, slowly increasing the information and the number of decision rules stored in the computer. The final product, called DELTA, was able to "reason" much the same way an experienced locomotive engineer reasons. The new diagnostic technology enables a novice engineer or a technician to uncover a fault by spending only a few minutes at the computer terminal. The system can also *explain* to the user the logic of its advice, thus serving as a teacher. Furthermore, the system can lead users through the required repair procedures, presenting a detailed, computer-aided drawing of parts and subsystems and providing specific how-to instructional demonstrations.

The system is based on a flexible, humanlike thought process, rather than rigid procedures expressed in flowcharts or decision trees.

The system, which was developed on a minicomputer but operates on a microcomputer, is currently installed at every railroad repair shop served by GE, thus eliminating delays and boosting maintenance productivity. For further information, see Bonissone and Johnson [2].

3.4   Basic Concepts of Expert Systems

The CATS-1 example introduces the basic concepts of expert systems: expertise, experts, transferring expertise, inferencing rules, and explanation capability.

These concepts are defined in this section; the remainder of the chapter is then devoted to a more detailed description and discussion of them and their role in ES.

Expertise

Expertise is the extensive, task-specific knowledge acquired from training, reading, and experience. The following types of knowledge are examples of what expertise includes:

- □ Facts about the problem area
- □ Theories about the problem area
- □ Hard-and-fast rules and procedures regarding the general problem area
- □ Rules (heuristics) of what to do in a given problem situation (i.e., rules regarding problem solving)
- □ Global strategies for solving these types of problems
- □ Meta-knowledge (knowledge about knowledge)

These types of knowledge enable experts to make better and faster decisions than nonexperts in solving complex problems. It takes a long time (usually several years) to become an expert, and novices become experts only incrementally.

Experts

It is difficult to define what an **expert** is because we actually talk about degrees or levels of expertise. (The question is how much expertise should a person possess before qualifying as an expert.) Nevertheless, it has been said that nonexperts outnumber experts in many fields by a ratio of 100 to 1. Distribution of expertise appears to be of the same shape regardless of the type of knowledge being evaluated. Figure 3.2 represents a typical distribution of expertise. The top tenth (decile) performs three times better than the average, and thirty times better than the lowest tenth. This distribution suggests that the overall effectiveness of human expertise can be significantly increased (up to 200 percent) if we can somehow make top-level expertise available to other decision makers.

Typically, human expertise includes a constellation of behavior that involves the following activities:

- □ Recognizing and formulating the problem
- □ Solving the problem quickly and properly
- □ Explaining the solution
- □ Learning from experience
- □ Restructuring knowledge
- □ Breaking rules
- □ Determining relevance
- □ Degrading gracefully

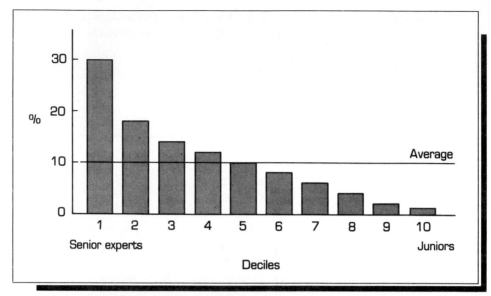

FIGURE 3.2 Distribution of Expertise: Percent Successes Achieved per Decile (*Source:* Adapted from N.R. Augustine, "Distribution of Expertise," *Defense Systems Management* [Spring 1979].)

Experts can take a problem stated in some arbitrary manner and convert it to a form that lends itself to a rapid and effective solution. Problem-solving ability is necessary, but not sufficient by itself. Experts should be able to explain the results, learn new things about the domain, restructure knowledge whenever needed, break rules whenever necessary (i.e., know the exceptions to the rules), and determine whether their expertise is relevant. Finally, experts "degrade gracefully," meaning that as they get close to the boundaries of their knowledge, they gradually become less proficient at solving problems. All these activities must be done efficiently (quickly and at low cost) and effectively (with high-quality results).

To mimic the human expert, it is necessary to build a computer that exhibits all these characteristics. To date (1992), work in ES has primarily explored the second and third of these activities (solving problems and explaining the solutions).

Transferring Expertise

The objective of an expert system is to transfer expertise from an expert to a computer and then on to other humans (nonexperts). This process involves four activities: knowledge acquisition (from experts or other sources), knowledge representation (in the computer), knowledge inferencing, and knowledge transfer to the user. The knowledge is stored in the computer in a component called a knowledge base. Two types of knowledge are distinguished: *facts* and *procedures* (usually rules) regarding the problem domain.

Inferencing

A unique feature of an expert system is its ability to reason. Given that all the expertise is stored in the knowledge base and that the program has accessibility to databases, the computer is programmed so that it can make inferences. The inferencing is performed in a component called the **inference engine,** which includes procedures regarding problem solving.

Rules

Most commercial ES are **rule-based systems**; that is, the knowledge is stored mainly in the form of rules, as are the problem-solving procedures. A rule in the CATS-1 example may look like this: "*IF*, the engine is idle, and the fuel pressure is less than 38 psi, and the gauge is accurate, *THEN*, there is a fuel system fault." There are about 600 such rules in the CATS-1 system. Recently, a frame representation (Chapter 6) is complementing the rule representation (in some applications).

Explanation Capability

Another unique feature of an ES is its ability to explain its advice or recommendations and even to justify why a certain action was not recommended. The explanation and justification is done in a subsystem called the **justifier,** or the **explanation subsystem.** It enables the system to examine its own reasoning and to explain its operation.

The characteristics and capabilities of ES make them different from conventional systems. For a comparison, see Table 3.1.

3.5   Structure of Expert Systems

Expert systems are composed of two major parts: the **development environment** and the **consultation** (runtime) **environment** (Figure 3.3). The development environment is used by the ES builder to build the components and to introduce knowledge into the knowledge base. The consultation environment is used by a nonexpert to obtain expert knowledge and advice.

The following components may exist in an expert system:

- Knowledge acquisition subsystem
- Knowledge base
- Inference engine
- Blackboard (workplace)

□ User interface
□ Explanation subsystem (justifier)
□ Knowledge refining system

Most existing expert systems do not contain the knowledge refinement component. There are also large variations in the content and capabilities of each component. These components are underlined in Figure 3.3, which also shows the relationships among the components. A brief description of each component follows.

Knowledge Acquisition Subsystem

Knowledge acquisition is the accumulation, transfer, and transformation of problem-solving expertise from some knowledge source to a computer program for constructing or expanding the knowledge base. Potential sources of knowledge include human experts, textbooks, databases, special research reports, and pictures.

Acquiring knowledge from experts is a complex task that frequently creates a bottleneck in ES construction. The state of the art today requires a **knowledge engineer** to interact with one or more human experts in building the knowledge

TABLE 3.1 Comparison of Conventional Systems and Expert Systems

Conventional Systems	Expert Systems
Information and its processing are usually combined in one sequential program	Knowledge base is clearly separated from the processing (inference) mechanism (i.e., knowledge rules separated from the control)
Program does not make mistakes (programmers do)	Program may make mistakes
Do not (usually) explain why input data are needed or how conclusions were drawn	Explanation is a part of most ES
Changes in the program are tedious	Changes in the rules are easy to accomplish
The system operates only when it is completed	The system can operate with only a few rules (as the first prototype)
Execution is done on a step-by-step (algorithmic) basis	Execution is done by using heuristics and logic
Need complete information to operate	Can operate with incomplete or uncertain information
Effective manipulation of large databases	Effective manipulation of large knowledge bases
Representation and use of data	Representation and use of knowledge
Efficiency is a major goal	Effectiveness is the major goal
Easily deal with quantitative data	Easily deal with qualitative data
Capture, magnify, and distribute access to numeric data or to information	Capture, magnify, and distribute access to judgment and knowledge

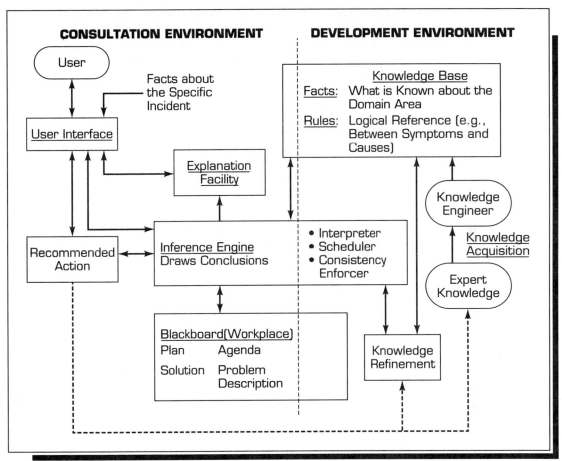

FIGURE 3.3 Structure of an Expert System

base. Typically, the knowledge engineer helps the expert structure the problem area by interpreting and integrating human answers to questions, drawing analogies, posing counterexamples, and bringing to light conceptual difficulties. The acquisition process, its supports, and its problems will be discussed in Chapter 4.

Knowledge Base

The knowledge base contains knowledge necessary for understanding, formulating, and solving problems. It includes two basic elements: (1) facts, such as the problem situation and theory of the problem area and (2) special heuristics, or rules that direct the use of knowledge to solve specific problems in a particular domain. (In addition, the inference engine includes *standard* problem-solving and decision-making rules.) The heuristics express the informal judgmental knowledge in an application area. Global strategies, which can be both heuristics and a part of the theory of the problem area, are usually included in the knowledge base. Knowledge, not mere facts, is the primary material of expert systems. The information in the knowledge base is incorporated into a computer program by a process called **knowledge representation,** which will be discussed in Chapter 5.

Inference Engine

The "brain" of the ES is the inference engine, also known as the *control* structure or the rule interpreter (in rule-based ES). This component is essentially a computer program that provides a methodology for reasoning about information in the knowledge base and in the "blackboard," and for formulating conclusions. This component provides directions about how to use the system's knowledge by developing the agenda that organizes and controls the steps taken to solve problems whenever consultation is performed.

The inference engine has three major elements:

□ An *interpreter* (rule interpreter in most systems), which executes the chosen agenda items by applying the corresponding knowledge base rules
□ A *scheduler*, which maintains control over the agenda. It estimates the effects of applying inference rules in light of item priorities or other criteria on the agenda.
□ A *consistency enforcer*, which attempts to maintain a consistent representation of the emerging solution

Blackboard (Workplace)

The **blackboard** is an area of working memory set aside for the description of a current problem, as specified by the input data; it is also used for recording intermediate results. The blackboard records intermediate hypotheses and decisions. Three types of decisions can be recorded on the blackboard: (1) *plan—* how to attack the problem, (2) *agenda—*potential actions awaiting execution, and (3) *solution—*candidate hypotheses and alternative courses of action that the system has generated thus far.

Blackboards exist only in some systems. The use of the blackboard approach is especially popular when several experts team up in solving one problem (see Chapter 14).

Let's consider an example. When your car fails, you enter the symptoms of the failure into the computer for storage in the blackboard. As the result of an intermediate hypothesis developed in the blackboard, the computer may then suggest that you do some additional checks (e.g., see if your battery is connected properly) and ask you to report the results. Again, this information is recorded in the blackboard.

User Interface

Expert systems contain a language processor for friendly, problem-oriented communication between the user and the computer. This communication could best be carried out in a natural language, and in some cases it is supplemented by menus and graphics. This topic will be discussed in Chapters 8 and 14.

Explanation Subsystem (Justifier)

The ability to trace responsibility for conclusions to their sources is crucial both in the transfer of expertise and in problem solving. The explanation subsystem can trace such responsibility and explain the ES behavior by interactively answering questions such as the following:

- □ *Why* was a certain question asked by the expert system?
- □ *How* was a certain conclusion reached?
- □ *Why* was a certain alternative rejected?
- □ *What* is the plan to reach the solution? For example, what remains to be established before a final diagnosis can be determined?

Knowledge Refining System

Human experts have a **knowledge refining** system; that is, they can analyze their own performance, learn from it, and improve it for future consultations. Similarly, such evaluation is necessary in computerized learning so that the program will be able to analyze the reasons for its success or failure. This could lead to improvements that result in a better knowledge base and more effective reasoning. Such a component is not available in commercial expert systems at the moment, but it is being developed in experimental ES in several universities and research institutions (see Chapter 19).

3.6 The Human Element in Expert Systems

At least two humans, and possibly more, participate in the development and use of an expert system. At a minimum there is an expert and a user. Frequently, there is also a knowledge engineer and a system builder. Each has a role to play.

The Expert

The expert, commonly referred to as the domain expert, is a person who has the special knowledge, judgment, experience, and methods along with the ability to apply these talents to give advice and solve problems. It is the domain expert's job to provide knowledge about how he or she performs the task that the knowledge system will perform. The expert knows which facts are important and understands the meaning of the relationships among facts. In diagnosing a problem with an automobile's electrical system, for example, an expert mechanic knows that fan belts can break and cause the battery to discharge. Directing a novice to check the fan belts and interpreting the meaning of a loose or missing belt are examples of expertise. When more than one expert is used, situations can become difficult if the experts disagree.

Usually, the initial body of knowledge, including terms and basic concepts, is documented in textbooks, reference manuals, sets of policies, or a catalog of products. However, this is not sufficient for a powerful ES. Not all expertise can be documented because most experts are unaware of the exact mental process by which they diagnose or solve a problem. Therefore, an interactive procedure is needed to acquire additional information from the expert to expand the basic knowledge. This process is fairly complex and usually requires the intervention of a knowledge engineer.

The Knowledge Engineer

The knowledge engineer helps the expert(s) structure the problem area by interpreting and integrating human answers to questions, drawing analogies, posing counterexamples, and bringing to light conceptual difficulties. He or she is usually also the system builder. The shortage of experienced knowledge engineers is a major bottleneck in ES construction. To overcome this bottleneck, ES designers are using productivity tools (e.g., special editors), and research is being conducted on building systems that will bypass the need for knowledge engineers.

The User

Most computer-based systems have evolved in a single-user mode. In contrast, an ES has several possible types of users:

- A nonexpert client seeking direct advice. In such a case the ES acts as a *consultant* or *advisor*.
- A student who wants to learn. In such a case the ES acts as an *instructor*.
- An ES builder who wants to improve or increase the knowledge base. In such a case the ES acts as a *partner*.
- An expert. In such a case the ES acts as a *colleague*.

For example, an ES can provide a "second opinion," so the expert can validate his or her judgment. An expert can also use the system as an assistant to carry on routine analysis or computations or to search for and classify information.

Users may not be familiar with computers and may lack in-depth knowledge in the problem domain. Many, however, have an interest in making better and possibly cheaper and faster decisions by using expert systems. The domain expert and the knowledge engineer should anticipate users' needs and limitations when designing ES.

The capabilities of ES were developed to save users time and effort. Therefore, unlike more traditional computer systems, ES provide *direct* answers to questions, not merely information and support. Furthermore, ES address the need to teach and train nonexperts. In addition, experts can improve their expertise through the use of ES (e.g., by discovering combinations of facts not previously considered). Finally, ES can be used as a knowledge assistant to experts by executing tedious tasks like searches and computations.

Other Participants

Several other participants may be involved in ES. For example, a *system builder* may assist in integrating the expert system with other computerized systems. A *tool builder* may provide generic or build specific tools. *Vendors* may provide tools and advice, and *support staff* may provide clerical and technical help. The various participants and their roles are demonstrated in Figure 3.4. Notice that several roles can be executed by one person. For example, some systems include only an expert and a user while others include only a system builder an expert and a user.

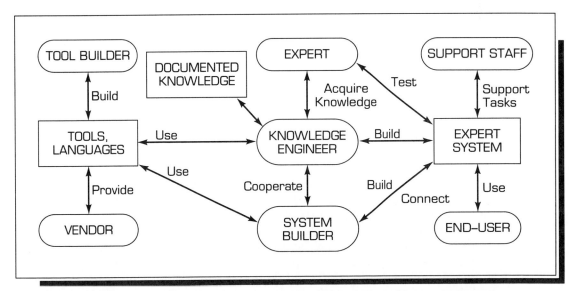

FIGURE 3.4 Participants in Building Expert Systems and Their Roles (*Source:* Modified from D. A. Waterman, *A Guide to Expert Systems* [Reading, Mass.: Addison-Wesley, 1985].)

3.7   How Expert Systems Work

Three major activities are part of ES construction and use: development, consultation, and improvement.

Development

The development of an expert system involves the construction of the knowledge base by acquiring knowledge from experts and/or from documented sources. The knowledge is separated into *declarative* (factual) and *procedural* aspects. Development activity also includes the construction (or acquisition) of an inference engine, a blackboard, an explanation facility, and any other required software, such as interfaces. The major participants in this activity are the domain expert, the knowledge engineer, and possibly information system programmers (especially if there is a need to interface with other computer programs). The knowledge is represented in the knowledge base in such a way that the system can draw conclusions by emulating the reasoning process of human experts.

The process of developing ES can be lengthy (see Chapter 12). A tool that is frequently used to expedite development is called the *ES shell*. ES shells include all the generic components of an ES, but they do *not* include the knowledge. EMYCIN (Figure 3.1) is a shell constructed by taking MYCIN minus its knowledge. (The letter *E* in EMYCIN stands for empty, namely EMYCIN without the knowledge is MYCIN.)

Consultation

Once the system is developed and validated, it is transferred to the users. When users want advice, they come to the ES. The ES conducts a bidirectional dialogue with the user, asking her or him to provide facts about a specific incident. After accepting the user's answers, the ES attempts to reach a conclusion. This effort is made by the inference engine, which "decides" which heuristic search techniques should be used to determine how the rules in the knowledge base are to be applied to the problem. The user can ask for explanations. The quality of the inference capability is determined by the knowledge representation method used and by the power of the inference engine.

Because the user is usually a computer novice, the ES must be very easy to use. At the present state of the technology, the user must sit by the computer terminal and type in the description of the problem (future ES will use voice input). The ES asks questions and the user answers them; more questions may be asked and answered; and, finally, a conclusion is reached. The consultation environment is also used by the builder during the development phase to test the system. At that time, the interface and the explanation facility may be tested.

Improvement

Expert systems are improved several times through a process called **rapid prototyping** during their development (see Chapter 12).

3.8   An Expert System at Work

Let's look at a simple rule-based expert system programmed with EXSYS the development shell (see Chapter 13). This is a typical consultation with a system called *Select Auto*. The opening statement follows:

Select Auto is an expert system designed to assist a user to make
a right decision of buying a new car. It will review prospective cars
that match with the users' needs and preference.

Now the consultation continues. User's answers are in boldface characters.

The car is made in
1   the United States
2   foreign countries
3   don't know
1

In this menu-driven consultation the user selected answer number 1.

Quality is
1   the highest concern
2   of high concern
3   of moderate concern
4   don't know
1

The computer keeps asking questions. The user may want to know *why* specific information is needed by the computer.

Price of the car is
1   important
2   unimportant
3   don't know
WHY

The computer will display the rule(s) in which price is a factor. This is part of the explanation capability. Rules can be presented either in plain English or in the way they are programmed. For example, EXSYS will show rule 5 (and possibly other related rules).

```
RULE NUMBER: 5
IF:
(1)  Price of a car is important
and
(2)  The payment is in installments
THEN:
The monthly payment is determined
```

Now, the user answers the question.

```
Price of a car is
1    important
2    unimportant
3    don't know
1
```

The computer will ask more questions. Later on we will explain why and when questions are being asked. Here are some typical questions with a user's selection shown.

```
The monthly payment is no more than
1    $100
2    $150
3    $200
4    $250
5    $300
4

Front seat is
1    important
2    unimportant
1

Acceleration is
1    strong
2    moderate
3    don't know
2

Engine is
1    between 1000–1500 cc
2    between 1501–2000 cc
3    over 2000 cc
4    don't know
2
```

Notice that "don't know" is an option. Expert systems can work with fuzzy or incomplete information just as human experts do.

```
Reliability of a car is
1      of high concern
2      of concern
3      of less concern
4      not sure
4
```

The computer will ask some more questions.

```
The most considered factor in making
a decision to buy a car is
1      price
2      fuel economy
3      comfort and convenience
4      performance of a car
5      safety
6      reliability
7      quality
8      don't know
1, 7
```

Here again, the user gave an indirect answer, stating that *both* price and quality are most important.

Once all questions are answered the computer will make a statement like this:

```
The following are the automobiles most likely to suit your
stated needs. If no selection has been made, it is most
likely the result of the fact that there does not exist an
automobile with all the attributes you desire. Should this
occur readjust your criteria and try again.
```

In our case this is exactly what happened. Therefore, the computer allowed the user to *change* the answers to the questions. This is done by displaying the questions and the answers.

```
1      The car is made in the United States
2      Quality is the highest concern
3      The price of the car is important
4      The monthly payment is no more than $250.00
5      The front seat is important
6      Acceleration is moderate
7      Engine is between 1501–2000 cc
8      Reliability is not sure
9      The most considered factors are price and quality
```

We changed the first answer from a car made in the United States to one made in a foreign country. This time we were advised that two cars are recommended.

Values based on −100 to +100 system	VALUE
1 Toyota Corolla	51
2 Renault Alliance	23

Since 100 points can be considered as the highest possible recommendation, neither car is really highly recommended. (We will explain later how the "value" is computed.) So we can now change our requirement again.

The user may ask *how* a certain recommendation has been derived. The computer will display all the rules that were used in deriving the recommendation.

3.9   Problem Areas Addressed by Expert Systems

Expert systems can be classified in several ways. One way is a generic categorization that uses the general problem areas they address. For example, diagnosis can be defined as "inferring system malfunctions from observations." Diagnosis is a generic activity executed in medicine, organizational studies, computer operations, and so on. The generic categories of expert systems are listed in Table 3.2. Some ES belong to two or more of these categories. A brief description of each category follows.

TABLE 3.2   Generic Categories of Expert Systems

Category	Problem Addressed
Interpretation	Inferring situation descriptions from observations
Prediction	Inferring likely consequences of given situations
Diagnosis	Inferring system malfunctions from observations
Design	Configuring objects under constraints
Planning	Developing plans to achieve goal(s)
Monitoring	Comparing observations to plans, flagging exceptions
Debugging	Prescribing remedies for malfunctions
Repair	Executing a plan to administer a prescribed remedy
Instruction	Diagnosing, debugging, and correcting student performance
Control	Interpreting, predicting, repairing, and monitoring system behaviors

Interpretation systems infer situation descriptions from observations. This category includes surveillance, speech understanding, image analysis, signal interpretation, and many kinds of intelligence analysis. An interpretation system explains observed data by assigning them symbolic meanings describing the situation.

Prediction systems include weather forecasting, demographic predictions, economic forecasting, traffic predictions, crop estimates, and military, marketing, or financial forecasting.

Diagnostic systems include medical, electronic, mechanical, and software diagnosis. Diagnostic systems typically relate observed behaviorial irregularities to underlying causes.

Design systems develop configurations of objects that satisfy the constraints of the design problem. Such problems include circuit layout, building design, and plant layout. Design systems construct descriptions of objects in various relationships with one another and verify that these configurations conform to stated constraints.

Planning systems specialize in problems of planning like automatic programming. They also deal with short- and long-term planning in areas such as project management, routing, communications, product development, military applications, and financial planning.

Monitoring systems compare observations of system behavior with standards that seem crucial for successful goal attainment. These crucial features correspond to potential flaws in the plan. Many computer-aided monitoring systems exist for topics ranging from air traffic to fiscal management tasks.

Debugging systems rely on planning, design, and prediction capabilities to create specifications or recommendations for correcting a diagnosed problem.

Repair systems develop and execute plans to administer a remedy for some diagnosed problems. Such systems incorporate debugging, planning, and execution capabilities.

Instruction systems incorporate diagnosis and debugging subsystems that specifically address the student as the focus of interest. Typically, these systems begin by constructing a hypothetical description of the student's knowledge that interprets his or her behavior. They then diagnose weaknesses in the student's knowledge and identify appropriate remedies to overcome the deficiencies. Finally, they plan a tutorial interaction intended to deliver remedial knowledge to the student.

Control systems adaptively govern the overall behavior of a system. To do this, the control system must repeatedly interpret the current situation, predict the future, diagnose the causes of anticipated problems, formulate a remedial plan, and monitor its execution to ensure success.

Not all the tasks that are usually found within each of the preceding ten categories are suitable for expert systems. Some guidelines for task selection are presented in Chapter 12. Table 3.3 attempts to answer, in general terms, this question: What tasks are suitable for expert systems?

TABLE 3.3   What Tasks Are Suitable for Expert Systems?

Too Easy (Use Conventional Software)	Just Right	Too Hard (Requires Human Intelligence)
Payroll, Inventory	Diagnosing and troubleshooting	Designing new tools or a cover for a magazine
Simple tax returns	Analyzing diverse data	Stock market predictions
Decision trees	Production scheduling	Discovering new principles
Database management	Equipment layout	Everyday language
Mortgage computations	Advise on tax shelters	"Commonsense" problems
Regression analysis	Determine type of statistical analysis	Developing new statistical tests
Facts are known precisely; they are reduced to numbers.	Facts are known but not precisely; they are stated as ideas	Requires innovation or discovery or "common sense"
Expertise is cheap.	Expertise is expensive but available.	Expertise is not available, or nobody knows enough to be an expert.

Source: Based on M. Van Horn, *Understanding Expert Systems* (Toronto: Bantam Books, 1986).

3.10   Benefits of Expert Systems

ES can provide major benefits to users (e.g., see Appendix B at the end of this chapter). Some of the *potential* benefits are discussed next.

Increased Output and Productivity.   ES can work faster than humans. For example, XCON (see Appendix C) has enabled DEC to increase fourfold the throughput of VAX configurating orders. Increased output means fewer workers needed and reduced costs.

Increased Quality.   ES can increase quality by providing consistent advice and reducing error rate. For example, XCON reduced the error rate of configurating computer orders from 35 to 2 percent.

Reduced Downtime.   Many operational ES (e.g., the CATS-1 system described earlier) are used for diagnosing malfunctions and prescribing repairs. By using ES it is possible to reduce downtime significantly. For example, one day of lost time on an oil rig can cost as much as $250,000. A system called Drilling Advisor was developed to detect malfunctions in oil rigs. This system saved a considerable amount of money for the company involved by cutting down the downtime.

Capture of Scarce Expertise. The scarcity of expertise becomes evident in situations where there are not enough experts for a task, the expert is about to retire or leave a job, or expertise is required over a broad geographic location. Typical systems that capture scarce expertise are CATS-1, Campbell Soup's ES (see Chapter 20) and TARA (see Box 3.1).

Flexibility. ES can offer flexibility in both the services and manufacturing industries. For example, DEC tries to make each VAX order fit the customer's needs as closely as possible. Before XCON, DEC found it increasingly difficult to do this because of the variety of customer requests.

Easier Equipment Operation. ES makes complex equipment easier to operate. For example, STEAMER is an ES intended to train inexperienced workers to operate complex ship engines. Another example is an ES developed for Shell Oil Co. (by Intelligent Terminal Ltd.) to train people to use complex FORTRAN routines.

Elimination of the Need for Expensive Equipment. In many cases a human must rely on expensive instruments for monitoring and control. ES can perform the same tasks with lower-cost instruments because of their ability to investigate more thoroughly and quickly the information provided by instruments. DENDRAL is an example of such an ES.

Operation in Hazardous Environments. Many tasks require humans to operate in hazardous environments. The ES may enable humans to avoid such environments. This characteristic is extremely important in military conflicts; it can also enable workers to avoid hot, humid, or toxic environments, such as a nuclear power plant that has malfunctioned (see Box 3.1).

Accessibility to Knowledge and Help Desks. Expert systems make knowledge (and information) accessible. People can query systems and receive advice. One area of applicability is support of help desks (see Chapter 20). Another is the support of any advisory service (see Box 3.2).

Reliability. ES are reliable. They do not become tired or bored, call in sick, or go on strike; and they do not talk back to the boss. ES also consistently pay attention to all details and so do not overlook relevant information and potential solutions.

Increased Capabilities of Other Computerized Systems. Integration of ES with other systems makes the other systems more effective: they cover more applications, work faster, and produce higher quality results.

Integration of Several Experts' Opinions. In certain cases, ES forces us to integrate the opinions of several experts and thus may increase the quality of the advice.

Ability to Work with Incomplete or Uncertain Information. In contrast to conventional computer systems, ES can, like human experts, work with

---

Box 3.1: Innovative Expert Systems—A Sampling

Of the many innovative expert systems on the market, the following are of particular interest.

TARA: An Intelligent Assistant for Foreign Traders: Foreign exchange currency traders cannot afford to think over multimillion dollar situations for long. In real time, they must examine large quantities of data; consider historical trends; determine what is relevant; and, many times in the course of a day, make the ever-critical decision to buy or sell. It is a high-risk, high-reward job of prediction where even the best traders are pleased with being right 60 percent of the time. At Manufacturers Hanover Trust an expert system called the Technical Analysis and Reasoning Assistant (TARA) was built to assist foreign currency traders. *Source:* Schorr and Rappaport [15].

Soviet Union Trade Adviser: This system provides advice about doing business and marketing in the Soviet Union. The advice ranges from assessing the probability of obtaining an export license (in the United States) to information about demand and products in the USSR. (See Chapter 20 for details.)

Managing Toxicological Studies: This system helps in identifying computing resources (and their costs) that support toxicological research programs for assessing the risks posed by toxic chemicals in an effort to reduce human health hazards. *Source:* H. Berghel, et al., "An Expert System for Managing Toxicological Studies," *Expert Systems: Planning, Implementation, Integration* (Spring 1991).

Analyst: An Advisor for Financial Analysis for Automobile Dealerships: One of the services General Motors (GM) offers to approximately 12,000 domestic GM dealerships (and affiliates) is inventory financing. This service is also known as wholesale, or "floor-plan," financing. In exchange for funds, dealers must adhere to a set of rules, the most important of which is to promptly pay GM as vehicles are sold. Adherence is analyzed at least annually. The process of analyzing a dealership is, in essence, financial risk analysis. An expert system was developed to expedite analysis, specifically to predict a dealership's likely performance until the next scheduled review. The system also recommends credit lines and suggests ways to reduce risk. *Source:* Schorr and Rappaport [15].

Box 3.2: Expert System Advises Students

From semester to semester, students are plagued with decisions about which courses to take, and even what to do after graduation. This semester's no different.

But Eastern Illinois University's students may find those decisions a little bit easier to handle with the Siggi-Plus computer system at Eastern's Counseling Center. This program's main function is to help students with undecided majors choose what will best suit their own personal needs by having them enter information about themselves. The computer asks what work experience the student has had thus far, what the student values most about a job, and what extracurricular activities and interests the student enjoys. Then it produces a printout of careers to consider based on all of these factors.

The biggest benefit of this system is that it gives the student a much broader outlook than did the old program (called Discover). In the past, all students had to do to get a career listing from Discover was take an interest test. The information provided, however, did not take into account the student's actual job abilities.

"I sang in a choir as a boy, and had much interest in music," counselor Bud Sanders said. "With Discover I would most likely be told to pursue a career in music. Unfortunately, I do not have the abilities to do this. Siggi-Plus would recognize both of these factors, and give me a more accurate listing."

Siggi-Plus is not only aimed at students with undecided majors, though. It is also beneficial to students on academic probation or to those who believe they are in the wrong major.

incomplete information. The user can respond with a "don't know" or "not sure" answer to one or more of the system's questions during a consultation, and the expert system will still be able to produce an answer, although it may not be a certain one. ES do not have to be complete in the same way in which a set of FORTRAN IF-statements do. They can also deal with probabilities, as long as the inference engine can cope with them.

Provision of Training. ES can provide training. Novices who work with ES become more and more experienced. The explanation facility can also serve as a teaching device, and so can notes that may be inserted in the knowledge base.

Enhancement of Problem Solving. ES enhance problem solving by allowing the integration of top experts' judgment into analysis. They also increase users' understanding through explanation. ES can be used to support the solution of difficult problems. For example, an ES called Statistical Navigator was developed to help novices use complex statistical computer packages.

Ability to Solve Complex Problems. Expert systems may, one day, solve problems whose complexity exceeds human ability. Already some ES are able to solve problems where the required scope of knowledge exceeds that of any one individual. However, these problems must be in a narrow domain.

Knowledge Transfer to Remote Locations. One of the greatest potential benefits of ES is its ease of transfer across international boundaries. This can be extremely important to developing countries that cannot pay for knowledge delivered by human experts. An example of such a transfer is an eye-care ES developed at Rutgers University (by Kulikowski) in conjunction with the World Health Organization. The program has been implemented in Egypt and Algeria, where serious eye diseases are prevalent but eye specialists are rare. The program is rule based, runs on a micro, and can be operated by a nurse, a physician's assistant, or a general practitioner. The program diagnoses the disease and then recommends a treatment.

3.11   Problems and Limitations of Expert Systems

Available ES methodologies are not straightforward and effective, even for applications in the generic categories (see Table 3.2). For applications of even modest complexity, some ES code, especially for systems constructed with programming languages, is generally hard to understand, debug, extend, and maintain. Here are some factors and problems that have slowed down the commercial spread of ES:

□ Knowledge is not always readily available.
□ Expertise is hard to extract from humans.
□ The approach of each expert to situation assessment may be different, yet correct.
□ It is hard, even for a highly skilled expert, to abstract good situational assessments when he or she is under time pressure.
□ Users of expert systems have natural cognitive limits. Humans see what they are prepared to see, often only what falls within a narrow attention span.
□ ES work well only in a narrow domain, in some cases in very narrow domains.
□ Most experts have no independent means of checking whether their conclusions are reasonable.

□ The vocabulary, or jargon, that experts use for expressing facts and relations is frequently limited and not understood by others.

□ Help is frequently required from knowledge engineers who are rare and expensive—a fact that could make ES construction rather costly.

□ Lack of trust by end-users may be a barrier to ES use.

□ Knowledge transfer is subject to a host of perceptual and judgmental biases.

An interesting way to examine ES limitations is to review the generic areas where ES were found to be successful and point out the major difficulties encountered in each category (Table 3.4).

Last, but not least, is the fact that expert systems may not be able to arrive at conclusions (especially in early stages of system development). For example,

TABLE 3.4   Representative Tasks of Experts and Their Difficulties

Task	Difficulties
Interpretation: Analysis of data to determine their meaning	□ Data are often "noisy" and full of errors □ Data values may be missing
Diagnosis: Faultfinding in a system based on interpretation of data	□ Faults can be intermittent □ Symptoms of other faults may interfere □ Data contain errors or are inaccessible □ Diagnostic equipment may be unreliable
Monitoring: Continuously interpreting signals and flag for intervention	□ When to flag often depends on context □ Signal expectations vary with the time/situation
Prediction: Forecasting from past and present	□ Integration of incomplete information □ Account for multiple possible futures □ Contingencies for uncertainties □ Diversity of data, often contradicting data
Planning: Creating a plan to achieve goals	□ Many alternative courses of action □ Overwhelming volume of details □ Interactions between plans and subgoals □ Planning context is only approximately known
Design: Making specifications to create objects for satisfying particular requirements	□ Difficulty in assessing consequences □ Several conflicting constraints □ Interaction among subdesigns

Source: Adapted from M. Stefik, et al., "The Organization of Expert Systems, A Tutorial," *Artificial Intelligence* (March 1982).

even the fully developed XCON cannot fulfill about 2 percent of the orders presented to it. In addition, expert systems do make mistakes (see Box 3.3).

These limitations clearly indicate that today's ES fall short of generally intelligent human behavior. Several of these limitations will diminish or disappear with technological improvements over time.

Box 3.3: Expert Systems Make Mistakes

Whereas conventional programs are designed to produce the correct answer every time, expert systems are designed to behave like experts, who usually produce correct answers but sometimes produce incorrect ones. John McDermott, describing the development of an ES for configuring minicomputer systems for the Digital Equipment Corp., neatly summarizes the problem:

> I have hammered on the theme that a knowledge-based program must pass through a relatively lengthy apprenticeship stage and that even after it has become an expert, it will, like all experts, occasionally make mistakes. The first part of this message got through, but I suspect the second has not. My concern then, is whether this characteristic of expert systems is recognized. Will Digital (or any other large corporation) be emotionally prepared to give a significant amount of responsibility to programs that are known to be fallible?

At first glance it would seem that conventional programs have a distinct advantage over ES in this regard. However, the advantage is an illusion. Conventional programs that perform complex tasks, like those suitable for expert systems, may result in mistakes. But their mistakes will be very difficult to remedy because the strategies, heuristics, and basic assumptions on which these programs are based will not be explicitly stated in the program code. Thus, they cannot be easily identified and corrected. ES, like their human counterparts, make mistakes. But unlike conventional programs, they have the potential to learn from their errors. With the help of skillful users, ES can be made to improve their problem-solving abilities on the job. Furthermore, the programming job required to make improvements is much simpler than that required in most conventional systems.

(*Source:* D.A. Waterman, *A Guide to Expert Systems* [Reading, Mass.: Addison-Wesley, 1985].)

3.12   Types of Expert Systems

Expert systems appear in many varieties. The following classifications of ES are not exclusive, that is, one ES can appear in several categories.

Expert Systems Versus Knowledge-based Systems. According to this classification, an ES is one whose behavior is so sophisticated that we would call a person who performed in a similar manner an expert. MYCIN and XCON are good examples. Highly trained professionals diagnose blood diseases (MYCIN) and configure complex computing equipment (XCON). These systems truly attempt to emulate the best human experts.

In the commercial world, however, systems are emerging that can perform effectively and efficiently tasks for whose execution you really do not need an expert. Such small systems are referred to as **knowledge-based systems**[3] (also known as advisory systems, knowledge systems, intelligent job aid systems, or operational systems). As an example, let us look at a system that gives advice on immunizations recommended for travel abroad. The advice depends on many attributes such as the age, sex, and health of the traveler and the country of destination. One needs to be knowledgeable to give such advice, but one need not be an expert. In this case, practically *all* the knowledge that relates to this advice is documented in a manual available at most public health departments (in only 1 or 2 percent of the cases it is necessary to consult a physician). Another example is supporting help desks (see Chapter 20).

The distinction between the two types may not be so sharp when it comes to reality. Many systems involve both documented knowledge and undocumented expertise. Basically it is a matter of *how much* expertise is included in the systems that classifies them in one category or the other.

Knowledge systems can be constructed more quickly and cheaply than expert systems, as will be demonstrated in Chapters 4 and 12.

Rule-based Expert Systems. Many commercial ES are rule based, because the technology of rule-based systems is relatively well developed. In such systems the knowledge is represented as a series of production rules (see Chapter 5). The classic example of a rule-based ES is MYCIN (see Appendix C). Many commercial systems can be considered as descendants of MYCIN.

Frame-based Systems. In these systems, the knowledge is represented as frames, a representation of the object-oriented programming approach (see Chapter 5).

---

[3] This terminology is not widely accepted as yet. Therefore the terms *expert systems* and *knowledge-based systems* are frequently used interchangeably.

Hybrid Systems. These systems include several knowledge representation approaches, at minimum frames and rules, but usually much more.

Model-based Systems. **Model-based systems** are structured around a model that simulates the structure and function of the system under study. The model is used to compute values which are compared to observed ones. The comparison triggers action (if needed) or further diagnosis. These computer systems will be discussed in Chapter 6.

Systems Classified by Their Nature. Buchanan and Shortliffe [4] distinguish several types of ES. One type deals with *evidence gathering*. The system leads the user to a structured selection from among a reasonable number of possible outcomes or actions. (A "reasonable" number might be dozens or hundreds; it would not be tens of thousands or more.) This evidence-gathering type of ES is the one being most widely developed today. The problems that are treated by this type of ES are called "classification problems." The process of dealing with such problems is described as follows by Buchanan and Shortliffe:

> The system solves problems by precisely classifying what the problem is and then retrieving the solution to this class of problem. For example, the problem of repairing an automobile can be viewed as the problem of precisely classifying the problem: "it is a charging system failure caused by one or more shorted diodes in the alternator." Once the problem is classified precisely, the repair or advice is clear.

Another example of this type of ES is a system that interrogates a designer about the configuration of a device, selects a design template and tailors it to the designer's needs, builds a source file of the information, and ships it to a CAD/CAM system. That system then prepares a blueprint for engineering.

A second type is a *stepwise refinement* system. It deals with a large number of possible outcomes by means of successive levels of detail.

A third type of system is *stepwise assembly*, where the subject domain can have an extremely large number of possible outcomes. Such a system requires a lot of interaction with the user, so that the user's intelligence can help steer the system in the right direction for a solution. A special case of this type is called a *catalog selection*. This system deals with problems like choosing the right chemical, steel, or auto parts from a catalog of choices. Users know the characteristics of the problem but lack the knowledge of the catalog or the relationships between the problem and item in the catalog. An example is Boeing's documentation maintenance system.

Ready-made (Turnkey) Systems. ES can be developed to meet the particular needs of a user (custom-made), or they can be purchased as ready-made packages for any user. **Ready-made systems** are similar to application packages like an accounting general ledger or project management in operations management. Ready-made systems enjoy the economy of mass production and therefore arc considerably less expensive than customized systems. They also can be used as soon as they are purchased. Unfortunately, ready-made systems are very general in nature, and the advice they render may not be of value to a user involved in a complex situation. Ready-made systems started to appear on the market in 1983. Most of them are sold for microcomputers only.

Ready-made ES are not popular yet. However, as time passes, their performance will improve and they will probably become as widespread as other CBIS application packages. (For further discussion and examples see Chapter 20.)

Real-Time Expert Systems. **Real-time systems** are systems in which there is a strict time limit on the system's response time, which must be *fast enough* for use to control the process being computerized. In other words, the system *always* produces a response by the time it is needed. (This topic is discussed in Chapter 14.)

To learn about other classifications schemes refer to Coursey and Shangraw [5] and Meyer and Curley [9].

Chapter Highlights

- □ Expert systems imitate the reasoning process of experts for solving difficult problems.
- □ A predecessor of ES was the General-purpose Problem Solver (GPS). The GPS (and similar programs) failed because they attempted to cover too much and ignored the importance of the specific knowledge required.
- □ The power of an ES is derived from the specific knowledge it possesses, and not from the particular knowledge representation and inference schemes it employs.
- □ Expertise is a task-specific knowledge acquired from training, reading, and experience.
- □ Experts can make fast and good decisions regarding complex situations.
- □ Most of the knowledge in organizations is possessed by a few experts.
- □ Expert system technology attempts to transfer knowledge from experts and documented sources to the computer and make it available for use by nonexperts.
- □ The most popular method of knowledge representation is rules. However, frame representation, which is based on object-oriented programming, is becoming popular.
- □ The reasoning capability in expert systems is provided by an inference engine.
- □ The knowledge in ES is separated from the inferencing (processing).
- □ Expert systems provide limited explanation capabilities.
- □ A distinction is made between a development environment (building an ES) and a consultation environment (using an ES).

□ The major components of an ES are the knowledge acquisition subsystem, knowledge base, inference engine, blackboard, user interface, and explanation subsystem.

□ Future expert systems will have a knowledge refinement component.

□ The knowledge engineer captures the knowledge from the expert and programs it into the computer.

□ Although the major user of the ES is a nonexpert, other users (such as students, ES builders, and even experts) may utilize ES.

□ Knowledge can be declarative (facts) or procedural.

□ Expert systems are being improved in an iterative manner using a process called rapid prototyping.

□ The ten generic categories of ES are: interpretation, prediction, diagnosis, design, planning, monitoring, debugging, repair, instruction, and control.

□ Expert systems can provide many benefits. The most important are improvement in productivity and/or quality, preservation of scarce expertise, enhancing other systems, coping with incomplete information, and providing training.

□ Although there are several limitations to the use of expert systems, some of them will disappear with improved technology.

□ Expert systems, just as human experts, can make mistakes.

□ Some make a distinction between expert systems, where most of the knowledge comes from experts, and knowledge systems, where the majority of the knowledge comes from documented sources.

□ Some ES are available as ready-made systems; they render generic advice for standard situations.

□ Expert systems can also be provided in a real-time mode.

Key Terms

blackboard
consultation environment
development environment
domain
expert
expertise
expert system
explanation subsystem

General-purpose Problem Solver
inference engine
justifier
knowledge acquisition
knowledge engineer
knowledge refining
knowledge representation

knowledge-based system
model-based system
rapid prototyping
ready-made system
real-time system
rule-based system

Questions for Review

1. List three capabilities of ES.
2. Why did the General-purpose Problem Solver fail?

3. Explain this statement: "The power of an ES is derived from the specific knowledge it possesses, not from the particular formulas and inference schemes it employs."
4. Explain how ES can distribute (or redistribute) the available knowledge in an organization.
5. List the types of knowledge included in expertise.
6. From Figure 3.2, estimate the percentage of knowledge possessed by the top 30 percent of experts (percent success achieved by deciles 1, 2, and 3).
7. List and describe the eight activities that human experts perform. Which activities are performed well by current expert systems?
8. Define the ES development environment and contrast it with the consultation environment.
9. List and define the major components of an ES.
10. What is the difference between knowledge acquisition and knowledge representation?
11. What is the role of a knowledge engineer?
12. A knowledge base includes facts and rules. Explain the difference between the two.
13. Which component of ES is mostly responsible for the reasoning capability?
14. List the major components of the inference engine.
15. What are the major activities performed in the ES blackboard (workplace)?
16. What is the function of the justifier?
17. List four types of potential users of ES.
18. List the ten generic categories of ES.
19. Describe some of the limitations of ES.
20. What is a ready-made ES? (Define and give an example.)

Questions for Discussion

1. It is said that reasoning ability, powerful computers, inference capabilities, and heuristics are necessary but not sufficient for solving real problems. Why?
2. Comprehensive knowledge representation theories and associated general-purpose systems added to the capabilities listed in question 1 were helpful but still not sufficient. Why?
3. Review the CATS-1 case. What are the major lessons learned? What kind of ES is CATS-1 (according to Table 3.2)? What are the major advantages of this system?
4. A major difference between a conventional decision support system and ES is that the former can explain a "how" question whereas the latter can also explain a "why" question. Discuss.
5. Explain how the major components of the inference engine relate to the major components of the blackboard.
6. Why is it so difficult to build a component that will automatically refine knowledge?

7. Explain the relationship between development environment and consultation (runtime) environment.
8. What kind of mistakes do ES make and why? Why is it easier to correct mistakes in ES than in conventional programs?
9. Table 3.2 provides a list of ten categories of ES. Compile a list of twenty examples, two in each category, from the various functional areas in an organization (accounting, finance, production, marketing, personnel, etc.).
10. Review the limitations of ES discussed in the chapter. From what you know, which of these limitations are the most likely to remain as limitations in the year 2100? Why? (See Chapters 18 and 19 for some insights.)
11. A ready-made ES is selling for $10,000. Developing one will cost you $50,000. A ready-made suit costs you $100; a tailored one will cost you $500. Develop an analogy between the two situations and describe the markets for the ready-made and the customized products.
12. Which generic category of ES best fits the following statements?
    a. Computer-controlled fuel injection system in a satellite
    b. Advice to farmers on what fertilizer to use
    c. Instructions on how to handle a computer with problems.

Exercise: Can an ES Enhance the Image of a Bank?

First, a reporter's opinion regarding an ES used by a bank for loan approval is given. A counterargument follows.[4] Read the arguments of both sides and express your opinion. Can you reconcile the different arguments?

Against ES. If you saw the classic science fiction film *2001: A Space Odyssey*, you might remember the astronaut saying, "Open the pod bay door, HAL." That was the computer's name, the HAL 2000. HAL replies, "I'm sorry, Dave, I can't do that."

HAL could say things like that. He had artificial intelligence. Well, there's a computer in your future. When you go into the bank to ask for a loan, it might just say to you, "I'm sorry, Dave, I can't do that." The First National Bank of Chicago is experimenting with a special artificial intelligence software program that supposedly is able to reason and make decisions just like a human banker.

That's how the bank AI programs are supposed to work. Experienced bankers feed all their knowledge and criteria for making loans into a computer. They program the computer with the various criteria they use to make lending decisions. The AI program then has about 150 rules on how to make lending decisions.

---

[4] The first argument is condensed from an article in *The Orange County Register*, February 17, 1986. The second is from M. Van Horn, *Understanding Expert Systems* (Toronto: Bantam Books, 1986), p. 194.

When you come in for a loan, the younger or less experienced lending officer types your information into the system. Then the computer asks some questions to clarify a few points. Then it decides whether you get the loan.

Using AI to diagnose illnesses, locate petroleum deposits, or play chess (as many of the programs are designed to do) seems like a sensible thing. But making a loan is based on a list of criteria, such as that the bank wants to "reduce its exposure to risk."

That strikes me as pretty cold, but it's exactly the reason I take a dim view of AI computers in banking. Banks have been trying to shake that cold, impersonal image they had for years by taking out the steel bars at the teller windows and developing a business style that is more sensitive to customers. Now, along comes this cold, calculating computer that will never understand, or be able to take into account, somebody's personal situation. A couple with a new child on the way won't get a home improvement loan for a room addition because the computer says the bank wants to "reduce its exposure" to those kinds of loans.

Computers can't think, they can't feel, and so far, they cannot reason. Don't get me wrong; I like computers, and I use them every day. But it's how they're used that's important. AI programs could be used to find reasons to say "yes" when people want a loan. They could be used to help people solve complex personal financial planning problems. I'd like to see the bankers realize that their AI programs ought to be designed to say, "Sure, Dave, I'd be happy to open the pod bay door."

For ES. Many banks are busily developing ES that capture the experience of their top loan officers in sizing up loan applicants. These capture not just the formulas loan officers use to analyze the applicant's financial statements and the condition of the applicant's industry, but also all the subjective factors—the loan officers' "sixth sense"—which lead them to grant a loan to an applicant who looks questionable on paper, or to turn down an applicant who looks good. These allow junior loan officers to draw on the expertise of the most successful lenders as advisory systems.

Furthermore, loan officers must have at their fingertips an enormous amount of constantly changing data—on industry conditions, interest rates, tax law, credit ratings of the applicant's customers, and so on. Systems that make available the latest data, coupled with heuristic rules, are providing a service that easily pays for itself and provides better service to the clients.

There is a concern that lenders would put too much reliance on the dumb system and lose the human element. But from experience so far, the reality seems the opposite. Bankers who are unsure of their ability to make good decisions tend to be too conservative and to turn down potentially good loans. This costs the bank just as much as granting poor loans. So these expert loan advisers allow more people to make better decisions. As a result, banks keep their clients happy and improve their own profitability.

References and Bibliography

1. Augustine, N.R. "Distribution of Expertise." *Defense Systems Management* (Spring 1979).
2. Bonissone, P.P., and H.E. Johnson, Jr. "Expert System for Diesel Electric Locomotive Repair." *Human Systems Management* 4 (1985).
3. Bowerman, R.G., and D. Glover. *Putting Expert Systems into Practice.* New York: Van Nostrand Reinhold Co., 1988.
4. Buchanan, B.G., and E.H. Shortliffe, eds. *Rule-Based Expert Systems.* Reading, Mass.: Addison-Wesley, 1984.
5. Coursey, D.H., and R.G. Shangraw. "Expert System Technology for Managerial Applications: A Typology." *Public Productivity Review* 12 (Spring 1989).
6. Feigenbaum, E., et al. *The Rise of the Expert Company.* New York: Times Books, 1988.
7. Hertz, D.B. *The Expert Executive.* New York: John Wiley & Sons, 1988.
8. Holsapple, C.W., and A.B. Whinston. *Business Expert Systems.* Homewood, Ill.: Richard D. Irwin, 1987.
9. Meyer, M.H., and K.F. Curley. "Expert System Success Models." *Datamation* (September 1, 1989).
10. Monger, R.F. "AI Applications: What's Their Competitive Advantage?" *Journal of Information Systems Management* (Summer 1988).
11. Newell, A., and H. Simon. *Human Problem Solving.* Englewood Cliffs, N.J.: Prentice-Hall, 1973.
12. Parsaye, K., and M. Chignell. *Expert Systems for Experts.* New York: John Wiley & Sons, 1988.
13. Robinson, J.A. "The Generalization Resolution Principle." In *Machine Intelligence,* vol. 3, D. Michie, ed. New York: Elsevier, 1986.
14. Savory, S.E. *Expert Systems in the Organization.* New York: John Wiley & Sons, 1988.
15. Schorr, A., and A. Rappaport. *Innovative Applications of Artificial Intelligence.* Menlo Park, Calif.: AAAI Press, 1989.
16. Stefik, M., et al. "The Organization of Expert Systems, A Tutorial." *Artificial Intelligence* (March 1982).
17. Sviokla, J.J. "An Examination of the Impact of Expert Systems on the Firm: The Case of XCON." *MIS Quarterly* (June 1990).
18. Turban, E., and P. Watkins, eds. *Applied Expert Systems.* Amsterdam: North Holland, 1988.
19. Van Horn, M. *Understanding Expert Systems.* Toronto: Bantam Books, 1986.
20. Waterman, D.A. *A Guide to Expert Systems.* Reading, Mass.: Addison-Wesley, 1985.
21. Waterman, D.A. "How Do Expert Systems Differ from Conventional Programs?" *Expert Systems* (January 1986).

Appendix A: Systems Cited in Chapter

System	Vendor (Developer)	Description
AGE	Stanford University (Stanford, Calif.)	It is an ES development tool that helps the builder to select a framework, design a rule language, and assemble parts into a system (different architectures, including a blackboard).
DENDRAL	Stanford University (Stanford, Calif.)	It infers the molecular structure of unknown compounds from mass spectral and nuclear magnetic response data. The system uses a special algorithm to systematically enumerate all possible molecular structures; it uses chemical expertise to prune this list of possibilities to a manageable size. Knowledge in DENDRAL is represented as a procedural code.
EURISKO	Stanford University (Stanford, Calif.)	It learns new heuristics and new domain-specific definitions of concepts in a problem domain. The system can learn by discovery in a number of different problem domains, including VLSI design. EURISKO operates by generating a device configuration, computing its input/output behavior, assessing its functionality, and then evaluating it against other comparable devices.
META-DENDRAL	Stanford University (Stanford, Calif.)	It helps chemists determine the dependence of mass spectrometric fragmentation on substructural features. It does this by discovering fragmentation rules for given classes of molecules. META-DENDRAL first generates a set of highly specific rules that account for a single fragmentation process in a particular molecule. Then it uses the training examples to generalize these rules. Finally, the system reexamines the rules to remove redundant or incorrect rules.
STEAMER	U.S. Navy in cooperation with Bolt, Beranek, and Newman (Cambridge, Mass.)	It is an intelligent CAI that instructs Navy personnel in the operation and maintenance of the propulsion plant for a 1078-class frigate. The system can monitor the student executing the boiler light-off procedure for the plant, acknowledge appropriate student actions, and correct inappropriate ones. The system works by tying a simulation of the propulsion plant to a sophisticated graphic interface program that displays animated color diagrams of plant subsystems. The student can manipulate simulated components like valves, switches, and pumps, and observe the effects on plant parameters, such as changes in pressure, temperature, and flow. STEAMER uses an object-oriented representation scheme.
XSEL	Digital Equipment Corp.	See description in Appendix C.

Appendix B: Application Note[*]

Gordon Campbell can smile now when he tells of the time he was asked to change 75 percent of an application he had just finished developing. Campbell, technical planning manager for the state of Washington's Department of Labor and Industries, not only had to rewrite the application, but had to complete the changes in two days.

In years past, a request for such massive changes in two days was unheard of. But more and more these days, industry is turning to expert systems technology to develop and maintain rapidly changing or logically complex business applications.

"Using the Aion Development System (ADS), we made all of those changes within the normal working environment and had it done on time," Campbell said. "Nobody had to work overtime. It was easy to change things."

As a result of ADS, there have already been quite a few changes at Washington's Department of Labor and Industries, one of the largest industrial insurance carriers in the country. The department provides insurance to 1,200 employer-customers, who employ 1.6 million workers in the state.

One of Campbell's first projects was developing a Claims Manager Training prototype to help improve consistency in the claims department, which had a high turnover of claims managers. The system was designed to alleviate this problem by capturing the expertise of the more experienced managers and then providing an online tutorial for new staff. The prototype was completed in six months, six weeks ahead of schedule.

"A lot of credit goes to the (Aion) development environment," said Campbell, who has 27 years of experience in conventional programming. "It was an easy environment for our staff person, a COBOL and IBM-mainframe programmer, to pick up."

But one of the most exciting advantages of ES technology is the ability to quickly create a prototype system and then evaluate it. This is one of the most significant differences between ES technology and conventional methods for developing systems.

"If it doesn't meet the criteria, you can scrap the whole system," Campbell said. "In conventional systems I've been involved with, you don't ever get to the point where you say, well, we've spent six months on the system. It's not something we should build a system for. After a certain point, you never ask yourself whether an investment should have been made in the system. You just implement it."

Expert systems allow programmers to easily make changes without penalty. Programmers aren't restricted by procedural structure, because new rules can be entered, changed, and tested as the application is developed.

---

[*]This application was derived from publicly disclosed information of the Aion Corp., Palo Alto, Calif.

Campbell's group has also developed a stand-alone self-study program to teach programmers about expert systems and how to build them. Another expert system advises computer operators how to diagnose and correct a program's problems about 90 percent of the time. The expert system application lets them bring the system back faster, and also eliminates the cost of calling in an expert.

Currently in the prototype stage is the Vocational Rehabilitation Early Assessment (VREA) system, which quickly determines whether claimants are candidates for vocational rehabilitation. The result is better case assignments, which in turn results in a higher rate of people returning to work and thus reduces the length of time they're collecting disability benefits. And that benefits the state of Washington's Department of Labor and Industries.

Appendix C: Classic Expert Systems

MYCIN

Each year 2 million people get sick while in hospitals recovering from something else; and perhaps 50,000 of them die. The cause is hospital-borne infections. These may develop unnoticed, and when discovered they need to be diagnosed quickly. MYCIN, which is considered the granddaddy of ES, was developed to aid physicians in diagnosing meningitis and other bacterial infections of the blood and to prescribe treatment. Specifically, the system's objective is to aid physicians during a critical 24–48-hour period after the detection of symptoms, a time when much of the decision making is imprecise because all the relevant information is not yet available. Early diagnosis and treatment can save a patient from brain damage or even from death.

MYCIN was developed at Stanford Medical School in the 1970s by Dr. Edward H. Shortliffe. The program's record of correct diagnoses and prescribed treatments has equaled the performance of top human experts.

MYCIN introduced several features that have become the hallmarks of ES:

□ *Rule-based knowledge representation:* The knowledge base consists of about 500 IF-THEN inference rules. For example:
    IF   1. The infection that requires therapy is meningitis, and
           2. The patient has evidence of serious skin or soft tissue infection, and
           3. Organisms were not seen on the stain of the culture, and
           4. The type of infection is bacterial
    THEN There is evidence that the organism (other than those seen on cultures or smears) that might be causing the infection is *Staphylococcus coagpos* (0.75), or *Streptococcus* (0.5).

□ *Probabilistic rules:* Many of the rules include a *chance* option that allows the system to reach plausible conclusions from uncertain evidence. The chance figures in the rules are expressed as certainty factors. (See Chapter 7 of this text.)

□ *Backward chaining method:* The program executes an exhaustive *backward chaining* search (see Chapter 6) for a diagnosis, augmented by a numeric heuristic function.

□ *Explanation:* MYCIN can explain its reasoning. The user (a physician) can interrogate it in various ways—by inquiring *why* the ES asked a particular question or *how* it reached an intermediate or final conclusion. Because each rule is a semi-independent package of knowledge, the user can easily trace the rules that led to a certain question or conclusion.

□ *User-friendly system:* MYCIN is very easy to use. The required training is minimal. The entire dialogue is conducted in plain English.

In a typical consultation session, the physician conducts an interactive dialogue with MYCIN about a particular patient. He or she provides information (e.g., symptoms, patient's characteristics) and responds to questions generated by the ES. The user can also apply *certainty factors* to qualify the answers. MYCIN examines approximately a hundred potential diagnoses. Once the diagnosis is completed, a drug treatment is prescribed.

Because physicians have the final responsibility for treatment, transparency in the system is essential. By typing "RULE," the user obtains an English-language explanation of the last rule executed. Typing "WHY" triggers a back-trace of the inference process that fired the system's last question. Repeated use of RULE and WHY activates further backtracing. A sample consultation with MYCIN is shown next:

MYCIN: What is the infection?
Physician: Endarteritis [an inflammation of the inner layer of an artery that can be caused by a number of agents].
MYCIN: Is organism-1 a rod or a coccus? [This question will narrow the range of possible agents for the disease.]
Physician: Rod.

MYCIN then asks additional questions about laboratory test results to help determine what organisms might be causing the disease. When it has reached its conclusion, it will recommend a particular drug therapy to combat the organism or organisms involved. So that the physician will trust MYCIN's conclusions, the program is designed to answer questions about its reasoning. For example:

Physician: How did you decide that organism-1 is *E. coli?*
MYCIN: I used rule 084 to conclude that organism-1 is *E. coli.* This gave a cumulative certainty factor of 0.51. [The physician can question further, either by looking at the text of the rule involved, or by questioning its antecedents.]

XCON (Expert VAX System Configuration)

Digital Equipment Corp. (DEC) has always offered its customers a wide range of minicomputer system configurations. It is not uncommon to have thousands of customer orders on hand, each one involving different needs and specifications. This wide range of combinations creates a complex business environment involving many interdependent decisions and tasks for processing the orders, scheduling the necessary manufacturing and other operations, and distributing computer system orders to the customer in a timely manner.

Until XCON became available, the computer system configuration task was accomplished manually. Technical editors in manufacturing reviewed all customer orders for technical correctness and order completeness. This was an extremely difficult task that required many knowledgeable people. Traditional work methods did not yield the accurate, cost-effective, fast response that XCON provides.

Most of the computer system orders that customers send to DEC have unique specifications (many line items per order). The development of XCON represented a very significant tool for managing the complexity of DEC's business. A dramatic increase in productivity of the technical editors has occurred as a result of the effective use of XCON in the manufacturing environment. XCON is a rule-based system with several thousand rules, implemented in OPS5, a general-purpose, rule-based language (see Chapter 13).

When XCON was first installed for the configuration of the VAX 11/750 and 11/780 computers, the system had limited capability and knowledge. Therefore, much interaction was required with the technical editors to increase the system's expertise. The results, however, are astonishing. Traditionally trained manufacturing technical editors required twenty to thirty minutes to configure each system order. In contrast, XCON can configure extremely complex system orders in less than a minute. It also provides additional functions and capabilities not formerly performed by the traditional technical editors, such as (1) defining the exact cable length for all cables required between each system component, and (2) providing the vector addresses calculation for the computer bus options.

By 1985 all VAX family system orders in U.S. and European plant operations were configured by XCON. As the workload increased in the system manufacturing plants, no additional technical editors were hired because of the increase in productivity and capacity provided by XCON.

In the past, a large portion of the system orders scheduled for the factory floor had numerous configuration errors and lacked completeness; with XCON, VAX orders have accurate configurations 98 percent of the time (compared with 65 percent in the manual system). Manufacturing operation benefits from accurate system configurations include (1) an increased throughput order rate, (2) fewer shipments delayed because of system configuration errors, and (3) better use of materials on hand.

When numerous line item changes occur on customer orders already scheduled in the manufacturing process, XCON provides a tool to save time, increase output per person, and lower manufacturing costs.

Redeployment of DEC's highly skilled senior technicians has occurred, allowing them to address more technically difficult tasks. Cost savings to DEC are estimated at about $15 million each year. Plant management, extremely satisfied with the emerging artificial intelligence methodologies, is participating in this pioneering effort with great enthusiasm.

The company is developing related ES. Figure 3C.1 shows the expansion to XSEL, XSITE, and several other related systems. XSEL is a system that checks orders for consistency, such as making sure that power supplies match the equipment being shipped. XSITE provides a site plan for the customer's machine room and lists the equipment needed. Other systems are ISA, to aid scheduling; IMACS, to aid manufacturing; ILRPS, to aid long-range planning; IPMS, to aid in project management; and ICSR, to aid in customer service.

DEC's experience provides a good argument for the use of expert systems. Without the flexibility and modular organization inherent in the rule-based ES approach, developers would have been hard-pressed to maintain the incremental growth needed to support DEC's changing product lines.

For more information about XCON see V. Barker and D. O'Connor, "Expert Systems for Configuration at Digital, XCON and Beyond," *Communications of ACM* (March 1989) and J. J. Sviokla, "An Examination of the Impact of Expert Systems on the Firm: The Case of XCON," *MIS Quarterly* (June 1990).

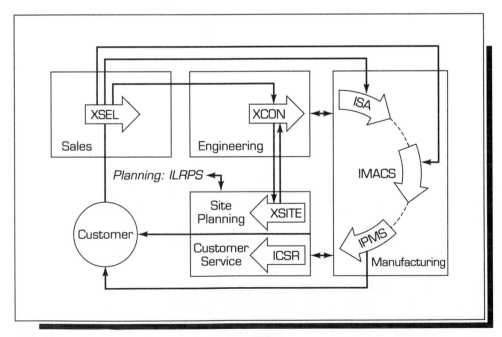

FIGURE 3.C1 Expert Systems Network at DEC

Part 2

Knowledge Engineering

Artificial intelligence applications process knowledge. The theoretical fundamentals of knowledge processing, which is also called knowledge engineering, are described in Part 2. The result of the process is a knowledge base—an essential part of most AI applications.

Knowledge engineering involves several tasks. First, knowledge is collected (from people or from documented sources) in a process called knowledge acquisition (Chapter 4). Acquisition can be done manually and with some degree of automation. Then the acquired knowledge is organized into a knowledge base. In many systems knowledge representation (Chapter 5) involves IF-THEN rules, but other representations are available (e.g., frames).

Making use of the represented knowledge is done through reasoning, or inferencing, procedures (Chapter 6), which are closely related to the manner in which knowledge is represented. For the most part, knowledge is processed under assumed certainty; however, in some cases it is processed under assumed risk or uncertainty. Several procedures are available for treating uncertain knowledge and they are presented in Chapter 7.

Chapter 4

Knowledge Acquisition and Validation

Knowledge acquisition can be viewed as the process of extracting, structuring, and organizing knowledge from one or more sources. This process has been identified by many researchers and practitioners as a (or even as *the*) bottleneck that currently constrains the development of expert systems and other AI systems. This chapter, which attempts to present the most important issues and topics in knowledge acquisition, is divided into the following sections:

4.1 Knowledge Engineering

The activity of **knowledge engineering** has been defined by Feigenbaum and McCorduck [14] as:

> the art of bringing the principles and tools of AI research to bear on difficult applications problems requiring experts' knowledge for their solutions. The technical issues of acquiring this knowledge, representing it, and using it appropriately to construct and explain lines-of-reasoning are important problems in the design of knowledge-based systems. The art of constructing intelligent agents is both part of and an extension of the programming art. It is the art of building complex computer programs that represent and reason with knowledge of the world.

Knowledge engineering can be viewed from two perspectives: narrow and wide. According to the narrow perspective, knowledge engineering deals with knowledge acquisition, representation, validation, inferencing, explanation, and maintenance. Alternatively, according to the wide perspective the term describes the *entire process* of developing and maintaining AI systems. In this book the narrow definition is being used.

Knowledge engineering involves the cooperation of human experts in the domain who work with the knowledge engineer to codify and make explicit the rules (or other procedures) that a human expert uses to solve real problems. Often the expert uses rules applied almost subconsciously. Usually, the program is developed in what may seem a hit-or-miss method. As the knowledge is refined by using the emerging program, the expertise of the system increases. Similarly, as more knowledge is incorporated into the program, the level of expertise rises.

Knowledge engineering usually has a synergistic effect. The knowledge possessed by human experts is often unstructured and not explicitly expressed. The construction of a knowledge base aids the expert to articulate what he or she knows. It can also pinpoint variances from one expert to another (if several experts are being used).

A major goal in knowledge engineering is to construct programs that are modular in nature, so that additions and changes can be made in one module without affecting the workings of other modules. (This is not necessarily the same as the concept of structured programming. Here, the concept of modularity refs to separation of knowledge structures from control mechanisms.) A second major goal is obtaining a program that can explain why it did what it did and justify how it did it.

The success of AI systems depends not only on the knowledge acquired but also on how the knowledge is represented in the computer. The representation then determines the manner in which inference (or reasoning) is executed.

The Knowledge Engineering Process

The knowledge engineering process includes five activities:

Knowledge Acquisition. **Knowledge acquisition** involves the acquisition of knowledge from human experts, books, documents, sensors, or computer files. The knowledge may be specific to the problem domain and the problem-solving procedures, or it may be general knowledge (e.g., knowledge about business), or it may be **metaknowledge** (knowledge about knowledge). By the latter, we mean information about how experts use their knowledge to solve problems.

Knowledge Representation. The acquired knowledge is organized in an activity called knowledge representation. This activity involves preparation of a "knowledge map" and encoding the knowledge in the knowledge base.

Knowledge Validation. The knowledge in the knowledge base is validated and verified (e.g., by using test cases) until its quality is acceptable.

Inference. This activity involves the design of software that will enable the computer to make inferences based on the knowledge, and then provide advice to the user on specific issues.

Explanation and Justification. This activity involves the design and programming of an explanation capability; for example, programming the ability to answer questions like *why* a specific piece of information is needed by the computer or *how* a certain conclusion was derived by the computer.

The process of knowledge engineering and the interrelationships among these activities is shown in Figure. 4.1. The topics of knowledge acquisition and validation are discussed in this chapter. The other activities are presented in subsequent chapters.

4.2 Scope of Knowledge

Knowledge acquisition is the extraction of knowledge from sources of expertise and its transfer to the knowledge base, and sometimes to the inference engine. Acquisition is actually done throughout the entire development process.

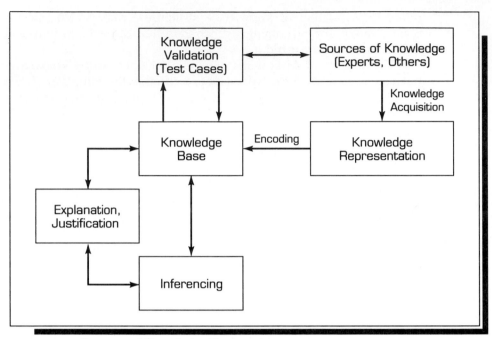

FIGURE 4.1   Process of Knowledge Engineering

Knowledge is a collection of specialized facts, procedures, and judgment rules. Some types of knowledge used in AI are shown in Figure 4.2. These types of knowledge may come from one source or from several sources.

Sources of Knowledge

Knowledge may be collected from many sources. A representative list of sources includes books, films, computer databases, pictures, maps, flow diagrams, stories, songs, or observed behavior. These sources can be divided into two types: *documented* and *undocumented*. The latter resides in people's minds. Knowledge can be identified and collected by using any of the human senses. Knowledge can also be identified and collected by machines.

The multiplicity of sources and types of knowledge contribute to the complexity of knowledge acquisition. This complexity is only one reason why it is difficult to acquire knowledge.

Levels of Knowledge

Knowledge can be represented at different levels. The two extremes are **shallow knowledge** (surface) and **deep knowledge.**

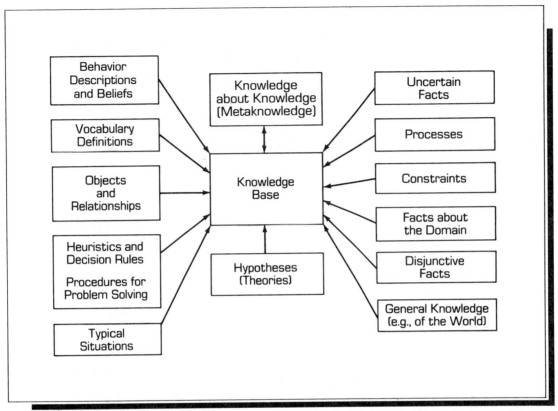

FIGURE 4.2 Types of Knowledge to be Represented in the Knowledge Base (*Source:* Adapted from R. Fikes and T. Kehler, "The Role of Frame-Based Representation in Reasoning," *Communications of ACM* [September 1985].)

Shallow Knowledge. Shallow knowledge refers to representation of only surface level information that can be used to deal with very specific situations. For example, if you don't have gasoline in your car, the car won't start. This knowledge can be shown as a rule:

If gasoline tank is empty → then car will not start.

The shallow version represents basically the input-output relationship of a system. As such, it can be ideally presented in terms of IF-THEN types of rules.

Shallow representation is limited. A set of rules by itself may have little meaning to the user. It may have little to do with the manner in which experts view the domain and solve problems. This may limit the ability of the system, for example, to provide appropriate explanations to the user. Shallow knowledge may also be insufficient in describing complex situations. Therefore, a deeper presentation is frequently required.

Deep Knowledge. Human problem solving is based on deep knowledge of a situation. Deep knowledge refers to the internal and causal structure of a system and considers the interactions among the system's components. Deep knowledge can be applied to different tasks and different situations. It is based on a completely integrated, cohesive body of human consciousness that includes emotions, common sense, intuition, etc. This type of knowledge is difficult to computerize. The system builder must have a perfect understanding of the basic elements and their interactions as produced by nature. To date, such a task has been found to be impossible. We may never be able to computerize deep knowledge, at its extreme.

It is possible, however, to implement a computerized representation that is *deeper* than shallow knowledge. To explain how this is done, let us return to the gasoline example. If we want to investigate at a deeper level the relationship between lack of gasoline and a car that won't start, we need to know the various components of the gas system (for example, pipes, pump, filters, and starter). Such a system is shown schematically in Figure 4.3.

To represent this system and knowledge of its operation, we use special knowledge representation methods such as semantic networks and frames (see Chapter 5). They allow the implementation of deeper-level reasoning such as abstraction and analogy. Reasoning by abstraction and analogy is an important expert activity. We can also represent the objects and processes of the domain of expertise at this level; the relations among objects are important. The control of frame or semantic network systems is usually much more involved than is control of surface systems, and control is implemented in a way that an explanation is much more difficult to produce.

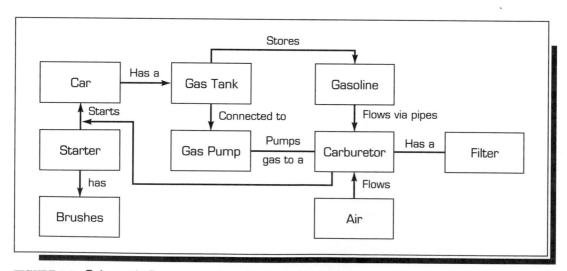

FIGURE 4.3 Schematic Representation of a Deep Knowledge

One type of expertise that has been represented with a deep-level approach is tutoring. The goal of tutoring is to convey to students a domain knowledge that is best represented at the deep level: concepts, abstractions, analogies, and problem-solving strategies.

Categories of Knowledge

Knowledge appears in various categories. The major ones are described next.

Declarative Knowledge. Declarative knowledge is a descriptive representation of knowledge. It tells us facts—*what* things are. It is expressed in a factual statement: "There is a positive association between smoking and cancer." Domain experts tell us about truths and associations. This type of knowledge is considered shallow, or surface-level, information that experts can verbalize. Declarative knowledge is especially important in the initial stage of knowledge acquisition.

Procedural Knowledge. Procedural knowledge considers the manner in which things work under different sets of circumstances. For example, "Compute the ratio between a price of a share and the earnings per share. If this ratio is larger than twelve, stop your investigation. Your investment is too risky. If the ratio is less than twelve, check the balance sheet." Thus, procedural knowledge includes step-by-step sequences and how-to types of instructions; it may also include explanations. Procedural knowledge involves automatic response to stimuli. It also may tell us how to use declarative knowledge and how to make inferences.

Semantic Knowledge. Semantic knowledge reflects cognitive structure that involves the use of the long-term memory. According to Tuthill [38] it is about

□ words and other symbols,
□ word/symbol meanings and usage rules,
□ word/symbol referents and interrelationships, and
□ algorithms for manipulating symbols, concepts, and relations.

Episodic Knowledge. Episodic knowledge is autobiographical, experimental information organized as a case or an episode. It is thought to reside in long-term memory, usually classified by time and place.

Metaknowledge. Metaknowledge means knowledge about knowledge. In AI, metaknowledge refers to knowledge about the operation of knowledge-based systems, that is, about its reasoning capabilities.

4.3   Difficulties in Knowledge Acquisition

In general, transferring information from one person to another is difficult. Several mechanisms can be used to conduct such a transfer—written words, voice, pictures, music—and not one of them is perfect.

Problems also exist in transferring any knowledge, even simple messages. Transferring knowledge in AI is even more difficult, and now we'll see why.

Problems in Transferring Knowledge

Expressing the Knowledge. To solve a problem a human expert executes a two-step process. First, the expert inputs information about the external world into the brain. This information is collected via sensors or is retrieved from memory. Second, the expert uses an inductive, deductive, or other problem-solving approaches on the information. The result (output) is a recommendation.

This process is *internal.* The knowledge engineer must ask the expert to be introspective about his or her (the expert's) decision-making process and about the inner experiences that are involved in it. It may be very difficult for the expert to express his or her experiences about this process, especially when the experiences are made up of sensations, thoughts, sense memories, and feelings. The expert is often unaware of the detailed process that he or she uses to arrive at a conclusion. Therefore, the expert may actually use different rules to solve real-life problems than he or she states in an interview.

Transfer to a Machine. Knowledge is transferred to a machine where it must be organized in a particular manner. The machine requires the knowledge to be expressed explicitly at a lower, *more detailed* level than humans use. Human knowledge exists in a compiled format. A human simply does not remember all the intermediate steps used by his or her brain in transferring or processing knowledge. Thus, there is a mismatch between computers and experts.

Number of Participants. In a regular transfer of knowledge there are two participants (a sender and a receiver). In AI there could be as many as four participants (plus a computer): the expert, the knowledge engineer, the system designer (builder), and the user. Sometimes there are even more participants (e.g., programmers and vendors). These participants have different backgrounds, use different terminology, and possess different skills and knowledge. The experts, for example, may know very little about computers, while the knowledge engineer may know very little about the problem area.

Structuring the Knowledge. In AI it is necessary to elicit not only the knowledge, but also its structure. We have to *represent* the knowledge in a structured way (e.g., as rules).

Other Reasons. Several other reasons add to the complexity of transferring the knowledge:

- □ Experts may lack time or may be unwilling to cooperate.
- □ Testing and refining knowledge is complicated.
- □ Methods for knowledge elicitation may be poorly defined.
- □ System builders have a tendency to collect knowledge from one source, but the relevant knowledge may be scattered across several sources.
- □ Builders may attempt to collect documented knowledge rather than use experts. The knowledge collected may be incomplete.
- □ It is difficult to recognize specific knowledge when it is mixed up with irrelevant data.
- □ Experts may change their behavior when they are being observed and/or interviewed.
- □ Problematic interpersonal communication factors may exist between the knowledge engineer and the expert.

Overcoming the Difficulties

Many efforts have been made recently to overcome some of these problems (for a comprehensive survey, see Boose [4]). For example, research on knowledge acquisition tools has begun to focus on ways to decrease the representation mismatch between the human expert and the program under development. One form of this research might be characterized as research on learning by being told. The attempt here is to develop programs capable of accepting advice as it would often be given to a human novice. In teaching a novice how to play the card game Hearts, an expert might advise the novice to "avoid taking the queen of spades." A human novice would be able to translate the advice into specific techniques or procedures that would result in not acquiring the queen of spades ("don't lead the ace or king of spades"). The ability of ES to make this kind of association is currently very limited.

Another method of easing the representation mismatch between an expert and a program is to allow the expert to converse with the system in a natural language. One step in this direction is to develop computer representations for knowledge that are easily represented in English-language equivalents. Several ES development software packages such as EXSYS, Level5 and VP Expert greatly simplify the syntax of the rules (in a rule-based system) to make them easier for an ES builder to create and understand without special training. Also, a natural language processor can be used to translate knowledge to a specific knowledge representation structure.

In addition, some of the difficulties may be lessened or eliminated with computer-aided knowledge acquisition tools and with extensive integration of the acquisition efforts (see Boose [4]).

Required Skills of Knowledge Engineers

The use of computers and special methods to overcome the difficulties requires qualified knowledge engineers. Listed here are some of the skills and characteristics that are desirable in knowledge engineers:

- Computer skills (hardware, programming, software)
- Tolerance and ambivalence
- Effective communication abilities—sensitivity, tact, and diplomacy
- Broad education
- Advanced, socially sophisticated verbal skills
- Fast-learning capabilities (of the domain)
- Understanding of organizations and individuals
- Wide experience in knowledge engineering
- Intelligence
- Empathy and patience
- Persistence
- Logical thinking
- Versatility and inventiveness
- Self-confidence

These requirements make knowledge engineers in *short supply* (and costly because of high salaries). Some of the automation developments described later attempt to overcome this problem.

4.4 Process of Knowledge Acquisition

The general process of knowledge acquisition can be viewed as being composed of five stages (Hayes-Roth et al.) [19]. These stages are explained here and shown in Figure 4.4.

1. *Identification:* During this stage the problem and its major characteristics are identified. The problem is broken into subproblems (if necessary), the participants (experts, users, etc.) are identified, and the resources are outlined. The knowledge engineer learns about the situation, and all agree on the purpose of the AI application.
2. *Conceptualization:* The knowledge relevant to the decision situation can be quite diversified. Therefore, it is necessary to determine the concepts and relationships used. These and several other questions are answered during conceptualization such as: Which information is used and how can it be represented in the knowledge base? Are rules a good representation medium? How is certain knowledge to be extracted?
3. *Formalization:* Knowledge is acquired for representation in the knowledge base. The manner in which knowledge is organized and represented could determine the acquisition methodology. For example, in rule-

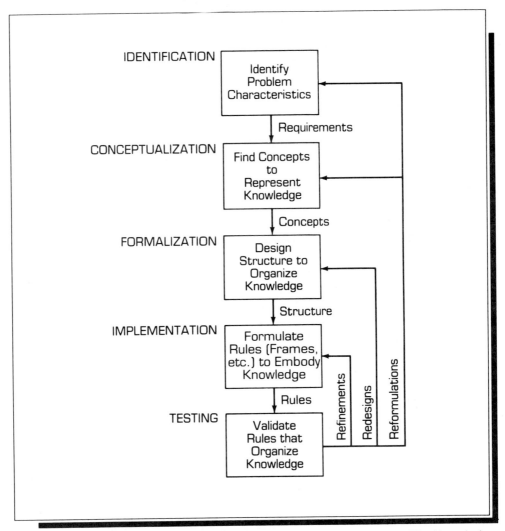

FIGURE 4.4 Stages of Knowledge Acquisition (*Source*: F. Hayes-Roth, "The Knowledge-Based Expert System: A Tutorial," *Computer* [September 1984], © 1984, IEEE.)

based systems the knowledge must be organized in terms of rules. In this stage knowledge acquisition is actually mixed with knowledge representation. Here, the various software and hardware pieces are also examined. This stage is very difficult because it includes the extraction of knowledge from experts.

4. *Implementation:* This stage involves the programming of knowledge into the computer. However, refinements of the knowledge are made with additional acquisitions or changes. A prototype ES is developed at this stage.

5. *Testing:* In the final stage, the knowledge engineer tests the system by subjecting it to examples. The results are shown to the expert and the rules or the frames are revised if necessary. In other words, the validity of the knowledge is examined.

As you can see in Figure 4.4, each stage involves a circular procedure of iteration and reiteration (i.e., the knowledge engineer reformulates, redesigns, and refines the system constantly). In addition, rules (or other representations of knowledge) are added and deleted periodically. During the entire time, the knowledge engineer works closely with the domain expert.

TABLE 4.1 Preliminary and Detailed Issues in Knowledge Acquisition

Preliminary Issues

Basic ("primitive") concepts and terms

Inputs to the problem; which of them are difficult to obtain?

Typical solutions (outputs) to the problem; what are their characteristics?

Sources of knowledge to be used

Methods of knowledge acquisition

Decomposition of the problem (if needed)

Process to be used

Implementation strategies (and problems) of proposed solutions

Detailed Issues

Specific input data; where they come from and how they are organized and which ones are difficult to obtain

Interrelationship between data items; how they relate to decision rules

Relative importance and validity of data

Degree of certainty of the data (inputs, outputs) and the expert's strength of belief in data, rules, and output

Underlying assumptions, strategies, and conclusions

Constraints

Conflicts, exceptions to rules, and conflict resolutions

Reasoning process; the types of inferences

Expert's responses to changes in the system or its environment

Measures of performance (of the outcome)

Degree of complexity of the problem

Relationship to solutions of other experts

Source: Adapted from A. Hart, *Knowledge Acquisition for Expert Systems* (New York: McGraw-Hill, 1986) and D. D. Wolfgram, et al., *Expert Systems* (New York: John Wiley & Sons, 1987).

The execution of these stages can be lengthy and tedious. Many experts are usually not explicitly aware of conceptualization and modeling. Therefore, the knowledge engineer needs to clarify the identification and conceptualization stages. Representative issues that need to be clarified are shown in Table 4.1. They are usually divided into stages: preliminary and detailed issues. For example, a preliminary issue is a list of sources of knowledge that are going to be used, or a decision on what method to use. Once we determine the preliminary issue, we must deal with details, for example, the kind of constraints that exist on each source of knowledge.

4.5 Methods of Knowledge Acquisition: An Overview

The basic model of knowledge engineering portrays teamwork in which a knowledge engineer mediates between the expert and the knowledge base. The knowledge engineer elicits knowledge from the expert, refines it with the expert, and represents it in the knowledge base. The **elicitation of knowledge** from the expert can be done manually or with the aid of computers. Most of the manual elicitation techniques have been borrowed (but frequently modified) from psychology or from system analysis. These elicitation methods are classified in different ways and appear under different names.

The methods described in this book are classified in three categories: manual, semiautomatic, and automatic. The major methods discussed are shown in Figure 4.5.

Manual methods are basically structured around some kind of interview. The knowledge engineer elicits knowledge from the expert and/or other sources and then codes it in the knowledge base. The process is shown in Figure 4.6. The three major manual methods are interviewing (structured, semistructured, unstructured), tracking the reasoning process, and observing. Manual methods are slow, expensive, and sometimes inaccurate. Therefore, there is a trend to automate the process as much as possible.

Semiautomatic methods are divided into two categories: (1) those that are intended to support the experts by allowing them to build knowledge bases with little or no help from knowledge engineers (Figure 4.7), and (2) those that are intended to help the knowledge engineers by allowing them to execute the necessary tasks in a more efficient and/or effective manner (sometimes with only minimal participation by an expert).

In automatic methods the role of both the expert and/or the knowledge engineer is minimized or even eliminated. For example, the induction method of Figure 4.8 can be administered by any builder (e.g., a system analyst). The role of the expert is minimal (limited to validation) and there is no need for a knowledge engineer. The term *automatic* may be misleading. There is always going to be a human builder, but there may be little or no need for a knowledge engineer and an expert.

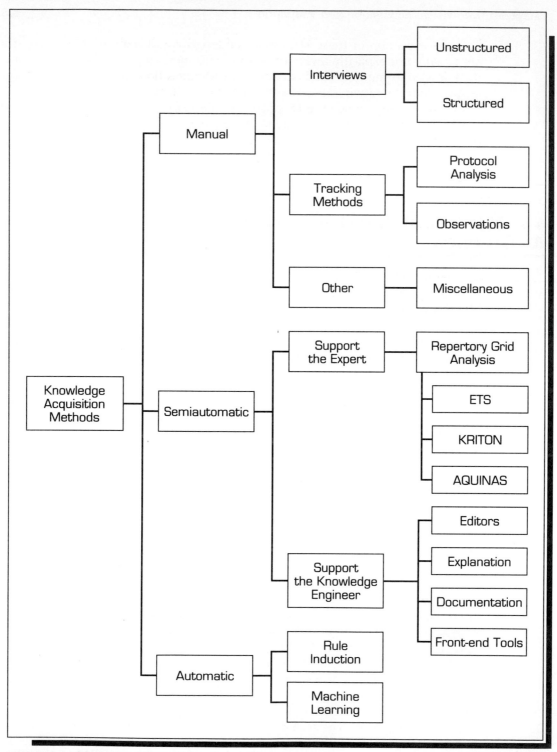

FIGURE 4.5 Methods of Knowledge Acquisition

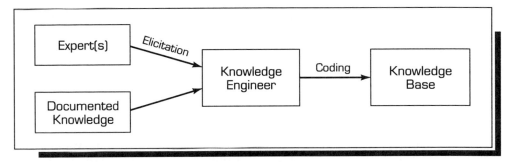

FIGURE 4.6   Manual Methods

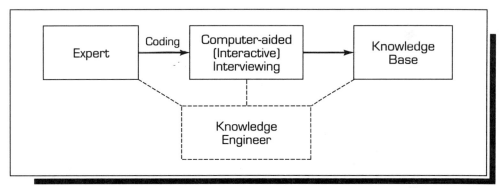

FIGURE 4.7   Expert-driven Knowledge Acquisition; broken lines designate optional interactions

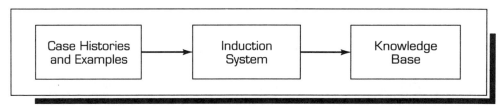

FIGURE 4.8   Induction

4.6   Interviews

The most commonly used form of knowledge acquisition is face-to-face **interview analysis.** It is an explicit technique and it appears in several variations. It involves a direct dialogue between the expert and the knowledge engineer. Information is collected with the aid of conventional instruments (such as tape recorders or questionnaires), and it is subsequently transcribed, analyzed, and coded.

In the interview, the expert is presented with a simulated case, or if possible, with an actual problem of the sort that the ES will be expected to solve. The expert is asked to "talk" the knowledge engineer through the solution. Sometimes this method is referred to as the **walkthrough** method. One variant of the interview approach begins with no information at all being given to the expert. Any facts that the expert requires must be asked for explicitly. By doing this, the expert's path through the domain may be made more evident, especially in terms of defining the input an ES would require.

The interview process can be tedious, and it requires that the knowledge engineer possess a multitude of skills (e.g., communication, conceptualization). It also places great demands on the domain expert, who must be able not only to demonstrate expertise but also to express it. On the other hand, it requires little equipment, it is highly flexible and portable, and it can yield a considerable amount of information if the knowledge engineer is highly trained. Two basic types of interviews can be distinguished: unstructured (informal) and structured.

Unstructured Interviews

Many knowledge acquisition interviews are conducted informally, usually as a starting point. Starting informally saves time; it helps to get quickly to the basic structure of the domain. Usually it is followed by a formal technique. (Actually, you may not want too much information too early because of the many changes and refinements that normally take place.)

Developers might be tempted to think of knowledge acquisition simply as a knowledge engineer talking to experts about their tasks. The knowledge engineer's role is to ask spontaneous questions. Unstructured interviews are seldom this simple. In fact, they may present the knowledge engineer with some very problematic aftereffects.

Unstructured interviewing, according to McGraw and Harbison-Briggs [27], seldom provides complete or well-organized descriptions of cognitive processes. First, they observed that the expert system domains are generally complex; thus, the knowledge engineer *and* the expert must actively prepare for interview situations. Unstructured interviews generally lack the organization that would allow this preparation to transfer effectively to the interview itself. Second, domain experts usually find it very difficult to express some of the more important elements of their knowledge. Third, domain experts may interpret the lack of structure as requiring little preparation on their part prior to the interview. Fourth, data acquired from an unstructured interview are often unrelated, exist at varying levels of complexity, and are difficult for the knowledge engineer to review, interpret, and integrate. A fifth problem cited by McGraw and Harbison-Briggs concerns training. Because of a lack of training and experience, few knowledge engineers can conduct an efficient unstructured interview. Thus, knowledge engineers appear disorganized and may unwittingly allow the expert to have low confidence in the knowledge engineer. This may decrease the rapport needed to work together on a large-scale development effort. Finally and most importantly, unstructured situations generally do not facilitate the acquisition of *specific* information for experts.

Example. Here is a simple example (provided by D. King of Teknowledge, Inc.) of knowledge acquisition for the topic of helping novices use the Statistical Analysis System (SAS) computer package. The dialogue between the expert and the knowledge engineer (KE) may look like this:

EXPERT: Yesterday I talked with a typical novice. He couldn't get started because he didn't understand the DATA step. That's generally a first step and people often forget it.

KE: What did this novice need in the DATA step?

EXPERT: Well, he needed one and it was missing. There are about five different kinds of DATA steps. I recommended a simple fixed-field input and suggested he put the data in the deck rather than in a separate file. By doing that, it cuts down on the complexity of the JCL.

KE: JCL?

EXPERT: JCL is job control language, a nasty set of instructions mostly for file handling. If the data are elsewhere, then a line of JCL must be prepared that says where the data file is and how it is formatted.

KE: We may need to talk more about JCL, but for now, let's return to the man yesterday and his need for a DATA step. Why did you suggest a fixed-format DATA step?

EXPERT: Mostly because his data set was simple. Fixed-format requires the person to refine his data and organize them neatly in rows and columns. Free-field input in the DATA step seems easier to novices, but the possibility of error is greater and finding mistakes in a free-field data set is difficult.

KE: When you say that this man's data set was simple, what do you mean?

EXPERT: There were fewer than a hundred records and only about fifteen variables. There also were no missing data and no complexity in the cases. Last week I talked with a woman who couldn't decide what a record was. She had scores for people who were in classrooms that were nested in schools. She wanted to study school differences. That's not a simple data set.

By interviewing the expert, the knowledge engineer slowly, step-by-step, learns what is going on. Then he or she builds a representation of the knowledge in the expert's terms.

The process of knowledge acquisition involves uncovering the attributes of the problem to which the expert pays attention (e.g., the DATA step, fixed-field input) and making explicit the thought process (usually expressed as rules) that the expert uses to interpret these attributes.

This type of interview is most common. It appears in several variations. In addition to the "talkthrough" one can ask the expert to "teachthrough" or "readthrough." In a teachthrough the expert acts as an instructor and the knowledge engineer as a student. The expert not only tells *what* he or she does, but also explains *why* and, in addition, instructs the knowledge engineer in the skills and strategies needed to perform the task. In a readthrough approach the expert is asked to instruct the knowledge engineer *how* to read and interpret the documents which are used for the task.

Structured Interviews

The **structured interview** is a systematic goal-oriented process. It forces an organized communication between the knowledge engineer and the expert. The structure reduces the interpretation problems inherent in unstructured interviews, and it allows the knowledge engineer to prevent the distortion caused by the subjectivity of the domain expert. Structuring an interview requires attention to a number of procedural issues, which are summarized in Table 4.2.

Because of the specific nature of each interview, it is difficult to provide good guidelines for the entire interview process. Therefore, interpersonal communication and analytical skills are important. There are, however, several guidelines, checklists, and instruments that are fairly generic in nature. An example is provided in Table 4.3.

Interviewing techniques, though very popular, do have many disadvantages. They range from inaccuracies in collecting information to biases introduced by the interviewer (see references 26, 27, 29, and 31).

TABLE 4.2 Procedures for Structured Interviews

☐ The knowledge engineer studies available material on the domain to identify major demarcations of the relevant knowledge.

☐ The knowledge engineer reviews the planned expert system capabilities. He or she identifies targets for the questions to be asked during the knowledge acquisition session.

☐ The knowledge engineer formally schedules and plans (using a form) the structured interviews. Planning includes attending to physical arrangements, defining knowledge acquisition session goals and agendas, and identifying or refining major areas of questioning.

☐ The knowledge engineer may write sample questions, focusing on question type, level, and questioning techniques.

☐ The knowledge engineer ensures that the domain expert understands the purpose and goals of the session and encourages the expert to prepare prior to the interview.

☐ During the interview the knowledge engineer follows guidelines for conducting interviews.

☐ During the interview the knowledge engineer uses *directional control* to retain the interview's structure.

Source: Condensed from K. L. McGraw and B. K. Harbison-Briggs, *Knowledge Acquisition, Principles and Guidelines* (Englewood Cliffs, N.J.: Prentice-Hall, 1989).

TABLE 4.3 Sample Guidelines for Manual Note Taking

☐ Before the interview, tell the expert that you will be taking notes and how you expect to use them. This provides an opportunity to diffuse an expert's hesitation about having his or her ideas recorded.

☐ Maintain eye contact as much as possible during the note-taking intervals.

☐ Do not cue the expert as to what is or is not important by furiously scribbling in response to an answer. Maintain as steady a level of note-taking activity throughout the interview as is possible.

☐ To make the expert feel more at ease, allow him or her to view the notes instead of trying to hide them.

☐ Code the notes to phases or sections of the interview to help you restructure the interview as you are refining your notes.

☐ Review the notes soon (within twenty-four to forty-eight hours) after the interview to aid your recall.

In summary, interviews are important techniques, but they must be planned carefully, and the interview results *must* be subjected to thorough verification and validation methodologies. Interviews are sometimes replaced by tracking methods. Alternatively, they can be used to supplement tracking or other knowledge acquisition methods.

4.7 Tracking Methods

Process tracking refers to a set of techniques that attempt to *track* the reasoning process of an expert. It is a popular approach among cognitive psychologists who are interested in discovering the expert's "train of thought" while he or she reaches a conclusion.

The knowledge engineer can use the tracking process to find what information is being used and how it is being used. Tracking methods can be informal or formal. The most common formal method is protocol analysis.

Protocol analysis, particularly a set of techniques known as verbal protocol analysis, is a common method by which the knowledge engineer acquires detailed knowledge from the expert. A protocol is a record or documentation of the expert's step-by-step information processing and decision-making behavior. In this method, which is similar to interviewing but more formal and systematic, the expert is asked to perform a real task and to verbalize his or her thought process. The expert is asked by the knowledge engineer to "think aloud" while performing the task or solving the problem under observation. Usually, a recording is made as the expert thinks aloud; it describes every aspect of the information processing and decision-making behavior. This recording then becomes a record, or protocol, of the expert's ongoing behavior. Later, the

TABLE 4.4 Procedure of
Protocol Analysis

Provide the expert with a full range of information normally associated with a task.

Ask the expert to verbalize the task in the same manner as would be done normally while verbalizing his or her decision process and record the verbalization on tape.

Make statements by transcribing the verbal protocols.

Gather the statements that seem to have high information content.

Simplify and rewrite the collected statements and construct a table of production rules out of the collected statements.

Produce a series of models by using the production rules.

Source: J. Kim and J. F. Courtney, "A Survey of Knowledge Acquisition Techniques and Their Relevance to Managerial Problem Domains," *Decision Support Systems* 4 (October 1988), p. 273.

recording is transcribed for further analysis (e.g., to deduce the decision process) and coded by the knowledge engineer. For further details see Ericsson and Simon [13] and Wolfgram et al. [40].

In contrast with interactive interview methods, a protocol analysis involves mainly a one-way communication. The knowledge engineer prepares the scenario and plans the process. During the session the expert does most of the talking as he or she interacts with data to solve the problem. Concurrently, the knowledge engineer *listens* and records the process. Later, he or she must be able to analyze, interpret, and structure the protocol into knowledge representation for a review by the expert.

The process of protocol analysis is summarized in Table 4.4 and its advantages and limitations are presented in Table 4.5.

TABLE 4.5 Advantages and Limitations of Protocol Analysis

Advantages	Limitations
Expert consciously considers decision-making heuristics	Requires that expert be aware of why he or she makes a decision
Expert consciously considers decision alternatives, attributes, values	Requires that expert be able to categorize major decision alternatives
Knowledge engineer can observe and analyze decision-making behavior	Requires that expert be able to verbalize the attributes and values of a decision alternative
Knowledge engineer can record, and later analyze with the expert, key decision points	Requires that expert be able to reason about the selection of a given alternative
	Subjective view of decision making
	Explanations may not track with reasoning

Source: K. L. McGraw and B. K. Harbison-Briggs, *Knowledge Acquisition, Principles and Guidelines* (Englewood Cliffs, N.J.: Prentice-Hall, 1989), p. 217.

4.8 Observations and Other Manual Methods

Observations

In some cases it may be possible to observe the expert at work in the field. In many ways this is the most obvious and straightforward approach to knowledge acquisition. The difficulties involved should not, however, be underestimated. For example, most experts advise several people simultaneously. The observations being made thus cover all other activities as well. Therefore, large quantities of data are being collected from which only a little is useful. In particular, if recordings and/or videotapings are made, the cost of transcribing from large quantities of tape or video should be carefully considered.

Observations, which can be viewed as a special case of protocols, are of two types: motor and eye movement. In the first type the expert's *physical* performance of the task (e.g., walking, reaching, talking) is documented. In the second type a record of where the expert fixes his or her gaze is being made. Observations are used primarily as a way of supporting verbal protocols. They are generally expensive and time consuming.

Other Manual Methods

Many other manual methods can be used to elicit knowledge from experts. A representative list is given here; for complete discussion see Diaper [10].

- *Case analysis:* Experts are asked how they handled specific cases in the past. Usually this method involves analyzing documentation. In addition to the experts, other people (e.g., managers, users) may be questioned.
- *Critical incident analysis:* In this approach only selected cases are investigated, usually those that are memorable, difficult, or of a special interest. Both experts and others may be questioned.
- *Commentaries:* In this method the knowledge engineer asks experts to give a running commentary on what they are doing. This method can be supported by videotaping the experts in action or by asking an observer to do the commentary.
- *Conceptual graphs:* Diagrams and other graphic methods can be instrumental in supporting other acquisition methods.
- *Brainstorming:* This method can be used to solicit the opinion of multiple experts. The method helps to generate ideas.
- *Prototyping:* Working with a prototype of the system is a powerful approach to induce experts to contribute their knowledge. Experts like to criticize systems. Changes may be made instantly.
- *Multidimensional scaling:* The complex technique of **multidimensional scaling** identifies various dimensions of knowledge and then places the knowledge in a form of a distance matrix. By using least-squares fitting regression, the various dimensions are analyzed, interpreted, and integrated.

□ *Johnson's hierarchial clustering:* This is another scaling method, but it is much simpler to implement and therefore is used more. It combines related knowledge elements into clusters (two elements at a time).
□ *Simulation*
□ *Concept sorting*
□ *Task analysis*

4.9   Expert-driven Methods

In the previous methods the major role of knowledge acquisition was played by the knowledge engineer, whose skills determined the quality of the knowledge base. However, knowledge engineers typically lack knowledge about the domain, their services are expensive, and they may have problems communicating with experts. As a result knowledge acquisition may be a slow process with many iterations (for verification and learning purposes). The process, then, is usually slow, expensive, and even unreliable because the experts may find it difficult to contribute their knowledge via the knowledge engineering process.

Perhaps experts should be their own knowledge engineers, encoding their own expertise into computers. Such expert-driven arrangements could solve some of the difficulties described earlier as well as result in less "noise" being introduced into the knowledge base. The role of knowledge engineers will be reduced and the acquisition process will be drastically expedited.

According to Kim and Courtney [23] the following assumptions are necessary to implement such an arrangement:

□ The expert can identify the variables and the relationships among them.
□ The expert can learn and use the encoding interface.
□ The expert can use computer-aided techniques for executing the process, when needed.
□ The expert can structure a refinable model by using a structured approach to the domain.
□ The inevitable loss of transparency in encoded knowledge is acceptable if the expert can assure the performance of the model.

Two approaches to expert-driven systems are available: manual and computer aided (semiautomatic).

Manual Method: Expert's Self-reports

Sometimes it is possible to elicit knowledge from experts manually by using a self-administered questionnaire or an organized report. Open-ended questionnaires are appropriate for knowledge discovery in which high-level concepts are usually the result. Close-ended (or forced-answer) questionnaires are more structured and easy to fill in, but the knowledge collected is limited. In addition to questionnaires, experts may be asked to log their activities, prepare a one-hour introductory lecture, or produce reports about their problem-solving activities.

Experts' reports and questionnaires exhibit a number of problems according to Wolfgram et al. [40].

1. They essentially require the expert to act as a knowledge engineer, without a knowledge engineer's training.
2. The reports tend to have a high degree of bias; they typically reflect the expert's opinion concerning how the task "should be done" rather than "how it is really done."
3. Experts will often describe new and untested ideas and strategies they have been contemplating but still have not included in their decision-making behavior. Thus, there is a mixture of past experience, actual behavior, and "ideal future" behavior.
4. Experts' reports are time-consuming efforts, and the experts lose interest rapidly. The quality of information attained will rapidly decrease as the report progresses.
5. Experts must be proficient in flowcharting or other process-documenting techniques.
6. Experts may forget to specify certain pieces of knowledge (which may result in ambiguity).
7. Experts are likely to be fairly vague about the nature of associations among events (which may result in an indeterminate bias).

Given these caveats, under certain conditions such as the inaccessibility of an expert to the knowledge engineer, expert reports and self-questionnaires may provide useful preliminary knowledge discovery and acquisition.

Some of the limitations of the manual approach can be removed if a computer is used to support the process.

Computer-aided Approaches

The purpose of computerized support to the expert is to reduce or eliminate the potential problems discussed, especially those of indeterminate bias and ambiguity (see Kim and Courtney [23]). These problems dominate the gathering of information for the initial knowledge base and the interactive refinements of this knowledge. A smart knowledge acquisition tool needs to be able to add knowledge incrementally to the knowledge base and refine or even correct existing knowledge.

Visual modeling techniques are often used to construct the initial domain model. The objective of the visual modeling approach is to give the user the ability to visualize real-world problems and to manipulate elements of it through the use of graphics. Kearney [22] indicates that diagrams and drawings are useful in representing problems; they serve as a set of external memory aids and reveal inconsistencies in an individual's knowledge.

Several tools can be used by experts (for a survey see Boose and Gaines [6]). Of a special interest are those methods that are based on repertory grid analysis, a topic presented next.

4.10   Repertory Grid Analysis

Experience is often based on perception, insight, and intuition. Therefore, many experts have difficulties in expressing their line of reasoning. Experts may also be confused between facts and factors that actually influence decision making. To overcome these and other limitations of knowledge acquisition by gaining insight into the expert's mental model of the problem domain, a number of elicitation techniques have been developed. These techniques, derived from psychology, use an approach called the *classification interview*. Since they are fairly structured, when applied to AI technologies, these methods are usually aided by a computer. The primary method is **repertory grid analysis** (RGA).

Basis for the Grid

The RGA is based on Kelly's model of human thinking called Personal Construct Theory. According to this theory each person is viewed as a "personal scientist" who seeks to predict and control events by forming theories, testing hypotheses, and analyzing results of experiments. Knowledge and perceptions about the world (or about a domain or a problem) are classified and categorized by each individual as a personal, perceptual model. Based on the model developed, each individual is able to anticipate and then act on the basis of these anticipations.

This personal model matches our view of an expert at work; it is a description of the development and use of the expert's knowledge, and therefore it is suitable for expert systems as suggested by Hart [18]. The RGA is a method of investigating such a model.

How the RGA Works

The RGA combines several processes. First, the expert identifies the *important objects* in the domain of expertise. For example, computer languages (LISP, C, COBOL) are objects in the case of a need to select a computer language. This identification is done in an interview.

Second, the expert identifies the important attributes that are considered in making decisions in the domain. For example, availability and ease of programming are important in the case of selecting a computer language.

Third, for each attribute the expert is asked to establish a bipolar scale with distinguishable characteristics (traits) and their opposites. For example, in the case of selecting computer languages the information shown in Table 4.6 may be included.

TABLE 4.6 RGA Input for Selecting a Computer Language

Attributes	Trait	Opposite
Availability	Widely available	Not available
Ease of programming	High	Low
Training time	Low	High
Orientation	Symbolic	Numeric

Fourth, the interviewer picks any three of the objects and asks: What attributes and traits distinguish any two of these objects from the third? For example, if a set includes LISP, PROLOG, and COBOL, the expert may point to "orientation." Then the expert will tell that the LISP and PROLOG are symbolic in nature (getting three points each), while COBOL is numeric (one point). This step continues for several triplets of objects. The answers are recorded in a grid as shown in Table 4.7. The numbers inside the grid designate the value assigned to each attribute for each object (a scale of 1 to 3 or 1 to 5 is usually used; in this case, 1 to 3).

Once the grid is completed, the expert may change the ratings inside the box. The grid can be used afterward to make recommendations in situations where the importance of the attributes is known. For example, in a simplistic manner, it can be said that if numeric orientation is very important, then, COBOL is the recommended language.

Use of RGA in Expert Systems

A number of knowledge acquisition tools have been developed based on the RGA (e.g., see Boose [4]). These tools are aimed at helping in the conceptualization of the domain. Three representative tools are ETS, KRITON, and AQUINAS.

Expertise Transfer System. **Expertise Transfer System** (ETS) is a computer program that interviews experts and helps them build expert systems. ETS interviews experts to uncover vocabulary conclusions, problem-solving traits, trait structures, trait weights, and inconsistencies. It has been utilized to

TABLE 4.7 Example of a Grid

Attribute	Orientation	Ease of Programming	Training Time	Availability
Trait Opposite	Symbolic (3) Numeric (1)	High (3) Low (2)	High (1) Low (3)	High (3) Low (1)
LISP	3	3	1	1
PROLOG	3	2	2	1
C	2	3	2	2
COBOL	1	2	1	3

construct prototypes rapidly (often in less than two hours for very small ES), to aid the expert in determining if there is sufficient knowledge to solve the problem, and to create knowledge bases for a variety of different ES shells from its own internal representation. An improved version of ETS called NeoETS has been developed to expand the capabilities of ETS. The method is limited to classification-type problems. For details see Boose [3].

KRITON. KRITON is a system that attempts to automate the use of the repertory grid approach. First it conducts interviews with experts; then it analyzes protocols and documents by interacting with the experts. The expert, based on key word statistics, selects portions of texts for propositional analysis using the same tools used in protocol analysis. Since documents are normally not as problem-oriented as protocols, the expert adds goal information to the results of the analysis. Should experiments with this system be successful, it can replace a knowledge engineer, resulting in a true breakthrough in AI applications. For further details see Diederich et al. [11].

AQUINAS. AQUINAS is a very complex tool (see Boose and Bradshaw [5]) that extends the problem solving and knowledge representation of ETS by allowing experts to structure knowledge in hierarchies. A set of heuristics has been defined and incorporated in the Dialog Manager, a subsystem of AQUINAS, to provide guidance in the knowledge acquisition process to domain experts and knowledge engineers.

Finally, the Auto-Intelligence tool (see section 4.12) is based on the RGA. It was the first commercial tool to combine the repertory grid approach with rule induction.

4.11   Supporting the Knowledge Engineer

A number of acquisition and encoding tools greatly reduce the need for the time (and/or skill level) of the knowledge engineer. Nevertheless, the knowledge engineer in such a case still plays an important role in the process as shown in Figure 4.9. The figure depicts the major tasks of the knowledge engineer:

- Advise the expert on the process of interactive knowledge elicitation
- Manage the interactive knowledge acquisition tools, setting them up appropriately
- Edit the unencoded and coded knowledge base in collaboration with the expert
- Manage the knowledge encoding tools, setting them up appropriately
- Validate the application of the knowledge base in collaboration with the expert
- Train the clients in the effective use of the knowledge base in collaboration with the expert by developing operational and training procedures

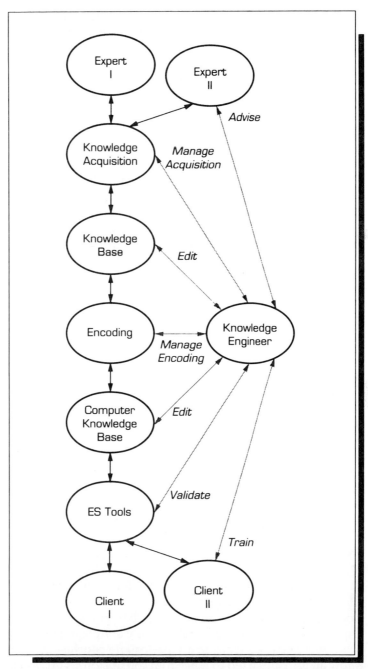

FIGURE 4.9 Knowledge Engineers' Roles in Interactive Knowledge Acquisition (*Source:* Adapted from B. R. Gaines "Knowledge Acquisition: Development and Advances," in *Expert Systems and Intelligent Manufacturing*, M. D. Oliff, ed. [New York: Elsevier, 1988].)

This use of interactive elicitation can be combined with manual elicitation and with the use of the interactive tools by the knowledge engineer. The knowledge engineer can (1) directly elicit knowledge from the expert and (2) use interactive elicitation tools to enter knowledge into the knowledge base.

Knowledge Acquisition Aids

Several types of tools have been developed for supporting knowledge acquisition. Some representative examples follow.

Editors and Interfaces. Use of a text editor or a special knowledge-base editor can facilitate the task of entering knowledge into the system and decrease the chance of errors. A good editor provides smooth user interfaces that facilitate instruction and display information conveniently. The editor checks, for example, syntax and semantics for completeness and consistency. The rule editor of EXSYS is an example of one that simplifies rule input and testing. A spelling and a grammar checker can also be used to detect errors.

Explanation Facility. The explanation subsystem serves not only the user but also the knowledge engineer and the expert in refining and improving the knowledge base. In addition to general-purpose devices (such as debugging and trace mechanisms), there are specially constructed explanation facilities, which can trace, for example, the chain of reasoning after it has been completed.

Revision of the Knowledge Base. Changes in the knowledge base can be made by selecting an appropriate revision from a set of possibilities. To avoid introducing new bugs or inconsistencies with the existing knowledge base, aids such as a semantic consistency checker or automated testing can be used.

Pictorial Knowledge Acquisition (PIKA). PIKA is a graphics editor whose output is a collection of structured graphic objects that can be combined to support a multilevel interface (see Freiling et al. [15]).

Example of a Knowledge Acquisition Aid. A classic program called TEIRE-SIAS (see Hayes-Roth et al. [19]), was developed to assist knowledge engineers in the creation (or revision) of rules for a specific ES while working with the EMYCIN shell. The program uses a natural language interface to assist the knowledge engineer in testing and debugging new knowledge. It provides an expanded explanation capability. For example, if system builders find that a set of knowledge rules leads to an inadequate conclusion, they can have TEIRESIAS show all the rules used to reach that conclusion. With the rule editor, adjustments can easily be made. To expedite the process, TEIRESIAS translates each new rule, which is entered in natural language, into LISP. Then it retranslates the rule into natural language. The program thus can point out inconsistencies, rule conflicts, and inadequacies.

Integrated Knowledge Acquisition Aids

Most of the preceding tools and many others were designed separately on the assumption that they will be used by a specific ES participant (e.g., the expert) for the execution of a specific task. In reality, however, participants may play multiple roles or even exchange roles. Therefore, there is a trend to integrate the acquisition aids. For an overview of such integration tools see Gaines [16]. Examples of such tools are Auto-Intelligence, which will be described in section 4.12, and KADS, which is described next.

Knowledge Acquisition and Documentation System (KADS). The purpose of these techniques, which were developed at the University of Amsterdam, is to aid the knowledge engineer in acquiring, structuring, analyzing, and documenting expert knowledge. KADS is known to be very successful in increasing the knowledge engineer's productivity.

Front-end Tools

Knowledge needs to be coded in a specific manner in various knowledge-based tools. In an attempt to automate the coding, various tools have been developed. For example, Knowledge Analysis Tool (KAT) converts knowledge to a specific rule format for a tool called Level5 (see Chapter 13). NEXTRA is a similar tool that helps the knowledge engineer to code rules in a product called Nexpert Object (see Chapter 13).

4.12 Induction

The elicitation methods presented so far in this chapter are labor intensive. The two major participants are the knowledge engineer, who is difficult to get and is highly paid, and the domain expert, who is usually busy and frequently uncooperative. Therefore, manual and even the semiautomatic elicitation methods are both slow and expensive. In addition, they exhibit some other deficiencies:

- It is difficult to validate the acquired knowledge.
- There is frequently weak correlation between verbal reports and mental behavior.
- In certain situations experts are unable to provide an overall account of how their decisions are made.
- The quality of the system depends too much on the quality of the expert and the knowledge engineer.
- The expert does not understand the AI technology.
- The knowledge engineer does not understand, in many cases, the nature of the business.

Thus it makes sense to develop knowledge acquisition methods that will reduce or even eliminate the need for these two participants. These methods, which are described as *computer-aided* knowledge acquisition, or automated knowledge acquisition, vary in their objectives, some of which are listed here:

- Increase the productivity of knowledge engineering (reduce the cost)
- Reduce the skill level required from the knowledge engineer
- Eliminate (or drastically reduce) the need for an expert
- Eliminate (or drastically reduce) the need for a knowledge engineer
- Increase the quality of the acquired knowledge

Two major topics are frequently covered under automated knowledge acquisition: machine learning (which will be discussed in Chapter 19) and **rule induction,** which is presented next.

Automated Rule Induction

Induction means a process of reasoning from the specific to the general. In ES terminology it refers to the process in which rules are generated by a computer program from example cases.

A rule-induction system is given examples of a problem (called a *training set*) where the outcome is known. After it has been given several examples (the more the better), the rule induction system can create rules that fit the example cases. The rules can then be used to assess other cases where the outcome is not known. The heart of a rule-induction system is an algorithm, which is used to induce the rules from the examples (see Box 4.1).

Box 4.1: Induction Algorithms

Induction methods use various algorithms to convert a knowledge matrix of attributes, values, and selections to rules. Such algorithms vary from statistical methods to neural computing.

A popular induction algorithm is ID3. ID3 first converts the knowledge matrix into a decision tree. Irrelevant attributes are eliminated and the relevant attributes are organized in an efficient manner. For more information on ID3 consult pages 406–410 of Cohen and Feigenbaum [9].

An example of a simplified rule induction can be seen in the work of a loan officer in a bank. Requests for loans include information about the applicants such as income level, assets, age, and the number of dependents. These are the *attributes*, or characteristics, of the applicants. If we log several example cases, each with its final decision, we will find a situation that resembles the data in Table 4.8.

TABLE 4.8 Cases for Induction

| | Attributes | | | | |
| | | | | | |
Applicant	Annual Income ($)	Assets ($)	Age	Number of Dependents	Decision
Mr. White	50,000	100,000	30	3	Yes
Ms. Green	70,000	None	35	1	Yes
Mr. Smith	40,000	None	33	2	No
Ms. Rich	30,000	250,000	42	0	Yes

From these cases it is easy to infer the following three rules:

1. If income is $70,000 or more, approve the loan.
2. If income is $30,000 or more, age is at least forty, assets are above $249,000, and there are no dependents, approve the loan.
3. If income is between $30,000 and $50,000 and assets are at least $100,000, approve the loan.

Advantages of Rule Induction. One of the leading researchers in the field, Donald Michie, has pointed out that only certain types of knowledge can be properly acquired using manual knowledge acquisition methods like interviews and observations. These are cases in which the domain of knowledge is certain, small, loosely coupled, or modular. As the domain gets bigger and more complex, experts become unable to explain how they operate. They can, however, still supply the knowledge engineer with suitable examples of problems and solutions. Using rule induction allows ES to be used in more complicated, and more commercially rewarding, fields (see Michie [31]).

Another advantage is that the builder does not have to be a knowledge engineer. He or she can be the expert or a system analyst. This not only saves time and money, but it also solves the difficulties of dealing with the knowledge engineer who is an outsider unfamiliar with the "business."

Machine induction also offers the possibility of deducing new knowledge. It may be possible to list all the factors that influence a decision, without understanding their impacts, and to induce a rule that works successfully.

Once rules are generated they are reviewed by the expert and modified if necessary. A big advantage of rule induction is that it enhances the thinking process of the expert.

Difficulties in Implementation. Despite the advantages, several difficulties exist with the implementation of rule induction:

  □ Some induction programs may generate rules that are not easy for a human to understand, because the way in which they classify a problem's attributes and properties may not be in accordance with the way that a human would do it.

□ Rule-induction programs do not select the attributes. An expert still has to be available to specify which attributes are significant; for example, the important factors in approving a loan. Rule-induction systems also do not help discover that two or more attributes may be functionally or causally related and not independent of each other. Use of redundant attributes can create biased and incorrect rules.

□ The search process in rule induction is based on special algorithms that generate efficient decision trees, which reduce the number of questions that must be asked before a conclusion is reached. Several alternative algorithms are available and they vary in their processes and capabilities (e.g., general versus specific).

□ The method is good only for rule-based, classification-type problems, especially of the yes-or-no types. (However, many problems can be rephrased or split so that they fall into the classification category.)

□ The number of attributes must be fairly small. With more than fifteen attributes there may be a need for a large computer. The upper limit on the number of attributes is approached very quickly.

□ The number of "sufficient" examples that is needed can be very large.

□ The set of examples must be "sanitized"; for example, cases that are exceptions to rules must be removed. (Such exceptions can be determined by observing inconsistent rules.)

□ The method is limited to situations under certainty (deterministic).

□ A major problem with the method, according to Hart [18], is that the builder does not know in advance whether the number of examples is sufficient and whether the algorithm is good enough. To be sure of this would presuppose that the builder had some idea of the "solution"; the reason for using induction in the first instance is that the builder *does not know* the solution, but wants to discover it by using the rules.

Because of these limitations, the induction method is used to provide a first prototype; then it is translated into something more robust and handcrafted into an improved system.

Software Packages. Several induction software packages are available on the market both for personal computers and for larger computers. Here are some representative packages:

□ 1st-CLASS (personal computer)
□ TIMM (larger computer)
□ Rule Master (personal computer and larger)
□ EX-Tran 7 (personal computer and larger)
□ Knowledgeshaper (workstation and mainframe)
□ BEAGLE (personal computer and larger)
□ Level5 (personal computer)
□ VP Expert (personal computer)

Most of these programs not only generate rules, but also check them for possible logical conflict. Furthermore, some of them can be used as ES shells; that is, they can be used to generate the rules for the knowledge base and then to construct an ES that uses this knowledge.

Interactive Induction

The major objective of rule induction methods and software, as described earlier, is to eliminate or drastically reduce the need for both the expert and the knowledge engineer. The tools are fairly simple so they can be used with little training. In many cases, however, it is advisable to use a knowledge engineer, even if the rules are induced automatically.

The combination of an expert supported by a computer is labeled **interactive induction.** An attempt to automate some tasks of the knowledge engineer will be shown in the next section. However, one interesting attempt that combines induction and interactive acquisition can be found in a tool called Auto-Intelligence (IntelligenceWare, Inc., Los Angeles).

Auto-Intelligence captures the knowledge of an expert through interactive interviews, distills the knowledge, and then automatically generates a rule-based knowledge base. An important part of the interaction with Auto-Intelligence is a structure discovery, during which the *system* interviews the expert prior to classifying the information and distilling knowledge by induction.

Structure is discovered by utilizing special deductive question-generation techniques based on repertory grids, multidimensional scaling, and data classification. These techniques help experts think about problems locally and piece by piece, thus gradually revealing their expertise.

Auto-Intelligence builds ES for structured selection or heuristic classification tasks in which an expert makes decisions and selects among a number of choices based on available criteria. Examples of heuristic classification tasks include diagnosis, investment selection, situation assessment, and so forth. Auto-Intelligence interacts with experts (without knowledge engineers); it helps them bypass their cognitive defenses and biases and identify the important criteria and constructs used in decision making. For details, see Parsaye [35].

4.13   Selecting an Appropriate Method

Several years ago the objectives of an ideal knowledge acquisition system were outlined by Hill et al. [20]:

□ Direct interaction with the expert without intervention by a knowledge engineer
□ Applicability to unlimited, or at least a broad class of, problem domains
□ Tutorial capabilities to eliminate the need for prior training of the expert

□ Ability to analyze work in progress to detect inconsistencies and gaps in knowledge

□ Ability to incorporate multiple sources of knowledge

□ A human interface (i.e., a natural conversation) that will make the use of the system enjoyable and attractive

□ Ability to interface easily with different expert system tools as appropriate to the problem domain

To attain these objectives it is necessary to automate the process. However, automatic knowledge acquisition methods, known also as *machine learning*, (see Chapter 19), are presently limited in their capabilities. Nevertheless, diligent efforts on the part of researchers, vendors, and system builders are helping to slowly approach these objectives. Best results can be achieved in acquisition of knowledge that is difficult to acquire manually (e.g., large databases). In the interim, acquisition will continue to be done manually in most cases, but it will be supported by productivity improvement aids.

While such improvements are being made, it is necessary to recognize the existence of different types of knowledge, and the fact that they can be best elicited by different techniques and computerized aids. Furthermore, in some systems it is best to employ several techniques jointly. Unfortunately, this is not a simple task (one day we will see an expert system that will advise us on this matter). Since the knowledge is collected for the purpose of representing it, representation may have a major impact on the selected method(s). Ideally, one should start with preliminary knowledge acquisition (e.g., using informal interviews), then decide on a representation technique based on the type of knowledge collected, and only then determine the elicitation method. Sometimes, the representation method could be changed once the prototype is in progress; however, this is also true of the knowledge acquisition method.

Several experts on knowledge acquisition have made suggestions about how to select an appropriate method. An example of such a suggestion is to relate the categories of knowledge (described in section 4.2) to the various acquisition techniques. Such a proposal is shown in Table 4.9. Even though this matching, which was proposed by McGraw and Harbison-Briggs [27] may work in some cases, it is not necessarily good for all cases. The experience and judgment of the knowledge engineer will dictate what is the best method for each specific situation.

4.14   Knowledge Acquisition from Multiple Experts

An important element in the development of an ES is the identification of experts. This is a complicated task in the real-world environment, perhaps because often so many support mechanisms are used by practitioners for certain tasks (questionnaires, informal and formal consultations, texts, etc.). Together

TABLE 4.9 Correlating Knowledge Type and Acquisition Technique

Knowledge	Activity	Suggested Technique
Declarative knowledge	Identifying general (conscious) heuristics	Interviews
Procedural knowledge	Identifying routine procedures/tasks	Structured interview Process tracing (Tracking) Simulations
Semantic knowledge	Identifying major concepts/vocabulary	Repertory grid Concept sorting
Semantic knowledge	Identifying decision-making procedures and heuristics (unconscious)	Task analysis Process tracing
Episodic knowledge	Identifying analogical problem-solving heuristics	Simulations Process tracing

Source: K. L. McGraw and B. K. Harbison-Briggs, *Knowledge Acquisition, Principles and Guidelines* (Englewood Cliffs, N.J.: Prentice-Hall, 1989).

these support mechanisms contribute to the high quality of professional output. They may also, however, tend to make it difficult to identify a knowledge "czar" whose estimates, process, or knowledge are clearly superior to what the system and mix of staff, support tools, and consulting skills produce in the rendering of normal client service.

The usual approach to this problem is to build ES for a very narrow domain in which expertise is clearly defined. In such a case it is easy to find one expert. However, even though many ES have been constructed with one expert—an approach that is advocated as a good strategy for ES construction—there could be a need for **multiple experts,** especially when more serious ES are being constructed or when expertise is not particularly well defined.

The major purposes of using multiple experts are (1) to broaden the coverage of proposed solutions (i.e., the solutions complement each other) and (2) to combine the strengths of different approaches of reasoning. Table 4.10 lists benefits and problems with multiple experts.

When multiple experts are used, there are often differences of opinion and conflicts that have to be resolved. This is especially true when developing knowledge bases from multiple sources, where these systems address problems that involve the use of subjective reasoning and heuristics. Conflicts can arise due to a lack of knowledge of a certain aspect of the problem or as a result of statistical uncertainty (e.g., different experts may assign different event outcome probabilities while observing the same evidence). Experts may also follow different lines of reasoning derived from their background and experience, which could lead to conflicting solutions. Sometimes multiple lines of reasoning can be used to combine the strengths of the proposed solutions and/or to assure a complete coverage of the domain.

TABLE 4.10   Benefits of and Problems with Participation of Multiple Experts

Benefits	Problems
On the average, fewer mistakes by a group of experts than by a single expert	Groupthink phenomena
Several experts in group eliminate need for using a world-class expert (who is difficult to get and expensive)	Fear on the part of some domain experts of senior experts or a supervisor
	Compromising solutions generated by a group with conflicting opinions
Wider domain than a single expert's	Waste of time in group meetings
Synthesis of expertise	Lack of confidentiality (fear of expressing ideas)
Enhanced quality from synergy among experts	Difficulties in scheduling
	Dominating experts (controlling, not letting others speak)

Other related issues are identifying different aspects of the problem and matching them with different experts, integrating knowledge from various experts, assimilating conflicting strategies, personalizing community knowledge bases, and developing programming technologies to support these issues.

Multiple Expert Scenarios

Four possible scenarios, or configurations, of multiple experts exists (see McGraw and Harbison-Briggs [27]): individual experts, primary and secondary experts, small groups, and panels.

Individual Experts. In this case several experts contribute knowledge individually. Using multiple experts in this manner relieves the knowledge engineer from the stress associated with multiple expert teams. However, this approach requires that the knowledge engineer have a means of resolving conflicts and handling multiple lines of reasoning.

Primary and Secondary Experts. In this case a primary expert is responsible for validating information retrieved from other domain experts. Knowledge engineers may consult the primary expert at the beginning of the program for guidance in domain familiarization, refinement of knowledge acquisition plans, and the identification of individuals who may be asked to serve as secondary experts. The primary expert is consulted periodically to review the results of knowledge acquisition sessions.

Small Groups. In this case several experts are consulted, together, and asked to provide agreed-upon information. Working with small groups of experts allows the knowledge engineer to observe (1) alternate approaches to the solution of a problem and (2) the key points made in solution-oriented discussions among experts.

Panels. To meet goals for verification and validation of ongoing development efforts, some programs choose to establish a council of experts. These individuals typically meet together at times scheduled by the developer for the purpose of reviewing knowledge base efforts, content, and plans. In many cases, the functionality of the expert system itself is tested against the expertise of such a panel.

These scenarios determine, in part, the method to be used for handling multiple expertise.

Methods of Handling Multiple Expertise

Several major approaches to the issue of integrating experts' opinions have been defined by Alexander and Evans [1]:

- ☐ Blend several lines of reasoning through consensus methods
- ☐ Use an analytical approach
- ☐ Keep the lines of reasoning distinct and select a specific line of reasoning based on the situation
- ☐ Automate the process
- ☐ Decompose the knowledge acquired into specialized knowledge sources (blackboard systems)

Now a brief description of each method follows.

Consensus Methods. Consensus in small groups can be reached in several ways using methodologies borrowed from behavioral sciences such as group dynamics. Each expert is provided information on the judgment of the other experts within the group and is provided an opportunity to revise his or her judgment based on this information. The interaction could include a face-to-face meeting of the experts, or the experts' identities might be concealed from each other to avoid personality influences. The following activities are some acceptable techniques for achieving consensus: the nominal-group technique, brainstorming, Delphi, consensus decision making, and computer-supported cooperative work. For further discussion and references see McGraw and Harbison-Briggs [27].

Generic consensus methods may not be effective in knowledge acquisition because experts are very much opinionated, and because the process may be too expensive for implementation.

Analytical Approaches. An analytical approach can be appropriate when the expertise involves numeric values (such as assessment of probabilities). Methods borrowed from the literature on multiple-criteria decision making can be used. Several attempts have been made to develop a "group probability" as a weighted aggregation of individual probability assessments. For details, see Alexander and Evans [1]. This topic is revisited when we discuss uncertainty and fuzziness (Chapter 7).

Specific Lines of Reasoning. According to this procedure, which was developed by LeClair [25], multiple lines of reasoning are allowed to coexist without unwanted interactions that could compromise an expert's advice. Hence, a deduction obtained through one expert's line of reasoning would not be used in the reasoning process of another expert.

Once multiple lines of reasoning are accommodated in the expert system, the system should attempt to select a line of reasoning based on the characteristics of each situation. The goal is not to achieve a consensus solution, but to select the most appropriate solution. LeClair achieves this by introducing information specific to the decision situation; the expert system then *automatically* selects a line of reasoning using this information. The basis for this approach is that each expert's line of reasoning is founded on his or her unique experiences in the problem domain and therefore represents a distinct philosophy regarding the problem domain.

Automated Processes. The previous method uses an automated approach for selecting a line of reasoning. Once multiple lines of reasoning are programmed and accommodated in the knowledge base, however, an attempt can also be made to automate the *entire process*. Expert Ease (an early ES shell, which currently sells under the name Expert One) allows for the input of multiple lines of reasoning. Once the multiple lines of reasoning have been input, the system determines the most efficient way (using the theory of entropy, or uncertainty reduction) to reach the solution. However, it is difficult to discern what line of reasoning is followed, since the system blends the multiple lines of reasoning together in attempting to find the most efficient route to a solution. Another negative aspect of Expert Ease is that it does not accommodate conflicts in lines of reasoning. When a conflict does occur, it simply avoids the problem by selecting the first occurrence of the conflicting rule.

Blackboard Systems. Blackboard systems maximize independence among knowledge sources by appropriately dividing the problem domain. In this approach expertise is divided among subdomains (one expert for each subdomain) and the experts cooperate to solve the problem. Interaction is kept to a minimum. Any interaction among experts can be handled in several ways. For example, conclusions of the different knowledge sources can be posted on a "blackboard" available to all knowledge sources. The knowledge sources have a condition and an action part. The condition component specifies the situations under which a particular knowledge source could contribute to an activity. A scheduler, or an event manager, controls the progress toward a solution in blackboard systems by determining which knowledge source to schedule next or which problem subdomain to focus on. For further details see Nii [33] and Chapter 14.

4.15   Validation and Verification
of the Knowledge Base

Knowledge acquisition involves quality control aspects that appear under the terms *evaluation, validation,* and *verification.* (This topic is related to the topic of validation of knowledge-based systems which is discussed in Chapter 13.) These terms are frequently confused, mixed up, or used interchangeably. We use the definitions provided by O'Keefe et al. [34].

Evaluation is a broad concept. Its objective is to assess an AI system's *overall value.* In addition to assessing acceptable performance levels, it analyzes whether the system would be usable, efficient, and cost-effective. This topic will be revisited in Chapter 16 on implementation.

Validation is the part of evaluation that deals with the *performance* of the system (e.g., as it compares to the expert's). Simply stated, validation refers to building the "right" system, that is, substantiating that a system performs with an acceptable level of accuracy.

Verification refers to building the system "right," that is, substantiating that the system correctly implements its specifications.

In the realm of ES these activities are dynamic, since they must be repeated each time that the prototype is changed.

In terms of the knowledge base, it is necessary to assure that we have the *right* knowledge base, that is, that the knowledge is valid. It is also essential to assure that the knowledge base was constructed properly (verification).

The validation and verification of the knowledge base should be conducted several times during the system's life cycle. Benbasat and Dhaliwal [2] have developed a framework for such validation.

In executing these quality control tasks, we are dealing with several activities and concepts. These are listed in Table 4.11.

Automated verification of knowledge is offered in the Auto-Intelligence product described earlier. Verification is conducted by measuring the system's performance, and it is limited to classification cases with probabilities. It works as follows: When an ES is presented with a new case to classify, it assigns a confidence factor to each selection. By comparing these confidence factors with those provided by an expert, one can measure the *accuracy* of the ES as it is reflected in each case. By performing comparisons on many cases one can arrive at an overall measure of performance of the ES. For details see Parsaye [35].

TABLE 4.11 Measures of Validation

Measure (Criteria)	Description
Accuracy	How well the system reflects reality; how correct the knowledge is in the knowledge base
Adaptability	Possibilities for future development, changes
Adequacy (or Completeness)	Portion of the necessary knowledge that is included in the knowledge base
Appeal	How well the knowledge base matches intuition and stimulates thought and practicability
Breadth	How well the domain is covered
Depth	Degree of the detailed knowledge
Face validity	Credibility of knowledge
Generality	Capability of a knowledge base to be used with a broad range of similar problems
Precision	Capability of the system to replicate particular system parameters; consistency of advice; coverage of variables in knowledge base
Realism	Accounting for relevant variables and relations; similarity to reality
Reliability	Fraction of the ES predictions that are empirically correct
Robustness	Sensitivity of conclusions to model structure
Sensitivity	Impact of changes in the knowledge base on quality of outputs
Technical and operational validity	Goodness of the assumed assumptions, context, constraints, and conditions, and their impact on other measures
Turing Test	Ability of a human evaluator to identify if a given conclusion is made by an ES or by a human expert
Usefulness	How adequate the knowledge is (in terms of parameters and relationships) for solving correctly
Validity	Knowledge base's capability of producing empirically correct predictions

Source: Adapted from B. Marcot, "Testing Your Knowledge Base," *AI Expert* (August 1987).

4.16 Analyzing, Coding, Documenting, and Diagramming

The collected knowledge must be analyzed, coded, and documented. The manner in which these activities takes place depends on the methods of acquisition and representation. The following example (based on Wolfgram et al. [40]) illustrates some of the steps in this process. It deals with knowledge acquired with the use of verbal protocols and includes four steps.

Transcription. First, a complete transcription of the verbal report is made, including not only the expert's utterances, but also those of the knowledge engineer and any other distractions or interferences that may have occurred during the session.

Phrase Indexing. Second, a phrase index is compiled by breaking up the transcription into short phrases, each identified by an index number. Each phrase should correspond to the knowledge engineer's assessment of what constitutes a piece of knowledge, that is, a single task, assertion, or data collection process by the expert.

Knowledge Coding. Third, knowledge is coded. This activity attempts to classify the knowledge. One useful classification is to distinguish between descriptive and procedural knowledge. *Descriptive knowledge* relates to a specific object. It includes information about the meaning, roles, environment, resources, activities, associations, and outcomes of the object. *Procedural knowledge* relates to the procedures employed in the problem-solving process (e.g., information about problem definition, data gathering, the solution process, and evaluation criteria). Each piece of knowledge is indexed according to the appropriate category and subcategory.

Documentation. Fourth, the knowledge should be properly organized and documented. One way of organizing the documentation is to divide it into four parts: comprehensive domain listing, descriptive knowledge, procedural knowledge, and glossary. Certainly, the documented knowledge should be maintained and updated properly. The documentation should be done in a consistent manner. Forms can be used, and some vendors of ES provide their clients with necessary forms.

Knowledge Diagramming. **Knowledge diagramming** is a graphic approach to improving the process of knowledge acquisition. It consists of hierarchical, top-down descriptions of the major types of knowledge used to describe facts and reasoning strategies for problem-solving in expert systems. These types are objects, events, performance, and metaknowledge. Diagramming also describes the linkages and interactions among the various types of knowledge. As knowledge is acquired, the diagrams support the analysis and planning of subsequent acquisitions. The process is similar to diagramming in system analysis; by acting as a high-level representation of knowledge, the *productivity* of the builders and the *quality* of the system can be increased.

Hierarchical diagramming ends with a primitive level that cannot be decomposed. The decomposition in all levels is diagrammed to provide a partitioned view of events and objects. A special knowledge representation language called KRL (Knowledge Representation Language) is used in the process. Graphic techniques augment the scope, understanding, and modularity of knowledge.

Knowledge diagramming can be used to manage acquisition very effectively when it is tied to the five-stage model of knowledge acquisition (see Figure 4.4). A special expert system called INQUEST has been developed using this approach. For information about this system and knowledge diagramming in general, see Hillman [21].

4.17   Numeric and Documented Knowledge Acquisition

Acquisition of Numeric Knowledge

Traditional knowledge acquisition methods are designed to deal mainly with symbolic representation of knowledge. Drake and Hess [12] claim that a special approach is needed to capture numeric knowledge. They suggest complementing symbolic knowledge acquisition with a numeric one. Drake and Hess present a methodology called *abduction,* which handles numeric, complex, and uncertain relationships.

The methodology is implemented in a hybrid knowledge acquisition process (Figure 4.10). A special tool to support the numeric process is AIM Problem Solver.

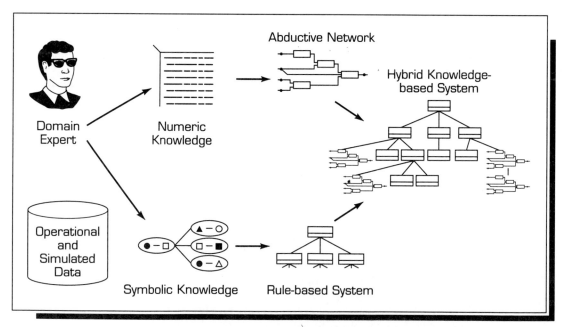

FIGURE 4.10 Hybrid Development Process for Knowledge-based Systems (*Source:* K. C. Drake and P. Hess. Abduction. *PC AI.* 1990. p. 61. Courtesy of AbTech Corp., Charlottesville, Va.)

Acquisition of Documented Knowledge

In many cases knowledge can be acquired from other sources in addition to, or instead of, human experts. The major advantage of this approach is that there is no need to use an expert. The approach is used in knowledge-based systems where the concern is to handle a large or complex amount of information rather than world-class expertise. Searching through corporate policy manuals or catalogs is an example of such a situation.

At present, very few methodologies deal with knowledge acquisition from documented sources. The approach has, however, a great potential for automation. Documented knowledge of almost any type can be easily (and inexpensively) transferred to a computer's database. The analysis of the knowledge can then be done manually, but it can also be done with the use of AI technologies (perhaps a combination of a speech understanding and expert systems). Thus, expert systems may be used to build other expert systems.

Expert systems can scan databases and digitize books, journals, and magazines, and this capability is increasing. Data stored in another computer system could be retrieved electronically to create or update the knowledge base of the expert system, all without the intervention of a knowledge engineer or an expert.

Chapter Highlights

- ☐ Knowledge engineering involves acquisition, representation, reasoning (inference), and explanation of knowledge.
- ☐ Knowledge is available from many sources, including those that are documented and those that are undocumented (experts).
- ☐ Knowledge can be shallow, describing a narrow input-output relationship, or deep, describing complex interactions and a system's operation.
- ☐ The many types of knowledge can be classified in several ways.
- ☐ Knowledge acquisition, especially from human experts, is a difficult task due to several communication and information processing problems.
- ☐ Many methodologies have been devised to improve knowledge acquisition. They range from automation to programming aids in knowledge representation.
- ☐ The process of knowledge acquisition is composed of five stages: identification, conceptualization, formalization, implementation, and testing.
- ☐ The methods of knowledge acquisition can be divided into manual, semiautomated, and automated.
- ☐ The primary manual approach is interviewing. Interviewing methods range from completely unstructured to highly structured.
- ☐ The reasoning process of experts can be tracked by several methods. Protocol analysis is the primary method used in AI.

□ Although it is possible to observe experts in action, this approach is limited in scope.

□ Attempts are being made to reduce or even eliminate the role of the knowledge engineer by providing experts with manual and/or computerized tools for knowledge acquisition. Such tools require training the experts not only in the use of the tools but also in the entire process of knowledge acquisition.

□ The repertory grid analysis (RGA) is the most applied method of semiautomated interviews used in AI. Several software packages that use RGA improve the knowledge acquisition process.

□ Many productivity tools are available for knowledge acquisition (e.g., editors, interfaces, diagramming).

□ Rule induction is a popular method that automates the knowledge acquisition process when knowledge is expressed in terms of rules in classification-type problems. Several commercial packages are available for the execution of the process.

□ Rule induction examines historical cases and generates the rules that were used to arrive at certain recommendations.

□ Rule induction can be used by a system engineer, an expert, or any other system builder.

□ Several procedures are available for selecting an appropriate method of knowledge acquisition for any special situation. (Take them as advice only. Some of them will give you contradicting suggestions.)

□ There are benefits as well as limitations and problems in using several experts to build a knowledge base.

□ The four possible scenarios for use of multiple expertise are individual experts, primary and secondary experts, small groups, and panels.

□ The major methods of dealing with multiple experts are consensus methods, analytical approaches, selection of an appropriate line of reasoning, automation of the process, and a blackboard system.

□ Validation and verification of the knowledge base are critical success factors in AI implementation.

□ More than a dozen specific measures are available to determine the validity of knowledge.

□ Automated knowledge acquisition methods are easier to validate and verify.

□ Knowledge collected must be analyzed and coded prior to its representation in the computer.

Key Terms

deep knowledge	Expertise Transfer System	induction
elicitation of knowledge	interactive induction	knowledge acquisition
evaluation	interview analysis	knowledge diagramming

knowledge engineering   protocol analysis   walkthrough
multidimensional   repertory grid analysis   validation
   scaling   rule induction   verification
multiple experts   shallow knowledge
metaknowledge   structured interview

Questions for Review

1. Define knowledge engineering.
2. What are the steps in the knowledge engineering process?
3. What is metaknowledge?
4. Define knowledge acquisition and contrast it with knowledge representation.
5. List several sources of knowledge.
6. What is the difference between documented and undocumented knowledge?
7. Compare declarative and procedural knowledge.
8. Give four reasons why knowledge acquisition is difficult.
9. What are the major desired skills of a knowledge engineer?
10. Name the five stages in the knowledge acquisition process.
11. Describe the process of protocol analysis.
12. What is repertory grid analysis?
13. Describe the process of observing an expert at work.
14. What is the major advantage of using documented knowledge?
15. Briefly discuss three deficiencies of manual knowledge acquisition.
16. Describe the process of automated rule induction.
17. List the major difficulties of knowledge acquisition from multiple experts.
18. Briefly discuss the five major approaches to knowledge acquisition from multiple experts.
19. Describe the four possible scenarios of multiple experts.
20. Define evaluation, validation, and verification of knowledge.

Questions for Discussion

1. Discuss the major tasks performed by knowledge engineers.
2. Define and contrast shallow and deep knowledge.
3. Assume that you are to collect knowledge for one of the following systems:
   a. Advisory system on equal opportunity hiring situation in your organization
   b. Advisory system on investment in residential real estate
   c. Advisory system on how to prepare your federal tax return (Form 1040)
   What sources of knowledge would you consider? (Consult Figure 4.2.)
4. Why is knowledge acquisition considered by many as the most difficult step in knowledge engineering?
5. Discuss the major advantages of rule induction. Give an example that illustrates the method and point to a situation where you think it will be most appropriate.

6. Discuss the difficulties of knowledge acquisition from several experts. Describe a situation that you are familiar with where there could be a need for several experts.
7. Transfer of knowledge from a human to a machine to a human is said to be a more difficult task than a transfer from a human to a human. Why?
8. Explain the importance of conceptualization and list some of the detailed issues that are involved.
9. What are the major advantages and disadvantages of interviews based on example problems?
10. Compare and contrast protocol analysis to interviews based on example cases.
11. What are the major advantages and disadvantages of working with a prototype system for knowledge acquisition?
12. Why is repertory grid analysis so popular? What are its major weaknesses?
13. What are the major advantages and disadvantages of the observation method?
14. Discuss some of the problems of knowledge acquisition through the use of expert reports.
15. What are the present and future benefits of knowledge acquisition through an analysis of documented knowledge? What are its limitations?
16. Why are manual elicitation methods so slow and expensive?
17. Why can the case analysis method be used as a basis for knowledge acquisition?
18. What are the advantages of rule induction as an approach to knowledge acquisition?
19. What are the major benefits of Auto-Intelligence (or similar products) over a conventional rule induction package?
20. Discuss how some productivity improvement tools can expedite the work of the knowledge engineer.
21. Give an example for which an automated approach to knowledge acquisition from multiple experts would be feasible.
22. Explain why it is necessary to both verify and validate the content of the knowledge base. Who should do it?
23. Why is it important to have the knowledge analyzed, coded, and documented in a systematic way?
24. What are the major advantages of acquiring knowledge through a knowledge engineer?
25. Compare and contrast semantic and episodic knowledge.
26. Knowledge engineers are compared to system analysts. Why?
27. Discuss the conditions that are necessary to assure success when an expert is his or her own knowledge engineer.

Exercises

1. Fill in the accompanying table with regard to the type of communication between the expert and the knowledge engineer. Use the following symbols: Y = yes, N = no, H = high, M = medium, L = low.

TABLE 4A

Method	Type of Communication				
	Face-to Face Contact	Written Communications	Continuing for a Long Time	Time Spent by Expert	Time Spent by Knowledge Engineer
Interview analysis					
Observations of experts					
Questionnaires and expert report					
Analysis of documented knowledge					

2. Evaluate the current success of automated rule induction and interactive methods in knowledge acquisition. Use the accompanying table. Then, comment on the major limitation of each method.

TABLE 4B

Method/Tool	Time of Expert	Time of Knowledge Engineer	Skill of Knowledge Engineer
Rule induction			
Auto-Intelligence			
Smart editors			
Expertise Transfer System			

3. Read this knowledge acquisition session and complete the exercises that follow it.

KNOWLEDGE
ENGINEER
(KE): You have the reputation for finding the best real estate properties for your clients. How do you do it?

EXPERT: Well, first I learn about the clients' objectives.

KE: What do you mean by that?

EXPERT: Some people are interested in income, others in price appreciation. There are some speculators, too.

KE: Assume that somebody is interested in price appreciation. What would your advice be?

EXPERT: Well, I will find first how much money the investor can put down and to what degree he or she can subsidize the property.

KE: Why?

EXPERT: The more cash you put as downpayment, the less subsidy you will need. Properties with high potential for price appreciation need to be subsidized for about two years.

KE: What else?

EXPERT: Location is very important. As a general rule I recommend looking for the lowest-price property in an expensive area.

KE: What else?

EXPERT: I compute the cash flow and consider the tax impact by using built-in formulas in my calculator.

    a. List the heuristics cited in this interview.
    b. List the algorithms mentioned.

4. Examination of admission records of Pacifica University showed the admission cases listed in Table 4C.

TABLE 4C

Case #	GMAT	GPA	Decision
1	510	3.5	Yes
2	620	3.0	Yes
3	580	3.0	No
4	450	3.5	No
5	655	2.5	Yes

    a. Assume that admission decisions are based only on the scores of GMAT and GPA. Find, by induction, the rules used. Subject all five cases to the rules generated; make sure they are consistent with the rules.
    b. Assume that only *two* rules were used. Can you identify these rules?

5. Give an example of shallow and deep knowledge in an area of your interest.

References and Bibliography

1. Alexander, S.M., and G.W. Evans. "The Integration of Multiple Experts: A Review of Methodologies." In *Applied Expert Systems*, E. Turban and P. Watkins, eds. Amsterdam: North Holland, 1988.
2. Benbasat, I., and J.S. Dhaliwal. "A Framework for the Validation of Knowledge Acquisition." *Knowledge Acquisition* 1 (1989).
3. Boose, J.H. *Expertise Transfer for Expert Systems Design.* New York: Elsevier, 1986.

4. Boose, J.H. "A Survey of Knowledge Acquisition Techniques and Tools." *Knowledge Acquisition* 1 (March 1989).

5. Boose, J.H., and J.M. Bradshaw. "A Knowledge Acquisition Workbench for Eliciting Decision Knowledge." In *Proceedings, 20th HICSS*. Hawaii, January 1987.

6. Boose, J.H., and B.R. Gaines, eds. *The Foundations of Knowledge Acquisition*. New York: Academic Press, 1990.

7. Braun, R. "Expert System Tools for Knowledge Analysis." *AI Expert* (October 1989).

8. Brule, J.F., and A. Blount. *Knowledge Acquisition*. New York: McGraw-Hill, 1989.

9. Cohen, P.R., and E.A. Feigenbaum. *The Handbook of Artificial Intelligence,* vol. 3. Reading, Mass.: Addison-Wesley, 1982.

10. Diaper, D., ed. *Knowledge Elicitation*. New York: Ellis Horwood, 1989.

11. Diederich, J., et al. "Kriton: A Knowledge Acquisition Tool for Expert Systems." *International Journal of Man-Machine Studies* (January 1987).

12. Drake, K.C., and P. Hess. "Abduction, A Numeric Knowledge Acquisition Approach." *PC AI* (September/October 1990).

13. Ericsson, K.A., and H.A. Simon. *Protocol Analysis, Verbal Reports and Data*. Cambridge, Mass.: MIT Press, 1984.

14. Feigenbaum, E., and P. McCorduck. *The Fifth Generation*. Reading, Mass.: Addison-Wesley, 1983.

15. Freiling, M., et al. "Starting a Knowledge Engineering Project: A Step by Step Approach." *AI Magazine* (Fall 1985).

16. Gaines, B.R. "Knowledge Acquisition: Development and Advances." In *Expert System and Intelligent Manufacturing*, M.D. Oliff, ed. New York: Elsevier, 1988.

17. Gray, N.A.B. "Capturing Knowledge through Top-Down Induction of Decision Trees." *IEEE Expert* (June 1990).

18. Hart, A. *Knowledge Acquisition for Expert Systems*. New York: McGraw-Hill, 1986.

19. Hayes-Roth, F., et al. *Building Expert Systems*. Reading, Mass.: Addison-Wesley, 1983.

20. Hill, R.B., D.C. Wolfgram, and D.E. Broadbent. "Expert Systems and the Man Machine Interface." *Expert Systems* (October 1986).

21. Hillman, D. "Bridging Acquisition and Representation." *AI Expert* (November 1988).

22. Kearney, M. "Making Knowledge Engineering Productive." *AI Expert* (July 1990.

23. Kim, J., and J.F. Courtney. "A Survey of Knowledge Acquisition Techniques and Their Relevance to Managerial Problem Domains." *Decision Support Systems* 4 (October 1988).

24. Kitzmiller, C.T., and J.S. Kowalik. "Coupling Symbolic and Numeric Computing in KB Systems," *AI Magazine* (Summer 1987).

25. LeClair, S.R. "A Multiple-Expert Knowledge System Architecture for Manufacturing Decision Analysis," Ph.D. diss., Arizona State Univ., 1985.

26. Liang, T.P., et al. *Automated Knowledge Acquisition*, San Mateo, Calif.: Morgan Kaufman, 1992.

27. McGraw, K.L., and B.K. Harbison-Briggs. *Knowledge Acquisition, Principles and Guidelines*. Englewood Cliffs, N.J.: Prentice-Hall, 1989.

28. McGraw, K.L., and M. Seale. "Knowledge Elicitation with Multiple Experts: Considerations and Techniques." *Artificial Intelligence Review* 2 (no. 1, 1988).

29. McGraw, K.L., and C.R. Westphal, eds. *Readings in Knowledge Acquisition*. New York: Ellis Horwood, 1990.

30. Marcot, B. "Testing Your Knowledge Base," *AI Expert* (August 1987).

31. Michie, D., ed. *Introductory Readings in Expert Systems*. New York: Gordon & Breach, 1984.

32. Nguyen, T.A., et al. "Knowledge Base Verification." *AI Magazine* (Summer 1987).

33. Nii, P.H. "Blackboard Systems." *AI Magazine* 7 (no. 3, 1986).

34. O'Keefe, R.M., et al. "Validating Expert System Performance." *IE Expert* (Winter 1987).

35. Parsaye, K. "Acquiring and Verifying Knowledge Automatically." *AI Expert* (May 1988).

36. Prerau, D.S. "Knowledge Acquisition in the Development of a Large Expert System." *AI Magazine* (November 1988).

37. Prietule, M.J., and H.A. Simon. "The Experts in Your Midst." *Harvard Business Review* (January-February 1989).

38. Tuthill, G.S. *Knowledge Engineering*. Blue Ridge Summit, Pa.: TAB Books, 1990.

39. Weiss, S., and C. Kulikowski. *Computer Systems That Learn Techniques from Statistics, Neural Nets, Machine Learning and Expert Systems*. San Mateo, Calif.: Morgan Kaufman, 1989.

40. Wolfgram, D.D., et al. *Expert Systems*. New York: John Wiley & Sons, 1987.

Chapter 5

Knowledge Representation

Once knowledge is acquired it needs to be organized. The software program that hosts the knowledge is called a knowledge base. Similar to a database, a knowledge base can be organized in several different configurations (or schemes). Knowledge bases are organized differently from databases to facilitate fast inferencing (or reasoning) from the knowledge. The topics in this chapter are divided into these sections:

5.1   Introduction

Most artificial intelligence systems are made up of two basic parts: a knowledge base and an inference mechanism (engine). The knowledge base contains facts about objects in the chosen domain and their relationships. Most AI programs focus on a specific domain or sphere of interest. The knowledge base can also contain concepts, theories, practical procedures, and their associations. The knowledge base forms the system's source of intelligence and is used by the inference mechanism to reason and draw conclusions.

The inference mechanism is a set of procedures that are used to examine the knowledge base in an orderly manner to answer questions, solve problems, or make decisions within the domain. Much of the inference knowledge is generic and it can be used to solve many different problems, especially if they have a similar structure. For example, in diagnosing malfunctions in a human, a machine, or an organization, we may use the same problem-solving procedures, and all can be constructed with the same inference engine.

Knowledge can be organized in one or more configurations (termed *schemes*). This is analogous to a database that can be organized as relational, hierarchical, or network. Furthermore, the knowledge in the knowledge base may be organized differently from that in the inference engine.

A variety of **knowledge representation** schemes have been developed over the years. They share two common characteristics. First, they can be programmed with existing computer languages and stored in memory. Second, they are designed so that the facts and other knowledge contained within them can be used in reasoning. That is, the knowledge base contains a data structure that can be manipulated by an inference system that uses search and pattern-matching techniques on the knowledge base to answer questions, draw conclusions, or otherwise perform an intelligent function.

Because there are so many different knowledge representation schemes, this chapter can be only an introduction—a survey of the most popular methods used throughout the AI field. You are introduced to the whole scope of techniques as a sound base for more detailed study.

In later chapters on AI programming languages and tools, and in the programming experiences that you will gain, you will see how some of these knowledge representation schemes are implemented in real programs.

5.2   Knowledge Representation Methods: An Overview

Knowledge captured from experts and other sources must be organized in such a fashion that a computer inferencing program will be able to access this knowledge whenever needed and draw conclusions. There are several methods of representing knowledge in AI. Many of these are pictorial representations. Carrico et al. [5] list seven benefits of pictorial representations:

1. Validation through enhanced, uniform communication between development team and users
2. Testing and debugging system logic because of clean design and documentation
3. Completeness because methodologies encourage complete documentation and quality assurance reviews with users
4. Accuracy of solutions because of documented and tested logic
5. Ease of maintenance because reduced effort is needed to understand and interpret someone else's code
6. Programming productivity through enhanced, uniform communication and documentation
7. Ease in coding system because of structured approach

There are two general types of knowledge representations: those that support analysis and those that are used in actual coding. The relationship between the two types and the rest of the knowledge engineering process is shown in Figure 5.1.

Knowledge analysis techniques are usually used to support knowledge acquisition during scope establishment and initial knowledge gathering. Most of these techniques are pictorial. They help in the preliminary analysis of knowledge. The knowledge, once organized, is ultimately coded in one (or more) of the coding techniques. Typical analysis techniques are semantic networks, scripts, lists, decision trees, and decision tables.

The working code of a knowledge-based system is usually represented either in the form of production rules or as frames. A **frame** (see section 5.9) represents *all* relevant knowledge about a particular object in one data structure. Knowledge recorded in any of the analysis techniques can be easily translated into rules or frames. For example, there are software tools that assimilate decision tables to rules or convert decision trees to rules.

This chapter explores the major knowledge representation techniques.

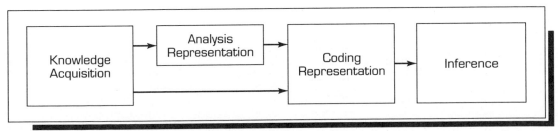

FIGURE 5.1 Knowledge Representation Techniques

5.3   Representation in Logic

Perhaps the oldest form of knowledge representation is logic, the scientific study of the process of reasoning and the system of rules and procedures that aid in the reasoning process. Logic is considered to be a subdivision of philosophy. The development and refinement of its processes are generally credited to the ancient Greeks.

The general form of any logical process is illustrated in Figure 5.2. First, information is given, statements are made, or observations are noted. These form the inputs to the logical process and are called *premises*. The premises are used by the logical process to create the output which consists of conclusions called *inferences*. With this process, facts that are known to be true can be used to derive new facts that also must be true.

For a computer to perform reasoning using logic, some method must be used to convert statements and the reasoning process into a form suitable for manipulation by a computer. The result is what is known as *symbolic*, or *mathematical, logic*. It is a system of rules and procedures that permit the drawing of inferences from various premises using a variety of logical techniques.

The two basic forms of computational logic are **propositional logic** (or propositional calculus) and **predicate logic** (or predicate calculus). The term *calculus* here does not refer to the differential and integral calculus which we ordinarily associate with the term. Instead, calculus simply refers to a system for computing.

Propositional Logic

A proposition is nothing more than a statement that is either true or false. Once we know what it is, it becomes a premise that can be used to derive new propositions or inferences. Rules are used to determine the truth (T) or falsity (F) of the new proposition.

In propositional logic we use symbols such as letters of the alphabet to represent various propositions, premises, or conclusions. For example, consider the propositions used as follows in this simple deductive process:

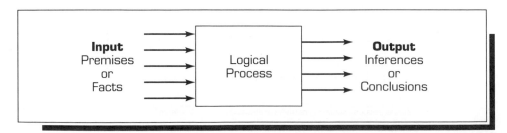

FIGURE 5.2 Using Logic to Reason

Statement: A = The mail carrier comes Monday through Saturday.
Statement: B = Today is Sunday.
Conclusion: C = The mail carrier will not come today.

Single, simple propositions like these are not very interesting or useful. Real-world problems involve many interrelated propositions. To form more complex premises, two or more propositions can be combined using logical connectives. These connectives or operators are designated as AND, OR, NOT, IMPLIES, and EQUIVALENT. The meanings of each of these connectives and the symbols used to represent them are given in Figure 5.3.

These symbols are the same as those used in Boolean algebra. In fact, because propositional logic involves only the truth or falsity of propositions, Boolean algebra and all of the related techniques used in analyzing, designing, or simplifying binary logic circuits can be used in propositional logic.

Connectives are used to join or modify propositions to make new propositions. Some examples will show what we mean.

NOT. A truth table can be used to show all possible combinations of this connective.

A = It is raining today.
NOT A = It is not raining today.

A	NOT A
T	F
F	T

This truth table shows that if proposition A is true, then NOT A is false. If proposition A is false, then NOT A is true.

Connective	Symbol
AND	∧, &, ∩
OR	∨, ∪, +
NOT	¬, ~
IMPLIES	⊃, →
EQUIVALENT	≡

FIGURE 5.3 Logical Connectives, or Operators, and Their Symbols

AND. When the AND connective is used to combine two propositions, the resulting new proposition is true only if both of the original propositions are true.

> D = The car is black.
> E = The car has a six-cylinder engine.
> F = The car is black AND has a six-cylinder engine.
> F = D AND E

In this case, F is true only if D AND E are true.

OR. When the OR connective is used to combine propositions, the new proposition is true if either one or both of the original propositions are true.

> P = The moon is a satellite.
> Q = The earth is a satellite.
> R = P OR Q—The moon OR the earth is a satellite.

A truth table can be used to illustrate all possible combinations of the OR connective.

P	Q	R
F	F	F
F	T	T
T	F	T
T	T	T

You can see that the new proposition R is true if P is true, Q is true, or both P and Q are true.

This form of OR is known as the *inclusive* OR (see Chapter 18). Another form of the OR connective is the *exclusive* OR which means that either one proposition (P OR Q) or the other is true, but not both.

IMPLIES. The IMPLIES connective means that if proposition A is true, then proposition B is also true. The truth of A implies the truth of B:

$$A \rightarrow B$$
Example: A = The car's engine is defective.
B = I cannot drive today.
C = A IMPLIES B

Another way to explain IMPLIES is to use an IF-THEN arrangement. In this example, we can say that IF the car's engine is defective, THEN I will not drive today.

This truth table illustrates the IMPLIES function.

A	B	C
F	F	T
F	T	T
T	F	F
T	T	T

The IMPLIES function is somewhat difficult to understand. The way to look at this is that the new proposition C is true if A is false OR B is true. Written logically, this is NOT A, OR B. You can see that B is true in the second and fourth entries in the truth table. A is false in the first and second entries. As a result, the first, second, and fourth entries are true. The only time C is false is when A is true and B is false: A AND NOT B.

By using symbols for the various propositions and relating them with connectives, a complete set of premises with resulting conclusions can be expressed. The resulting symbolic expression looks very much like a math formula. It can then be manipulated using the rules of propositional logic or Boolean algebra to infer new conclusions. The truth or falsity of a conclusion can be determined from a wide variety of premises.

Predicate Calculus

Although propositional logic is a knowledge representation alternative, it is not very useful in artificial intelligence. Since propositional logic deals primarily with complete statements and whether they are true or false, its ability to represent real-world knowledge is limited. (It cannot make assertions about the individual elements that make up the statements.) Consequently, AI uses *predicate logic* instead.

Predicate logic is a more sophisticated form of logic that uses all the same concepts and rules of propositional logic. It gives added ability to represent knowledge in finer detail. Predicate logic permits you to *break a statement down into component parts, namely an object, a characteristic of the object, or some assertion about the object.* Predicate calculus allows you to separate a statement or proposition into the objects about which something is being asserted and the assertion itself. In addition, predicate calculus lets you use variables and functions of variables in a symbolic logic statement. The result is a more powerful knowledge representation scheme that is far more applicable to practical problem solving on a computer. Predicate calculus is the basis for the AI language called PROLOG (programming in logic).

In predicate calculus, a proposition is divided into two parts, the arguments (or objects) and the predicate (or assertion). The arguments are the individuals or objects about which an assertion is made. The predicate is the assertion made about them. In a common English language sentence, objects and individuals are nouns that serve as subjects and objects of the sentence. For further details refer to Winston [18]. Once knowledge is organized as either prepositional or predicate logic, it is ready for inferencing. (Inferencing with logic will be discussed in Chapter 6.)

5.4 Semantic Networks

One of the oldest and easiest-to-understand knowledge representation schemes is the **semantic network,** or semantic net, which is composed of *nodes* and *links*. Semantic networks are basically graphic depictions of knowledge that show hierarchical relationships between objects.

A simple semantic network is shown in Figure 5.4. It is made up of a number of circles, or nodes, which represent objects and descriptive information about those objects. Objects can be any physical item such as a book, car, desk, or even a person. Nodes can also be concepts, events, or actions. A concept might be Ohm's Law, an event such as a picnic or an election, or an action such as building a house or writing a book. Attributes of an object can also be used as nodes. These might represent size, color, class, age, origin, or other characteristics. In this way, detailed information about objects can be presented.

The nodes in a semantic network are also interconnected by links, or arcs. These arcs show the *relationships* between the various objects and descriptive factors. Some of the most common arcs are of the is-a or has-a type. Is-a, usually just designated as isa, is used to show class relationship, that is, that an object belongs to a larger class or category of objects. Has-a links are used to identify characteristics or attributes of the object nodes. Other arcs are used for definitional purposes.

Now refer to the example in Figure 5.4. As you can see, the central figure in the domain of knowledge is a person called Sam. One link shows that Sam is a man and that man is a human being or is part of a class called humans. Another arc from Sam shows that he is married to Kay. Additional arcs show that Kay is a woman and that a woman is, in turn, a human being. Other links show that they have a child, Joe, who is a boy and goes to school.

Some nodes and arcs show other characteristics about Sam. For example, he is a vice president for Acme, a company that is a subsidiary of Ajax, a large corporation. We also see that Sam plays golf, which is a sport. Further, Sam owns a Mercedes Benz whose color is silver. We also see that Mercedes Benz is a type of car that is made in Germany.

One of the most interesting and useful facts about a semantic network is that it can show **inheritance.** Since the semantic network is basically a hierarchy, the various characteristics of some nodes actually inherit the characteristics of others. As an example, consider the links showing that Sam is a man and a

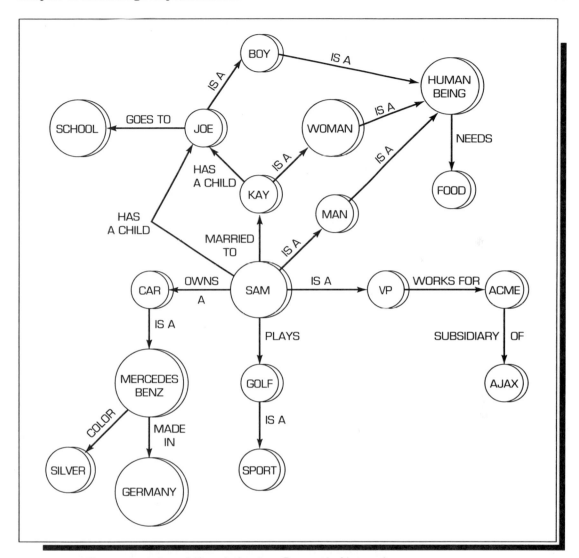

FIGURE 5.4 Representation of Knowledge in a Semantic Network

man is, in turn, a human being. Here, Sam inherits the property of human being. We can ask the question, "Does Sam need food?" Because of the inheritance links, we can say that he needs food if human beings need food.

Another example of inheritance is the relationship between Acme for whom Sam works and its parent corporation, Ajax. Again we can ask the question, "Does Sam work for the Ajax Corporation?" The answer is yes, because Ajax owns Acme. This inheritance characteristic of semantic networks makes it possible to make a variety of deductions from the information provided.

The amount of detail that you include in a semantic network depends on the kinds of problems that must be solved. If the problems are general, less detail is required. If the problems involve a lot of nitty-gritty, more explanation must be given in the original network. For example, the link showing that Sam owns a car might be expanded to show that he owns many other things. Figure 5.5 illustrates the idea. Here, Sam is linked to a new node called "owns."

Another example involves the attributes of various objects in the network. For example, suppose that we want to show the ages of Sam and Kay. This could be done by the network shown in Figure 5.6a. The ages are given as numeric values in related nodes. A more flexible way of representing this information is given in Figure 5.6b. Here, we assign both Sam and Kay an age node. The age node, in turn, is given the actual value. This representation is much better because a factor such as age will change. Furthermore, we can show the relationship between ages better in this format. The "greater than" link accomplishes that.

Although the semantic network is graphic in nature, it does not appear this way in a computer. Instead, the various objects and their relationships are stated in verbal terms, and these are programmed into the computer using one of several different kinds of languages. Searching semantic networks (especially large ones) may be difficult. Therefore, the technique is used mainly for analysis

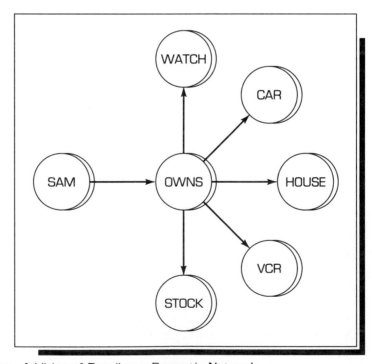

FIGURE 5.5 Addition of Detail to a Semantic Network

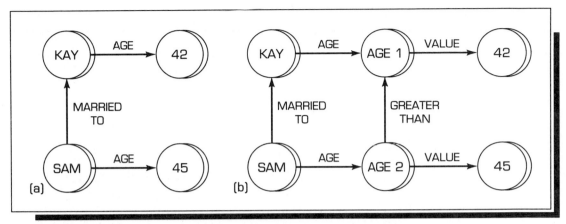

FIGURE 5.6 Expansion of the Knowledge in a Semantic Network

purposes. Then, a transformation to rules or frames is executed. Semantic nets are used basically as a visual representation of relationships, and they can be combined with other representation methods. Their major advantages and limitations are summarized in Table 5.1.

TABLE 5.1 Advantages and Limitations of Semantic Networks

Advantages
The semantic net offers flexibility in adding new nodes and links to a definition as needed. The visual representation is easy to understand.
The semantic net offers economy of effort since a node can inherit characteristics from other nodes to which it has an is-a relationship.
The semantic net functions in a manner similar to that of human information storage.
Since nodes in semantic nets have the ability to inherit relationships from other nodes, a net can support the ability to reason and create definition statements between nonlinked nodes.

Limitations
No standards exist for the definition of nodes or relationships between and among nodes.
The power of inheriting characteristics from one node to another offers potential difficulties with exceptions.
The perception of the situation by the domain expert can place relevant facts at inappropriate points in the network.
Procedural knowledge is difficult to represent in a semantic net, since sequence and time are not explicitly represented.

Source: G. S. Tuthill, *Knowledge Engineering: Concepts and Practices for Knowledge-based Systems* (Blue Ridge Summit, PA.: TAB Books, 1989).

5.5   Scripts

A **script** is a knowledge representation scheme similar to a frame, but instead of describing an object, the script describes a *sequence of events*. Like the frame, the script portrays a stereotyped situation. Unlike the frame, it is usually presented in a particular context. To describe a sequence of events, the script uses a series of slots containing information about the people, objects, and actions that are involved in the events.

Some of the elements of a typical script include entry conditions, props, roles, tracks, and scenes. The *entry conditions* describe situations that must be satisfied before events in this script can occur or be valid. *Props* refer to objects that are used in the sequence of events that occur. *Roles* refer to the people involved in the script. The result is conditions that exist after the events in the script have occurred. *Track* refers to variations that might occur in a particular script. And finally, *scenes* describe the actual sequence of events that occur.

A typical script is shown in Figure 5.7. It is a variation of the well-known restaurant example that has been used in AI to show how knowledge is represented in script format. Going to a restaurant is a stereotyped situation with predictable entry conditions, props, roles, and scenes. As you can see, such a script accurately describes what occurs in almost every fast-food restaurant situation. The scenes are miniscripts within the main script that describes the various subdivisions of the entire process. Note the optional scene that describes a take-out situation rather than an eat-in situation. Another option may be a drive-through scene. Finally, note the results.

A script is useful in predicting what will happen in a specific situation. Even though certain events have not been observed, the script permits the computer to predict what will happen to whom and when. If the computer triggers a script, questions can be asked and accurate answers derived with little or no original input knowledge. Like frames, scripts are a particularly useful form of knowledge representation because there are so many stereotypical situations and events that people use every day. Knowledge like this is generally taken for granted, but in computer problem-solving situations, such knowledge must often be simulated to solve a particular problem using artificial intelligence.

To use the script, you store knowledge in the computer in symbolic form. This is best done using LISP or another symbolic language. You can then ask questions about various persons and conditions. A search and pattern-matching process examines the script for the answers. For example, what does the customer do first? Well, he parks the car, then goes into the restaurant. Whom does he pay? The server, of course. The whole thing is totally predictable.

Script representation is interrelated with case-based reasoning, as will be seen in Chapter 6.

Restaurant Script

Track: Fast-food restaurant
Roles: Customer (C)
        Server (S)
Props: Counter
        Tray
        Food
        Money
        Napkins
        Salt/Pepper/Catsup/Straws
Entry Conditions: Customer in hungry.
                   Customer has money.

Scene 1: Entry
- Customer parks car.
- Customer enters restaurant.
- Customer waits in line at the counter.
- Customer reads the menu on the wall and makes a decision about what to order.

Scene 2: Order
- Customer gives order to server.
- Server fills order by putting food on tray.
- Customer pays server.

Scene 3: Eating
- Customer gets napkins, straws, salt, etc.
- Customer takes tray to an unoccupied table.
- Customer eats food quickly.

Scene 3A (option): Take–out
- Customer takes food and exits.

Scene 4: Exit
- Customer cleans up table.
- Customer discards trash.
- Customer leaves restaurant.
- Customer drives away.

Results:
- Customer is no longer hungry.
- Customer has less money.
- Customer is happy.*
- Customer is unhappy.*
- Customer is too full.*
- Customer has upset stomach.*

* Options

FIGURE 5.7 Typical Script

5.6   Object, Attributes, and Values

A common way to represent knowledge is to use objects, attributes, and values, the **O-A-V triplet.** *Objects* may be physical or conceptual. *Attributes* are the characteristics of the objects. *Values* are the specific measures of the attributes in a given situation. Table 5.2 presents several O-A-V triplets. An object may have several attributes. An attribute itself may be considered as a new object with its own attributes. For example, in Table 5.2 a bedroom is an attribute of a house but also an object of its own. O-A-V triplets are used both in frame and semantic network representations.

The O-A-V triplet can be viewed as a variation of either frames or semantic networks. For example, the representation of Figure 5.4 includes a segment which is shown in Figure 5.8. We added to this segment the O-A-V triplet. Thus, objects and values are designated as nodes, while attributes are designated as arcs. The O-A-V triplet can be used in both static and dynamic presentations (in dynamic presentations the object value portions can change). O-A-V triplets can be used to show order and relationships by using a tree structure. For example, they can show inheritance, causal relationships, or part-to-subpart links.

5.7   Lists and Trees

Lists and trees are simple structures used for representing *hierarchical knowledge.*

Lists

A **list** is a written series of related items. It can be a list of names of people you know, things to buy at the grocery store, things to do this week, or products in a catalog.

Lists are normally used to represent knowledge in which objects are grouped, categorized, or graded according to rank or relationship. Objects are first divided into groups or classes of similar items. Then, their relationships

TABLE 5.2   Representative O-A-V Items

Object	Attributes	Values
House	Bedrooms	2, 3, 4, etc.
House	Color	Green, white, brown
Admission to a university	Grade-point average	3.0, 3.5, 3.7, etc.
Inventory control	Level of inventory	15, 20, 30, etc.
Bedroom	Size	$9 \times 10'$, $6 \times 12'$, etc.

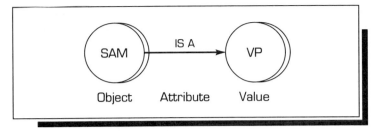

FIGURE 5.8 O-A-V Triplet Representation

are shown by linking them together. The simplest form is one list, but a hierarchy is created when two or more related lists are combined.

Figure 5.9 shows a generalized format for a list. The list has a name to identify it (List A) and two or more elements. You can see that an element in one list can be the name of another list containing subelements. One or more of the subelements can, in turn, be the name of another list and so on.

Another way to look at related lists is as an outline. An outline is nothing more than a hierarchical summary of some subject. The various segments of the outline are lists.

Decision Tables

Another method of knowledge representation is the **decision table,** which is organized in a spreadsheet format, using columns and rows. The table is divided

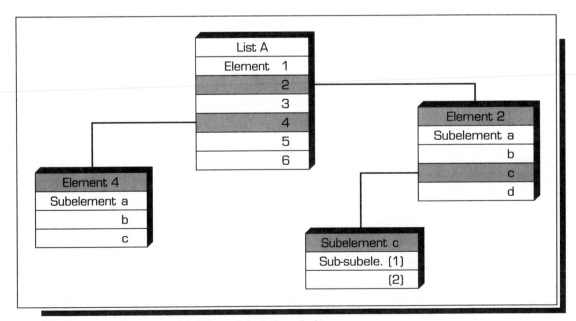

FIGURE 5.9 Lists Representing Hierarchical Knowledge

into two parts. First, a list of attributes is developed, and for each attribute all possible values are listed. Then, a list of conclusions is developed. Finally, the different configurations of attributes are matched against the conclusion. A simple example is shown in Figure 5.10.

Knowledge for the table is collected in knowledge acquisition sessions. Once constructed, the knowledge in the table can be used as input to other knowledge representation methods. It is not possible to make inferences with the domain tables by themselves, except when rule induction (see previous chapter) is used.

Decision tables are easy to understand and program. For further discussion see Carrico et al. [5].

Decision Trees

Decision trees are related to tables and are used frequently in system analysis (in non-AI systems). According to Carrico et al. [5], a decision tree may be thought of as a hierarchical semantic network bound by a series of rules. It couples search strategy with knowledge relationships. The trees are similar to the decision trees used in decision theory. They are composed of nodes representing goals and links representing decisions. The root of the tree is on the left and the leaves are on the right. All terminal nodes except the root node are instances of a primary goal.

Attributes								
shape	round	round	round	round	oblong	oblong	oblong	oblong
smell	acid	acid	sweet	sweet	sweet	sweet	acid	sweet
color	yellow	orange	yellow	red	yellow	yellow	orange	green
taste	sour	sweet	sweet	sweet	sweet	sweet	sour	sweet
skin	rough	rough	smooth	smooth	smooth	smooth	smooth	smooth
sees	yes	yes	yes	yes	yes	yes	yes	yes
Conclusions								
grapefruit	X							
orange		X						
apple			X	X				
banana					X			
pear						X		X
kumquat							X	

FIGURE 5.10 Decision Table Based on Dialogue with a Fruit Expert (*Source:* M. A. Carrico, et al., *Building Knowledge Systems: Developing and Managing Rule-based Applications.* New York: McGraw-Hill, 1989. Reprinted by permission of McGraw-Hill, Inc.)

Decision trees, like rules, depict a strong sense of cause and effect. Their major advantage is that they can simplify the knowledge acquisition process. Knowledge diagramming is frequently more natural to experts than formal representation methods (such as rules or frames). For further discussion see Gruber and Cohen [8]. Decision trees can easily be converted to rules. The conversion can be executed by a computer program (e.g., see Chapter 9 in Liang et al. [12]). The equivalence of a simple decision tree and a rule is shown in Figure 5.11. The problem depicted is fruit identification. Using heuristics, one starts by smelling the fruit; if it smells acidy then the fruit is known to be a citrus. A round shape will narrow the search to either an orange or grapefruit, etc.

There are several variations of decision trees. For example, the lists shown earlier can be shown as trees. Figure 5.12 represents the same knowledge shown in Figure 5.9 (nodes correspond to list names and arcs show the relationships).

Lists, and trees, are so commonly used to represent knowledge that you will deal with them regularly in virtually every area of AI. In fact, lists are so widely used that a special programming language has been created to deal with

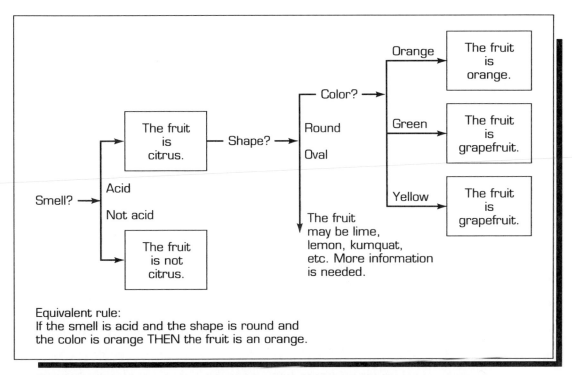

FIGURE 5.11 Decision Tree for Fruit Identification (*Source:* Based on M. A. Carrico, et al., *Building Knowledge Systems: Developing and Managing Rule-based Applications.* New York: McGraw-Hill, 1989. Reprinted by permission of McGraw-Hill, Inc.)

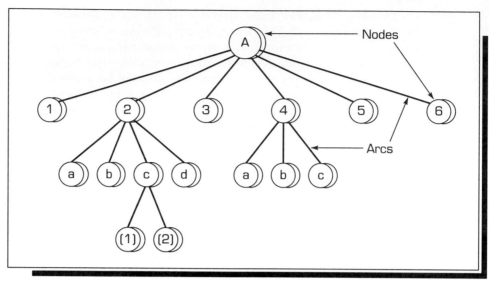

FIGURE 5.12   Tree Graph for Illustrating Hierarchical Knowledge

them. It is called LISP, for *list* processing. LISP is a main programming language for AI work (see Chapter 13).

5.8   Production Rules

Production systems were developed by Newell and Simon for their model of human cognition (see Chapter 3). The production systems are modular knowledge representation schemes that are finding increasing popularity in many AI applications. The basic idea of these systems is that knowledge is presented as **production rules** in the form of condition-action pairs: "IF this *condition* (or premise or antecedent) occurs, THEN some action (or result, or conclusion, or consequence) will (or should) occur. Consider these two examples:

1. IF the stoplight is red AND you have stopped, THEN a right turn is okay.
2. (This example from an internal control procedure includes a probability.) IF the client uses purchase requisition forms AND the purchase orders are approved and purchasing is segregated from receiving, accounts payable, AND inventory records, THEN there is strongly suggestive evidence (90 percent probability) that controls to prevent unauthorized purchases are adequate.

Each production rule in a knowledge base implements an autonomous chunk of expertise that can be developed and modified independently of other rules. When combined and fed to the inference engine, the set of rules behaves synergistically, yielding better results than that of the sum of the results of the individual rules. In reality, knowledge-based rules are not independent. They quickly become highly interdependent. For example, adding a new rule may conflict with an existing rule, or it may require a revision of attributes and/or rules.

The utility of production rules comes from the fact that the conditions for which each rule is applicable are made explicit and, in theory, the interactions between rules are minimized. In addition, the rules involve simple syntax and are flexible and easy to understand. Moreover, they enhance the explanation facility.

Production systems are composed of production rules, working memory, and a control. Such systems are useful as mechanisms for controlling the interaction between statements of declarative and procedural knowledge. Productions have been used in many ES, as well as in many commercially available ES development tools.

In addition, rules can be used as descriptive tools for problem-solving heuristics, replacing a more formal analysis of the problem. In this sense, the rules are thought of as incomplete but useful guides to make search decisions that can reduce the size of the problem space being explored. These rules are entered sequentially to the knowledge base by the builder.

Finally, rules can be viewed, in some sense, as a simulation of the cognitive behavior of human experts. According to this view, rules are not just a neat formalism to represent knowledge in a computer; rather, they represent a model of actual human behavior.

Rules may appear in different forms. Some examples follow:

- IF premise THEN conclusion: IF your income is high, THEN your chance of being audited by the IRS is high.
- Conclusion IF premise: Your chance of being audited is high IF your income is high.
- Inclusion of ELSE: IF your income is high OR your deductions are unusual, THEN your chance of being audited by the IRS is high, ELSE your chance of being audited is low.
- More complex rules: IF credit rating is high AND salary is more than $30,000, OR assets are more than $75,000, AND pay history is not "poor," THEN approve a loan up to $10,000, and list the loan in category "B." The action part may include additional information: THEN "approve the loan" and "refer to an agent."

The IF side of a rule may include dozens of IFs. The THEN side may include several parts as well.

Knowledge and Inference Rules

Two types of rules are common in AI: knowledge and inference. Knowledge **declarative rules** state all the facts and relationships about a problem. Inference

procedural rules, on the other hand, advise on how to solve a problem, given that certain facts are known.

For example, assume you are in the business of buying and selling gold. Knowledge rules may look like this:

☐ RULE 1: IF international conflict begins
                      THEN the price of gold goes up.
☐ RULE 2: IF inflation rate declines
                      THEN the price of gold goes down.
☐ RULE 3: IF the international conflict lasts more than seven days and IF it
                      is in the Middle East
                      THEN buy gold.

Inference rules may look like this:

☐ RULE 1: IF the data needed is not in the system
                      THEN request it from the user.
☐ RULE 2: IF more than one rule applies
                      THEN deactivate any rules that add no new data.

The following inference rule is designed to determine if an AND/OR node is satisfied:

☐ RULE 3: Determine if the node is satisfied without recourse to subgoals.
     If so, announce that the node is satisfied. Otherwise determine if the node
     is an AND node or an OR node, and then:
          3a: If the node is an AND node, use the AND procedure to determine
                  if the node is satisfied.
          3b: If the node is an OR node, use the OR procedure to determine if
                  the node is satisfied.

These types of rules are also called **metarules,** or rules about rules. They pertain to other rules (or even to themselves).

The knowledge engineer separates the two types of rules: *knowledge rules* go to the knowledge base, whereas *inference rules* become part of the inference engine. Note that the inference rules are *not* domain specific.

Advantages and Limitations of Rules

Rule representation is especially applicable when there is a need to recommend a course of action based on observable events. It has several major advantages:

☐ Rules are easy to understand. They are communicable because they are a
     natural form of knowledge.
☐ Inference and explanations are easily derived.
☐ Modifications and maintenance are relatively easy.

TABLE 5.3 Characteristics of Rule Representation

	First Part	**Second Part**
Names	Premise $\longrightarrow$ Antecedent $\longrightarrow$ Situation $\longrightarrow$ IF $\longrightarrow$	Conclusion Consequence Action THEN
Nature	Conditions, similar to declarative knowledge	Resolutions, similar to procedural knowledge
Size	Can have many IFs	Usually one conclusion
Statements	AND statements	All conditions must be true for a conclusion to be true.
	OR statements	If any of the OR statement is true, the conclusion is true.

□ Uncertainty is easily combined with rules.
□ Each rule is usually independent of all others.

The major limitations of rule representation are as follows:

□ Complex knowledge requires many, many (thousands of) rules. This may create problems in both using the system and maintaining it.
□ Builders like rules; therefore they try to enforce all knowledge into rules rather than looking for more appropriate representations.
□ Systems with many rules may have a search limitation in the control program. Some programs have difficulty in evaluating rule-based systems and making inferences.

The major characteristics of rules are summarized in Table 5.3.

5.9 Frames

Definitions and Overview

A frame is a data structure that includes all the knowledge about a particular object. This knowledge is organized in a special hierarchical structure that permits a diagnosis of knowledge independence.[1] Frames are basically an application of **object-oriented programming** for AI and ES. (For an overview of object-oriented programming, see Appendix A at the end of this chapter.)

[1]This section is based, in part, on Arcidiancono [1].

TABLE 5.4   Terminology for
Frames

Default	Instantiation
Demon	Master frame
Facet	Object
Hierarchy of frames	Slot
If needed	Value (entry)
instance of	

Each frame describes one *object*. To describe what frames are and how the knowledge is organized in a frame we need to use a special terminology, which is presented in Table 5.4. The specific terms will be defined as we encounter them.

Frames, as in frames of reference, provide a concise, structural representation of knowledge in a natural manner. In contrast to other representation methods, the values that describe one object are grouped together into a single unit called a frame. Thus, a frame encompasses complex objects, entire situations, or a management problem as a single entity. The knowledge is partitioned in a frame into slots. A slot can describe declarative knowledge (such as the color of a car) or procedural knowledge (such as "activate a certain rule if a value exceeds a given level"). The major capabilities of frames are summarized in Table 5.5.

A frame is a relatively large block or chunk of knowledge about a particular object, event, location, situation, or other element. The frame describes that object in great detail. The detail is given in the form of slots which describe the various attributes and characteristics of the object or situation.

Frames are normally used to represent stereotyped knowledge or knowledge built on well-known characteristics and experiences. We all have a great deal of commonsense knowledge and experiences stored away in our brains that we call on to analyze a new object or experience to solve a problem. Frames can be used to represent that kind of knowledge.

TABLE 5.5   Capabilities of Frames

Ability to clearly document information about a domain model, for example, a plant's machines and their associated attributes

Related ability to constrain the allowable values that an attribute can take on

Modularity of information, permitting ease of system expansion and maintenance

More readable and consistent syntax for referencing domain objects in the rules

Platform for building a graphic interface with object graphics

Mechanism that will allow us to restrict the scope of facts considered during forward or backward chaining

Access to a mechanism that supports the inheritance of information down a class hierarchy

Source: R.A. Edmonds, *The Prentice-Hall Guide to Expert Systems* (Englewood Cliffs, N.J.: Prentice-Hall, 1988) p. 102.

A frame provides a means of organizing knowledge in slots that contain characteristics and attributes. In physical form, a frame is somewhat like an outline with categories and subcategories. A typical frame describing an automobile is shown in Figure 5.13. Note the slots describing attributes such as name of manufacturer, model, origin of manufacturer, type of car, number of doors, engine, and other characteristics.

Content of a Frame

A frame includes two basic elements: slots and facets.

A **slot** is a set of attributes that describe the object represented by the frame. For example, in the automobile frame, there are weight and engine slots.

Each slot contains one or more **facets.** The facets (sometimes called subslots) describe some knowledge or procedures about the attribute in the slot. Facets may take many forms:

Automobile Frame

Class of: Transportation
Name of Manufacturer: Audi
Origin of manufacturer: Germany
Model: 5000 Turbo
Type of car: Sedan
Weight: 3300 lb.
Wheelbase: 105.8 inches
Number of doors: 4 (default)
Transmission: 3-speed automatic
Number of wheels: 4 (default)
Engine: (Reference Engine Frame)
 • Type: In-line, overhead cam
 • Number of cylinders: 5
Acceleration (procedural attachment)
 • 0–60: 10.4 seconds
 • Quarter mile: 17.1 seconds, 85 mph
Gas mileage: 22 mpg average (procedural attachment)

Engine Frame

Cylinder bore: 3.19 inches
Cylinder stroke: 3.4 inches
Compression ratio: 7.8 to 1
Fuel system: Injection with turbocharger
Horsepower: 140 hp
Torque: 160 ft/LB

FIGURE 5.13 Frame Describing an Automobile

□ *Values:* These describe the attributes such as blue, red, and yellow for a color slot.

□ *Default:* This facet is used if the slot is empty, that is, without any description. For example, in the car frame one default value is that the number of wheels on the car is four. It means that we can assume the car has four wheels unless otherwise indicated.

□ *Range:* Range indicates what kind of information can appear in a slot (e.g., integer numbers only, two decimal points, 0 to 100).

□ *If added:* This facet contains procedural information or attachments. It specifies an *action* to be taken when a value in the slot is *added* (or modified). Such procedural attachments are called *demons.*

□ *If needed:* This facet is used in a case when no slot value is given. It triggers, much like the if-added situation, a procedure that goes out and gets or computes a value.

□ *Other:* Slots may contain frames, rules, semantic networks, or any type of information.

Certain procedures can be attached to slots and used to derive slot values. For example, slot-specific heuristics are procedures for deriving slot values in a particular context. An important aspect of such procedures is that they can be used to direct the reasoning process. In addition to filling in slots, they can be triggered when a slot is filled.

In Figure 5.13, both acceleration and gas mileage are procedural attachments. They refer to a step-by-step procedure that would define how to acquire this information. For example, to determine acceleration, timing runs for both 0 to 60 mph and quarter-mile elapsed time and speed would be described. A procedural attachment to determine gas mileage would state a procedure for filling the gas tank, driving a certain number of miles, determining the amount of gasoline used, and then computing the gas mileage in terms of miles per gallon.

Hierarchy of Frames

Most AI systems use a collection of frames that are linked together in a certain manner. For example, Figure 5.14 illustrates five frames. Frame A is connected in a slot named is-a to frame B. The same frame also has a capacity slot that refers to a mixer (frame E) and a procedure (demon) which activates rule #36 when a second machine is added. Notice that these relationships create a hierarchy of frames. This hierarchy is not necessarily on a one-to-one basis. For example, frame A is formed from slots in frames A and C. Also, frame A is related to frames B, D, and E and to an independent rule.

Inheritance. The hierarchial arrangement of frames permits inheritance. Figure 5.15 shows a set of vehicles that are organized in a tree. The root of the tree is at the top, where the highest level of abstraction is represented. Frames at

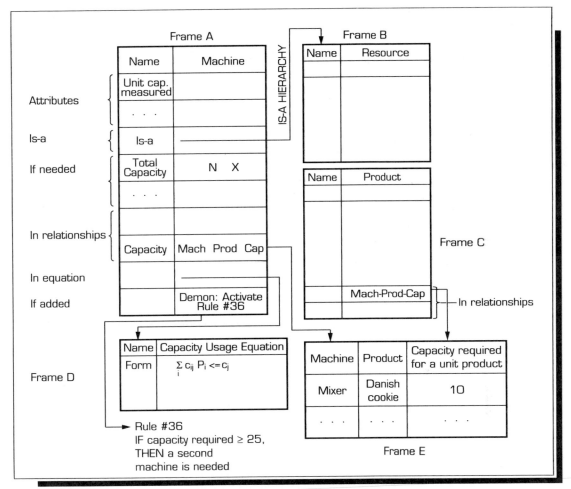

FIGURE 5.14 Hierarchy of Frames (*Source:* R. W. Blanning, "The Application of AI to Model Management," working paper, Owen Graduate School of Management, Vanderbilt Univ., 1988.)

the bottom are called leaves of the tree. The hierarchy permits inheritance of characteristics. Each frame usually inherits the characteristics of all related frames of *higher levels*. These characteristics are expressed in the internal structure of the frame.

Parent frames provide a more general description of the entities. The higher one is in the hierarchy, the more general is the description. Parent frames contain the attribute definitions. When we describe actual, physical objects, we **instantiate** the child's frame. The instances (child frames) contain actual values of the attributes. An example is shown in Figure 5.16.

Note that every parent is a child of a higher-level parent. In building a frame it is possible to have a frame where different slots are related to different

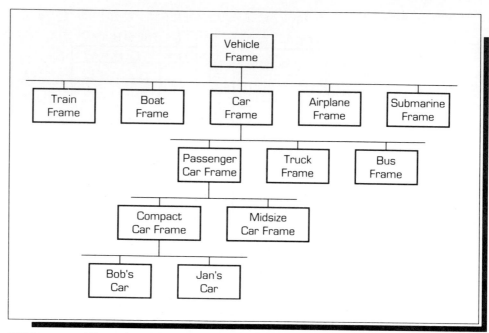

FIGURE 5.15   Hierarchy of Frames Describing Vehicles

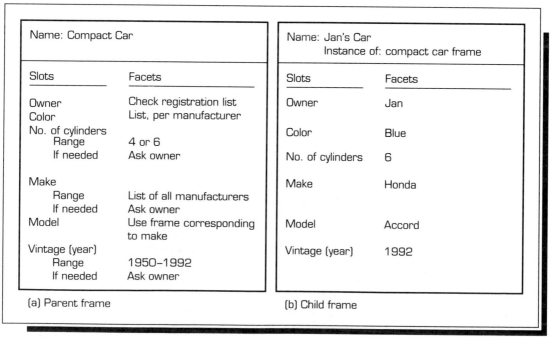

FIGURE 5.16   Parent and Child Frames

parents. The only frame without a parent is the one at the top of the hierarchy. This frame is called a master frame. It is the *root frame* and it has the most general characteristics.

Using Frames

A frame representation is based on the theory that previous situational experiences create certain expectations about objects and events associated with new situations. Frames provide frameworks within which new information can be interpreted. For example, based on previous experience, a chair is generally expected to be a kind of furniture with arms, legs, and a back. Expectations represent things that are always true about chairs and provide the context within which other objects can be interpreted. These expectations are represented as slots.

Obviously, before a frame can be used it must be identified as applicable to the current situation. Generally speaking, this can be done by matching the frame system against the facts in the knowledge base. The selected frame will be the one with the greatest number of lower-level slots filled in. Then, an attempt is made to fill in higher-level slots and if this fails, another frame is selected. For example, a "room" with very short walls and no windows or artificial light might better fit the "closet" frame than a "room" frame.

To use the frame system, the frame itself is programmed using an AI programming language. A slot hierarchy is set up, say using the LISP language, then addressed to derive the answer to a question. Special frame-based software development tools are also available. A tool is a program that helps a user create another program. Tools require no programming skill as they provide a preestablished format of slots that simply permit you to enter the various characteristics. Once the frames are stored in memory, various search and pattern-matching techniques are invoked to answer questions or otherwise make deductions from the knowledge available.

Inferencing with frames will be discussed in Chapter 6. The use of frame-based tools to build expert systems is demonstrated in Level5 Object, which supports this text.

5.10 Multiple Knowledge Representation

Knowledge representation should be able to support the tasks of acquiring and retrieving knowledge as well as subsequent reasoning. Several factors must be taken into account in evaluating knowledge representations for these three tasks:

- Naturalness, uniformity, and understandability of the representation
- Degree to which knowledge is explicit (declarative) or embedded in procedural code

□ Modularity and flexibility of the knowledge base
□ Efficiency of knowledge retrieval and the heuristic power of the inference procedure (Heuristic power is the reduction of the search space achieved by a heuristic mechanism.)

No single knowledge representation method is ideally suited by itself for all tasks (Table 5.6). When using several sources of knowledge simultaneously, the goal of uniformity may have to be sacrificed in favor of exploiting the benefits of **multiple knowledge representations,** each tailored to a different subtask. The necessity of translating among knowledge representations becomes a problem in such cases. Nevertheless, some recent ES shells use two or more knowledge representation schemes.

A rather successful combination of knowledge representation methods is that of production rules and frames. By themselves, production rules do not provide a totally effective representation facility for many ES applications. In particular, their expressive power is inadequate for defining terms and for describing domain objects and static relationships among objects.

The major inadequacies of production rules are in areas that are effectively handled by frames. A great deal of success, in fact, has been achieved by integrating frame and production-rule languages to form hybrid representation facilities that combine the advantages of both components. Systems such as KEE, Level5 Object, and Nexpert Object have shown how a frame language can serve as a powerful foundation for a rule language. The frames provide a rich structural language for describing the objects referred to in the rules and a

TABLE 5.6 Advantages and Disadvantages of Different Knowledge Representations

Scheme	Advantages	Disadvantages
Production rules	Simple syntax, easy to understand, simple interpreter, highly modular, flexible (easy to add to or modify)	Hard to follow hierarchies, inefficient for large systems, not all knowledge can be expressed as rules, poor at representing structured descriptive knowledge
Semantic networks	Easy to follow hierarchy, easy to trace associations, flexible	Meaning attached to nodes might be ambiguous, exception handling is difficult, difficult to program
Frames	Expressive power, easy to set up slots for new properties and relations, easy to create specialized procedures, easy to include default information and detect missing values	Difficult to program, difficult for inference, lack of inexpensive software
Formal logic	Facts asserted independently of use, assurance that all and only valid consequences are asserted (precision), completeness	Separation of representation and processing, inefficient with large data sets, very slow with large knowledge bases

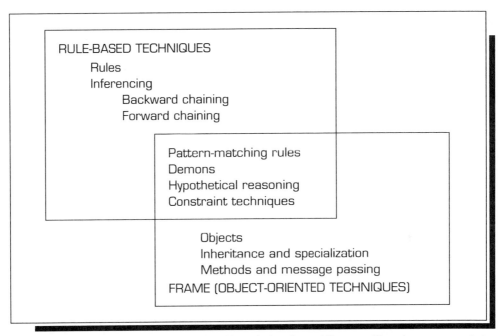

FIGURE 5.17 Two Basic Techniques in Knowledge-based System Development and the Programming Techniques that Emerged from the Combination of the Technologies (*Source:* P. Harmon, "Object-oriented Systems," *Intelligent Software Strategies* [September 1990].)

supporting layer of generic deductive capability about those objects that does not need to be explicitly dealt with in the rules. Frame taxonomies can also be used to partition, index, and organize a system's production rules. This capability makes it easier for the domain expert to construct and understand rules, and for the system designer to control when and for what purpose particular collections of rules are used by the system. For a detailed overview of frames and rule integration see Thuraisingham [16].

An example of combining rule-based representation and frame representation is given by Harmon [9]. As shown in Figure 5.17, the integration allows the creation of pattern-matching rules that can increase the speed of search. The integration allows much more complex representation than can be made when pure frames are used, even when tools such as C++ are utilized.

More recently, knowledge representation researchers have become increasingly concerned with the need to formally understand the representational adequacy of various knowledge representation schemes. When various knowledge representations are "recast" in terms of logic, they can be compared and the strengths and weaknesses of logic for knowledge representations can be better understood. These investigations have already led to a better understanding of knowledge representation and to the development of logic than can handle incompleteness and default reasoning.

Chapter Highlights

□ The two main parts of any AI system are a knowledge base and an inferencing system.

□ The knowledge base is made up of facts, concepts, theories, procedures, and relationships representing real-world knowledge about objects, places, events, people, and so on.

□ The inference engine, or thinking mechanism, is a method of using the knowledge base, that is, reasoning with it to solve problems.

□ Pictorial representation of knowledge has many benefits (a picture is worth a thousand words).

□ Knowledge representation methods are used either for acquisition and analysis and/or for coding.

□ To build the knowledge base, a variety of knowledge representation schemes are used including logic, lists, semantic networks, frames, scripts, and production rules.

□ Logic is a set of rules and procedures used in reasoning.

□ Propositional logic is a system of using symbols to represent and manipulate premises, prove or disprove propositions, and draw conclusions.

□ Predicate calculus is a type of logic used to represent knowledge in the form of statements that assert information about objects or events and apply them in reasoning.

□ The following operators are used frequently in logic: OR, NOT, AND, and IMPLIES.

□ Semantic networks are graphic depictions of knowledge that show relationships (arcs) between objects (nodes); common relationships are is-a, has-a, owns, made from, etc.

□ A major property of networks is the inheritance of properties through the hierarchy.

□ Semantic networks are excellent in supporting system analysis, demonstrating changes, and showing inheritance relationships.

□ The major limitations of semantic networks are the difficulties in representing procedural knowledge and the lack of formalized structure.

□ Scripts describe an anticipated sequence of events (like a story); they indicate the participants, the actions, and the setting.

□ A common way to represent hierarchical knowledge is to use lists.

□ Hierarchical knowledge can also be represented visually with graphs called trees.

□ Decision trees and tables are frequently used in conjunction with other representation methods. They help to organize the knowledge acquired before it is coded.

□ Production rules are two-part statements consisting of a premise and a conclusion. They also may state a situation and a corresponding action.

□ Production rules take the form of an IF-THEN statement such as: IF you drink too much, THEN you should not drive.

□ There are two types of rules: declarative (describing facts) and procedural (inference).

□ Rules are easy to understand and inferences can be easily derived from them.

□ Complex knowledge may require tens of thousands of rules, which may create problems in both search and maintenance. Also, some knowledge cannot be represented in rules.

□ A frame is a holistic data structure based on object-oriented programming technology.

□ Frames are composed of slots that may contain different types of knowledge representation (e.g., rules, scripts, formulas).

□ Frames can show complex relationships, graphic information, and inheritance in a concise manner. Their modular structure helps in inferences and maintenance.

□ Frames are not as simple as rules to understand and are more difficult to code and program.

□ Integrating several knowledge representation methods is gaining popularity due to decreasing software costs and increasing capabilities.

Key Terms

decision table	list	procedural rule
decision tree	metarule	production rule
declarative rule	multiple knowledge	propositional
demon	representation	logic
facet	object-oriented	script
frame	programming	semantic network
inheritance	O-A-V triplet	slot
instantiation	predicate logic	
knowledge	(calculus)	
representation		

Questions for Review

1. What do we mean by knowledge representation?
2. What are some of the benefits of pictorial representation?
3. List the major knowledge representation methods.
4. What is propositional logic? Give an example.
5. What is the meaning of IMPLIES in logic?
6. Define a semantic network.
7. List two advantages and two limitations of semantic networks.
8. Define O-A-V.
9. Define a "list" and give an example.
10. What is a production rule? Give an example.

11. What are the basic parts of a production rule? List several names for each part.
12. Define and contrast declarative and procedural knowledge.
13. What is an inference rule?
14. List two advantages and two disadvantages of rule representation.
15. Describe a frame. Give an example of a frame for sailboat or for kitchen.
16. What is an instantiation of a frame?
17. List three types of facets of a frame and explain their meaning.
18. What is a demon and what is its role in frames?
19. What is a slot in a frame?

Questions for Discussion

1. Give an example that illustrates the difference between propositional logic and predicate calculus.
2. Give examples of production rules in three different functional areas (e.g., marketing, accounting).
3. Why is frame representation considered more complex than production-rule representation? What are the advantages of the former over the latter?
4. It is said that multiple knowledge representation can be very advantageous. Why?
5. Compare knowledge representation to data representation in a database.
6. Provide an example that shows how a semantic network can depict inheritance.
7. Compare decision trees and decision tables. If you need to represent the knowledge of "identifying a bird," which presentation would you use and why? (Assume ten possible types of birds and ten possible attributes.)
8. Compare and contrast a knowledge and a procedural rule.
9. Review the benefits of frames over rules. In what cases would you use frames? (Give two examples.)
10. Explain this statement: Every parent is a child of a higher-level parent.
11. What are the major advantages of combining rules and frames?

Exercises

1. Construct a semantic network for the following situation: Mini is a robin; it lives in a nest which is on a pine tree in Ms. Wang's backyard. Robins are birds; they can fly and they have wings. They are an endangered species and they are protected by government regulations.
2. Write a frame that will describe the object robin, as described in the previous question.
3. Prepare a set of frames of an organization, given the following information:

   □ Company: 1,050 employees, $130 million annual sales, Jan Fisher is the president.

□ Departments: accounting, finance, marketing, production, personnel
□ Production department: five lines of production
□ Product: computers
□ Annual budget: $50,000 + $12,000 × number of computers produced
□ Materials: $6,000 per unit produced
□ Working days: 250 per year
□ Number of supervisors: one for each twelve employees
□ Range of number of employees: 400–500 per shift (two shifts per day). Overtime or part time on a third shift is possible.

4. Write a narrative of Figure 5.4.
5. Develop a script about shopping in a supermarket.
6. List attributes and values in the following objects: a lake, a stock market, a bridge, a car's engine. Use O-A-V representation.
7. Prepare a list for the following situation: a dining table with four chairs, four table cloths, and a vase with flowers.
8. Prepare a frame of a university that you know. Show two levels of hierarchies. Fill some slots, use a demon, and show at least one rule as it relates to a slot.
9. The following is a typical instruction set found in most cars' shop manuals (this one is based on Nissan's shop manual):

□ Topic: starter system troubles
□ Procedures: Try to crank the starter. If it is dead or cranks slowly, turn on the headlights. If the headlights are bright (or dim only slightly), the trouble is either in the starter itself, the solenoid, or in the wiring. To find the trouble, short the two large solenoid terminals together (not to ground). If the starter cranks normally, the problem is in the wiring or in the solenoid; check them up to the ignition switch. If the starter does not work normally check the bushings (see section 7-3 of the manual for instructions). If the bushings are good send the starter to a test station or replace it. If the headlights are out or very dim, check the battery (see section 7-4 for instructions). If the battery is okay, check the wiring for breaks, shorts, and dirty connections. If the battery and connecting wires are not at fault, turn the headlights on and try to crank the starter. If the lights dim drastically, it is probably because the starter is shorted to ground. Have the starter tested or replace it. (Based on Carrico et al. [5]).

Now translate the information into rules. (Can you do it in only six rules?)

References and Bibliography

1. Arcidiancono, T. "Computerized Reasoning," *PC Tech Journal* (May 1988).
2. Bench-Capon, T. *Knowledge Representation*. New York: Academic Press, 1990.
3. Brachman, R.J., and H.J. Levesque. *Readings in Knowledge Representation*. Palo Alto, Calif.: Morgan Kaufman, 1985.

4. Buchanan, G., and E.H. Shortliffe, eds. *Rule-Based Expert Systems.* Reading, Mass.: Addison-Wesley, 1984.

5. Carrico, M.A., et al. *Building Knowledge Systems: Developing and Managing Rule-based Applications.* New York: McGraw-Hill, 1989.

6. Edmonds, R.A. *The Prentice-Hall Guide to Expert Systems.* Englewood Cliffs, N.J.: Prentice-Hall, 1988.

7. Fikes, R., and T. Kehler. "The Role of Frame-Based Representation in Reasoning." *Communications of ACM* 28 (September 1985).

8. Gruber, T.R., and P.R. Cohen. "Design for Acquisition Principles of Knowledge System Design to Facilitate Knowledge Acquisitions." *International Journal of Man-Machine Studies* (no. 2, 1987).

9. Harmon, P. "Object-oriented systems." *Intelligent Software Strategies* (September 1990).

10. Khoshafian, S., and R. Abnous. *Object Orientation: Concepts, Languages, Databases, User Interface.* New York: John Wiley & Sons, 1990.

11. Kline, P.J., and S.B. Dalins. *Designing Expert Systems.* New York: John Wiley & Sons, 1989.

12. Liang, T.P., et al. *Automated Knowledge Acquisition Methods.* San Mateo, Calif.: Morgan Kaufman, 1992.

13. Owen, S. *Analogy for Automated Reasoning.* New York: Academic Press, 1990.

14. Ringland, G.A., and D.A. Duce. *Approaches to Knowledge Representation: An Introduction.* New York: John Wiley & Sons, 1988.

15. Stefik, M.J., et al. "Integrated Access-Oriented Programming into a Multiparadigm Environment." *IEEE Software* (January 1986).

16. Thuraisingham, B. "Rules to Frames and Frames to Rules." *AI Expert* (October 1989).

17. Tuthill, G.S. *Knowledge Engineering: Concepts and Practices for Knowledge-based Systems.* Blue Ridge Summit, Pa.: TAB Books, 1989.

18. Winston, P.H. *Artificial Intelligence,* 2nd ed. Reading, Mass.: Addison-Wesley, 1984.

Appendix A: Object-oriented Programming*

Object-oriented programming (OOP) is a novel way of thinking about data, procedures, and relationships among them. Some people view OOP as a unique programming language; others claim that it is *not* a programming language at all. OOP is a design principle that views descriptive and procedural attributes of an object as being associated with each individual object. Thus, each object

---

* This section is based, in part, on P. Harmon, et al. *Expert Systems Tools and Applications,* (New York: John Wiley & Sons, 1988) and on G.S. Howard, "Object-Oriented Programming Explained," *Journal of Systems Management* (July 1988).

TABLE 5A.1 Comparison of Traditional and Object-oriented Programming
Approaches

Traditional	Object-oriented
Procedures (routines)	Methods
Data	Instances (objects)
Procedure/invocation	Messages (events)
Data types	Classes
No inheritance	Inheritance
Programmer decides what to call when	System decides what to call when

Source: K. Hinsch et al., "Object-oriented Programming: Its Role in Computing," *Library Software Review* (January–February 1990).

can receive and send its own messages and perform independent actions (e.g., modify itself).

OOP features can be added to most existing programming languages for the purpose of increasing programmers' productivity as well as for making these languages more flexible. A comparison between traditional and OOP programming approaches is shown in Table 5A.1.

Benefits

OOP eliminates data dependency problems that exist in conventional programming. Thus, the complexity of information systems is dramatically reduced. Programmers' productivity can also be increased.

Frames

When AI programmers develop OOP environments, they tend to refer to objects as *frames*. Thus, when we talk about frame representation (see section 5.9 of the chapter), we essentially talk about using OOP in building knowledge bases.

Key Concepts

Several key concepts underlie OOP.

Objects. An object can be physical or it can be a concept or an event. It can be anything that we want to describe. For example, an object can be a car, a university, a course that you take, or a computer program. Objects are described

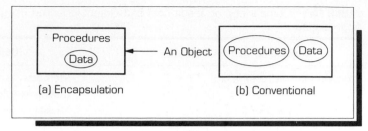

FIGURE 5A.1   Encapsulation Versus Conventional Organization

by a modular software program; that is, an object software is composed of several independent software units.

Encapsulation. Data (and other representations) are packaged inseparably in capsules that describe an object (Figure 5A.1).

Reusability. An object can be made sufficiently general and self-contained so it can be a component or a module that is "plugged in" when a system is programmed.

Inheritance. Objects inherit properties from other objects.

Multiple Inheritance. Inheritance can be singular or multiple.

Execution. In contrast to other programming languages that execute programming in a procedural, nonprocedural, functional (such as LISP), or logical (such as PROLOG) manner, in OOP a program execution is regarded as a physical model. Such a model simulates the behavior of either a real or an imaginary part of the world.

Messages, Methods, and Responses

Messages. An object can be accessed only by the private code surrounding the object. One reason to access an object is to send messages to it. Each message consists of a *selector*, which tells the object what to do with the message, and an *argument*. The argument is optional and its purpose is to explain, comment, provide instruction, or clarify the content of the message.

Methods. A method is a private procedure in an object that tells us what to do with the message and how to do it. In other words, it specifies what can be done with the object. Since each object owns its methods, objects respond differently to the same message. This is a powerful property of OOP. The object, based on the available knowledge, knows which is the most appropriate method to use.

Responses. Once a message has been received, the object sends a response to other objects or to the system, based on the selected method.

The World of Objects

Each object is considered a small world unto itself. It contains data and methods (procedures). It can receive and send messages. However, objects are related to other objects through a *hierarchy* of classes and subclasses of objects. Such a world is created by a process called *instantiation.*

Instantiation. In OOP, we may create objects by taking a copy of a preexisting object (called the parent), and then telling that object how it is to behave differently from the parent. For example, a parent object may be a "vehicle." By taking this object and adding a property "can fly," the vehicle becomes a new object, called "airplane." We refer to the airplane as a child (or offspring). We can create more objects from the vehicle (e.g., boat, car, train), and we can create objects from each of the new objects. For example, we can create a sailboat and a motorboat from a boat object. The process of creating new objects is called instantiation.

Another way to look at instantiation is simply by viewing it as *naming* the object or replacing variables by constants. For example, if the object is a bank account, then a balance of, say, $2,000 is an account instance; the balance is a variable. Once we place a value of 2,000, we instantiate the slot called value. If the object is a city, then Nashville is an instance of that object.

Classes and Inheritance. Organisms are grouped by biologists into classes and subclasses. For example, the class "animal" contains subclasses "bird" and "mammal." Classes inherit characteristics from their upper classes. A similar organization is available in OOP, as shown in Figure 5A.2.

When an object is created, it contains two parts. The left portion in Figure 5A.2 shows the new information unique to those objects. The right side shows information that points to the parent. Objects in lower levels inherit data and procedures from an upper level, except that private data and procedures are added. The ultimate source of data is the object at the top. It is called the class of all classes (or master object), and it has neither a parent nor private data. Everything held in common between a set of objects is the *class* of the objects.

When a message is sent to an object (say, the sailboat), it checks its private data and procedures to see how to handle the message. If it cannot find such information, it moves to its parent's private file and so on. This may continue, if needed, to the class of all classes whose data and procedures are shared with everybody else. This shared information is what we call the class of the objects.

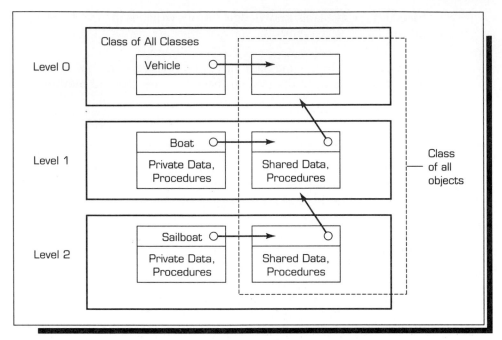

FIGURE 5A.2   Organization in Object-oriented Programming

OOP and Languages

OOP can be written in regular languages such as COBOL or BASIC. However, programming is usually done with special languages.

Smalltalk. Smalltalk is a programming environment within which the boundaries among operating systems, compilers, editors, utilities, data, and application programs become blurred. Hundreds of classes and methods are provided with an extensive use of icons, windows, and a mouse. Related products are Smalltalk-80 and Smalltalk V.

C++. C++ is a C implementation of OOP, specially suited for the UNIX environment. A similar product is Objective C.

LOOPS. LOOPS is a language for object-oriented representation. It also supports rule-based, access-oriented, and procedure-oriented representation methods. Its principal characteristic is the integration of its four programming schemes. For example, rules and rule sets are considered LOOPS objects. The support system contains display-oriented debugging tools, such as break packages and editors.

Other Languages. Many other languages have appeared on the market recently; see Wegner [9]. Some examples are Actor, Object Pascal, HyperTalk, and CLOS. For use of OOP in AI, see Retting et al. [4].

Access-oriented Programming

In *access-oriented programming*, gathering or sorting data can cause procedures to be invoked. This complements object-oriented programming. In object-oriented programming, when one object sends a message to another, the receiving object may change its data. Here, when one object changes its data, a message may be sent out. Access programs are composed of two parts: computing and monitoring the computations.

Figure 5A.3 shows a simulation of city street traffic (based on Stefik et al. [6]). The program includes objects such as city blocks, cars, emergency vehicles, and traffic lights that exchange messages to simulate traffic interactions. The display controller has objects for traffic *icons*, viewing transformations, and windows that display different parts of the city connected to the simulation objects by active values. The simulator represents the dynamics of traffic. The user can interact and control the view in the traffic windows. Access-oriented programming connects the simulation model with its numeric analysis to the graphic display. For example, when a light turns green, a message is sent to

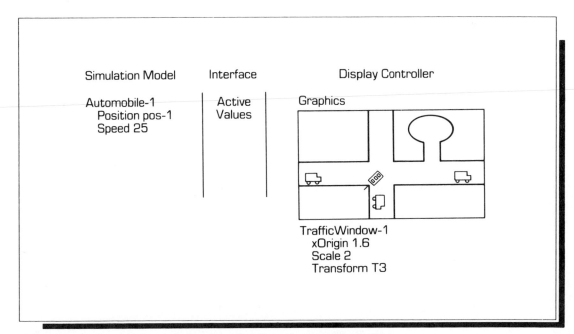

FIGURE 5A.3   Simulation of a City Street (*Source:* © 1986, IEEE.)

certain vehicles to move. The program computes the initial velocity and position. When the cars move, their position on the display is updated. The user can see the cars actually moving. Access-oriented and object-oriented programming provide interactive simulation and animation capabilities.

These representation methods are supported by special software (such as LOOPS) and can be combined with ES shells. An example of such a combination is KEE. For further details, see Stefik et al. [6].

Questions for Review

1. What is encapsulation? What is its major advantage?
2. Explain how OOP works with respect to messages.
3. What is a class of OOP?
4. How is OOP related to frames?
5. Relate access-oriented programming to object-oriented programming.

References and Bibliography

1. Hinsch, K. et al. "Object-oriented Programming: Its Role in Computing." *Library Software Review* (January–February, 1990).
2. Keene, S.E. *Object-oriented Programming in Common LISP.* Reading, Mass.: Addison-Wesley, 1989.
3. Pitta, J. "Object-oriented Processing." *Forbes* (March 19, 1990).
4. Retting, M., et al. "Object-oriented Programming in AI: New Choices." *AI Expert* (January 1989).
5. Shoemaker, S. "Train. Pas: An Example of Object-Oriented Programming." *PC AI* (September/October, 1990).
6. Stefik, M.J., et al. "Integrating Access-Oriented Programming into a Multi-paradigm Environment." *IEEE Software* (January 1986).
7. Tello, E.R. *Object-oriented Programming for AI.* Reading, Mass.: Addison-Wesley, 1988.
8. Thomas, D. "What's in an Object." *Byte* (March 1989).
9. Wegner, P. "Learning the (OOP) Language." *Byte* (March 1989).
10. Weiner, R.S., and L. Pinson. *Introduction to Object-oriented Programming in Smalltalk.* Reading, Mass.: Addison-Wesley, 1988.

Chapter 6

Inferences and Explanation

In Chapters 4 and 5, we saw how knowledge is acquired and then organized in the knowledge base. In this chapter, we consider the specific reasoning strategies that can be used to draw inferences. We also discuss the central strategies that can be used to guide a knowledge-based system on how to use the stored knowledge and how to communicate with the user. The following topics are addressed in this chapter:

6.1   Introduction

Once the knowledge base is completed it is ready for use. To do so, we need a computer program that will enable us to access the knowledge for the purpose of making inferences and decisions and for problem solving. This program is an algorithm that controls some reasoning process and it is usually referred to as the inference engine or the control program. In rule-based systems it is also referred to as the rule interpreter.

The control program directs the search through the knowledge base. The process may involve the application of inference rules in what is called pattern matching. The control program decides which rule to investigate, which alternative to eliminate, and which attribute to match. The most popular control programs are forward and backward chaining, which are described in this chapter (other methods were presented briefly in Chapter 2).

Before we examine the specific inferencing techniques used in AI, it might be interesting to see how people, which AI attempts to mimic, reason.

There are several ways in which people reason and solve problems. An interesting way to view the problem-solving process is one in which people draw on "sources of power." Lenat [11] identified nine such sources:

1. Formal methods—formal reasoning methods (e.g., logical deduction)
2. Heuristic reasoning—IF-THEN rules
3. Focus—common sense related toward more or less specific goals
4. Divide and conquer—dividing complex problems into subproblems
5. Parallelism—neural processors (perhaps a million) operating in parallel
6. Representation—ways of organizing pieces of information
7. Analogy—being able to associate and relate concepts
8. Synergy—the whole being greater than the sum of its parts
9. Serendipity—luck, or "fortuitous accidents."

These sources of power range from the purely deductive reasoning best handled by computer systems to inductive reasoning that is more difficult to computerize. Lenat believes that the future of AI lies in finding ways to tap those sources that have only begun to be exploited.

These sources of power are translated to specific reasoning or inference methods. The major inference and control approaches in AI are presented next.

6.2   Categories of Reasoning

Deductive Reasoning

Deductive reasoning is a process in which *general premises* are used to obtain a specific inference. Reasoning moves from a general principle to a specific conclusion. To illustrate this process, let's take a look at an example.

The deductive process generally begins with a statement of the premises and conclusions. It generally consists of three parts: a major premise, a minor premise, and a conclusion. Almost any problem or argument can be put into this form for deductive reasoning purposes:

Major premise: I do not jog when the temperature exceeds 90 degrees.
Minor premise: Today the temperature is 93 degrees.
Conclusion: Therefore, I will not jog today.

To use deductive reasoning, the problem must generally be formatted in this way. Once this format has been achieved, the conclusion must be valid if the premises are true. The whole idea is to develop new knowledge from previously given knowledge.

Inductive Reasoning

Inductive reasoning uses a number of established facts or premises to draw some general conclusion. An example will illustrate this process. Again, a statement is used to express the problem.

Premise: Faulty diodes cause electronic equipment failure.
Premise: Defective transistors cause electronic equipment failures.
Premise: Defective integrated circuits cause electronic equipment malfunction.
Conclusion: Therefore, defective semiconductor devices are a cause of electronic equipment failure.

The interesting thing about inductive reasoning is that the conclusion may be difficult to arrive at, or it may never be final or absolute. Conclusions can change if new facts are discovered. There will always be some uncertainty in the conclusion unless all possible facts are included in the premises, and this is usually impossible. As a result, the outcome of the inductive reasoning process will frequently contain some measure of uncertainty. That uncertainty will be reduced, however, as more facts or premises are used in the reasoning process. The more knowledge you have, the more conclusive your inferences can be.

Deductive or inductive approaches are used in logic, rule-based systems, and frames.

Analogical Reasoning

Analogical reasoning (which is natural to humans but still difficult to accomplish mechanically) assumes that when a question is asked, the answer can be derived by analogy. For example, if you ask, "What are the working hours of engineers in the company?" the computer may reason that engineers are white-collar employees. Because the computer *knows* that white-collar employees work from

9 to 5, it will infer that engineers work 9 to 5. This is an area of much research, and many new developments should be forthcoming. (For an overview see Eliot [5] and Vosniadou and Ortony [20]).

Analogical reasoning, according to Tuthill [19], is a type of verbalization of an internalized learning process. An individual uses processes that require an ability to recognize previously encountered experiences. Because analogical reasoning relates the present with the past in an attempt to relate unrelated objects or concepts, analogical reasoning is similar to commonsense reasoning. For example, a fisherman hooks a fish that fights in a familiar manner. The fisherman recalls the way a fish once ran and the feel of its tail against the line. The fish circled the boat and severed the line in kelp. As a result of that experience the fisherman now has an idea of how the present fish will fight, anticipates its actions, and lands the fish. Thus, the fisherman was able to relate a "feel" on the line to a past experience and a current condition.

The use of this approach has not been exploited yet in the AI field. However, case-based reasoning (see section 6.8) is an attempt to apply the approach to practical problems.

Formal Reasoning

Formal reasoning involves syntactic manipulation of data structures to deduce new facts, following prescribed rules of inference. A typical example is the mathematical logic used in proving theorems in geometry. Another example is the approach of predicate calculus, which is an effective symbolic representation and deductive technique (see section 6.3).

Procedural Numeric Reasoning

Procedural numeric reasoning uses mathematical models or simulation to solve problems. Model-based reasoning (see section 6.7) is an example of this approach.

Generalization and Abstraction

Generalization and abstraction can be successfully used with both logical and semantic representation of knowledge. For example, if we know that *all* companies have presidents and that *all* brokerage houses are considered companies, then we can infer and generalize that any brokerage house will have a president.

Similarly, if the computer knows that in a certain company all engineers are on a monthly salary, as are the accountants and the system analysts, eventually the computer might conclude that *all* professionals in the company are on a monthly salary.

Metalevel Reasoning

Metalevel reasoning involves "knowledge about what you know" (e.g., about the importance and relevance of certain facts). It could play a major role in developing future ES.

Which approach to use, and how successful the inference will be, depends to a great extent on which knowledge representation method is used. For example, reasoning by analogy can be more successful with semantic networks than with frames.

6.3   Reasoning with Logic

In the previous chapter, we discussed a logical system for expressing facts and knowledge in a symbolic form. What we really want to do is use that knowledge to make inferences. How do we employ this knowledge to answer questions, reason, or draw conclusions? We utilize various rules of inference to manipulate the logical expressions to create new expressions.

For executing either deductive or inductive reasoning, several basic reasoning rules allow the manipulation of the logical expressions to create new expressions. The most important rule is called **modus ponens.**

Modus Ponens. According to this procedure, if there is a rule "if A, then B," and if we know that A is true, then it is valid to conclude that B is also true. In the terminology of logic, we express this as:

$$[A \text{ AND } (A \rightarrow B)] \rightarrow B$$

A and $(A \rightarrow B)$ are propositions in a knowledge base. Given this expression, we can replace both propositions with the proposition B. In other words, we can use modus ponens to draw the conclusion that B is true if the first two expressions are true. Here's an example:

A: It is sunny.
B: We will go to the beach.
$A \rightarrow B$: If it is sunny, then we will go to the beach.

The first premise simply states that it is a sunny day. The second says we will go to the beach. Furthermore, A IMPLIES B. So if both A AND A IMPLIES B are true, B is true. Using modus ponens you can then deduce that we will go to the beach.

A different situation is the inference in the case that B is known to be false. This is called **Modus tollens.**

Modus Tollens. According to this procedure, when B is known to be false, and if there is a rule "if A, then B," it is valid to conclude that A is also false.

Resolution. **Resolution** is a method of discovering whether a new fact is valid, given a set of logical statements. It is a method of "theorem proving." It is applied to a class of well-formed formulas, called clauses. The resolution process, which can be computerized because of its well-formed structure, is applied to a pair of parent clauses to produce a derived new clause.

The procedure is a general automatic method for determining whether a theorem (hypothesis) follows from a given set of premises. The theorem to be proven is made negative and placed, together with the set of premises, in a clause. New clauses are derived, as needed, by using a resolution. For details see Winston [22].

Resolution is built into the PROLOG programming language. PROLOG permits you to solve problems by putting them in predicate calculus (see Chapter 5, section 5.3) form. Inferences are drawn automatically by the resolution algorithm that is part of PROLOG.

The importance of these procedures (which are used in production rule systems as well) is that they allow us to derive new facts from rules and known facts. Actually, all of this seems to be just common sense. Almost anyone can figure it out—except for a computer. Simple deduction like this comes naturally to our brains, but a computer must be told how to make simple inferences like modus ponens.

Numerous other techniques are used to make deductions from given premises or to prove the truth or falsity of a proposition. All of them require an extensive knowledge of logic and are complex in their implementation. Thus, they are beyond the scope of this book.

6.4   Inferencing with Rules: Forward and Backward Chaining

Inferencing with rules involves implementation of the modus ponens and other inferencing approaches described earlier. The inference mechanism in most commercial expert systems uses the modus ponens approach, which is reflected in the search mechanism with the rule interpreter. Consider the following example:

RULE 1: IF international conflict begins,
         THEN the price of gold goes up.

Let us assume that the ES knows that an international conflict just started. This information is stored in the "facts" (assertion) portion of the knowledge base. This means that the premise (IF side) of the rule is *true*. Using modus ponens, the conclusion (consequent) is then accepted as *true*. We say that Rule 1 "fires." Firing a rule occurs only when all of the rule's parts are satisfied (being either true or false). Then, the conclusion drawn is stored in the assertion base. In our case, the conclusion (the price of gold goes up) is added to the assertion base, and it could be used to satisfy the premise of other rules. The true (or false) values for either portion of the rules can be obtained by querying the user or by firing other rules. Testing a rule premise or conclusion can be as simple as matching a symbolic pattern in the rule to a similar pattern in the assertion base. This activity is referred to as **pattern matching.**

Every rule in the rule base can be checked to see if its premise or conclusion can be satisfied by previously made assertions. This process may be done in one of two directions, forward or backward, and it will continue until no more rules can fire, or until a goal is achieved.

Forward and Backward Chaining: An Overview

There are two approaches for controlling inference in rule-based ES: forward chaining and backward chaining (each of which has several variations). First, we shall provide an intuitive description of the two approaches; then we shall discuss them in detail.

Example 1. Suppose you want to fly from Denver to Tokyo and there are no direct flights between the two cities. Therefore, you try to find a chain of connecting flights starting from Denver and ending in Tokyo. There are two basic ways you can search for this chain of flights:

1. Start with all the flights that arrive at Tokyo and find the city where each flight originated. Then look up all the flights arriving at those cities and find where they originated. Continue the process until you find Denver. Because you are working backward from your goal (Tokyo), this search process is called **backward chaining** (or goal driven).
2. List all flights leaving Denver and mark their destination (intermediate) cities. Then look up all the flights leaving these intermediate cities and find where they land; continue the process until you find Tokyo. In this case, you are working forward from Denver toward your goal, so this search process is called **forward chaining** (or data driven).

This example also demonstrates the importance of heuristics in expediting the search process. Going either backward or forward, you can use heuristics to make the search more efficient. For example, in the backward approach you can look at flights that go only eastward. Depending on the goals of your trip (e.g., minimize cost, minimize travel time, maximize stopovers), you can develop additional rules to expedite the search even further.

Example 2. Suppose your car will not start. Is it because you are out of gas? Or is it because the starter is broken? Or is it because of some other reason? Your task is to find out why the car won't start. From what you already know (the *consequence:* the car won't start), you go *backward* trying to find the *condition* that caused it. This is a typical application of ES in the area of diagnosis (i.e., the conclusion is known and the causes are sought).

A good example of *forward* chaining is a situation in which a water system is overheating. In this case the goal is to predict the most likely result. After reviewing the rules and checking additional evidence, you can finally find the answer. In forward chaining, you start with a *condition,* or a symptom, which is given as a fact.

As will be shown later, the search process in both cases goes through a set of knowledge rules. After determining which rules are true and which are false, the search will end in a finding (we hope). The word *chaining* signifies the linking of a set of pertinent rules.

The search process is directed by an approach sometimes referred to as **rule interpreter,** which works as follows:

- □ In forward chaining, if premise clauses match the situation, then the process attempts to assert the conclusion.
- □ In backward chaining, if the current goal is to determine the fact in the conclusion, then the process attempts to determine whether the premise clauses match the situation.

Backward Chaining

Backward chaining is a *goal-driven* approach in which you start from an expectation of what is to happen (hypothesis), then seek evidence that supports (or contradicts) your expectation. Often this entails formulating and testing intermediate hypotheses (or subhypotheses).

Hypothesis: Total sales are down because of the cold weather.
Subhypothesis: Sales are relatively lower in the northern states.

Now, consider the northern states and compare the sales there with the sales of the remaining states so that the hypothesis can either be accepted or rejected.

On a computer, goal-driven reasoning works the same way. The program starts with a goal to be verified as either true or false. Then it looks for a rule that has that goal in its *conclusion.* It then checks the *premise* of that rule in an attempt to satisfy this rule. It checks the assertion base first. If the search there fails, the ES looks for another rule whose conclusion is the same as that of the premise of the first rule. An attempt is then made to satisfy the second rule. The process continues until all the possibilities that apply are checked or until the first rule is satisfied.

Example. Here is an example of an investment decision. The following variables are involved:

A = Have $10,000
B = Younger than thirty
C = Education at college level

       D = Annual income of at least $40,000
       E = Invest in securities
       F = Invest in growth stocks
       G = Invest in IBM stock

Each of these variables can be answered as true (yes) or false (no).

The facts: Let us assume that an investor has $10,000 (i.e., A is true) and she is twenty-five years old (B is true). She would like advice on investing in IBM stock (yes or no for the *goal*).

The rules: Let us assume that our knowledge base includes these five rules:

    R1: IF a person has $10,000 and she has a college degree, THEN she should invest in securities.
    R2: IF a person's annual income is at least $40,000 and she has a college degree, THEN she should invest in growth stocks.
    R3: IF a person is younger than thirty and if she is investing in securities, THEN she should invest in growth stocks.
    R4: IF a person is younger than thirty, THEN she has a college degree.
    R5: IF a person wants to invest in growth stock, THEN the stock should be IBM.

These rules can be written as:

    R1: IF A, Then C THEN E.
    R2: IF D and C, THEN F.
    R3: IF B and E, THEN F.
    R4: IF B, THEN C.
    R5: IF F, THEN G.

Our goal is to find whether or not to invest in IBM stock.

Starting point: In backward chaining we start by looking for a rule that includes the goal (G) in its *conclusion* (THEN) part. Since rule 5 is the only one that qualifies, we start with it. If several rules include G, then the inference engine will follow procedure to handle the situation.

Step 1: Try to accept or reject G. The ES goes now to the *assertion base* to see if G is there. At the present time, all we have in the assertion base is:

    A is true.
    B is true.

Therefore, the ES will proceed to step 2.

Step 2: R5 says that if it is *true* that we invest in growth stocks (F), THEN we should invest in IBM (G). If we can conclude that the premise of R5 is true or false, then we have solved our problem. However, we do not know if F is true. What shall we do now? Note that F, which is the *premise* of R5, is also the *conclusion* of R2 and R3. Therefore, to find out if F is true, we must check these two rules.

Step 3: We try R2 first (arbitrarily); if both D and C are true, then F is true. Now we have a problem. D is not a conclusion of any rule, nor is it a fact. The computer can then either move to another rule or try to find if D is true by asking the investor for whom the consultation is given if her annual income is above $40,000.

What the ES will do depends on the procedures in the inference engine. Usually a user is going to be asked for additional information *only* if the information is not available or it cannot be deduced.

We abandon R2 and return to the other rule, R3. This action is called **backtracking** (i.e., knowing that we are in a dead end, we try something else. The computer must be preprogrammed to handle backtracking).

Step 4: Go to R3, test B and E. We know that B is true, because it is a given fact. To prove E, we should go to R1, where E is the conclusion.

Step 5: Examine R1. It is necessary to find if A and C are true. A is true because it is a given fact. To test C, it is necessary to test rule R4 (where C is the conclusion).

Step 6: Rule R4 tells us that C is true (because B is true). Therefore, C becomes a fact (added to the assertion base).

Step 7: If C is true, then E is true, which validates F, which validates our goal (i.e., the advice is to invest in IBM). A negative response to any of the preceding statements would result in a "do not invest in IBM stock."

Notice that during the search the ES moved from the THEN part to the IF part to the THEN part, etc. (Figure 6.1). This is a typical search pattern in *backward chaining.* As will be seen next, the forward chaining starts with the IF part, moves to the THEN part, then to another IF, and so on. Some systems allow a change in the direction of the search during midcourse; that is, they will go from a THEN to THEN (or from IF to IF) if needed.

For another example of backward chaining, see Appendix A at the end of this chapter.

Forward Chaining

Forward chaining is a *data-driven* approach. In this approach we start from available information as it comes in, or from a basic idea, then try to draw conclusions.

The computer analyzes the problem by looking for the facts that match the IF portion of its IF-THEN rules. For example, if a certain machine is not working, the computer checks the electricity flow to the machine. As each rule is tested, the program works its way toward a conclusion.

Example. Let us use the same example that we introduced in backward chaining. Here we reproduce the rules:

R1: IF A and C, THEN E.
R2: IF D and C, THEN F.

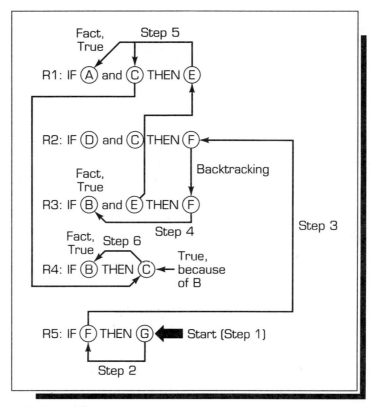

FIGURE 6.1 Backward Chaining

R3: IF B and E, THEN F.
R4: IF B, THEN C.
R5: IF F, THEN G.

and the facts:

A is true (have $10,000) and
B is true (the investor is younger than 30)

Start: Since it is known that A and B are true, the ES starts with one of them (takes A first) and looks for a rule that includes an A in the IF side of the rule. In our case, this is R1. It includes E in its conclusion.

Step 1: The system attempts to verify E. Since A is known (fact, in the assertion base), it is necessary to test C in order to conclude about E. The system tries to find C in the assertion base. Since C is not there, the ES moves to a rule where C is in the THEN side. This is R4.

Step 2: The system tests R4. C is true because it is matched against B, which is known to be true, in the assertion base. Therefore, C is added to the assertion base as being true.

Step 3: Now R1 fires and E is established to be true. This leads to R3 where E is in the IF side.

Step 4: Since B and E are known to be true (they are in the assertion base), then R3 fires, F is established to be true in the assertion base.

Step 5: Now R5 fires (since F is in its IF side) which establishes G as true. So the expert systems will recommend an investment in IBM stock.

We have seen that an antecedent-consequence rule system can run forward or backward, but which one is better? The answer depends on the purpose of the reasoning and the shape of the search space. For example, if the goal is to discover all that can be deduced from a given set of facts, the system should run forward. In some cases, the two strategies can be mixed (bidirectional).

The execution of the forward and/or backward chaining is done with the aid of a rule interpreter. Its function is to examine production rules to determine which one(s) is capable of being fired and then to fire the rule. The *control strategy* of the rule interpreter (e.g., the backward chaining) determines how the appropriate rules are found and when to apply them.

Inferencing with rules (as well as with logic) can be very effective, but there are some obvious limitations to these techniques. One reason for this is summarized by the familiar axiom that there is an exception to every rule. For example, consider the following argument:

Proposition 1: Birds can fly.
Proposition 2: An ostrich is a bird.
Conclusion: An ostrich can fly.

The conclusion is perfectly valid but false; ostriches do not cooperate. For this reason, as well as for increased efficiency of the search, we use other inferencing methods.

6.5   The Inference Tree

The **inference tree** (also goal tree, or logical tree) provides a schematic view of the inference process. It is similar to a decision tree. Note that each rule is composed of a premise and a conclusion. In building the inference tree the premises and conclusions are shown as nodes. The branches connect the premises and the conclusions. The operators AND and OR are used to reflect the structures of the rules. There is no deep significance to the construction of such trees—they just provide a better insight into the structure of the rules.

Figure 6.2 presents the logical tree of the example that we used in the previous section. By using the tree, we can visualize the process of inference and movement along the branches of the tree. This is called *tree traversal.* To traverse an AND node, we must traverse all the nodes below it. To traverse an OR node, it is enough to traverse just one of the nodes below.

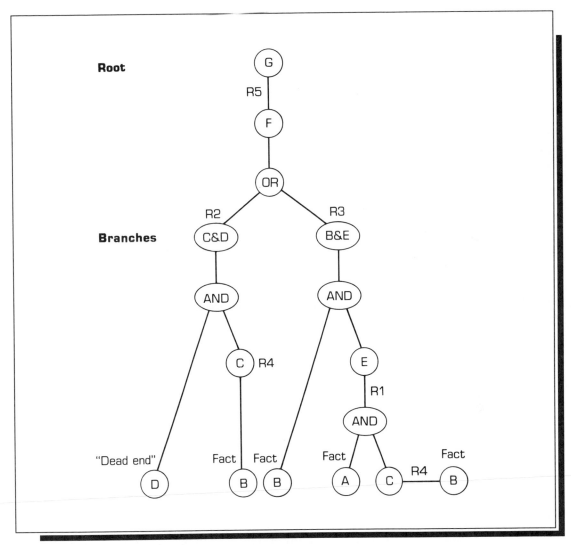

FIGURE 6.2 Inference Tree, Backward Chaining

The inference tree is constructed upside down: the root is at the top and the branches point downward. The tree ends with "leaves" at the bottom. (It can also be constructed from the left to the right, much like a decision tree.)

Inference trees are composed basically of clusters of goals like those in Figure 6.3. Each goal may have subgoals (children) and a supergoal (parent). The top goal (root goal) does not have a parent; the bottom goals (leaves) are facts or dead ends, and they do not have children.

Single inference trees are always a mixture of AND nodes and OR nodes; they are often called AND/OR trees. (More complicated trees involve several

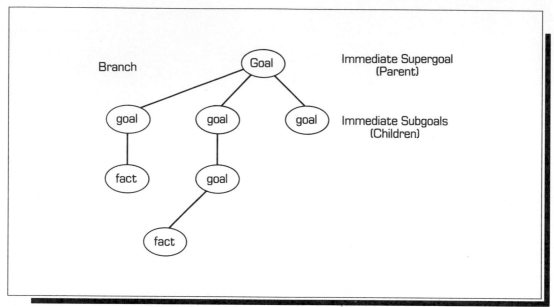

FIGURE 6.3   Goals and Subgoals

goals and additional parts of a rule such as ELSE). The AND node signifies a situation in which a goal is satisfied only when *all* its immediate subgoals are satisfied. The OR node signifies a situation in which a goal is satisfied when *any* of its immediate goals is satisfied. When enough subgoals are satisfied to achieve the primary goal, the tree is said to be *satisfied*. The inference engine contains procedures for expressing this process as a backward and/or forward chaining. These procedures are organized as a set of instructions involving inference rules. They aim at satisfying the inference tree and collectively contribute to the process of goal (problem) reduction. For further discussion see Winston [22].

The inference tree has another big advantage; it provides a guide for answering the *why* and *how* questions in the explanation process. The *how* question is asked by users when they want to know how a certain conclusion has been reached. The computer follows the logic in the inference tree, identifies the goal (conclusion) involved in it and the AND/OR branches, and reports the immediate subgoals. The *why* question is asked by users when they want to know why the computer requests certain information as input. To deal with why questions, the computer identifies the goal involved with the computer-generated query and reports the immediate subgoals.

A similar graphic presentation to an inference tree is the inference network (net). An inference net shows the inference process together with the rules that are being used. For further details, see Winston [22].

6.6   Inferencing with Frames

Reasoning with frames is much more complicated than reasoning with rules. The slot provides a mechanism for a kind of reasoning called *expectation-driven processing*. Empty slots (i.e., unconfirmed expectations) can be filled, subject to certain conditioning, with data that confirm the expectations. Thus, frame-based reasoning looks for confirmation of expectations and often just involves filling in slot values.

Perhaps the simplest way to specify slot values is by default. The default value is attached loosely to the slot so as to be easily displaced by a value that meets the assignment condition. In the absence of information, however, the default value remains attached and expressed.

The reasoning process that takes place with frames is essentially the seeking of confirmation of various expectations. This amounts to filling in the slots and verifying that they match the current situation. With frames, it is easy to make inferences about new objects, events, or situations because the frames provide a base of knowledge drawn from previous experience.

The reasoning in frames can be executed in different ways. Two most common ways are using rules and employing hierarchial reasoning.

Using Rules

A rule can reason about the characteristics of a frame by referring to its slot values. The following is an example (provided by Walters and Nielsen [21], p. 226).

Example. A route must be planned for driving to a certain destination where a bridge must be avoided if the vehicle is too heavy. A rule such as the following might be placed in the knowledge base:

> RULE 1: IF   WEIGHT of MY-FORD > 3,000 pounds
>   THEN   take DETOUR around RICKETY BRIDGE

If the value of the WEIGHT slot of the frame MY-FORD is greater than 3,000 pounds, then the plan should include a detour around the rickety bridge.

Rules can be used to process the structural knowledge contained in a taxonomy. The following rule, which might be one of a set for determining at what type of service station the driver should stop to refuel the car, is illustrative:

> RULE 2: IF   ?VEHICLE is MEMBER-OF AUTOMOBILES
>   AND   ?VEHICLE has-a ?ENGINE
>   AND   ?ENGINE is MEMBER-OF DIESEL
>   THEN   set REFUEL of ?VEHICLE to TRUCKSTOP

On the first line the inference engine attempts to instantiate the variable ?VEHICLE with every frame, but only those instantiations that are members of the class AUTOMOBILES are kept. At this point, several vehicles might qualify, so several instances of the rule would be established (e.g., with vehicle-2). The second line instantiates the variable ?ENGINE with any frame that ?VEHICLE points to with a has-a relation. Thus, if vehicle-2 had an engine and, say, a fuel-tank, the rule would be instantiated twice—once with ?VEHICLE = vehicle-2 and ?ENGINE = ENGINE and once with ?VEHICLE = vehicle-2 and ?ENGINE = FUEL-TANK.

The third line of the rule then throws out any instantiation of the rule for which ?ENGINE is not a member of the class DIESEL. The fourth line then sets the slot REFUEL of the associated vehicle to the value TRUCKSTOP.

Reasoning with a knowledge taxonomy is not the exclusive province of rules, *although many frame-based systems are rule-based knowledge extensively*. However, procedural knowledge of the type found in blackboard systems (see Chapter 14) *can process frame-based knowledge* quite efficiently.

Using Hierarchial Reasoning

According to **hierarchial reasoning,** certain alternatives, objects, or events can be *eliminated* at various levels of the search (reasoning) hierarchy. For example, at one level there might be a rule:

> RULE: IF   MANUFACTURER of ?VEHICLE is FORD
> THEN   ?VEHICLE is NOT MEMBER-OF DIESEL

Assuming Ford does not manufacture any diesel engines, a single rule at this level can eliminate a number of class and subclass possibilities. For details and other methods of elimination see Walters and Nielsen [21].

6.7   Model-based Reasoning[1]

Model-based reasoning is based on knowledge of the structure and behavior of the devices the system is designed to understand. Model-based systems are especially useful in diagnosing equipment problems. The systems include a model of the device to be diagnosed that is then used to identify the cause(s) of the equipment's failure. Because they draw conclusions directly from knowledge of a device's structure and behavior, model-based expert systems are said to reason from "first principles."

The Hardware Troubleshooting Group in MIT's AI lab assesses the use of model-based ES to diagnose malfunctioning computers. The group uses a

---

[1]Based, in part, on Mishkoff [13].

computer-repair scenario to contrast the rule-based with the model-based approaches. First, the rule-based approach:

> Consider the likely behavior of an engineer with a great deal of repair experience. He or she simply stares briefly at the console, noting the pattern of lights and error message, then goes over to one of the cabinets, opens it, raps sharply on one of the circuit boards inside, and restarts the machine.

The diagnostic process used in this episode represents the approach that is incorporated in a rule-based expert system. A knowledge engineer formalizes the reasoning process that an expert uses to discover the source of the problem and encodes that procedure in a series of production rules.

A model-based approach, on the other hand, is represented by a scenario such as the following:

> Consider a new engineer who has just completed training. He or she carefully notes the symptoms, gets out a thick book of schematics, and spends the next half hour pouring over them. At last he or she looks up, goes over to one of the cabinets, opens it, raps sharply on one of the circuit boards inside, and restarts the machine.

Although in this example the rule-based and model-based approaches resulted in the same actions, the *procedures* used to arrive at the conclusions were very different. Because the novice engineer in the latter scenario could not rely on his or her expertise to diagnose and repair the computer, he or she had to refer to documentation that explained how the computer worked. Similarly, a model-based system depends on knowledge of the structure and behavior of a device, rather than relying on production rules that represent expertise.

One especially attractive feature of a model-based ES is its "transportability." A rule-based ES that incorporates an expert's knowledge of troubleshooting problems with a particular computer might be of no value for repairing a different kind of computer. On the other hand, if a model-based ES included a thorough working knowledge of digital electronic computer circuits, it theoretically could be used to diagnose the problem of *any* computer.

Example. An example of model-based reasoning is given by Fulton and Pepe [6]. Their systems are implemented by NASA at the Kennedy Space Center for troubleshooting (diagnosing failures). Rule-based systems are not effective in situations where there is a mass of sensor information. Such systems cannot make the necessary association between the set of sensor data and the fault.

The model-based system includes a model that simulates the structure and function of the machinery under diagnosis. Instead of reasoning only from observable values, those systems reason from first principles; that is, the systems know the machinery's internal processes. The systems can *compute* which state the machine is in rather than attempting to match such a state against complex symptoms (which a rule-based system will do).

Once signals are received from the sensors, the expert system activates a simulation program that generates predicted values. These are compared against the information provided by the sensors. As long as the actual data are within the range of the predicted values (the "tolerance"), nothing is done. If the actual data are outside the tolerance, a diagnosis is automatically performed. The result of the diagnosis may activate control commands to prevent the system from entering a dangerous state. This mode of reasoning is very important in intelligent robots (see Chapter 11).

The models used in this type of reasoning can be either **mathematical models** or **component models.** For example, a mathematical model can simulate the function of a grandfather clock, taking into account the oscillator length, gear size, and so forth. The model can predict the position of the hands after a specific time interval; and with more complexity, can diagnose why the clock is too fast (or too slow). In contrast, a component model contains a functional description of all components and their interactions. As the clock ticked, each component would alter itself, propagate its final position to the relevant components, then allow them to alter their positions.

Special model-based tools are available (they usually involve frames). They are especially helpful in inferencing that involves monitoring production processes (and taking appropriate actions) and diagnosing. A necessary condition for model-based reasoning is the creation of a *complete* and *accurate* model of the system under study. The approach is especially useful in real-time systems (see Chapter 14). For further details see Davis and Hamscher [3].

Generally speaking, model-based representations are combined with other representation and inference techniques to achieve a synergistic effect. Two types of model-based systems are available: **static representations,** which deal with situations that are relatively stable (e.g., diagnosis), and **dynamic representations,** which deal with situations involving variability. For details and examples, see Walters and Nielsen [21].

6.8   Case-based Reasoning

Basics

The basic idea of **case-based reasoning** is to adapt solutions that were used to solve old problems and use them for solving new problems. One variation of this approach is the rule-induction method described in Chapter 4. In rule induction the computer examines historical cases and generates rules, which then are chained (forward or backward) to solve problems. Case-based reasoning, on the other hand, (according to Riesbeck and Schank [16]), follows a different process; it

  ☐ finds those cases in memory that solved problems similar to the current problem, and

□ adapts the previous solution or solutions to fit the current problem, taking into account any difference between the current and previous situations.

Finding relevant cases involves

□ characterizing the input problem, by assigning the appropriate features to it,
□ retrieving the cases from memory with those features, and
□ picking the case or cases that match the input best.

The basic justification for the use of case-based reasoning according to Riesbeck and Schank is that human thinking does not use logic (or reasoning from first principle). It is basically a processing of the right information retrieved at the right time. So the central problem is the identification of pertinent information whenever needed. This is done in case-based reasoning with the aid of scripts.

Scripts. As you may recall from Chapter 5, scripts describe a well-known sequence of events. For example, recall the script that describes what happens when you enter a restaurant. If a script is available, then you don't have to think much in an attempt to infer the intentions of a waitress. These intentions are either documented in the script or can be inferred from there easily. Therefore, in many cases, it is possible to say that reasoning is no more than applying scripts. The more scripts available to us, the less thinking we need to do. All that is necessary is finding the right script to use. Riesbeck and Schank [16] postulate that given a choice between thinking hard (reworking the problem) and applying an old script, people will choose the script every time. Scripts are found in historical cases, which reflect human experience. The experience can be that of the decision makers or that of others. Case-based reasoning is the essence of how people reason from experience.

Case-based reasoning has been proposed as a more psychologically plausible model of the reasoning of an expert than a rule-based model. A theoretical comparison of the two was made by Riesbeck and Schank [16] and a summary is provided in Table 6.1.

Advantages. Case-based reasoning has several potential benefits; they are summarized in Table 6.2.

Process of Case-based Reasoning

The process of case-based reasoning is shown graphically in Figure 6.4. Boxes represent processes and ovals represent knowledge structure. The major steps in the process are described beginning on page 227 (reprinted from Slade [18]).

TABLE 6.1 Comparison of Case-based and Rule-based Reasoning

Criterion	Rule-based Reasoning	Case-based Reasoning
Knowledge unit	Rule	Case
Granularity	Fine	Coarse
Knowledge acquisition units	Rules, hierarchies	Cases, hierarchies
Explanation mechanism	Backtrace of rule firings	Precedent cases
Characteristic output	Answer, plus confidence measure	Answer, plus precedent cases
Knowledge transfer across problems	High, if backtracking Low, if deterministic	Low
Speed as a function of knowledge base size	Exponential, if backtracking Linear, if deterministic	Logarithmic, if index tree balanced
Domain requirements	Domain vocabulary Good set of inference rules Either few rules or Rules apply sequentially Domain mostly obeys rules	Domain vocabulary Database of example cases Stability—a modified good solution is probably still good Many exceptions to rules
Advantages	Flexible use of knowledge Potentially optimal answers	Rapid response Rapid knowledge acquisition Explanation by examples
Disadvantages	Computationally expensive Long development time Black-box answers	Suboptimal solutions Redundant knowledge base

Source: Courtesy of Marc Goodman, Cognitive Systems, Inc. Based on: M. Goodman, "PRISM: A Case-Based Telex Classifier," in *Innovative Applications of Artificial Intelligence*, vol. 11, A. Rappaport and R. Smith, eds. (Cambridge, Mass: MIT Press, 1990).

TABLE 6.2 Advantages of Case-based Reasoning

Knowledge acquisition is improved: easier to build, simpler to maintain, less expensive to develop and support.

Processing time is faster.

Existing data and knowledge are leveraged.

Complete formalized domain knowledge (which is required with rules) is not required.

Experts feel better discussing concrete cases (not general rules).

Explanation becomes easier. Rather than showing many rules, a logical sequence can be shown.

Acquisition of new cases is easy (can be automated). (For an example of knowledge acquisition of cases, see diPiazza and Helsabeck [4].)

Learning can occur from both success and failures.

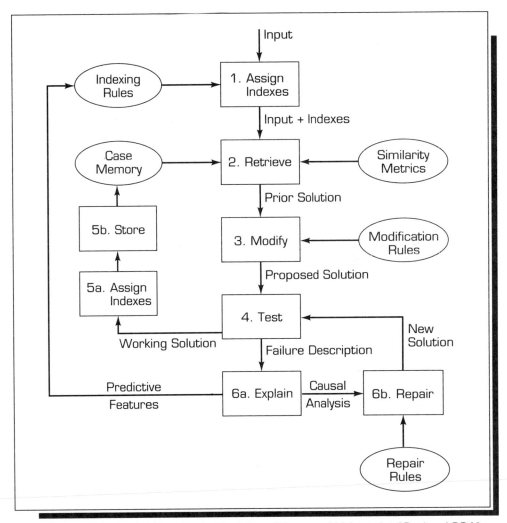

FIGURE 6.4   Case-based Reasoning Flowchart (*Source: AI Magazine* [Spring 1991], p. 46; based on C. K. Riesback and R. L. Schank, *Inside Case-based Reasoning* [Hillsdale, N.J.: Lawrence Erlbaum Associates, 1989], p. 32. Copyright © 1989, American Association for Artificial Intelligence. All rights reserved.)

1. Assign Indexes: Features of the new event are assigned as indexes characterizing the event. For example, our first air shuttle flight might be characterized as an airplane flight.

2. Retrieve: The indexes are used to retrieve a similar past case from memory. The past case contains the prior solution. In our example, we might be reminded of a previous airplane trip.

3. Modify: The old solution is modified to conform to the new situation, resulting in a proposed solution. For our airplane case, we would make appropriate modifications to account for changes in various features such as destination, price, purpose of the trip, departure and arrival times, weather, and so on.

4. Test: The proposed solution is tried out. It either succeeds or fails. Our airplane reminding generates certain expectations.

5. Assign and Store: If the solution succeeds, then assign indexes and store a working solution. The successful plan is then incorporated into the case memory. For a typical airplane trip there will be few expectation failures and, therefore, little to make this new trip memorable. It will be just one more instance of the airplane script.

6. Explain, Repair, and Test: If the solution fails, then explain the failure, repair the working solution, and test again. The explanation process identifies the source of the problem. The predictive features of the problem are incorporated into the indexing rules to anticipate this problem in the future. The failed plan is repaired to fix the problem, and the revised solution is then tested. For our air shuttle example, we realize that certain expectations fail. We learn that we do not get an assigned seat and that we do not have to pay ahead of time. We might decide that taking the air shuttle is more like riding on a train. We can then create a new case in memory to handle this new situation and identify predictive features so that we will be reminded of this episode the next time we take the shuttle.

In support of this process are the following types of knowledge structures, represented by ovals in the figure:

Indexing Rules: Indexing rules identify the predictive features in the input that provide appropriate indexes in the case memory. Determining the significant input features is a persistent problem . . .

Case Memory: Case memory is the episodic memory, which comprises the database of experience.

Similarity Metrics: If more than one case is retrieved from episodic memory, the similarity metrics can be used to decide which case is more like the current situation. For example, in the air shuttle case, we might be reminded of both airplane rides and train rides. The similarity rules might initially suggest that we rely on the airplane case.

Modification Rules: No old case is going to be an exact match for a new situation. The old case must be modified to fit. We require knowledge about what kinds of factors can be changed and how to change them. For the airplane ride, it is acceptable to ride in a different seat, but it is usually not advisable to change roles from passenger to pilot.

Repair Rules: Once we identify and explain an expectation failure, we must try to alter our plan to fit the new situation. Again, we have rules for what kinds of changes are permissible. For the air shuttle, we recognize that paying for the ticket on the plane is an acceptable change. We can generate an explanation that recognizes an airplane ride as a type of commercial transaction and suggests that there are alternative acceptable means of paying for services.

Uses, Issues, Applications

Case-based reasoning can be used on its own or it can be combined with other reasoning paradigms. Table 6.3 provides some guidelines. Target application domains, according to Cognitive Systems, Inc., are listed below:

- Tactical planning
- Political analysis

TABLE 6.3   When to Use Case-based Reasoning

Domain cannot be formalized with rules because:
  — domain has weak or unknown causal model
  — domain has underdefined terms
  — contradictory rules apply in different situations
Application requires complex output, e.g., battle plans
Domain is already precedent-based, e.g., law, medical diagnosis, claims settlement
Domain formalization requires too many rules
Domain is dynamic, requiring rapid acquisition of solutions to new problem types
Domain task benefits from records of past solutions, to reuse successful ones and avoid bad ones

---

Source: Courtesy of Marc Goodman, Cognitive Systems, Inc. Based on: M. Goodman, "PRISM: A Case-Based Telex Classifier," in *Innovative Applications of Artificial Intelligence*, vol. 11, A. Rappaport and R. Smith, eds. (Cambridge, Mass: MIT Press, 1990).

□ Situation assessment
□ Legal planning
□ Diagnosis
□ Fraud detection
□ Design/configuration
□ Message classification

Case-based reasoning is a new field (started in the mid-1980s) with little practical experience. Therefore, issues and problems may be anticipated. Slade [18] raises the following issues and questions regarding case-based implementation:

□ The quality of the results is heavily dependent on the indexes used.
□ Automatic case-adaptation rules can be very complex.
□ The case base may need to be expanded as the domain model evolves, yet much analysis of the domain may be postponed.
□ What makes up a case? How can we represent case memory?
□ How is memory organized? What are the indexing rules?
□ How does memory function in retrieval of relevant information?
□ How can we adapt old solutions to new problems? What are the similarity metrics and the modification rules?
□ How can we learn from mistakes? What are the repair rules?

Example of Application. This example was provided by Goodman [7]. The application was constructed by Cognitive Systems, Inc., using their case-based reasoning shell. The purpose of the application is to classify incoming telex messages in a bank into one of 109 categories so that they can be processed faster. Also, by proper classification, the receiver can quickly identify if there are some missing data. This application is related to natural language processing (Chapter 8). The example includes eight steps:

□ *Step 1:* Collection of messages. Messages are collected as they come and are given names. The **case library** consists of over 10,000 sample messages.

□ *Step 2:* Expert establishes a hierarchy of telex classifications based on content. Overall, there are 109 types of messages.

□ *Step 3:* An expert matches the messages in the case library against the 109 categories.

□ *Step 4:* Formulas are used to create *abstract features*, which can either be used to predict a classification or as the classification to be predicted. (For example, a formula determines whether a message is or is not a money transfer.)

□ *Step 5:* Lexical patterns, consisting of words, phrases, abbreviations, and synonyms, are established for the domain. These patterns are used to tokenize each message.

□ *Step 6:* Each case in the library is then fully represented; that is, its classification, formulas, and features are summarized on one page.

□ *Step 7:* By using the case-based reasoning shell, the domain expert applies special techniques to identify possible features that may be important in determining the message category. At the moment (1992), three commercial shells are available (from Cognitive Systems, Inc., Inference Corp., and Esteem Software, Inc.)

□ *Step 8:* An incoming message's classification is determined (automatically) by matching the incoming case with similar cases from the case library. Explanations for the match are automatically provided.

6.9 Explanation and Metaknowledge

Explanation

Human experts are often asked to explain their views, recommendations, or decisions. If ES are to mimic humans in performing highly specialized tasks, they need to justify and explain their actions as well. An explanation is an attempt by an ES to clarify its reasoning, recommendations, or other actions (e.g., asking a question). The part of an ES that provides explanations is called an **explanation facility** (or **justifier**). The explanation facility has several specific purposes:

□ Make the system more intelligible to the user.

□ Uncover the shortcomings of the rules and knowledge base (debugging the systems by the knowledge engineer).

□ Explain situations that were unanticipated by the user.

□ Satisfy psychological and/or social needs by helping a user feel more assured about the actions of the ES.

□ Clarify the assumptions underlying the system's operations, both to the user and the builder.

□ Conduct sensitivity analyses (Using the explanation facility, the user can predict and test the effects of changes on the system.).

Explanation in rule-based ES is usually associated with some form of tracing the rules that are fired during the course of a problem-solving session. This is about the closest to a real explanation that today's systems can come, given that their knowledge is usually represented almost exclusively as rules that do not include basic principles necessary for a human-type explanation.

Programs like MYCIN replay the exact rule used when asked for an explanation. DIGITAL ADVISOR is a slight improvement over this. Instead of feeding back the rule verbatim, the ADVISOR determines the generic principle that the rule is based on (at that point in the consultation) and displays that general principle.

In developing large ES, the need for a good explanation facility is essential. Large ES always include more facts and rules than one can easily remember. Often, a new rule added during ES development will interact with other rules and data in unanticipated ways and will make the ES display strange behavior.

Explanation is an extremely important function since understanding depends on explanation (thus making implementation of proposed solutions easier). To understand an event or a situation, you have to explain to yourself exactly what is going on, the role of every participant, and their actions. You need to know the goals of the participants, their intentions, and their potential behavior. Thus, constructing explanations can become a very complex task, especially when done by machines. For this reason most existing explanation facilities provide only two basic types of explanation: the *why* and the *how*.

Why Explanations. A typical *why* question is posed by the user to the computer after the computer asks the user to provide some information. For example, in an investment example (section 6.4) we may have the following dialogue:

COMPUTER: What is your annual income?
    CLIENT: Why? (Why do you need to know?)
COMPUTER: In checking R2, I need to know if your income is above $40,000. If this is true, I will conclude that because you have a college degree, you should invest in growth stocks.

The ES asks for this input when it is unable to find it in the conclusion part of any rule! In the example cited, the computer actually backtracked to another rule and successfully arrived at a final conclusion.

How Explanations. The typical *how* question is posed by users when they would like to know how a certain conclusion or recommendation was reached. Simple systems are limited to the final conclusion. More complex systems can handle intermediate conclusions as well. The system can explain why a certain rule was fired; that is, it shows the chain of rules used to reach the conclusion. In the investment problem the *how* explanation may look like this:

COMPUTER: Invest in IBM stocks.
    CLIENT: How? (How was the conclusion reached?)

COMPUTER: Given that you have $10,000 to invest and you are younger than thirty, then according to rule 4 you have a college degree. If this is the case, then according to R1 you should invest in securities. For a young investor like you, according to R3, you should invest in growth stocks if you are going to invest at all. Finally, in your case, according to R5, if you need to invest in growth stocks, then IBM is your best bet.

The *why* and *how* explanations can show the rules as they are written (usually as a reply to a LIST or some other command).

Other Explanations. Some sophisticated ES can provide other explanations. For example, some systems provide a limited *why not* capability. Let us assume that the system selected IBM as a growth stock. The user may ask "Why not GE?" and the system may answer, "Because the annual growth rate of GE is only 7 percent, whereas that of IBM is 11 percent, using rule 78."

This example illustrates a possible connection between the ES and a regular database. In order to provide explanations, the computer may need to go to a database.

Explanation in non-rule-based systems is much more difficult than in rule-based ones because the inference procedures are more complex. For an overview of the topic of explanation see Moore et al. (14).

Metaknowledge

The system's knowledge about how it reasons is called metaknowledge, or knowledge about knowledge. The inference rules presented earlier are a special case of metaknowledge. Metaknowledge allows the system to examine the operation of the descriptive (declarative) and procedural knowledge in the knowledge base.

Explanation can be viewed as another aspect of metaknowledge. In the future, metaknowledge will allow ES to do even more. They will be able to create the rationale behind individual rules by reasoning from first principles. They will tailor their explanations to fit the requirements of their audience. And they will be able to change their own internal structure through rule correction, reorganization of the knowledge base, and system reconfiguration.

There are different methods for generating explanations. An easy way to do them is to preinsert pieces of English text in the system. For example, each question that could be asked by the user may have an answer test associated with it. This is called a **static explanation.** Several problems are associated with static explanations. For example, all questions and answers must be anticipated in advance. For large systems this is very difficult. The system also has essentially no idea about what it is saying. In the long run, the program may be modified without changing the text, thus causing inconsistency.

A better form of explanation is a **dynamic explanation,** which is reconstructed according to the execution pattern of the rules. In this method the system reconstructs the reasons for its actions as it evaluates rules.

Most existing explanations fail to meet some of the objectives and requirements listed earlier. The following are some thoughts on this topic (provided by Kidd and Cooper [10]):

The explanation facility of most ES consists of printing out a trace of the rules being used. Explanation is not treated as a task that requires intelligence in itself. If ES are to provide satisfactory explanations, future systems must include not only knowledge of how to solve problems in their respective domains but also knowledge of how to effectively communicate to users their understanding of this problem-solving process. Obviously, the relative balance of these two types of knowledge will vary according to the primary function of the system. Constructing such knowledge bases will involve formalizing the heuristics used in providing good explanations.

With current ES, much of the knowledge vital to providing a good explanation (e.g., knowledge about the system's problem-solving strategy) is not expressed explicitly in rules. Rather, it is implicit in the ordering of certain rule clauses or the way certain hypotheses are linked (i.e., there is a mass of implicit knowledge underpinning each rule and the way groups of rules are structured). Kidd and Cooper have recorded dialogues between experts and their clients in various domains and have found that rules of the form "IF . . . THEN . . . BECAUSE . . ." are used extensively in explanations. Explanations can also be supported graphically.

The purely rule-based representation may be difficult to grasp, especially when the relationships between the rules are not made explicit in the explanation. Kidd and Cooper have developed an explanation facility that can show the inference tree and the parts of it that are relevant to specific queries, thus overcoming some of the deficiencies cited earlier.

6.10   Topics in Reasoning

In addition to the topics discussed in this chapter, several other topics need to be considered in ES development. They will be discussed briefly next.

Monotonic Versus Nonmonotonic Reasoning. Most existing ES deal with static, or **monotonic reasoning.** In such cases, if one can prove a statement from more basic facts, the statement remains true regardless of what other information is added. However, in real life we frequently deal with situations that are not static: a particular situation (fact) can change as new information is added. These are nonmonotonic situations. For example, production planning and control could involve nonmonotonic reasoning.

Shallow and Deep Representation of Knowledge. Rule-based representation is considered to be very limited compared with frames and networks. Therefore, the former is classified as **shallow representation** (or surface), whereas the latter are considered as providing **deep representation.**

Frame-based and network-based approaches allow the implementation of "deeper-level" reasoning such as abstraction and analogy. Reasoning by abstraction and analogy is an important expert activity. The objects and processes of the domain of expertise can also be represented at this level. The relations among objects are important. Deep-representation ES perform inference using relations represented by networks or frames. The control of frame or semantic-net systems is usually much more involved than with surface systems and is implemented in a way that an explanation is much more difficult to produce.

One type of expertise that has been represented with a deep-level approach is tutoring. The goal is to convey to students a domain knowledge that is best represented at the deep level: concepts, abstractions, analogies, and problem-solving strategies.

Conflict Resolution. **Conflict resolution** refers to a situation in which the computer needs to select a rule from several rules that apply. For example, suppose we have two rules that look like this:

R1: If a person is old, THEN . . .
R2: If a person is over 65, THEN . . .

We may instruct the computer to select the second rule because it is more specific.

Similarly, the computer may be instructed to ignore confidence levels if they are below 0.2.

Conflict resolution instructions are stored in the inference engine and they can be found in several ES development tools.

Metarules. Conflict resolution is done in many cases by introducing inference rules, for example, deciding about which rules to use next. In such a case, we deal with **metarules,** or rules about rules.

Inference engines that include metarules are more complex than those that do not. Furthermore, it is worth noting that metarules also make the knowledge base harder to read and understand. This is so because one metarule potentially affects the sequence in which all other rules are called; the effect of a metarule is distributed throughout the rest of the knowledge base.

Pattern Matching. A special technique for inferencing, called pattern matching, works with semantic networks, frames, or rules. In the AI context, a pattern is a type of standardized, simplified frame. Many of the details that might be present in a specific frame in a knowledge base are not present in a pattern, but patterns can be far more powerful. For example, the specific frame for a car might include its color. A pattern for a car would include only the essential description of the car (e.g., sedan or sport). If an unknown vehicle is compared with the specific frame for a known car, the color stored there would be detected as a difference and could cause an error. The car pattern would identify the unknown vehicle as a car *regardless* of color, provided it fits the rest of the description.

Patterns can take many forms. In the car example the pattern is a kind of stereotypical frame that could be used to fill in the details of another frame that is incomplete, but otherwise matches the stereotype. Pattern matching also can be used to invoke heuristics and thus limit the amount of time the computer spends searching through its rules and testing them on a given problem.

Pattern matching also plays an important role in systems that use natural language processing, machine vision, and speech recognition.

The quality of development tools is frequently recognized by their pattern-matching capability. For example, a tool called OPS5 has a powerful capability that permits quite complex patterns to be efficiently processed and matched.

Semantic Networks. As stated earlier, semantic networks are used more for knowledge organizations than for inferencing. However, it is possible to reason with semantic networks.

Once a semantic network has been constructed, it can be used for problem solving. For example, you can ask questions about the domain represented by the network. Usually the network will provide the answers. For example, in viewing Figure 5.4 (Chapter 5), we can ask the question, "Who is Sam married to?" Of course, the "married to" link shows that he is married to Kay. Or you might ask, "Does Sam have any children?" Of course, the link "has child" to son Joe shows that he does. We could also ask, "What sport does Sam play?" the "plays" link to golf provides the answer. The computer searches forward or backward through the arcs from a starting node to seek the answers.

The graphic network is translated into a computer program. To conduct a search, a starting point is given at some particular node. This starting point is usually determined by a question. The computer then uses various search and pattern-matching techniques to look through the network structure to identify the desired objects and determine their relationship as posed by the question.

Blackboard Approach. For cases involving multiple sources of expertise or multiple reasoning, the blackboard architecture can be used. Expertise is divided among subdomains, and different reasoning techniques can be used in each subdomain. The blackboard is used, then, to integrate the various lines of reasoning. For further details, see Chapter 14.

Which Reasoning Process to Use? The development of an expert system involves building a knowledge base.[2] The true power of an expert system is in effective management of the reasoning process by utilizing the appropriate

---

[2]This material is condensed from Kameny et al. [9]. The research was published by RAND Corp. The research was supported by the Department of Defense and it is in the public domain.

components of the knowledge base and the inference engine. Several paradigms for controlling the inferencing process are available and each has its advantages and disadvantages. Most expert system shells provide only one or just a few of the paradigms. Only in the largest and most expensive expert system shells will we find an integrated set of most or all of the current paradigms.

Forward chaining and backward chaining are most popular paradigms. In each case conflict resolution, deciding which of the rules currently ready to fire should be next to execute, plays an important part. Some systems offer user hooks to augment the rule-scheduling process. Others provide the knowledge engineer with syntactic tools for controlling the order of rule execution, for example, shortest rule next, first rule entered next, and rule priority.

The expressiveness of the rule language is directly related to the power of the expert system. The rule language is a combination of patterns and operators. The pattern matching capabilities of the rule-matching system and the complexity of pattern expressions enhance the rule expressiveness. The rule operators—such as iteration, conjunction, negation, disjunction, and logical dependency—support the construction of complex rules. As rule languages grow in complexity, the old technique of estimating the size of an expert system by rule count becomes less and less valid.

The style of interactive expert system reasoning has led to the development and support of several new reasoning paradigms. These paradigms were developed to support sound reasoning during the expert system development process without requiring the knowledge engineer to propagate all changes in the knowledge base and rule base.

Inheritance methods (e.g., frames), the first paradigm, propagate knowledge base changes within inheritance hierarchies in an attempt to maintain knowledge base consistency without requiring the user to update all affected fields. The second paradigm, **truth maintenance,** is a generalization of inheritance. Inheritance was not powerful enough by itself to support the logical consistency of the knowledge base. Truth maintenance systems include sophisticated inheritance components and rule base components to attempt the difficult task of *logical consistency* (see Chapter 19 for details).

The next paradigm, **hypothetical reasoning,** is a different approach to the truth maintenance issue. It allows the user to specify the tentative nature of a hypothesis. This style of reasoning, often called what-if reasoning, allows the knowledge engineer to establish fixed points in the knowledge base to reason from and to mark information that is added to the first knowledge base as potentially temporary. If the what-if path turns out to be correct, some expert system shells offer a *believe operator* to permanently incorporate the knowledge base changes.

Reasoning with Uncertainty. In many cases reasoning is done in an uncertain environment. In such a case, the methodologies described in this chapter need to be supplemented with procedures to handle the uncertainties. These methodologies are the subject of the next chapter.

Chapter Highlights

- Several methods can direct search and reasoning. The major ones are chaining (backward and forward), model-based reasoning, and case-based reasoning.
- Analogical reasoning relates past experiences to a current case.
- Modus ponens is a reasoning procedure that says that in an IF-THEN rule, if one part is true, so is the other.
- Testing rules to find if they are true or false is based on a pattern-matching approach.
- In backward chaining the search starts from a goal. You seek evidence that supports (or contradicts) the acceptance of your goal.
- In forward chaining the search starts from the data (evidence) and tries to arrive at a conclusion.
- The chaining process can be described graphically by an inference tree.
- Inferencing with frames is frequently done with the use of rules.
- In model-based reasoning, a model describes the system. Experimentations are conducted using a what-if approach to solve the problem.
- Model-based approaches may involve either mathematical models or (and) component-type models.
- Case-based reasoning is based on experience with similar situations.
- In a case-based reasoning the attributes of an existing case are compared against critical attributes derived from cases stored in the case library.
- Two types of explanations exist in most ES: the *why* question, which requests an explanation of why certain information is needed, and the *how* question.
- The purpose of the *how* question is to find how a certain conclusion was arrived at by the computer.
- Metaknowledge is knowledge about knowledge. It is especially useful in generating explanations.
- Explanation can be static, in which case a canned response is available for a specific configuration.
- Explanation can be dynamic, in which case the explanation is reconstructed according to the execution pattern of the rules.
- In using chaining it is frequently necessary to resolve potential conflicts between rules.
- Metarules are rules about rules.

Key Terms

analogical reasoning	case library	deep presentation
backtracking	component model	dynamic explanation
backward chaining	conflict resolution	dynamic representation
case-based reasoning	deductive reasoning	explanation facility

firing a rule   justifier   procedural (numeric)
forward chaining   mathematical model   reasoning
generalization and   metaknowledge   resolution
   abstraction   metarule   rule interpreter
hierarchial reasoning   model-based reasoning   script
hypothetical reasoning   modus ponens   shallow presentation
inductive reasoning   modus tollens   static explanation
inference tree   monotonic reasoning   static representation
inheritance methods   pattern matching   truth maintenance

Questions for Review

1. List the nine "sources of power." How are they related to problem solving?
2. Define deductive reasoning and contrast it with inductive reasoning.
3. What is meant when we say that a rule "fires"?
4. Define pattern matching. Explain how it is used in rule chaining.
5. Explain why backward chaining is considered goal driven.
6. Explain why forward chaining is considered data driven.
7. Explain the difference between an AND and an OR question.
8. Define backward chaining and contrast it with forward chaining.
9. Define an inference tree. What is its major purpose?
10. Explain this statement: Reasoning with frames may involve hierarchial reasoning.
11. Define model-based reasoning.
12. Define case-based reasoning.
13. List five advantages of case-based reasoning.
14. Review the case-based reasoning processing. Briefly discuss each step.
15. List some of the purposes of the explanation capability.
16. Explanation in current expert systems is done by tracing the rules. Discuss how this is done.
17. What is the *why* question? What is a typical answer to this question?
18. What is the *how* question? What is a typical answer to this question?
19. What is metaknowledge? How is it related to the explanation facility?
20. Define static explanation.
21. Define conflict resolution.
22. Define metarules.

Questions for Discussion

1. Describe analogical reasoning. How is it related to case-based reasoning?
2. Compare modus ponens with modus tollens. Why is the former used more?
3. It is said that chaining (backward, forward) is an implementation of modus ponens. Why?

4. Relate metaknowledge to metarules. Explain how metarules work. How do they relate to inference rules?
5. Discuss the major deficiencies of existing explanation facilities. Organize your discussion as a comparison with a potential explanation given by a human.
6. The explanation facility serves the user as well as the developer. Discuss the benefits derived by each.
7. If you had a dialogue with a human expert, what questions besides "Why?" and "How?" would you be likely to ask? Give examples.
8. It is said that reasoning with frames almost always involves rules. Explain why.
9. What is meant by "reasoning from first principles"? Give an example. Give an example of reasoning *not* from a first principle.
10. Summarize the major advantages of model-based reasoning. When would you use it?
11. Comment on this statement: "An understander of the world is an explainer of the world."
12. Describe the relationship between metaknowledge and explanations.
13. Explain how conflict resolution is used in a rule-based system.
14. Explain the basic premise of case-based reasoning.
15. Explain the relationship between scripts and case-based reasoning.
16. Compare and contrast rule-based versus case-based reasoning.
17. Which applications are most suitable for case-based reasoning? Why?
18. List and discuss some of the potential problems with case-based reasoning.

Exercises

1. You are given a set of rules for this question: Should we buy a house or not?

   R1: IF inflation is low
       THEN interest rates are low
       ELSE interest rates are high
   R2: IF interest rates are high
       THEN housing prices are high
   R3: IF housing prices are high
       THEN do not buy a house
       ELSE buy it

   a. Run a backward chaining with a high inflation rate as given.
   b. Run a forward chaining with a low inflation rate as given.
   c. Prepare an inference tree for the backward chaining case.
2. You are given an ES with the following rules:

   R1: IF interest rate falls
       THEN bond prices increase

R2: IF interest rate increases
     THEN bond prices decline
R3: IF interest rate is unchanged
     THEN bond prices remain unchanged
R4: IF the dollar rises (against other currencies)
     THEN interest rate declines
R5: IF the dollar falls
     THEN interest rate increases
R6: IF bond prices decline
     THEN buy bonds

a. A client just observed that the dollar exchange rate is falling. He wants to know whether to buy bonds. Run a forward and a backward chaining and submit a report to him.
b. Prepare an inference tree for the backward chaining you did.
c. A second client observed that the interest rates are unchanged. She asks for advice on investing in bonds. What will the ES tell her? Use forward chaining.

3. Assume you plan to drive from New York to Los Angeles to arrive midafternoon for an appointment. You want to drive no more than two hours the day you arrive, but on other days, you're willing to drive eight to ten hours. One logical way to approach this problem is to start at Los Angeles, your goal, and work backward. You would first find a place about two hours from Los Angeles for your final stopover before arrival, then plan the rest of your trip by working backward on a map until your route is completely planned. You have a limited number of days to complete the trip.

   How would you analyze the problem starting from New York? What are the major differences? Which approach would you use? Why?

4. You are given an expert system with seven rules pertaining to interpersonal skills for a job applicant:

R1: IF the applicant answers questions in a straightforward manner
     THEN he is easy to converse with
R2: IF the applicant seems honest
     THEN he answers in a straightforward manner
R3: IF the applicant has items on his resume that are found to be untrue
     THEN he does not seem honest
     ELSE he seems honest
R4: IF the applicant is able to get an appointment with the executive assistant
     THEN he is able to strike up a conversation with the executive assistant
R5: IF the applicant struck up a conversation with the executive assistant
     and the applicant is easy to converse with
     THEN he is amiable
R6: IF the applicant is amiable
     THEN he has adequate interpersonal skills
R7: IF the applicant has adequate interpersonal skills
     THEN he will get the job

a. It is known that the applicant answers questions in a straightforward manner. Run a backward chaining analysis to find if the applicant will get the job or not.

b. Assume that the applicant does not have any items on her resume that are found to be untrue and she is able to get an appointment with the executive assistant. Run a *forward* chaining analysis to find out if she will get the job.

c. We just discovered that the applicant was able to get an appointment with the executive assistant. It is also known that she is honest. Does she have interpersonal skills, or not?

   Note: a, b, and c are *independent* incidents.

5. Given the following two sets of statements and conclusions, what type of reasoning was used to arrive at the conclusions?

   Case a: Students that do not study do not pass exams.
   Nancy is a student.
   Nancy did not study.
   Conclusion: Nancy will not pass her exam.

   Case b: Jack did not study for the exam.
   Jack is a student.
   Jack did not pass the exam.
   Conclusion: Students who do not study, do not pass exams.

6. Review the message classification example in the case-based section of the chapter. Compare the eight steps to Figure 6.4 and discuss.

References and Bibliography

1. Bareiss, R. *Exemplar-Based Knowledge Acquisition.* New York: Academic Press, 1989.

2. Blasius, K.H., and H. Burckert, eds. *Deduction Systems in Artificial Intelligence.* New York: Ellis Horwood, 1989.

3. Davis, R., and W. Hamscher. "Model-Based Reasoning: Troubleshooting." In *Exploring AI: Survey Talks from the National Conference on AI,* H.E. Shrobe, ed. San Mateo, Calif.: Morgan Kaufman, 1988.

4. diPiazza, J.S., and F.A. Helsabeck. "Laps: Cases to Models to Complete Expert Systems." *AI Magazine* (Fall 1990).

5. Eliot, L.B. "Analogical Problem Solving and Expert Systems."*IEEE Expert* (Summer 1986).

6. Fulton, S.L., and C.O. Pepe. "An Introduction to Model-based Reasoning." *AI Expert* (January 1990).

7. Goodman, M. "PRISM: A Case-Based Telex Classifier." In *Innovative Applications of Artificial Intelligence,* vol. 11, A. Rappaport and R. Smith, eds. Cambridge, Mass.: MIT Press, 1990.

8. Hammond, K.J. *Case-Based Planning*. New York: Academic Press, 1989.

9. Kameny, I., et al. *Guide for the Management of Expert Systems Development*. Santa Monica, Calif.: RAND Corp., 1989.

10. Kidd, A.L., and M.B. Cooper. "Man-Machine Interface Issues in the Construction and Use of an Expert System." *International Journal of Man-Machine Studies* 22 (1985).

11. Lenat, D.B. "The Ubiquity of Discovery." *Artificial Intelligence* 19 (no. 2, 1982).

12. Liang, T.P., and E. Turban, eds. *Case-Based Reasoning*, a special issue of *Expert Systems with Applications*, 1992.

13. Mishkoff, H.C. *Understanding Artificial Intelligence*. Dallas: Texas Instruments, 1985. (republished by H.W. Sams, 1988)

14. Moore, J.D., et al. "Explanation in Expert Systems—A Survey." In *Proceedings, The First International Symposium on Expert Systems in Business, Finance, and Accounting*. Univ. of Southern California, Los Angeles, September 1988.

15. Nagao, M. *Knowledge and Inference*. New York: Academic Press, 1990.

16. Riesbeck, C.K., and R.L. Schank. *Inside Case-based Reasoning*. Hillsdale, N.J.: Lawrence Erlbaum Associates, 1989.

17. Ringland, G.A., and D.A. Duce. *Approaches to Knowledge Representation: An Introduction*. New York: John Wiley & Sons, 1988.

18. Slade, S. "Case-based Reasoning: A Research Paradigm." *AI Magazine* (Spring 1991).

19. Tuthill, G.S. *Knowledge Engineering*. Blue Ridge Summit, Pa.: TAB Books, 1990.

20. Vosniadou, S., and A. Ortony, eds. *Similarity and Analogical Reasoning*. Cambridge, Mass.: Cambridge Press, 1989.

21. Walters, J., and N.R. Nielsen. *Crafting Knowledge Based Systems*. New York: John Wiley & Sons, 1988.

22. Winston, P.H. *Artificial Intelligence*, 2nd ed. Reading, Mass.: Addison-Wesley, 1984.

APPENDIX A: Example of a Goal-directed Search

In this example, the program identifies a goal, that is, to answer the question in the upper box of Figure 6A.1. Then it scans the rules to find which ones will give the answer to this question (i.e., the "value" of A). Rule 3 of those given here is the one chosen because its consequent gives the answer to the question. But to apply this rule, the program will need three pieces of information: A1, B, and A2. The program will check if these pieces of information are in the assertion base. If they are not, the new goal becomes to find the values of A1, B, and A2 by using rules R1 and R2, and asking the user for the value of B. The same procedure is then applied to rules 1 and 2 until all the information

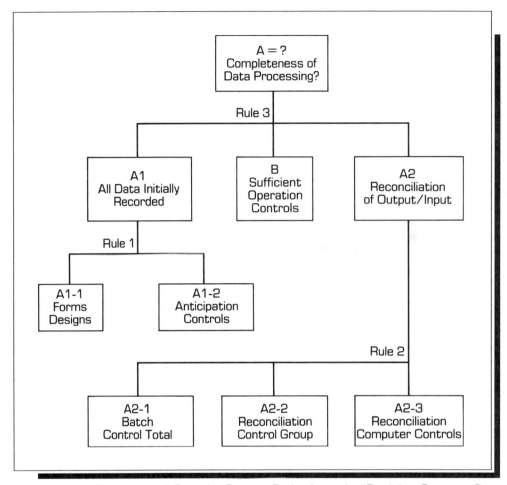

FIGURE 6A.1 Goal-directed Search (*Source:* Bedard, et al., "Decision Support Systems and Auditing," working paper no. 49, Univ. of Southern California, Los Angeles, 1983.)

necessary to apply the rules is found in the knowledge base. The value of it is then determined (see THEN below).

RULE 1: IF   system makes use of specially designed form
               AND
               anticipation controls are present
      THEN the method used to ensure that all data are initially
               recorded and identified is good
RULE 2: IF   system makes use of batch control totals
               AND
               the batch totals are reconciled by the control group

                    OR
                    the batch totals are reconciled by the computer
          THEN the controls that ensure that the input is reconciled are
                    good
RULE 3: IF   the methods used to ensure that all data are initially
                    recorded and identified are good
                    AND
                    the operation controls are sufficient
                    AND
                    the controls that ensure that the input and output are
                    reconciled are good
          THEN the quality of the system of controls to ensure the
                    completeness of data processed by the computer is good

Chapter 7

Uncertainty in Knowledge-based Systems

The construction of the knowledge base and the establishment of the reasoning procedures discussed so far were made under an assumed certainty. In reality, however, we often deal with situations in which the knowledge is inexact. Knowledge-based systems that aim at mimicking human behavior should be able to reason with uncertain knowledge or information. To handle such situations, it is necessary to supplement the knowledge representation and inferencing methods discussed in the previous two chapters with procedures to handle uncertainty. These topics will be discussed here:

7.1   Introduction

One of the basic assumptions made in the previous chapters was that every rule can have only one of two truth values (i.e., it is either true or false). In this sense, our previous discussion forced us to be exact about the truth of statements.

However, human knowledge is often inexact. Sometimes we are only partially sure about the truth of a statement and still have to make educated guesses to solve problems. Some concepts or words are inherently inexact. For instance, how can we exactly determine if someone is tall? The concept *tall* has a built-in form of inexactness. Moreover, we sometimes have to make decisions based on partial or incomplete data.

One source of uncertainty occurs when a user cannot provide a definite answer when prompted for a response. For example, when asked to provide a choice between responses B or C, the user may respond that he or she is 30 percent sure of B and 70 percent sure of C.

Another source of uncertainty stems from imprecise knowledge. In many situations, a set of symptoms can help indicate a particular diagnosis without being conclusive.

Yet another source of uncertainty is incomplete information. The information (or some parts of it) is simply not available or is too expensive or time consuming to obtain.

To deal with inexact knowledge in knowledge-based systems, it is necessary to understand how people process uncertain knowledge (see Hink and Woods [4]). In addition, in AI there is a need for inexact inference methods because we often have many inexact pieces of data and knowledge that need to be combined.

Several approaches are available to deal with uncertainty; none is clearly superior in all cases to all others. Most of the approaches are related to mathematical and statistical theories such as Bayesian statistics, Dempster and Shafer's belief functions, and fuzzy sets. Four ways of representing uncertain information in ES are presented here:

- □ Probabilities (Bayesian approach)
- □ Certainty factors
- □ Theory of evidence
- □ Fuzzy logic

Other approaches such as the use of neural computing (Chapter 18) and genetic algorithms (Chapter 19) are extremely promising but are still in a research stage.

7.2   Issues and Approaches in Uncertainty

The term **uncertainty** has several meanings. According to *Webster's New World Dictionary of the American Language*, uncertainty means doubt, dubious, questionable, not surely, or problematical. Uncertainty ranges in implication from a mere lack of absolute sureness to such vagueness as to preclude anything more than guesswork. In decision theory, there is a distinction between decision making under uncertainty and under risk. In both cases, one is not sure about the results of a decision. However, in the case of risk, one can assess the probabilities of the results happening, whereas in the case of uncertainty, one only knows what the possible results are going to be but cannot assess their probabilities. In AI uncertainty includes both terms plus more, as will be shown next.

Uncertainty in AI

In AI, the term *uncertainty* (also referred to as *approximate reasoning* or *inexact reasoning*) refers to a wide range of situations where the relevant information is deficient in one or more of the following ways:

  □ Information is partial.
  □ Information is not fully reliable (e.g., unreliable observation of evidence).
  □ Representation language is inherently imprecise.
  □ Information comes from multiple sources and it is conflicting.
  □ Information is approximate.
  □ Non-absolute cause-effect relationships exist.

In numeric context, uncertainty can be viewed as a value with a known error margin. When the possible range of values for a variable is *symbolic* rather than *numeric*, uncertainty can be represented in terms of qualitative expressions or by using fuzzy sets with a corresponding membership function. (See sections 7.3 and 7.7).

Dealing with Uncertainty

Uncertainty in AI is treated as a three-step process (according to Kanal and Lemmer [7], and Parsaye and Chignell [22]) as shown in Figure 7.1. In step 1 an expert provides inexact knowledge, that is, in terms of rules with likelihood values. These can be numeric (e.g., a probability value), graphic, or symbolic ("it is most likely that . . .").

In step 2 the inexact knowledge of the basic set of events can be directly used to draw inferences in simple cases (step 3). However, in many cases the various events are interrelated. Therefore, it is necessary to combine the information provided in step 1 into a global value for the system. Several methods can be used for such an integration. The major methods to be discussed here are probabilities, theory of evidence, certainty factors, and fuzzy sets.

In step 3 the purpose of the knowledge-based system is to draw inferences. These are derived from the inexact knowledge of step 1 and/or step 2, and usually they are implemented with the inference engine. Working with the

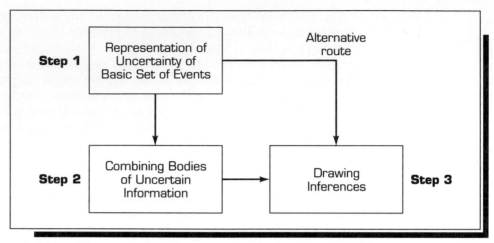

FIGURE 7.1   Three-step Process for Dealing with Uncertainty in AI

inference engine, experts can adjust the input they give in step 1 after viewing the results in steps 2 and 3.

Approaches to Treatment of Uncertainty

The methods of treating uncertainty in AI can be divided into two basic categories:

1. *Parallel certainty inference techniques*: In this type of approach knowledge is either treated as an exact (although it is not) or a parallel process determining the amount of uncertainty associated with the conclusion (inferences). Three methods are discussed in this chapter: Bayesian probability theory, certainty factors, and the Dempster-Shafer theory of evidence.
2. *Uncertainty structuring techniques*: These techniques attempt to formalize (structure) uncertain knowledge. Three methods are presented in this text: fuzzy sets/fuzzy logic, neural nets (Chapter 18), and genetic algorithms (Chapter 19).

7.3   Representation of Uncertainty

The three basic methods of representing uncertainty are numeric, graphic, and symbolic.

Numeric

The most common method of representing uncertainty is numeric using a scale with two extreme numbers. For example, 0 may be used to represent complete uncertainty while 1 or 100 represents complete certainty. Although such representation seems to be easy to some people (maybe because it is similar to representation of probabilities), it is very difficult for others. One reason why experts have difficulty in quantifying uncertainty is that most of our early education was done emphasizing an environment of certainty. For example, when we learned mathematics we were asked to find the time it takes to travel between two cities 200 miles apart, traveling at 50 miles per hour. In reality, the speed may vary considerably depending on traffic and weather conditions.

In addition to the difficulties of using numbers, there are problems with cognitive biases. For example, experts figure the numbers from their own experience and are influenced by their own perceptions. For a discussion of these biases, see Parsaye and Chignell [22]. Finally, people may be inconsistent in providing numeric values at different times.

Graphic

Although many experts can describe uncertainty in terms of numbers, such as "it is 85 percent certain that . . .," some have difficulties in doing so. By using horizontal bars, for example, it is possible to assist experts in expressing their confidence in certain events. Such a bar is shown in Figure 7.2. Experts are asked to place markers somewhere on the scale. Thus, expert A may express very little confidence in the likelihood of inflation, whereas expert B is more confident that inflation is coming.

The confidence scale of Figure 7.2 can be changed to include numbers. Two possible scales are shown in Figure 7.3. Part a shows a typical probability-like presentation of confidence, whereas part b shows a scale built around zero. Option a is used by the ES shells Level5 and VP Expert. The classic EMYCIN shell uses the −1 to 1 scale, while EXSYS uses several scales including −100 to +100.

Even though graphic presentation is preferred by some experts, the graphs are not as accurate as numbers. Another problem is that most experts do not have experience in marking graphic scales (or setting numbers on the scale).

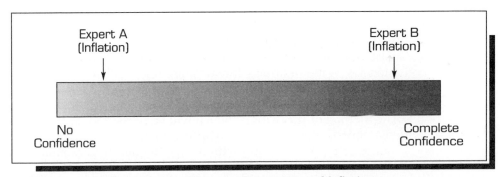

FIGURE 7.2 Confidence Scale about the Occurrence of Inflation

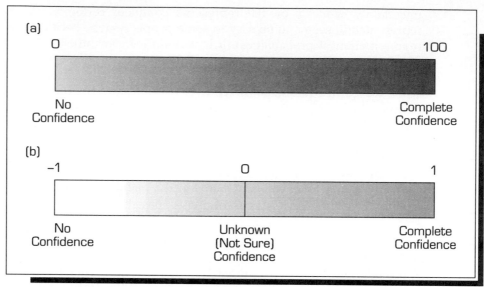

FIGURE 7.3 Two Types of Confidence Scales: (a) Probability-like Scale and (b) Scale Built Around Zero

Many experts, especially managers, prefer ranking over either graphic or numeric methods.

Symbolic

There are several ways to represent uncertainty by using symbols. Many experts use a *Likert scale* approach to express their opinion. For example, an expert may be asked to assess the likelihood of inflation on a five-point scale: very unlikely, unlikely, neutral, likely, and very likely. *Ranking* is a very popular approach among experts with nonquantitative preferences. Ranking can be either ordinal (i.e., listing items by the order of their importance) or cardinal (ranking complemented by numeric values). Managers are especially comfortable with ordinal ranking. When the number of items to be ranked is large, people may have a problem with ranking and also tend to be inconsistent. One method that can be used to alleviate this problem is a pair-wise comparison combined with a consistency checker; that is, rank the items, two at a time, and check for consistencies. A methodology for such ranking is called the **analytical hierarchy process** (see Saaty [25]). Software called Expert Choice can be used to execute the process. For further discussion of ranking, see Parsaye and Chignell [22].

The method of fuzzy logic, which will be presented later, includes a special symbolic representation combined with numbers.

Symbolic representation methods are frequently combined with numbers or are converted to numeric values. For example, it is customary to give weight of one to five to the five options in a Likert-like scale.

7.4   Probability and the Bayesian Approach

The Probability Ratio

The degree of belief of confidence in a premise or a conclusion can be expressed as a probability. Probability is the chance that a particular event will occur (or not occur). It is a ratio computed as follows:

$$P(X) = \frac{\text{Number of outcomes favoring the occurrence of}}{\text{Total number of events}}$$

The probability of X occurring, stated as $P(X)$, is the ratio of the number of times X occurs to the total number of events that take place.

Multiple probability values occur in many systems. For example, a rule may have three parts to its antecedent, each with a probability value. The overall probability of the rule can be computed as the product of the individual probabilities, if the parts of the antecedent are independent of one another. In a three-part antecedent, the probabilities may be 0.9, 0.7, and 0.65. The overall probability is

$$P = (0.9)(0.7)(0.65) = 0.4095$$

The combined probability is about 41 percent. But this is true only if the individual parts of the antecedent do not affect or interrelate to one another.

Sometimes one rule references another. Here, the individual rule probabilities can propagate from one to another. So we need to evaluate the total probability of a sequence of rules or a path through the search tree to determine if a specific rule fires. Or, we may be able to use the combined probability to predict the best path through the search tree.

In knowledge-based systems several approaches for combining probabilities exist. For example, probabilities can be multiplied (i.e., joint probabilities) or averaged out (using a simple or a weighted average); in other instances, only the highest or lowest values are considered. In all such cases, rules and events are considered independent of each other. If there are dependencies in the system, the Bayes extension theorem can be employed.

The Bayesian Extension

Bayes theorem is a mechanism for combining new and existent evidence usually given as subjective probabilities. It is used to *revise* existing **prior probabilities** based on new information. The results are called **posterior probabilities.**

In the simplest possible case we have two probabilities, one for event A and one for event B:

$$P(A/B) = \frac{P(B/A * P(A)}{P(B/A)\,P(A) + P(B/\text{ not A}) * P(\text{not A})}$$

where: $P(A/B)$ = probability of event A occurring, given that B has already occurred (posterior probability); $P(A)$ = probability of event A occurring (prior probability); $P(B/A)$ = additional evidence of B occurring, given A; and $P(\text{not A})$ = A is not going to occur, but another event is $P(A) + P(\text{not A}) = 1$.

If we extend the formula to n events (or hypotheses) we get (for the ith item):

$$P(A_i/B) = \frac{P(A_i) * P(B/A_i)}{P(B/A_1) * P(A_1) + \cdots P(B/A_n) * P(A_n)}$$

where: $P(A_1) + P(A_2) + \cdots P(A_n) = 1$.

The Bayesian theory is based on the following assumptions:

- Mutually exclusive hypotheses
- Conditionally independent evidence
- Completely enumerated set of hypotheses

The theory is good for well-structured situations in which all the data are available and the assumptions are satisfied. Unfortunately, these conditions do not occur in reality very often. The procedure cannot deal with qualitative presentation of knowledge or with ignorance ("don't know"). Additionally, a major difficulty is the acquisition of the prior probabilities as well as that of the new evidence.

The Bayesian approach is based on **subjective probabilities;** a subjective probability is provided for each proposition. If E is the evidence (sum of all information available to the system), then each proposition (P) has associated with it a value representing the probability that P holds in the light of all the evidence E, derived by using Bayesian inference. Bayes' theorem provides a way of computing the probability of a particular event given some set of observations we have already made. The main point here is not how this value is derived, but that what we know or have inferred about a proposition is represented by a single value for its likelihood.

Two criticisms may be advanced against this approach. The first is that the single value does not tell us much about its precision, which may be very low when the value is derived from uncertain evidence. To say that the probability of a proposition being true in a given situation is 0.5 (in a range of 0 to 1) usually refers to an *average* figure that is true within a given range. For example, 0.5 plus or minus 0.001 is completely different from 0.5 plus or minus 0.3, yet both may be reported as 0.5. The second criticism is that the single value combines the evidence for and against a proposition without indicating how much there is of each.

The subjective probability expresses the "degree of belief," or how strongly a value or a situation is believed to be true.

The Bayesian approach, with or without new evidence, can be diagrammed as a network.

7.5 Dempster-Shafer Theory of Evidence

The Dempster-Shafer **theory of evidence** is a well-known procedure for reasoning with uncertainty in artificial intelligence. (For details see Shafer [27] and Kanal and Lemmer [7].) It can be considered an extension of the Bayesian approach.

The Dempster-Shafer approach distinguishes between uncertainty and ignorance by creating **belief functions.** Belief functions allow us to use our knowledge to bound the assignment of probabilities when these may be unavailable.

The procedure indicates the expert belief in a hypothesis given a piece of evidence. It may include the Bayesian approach when a probability interval is limited to a single point. Thus, the method shares several properties of the Byesian approach. For example, in both methods the sum of the probabilities of a set of hypotheses is one. Even though the Dempster-Shafer approach gives us methods of computing these various belief parameters, their great complexity adds to the computational cost.

The Dempster-Shafer approach is especially appropriate for combining expert opinions, since experts do differ in their opinions with a certain degree of ignorance and, in many situations, at least some **epistemic information** (i.e., one that was constructed from vague perceptions). The Dempster-Shafer approach can be used to handle epistemic information as well as ignorance or lack of information. Unfortunately, the theory assumes that the sources of information to be combined are statistically *independent* of each other. In reality, there are many cases in which the knowledge of experts is overlapping; that is, there are dependencies among sources of information. For such cases the Ling and Rudd extensions are necessary.

The Ling and Rudd models extend the work of Dempster-Shafer to handle dependencies among experts or among hypotheses. Two extensions are proposed. First, the approach combines the opinions of dependent experts where the opinions can be presented as simple support functions. Second, the authors developed a method for combining more complex opinions of experts where problems of high-order dependencies exist. For details see Ling and Rudd [13].

7.6   Theory of Certainty (Certainty Factors)

Certainty Factors and Beliefs

Bayesian methods are based on the assumption that an uncertainty is the probability that an event (or fact) is true or false. In the **certainty theory**, as well as in fuzzy logic, uncertainty is represented as a *degree of belief*. In any nonprobabilistic method of uncertainty one needs to go through two steps. First, it is necessary to be able to express the degree of belief. Second, it is necessary to manipulate (e.g., combine) degrees of belief during the use of knowledge-based systems.

Certainty theory relies on the use of **certainty factors.** Certainty factors (CF) express belief in an event (or fact, or hypothesis) based on evidence (or the expert's assessment). There are several methods of using certainty factors in handling uncertainty in knowledge-based systems. One way is to use a 100 for absolute truth (complete confidence) and 0 for certain falsehood. These certainty factors are not probabilities. For example, when we say there is a 90 percent chance for rain, then there is either rain (90 percent) or no rain (10 percent). In a nonprobabilistic approach, we can say the certainty factor rain = 90 means that it is very likely to rain. Thus, certainty factors *do not* have to sum up to 100.

Bayesian and probability theories assume that the sum of probabilities must total 1. Thus, for example, if an expert believes that there is a 75 percent (0.75) chance for an event to occur, there is a 25 percent (0.25) chance that this event will not occur. In reality, this may not be the case. The expert may have no feeling at all about what is not going to occur. Thus, certainty theory introduces the concepts of *belief* and **disbelief**. These concepts are independent of each other and so cannot be combined as probabilities, but they can be combined according to the following formula:

$$CF\,[P,E] = MB\,[P,E] - MD\,[P,E]$$

where

$$
\begin{aligned}
CF &= \text{certainty factor} \\
MB &= \text{measure of belief} \\
MD &= \text{measure of disbelief} \\
P &= \text{probability} \\
E &= \text{evidence, or event}
\end{aligned}
$$

Another assumption of the certainty theory is that the knowledge content of rules is much more important than the algebra of confidences that holds the system together. Confidence measures correspond to the information evaluations that human experts attach to their conclusions, for example, "it is probably true" or "it is highly unlikely."

Combining Certainty Factors

Certainty factors can be used to combine different estimates of experts in several ways. Before using any ES shell make sure that you understand how certainty factors are combined (for an overview see Kopcso et al. [10]). The most acceptable way of combining them in rule-based systems is the approach used in EMYCIN. According to this approach, we can distinguish between the two cases as described next.

Combining Several Certainty Factors in One Rule. Consider this rule with an AND operator:

IF inflation is above 5 percent, CF = 50 percent (A), and
IF unemployment rate is above 7 percent, CF = 70 percent (B), and
IF bond prices decline, CF = 100 percent (C)
THEN stock prices decline

For this type of rule, for the conclusion to be true, all IFs must be true. However, since several CFs are involved, the CF of the conclusion will be the *minimum* CF on the IF side:

$$CF (A, B, \text{ and } C) = \text{minimum } [CF(A), CF(B), CF(C)]$$

In our case, the CF for stock prices to decline will be 50 percent. In other words, the chain is as strong as its weakest link.

Now look at this rule with an OR operator:

IF inflation is low, CF = 70 percent; or
IF bond prices are high, CF = 85 percent
THEN stock prices will be high

In this case it is sufficient that only *one* of the IFs is true for the conclusion to be true. Thus, if *both* IFs are believed to be true (at their certainty factor) then the conclusion will have a CF with the *maximum* of the two:

$$CF (A \text{ or } B) = \text{maximum } [CF (A), CF (B)]$$

In our case, CF = 0.85 for stock prices to be high. Note that both cases hold for any number of IFs.

Combining Two or More Rules. When we have a knowledge-based system with several interrelated rules, each of which has the same conclusion but a different certainty factor, then each rule can be viewed as a piece of evidence that supports the joint conclusion. To calculate the certainty factor (or the confidence) of the conclusion, it is necessary to combine the evidences. This is done according to the following procedure (as used in MYCIN).

Let's assume there are two rules:

R1: IF the inflation rate is less than 5 percent
   THEN stock market prices go up (CF = 0.7)
R2: IF unemployment is less than 7 percent,
   THEN stock market prices go up (CF = 0.6)

Now, let's assume it is predicted that next year the inflation rate will be 4 percent and unemployment will be 6.5 percent (i.e., we assume that the premises of the two rules are true). The combined effect is to be computed in the following way:

$$CF(R1,R2) = CF(R1) + CF(R2)[1 - CF(R1)]; \text{ or}$$
$$CF(R1,R2) = CF(R1) + CF(R2) - CF(R1) * CF(R2)$$

In probabilistic terms, when we combine two dependent probabilities (joint probabilities) we get:

$$CF(R1,R2) = CF(R1) * CF(R2)$$

Here, we deleted this value from the sum of the two certainty factors, assuming an *independent* relationship between the rules.

Example: Given CF(R1) = 0.7 AND CF(R2) = 0.6, then:
    CF(R1,R2) = 0.7 + 0.6(1 − 0.7) = 0.7 + 0.6(0.3) = 0.88

That is, the ES will tell us that there is an 88 percent chance that stock prices will increase.

Note: If we just added the CFs of R1 and R2, their combined certainty would be too large. We modify the amount of certainty added by the second certainty factor by multiplying it by (1 − the first certainty factor). Thus the greater the first CF, the less certainty is added by the second. But additional factors always add some confidence.

For a third rule to be added, the following formula may be used:

$$CF(R1,R2,R3) = CF(R1,R2) + CF(R3)\,[1 - CF(R1,R2)]$$

Assume a third rule is added:

R3: IF bond price increases
    THEN stock prices go up (CF = 0.85)

Now, assuming all rules are true in their IF part, the chance that stock prices will go up is:

$$CF(R1,R2,R3) = 0.88 + 0.85\,(1 - 0.88) = 0.88 + 0.85\,(.12) = 0.982$$

That is, there is a 98.2 percent chance that stock prices will go up. Note that CF(R1,R2) was computed earlier as 0.88. For more rules, we apply the same formula incrementally.

In this case it is sufficient that only *one* of the IFs is true for the conclusion to be true. Thus, if *both* IFs are believed to be true (at their certainty factor), then the conclusion will have a CF with the *maximum* of the two.

$$CF(A \text{ or } B) = \text{maximum }[CF(A),\ CF(B)]$$

In our case, CF = 0.85 for stock prices to be high. Note that both cases hold for any number of IFs.

7.7 Fuzzy Logic

Some AI programs exploit the technique of approximate reasoning. This technique, which uses the mathematical theory of **fuzzy sets** (e.g., see Zadeh [32] and Negoita [18]), simulates the process of normal human reasoning by allowing the computer to behave less precisely and logically than conventional computers do.

Uncertainty and approximation, often the nemesises of managers, are deliberately being programmed into computers. Does this mean that computers are going to be as confused in their "thinking" as people sometimes are? Quite the contrary. They will make more intelligent decisions. Software programs are being developed that use a natural language, with heavy emphasis on qualifying adjectives and adverbs such as *usually, highly unlikely, not very, probable,* and *marginal.*

The thinking behind this approach is that decision making isn't always a matter of black and white, true or false; it often involves gray areas and the term *maybe.* In fact, creative decision-making processes are unstructured, playful, contentious, and rambling.

Fuzzy logic can be advantageous for the following reasons:

☐ *It provides flexibility.* Rigid thinking can often lead to unsatisfactory conclusions. You've locked yourself into a set pattern. Make allowances for the unexpected and you can shift your strategy whenever necessary.

☐ *It gives you options.* If you're confronted with a number of possibilities, you'll need to consider them all. Then, using facts *and* intuition ("highly unlikely" or "very good"), you can make an educated guess. Even computers are learning to use such rules of thumb.

☐ *It frees the imagination.* At first you may feel that something simply can't be done—all the facts conspire against it. Why not try asking yourself, "What if . . .?" Follow another avenue and see where you end up. You may make a better decision.

☐ *It's more forgiving.* When you're forced to make black or white decisions, you cannot afford to be wrong, because when you're wrong, you lose completely. The other way is more forgiving. If you figure something is 80 percent gray, but it turns out to be 90 percent gray, you're not going to be penalized very much.

☐ *It allows for observation.* Literal-minded computers have been known to come up with some peculiar results. For example, when one user instructed her computer to come up with information on smoking in the workplace, the computer diligently churned out an article on a salmon-processing plant. A little fuzzy logic might have helped the computer make a more intelligent choice.

Let's look at an example of a fuzzy set that describes a tall person. Suppose people are asked to define the minimum height that a person must attain before being considered "tall." The answers could range, say, from 5'10" to 6'2". The distribution of answers may look like this:

Height	Proportion Voted for
5'10"	0.05
5'11"	0.10
6'	0.60
6'1"	0.15
6'2"	0.10

Let's assume that Jack is 6 feet tall. In probability theory we can use the cumulative probability and say that there is a 75 percent chance that Jack is tall.

In fuzzy logic we say: Jack's degree of membership within the set of tall people is 0.75. The difference is that in probability terms Jack is perceived to be either tall or not tall and we are not sure completely whether he is tall or not. By contrast, in fuzzy logic we agree that Jack is more or less tall. Then, we can assign a membership function to show the relationship of Jack to the set of tall people (the fuzzy logic set):

$$\langle \text{Jack, } 0.75 \rangle \equiv \text{Tall}$$

This can be expressed in a knowledge-based system as Jack is tall (CF = 75). An important difference from probabilities is that related membership does *not* have to total 1. For example, the statement Jack is short, CF = 15, indicates that the combination is only 90. In probability theory if the probability that Jack is tall is 75 percent, then the probability that he is not tall (i.e., he is short—assuming only two events), must be 25 percent.

In contrast to certainty factors that include two values (e.g., the degree of belief and disbelief), fuzzy sets use a spectrum of possible values. Fuzzy logic has not been used much in ES in the past because it is more complex to develop, it requires more computing power, and it is more difficult to explain to users.

Fuzzy Logic in Rule-based Systems

In a regular rule-based system, a production rule has no concrete effect at all unless the data completely satisfy the antecedent of the rule. The operation of the system proceeds sequentially, with one rule firing at a time; if two rules are simultaneously satisfied, a conflict resolution policy is needed to determine which ones takes precedence.

In a fuzzy rule-based system, in contrast, *all* rules are executed during each pass through the system, but with strengths ranging from "not at all" to "completely," depending on the relative degree to which their fuzzy antecedent propositions are satisfied by the data. If the antecedent is satisfied exceptionally well, the result of the rule firing is an assertion that exactly matches the consequent proposition of the rule. If the antecedent fuzzy proposition is only partially satisfied, the result is an assertion resembling the consequent, but made vague in proportion to the fuzziness of the match. If the antecedent is not satisfied at all, the result of the rule firing is a null proposition that puts no restrictions on the possible values of the variables in the consequent.

Applications and Software

Fuzzy logic is difficult to apply when the evidence is provided by people. The problems stem from linguistic vagueness to difficulties in supplying the definitions needed. The approach is useful for inference rules that use natural

---

Box 7.1: Fuzzy Logic Applications

Regulating Automatic Braking systems in cars
Autofocusing in cameras
Automating the operation of laundry machines
Building environmental controls
Controlling the motion of trains
Indentifying the dialect of killer whales
Inspecting beverage cans for printing defects
Keeping the shuttle vehicles in one place in space
Matching golf clubs to customer's swings
Trading stocks on the Japanese Nikke stock exchange
Regulate water temperature in shower-heads
Controlling the amount of oxygen in cement kilns
Increasing accuracy and speed in industrial quality control applications

---

languages and for cases where boundaries are hard to define, but where a set can be defined. One example where fuzzy logic is being used extensively is in consumer products where the input is provided by sensors rather than by people. Some examples are air conditioners, cameras, dishwashers, and microwaves. (See Box 7.1.)

Fuzzy sets can be processed with special software packages such as the following representative examples:

☐ Fuzzy C Compiler (Togai Infralogic Inc.): This product takes text file specifications of computer programs called fuzzy associative memory, a program that processes fuzzy sets, and creates appropriate data structures and source code in C.

☐ TILSHELL (Togai Infralogic Inc.): This product is a complete development environment featuring window-driven editors for quickly developing the necessary text files. Limited fuzzy logic capabilities are available in the following ES shells: Gensym, Guru, and OPS-2000.

7.8 A Note on Uncertainty

Although uncertainty is widespread in the real world, its treatment in the practical world of AI is very limited. As a matter of fact, many real-life knowledge-based systems completely avoid the issue of uncertainty. People feel that representation of uncertainty is not necessary to deal with uncertain knowledge. Why is this so?

The answer given by practitioners is very simple. Even though they recognize the problem of uncertainty, they feel that none of the methods available are accurate or consistent enough to handle the situation. As a matter of fact, some knowledge engineers have experimented with several proposed methods for dealing with uncertainty and either found no significant difference from treating the situation under assumed certainty, or found large differences among the results when using these methods. Does this mean that **uncertainty avoidance** is the best approach and this chapter should be deleted from this book? Certainly not!

Uncertainty is a serious problem. Avoiding it may not be the best strategy. Instead, we need to improve the methods for dealing with uncertainty (e.g., the Ling and Rudd extension to the theory of evidence). Theoreticians must realize that many of the concepts presented in this chapter are foreign to many practitioners. Even structured methods, such as the Bayesian formula, seem extremely strange and complex to many people.

Chapter Highlights

- □ Knowledge may be inexact and experts may be uncertain at times.
- □ Uncertainty can be caused by several factors ranging from incomplete to unreliable information.
- □ Uncertainty can be handled in AI in several ways, none of which is perfect.
- □ AI treats uncertainty as a three-step process: First uncertainty is represented, then it is combined, and finally inferences are drawn.
- □ Four major methods can be used to combine uncertainty: probability (Bayesian), certainty factors, theory of evidence, and fuzzy sets.
- □ Three basic methods can be used to represent uncertainty: numeric (probability-like), graphic, and qualitative.
- □ Several possibilities of using subjective probabilities exist; they include averaging probabilities, multiplying probabilities, and using the Bayesian formula.
- □ The Bayesian formula combines initial estimated probabilities with additional information (evidence).
- □ Subjective probabilities refer to assessments of situations based on personal experience and judgment.
- □ The theory of evidence allows use of probability-like analysis without exact probabilities. It can even handle situations involving ignorance and lack of information.
- □ Certainty theory is based on degrees of belief. In contrast to probabilities, degrees of belief do not have to total one, and they can be expressed over a variety of scales. They are similar to probabilities in their representation along a continuum ranging from no belief to total belief.

□ A certainty factor expresses the degree of belief.

□ Disbelief expresses a feeling of what is *not* going to occur.

□ Certainty theory combines evidence available in one rule by seeking the *lowest* certainty factor when several certainty factors are added, and the *highest* certainty factor when either one of several factors is used to establish evidence.

□ Certainty theory uses a special formula to combine evidences available in two or more rules.

□ Fuzzy logic represents uncertainty by using fuzzy sets.

□ Fuzzy logic is based on two premises: First, people reason using vague terms (e.g., *tall, young, beautiful*). Boundaries between classes are vague and are subject to interpretation. Second, human quantification is frequently fuzzy.

□ Fuzzy sets create sets whose boundaries are well defined and they assign membership values to those items that cannot be defined precisely.

□ Fuzzy logic is being applied to a great degree in control systems where evidence is collected by sensors.

Key Terms

Analytical hierarchy process	epistemic information	prior probability
Bayesian theorem	fuzzy logic	subjective probability
belief function	fuzzy set	theory of evidence
certainty factor	inexact (approximate)	(Dempster-Shafer)
certainty theory	reasoning	uncertainty
disbelief	posterior probability	uncertainty avoidance

Questions for Review

1. Define uncertainty (approximate reasoning).
2. Why can knowledge be inexact?
3. Review the general process of dealing with uncertainty.
4. Provide an example that shows why numeric presentation of uncertainty is difficult or even impossible.
5. What are the advantages of the graphic representation of uncertainty? What are the disadvantages?
6. Qualitative methods such as multiple choice (Likert scale) and ranking are popular among experts. Why do they like these methods?
7. What is the major function of the Bayes theorem (formula)?
8. What is the purpose of the theory of evidence (Dempster-Shafer)?
9. What is the role of belief functions in the theory of evidence?
10. What is a degree of disbelief? Give an example.
11. Why does one select a *minimum* value when using AND operator and a *maximum* value when using OR operator in combining certainty factors?

12. What are the basic premises on which the fuzzy logic approach is based?
13. What are the major advantages of fuzzy logic? What are the major disadvantages?

Questions for Discussion

1. Describe sources of uncertainty and provide examples.
2. What are some of the potential problems with qualitative methods of representing uncertainty?
3. What is the purpose of using a method such as the analytical hierarchy process?
4. Certainty factors are popular in rule-based systems. Why is this so? What unique features does the theory of uncertainty provide?
5. Fuzzy thinking is said to be advantageous for five reasons. List the reasons and provide an example to support each. If you disagree with a reason, explain why.
6. Give an example in which a detective transforms uncertainty into certainty. Compare it to the work of physicians. What approaches do they use?

Exercises

1. You are given these rules:

   R1: IF inflation is high
       THEN unemployment is high
   R2: IF inflation is high and the interest rate is high
       THEN stock prices are low
   R3: IF the gold price is high or dollar exchange is low
       THEN stock prices are low
   R4: IF gold price is high
       THEN unemployment is high

   Conduct the following computations and list the rules used.
   a. The certainty factor for high inflation is 0.8 and for high interest rates it is 0.6. Find the certainty factor for stock prices.
   b. The certainty factor for a high gold price is 0.5 and that for a low dollar exchange rate is 0.7. Find the certainty factor for stock prices.
   c. Given all the information in parts a and b, figure the certainty factor for low stock prices and for high stock prices.
   d. Figure the certainty factor for a high unemployment rate given that the inflation rate is high and the gold price is high. (Use the data in parts a and b.)

2. You are given three rules:

R1: IF blood test results = 'yes'
    THEN there is 0.8 evidence that disease is 'malaria'
R2: IF in malaria zone = 'yes'
    THEN there is 0.5 evidence that disease is 'malaria'
R3: IF bit by flying bug is 'true'
    THEN there is 0.3 evidence that disease is 'malaria'

What certainty factors will be computed for having malaria by the expert system if:
a. the first two rules are considered
b. all three rules are considered
3. You are given these rules:

R1: If you study hard, then you will receive an A in the course. CF = 0.82.
R2: If you understand the material, then you will receive an A in the course. CF = 0.85.
R3: If you are very smart, then you will receive an A in the course. CF = 0.90.

a. What is the chance of getting an A in the course if you study hard and understand the material?
b. What is the chance of getting an A in the course if all premises of the rules are true?
4. Uncertainty avoidance is a viable strategy, and it is used by many builders of knowledge-based systems. Review the literature and/or conduct an interview with a builder. Prepare statements *for* and *against* uncertainty avoidance.
5. Express the following statements in terms of fuzzy sets:
a. The chance for rain is 80 percent today. (rain? no rain?)
b. Mr. Smith is sixty years old (young?)
c. The salary of the president of the United States is $200,000 per year. (high? very high?)
d. The latest survey of economists indicates that they believe that the recession will bottom in April (20 percent), in May (30 percent), or in June (22 percent).

References and Bibliography

1. Buxton, R. "Modeling Uncertainty in Expert Systems." *International Journal of Man-Machine Studies* 31 (1989).
2. Caudill, M. "Using Neural Nets: Fuzzy Decisions." *AI Expert* Part I (December 1989) and Part II (April 1990).
3. Eliot, L.B. "Analogical Problem Solving and Expert Systems." *IEEE Expert* (Summer 1986).

4. Hink, R.F., and D.L. Woods. "How Humans Process Uncertain Knowledge: An Introduction for Knowledge Engineers." *AI Magazine* 8 (Fall 1987):41–53.

5. Horvitz, E., et al. "Decision Theory in Expert Systems and Artificial Intelligence." *International Journal of Approximate Reasoning* 2 (1988).

6. Johnson, R.C. "The Fuzzy Feeling." *Datamation* (July 15, 1989).

7. Kanal, L., and J. Lemmer. *Uncertainty in Artificial Intelligence.* Amsterdam: North Holland, 1986.

8. Karr, C. "Genetic Algorithms for Fuzzy Controllers." *AI Expert* (February 1991).

9. Klir, G., and T. Folger. *Fuzzy Sets, Uncertainty and Information.* Englewood Cliffs, N.J.: Prentice-Hall, 1988.

10. Kopcso, D., et al. "A Comparison of the Manipulation of Certainty Factors by Individuals and Expert Systems Shells." *Journal of Management Information Systems* (Summer 1988).

11. Lamberti, O., and W.A. Wallace. "Presenting Uncertainty in Expert Systems: An Issue of Information Portrayal." *Information and Management* 13 (1987).

12. Lindley, D.V. "The Probability Approach to the Treatment of Uncertainty in Artificial Intelligence and Expert Systems." *Statistical Science* 2 (no. 1, 1987).

13. Ling, X., and W.G. Rudd. "Combining Opinions from Several Experts." *Applied AI* 3 (1989).

14. Magill, W.G.W., and A.L. Stewart. "Uncertainty Techniques in Expert Systems Software." *Decision Support Systems* (January 1991).

15. Moore, J.D., et al. "Explanation in Expert Systems—A Survey." In *Proceedings, The First International Symposium on Business, Finance, and Accounting.* Univ. of Southern California, Los Angeles, September 1988.

16. Morawski, P. "Programming Bayesian Belief Networks." *AI Expert* (August 1989).

17. Neapolitan, R.E. *Probabilistic Reasoning in Expert Systems.* New York: John Wiley & Sons, 1990.

18. Negoita, C.F. *Expert Systems and Fuzzy Systems.* Menlo Park, Calif: Benjamin-Cummings, 1985.

19. Ng, K.C., and B. Abramson. "Uncertainty Management in Expert Systems." *IEEE Expert* (April 1990).

20. Nilesson, N.J. "Probabilistic Logic." *Artificial Intelligence* 28 (1986).

21. Osborn, P.B., and W.H. Zickefoose. "Building Expert Systems from the Ground Up." *AI Expert* (May 1990).

22. Parsaye, K., and M. Chignell. *Expert Systems for Experts.* New York: John Wiley & Sons, 1988.

23. Pearl, J. *Probabilistic Reasoning in Intelligent Systems: Networks of Plausible Inference.* San Mateo, Calif: Morgan Kaufman, 1988.

24. Rothman, P. "Selecting an Uncertainty Management Systems." *AI Expert* (July 1989).

25. Saaty, T.S. *Decision Making: The Analytical Hierarchy Process*. Pittsburgh: Univ. of Pittsburgh Press, 1988.

26. Schwartz, T.J. "Fuzzy Systems in the Real World." *AI Expert* (August 1990).

27. Shafer, G. *A Mathematical Theory of Evidence*. Princeton, N.J.: Princeton Univ. Press, 1976.

28. Sombe, L. *Reasoning Under Incomplete Information in Artificial Intelligence*. New York: John Wiley & Sons, 1990.

29. Whalen, T. "Fuzzy Knowledge Based Systems in Management." *Human Systems Management* (no. 4, 1984).

30. Zadeh, L.A. "A Simple View of the Dempster-Shafer Theory of Evidence and Its Implication for the Rule of Combination." *AI Magazine* (Summer 1966).

31. Zadeh, L.A. "Common-Sense Knowledge Representation Based on Fuzzy Logic." *IEEE Computer* (October 1983).

32. Zadeh, L.A. "Coping with the Imprecision of the Real World." *Communications of ACM* (April 1984).

33. Zimmerman, H. "Fuzzy Sets." In *Decision Making and Expert Systems*. Norwell, Mass.: Kluwer Academic, 1987.

Appendix A: ES Shells and Uncertainty

This appendix shows how different expert system shells handle uncertainty.*
EMYCIN is the classic ES shell (see Chapter 13).

$$-1 \leq CF \leq +1$$

IF, $CF1 \geq 0$, $CF2 \geq 0$
   THEN, $CFX = CF1 + CF2 - CF1*CF2$

IF, $CF1 < 0$, $CF2 < 0$
   THEN, $CFX = CF1 + CF2 + CF1*CF2$

IF, CF1 and CF2 have different signs

$$\text{THEN, } CFX = \frac{CF1 + CF2}{1 - MIN\,(|CF1|, |CF2|)}$$

EXSYS is a small rule-based shell. There are two options:
1. Use a scale of 0 through 10, actually 1 through 9; using 0 and 10 will lock the values as either completely true or completely untrue.

---

*According to D. Kopcso, et al., "A Comparison of the Manipulation of Certainty Factors by Individuals and Expert System Shells," *Journal of Management Information Systems* (Summer 1988). For additional information see W. G. W. Magill and A. L. Stewart, "Uncertainty Techniques in Expert Systems Software," *Decision Support Systems* (January 1991).

CF = 0, 1, 2, . . . , 10
IF, either CF1 or CF2 = 0 or 10
  THEN, CFX is the first 0 or 10 found
  ELSE, CFX = AVG(CF1, CF2)

2. Use a -100 to $+100$ scale; three suboptions are available
  a. Average the certainty factors:

$$-100 \leq CF \leq 100$$
CFX = AVG(CF1, CF2)

  b. Multiply the certainty factors (similarly to a joint probability):

$$-100 \leq CF \leq 100$$
IF, CF1 $\geq$ 0 AND CF2 $\geq$ 0
  THEN, CFX = CF1 $*$ CF2/100
  ELSE, UNDEFINED

  c. Use a certainty-factors-like approach:

$$-100 \leq CF \leq 100$$
IF, CF1 $\geq$ 0 AND CF2 $\geq$ 0
  THEN, CFX = 100 $-$ (100 $-$ CF1)$*$(100 $-$ CF2)/100
  ELSE, UNDEFINED

VP Expert is a small shell.

$0 \leq CF \leq 100$
CFX = CF1 + CF2 $-$ CF1 $*$ CF2/100

Part 3

AI Technologies

In addition to expert systems, several other applied AI technologies are being commercialized. Most applications are integrated with other AI technologies or with conventional computerized technologies. Four AI technologies are presented in Part 3. We start with natural language processing (Chapter 8). This process enables users to communicate with computers in a natural language (such as English). Currently, it is used primarily as a front-end (access) to databases, expert systems, conventional applications, robots, and so on. A natural ally of natural language processors is speech (voice) understanding. This technology, which is described in Chapter 9, has only limited applicability today, but it will be of tremendous value in the future. A third technology, computer vision (Chapter 10), was developed first for military applications. Now we see extensive use of machine vision for tasks ranging from quality control to serving as a robot's eyes. Robots (Chapter 11), especially intelligent ones, can use all other AI technologies. For example, you can command a robot by voice, and instead of using a structured command language, you can use a natural language processor to ease the communication between you and the machine.

267

Chapter 8

Natural Language Processing

Natural language processing refers to communicating with a computer in a natural language (say, English or Japanese) rather than using special commands, syntax, or menus. AI-based programs allow a computer to understand and generate natural language. With natural language processing, it is much, much easier to communicate with computers. Also, natural language processing can be applied as a productivity tool in applications ranging from summarization of news to translation from one language to another. The following specific topics are discussed in this chapter:

8.1 Introduction

After expert systems, natural language processing is the largest application for artificial intelligence. **Natural language processing** (NLP) refers to artificial intelligence methods of communicating with a computer in a natural language such as English or whatever language is spoken. Today, although we use natural language processing, we still do not *speak* with the computer; rather, we type in terse commands by keyboard or enter programs in a special language for creating software. In the future, such communication will be done in voice (see Chapter 9). In responding to a user, the computer outputs symbols or short cryptic notes of information or direction. An error message is a good example.

To use a computer properly, we must learn the commands, languages, and jargon. This usually takes considerable time and practice. It is the main reason why computers have been called unfriendly. Menus and icons with pointing devices like mice, light pens, and touch screens help, of course, but they are not perfectly natural.

Many problems could be minimized or even eliminated if we could communicate with the computer in our own language. No special commands or languages would have to be learned or used. We would simply type in directions, instructions, or information in any convenient form. The computer would be smart enough to interpret the input regardless of its format (Figure 8.1).

Natural language processing could also help us cope with **information overload**. Books and other printed sources, television, radio, and human

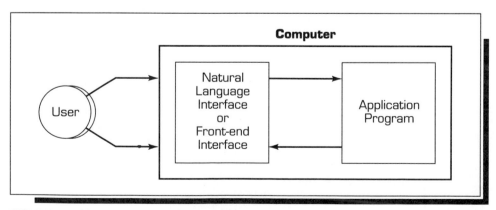

FIGURE 8.1 Natural Language Interface

conversation bombard us daily. There is so much information available that we have no good way to absorb it all and use it. As a result, a lot of good information goes to waste.

Information overload is frustrating and wasteful, but there are ways to deal with it. Once information is collected, it can be sorted, categorized, and otherwise organized to provide access to it. The information may be put into a **database management system** or into a knowledge base.

Database management systems and expert systems both provide a means of accessing information and knowledge, but often they involve difficult computer techniques. Special query languages are required to obtain information from a database. Most expert systems have a less than optimum user interface. In both cases, natural language processing would make such systems much easier to use.

To understand a natural language inquiry, a computer must have knowledge to analyze, then interpret the input. It must understand grammar and the definitions of words. It must also have significant (sometimes very large) amounts of general, commonsense, world knowledge, which is sometimes needed to understand even the simplest sentences used commonly by people. The computer needs a general dictionary and general inference algorithms. In addition to the general knowledge base, a natural language processing system must have a large domain-specific (and even task-specific) knowledge base. This base should contain, like the general knowledge base, terms and algorithms, but they must be domain specific (e.g., "patients," "drugs," methods to calculate drug doses, etc.).

These different knowledge bases can be built and handled, of course, using the same tools. AI techniques can represent this internal knowledge and process the inputs. Conventional search and pattern-matching techniques can be used along with the knowledge to provide understanding. Once the computer understands the input, it can take the desired action.

Once the computer takes action, it usually provides some output. In most cases it is desirable to provide that output in natural language. For that reason, the computer must be able to generate appropriate natural language; the easiest way to do this is to provide the computer with canned sentences, phrases, paragraphs, or other outputs. When a particular input is detected, an appropriate output response is accessed and delivered. More sophisticated techniques for generating natural language output are also available.

In this chapter we are going to discuss natural language processing software, the programs that understand natural language inputs and generate outputs. We will also cover the practical applications of such software.

8.2 Vocabulary and Issues

Let's take a minute to explain some of the terminology we will be using in this chapter.

Vocabulary

Language is a system for communication. It embodies both verbal and written expression to help us communicate our thoughts and feelings. Language uses a wide range of sounds, signs, and symbols to create words, sentences, paragraphs, and other media. Whether written or spoken, language is the medium we use for expressing and organizing what we know, think, and feel.

Most **natural languages** are not deliberately invented or designed. They have evolved over the centuries as human beings learned to communicate with one another. In fact, most languages continue to evolve as society changes, as new technological developments occur, and as changes in customs dictate.

Formal languages are artificial or contrived languages deliberately developed for a special purpose. A good example is a computer language. If used properly, the language will permit a limited form of communication between people and computers.

Linguistics is the study of how languages are structured and used. A linguist, for example, is a person who specializes in the study of languages. Linguists conduct research to organize all of the symbols, words, phrases, rules, and procedures of a language in an effort to record what it is and how it should be used.

A *vocabulary* consists of the words and phrases used in a particular language. As part of the study of language, linguists identify all of the commonly used words and phrases and organize them into a **lexicon**. A lexicon is nothing more than a dictionary that lists all of the words of a language alphabetically. A dictionary specifies the correct spelling and punctuation of the words and gives their definitions and pronunciation. A *glossary* is a subset of a dictionary which defines words, terms, or phrases in a special field of interest.

The system of rules for putting words together to form complete sentences and thoughts is called *grammar*. Grammar is composed of two basic parts: syntax and semantics. *Syntax* refers to the way in which words are assembled to form phrases and sentences. It is that branch of grammar that deals with the mixing and sequencing of different kinds of words in the language such as nouns, verbs, adjectives, and so on. Syntax is a method of putting words in a specific order so they will have the correct form according to the language.

Semantics refers to meaning in language. It is the study of relationships between words and the way they are assembled to represent a particular thought. Semantics provides us with ways of analyzing and interpreting what is being said. Keep in mind that meaning is also a function of syntax. The way words are used and ordered very much determines the meaning of the combination.

When we form sentences in a certain way and use specific words, we are referring to a certain *model* of the world that we have in mind. The mapping between a sentence and the conceptual mental model is the role of semantics.

We usually speak or write in complete sentences. Each sentence expresses one complete thought. We then string the sentences together forming a paragraph to convey a particular idea. As a whole, the paragraph makes sense.

But if we pull one sentence out of the paragraph and look at it in isolation, its meaning may not be fully understood. We say that the sentence is out of context.

Context refers to the complete idea or thought surrounding any sentence in a paragraph. Together, all the sentences add up and make sense. Alone, each sentence contains only a piece of the whole and is often subject to interpretation. Much less interpretation is needed when the sentences are looked at together. Context clarifies meaning. It explains circumstances and relationships. Therefore, it is an important part of language and understanding.

Pragmatics refers to what people really mean by what they say or write. Often, we say or write one thing but mean another. You may ask what time it is, but you really mean am I late for the meeting. Pragmatics tries to get at the true meaning or feeling.

Both context and pragmatics play a major role in understanding. It is one thing to communicate, but another to know the real meaning of the message. Context and pragmatics fill in the gaps often left by syntax and semantics.

Important Issues

Many problems arise in applying natural language understanding. Natural language is inherently ambiguous. Unless we supply the program with all the needed clues through general world knowledge, domain-specific knowledge (e.g., mechanics), and task-specific knowledge (e.g., fixing cars), as well as the full context of the phrase or sentence, there might be too many potential interpretations to an innocent looking natural language clause. In addition, there are conversational conventions among humans. For example, the question, "Can you tell me the name of the most successful salesperson this month?" should not be answered with a "Yes." Such conventions must be considered when a natural language processing system is constructed.

There are several general sources of ambiguity in natural languages:

- □ Lexical ambiguity: For example, what does "sense" mean in this sentence? Is "bomb" a verb or a noun?
- □ Syntactic or structural ambiguity: "I saw the Grand Canyon flying to New York"; it is obvious to us who is flying, but not to the computer program. "Find the name of the best salesperson in this list and print it"; should the list or the name be printed?
- □ Vague semantics: "I got this video in the department store"; you probably mean that you bought it from the store. "Print the salary of programmers and analysts"—a total or per person?
- □ Elliptical phrases and other partial sentences: "John thinks vanilla"— seems unlikely, unless stated in response to, "What ice cream flavor does John prefer?"
- □ Anaphora and other context-sensitive ambiguous references: "The city council refused the demonstrators a permit because *they* feared [advocated]

violence." Note that choosing the bracketed verb would change our interpretation of *they*.

Sentences such as these need a great amount of general world knowledge to disambiguate. As we shall see when we discuss the issues of syntax and semantics in more detail, most real-world tasks do not need *all* of the general world knowledge we have. So an important primary task when considering an NLP system is to evaluate the complexity of the sentences the system will be expected to understand. This evaluation will greatly influence the choice of the software and hardware necessary for the particular application.

8.3 How Natural Language Processing Programs Work

Just how does a computer analyze natural language inputs, understand them, and then take appropriate action? The purpose of this section is to answer that question.

Presently, two major techniques are widely used in natural language processing programs. These are **key word search** and **syntactic** and **semantic analysis**. A third type, conceptual dependency, will be described briefly later.

We will take a look at each of these techniques to give you a taste of how a computer program can understand input text. Both the power and weakness of these techniques will become apparent. Before we begin, remember this assumption: In all of the examples here, we assume that the natural language input comes from the keyboard (rather than voice). The keyboard, of course, generates codes representing the various input characters, such as letters, numbers, punctuation marks, spaces, and special symbols. These characters are stored away in an input buffer, a part of memory set aside for input text. It is this string of characters stored in memory that our natural language processing programs will analyze and attempt to understand.

8.4 Key Word Analysis

The early natural language processing programs used key word analysis. The NLP program searches through an input sentence looking for key words or phrases. The program is able to identify, or "knows," only selected words and phrases. Once a key word or phrase is recognized, the program responds with specific canned responses.

Alternately, the program may actually construct a response based on a partial reply coupled with the key word or selected phrases from the input. The program recognizes very specific inputs which it uses to construct an output response or initiate some other action.

Process of Analysis

Figure 8.2 is a flowchart of the basic procedures that a key word NLP program uses to understand input sentences. The flowchart uses standard symbols: a rectangle represents some particular processing action carried out by a subroutine or segment of the program; a diamond represents a decision point with yes and no responses.

The program usually starts by displaying a message on the screen to elicit some input response from the user. The message may simply state that the program is ready to receive input. It could give you more personalized messages such as, "What can I do for you?" "Tell me your problems," or "What are your instructions?" You input a message. Your response is accepted by the program and stored in an input buffer.

Next, the program scans the input text searching for a key word. The program can tell where one word ends and another begins by looking for spaces and punctuation marks. As each word is identified, it is used in a **pattern-matching processing** which compares it to a list of prestored words and phrases. Every word or phrase that you want the program to be able to recognize must be prestored as part of the program.

Since you want the program to be able to respond to random natural language input, a considerable number of words will have to be stored if you wish to recognize the input text. For example, if you want the program to be able to recognize a specific word, you will also need to store variations or synonyms for that word. For example, a key word may be *father*. But since people call their fathers by many other names, you should include additional key words such as *Dad, Daddy, Poppa, Pa, the Old Man*, and so on.

Each word in the input text string is matched against those in the key word directory stored in the program. The diamond element in the flowchart labeled "keyword found?" has two output paths, depending on the outcome of this search. The first possibility is that no key word is located. If that is the case, the program is set up to respond with one or more stock messages. Some typical examples are "I don't understand," "Please rephrase your message," or some other output that will cause the user to enter a new or different message which contains a key word. This process may continue for several iterations until an appropriate word is recognized.

If a key word is located, it is flagged or marked so that it can be used to select an appropriate canned response or can be used in an assembled response. But before that is done, the input text string is continually scanned until all possible key words are found. For example, the second diamond in Figure 8.2 asks the question "more key words?" If there are (yes), the search continues. There may be several key words in the input. The program continues to scan all of the words in the input string to match against those in the key word directory.

If no more key words are found, the next step occurs. An appropriate output response is selected or developed and sent to the user. There are several different ways in which this is done. The simplest method, of course, is by

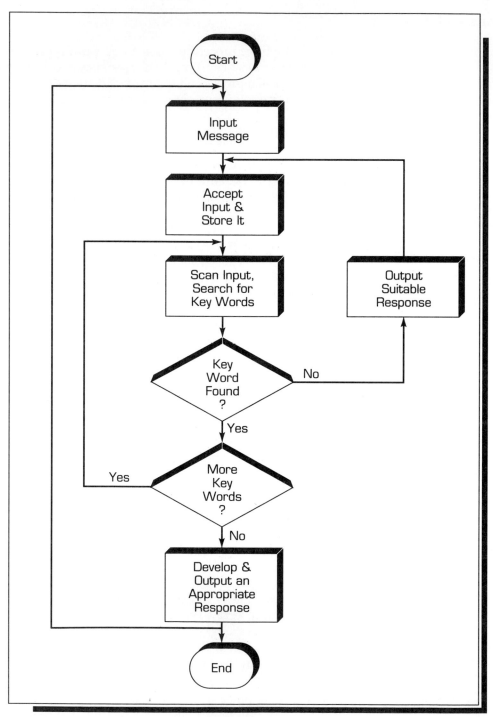

FIGURE 8.2 Process of Key Word Analysis

relating the key word to a specific standard response stored in the program. The key word triggers the use of that response. The program branches to a subroutine where that particular response is stored, and it is outputted to the user.

In other cases, some additional processing may take place to develop, at least partially, the output response. For example, a portion of the input text, be it a word or phrase, might be remembered by the program and then combined with a preprogrammed portion to form a complete response. In another situation, selected key words will be recognized so that some special processing takes place. The words *I* or *me*, for instance, are recognized in the input string and this signals the program to respond with the word *you*. The user may input something like "I want to know more about computers." The NLP program recognizes the "I" and knows to include a "you" in the response, such as "Why do you want to know more about computers?" As you can imagine, there are all kinds of possibilities depending on what the key words are and what output messages are appropriate.

A Program at Work: ELIZA

To give you an even better feel for how key word matching programs work, let's take a look at a real-world example. One of the most widely known and discussed key word matching programs is called ELIZA. ELIZA was written by Joseph Weizenbaum of MIT in the mid-1960s. It was not written to demonstrate natural language processing. Instead, its purpose was to show how computers could be used to exhibit a certain amount of intelligence but without any true understanding. Weizenbaum created one of the most talked about programs ever developed. He showed what has proved to be a very effective natural language processing technique that is still widely used.

ELIZA is named after Eliza Doolittle of *Pygmalian* and *My Fair Lady* fame. The program itself is designed to act like a nondirective psychiatrist. Such psychiatrists ask you to tell them about your problem, then respond occasionally to draw you out. The idea is that you will talk yourself through the problem to a solution or decision.

Many spin-offs or variations of this program have been created. To see what the program is like, refer to Figure 8.3. The computer's responses are in uppercase letters. The program opens by having you state your problem. Of course, you can respond with almost anything. Read through the basic conversation in Figure 8.3; then let's talk about it.

This is a listing of a real conversation. It shows the power of ELIZA to create the illusion of a real dialogue, but it also shows its weaknesses. The first weakness appears several lines down with the response, "Well, it is not my problem exclusively. . . ." ELIZA thinks the problem is "exclusively."

Later on, things get a bit muddy with the statement "Well, sure but not AI." ELIZA's response is "earlier you said your problem." It is clear that the program doesn't really understand.

HOW DO YOU DO.
PLEASE TELL ME YOUR PROBLEM.

My problem is artificial intelligence.
YOUR PROBLEM IS ARTIFICIAL INTELLIGENCE—THAT'S INTERESTING.

Well actually, the real problem is a subfield of artificial intelligence called
natural language.
I AM NOT SURE I UNDERSTAND YOU FULLY.

That is the problem, getting a program to understand.
PLEASE GO ON.

How can I get a program to comprehend what I tell it in plain English?
WHY DO YOU ASK?

That is the source of my problem.
WHY DO YOU SAY YOUR PROBLEM?

Well, it is not my problem exclusively, but I still have it.
DOES THE FACT THAT YOUR PROBLEM EXCLUSIVELY SUGGEST
ANYTHING ELSE TO YOU?

Not at all.
DOES THAT HAVE ANYTHING TO DO WITH THE FACT THAT YOUR
PROBLEM IS ARTIFICIAL INTELLIGENCE?

It sure does.
WHAT DOES THAT SUGGEST TO YOU?

If I understood AI well enough, I wouldn't have such a problem with natural
language understanding.

(continued)

FIGURE 8.3 Portion of a Real Conversation with the Key Word Matching Program
Called ELIZA

Nevertheless, ELIZA gives a good account of itself and displays a bit of wit
and humor as well. ELIZA's stored responses have been cleverly worded and
carefully matched to the key words. For example, if you should happen to state
that your problem is with your mother, father, sister, or brother, ELIZA will
respond with something like, "Tell me more about your family."

As for some typical canned responses, consider those that are outputted
when you respond with the words *yes* or *no*. If you type "yes" in answer to a
question, the program might respond with "You seem quite positive." If you
input a "no," the program may respond with "You are being a bit negative."
For the input term *yes*, ELIZA can respond with four possible outputs. In
addition to the one mentioned, it may also answer with "Are you sure?" "I
see," and "I understand." For very common key words such as *yes* and *no*, the
program contains multiple responses to avoid delivering the same reply each

DO YOU THINK IT'S LIKELY THAT YOU UNDERSTOOD AI WELL
ENOUGH?

No.
WHY NOT?

It is a tough subject.
YOU SEEM TO HAVE AVOIDED SPEAKING OF YOUR PARENTS
ALTOGETHER.

What the devil do my parents have to do with anything?
IS IT IMPORTANT TO YOU THAT YOUR PARENTS HAVE TO DO WITH
ANYTHING?

Well sure, but not AI.
EARLIER YOU SAID YOUR PROBLEM.

Yes.
YOU SEEM QUITE POSITIVE.

I'm not following you.
IS IT BECAUSE YOU ARE NOT FOLLOWING THAT YOU CAME TO ME?

Say what?
DOES THAT QUESTION INTEREST YOU?

This whole thing is getting ridiculous.
DO YOU FEEL STRONGLY ABOUT DISCUSSING SUCH THINGS?

I'm getting tired of your wimpy responses.
HOW LONG HAVE YOU BEEN GETTING TIRED OF MY WIMPY
RESPONSES?

time. This not only provides some variety, but also creates a better illusion of
understanding.

If more than one key word is recognized in an input statement, an
appropriate output response will be chosen according to a certain priority
structure set up within the program. Some key words are considered by the
program to be more important than others. The response to your input will be
triggered by the key word with the highest priority.

If the program does not identify a key word in the input sentence, it simply
outputs one of several possible noncommittal replies. The output may be
something like "I'm not sure I understand you fully" or "Please go on."

Of course, ELIZA knows all the little tricks to make you think it really does
understand, such as replacing the "I" in your input response with a "you" in
its own response. In addition, ELIZA has some special tricks to give you the

impression that it is intelligently analyzing your statements and responding to them. For example, ELIZA can store a brief word or phrase from one of your input statements and use it later. As an example, you might have stated earlier that your problem was your inability to afford a Mercedes. Later, during your conversation, when the subject or context may have changed, ELIZA will use that phrase in a statement such as this: "Does that have anything to do with the fact that you cannot afford a Mercedes?" It will do this if no key word is recognized. Such a response is clever, because it seems to prove that the program does have some intelligence because it did remember a previous part of the conversation and relate it back to you at another time. Many times the output expression seems meaningful regardless of what the previous discourse might have been.

ELIZA is an excellent demonstration of how key word matching can be used. However, it is not perfect. It often gives meaningless responses, and there are numerous ways that you can trick it. But for the most part, it is a remarkable demonstration of how a "stupid" program can give the illusion of intelligence.

Although key word matching programs are not perfect, they can be extremely useful. Even though the program doesn't really understand what you say, it can use its bag of tricks to make you think that it does. And this, in effect, often results in a useful outcome. For example, some natural language front-end interfaces for other computer programs, such as database management systems, use key word matching. The aim is not so much perfection as it is to generate some valuable outcome.

One important point about key word matching programs is the size of their vocabularies. The vocabulary is made up of all the key words and phrases that the program can identify. Most natural language understanding programs implemented with this technique have a limited vocabulary. It is limited by the program itself and in some cases by the amount of memory the computer may have. But typically, the vocabulary is limited because of the application. Most natural language interfaces, for example, are customized to a particular piece of software. As a result of the limited vocabulary, the number of appropriately stored responses or actions is also limited. It would be difficult to construct a general-purpose NLP program using key words, because the vocabulary would simply be too large. Furthermore, even if sufficient storage space were available, the search time would be extremely long, making the computer's response sluggish if not downright slow. The best approach is to limit the subject and customize the natural language interface to the application.

Note that ELIZA was expecting the user to mention his or her family at some point. The failure of this expectation led to ridiculous results. However, if indeed the conversation (and therefore its related vocabulary) were limited to only a subset of a psychiatric consultation scenario, namely, discussing emotions and family relations (as the original ELIZA was geared to do), the program would probably have made much more sense. This limitation of the domain of discourse is exploited in most of the domain- and task-specific natural language applications we will see.

8.5   Syntactic and Semantic Analysis

Although key word pattern matching is a widely used natural language technique, its usefulness is restricted because it simply cannot deal with the large variations in language that naturally occur. For that reason, AI researchers have looked for and developed more sophisticated ways of analyzing an input sentence and extracting meaning from it.

The most obvious and straightforward approach to the problem is to perform a detailed analysis of the syntax and semantics of an input statement. In this way, the exact structure of an input sentence and its meaning can be determined. Of course, this is easier said than done. Even sophisticated systems for analyzing syntax and semantics fall short of the job, because *there are too many words with multiple meanings* and an enormous number of ways to put those words together to form sentences.

Consider the following question phrased in five different ways:

1. How many nonstop flights are there from Phoenix to Boston?
2. Do you have any nonstop flights from Phoenix to Boston?
3. I would like to go from Phoenix to Boston without any layovers.
4. What planes leave Phoenix and get to Boston without stopping?
5. It's important that I find a nonstop Phoenix–Boston flight.

All the phrases just given request the same information, but they are syntactically dissimilar. An NLP can determine, through questions such as, "Do you mean to say . . .," exactly what the question is.

Yet, natural language processing systems that do a detailed analysis of syntax and semantics do a far better job than key word matchers, particularly if their application is restricted to a narrow domain. Today, most natural language systems use the syntactic and semantic analysis approach. The processes are varied and complex, so we will discuss only the basic procedures.

Basic Language Units

Before we get into the step-by-step details of natural language processors, let's take a look at the individual units of the input. First, the basic unit of the English language is the sentence. A sentence expresses a complete thought, asks a question, gives a command, or makes an exclamation. The sentence, of course, is made up of individual units known as words. The words have meaning, and when they are linked together in various ways, their relationships represent ideas, thoughts, and visual images.

The individual words, besides having a meaning of their own, also fall into various categories known as parts of speech. As you recall from your English classes, there are eight different parts of speech: nouns, pronouns, verbs, adjectives, adverbs, prepositions, conjunctions, and interjections. Every word is classified as one of these parts of speech.

The English language is tricky, however, because a word may have more than one meaning and can be classified as more than one kind of part of speech. A good example is the word *saw*. It can be a noun meaning a cutting tool. Or it can be a verb meaning "did see." The true meaning of a word depends on how it is used in the sentence, that is, how it is related to the other words. Words like this cause considerable difficulty for computer programs that attempt to analyze sentences and extract meaning.

Naturally, there is a complete system within the language that describes how the various parts of speech are to be put together to form complete sentences. These arrangements or structures are stated by specific rules and collectively are known as grammar. We won't attempt to define the full scope of grammar here as you probably already know a lot of it anyway. However, it must be said that a complete proper sentence is generally made up of two specific parts, a subject and a predicate. The subject, also referred to as a noun phrase, identifies a person, object, or thing that is the main focus of the sentence. The predicate, or verb phrase, states some action that the subject takes.

Of course, there are many variations of the noun phrase and verb phrase. Each can contain not only the basic noun or verb, but also adjectives, adverbs, pronouns, and prepositional phrases. In any case, both the noun phrase and the verb phrase must be present to form a complete legal sentence.

Although the sentence is the basic building block of language, we often communicate in incomplete sentences. Natural language processors are primarily designed to recognize complete sentences, but they must also deal with partial inputs. This phenomenon of using sentence fragments, short phrases, or even single words in a conversation is known as *ellipsis*. Such partial sentences are acceptable and they can be effective. We understand them because their meaning is inferred from the context of conversation. Ellipsis causes the natural language processing software to be even more complex. Neural computing (Chapter 18) can be used with NLP to overcome this problem.

Morphemes

To analyze an input sentence, the software first breaks down the sentence into individual words. The program scans the input stream looking for spaces and punctuation marks to identify the individual words. But syntactic and semantic analyzers often go one step farther. They may divide the input word into smaller units called **morphemes**. A morpheme is the smallest unit of language. A morpheme may be the word itself, in which case it is called a free morpheme. For example, the word *computer* is a morpheme. On the other hand, *computers* is made up of two morphemes, the basic or root word itself, *computer*, and the letter *s* added to the end, which indicates a plural. The *s* is a type of morpheme called a bound morpheme. Bound morphemes are usually prefixes and suffixes that are used on the root word to modify its meaning. A typical prefix may be the morpheme *un-* while typical suffixes might be *-ed* or *-ing*. There are many other variations. By subdividing words like this, it is much easier to analyze the word and tell how it is being used.

8.6   Natural Language Processing Systems

Figure 8.4 is a simplified block diagram of the major elements in a natural language processing program. The five major elements are the parser, the lexicon, the understander, the knowledge base, and the generator. Let's look at each of these major elements in detail.

Parser

The key element in a natural language system is the **parser**. The parser is a piece of software that analyzes the input sentence syntactically. Each word is isolated and its part of speech is identified. The parser then maps the words into a structure called the parse tree. The parse tree shows the meanings of all of the words and how they are assembled.

The entire parsing processing is analogous to the process of diagramming sentences, which you may have learned in an English class. The parser identifies the noun phrase and verb phrase and further breaks them down into other elements. This syntactic analysis is the first step toward trying to extract meaning from the sentence.

Recall that a sentence (S) is made up of a subject or noun phrase (NP) and a predicate or verb phrase (VP). We show this as:

$$S = NP + VP$$

The noun phrase could be a single noun, but it usually breaks down further into several additional parts of speech, such as an article (ART) or determiner (D) like *a* or *this*, and/or an adjective (ADJ) or two, and the main noun:

$$NP = D + ADJ + N$$

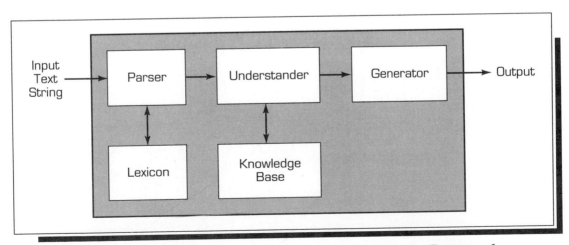

FIGURE 8.4   General Block Diagram of a Natural Language Understanding Program of the Syntactic-Semantic Analysis Type

The noun phrase may even have a prepositional phrase (PP) made up of a preposition (P) such as *of* or *with* and another determiner and noun:

$$PP = P + D + N$$

The verb phrase (VP) is made up of the verb (V) and often the object of the verb, which is usually another noun (N) and its determiner (D). A prepositional phrase (PP) may also be associated with the verb phrase:

$$VP = V + D + N + PP$$

Of course, there are many other variations.

The job of the parser is to examine each word in a sentence and create the parse tree that identifies all the words and puts them together in the right way. An example is illustrated in Figure 8.5. The sentence "Joan drove the new car to Bloomingdale's" is divided into its various parts. The parser begins by examining the word *Joan*. This is found to be a woman's name which is a noun. Next, the word *drove* is examined. This is revealed to be a verb. Then the word *the* appears to the parser. This is identified as a determiner. This process is continued as the parse tree is built.

A popular method of parsing is the *augmented transition network* (ATN). An ATN has discrete states or nodes that are linked by arcs. The arcs represent conditions that must be met to move from one state to another.

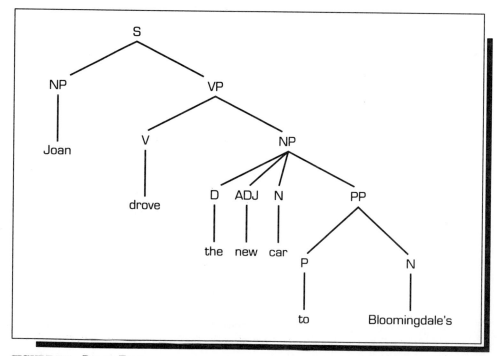

FIGURE 8.5 Parse Tree

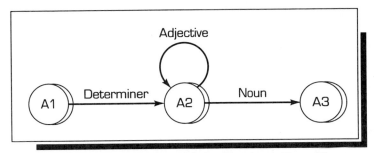

FIGURE 8.6 Augmented Transition Network for Parsing a Noun Phrase

A simple ATN is shown in Figure 8.6. This ATN is used to parse a noun phrase made up of a determiner (or article), one or more adjectives, and a noun. The start state is A1. To get to A2, the ATN looks for a determiner. It tests the first word to see if it is an article, such as *a, the,* or *this.* Assume we are parsing the phrase "the long, black car." The ATN looks *the* up in the lexicon and determines that it is indeed a determiner. The test for a determiner succeeds, so we move to the next state, A2.

Now the ATN looks at the next word in the sentence testing for an adjective. It finds *long,* and the test succeeds. But the ATN must be designed to look for more than one adjective so it does not change states. It simply loops back looking for another adjective. It finds *black.* It looks again at *car. Car* is not an adjective so the test finally fails.

Now the ATN looks for a noun, and it finds *car* so we move to the final state, A3. The phrase is then parsed. This simple ATN attaches to or references other ATNs to parse larger sentences or different types of sentences. It builds a data structure in memory that identifies all the words and their grammatical relationships.

Lexicon

The parser works closely with the lexicon in doing syntactic analysis. The lexicon contains all of the words that the program is capable of recognizing. As mentioned, the lexicon is (conceptually at least) composed of a *general* component as well as a *domain/task-specific* one.

The lexicon contains the correct spelling of each word and also designates its part of speech. For words that can have more than one meaning, the lexicon lists all of the various meanings permitted by the system. For instance, consider the word *can. Can* might be a verb indicating ability. It may also be a noun referring to a container. One of the ways to get around the problem of determining how the word is really used is to limit the lexicon entries to only those terms which are permitted by the system. If all possible combinations must be used, then the system must have some built-in segment that further determines how the word is used. Typically, this means that the word must first be related to other words in the sentence to determine its meanings. The more sophisticated NLP programs have such a capability.

Some parsers perform a morpheme analysis. They look at each input word and further subdivide it into its individual morphemes. The lexicon contains the various morphemes. In this way, a more precise meaning can be determined. Other natural language processing systems do not perform morpheme analysis, but instead store all possible variations of the root word. The overall result is basically the same.

The parser and the lexicon work together to pick apart a sentence and then create the parse tree—a new data structure that helps to get at the real meaning of the sentence. But even though the various parts of speech have been identified and the sentence has been fully analyzed syntactically, the computer still does not understand it. As a result, semantic analysis is necessary.

In operation, the parser is largely a pattern matcher. Once the individual word has been identified, the parser searches through the lexicon comparing each input word with all of the words stored there. If a match is found, the word is put aside along with the other lexical information, such as part of speech and meaning. The parser then goes on to analyze additional words and ultimately builds the parse tree.

During this process, the parser can also take care of general housekeeping activities such as misspelled words. Users may not know the spelling, or they may make typing errors when they key the input sentence. Consequently, most parsers have search routines to recognize spelling errors. Usually the spelling errors are typos and represent discrepancies in only one or two letters. The parser attempts to match the input word as closely as possible to those existing in the lexicon. The procedure may be to flag the misspelled word, notify the user, and ask for clarification. Detecting spelling errors commonly requires the ability to perform morpheme analysis by stripping the word of its prefixes and suffixes and looking for the morpheme in the lexicon.

Once the parse tree has been constructed, the system is ready for semantic analysis to obtain further meaning.

Understander and Knowledge Base

Semantic analysis is the function of the understander block in Figure 8.4. The **understander** works in conjunction with the knowledge base to determine what the sentence means. The knowledge base can be divided conceptually into two parts: the *general* knowledge base (general world knowledge and basic linguistic concepts) and the *domain/task-specific* knowledge base. The latter knows about entities and computational procedures specific to the application at hand.

To determine what is meant by an input sentence, the system must know things about words and how they are put together to form meaningful statements. The knowledge base is the primary means of understanding what has been said. As you already know, there are many different ways to implement a knowledge base. Production rules, semantic networks, frames, and scripts are all common methods for implementing natural language knowledge bases.

A lot of the knowledge contained in the general and domain-specific knowledge bases may be brought to bear at this point. This knowledge imposes constraints on possible interpretations of the parse tree, and disambiguates multiple, potentially feasible meanings.

The purpose of the understander is to use the parse tree to reference the knowledge base. Thus, the understander may answer a question using the knowledge base. If the input sentence is a statement, the understander determines meaning by looking up words and phrases in the knowledge base. Rules might be fired, frames or scripts referenced, or semantic nets searched. The understander can also draw inferences from the input statement. Many English sentences do not tell the whole story directly, but humans are able to infer the meaning from our general knowledge. This is also the case with more sophisticated natural language understanding systems.

As we shall see in the section about conceptual dependencies, understanding a sentence fully really means drawing all the implied inferences from it.

Generator

The generator uses the understood input to create a usable output. The understander creates another data structure that represents the meaning and understanding of the sentence and stores it in memory. That data structure can then be used to initiate additional action. If the NLP is part of a front-end interface, the data structure will be used to create special codes to control another piece of software. It may give the software commands to initiate some action. In a database management system, the generator would write a program in a query language to begin a search for specific information. In other systems, the action may be the generation of an output response such as a sentence or question.

In its simplest form, the natural language generator feeds standard, prestored output responses to the user based on the meaning extracted from the input. However, more sophisticated generators construct an original response from scratch.

In the model for a natural language processing system shown in Figure 8.4, individual blocks show the elements of the system and how they work together. They describe the system as first performing the syntactic analysis and then the semantic analysis. In practice, there are systems that work this way. However, much research and experimentation has shown that systems which combine the syntactic and semantic analysis have superior performance. In other words, as the syntax is being determined, semantic analysis also is being done. This helps to minimize ambiguity. Such integrated systems may have all of the blocks shown in Figure 8.4, but they are linked to communicate with one another on a word-by-word basis. In this way, the input statement is better understood and processing often takes place faster.

8.7   Conceptual Dependency

The **conceptual dependency** theory was developed by Roger Schank. It was implemented in many seminal works in natural language processing and generation executed by his students, mostly during the 1970s and 1980s at Yale University.

The main assumptions underlying the theory are that representations should facilitate inference, and the similarities in meaning should be reflected by similarities in representation. For instance, "Mary gave John a book" as compared to "Mary gave John a kiss" would need context-specific rules to interpret and would lead to complex inference models.

On the other hand, "John bought the book from Mary" means practically the same as "Mary sold John the book," at least with respect to questions like "Who has the book?" and "Who has the money?" From the point of view of most inferences, the two sentences have the same meaning and might use the same representation. The conceptual dependency representation, therefore, would usually not differentiate between these two sentences, though it would assign different representations to the two sentences.

In conceptual dependency theory, sixteen primitive "acts" are used to represent the full spectrum of natural language semantics. For example, the ATRANS Act describes an action involving transferring some OBJECT by an ACTOR from a SOURCE to a DESTINATION. The capitalized concepts are fixed slots in the ATRANS Act, possibly (but not necessarily) to be filled by a complete sentence. The inference to be drawn is that OBJECT is no longer at SOURCE but can be found at (or belong to) a DESTINATION.

In a similar vein, the PTRANS Act describes a physical movement by some ACTOR of some OBJECT from some SOURCE location to some DESTINATION location. It usually specifies an INSTRUMENT (say, a car) through which the action was carried out, as well as a possible TIME for the action (say, past). We can obviously draw some inferences regarding the position of OBJECT. We can also infer usually that a more primitive act was involved in the conceptual dependency. Other plausible (but not necessary) inferences are that an *ACT* was enabled by a certain *STATE* and resulted in another STATE. Such backward and forward inference chains can be formed automatically and are the simplest form of general, domain-independent inference. The inferences are not very specific and are usually only potentially feasible; more complex representations (which will not be discussed here) were used for more useful and efficient inferences.

The conceptual dependency intermediate representation can also be used to generate natural language sentences to be presented to the user.

8.8 Choosing and Applying NLP Systems

Issues in Design and Selection

Many issues need to be considered when implementing an NLP. The following topics are representative:

□ The typical elements embodied in the design of an NLP system usually can guide us when we are choosing a system for a specific application or when we are deciding whether to adapt a system for our domain and a specific task.

□ In general, we should first determine our expectations of the system, as well as the necessary vocabulary and the syntactic and semantic ranges the system should be able to handle. In some cases we may decide that our specifications cannot be fulfilled by present-day NLP technology. In many other cases, a very small subset of English or even a domain-specific language (including categories such as DRUG or PATIENT in addition to NOUN, etc.) might well suffice. Perhaps limiting the vocabulary to a restricted set of key words (e.g., well-defined commands) might completely avoid the need for the computer to understand natural language.

□ If considerable syntactic flexibility is expected, a much more complex system will be indicated and possibly will influence hardware choice.

□ An important consideration is whether the system needs to communicate with a human user or if it is sufficient to provide convenient interfaces to other software.

□ Vocabulary options such as synonyms, easy modification of meaning, multiple meanings, and other functions relevant to the application at hand must be taken into account.

□ The syntactic range expected from the system is an important element. Checking the agreement in number between subject and object; using quantifiers like *every*, conjunctions like *or*, and comparatives like *more*; using ellipses—all change the complexity of the required system.

□ Semantic range expected is important, too. Deciding which words in a sentence are modified by a quantifier calls for more than syntax and vocabulary. The query "a forty-year-old employee named Smith" really means "find an employee named Smith whose age is between forty and forty-one."

□ The link between the output of the parser and the application's model is the crucial aspect to consider when it is necessary to connect an NLP interface to existing software.

□ Since natural language has many sources of ambiguity, the system's method of handling ambiguities is crucial, in particular when the system cannot disambiguate between multiple meanings. (For instance, a system may paraphrase an ambiguous query and wait for the user's approval.)

Applications

Natural language processing programs have been applied in several areas. The most important are NLP interfaces, translation of a natural language to another natural language (e.g., English to German), translation of a computer language to another computer language, grammar analysis, and documents management (e.g., abstracting text, composing letters).

Now let's take a closer look at these important uses plus some other NLP applications. The value of an AI technique is directly proportional to its usefulness, and NLP ranks high with expert systems in user value.

8.9 Natural Language Interfaces and Software Tools

By far the most predominant use of NLP is interfaces, or **front-ends**, to other software packages. Such interfaces are used to simplify and improve the communication between the application program and the user. Many programs are complex and difficult to use. They require learning a special language or set of commands. This takes a lot of time and effort and frequently puts off the user. A natural language front-end helps overcome these problems.

The natural language front-end allows the user to operate the application program or development software with natural language. No special commands have to be learned. Once users understand the basic function of the software program, they can use everyday language to tap it. Even novice users can take advantage of the software.

Natural language front-ends make the software transparent to the user. Because users do not have to learn or worry about special languages or procedures, they can focus on the job, not the process of getting it done. Thus even computer illiterate managers, executives, and other busy people are able to use the computer. Furthermore, NLP can help open up the corporate mainframe database to users other than data processing programmers.

Access to Databases

Although natural language front-ends are being created for a wide variety of application programs, their most common use is with DBMS products, which store and retrieve huge files of data. Such files may be customer profiles, inventory items, or simply a variety of facts and figures. The easy part of using a DBMS is creating the files. The information to be stored is divided up into individual "chunks" generally known as records. Many records are used to create files. Many different kinds of files are combined to form the entire database. Although creating the database may be time consuming, it is not difficult. The difficulty arises in getting at and using the information stored there.

To access the information, the DBMS must be given instructions to tell it what kind of information to access. Different operations, including searching and sorting, may have to be performed to access the information. Some editing is also usually required to put the information into the desired output format. For example, if you wanted to tap a customer database and access all of the individuals whose last name is Smith and output them in zip code order, you would have to have some way to tell the DBMS to do this. Usually a special language called a query language is necessary. It is made up of special commands and instructions that are listed sequentially to form a program that will access the data you want in the format you want. This makes most DBMS products hard to use. Users who want and need the data do not have the expertise to create the program to get at the data. As a result, a programmer or some other computer-oriented person must do the job, which certainly limits the usefulness of the database.

Today, many DBMS software packages include a natural language front-end or offer one as an option. As a result, virtually anyone can sit in front of a computer and tap the database simply by keying in the details of what he or she wants as output. For example, to get the information mentioned earlier, all the user would have to type is the following: List all the customers named Smith in zip code order.

Software Tools

Some examples of software products follow.

INTELLECT. INTELLECT (AI Corp.) is one of the oldest and most widely used natural language front-ends. It is a complete natural language interface for large mainframe computers and was designed primarily to be used with DBMS products that operate in the IBM operating system environment.

In addition to being able to access data in a DBMS, INTELLECT allows the user to create databases using natural language. The built-in lexicon may be modified to fit a particular application. A lexicon editor allows the user to build and maintain special dictionaries for special uses. Unique words and their meanings or synonyms can be added to the lexicon. In this way, INTELLECT can be customized to the particular application.

In some cases, a natural language front-end attaches directly to the database. The natural language interface also can generate code in one of the numerous query languages used to access information in a DBMS. INTELLECT, for example, is available in a configuration which uses FOCUS, a query language for a large DBMS. INTELLECT allows the user to enter natural English-language statements and then converts them into the command structure of FOCUS which, in turn, accesses the desired data.

As an example of how INTELLECT might work, assume that a database has been created to keep track of the sales information on a company's products. The DBMS knows how many of the different kinds of products are sold each month in each of the sales regions. It also keeps track of monthly sales by individual salespeople. With all of this information on tap, a sales manager can access information quickly to get a picture of what is selling and what is not, who is performing and who is not. Such a DBMS can be very useful in finding problems and correcting them.

A sales manager may not be computer literate. But with a natural language front-end, the information can be tapped quickly from a database. For example, the sales manager could sit down at a terminal and key in the following message:

What are the sales of all products for February?

The natural language front-end converts this query into the code that will access that information. But there are some real subtleties in the inquiry. First, although the input states the month of the sales, it does not state the year. The sales manager obviously means the current year and, therefore, the computer must be set to anticipate this. Otherwise, it may simply come back to the user with a question asking what year.

This inquiry also assumes that the program knows which products the company makes. Again, large sophisticated systems have no problem in dealing with such information. Smaller less sophisticated systems, however, would simply ask which products the user wants to know about.

Once these preliminaries are out of the way, the computer will display the desired information. It might look something like this:

Sales for February 1991
Widgets 14,522
Whatchamacallits 7,918
Whizbangs 22,683

The sales manager may then make another inquiry such as:

Which sales region sold the most widgets?

Again, the interface has to assume several things, or it may ask for clarification. It must know which sales regions exist. In this case, assume that the country is divided into east, central, and western sales areas. The computer then looks up the sales for each of these regions on widgets and prints out the information:

East Coast:
Widgets 6,580

The important point is that the same question can be asked in several different ways. Yet, the computer will understand it.

INTELLECT is probably the best selling natural language interface for large mainframes (see Box 8.1 for typical applications); however, several other software companies offer such systems. Another system for large mainframes is EXPLORER (Cognitive Systems, Inc.). EXPLORER is a natural language front-end that is specifically customized to the database and the application.

RAMIS II ENGLISH. RAMIS II ENGLISH (Mathematica, Inc.) is another of the competitors to INTELLECT. It has been used successfully by the New York Stock Exchange to create a natural language interface for its large database of business practice regulatory information.

Box 8.1: Application of INTELLECT—British Gas

British Gas is a large natural gas provider; it serves 2 million customers in the United Kingdom. In less than three months, the company wrote twenty-five different management information systems with INTELLECT. The systems ranged from quality assurance and customer inquiry handling for stores to accounting and legal systems. Currently in preparation is a system for the personnel director which will allow a broad overview of staffing levels and requirements.

"It is as quick to use as any fourth-generation language on the market and is efficient in its use of machine resources," comments Dudley, the director of information systems. "We were also impressed by both the simplicity of the syntax and the privacy and access control aspects of the product."

The ultimate goal is for senior managers to be able to answer all their own inquiries using INTELLECT's capabilities themselves. New systems at British Gas are being designed to remove the need for regular printed reports and to enable users to produce their own information in the format they find most useful.

(*Source*: Publicly disclosed information of AI Corp.)

SPOCK. SPOCK (Frey Associates, Inc.), previously called Themis, is a natural language front-end available for Digital Equipment Corp.'s VAX family of minicomputers. The system is designed to interface with DEC DBMS/32 database software. Versions are also available to work with Data General's minicomputers, which use Oracle, a relational DBMS. Like most natural language front-ends, SPOCK comes with a basic vocabulary that can be added to or otherwise modified to better match the interface to the system and application.

Natural language front-ends are also available for DBMS products that run on personal computers. Most of these are designed to work with DBMS systems for the IBM personal computer and its compatibles. Let's take a closer look at several of them.

NaturalLink. NaturalLink (Texas Instruments) is another natural language front-end with a unique format. This front-end is menu driven; you don't even have to key in your own inquiry statements. Instead, NaturalLink already contains all of the acceptable words and phrases you can use in a valid inquiry. These word and phrase choices are displayed in windows on the screen. At the very top of the screen is the beginning phrase "I want to . . . ." By using the arrow keys, you can move a cursor around to highlight the desired words or phrases that express the inquiry you wish to make. Once the highlighted term is entered, it is automatically added to the beginning sentence. In this way, you build a query sentence that tells NaturalLink exactly what you want to do.

NaturalLink is designed to be used as a front-end to a number of popular application programs. These, of course, include the DBMS, but also popular spreadsheets, word processing packages, operating systems, and other programs. Facilities are included so that NaturalLink can be built and optimized for a specific application program. NaturalLink runs on Texas Instruments' own personal computers as well as the popular IBM personal computer and its compatibles.

BBN Parlance. BBN Parlance (BBN Labs, Inc.) is a natural language interface that enables access to relational database systems (e.g., Oracle) using various hardware types (usually large systems). The main benefit of Parlance is that it provides a sophisticated semantic range.

Embedded Interfaces

A major trend in natural language interfaces is to build them into the application program rather than making them extra-cost add-ons. Two good examples of **embedded systems** are Q&A and Paradox. Both contain built-in natural language interfaces which may be called on if desired. Lotus 1-2-3, version 3.2, also includes some NLP capabilities.

Q&A. Q&A (Symantec Corp.) is a basic file manager that contains modules for building files, accessing files, and generating an output report in a specific format. It also contains the natural language front-end called The Intelligent Assistant. The Intelligent Assistant parses common English questions and converts them into queries that the file manager can understand. A built-in vocabulary of several hundred words provides the lexical information for understanding the input query. Like CLOUT and other kinds of natural language interfaces, The Intelligent Assistant in Q&A may not understand your inquiry immediately if you use an input word or phrase that is not in the built-in dictionary. In this case, Q&A will come back to you and ask you to try again. To get closer to a successful input statement, you must rephrase your query using synonyms or different terms. Eventually, the front-end will understand and access the information you want.

   A unique feature of Q&A is that it paraphrases your input request to ensure that it fully understands what you want. Using the sales example given earlier, you may request the following:

Show the total 1985 sales for the Central Region

Q&A's Intelligent Assistant may come back with an inquiry that looks like this:

SHALL I DO THE FOLLOWING?
    CREATE A REPORT SHOWING THE AMOUNT OF SALES FOR THE CENTRAL
    REGION IN 1985?
    YES—CONTINUE   NO—CANCEL REQUEST

Paraphrasing verifies what you want to do. If the paraphrase is correct, simply type the letter Y for yes and data access will be completed. A no answer will cancel the request, and then you may change it or rephrase it.

The primary disadvantage of the Q&A system is that it is not a relational database. For that reason, it cannot initiate queries for multiple information items that are contained in separate files. It can only access information in one file at a time. Relational databases, on the other hand, permit several files to be open at a time to access multiple data items. For example, if the sales for widgets is in a separate file from sales for whizbangs, Q&A could not answer the question, "State the total sales of widgets and whizbangs." However, you could get the information by asking for the sales in separate inquiries.

Paradox. Paradox (Borland International, Inc.) is a *relational* DBMS with an AI technology based on the query by example approach developed by IBM. It does not have NLP capability, but it has an inference capability that allows users to retrieve information from the database with only a most cursory knowledge of its inner details. Users are presented with a graphic representation of an empty record in the database called the query table, which they fill in with data exemplary of the desired result of the search. By analyzing these entries, Paradox infers which information users are looking for and takes appropriate action by creating an answer table on a screen to display its findings. Users may stipulate which fields should be included in the report and/or make changes in the query table. Paradox provides two major advantages: ease of use and correct interpretation of the user's request. The program uses an heuristic query optimization approach to improve the efficiency of the database search.

Other Interfaces

Although natural language front-ends for DBMS products are the most common use of natural language processors, other popular software packages are expected to incorporate front-ends eventually. Spreadsheets, for example, would be easier to use if a natural language interface were available. Some such packages are available. An example is HAL (for human access language), which is now embedded in Lotus 1-2-3 (release 3.1 or newer). It is designed to interface with the Lotus 1-2-3 spreadsheet by allowing users to carry out the various program functions by simply typing in English-language commands.

Natural language front-ends for operating systems are another possibility. Such a program has been created using artificial intelligence techniques for the UNIX operating system. UNIX is a multiuser, multitasking operating system used mostly on larger minicomputers. However, versions such as XENIX are available for the larger personal computers. UNIX, an operating system originally developed by AT&T, is one of the most powerful and useful available. It is somewhat difficult to use, however, because of its complex command structure. A natural language front-end called UNIX Consultant has been developed that allows users to ask in English how to go about accomplishing specific actions in UNIX. For instance, to delete a file in the UNIX operating system, you must type "rm" followed by the file name. If you don't know how to do this, you may simply ask in English, "How do I eliminate a file?" UNIX Consultant will come back with an answer to your question. The program itself doesn't automatically implement the function, but it tells you how to do it.

Already several universal front-ends have been created. Typical of these are NaturalLink described earlier. Its menu-driven format is extremely flexible and adaptable to all kinds of application programs.

Even though natural language processing is nowhere near perfect, its level of development is high enough to provide a certain degree of usefulness. It is becoming more widely used every day. It is a major trend in application software and you can expect to see it continue to grow. As natural language processing research develops, further additions and improvements will be made.

Interfaces to Expert Systems

NLP is especially important to expert systems. All of the following activities profit greatly from a natural language interface: managing a dialogue with a nontechnical user; providing a consultation; explaining a recommendation in the user's terms, in particular the reasoning behind it; and finally, acquiring new knowledge using a knowledge engineer or even directly from a domain expert. For example, one of the earliest expert systems, Stanford University's MYCIN (providing treatment advice in the infectious disease domain—see Appendix C in Chapter 3) has a natural language interface which is especially useful in its question and answer mode. Language Craft (Carnegie Group, Inc.) provides a natural language interface to knowledge-based systems. It implements several unusual clause types. It is produced in LISP and is available for DEC machines and LISP workstations.

Integrating NLP and ES. As described earlier, NLP is being used as a front-end to databases. Such a combination requires extensive definitions of business terms in the NLP dictionary. Expert systems that already have knowledge about these terms in their knowledge bases can be added to, and therefore greatly increase the capabilities of, the system.

Figure 8.7 demonstrates a before-and-after structure of such a combination. Part *a* shows a typical use of a database with a DBMS; the user must know the DBMS language, which may take weeks of training. Part *b* adds NLP, which makes the communication easier yet very limited. The NLP dictionary must be prepared to understand a diversified natural language (e.g., business terminology) and to translate it to DBMS-limited commands.

The connection of NLP and a DBMS can be very difficult especially when large computers are involved. This is where ES can be of help. As shown in part *c*, an ES can improve communication by allowing the NLP to use the knowledge of the ES. A commercial product that combines ES and NLP

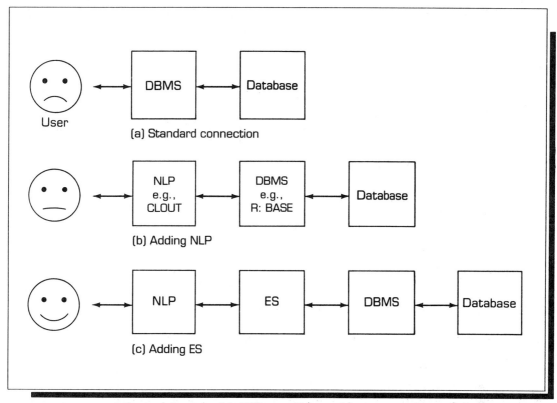

FIGURE 8.7 Ease of Communication with Different Types of Integrated Systems

is Conversational Advisory System. For further discussion of this topic see Harris (4).

Interfaces to Application Programs

NLP can be used as an interface for software application programs. For example, Security Pacific Bank developed an interface to its cash management system (called SPACIFICS). The system gives corporate clients of the bank the ability to monitor, manage, and initiate activities over communication channels, in plain English. Users do not need to learn a complex interface. The program can generate reports as well.

Other Tools for NLP

In addition to specific tools for databases and spreadsheets, there are more general-purpose NLP tools. One example is NL-Builder (Synchronetics, Inc.). This product, which is available for personal computers and minicomputers, is a shell that allows one to build a variety of natural language applications that range from message understanding to foreign language translation.

Limitations and Disadvantages

The advantages and benefits of natural language interfaces are relatively clear, but there are some disadvantages. First, natural language interfaces add cost and complexity to any system. A natural language front-end can cost upward of $50,000 on large mainframe systems. Minicomputer front-ends are much less expensive, but they still cost between $10,000 and $25,000 for a major system. Natural language interfaces for personal computers sell from $100 to $300 if they are not built in. Integrated systems add cost to the software regardless of their form.

Such systems also take up additional memory space. As a result, the computer on which they run must have more RAM than would be needed to run the application program alone.

Another disadvantage of a natural language interface is that it usually takes more time to access the data than other methods do. When standard commands or query languages are used to access information in a DBMS, an experienced programmer can get to the information quickly with a few simple keystrokes. Commands are short mnemonics that tell the DBMS or query language what to do. To get the information using natural language, a complete sentence has to be typed; in many cases multiple sentences have to be typed. Sometimes questions may not be immediately accepted and must be rephrased and keyed in again. All of this, of course, takes time. Then, the interface itself must interpret the question or sentence. It must search for key words, parse, activate the knowledge base, or otherwise go through gyrations to get to the data. Even though most front-ends are reasonably fast, some are sluggish at best.

Excessive access time may or may not be a disadvantage. With today's systems, increased time is the price one must pay for making that access easier and available to anyone.

8.10   Language Translation

One of the earliest proposed NLP applications was language translation. The language barrier has always been a problem in dealing with people from other countries. A language barrier also exists between human beings and machines. NLP is being used to break down those language barriers.

Natural Language to Natural Language

Many people would like to be able to read material published in other languages. Wide availability of general translations does not exist, and early computer scientists proposed the computer as a solution to the problem. In the late 1950s and early 1960s, language translation became a major computer project. It was heavily funded by the government, and the goal was to create a system that would translate Russian into English.

The Soviet Union launched the first satellite, Sputnik, back in 1957. The great concern in the United States was that the Soviet Union was far ahead of it technically and that massive programs should be instituted to correct this condition. Major funding programs were created to increase engineering and scientific education. Many felt that by making the Russian technical literature available to U.S. scientists and engineers, advancements could be expedited. As a result, the computer language translation project was highly regarded.

Early translation systems did nothing more than a word-for-word substitution. The translator looked up the Russian words in the input string, extracted their English-language equivalent from the dictionary, and made the substitution. Other minor adjustments were made to correct for differences in word sequencing; no other major changes were made.

The quality of such translations was incredibly poor. Typically, less than 50 percent of the translation was valid. The system simply could not deal with the wide variations in word meanings or the nuances and subtleties of language. Many of the translations were not only worthless, but hilarious. After considerable expense and effort, these early language translation programs were abandoned. For many years, no major language translation efforts were made. Yet basic research did continue.

Today, language translation has been reborn. With NLP, it is now possible to perform highly reliable translations of excellent quality. The translation task may be very complicated (see Box 8.2). These language translation systems use parse as described earlier. By analyzing the syntax and semantics of the sentence, translation accuracies of 80 percent or more can be achieved. If preceded by editing to simplify complicated sentence structures, accuracies of 90 percent or more can be achieved. Further improvements can be made by having a human translator polish the machine translation.

Today, there are many companies whose business is strictly performing language translations by computer. Translations are possible in most of the European languages, Arabic, and Japanese—to and from English. NLP is speeding up the translation process and, in many cases, costs significantly less than human translators. Even though some of the translations are still rough, they are in most cases acceptable simply because they are better than no translation at all.

One of the most interesting approaches to language translation is the concept of creating a special intermediate language generally referred to as an *interlingua*. The interlingua is an artificial language that contains symbols, rules, syntax, and logic so that any language can be converted to it. Using the interlingua, all translations would convert one language into the interlingua, which would then be retranslated into the final target language. Although such an interlingua has been used on a small scale, no one has yet developed an artificial language broad enough and useful enough to be used with all natural

Box 8.2: A Translating Challenge

The long word shown in the picture below is in the Thai language. It means "welcome to a beautiful Thailand." The symbols appear in four levels: low case, centered regular symbols (in the middle), and upper and lower small symbols.

ขอต้อนธับสู่ดวามสวยงามของเมืองไทยและ

Sometimes there are even five levels.

To begin with, it is difficult to place five levels in a computer. Furthermore, there are forty-six regular letters in the Thai alphabet which are combined to create very long words. Finally, the meaning of many words in Thai depends on the voice level at which these words are spoken.

Your challenge is to build an NLP system that will translate to and from Thai!

languages. There are such wide variations from one language to another that it is difficult to construct the interlingua. No one knows enough about the various languages to be able to develop a useful interlingua. For now interlingua remains a concept that one day may be implemented.

One of the largest translation efforts is taking place in Paris as part of the European Common Market project to enable interlingual document translation. The project uses an intermediate representation for French called "Conceptual Graphics"—an idea that can be viewed as an extension of conceptual dependency theory. It is implemented in PROLOG and in its first stage succeeded in translating from French to other languages and back to French, passing through the intermediate representation. One of the problems is that the intermediate representation is still too specific for directly generating from it natural language constructs in other languages.

Machine Language to Machine Language

If natural language processing techniques can be used to convert one natural language to another, then presumably they can also be used to convert one computer language to another. This is, in fact, the case. Artificial intelligence techniques based on NLP are now being applied widely to translation between different programming languages.

One of the problems that has plagued software development from the beginning is the inability to use a program written for one mainframe machine on another mainframe computer. This problem has its origin in the languages used by the two machines. In most cases, the languages are unique to the machines, thereby making the software unique to the machines. The problem has led to considerable duplication of effort and unnecessary software costs. There is an enormous waste of good software and a lot of "reinventing the wheel" going on because of the lack of transportability.

During the development of higher-level programming languages, some effort was made to standardize languages. Considerable effort was made, for example, with FORTRAN and COBOL. Yet, despite these standardization efforts, many different dialects of these languages exist. Total transportability is still not possible. However, the conversion of one dialect of FORTRAN to another dialect of FORTRAN is easier than converting between different languages. Still, the effort is considerable. Most programmers find that it is easier to write new software.

To make software more widely available, it would be desirable to have a standard language that all mainframe computers could understand. Unfortunately, this is not the case. Many different languages are available and programmers are free to choose the one they like best or that best fits the application. As a result, the lack of transportability and its resulting inefficiency continue.

As the shortage of programmers grows more acute and as software development costs rise, the transportability problem becomes more of an issue. Some solution is needed. This is particularly true with very large systems such as those used in the government and the military. Now, software developed for an older system must be totally rewritten and debugged when the computer system is upgraded to the newer, larger, and faster models. The costs of conversion are unacceptable in some cases; and so many government installations continue to use their very old computers. (Punch cards are still in use for data input in some places!)

Several companies are now developing special AI-based software that will perform automatic language translation. Similar forms of automated translators perform conversions from one dialect of a language to another. Systems are now available for FORTRAN, COBOL, and PL/1.

The more common conversion need is between two different languages. Numerous AI programs are being developed to make such translations. Two of the target output languages are Ada and C. Both of these are modern, advanced languages that are widely used in new software. Ada, for example, is a flexible language developed by the U.S. Department of Defense in an effort to standardize software for military applications. Most of the department's new software will be written in the Ada language, but the considerable existing base of software will have to be converted. Using automated NLP-like translators will save considerable time and effort.

Both Ada and C are essentially standardized languages. Although variations exist, there are fewer dialects and minimal differences between the two. For this reason, converting software to these two languages makes the programs easier to transport to a wider range of computers.

Automatic computer language translators are essentially the same techniques used in natural language understanding programs. Figure 8.8 is a block diagram of a typical system. As in other natural language systems, the parser decomposes the input statements of a language into its basic elements, producing a parse tree. Of course, the parser contains a built-in lexicon that recognizes various input terms. The parse tree is then translated into another format known as the generalized intermediate form (GIF) by a rule-based processor. This is an expert-system-like program that translates the parse tree made up of the input language instructions and commands and converts them to the GIF. The GIF is like an interlingua into which any language can be converted and vice versa.

Next, the GIF drives another rule-based processor, which effectively translates the GIF representation into the lines of code in the target language.

Software translators are a relatively new concept and only a few have been developed. They have, however, proven remarkably successful. As development continues, the process will be refined and new techniques will be uncovered. The result will be faster, easier, and lower-cost translations between the various languages. This should make software available for a wider range of computers and should greatly reduce software development expenses.

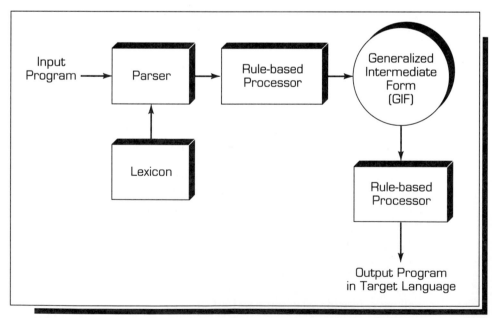

FIGURE 8.8 Block Diagram of a Computer Language Translation System

Machine Language to Natural Language

Another use for a natural language capability (this time using mainly the generator function) is providing means to translate a machine language representation to a natural language output. One example is an expert system built by Sedlock and associates to generate full-text English-language summaries to a large government database (Sedlock [11]). The system performs complex inferences using the information contained in the database. It is written in QUINTUS PROLOG and runs on a Sun workstation.

8.11   Grammar Analysis

Another application of natural language processing is grammar analysis. This is done with a special NLP program that converts poor writing to acceptable writing. Written communications in business are extremely important, but the quality of written business documents is generally poor. Even though we spend years in school learning English grammar, spelling, and word usage, many of us still write poorly. Special **grammar analyzer** programs can be used to process business communications and improve them.

To use a grammar analyzer, the user keys in a paragraph, memo, report, or other written document. Then the grammar analyzer takes over and performs a variety of functions. First, it checks spelling. Like most natural language processing programs, the grammar analyzer contains a rather large dictionary. In some cases, the dictionary has to be unusually large to analyze a wide range of business and technical communications.

In addition to checking spelling, the grammar analyzer looks for commonly misused words and phrases. It also analyzes unnecessarily long phrases and makes suggestions for shortening them to one word that means the same thing. For example, it might shorten the phrase *in view of the fact that* to the single word *since*. The analyzer also checks for subject and verb agreement, split infinitives, and sexist phrases. Even punctuation is checked.

Some grammar analyzing programs can determine reading level. Reading levels correspond to school grade levels. For example, text with a reading level of eighth grade is easier to read and comprehend than text at the twelfth-grade level. Reading level is generally computed by one of several formulas, which count the number of words per sentence and the number of multisyllabic words used in the sentence. The shorter the sentence and the fewer multisyllabic words used, the easier the text is to read. The grammar analyzer counts the words and syllables in a block of text and computes the reading level. You can then make adjustments to the text if reading level is important.

Some grammar analyzers also fully analyze each sentence; they break each word down into its part of speech and show the relationships among words. This is an easy job because they all create a parse tree which does this anyway. The grammar analyzer, in effect, diagrams the sentence for you. This allows a better representation of the sentence and more thorough analysis.

Perhaps the largest and most well-known grammar analyzer is Writer's Workbench. This system was originally developed at Bell Laboratories and is available for computer systems running the UNIX operating system. Writer's Workbench has been refined over the years and does an excellent job of improving writing. IBM has a similar system known as EPISTLE. Like Writer's Workbench, it does in-depth analysis of each sentence in the text and provides most of the functions mentioned earlier.

Several smaller grammar analyzers are available for personal computers. Naturally, they do not perform many functions. They do not have as large a dictionary and as a result are more limited. Nevertheless, they are useful for some applications. With the increased power of personal computers, their grammar analyzers will soon approach the capabilities of those for mainframes.

Grammar analyzers will not eliminate the need to take English grammar in school, but they will help to improve the quality of business writing (see Box 8.3). When they become more widely available, they will be useful in catching gross grammatical errors that embarrass the writer and have serious detrimental effects on the reader. Readers who know grammar and catch such errors usually are turned off by poor usage. As a result, a sale may be lost or the writer's original purpose may be obscured.

Box 8.3: Big Blue Pencil

"The cheese is made of green moon." Even a 5-year-old knows there's something wrong with that sentence, but the largest computers on earth can't identify it as nonsense. That's the problem Karen Jensen is grappling with. An IBM research scientist and linguist, she has spent the last 10 years of her life making Critique—IBM's grammatical-analysis software— understand English.

"Except for fine tuning, grammar parsers have already gone about as far as they can go," Jensen says. "The next frontier is true machine understanding. We've got to impart to computers an understanding of semantics and context." How? The best way, she says, is to use a grammar parser as strong as Critique's to break the sentence down into its essential elements, and then compare its components to a huge database. (The entire *Encyclopaedia Britannica* can already be stored on only one-fifth of a CD-ROM disk.) The computer would look up cheese in its "super-encyclopedia" and scan all the information for references to green or moon or anything similar. If it found none, it would question the sentence's validity. Prototypes based on this approach, Jensen says, will probably appear within five years.

(*Source*: S. Frankel, *The Washington Post*, April 29, 1990, p. D3.)

8.12 Document Management

Abstracting the News

An area in which natural language can be of immense value is the task of automatic indexing and retrieving of documents from a large amount of electronic textual data by actual content analysis rather than by key word search.

One such application of natural language processing is abstracting, which is basically the process of reading a block of text and summarizing the key points. Abstracting programs could be of major help in solving or at least minimizing the effect of information overload. For example, magazine articles could be fed to the abstracting system for a concise summary. Such an NLP program could reduce a four-page article to a paragraph that concisely sums up the main points and facts. The abstracting program boils down the input into a brief statement communicating all the key information. Such abstracting programs are available commercially especially for summarizing financial news. Systems have been designed to read a newspaper article and summarize it into a short paragraph. In addition to being able to read and understand the article, the program must contain sophisticated text generation software that can paraphrase the information (see Box 8.4).

The main problem with such programs is that to be useful over a wide range of subjects, they must have an enormous dictionary of input terms and a massive knowledge base. If the programs are constrained to specific subjects or fields, the abstracting process can be carried out successfully. It will be years before a general-purpose abstracting program will be available. Yet such a program will make our lives easier because it will allow us to assimilate a lot more information in less time (see Box 8.5).

Figure 8.9 (p. 308) illustrates the architecture of the SCISOR system discussed in Box 8.4. First newspaper stories, or questions about the stories that deal with corporate takeovers, are interpreted using the TRUMP (transportable understanding mechanism package) parser and semantic interpreter. Questions asked by users are parsed with the same understanding mechanism that was used for the input stories. The questions are stored along with the stories for future user modeling and to enable the system to answer a user's question when the answer comes along, if it was not known to the system at the time it was posed. After answers to input questions have been retrieved, they are passed to the KING (knowledge intensive generator) natural language generator for expression.

One system that uses NLP techniques to assist handling of a large mass of relatively uniform text documents is ATRANS (Cognitive Systems, Inc.)—a wire-message analysis package. The system, which is used in several banks including Chase-Manhattan in New York, extracts relevant information from unformatted wire messages and formats it according to one of several standards. Other packages from Cognitive Systems include, for instance, ACLASS, which

Box 8.4: GE's SCISOR Reads News

General Electric's Research and Development Center has developed a natural language system called SCISOR (System for Conceptual Information Summarization, Organization and Retrieval), which performs text analysis and question answering in a constrained domain. One application of this system is in analyzing financial news. Here this natural language processor automatically selects and analyzes stories about corporate mergers and acquisitions from an on-line financial service, Dow Jones. It is able to process news at 10 seconds per story. First it determines if the story is about a corporate merger or acquisition. Then it selects information such as the target, the suitor, and price per share. The system also allows the user to browse and to ask questions such as, "What was offered for Polaroid?" or "How much was Bruck Plastics sold for?" The schematic of this answer retrieval process is shown in the accompanying diagram.

This application demonstrates how natural language processors can be used in the knowledge acquisition mode by selecting specific types of articles from a universe of financial news. It also uses a processor as a database interface to permit questioning using ordinary language. Its effectiveness was demonstrated in testing when it proved to be 100% accurate in identifying all 31 mergers and acquisitions stories that were included in a universe of 731 financial news releases from the newswire source.

identifies message types and routes them appropriately, and LOCUS, which processes free-form credit letters. The ATRANS system is considered reliable, it saves human time, and it improves the accuracy of the formatted output due to its consistent operation.

CONSTRUE (Carnegie Group, Inc.) is a system that processes and classifies news messages automatically based on the product TCS (text categorization shell). CONSTRUE is used by Reuters Ltd. to read and classify economic and financial news into predefined categories. Within Reuters, the system is known as TIS (topic identification system) and is connected to two of the company's services. It has a high (96 to 99 percent) level of precision. Considerable savings in time and money are expected with the system, as well as better service (due to faster availability and higher consistency).

The TCS is marketed independently as a content-based online text categorization tool. Due to speed constraints, it uses an intermediate approach, that is, between key word search and NLP. Its main representation uses a set of IF-THEN rules after conversion of the input into an internal format.

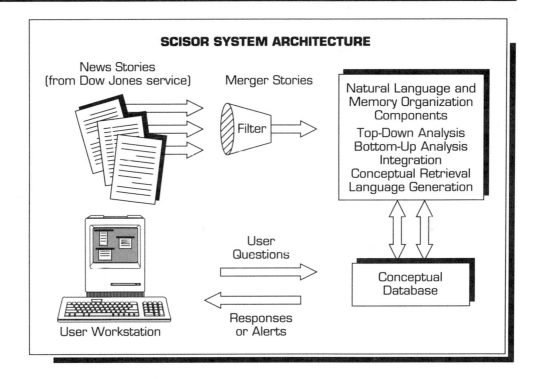

(*Source*: *Management Accounting*, October 1989, p. 35.)

Box 8.5: Intelligent Templates

Computers are beginning to help those who have difficulties in writing business letters or preparing simple legal documents. A new type of software using "intelligent templates" gives the user instant access to an expert. The program asks the user questions (e.g., specifics of the case or objectives). The answers are then used to prepare the necessary documents. The computer gives the user several choices and then a first draft, which can be edited.

An example is Home Lawyer (MECA Ventures). This software includes legal documents that range from promissory notes to lease forms. If you still want to see a lawyer, you can save time and money by bringing a draft document with you.

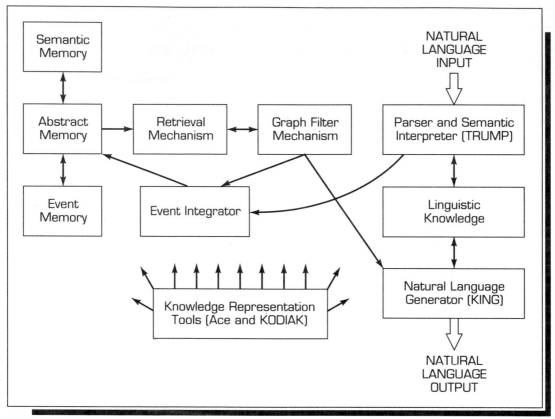

FIGURE 8.9   SCISOR System Architecture (*Source:* L. F. Rau, "Conceptual Information Extraction from Financial News," In *Proceedings, 21st HICSS*. Hawaii, January 1988, p. 504.)

All of these systems use a well-defined, restricted vocabulary and semantics. Within these boundaries, they operate efficiently, savings lots of time, energy, and money. Usually these systems are expended for even relatively simple NLP tasks using human text processors or generators. The applications of NLP are therefore expected to increase and diversify, especially when connected to a voice recognition interface.

Composing Letters

A process called intelligent correspondence generator, ICG (Cognitive Systems, Inc.) allows personalized letters to be written for customer service departments. In addition to having representative input, it draws information from the client's database file. A product called OMBUDSMAN now uses the ICG process. In composing a document, OMBUDSMAN executes the following five steps (Figure 8.10):

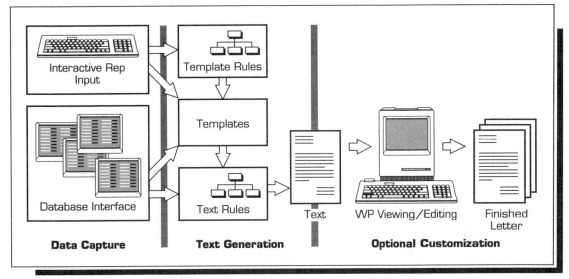

FIGURE 8.10 Functional Breakdown of OMBUDSMAN, a Product That Uses the Intelligent Correspondence Generator (ICG) in Composing Documents (*Source:* Cognitive Systems, Inc., New Haven, Conn.)

1. The user dialogue and the database interface collect the information that is needed to generate the document. This information is placed on the expert system blackboard.
2. Inference rules operate on the blackboard to organize the information and evaluate the situation.
3. Template rules determine the basic structure of the document to be generated.
4. Based on the template selected, generation rules perform lower-level text planning and realization, producing the specific text.
5. The final document is formatted and presented to the user via a word processor.

8.13   Voice (Speech) Understanding

A special AI field related to NLP is speech recognition. AI software can be created to allow a computer to respond to voice input. Voice, or speech, recognition uses an electronic process of converting voice input to a microphone into electronic signals that can be understood and used by the NLP system. Typically, voice recognition is a hardware process, but some advanced systems use AI software techniques. Thus natural language processing and voice recognition can be combined.

The output of the voice recognizer can be used to drive a natural language processing system so that a computer can be operated by voice. Instead of typing in natural language inquiries, all you do is speak into a microphone. The voice recognition equipment converts the sound waves into electronic signals that a natural language interface can understand. Then NLP takes over and interprets what is said and causes other actions to take place. Several commercial voice recognition systems are available, but like natural language processors, their vocabulary is limited. Nevertheless, they make it possible to operate a computer in an entirely new and easier way.

Relationships between NLP and speech recognition are described by White [16]. The field of speech recognition is described in detail in the next chapter of this book.

Chapter Highlights

- □ Most communication with computers is difficult because it takes place via special formal languages made up commands, symbols, and procedures.
- □ Natural language, such as English or German, refers to the system we use in verbal or written communication with others.
- □ A language is a system of symbols and rules which we use to express our ideas, thoughts, and feelings.
- □ Special artificial intelligence techniques known as natural language processing have been developed to allow human-machine communications to take place in a natural language.
- □ The main objective of a natural language processing program is to "understand" input and initiate some action.
- □ A common type of NLP program uses key word analysis. The input words are scanned and matched against internally stored "known" words. Identification of a key word causes some action to be taken.
- □ ELIZA, an early and famous key word matching program, acts like a nondirective psychiatrist.
- □ The most powerful NLP programs perform a syntactic and semantic analysis on an input sentence.
- □ The syntax, or grammar, of a sentence is determined by a program called a parser that breaks the sentence into its various parts of speech. The parser works in conjunction with a lexicon, or dictionary, of known words.
- □ The meaning of the parsed sentence is determined by semantic analysis, which is done by referencing a knowledge base that makes sense out of the various words.
- □ Some NLP programs contain a text generator that outputs canned statements or develops original replies in response to the natural language input. Sometimes the generator develops special codes to drive other software.
- □ The main application of NLP is in interfaces, or front-ends, to other software. These interfaces let anyone command a computer using natural language rather than a special language.

□ A principal use of natural language front-ends is on database management systems; however, they can be adapted to other types of software as well (e.g., spreadsheets).

□ Natural language add-on interfaces are available for mainframes, minicomputers, and personal computers. The trend is to build the NLP program into the software.

□ A major application of NLP is language translation, converting one natural language to another, thereby helping to overcome language barriers.

□ Translators are also available to convert one computer language to another; this allows programs to be more transportable.

□ Grammar analyzers examine input text to correct spelling and punctuation errors and to identify grammatical problems for the purpose of improving the quality of written documents.

□ NLP is used in abstracting articles or other documents to obtain a concise summary of key points.

Key Terms

conceptual dependency
database management
  system
embedded system
front-end
grammar analyzer
information overload
key word search

lexicon
morpheme
natural language
natural language
  interface
natural language
  processing
parser

pattern-matching
  processing
semantic analysis
syntactic analysis
understander

Questions for Review

1. Define a natural language and natural language processing.
2. What are the major advantages of NLP?
3. Distinguish between NLP and natural language generation.
4. What is meant by an elliptical phrase?
5. Explain how key word search works. What are its major limitations?
6. Explain how the program ELIZA provides answers to questions. What kind of pattern matching does it execute?
7. What is a morpheme?
8. Give an example of how the parser segregates a sentence.
9. Describe the functions of the lexicon.
10. Explain the roles of the understander and the knowledge base in NLP.
11. What is the role of the generator in NLP?
12. What is conceptual dependency? How can it be used in understanding a natural language?
13. What is the purpose of natural language interface?
14. Describe any disadvantages of natural language interfaces.
15. Explain how NLP can be used as a grammar analyzer.

Questions for Discussion

1. What is lexical ambiguity? Provide an example. Also give an example of vague semantics.
2. Obtain access to ELIZA and run a conversation with it. After about twelve to fifteen questions and answers, stop. What are the major limitations of ELIZA?
3. Why are language processing systems that analyze syntax and semantics far more effective than key word search?
4. Obtain NLP/DBMS software (e.g., CLOUT and R:BASE, Q&A). Try to use it. Compare with the use of a regular DBMS to the one supported by NLP.
5. Compare Paradox to Q&A. What are the major differences?
6. The use of NLP as an interface to database management systems is gaining popularity. Explain how NLP increases accessibility to databases.
7. How is the understander related to the lexicon?

References and Bibliography

1. Allen, J. *Natural Language Understanding*. Menlo Park, Calif.: Benjamin-Cummings, 1987.
2. Barnett, J., et al. "Knowledge and Natural Language Processing." *Communications of the ACM* (August 1990).
3. Green, G.M. *Pragmatics and Natural Language Understanding*. Hillsdale, N.J.: Lawrence Erlbaum Associates, 1989.
4. Harris, L.R. "The Natural-Language Connection: An AI Note." *Information Center* (April 1987).
5. Johnson, T. *Natural Language Computing: The Commercial Applications*. London: Ovum, 1985.
6. King, K.G., and R.W. Elliot. "In Plain English Please." *Journal of Accountancy* (March 1990).
7. McDonald, D.D., and L. Bolc. *Natural Language Generation Systems*. New York: Springer-Verlag, 1988.
8. "Natural Language." (Special Section) *Byte* 12 (December 1987):223–276.
9. Rau, L.F. "Conceptual Information Extraction from Financial News." In *Proceedings, 21st HICSS*. Hawaii, January 1988. Also in Trippi, R., and E. Turban, eds. *Investment Management Decision Support and Expert Systems*. New York: Van Nostrand Reinhold, 1990.
10. Schorr, H., and A. Rappaport. *Innovative Applications of Artificial Intelligence*. Menlo Park, Calif.: AAAI Press, 1989.
11. Sedlock, D. "The Natural Language Database Connection." *AI Expert* (July 1988).
12. Shwartz, S. *Applied Natural Language Processing*. Princeton, N.J.: Petrocelli Books, 1988.
13. Thomas, J. "A Primer on Speech Technologies." *IEEE Software* 7 (September 1990):91–92.

14. Trost, H., and E. Buchberger. "Datebank: How to Communicate with Your Database in German (and Enjoy It)." *Interc Comp* 2 (December 1990):67–81.

15. Waltz, D.L., ed. *Semantic Structures: Advances in Natural Language Processing.* Hillsdale, N.J.: Lawrence Erlbaum Associates, 1989.

16. White, G.M. "Natural Language Understanding and Speech Recognition." *Communications of ACM* (August 1990).

17. Wilks, Y., ed. *Theoretical Issues in Natural Language Processing.* Hillsdale, N.J.: Lawrence Erlbaum Associates, 1990.

18. Winston, T.W., et al. "Natural Language Query Processing." *AI Expert* (February 1989).

19. Zamora, A., and E.M. Zamora. "Development of NLP Systems from a Manager's Perspective." In *Managing Artificial Intelligence and Expert Systems*, D.A. De Salvo and J. Leibowitz, eds. Englewood Cliffs, N.J.: Yourdon Books/Prentice-Hall, 1990.

Chapter 9

Speech (Voice) Recognition and Understanding

Voice is a natural and convenient means for people to communicate. The purpose of speech (voice) recognition is to enable voice communication between people and computers. For this to happen the computer needs to recognize and understand the human voice. The AI area that supports such communication is called speech (or voice) recognition and it is the subject of this chapter. The following specific topics are covered:

9.1   Introduction

Speech (voice) recognition is the process by which the computer recognizes normal human speech. When a speech recognition system is combined with a natural language processing system, the result is an overall system that not only recognizes voice input but also *understands* it.

The speech recognition process allows us to communicate with a computer by speaking to it. The term *speech recognition* is sometimes applied only to the first part of the process: recognizing the words that have been spoken without necessarily interpreting their meanings. The other part of the process, in which the meaning of the speech is ascertained, is called **speech (voice) understanding.** It may be possible to understand the meaning of a spoken sentence without actually recognizing every word, and vice versa.

In this chapter we use the term *speech recognition* for both recognition and understanding (if applicable) of voice input to the computer. The speech recognition process is shown in Figure 9.1. The user speaks (usually via a microphone) to the computer. The computer recognizes the meaning of the words or conducts a preliminary recognition and sends it to an NLP device for further processing. Once recognized, words or sentences can be used in a variety of applications.

As we look at how speech recognition is accomplished in a computer, keep in mind that it is one of the most complex and difficult functions to implement. It involves a combination of sophisticated electronic hardware and a computer

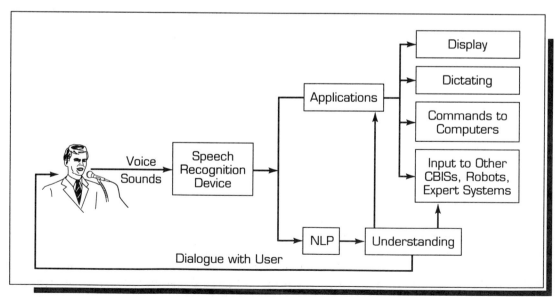

FIGURE 9.1   Process of Speech Recognition

capable of running advanced artificial intelligence software. In this chapter, we also will briefly discuss speech synthesis (generation) which is the process of converting information in the computer to voice output.

9.2   Glossary of Terms

Speech recognition has its own special terminology. The major terms given next are based on *AI Letter* (October 1985).

Dynamic programming is a path-finding algorithm (not to be confused with dynamic programming in operations research) that attempts to find the best alignment between two similar speech patterns.

Speaker-dependent recognition is a technique that requires each user to train the computer to recognize a specific vocabulary of spoken words.

Speaker identification is the process by which a computer can be taught to discriminate between human voices for security purposes.

Speaker-independent recognition is a function that recognizes a limited vocabulary of words spoken by anyone. Generally, the vocabulary is small and customized.

Speech analysis is the process by which sound is converted to digital signals. The two major techniques used to record sound are linear predictive coding (LPC) and adaptive pulse code modulation (ADPCM).

Speech playback is audible speech re-created from digitally stored data.

Speech recognition is the process by which a computer recognizes human speech and takes some action based on the spoken word. Recognition may be either speaker dependent or speaker independent.

Speech synthesis is the process by which human speech is reproduced from stored computer data. The speech may have been stored as digitized speech or as normal computer text. If the speech is reproduced from the textual data, it is commonly referred to as synthesis-by-rule, or text-to-speech.

Speech technology is a general term referring to the engineering techniques for implementing the five major speech capabilities used by computers to interact with humans: speech recognition, speaker identification, speech playback, speech synthesis, and speech analysis.

Training is the process by which a human teaches a computer to "understand" him or her. Normally, training consists of speaking each word of the vocabulary once to "enroll" the voice and at least two additional times to "update" the enrollment.

9.3   Advantages of Speech Recognition

The ultimate goal of speech recognition is to allow a computer to understand the natural speech of any human speaker at least as well as a human listener could understand it. In addition to being the most natural method of communication, speech recognition offers several advantages:

- □ *Ease of access:* Many more people can speak than can type. As long as communication with a computer depends on developing typing skills, many people may not be able to use computers effectively. Although natural language processing may help reduce the severity of the problem, it will not solve it completely.
- □ *Speed:* Even the most competent typists can speak more quickly than they can type. It is estimated that the average person can speak twice as fast as a proficient typist can type (150 versus 75 words per minute).
- □ *Manual freedom:* Communicating with a computer by typing occupies your hands and eyes. There are many situations in which computers might be useful to people whose hands and/or eyes are impaired or are otherwise occupied (product assemblers, pilots of military aircraft, and executives).
- □ *Remote access:* Many computers are set up to be accessed remotely by telephone. If a remote database includes speech recognition capabilities, you can retrieve information by issuing verbal commands into a telephone, or you can enter data via the telephone.
- □ *Accuracy:* Voice input (if properly interpreted by the computer) will have fewer errors than typed input. People err especially in typing names, codes, and complicated words.

Potential areas for application of speech recognition include the following: (1) medical—clinical-medical records, services for the handicapped; (2) entertainment and education—voice-controlled toys and interactive video games, teaching and training enhancements, language translation; (3) manufacturing process control—machine operation, quality assurance, package sorting; (4) office automation—data entry, automatic dictation, automatic transcription; and (5) security—voice-print identification, building access. We will discuss applications in detail in section 9.8.

9.4   Classifying the Technology

Speech recognizers can be classified in several different ways. First, there are systems that recognize individual words and connected words, and there are others that recognize continuous speech. Second, all systems can also be classified as either speaker dependent or speaker independent. Finally, systems can be classified by type of task and environment.

Recognition of Words and Continuous Speech

Individual-Word Recognizers. A **word recognizer,** as its title implies, is a speech recognition system that identifies individual words. Such systems are capable of recognizing only a small vocabulary of single words or possibly simple phrases. To give commands or enter data to a computer using one of these systems, you must state the input information in clearly definable single words given one after another. You should pause between the words; don't run them together.

Creating the hardware and software that will recognize human speech is difficult. The first practical speech recognizers were of the word recognition type. Early pioneering systems were even simpler in that they recognized only individual letters of the alphabet and numbers. Today, the majority of commercial word recognition systems are word recognizers. Most of them have a better than 95 percent recognition accuracy.

Connected-Word Recognizers. There have been attempts to extend word recognizers, which need unnatural pauses between words, to deal with connected words. The **connected-word recognizers** usually are speaker dependent and are restricted in vocabulary and syntax. They work well for a limited set of speech utterances, like digit strings, where words are pronounced similarly regardless of their position in the sentence. These techniques do not, however, extend to natural language sentences.

Continuous Speech Recognizers. **Continuous speech recognizers** attempt to recognize a continuous flow of words. You can speak to them in complete sentences; your input will be recognized and, when processed by NLP, understood. Continuous speech recognizers are far more difficult to build than word recognition systems. The difficulty lies in separating one word from another in a continuous phrase or sentence. When we speak, most of our words slur together in one continuous streak. It is difficult for a system to know where one word ends and another begins. Very sophisticated and complex techniques must be used to deal with continuous speech.

Today, few practical continuous speech systems are in use. Most systems are of the research and experimental type and run on very large and expensive computers. Many of them do not even operate in real time; that is, the information spoken is not recognized instantly as it is with word recognition systems. It may take many minutes for only a few seconds of speech to be analyzed and understood. Yet, progress is being made. Some practical continuous speech recognition systems are now on the market, but they have extremely limited vocabularies.

Speaker Dependency

A **speaker-dependent system** is one that has been customized to the voice of a particular individual. Because there is such a wide variation in speech quality from one person to another, it is difficult to build electronic and computer systems that will recognize *anyone's* voice. By limiting the system to the voice of one person, the system is not only simpler but also more reliable. The computer must be trained to recognize the voice of the particular individual.

Speaker-independent systems are those that anyone can use. The computer is not trained to recognize the voice of a specific person. Instead, the speech recognizer is designed to be as versatile as possible so that even though voice characteristics may vary widely from one speaker to another, the system can recognize them. Most speaker-independent systems are incredibly complex and costly. They also have very limited vocabularies.

A recent variation of speaker-independent systems is **speaker-adaptive systems.** Essentially, a speaker-adaptive system adjusts to the speech patterns of a specific speaker during a *short*, initial interactive training session.

Task Types and Environments

Another characteristic of speech recognition systems is the specific task for which they are intended. The size of the vocabulary that has to be recognized, the acoustic similarity between words in the domain of the task, and the grammar used by the user and accepted by the system are all important factors. For instance, the difficulty of grammar can range from a very constrained syntax to an almost natural language, context-sensitive grammar. The amount of constraint imposed by the grammar can be measured by the *perplexity* measure. This is a measure of the average number of words allowed at each node of the grammar. Early systems in the 1970s (e.g., HEARSAY of Carnegie-Mellon University) had a perplexity of less than 5. Such grammars enable a very low error rate. Increasing perplexity usually results in a significant loss of accuracy. However, only high-perplexity grammars can be used for tasks requiring free (or almost free) speech input (e.g., dictation).

Besides the device, speaker, and task characteristics, it is important to consider the environment in which the speech recognition system has to work. For example, noise type and noise level, position of the microphone, manner of users' speech, speed of speech, and general environmental circumstances are all factors that may affect the quality of speech recognition.

9.5   How Speech Recognition Systems Work

Converting Voice to Computer Language

All types of speech recognition systems use the same basic techniques. The voice input to the microphone produces an analog speech signal. Then an **analog-to-digital converter** converts the speech signal into binary words compatible with a digital computer. The binary version of the input voice is then stored in the system and compared to previously stored binary representations of words and phrases. The computer searches through the previously stored speech patterns and compares them one at a time to the current speech input. When a match occurs, recognition is achieved; the spoken word in binary form is then written on a video screen or passed along to a natural language understanding processor for additional analysis.

Training

Since most recognition systems are speaker dependent, it is necessary to train a system to recognize the dialect of each individual user. **Training** (also called **user enrollment**) involves asking each new user to provide at least one example of each word in the vocabulary. The computer shows a word on the screen, the user reads it aloud, and the computer digitizes the user's voice and stores it.

One problem with training is that the user is being asked to read the *entire* vocabulary in the database (sometimes twice). With a large system (10,000 to 15,000 words in certain domains), this can be a major task. One way around it is to ask the user to read aloud only a sample of the vocabulary (say, 500 to 1,000 words). Based on the sample, the machine can predict how the user will say a word it has never heard the user say.

Speaker-adaptive systems permit the computer to conduct the training during a short, initial interactive session. Such systems, of course, are more complex and expensive.

9.6   Word Recognizers

Now let's be more specific and look at a typical speaker-dependent word recognizer. Refer to Figure 9.2. Voice input is applied to a microphone. The electrical analog signal from the microphone is fed to an amplifier where it is increased in level. The amplifier will contain some kind of automatic gain control (AGC) to provide an output signal in a specific voltage range, even though the input signal may vary from weak to loud or anything between.

The analog signal representing a spoken word is a complex waveform that contains many individual frequencies. It may look something like that shown in Figure 9.3. Such complex waveforms are made of signals of individual frequencies of various amplitudes and phase relationships combined. The way to recognize the spoken word is to break that complex input signal into its component parts. This is usually done with a set of filters. A filter is an electronic circuit that passes or rejects frequencies in a certain range. In speech recognition equipment, bandpass filters (BPFs) are used. These filters pass on frequencies only in a certain frequency range; all others are rejected. In some simple systems, a minimum of three filters is used to pass the low-, medium-, and high-frequency components of the input signal. In more complex systems, as many as sixteen to thirty-two filters are used. Of course, the more filters that are used, the more precise the analysis of the signal and, therefore, the higher the probability of accurate recognition.

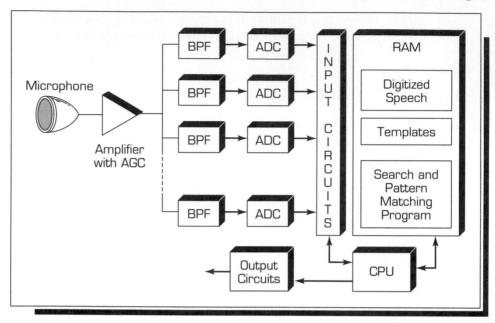

FIGURE 9.2   Speaker-dependent Word Recognizer

The filters themselves can be implemented in a variety of ways. In early systems, standard inductor-capacitor filters were used. Active filters using operational amplifiers with resistor-capacitor feedback networks have also been used. Today, however, switched-capacitor digital filters are widely used, simply because they can be implemented in integrated circuit form. They are smaller and less expensive than other types of filters.

The filter outputs are then fed to analog-to-digital converters (ADCs). The analog signals are thus translated into digital words. The analog-to-digital converter samples the filter outputs many times per second. Each sample

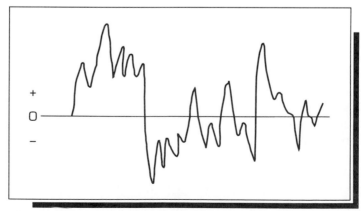

FIGURE 9.3   Analog Signal Representing a Spoken Word

represents a different amplitude of the signal as shown in Figure 9.4. Evenly spaced vertical lines designate the amplitude of the audio filter output at the instant of sampling. Each value is then converted to a binary number proportional to the amplitude of the sample. The ADCs feed input circuits controlled by the CPU. All of the digital values are stored in a buffer area in a large RAM. This digital information represents the spoken word. The CPU may now access the information in RAM and process it further.

The main linguistic information in normal speech is in the frequency range of 200 Hz to 7 kHz. Recognizing speech over telephone lines is more difficult since there is an inherent bandwidth limitation of 300 Hz to 3.3 kHz. Typically, voice sounds have a harmonic spectrum with sharp prominences (these are the resonant frequencies of the vocal tract, the *formats*), whereas voiceless sounds usually have a continuous spectrum with few peaks.

In speaker-dependent word recognition systems, the computer must first be taught to recognize the input words of a particular speaker. The speaker planning to use the system is asked to speak all of the words he or she plans to use so that they may be recorded by the system. As each word is stated, it is processed by the filters and analog-to-digital converters. The binary representation of each of these words becomes a **template,** or standard, against which future spoken words will be compared. The templates for each of the words are retained in memory. Some systems require that the speaker say each word multiple times so that multiple templates of the same word are created. Then, a special processing program generates the final template, which is an average of the multiple inputs.

Once all the templates are stored, the system can go into its active mode. Now it will recognize spoken words. As each word is spoken, it is processed and its binary equivalent is stored in RAM. Then the computer goes to work. A search routine begins looking through the templates and compares them to the binary input pattern. As you can imagine, even in speaker-dependent systems rarely is the input word said exactly the same way each time. There will be slight variations in amplitude or loudness of the signal. Furthermore,

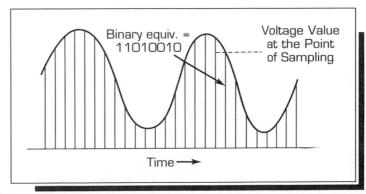

FIGURE 9.4 Sampling and Converting of Filter Outputs to Binary Form by an Analog-to-Digital Converter

the pronunciation of the word may take more or less time. The word may also be said at a different pitch, that is, with a higher or lower frequency. In any case, even if the word is said as similarly as possible each time, there will be variations. For that reason, there will never be a perfect match between the binary input word and the template. The search and pattern-matching program, therefore, is designed to look for the "best fit." The pattern-matching process uses statistical techniques to do this.

One pattern-matching technique causes all of the values of the binary input word to be subtracted from those in the corresponding values in the template. If the values are the same, the difference will be zero. Since the values won't perfectly match, the subtraction will produce some difference or error. The smaller the error, the better the match.

Once the computer searches its memory, comparing the templates to the spoken input word, at some point a best match will occur. It is at that point that the word is identified. A binary or ASCII version of that word may then be passed along to the video display or used in some other manner.

As you can see, a considerable amount of processing takes place before a word is recognized. The search process takes a considerable amount of time. Even though the CPU may be able to process at a high rate of speed, it must make many comparisons before recognition occurs. This means that high-speed processors are required.

In addition, memory sizes in word recognition systems must be large. Even though a spoken word may last only a few hundred milliseconds, that will translate into many thousands of binary words stored in memory. For the system to have a large vocabulary, a large RAM is necessary. Various data conversion techniques have been developed to reduce the number of binary words in a template.

An important issue that has to be addressed while matching templates is aligning words and templates correctly in time before computing the appropriate similarity score. This process is called **dynamic time warping.** It combines dynamic programming techniques with treatment of the time axis as an elastic band that can be stretched or shrunk to maximize overall similarity. This process recognizes that different speakers pronounce the same words at different speeds as well as elongate different parts of the same word. The process is especially important for the speaker-independent recognizers.

It is important to point out that the RAM and CPU shown in Figure 9.2 do not belong to a general-purpose computer. Instead, they are part of the speech recognition system itself. To minimize the computational burden on the computer to which the unit is attached, a *dedicated* RAM and CPU are used to handle the search, pattern matching, and other chores.

9.7 Continuous Speech Systems

Although continuous speech systems use the same basic techniques as individual word recognizers, they are more complex. They normally have larger vocabularies and a higher processing speed to achieve real-time recognition. The main problem in continuous recognition is that it is difficult to distinguish individual words. If the continuous speech is input as individual words with short pauses between them, the system will be far simpler and more reliable. A pause of 50 to 300 milliseconds is sufficient for the system to identify the beginnings and endings of adjacent words. However, if true continuous speech is to be processed, other approaches must be taken. In continuous speech, words are run together. In such cases more sophisticated processing techniques are needed.

One approach is to use phoneme rather than word analysis. A **phoneme** is the smallest recognizable unit of sound in a language. It is a family of closely related speech sounds (phones) represented by the same symbol. A typical phoneme is the pronunciation of an individual letter or group of letters to produce a distinctive sound. A phoneme is to the spoken word what letters of the alphabet are to the written word. There are approximately forty phonemes in the English language, and all English words are simply a continuous stream of phonemes.

Speech recognition systems that use phoneme analysis contain phoneme templates stored in RAM. The input words are converted into their binary form and then matched against these phonemes. As each phoneme is recognized, it is grouped with others in an effort to form words. The resulting combinations are then matched against known words in the system. Phoneme analysis is far more difficult and time consuming, but it produces superior results in continuous speech systems.

Another approach used in continuous speech systems is to attempt to predict which word will come after another. In certain systems where the input possibilities are limited, it is possible to anticipate the input and store many different variations of it. Once the first word in the speech is identified, the system goes along to predict which one of several words may follow next. This in turn leads to a prediction of the next word in sequence and so on. In this way, the entire input statement can be identified.

Because of the complexity of continuous speech techniques, it will be some time yet before general-purpose real-time systems are available. More research plus technology breakthroughs will be required to create usable systems. Today, a few very limited continuous speech systems are available, but word recognition units dominate because they are reliable and modestly priced.

A recent experimental system that introduced several new techniques is the SPHINX system (see Lee [8]) developed at Carnegie-Mellon University. The system is speaker adaptive and it accepts continuous speech. It has achieved speaker-independent word accuracies of 71, 94, and 96 percent with grammars of perplexity measures of 997, 60, and 20, respectively, using a 997-word vocabulary. These results are the best reported for such systems and comparable to the best speaker-independent results. The SPHINX system utilizes probabilistic modeling, new speech models, and adaptation of the probabilistic parameters to suit the actual speaker on hand by interpolating from a small number of adaptation sentences.

9.8   Applications of Speech Recognition

Many applications for speech recognition can be identified in industry, medicine, education, and services. The applications listed in the first part of this section intend to show the wide range of possibilities. In the second part, we will discuss a few applications in more detail.

General Applications

Earlier we said that one of the main benefits of speech input is that it frees the user's hands and eyes for other purposes. Consider a situation in which a computer controls various machines and processes in a factory. Users of such systems are frequently occupied with observing the process and manually handling materials or controlling other machines. In such cases, it is inconvenient to type commands to perform control functions on the computer. If a speech recognition system is used, the user can concentrate on observation and manual operations, yet still control the machinery by voice input commands.

Consider a situation where conveyor belts are used to transport goods from one place to another. During this process, a human operator may be examining or otherwise handling the objects being moved. It may be convenient to simply say "stop" rather than to push a button or type in a command on a computer to stop the conveyor belt. The movement of the conveyor belt could easily be restarted by simply saying "start."

Some airlines use voice control systems to sort baggage by destination. The baggage handler puts the luggage on a main conveyor belt, then states the name of the destination city into a microphone. The piece of luggage is then routed to the correct place by another belt.

Inventory control is another excellent application. In taking inventory, users must have their hands and eyes free to deal with the objects being counted. Voice input permits the object to be identified and counted verbally. This saves considerable time over keyboarding.

A major application of speech processing is in military systems. Voice control of weapons is an example. Again, any time that a user's hands and eyes must be free to perform other activities, speech recognition is of benefit. In combat, soldiers and sailors need all the help they can get.

Jet fighter pilots have their hands full flying planes, yet on most military aircraft in use today there are a number of computers that must be given commands and data. Often, a second person must be on board to handle such operations. But with reliable speech recognition equipment, pilots can give commands and information to the computers by simply speaking into their microphones.

Another relevant application of speech recognition, where verbal communication is the natural mode, is dictating free or almost-free text. A good example is a radiologist scanning hundreds of X-rays and other images while dictating conclusions to a speech-recognizing system connected to a word processor. The radiologist focuses his or her attention on the images rather than on typing text. Certain key words can be expanded automatically to predefine phrases (see section 9.10).

Speech recognition systems are also ideal for any application in which voice rather than a keyboard is normally used. For instance, voice recognition equipment could be used on computers for making airline and hotel reservations. A user would call up the airline reservation service and simply state a particular need to the computer. You could make a reservation, cancel a reservation, or make inquiries about schedules.

Speech recognition could also make large databases accessible by telephone. You would simply call up the database and state the desired information, and it would be provided to you via the telephone. A voice synthesizer converts the binary output data into a verbal response. A relevant example for using speech recognition over the telephone is an application (to be discussed in more detail in section 9.10) in which customers access their bank account, give instructions, and receive verbal responses—all over the telephone line.

A similar application is using speech recognition (and synthesis) over telephone lines for communicating with people, where binary data is not a viable alternative. For instance, an automatic call-handling system can record a caller's name, ask the called person whether he or she accepts the call, get a positive or negative answer, and act accordingly. Unless there is ambiguity beyond a certain level, no human operator needs to intervene.

An interesting application is to use voice where no other way is available to communicate between the person and the machine. For example, some severely disabled people are not able to use their hands at all, or not well enough, yet they can use their voice to control a computer which, in turn, controls a mechanical system that assists the person. An experimental system of this type is assisting quadriplegic patients to lead a productive life and to continue their work in their work environment. The speech recognition system is connected to a mobile robot arm.

Specific Applications

In this section, we review several examples of speech recognition applications. All of these systems are integrated with other computerized systems.

ANSER Banking Services System. ANSER (Nakatsu [11]), a system developed by the Japanese Nippon Telegraph and Telephone (NTT) Company, has been in use since 1981. It combines speaker-independent speech recognition with speech synthesis into a telephone information system that provides services for the banking industry. It has also been introduced in the stock brokerage industry.

The system has a sixteen-word vocabulary: ten digits and six control words (in Japanese). The database includes a large number of speaker variations. The average recognition accuracy for the sixteen-word vocabulary is 96.5 percent.

The system uses a modification of dynamic time warping (a staggered array) to cut down on computation.

In a typical dialogue, a user calls an ANSER center. The system asks the user to identify (by number) the required service, bank branch, account number, and the secret pass number. The user then accesses the customer's bank computer. The bank computer confirms the account and pass numbers, composes an answer, and returns it to ANSER, which converts it to a synthesized voice response.

Of Japan's 612 financial institutions, 583 offered the services by 1990. Total average traffic per month has been about 16 million calls, the peak being more than 1 million per day.

The ANSER system is accessed even more frequently nowadays through the popular medium of facsimile. Accessibility via personal computers and teletext is expected to increase soon. Future developments include larger vocabularies and continuous speech recognition to support even more sophisticated services.

AABS Telephone Calling Service. Another example of a speech recognition system working over the telephone lines, though for quite a different reason, is Northern Telecom's Automated Alternate Billing Service (AABS) system for collect calls, third-number-billed calls, and credit-card-billed calls (Lennig [10]).

In this application, the very nature of the task demands both communication over telephone lines and voice recognition. The system accepts, for instance, a collect call and records the caller's name. It dials the number and asks the called person whether he or she will accept a collect call from the (recorded) caller. The system then has to decide if the answer is yes, no, yes-equivalent, no-equivalent, or an "imposter" (unrecognized word or form). There is a trade-off between the false acceptance rate and the false recognition rate. Commonly the system is used with a false acceptance rate of less than 1 percent and a false rejection rate of less than 5 percent. The false acceptance rate is usually chosen to be less than the false rejection rate because false acceptance of a response triggers a substantially costlier action (unwanted billing or termination of a desired call).

The system has a very small vocabulary (basically *yes, no,* and equivalent forms), but it is speaker independent. It uses dynamic time warping and employs from 5 to 200 templates for different pronunciations of every word.

The system was implemented in May 1989 and has been used in thirty-six sites in the Ameritech and NYNEX regions. Customer satisfaction seems to be high due mainly to the sophisticated dialogue (using digital encoded voice) designed into the system and the excellent rejection rate of imposters.

Speech Interfaces for Medical Expert Systems. An important use of speech interfaces that is expected to expand in the future is interaction with expert systems. In particular, physicians often need decision support but are reluctant to type many details; the importance of an easy, user-friendly interface cannot be overemphasized in such situations.

Stanford University's medical informatics group has developed several speech interfaces for existent medical diagnostic expert systems (Shiffman et al. [14]). One of these is called OMR-DT; it includes a voice interface to the well-known expert system Quick Medical Reference (QMR), which performs diagnoses in internal medicine. Two main programs were developed.

The *Term Identifier* program uses the Voice Navigator XA Speech Recognition System, an isolated-word, speaker-independent recognizer (produced by Articulate Systems). The system requires a training session for each user. The Term Identifier program, which runs on a Macintosh computer under the HyperCard development tool, helps physicians navigate through a list of clinical and laboratory findings and enter only the relevant ones. This review process is important because the underlying expert system expects only certain terms (which are in its rule base).

Frame Browser is a program used to learn about the required vocabulary for the expert system, described as generic *frames* (e.g., abdominal pain), and the characteristics of and relationships among frames. It runs on a NEXT workstation and its interface is a speech recognition system called DS200 (from Speech Systems, Inc.). The system recognizes continuous speech, is speaker independent, and has a vocabulary of more than 38,000 words. It requires a dictionary and a grammar for each set of sentences it is expected to recognize. In the Frame Browser application, there is one dictionary of 700 words and three grammar packages that are switched according to the context.

The program identifies first the required generic frame name uttered by the user (e.g., abdominal pain); then it displays the generic frame or an instantiated version of it (e.g., intermittent or chronic abdominal pain). In one experiment, about 90 percent of the uttered frames were recognized, without any training, when physicians read names from a list they had not seen before.

Speech Recognition in Radiology. An interesting application that has been in use for several years is the generation of radiological reports by voice entry. The system has to recognize voice input from a radiologist who is examining various types of images (X-ray, ultrasound, CAT scan, etc.), expand certain key words into standard phrases, enable interactive correction of the output on a terminal, and finally produce an acceptable professional-quality output (a summary of the findings).

One example is the Kurzweil Voice Works Speech Recognition System which has a maximum capacity of between 5,000 and 10,000 words depending on their length (from Kurzweil Applied Intelligence, KAI). It incorporates a voice processor, the Acoustic Phonetic Analysis (also from KAI). The programs run on a 386 PC (equipped with 4MB RAM, 30MB disks, and a 80386 math coprocessor).

The application in radiology, called Voice Rad, requires a training process (at least two samples of each word to be used by the user).

The system includes an automatic adaptive feature that optimizes the recognition process. Certain "trigger phrases" can create whole lines or even reports. The system allows the use of linguistic knowledge, not just acoustic knowledge, to improve recognition. It does not recognize continuous speech, but it is capable of recognizing connected words (linked phrases) such as *there are* or *seen at this time* if these are included in the vocabulary. The system requires a 180-millisecond pause between words, which necessitates some behavioral adaptation, and an 18 to 53 percent longer dictating time (see Robbins et al. [13]).

The Kurzweil systems are being used in about 150 hospitals (late 1991) mainly in radiology, pathology, and emergency departments. Each system costs about $25,000.

9.9 Issues in Speech Recognition

Performance

The performance of speech recognition systems is expressed by the error rate. To assess the error rate one can measure word accuracy, sentence accuracy, and semantic accuracy. For a detailed discussion see Zue [16].

Reluctance to Use Voice Input

Even though voice input is now a practical reality for computers, many users are still more comfortable with standard keyboard entry. Despite the fact that speech is our primary method of communication, we have grown used to communicating with computers via a keyboard. We hesitate to use speech with computers for several reasons. First, it is necessary to speak slowly and clearly, which is not natural. Second, many people feel self-conscious about talking to a machine. For example, some people speak easily over the telephone, yet they become uncomfortable and tongue-tied when an answering machine is on the other end of the line. In the same way, many individuals are too self-conscious or embarrassed to use a dictating machine. Some people feel that it is abnormal to "speak to yourself." Such discomforts can be overcome; even so it does not appear likely that there will be a mass changeover from keyboard to voice input in the typical office environment in the near future. Perhaps that is good. Just imagine the confusion and interference in a large office when several individuals would be speaking to their computers simultaneously!

The Future

To date, voice recognition systems have not been widely used with computers. The primary reason is that such systems have been limited in their performance and they have been unreliable and costly. But today, through a combination of technological breakthroughs, speech recognition systems are overcoming these deficiencies. They are now a practical alternative for many limited applications (Table 9.1). While such systems are not perfect, their performance is

TABLE 9.1 Sample of Voice Technology Applications

Company	Applications
Scandinavian Airlines, other airlines	Answering inquiries about reservations, schedules, lost baggage, etc.
Citibank, many other banks	Informing credit-card holders about balances and credits; providing bank account balances and other information to customers
Delta Dental Plan (California)	Verifying coverage information
Federal Express	Requesting pickups
Illinois Bell, other telephone companies	Giving information about services; receiving orders
Domino's Pizza	Enabling stores to order supplies; providing price information
General Electric, Rockwell International, Austin Rover, Westpoint Pepperell, Eastman Kodak	Allowing inspectors to report results of quality assurance tests
Cara Donna Provisions	Allowing receivers of shipments to report weights and types of meats and cheeses
Weidner Insurance, AT&T	Conducting marketing research and telemarketing
Mellon Bank of Pennsylvania	Monitoring ATM malfunctions; dialing automatically for service
U.S. Dept. of Energy, Idaho National Engineering Laboratory, Honeywell	Notifying people in case of emergencies detected by sensors
New Jersey Dept. of Education	Notifying parents when students do not come to school; notifying parents about cancellation of classes
Kaiser-Permanente Health Foundation (HMO)	Calling patients to remind them of appointments; summarizing and reporting results
Car manufacturers	Activating radios, heaters, etc., by voice
Texoma Medical Center	Punching in and out by voice to payroll department
St. Elizabeth's Hospital	Prompting doctors in the emergency room to conduct all necessary tests; reporting of results by doctors
Wang Labs	Interpreting computerized analyses by voice
Hospital Corp. of America	Receiving and sending patient data by voice; searching for doctors; preparing schedules and medical records

TABLE 9.2 Speech
Recognition Software
Companies

Decillinix (Sunnyvale, Calif.)
Dragon Data Systems (Vancouver, B.C.)
Heuristics (Sunnyvale, Calif.)
Mountain Computer, Inc. (Scotts Valley, Calif.)
Peachtree Software (Atlanta, Ga.)
Speech Plus, Inc. (Mountain View, Calif.)
Supersoft (Champaign, Ill.)
Syntelect (Phoenix, Ariz.)
Tecmar, Inc. (Cleveland, Ohio)
Texas Instruments (Dallas, Tex.)
Votan, Inc. (Freemont, Calif.)
Votrax (Troy, Mich.)

excellent if their use is focused or constrained. Further developments are expected to bring significant improvements and cost reductions before the year 2000.

Speech Recognition Software

More than a dozen companies offer development tools for speech recognition and speech synthesis for both microcomputers and larger computers. Products change periodically. Companies that are active in marketing such products are listed in Table 9.2.

9.10   Speech Synthesis (Generation)

Speech synthesis, or **voice synthesis,** refers to the technology by which computers "speak." The synthesis of voice by computer differs from a simple playback of a prerecorded voice by either analog or digital means. As the term *synthesis* implies, the sounds that make up words and phrases are constructed electronically from basic sound components and can be made to form any desired voice pattern.

Voice synthesis has already come of age. Several good, commercially available voice synthesis packages work on limited domains and encompass phonetic rules. The "voices" generated today are generally flat, artificial voices that are obviously different from human voices, yet they are improving and are easily understandable.

Voice synthesis is not considered to be an AI technology; however, it can be integrated with AI technologies. Voice synthesis is now used in education, for dynamic and interactive queries (e.g., in banking), and for human interaction with technical instruments.

The quality of synthesized voice technology is currently very good, but it remains somewhat expensive. Anticipated lower costs and improved performance of the synthetic voice in the near future will encourage more widespread commercial applications. The opportunities for its use will encompass almost all applications that can provide an automated response to a user, for example, inquiries by employees about payroll and benefits. Several banks already offer a voice service to their customers; the service informs customers about their balance, about which checks were cashed, and so on. Another example is the answer provided when you request a telephone number. For an overview of the topic, see Lee et al. [9], Fink and Holen [3], and Gottesman [4].

Chapter Highlights

- □ Speech recognition technology is based on training the computer to match spoken words to certain patterns of sounds.
- □ Once speech is recognized, it can be further interpreted by a natural language processing program or it can be used directly in applications.
- □ The major advantages of speech recognition are ease of access, greater speed, freedom of hands and eyes, accessibility from remote locations (via telephone), and accuracy.
- □ Speech technology is most useful in situations where people use *very limited, standardized* vocabularies.
- □ Voice technology will have to accommodate normal speech patterns and very large vocabularies, at a reasonable cost, before it can be used extensively.
- □ Speech recognizers can deal with individual words, a small number of connected words, or with continuous speech (sentences and paragraphs).
- □ Voice technology can be speaker dependent, in which training of the computer is necessary, or speaker independent.
- □ Speech recognizers are influenced by the nature of the task (e.g., noise level).
- □ Training is done by showing the user words on the computer screen and asking him or her to read them aloud, at least once.
- □ Training of large vocabularies can be expedited by using only a small sample, or by doing the training during a very short interactive session.
- □ Voice is entered via a microphone; then it is converted to digital (binary) code and stored as templates. Using speech patterns, the computer matches spoken words against the templates.
- □ Continuous speech recognition is much more difficult to execute than word (discrete) recognition.
- □ Speech generation, or synthesis, refers to a non-AI technology by which computers "speak" (that is, convert information in the computer to voice).

Key Terms

analog-to-digital
  converter
connected word
  recognizer
continuous speech
  recognizer
dynamic time
  warping
phoneme

speaker-adaptive
  system
speaker-dependent
  system
speaker-independent
  system
speech synthesis
speech (voice)
  recognition

speech (voice)
  understanding
template
training (user
  enrollment)
voice synthesis
word recognizer

Questions for Review

1. Define speech recognition.
2. What is the difference between speech recognition and speech understanding?
3. What is the purpose of combining NLP with speech recognition?
4. List the major advantages of speech recognition.
5. Describe the difference between word and continuous speech recognizers.
6. List several elements in the environment that may affect the performance of speech recognition.
7. Explain why training is needed and how it is executed.
8. Trace the word recognition process in Figure 9.2. What are the roles of the RAM and CPU in this process?
9. What is the role of templates in speech recognition?
10. How is voice translated to a binary code?
11. Define phoneme and explain its role in speech recognition.
12. Explain speech generation (synthesis).

Questions for Discussion

1. Why is speech recognition considered AI technology?
2. Give several examples of how speech recognition can be applied today and list the benefit(s) in each case.
3. Why is a speaker-independent system preferred over a speaker-dependent one, and why is it so difficult to build?
4. It is said that voice synthesis is *not* AI technology. Why?
5. Describe some task characteristics that are important in speech recognition.
6. Speech recognition applications have been successful in hospitals. What are the major applications and why do you think they have been so successful?
7. The Japanese have developed a language translation system in which you can speak English on one side of the line while another person can speak

Japanese on the other side of the line. The speakers can understand each other even though each understands only one language. What AI technologies are being used in such a system?

8. Many people do not like to talk to machines, even to a telephone answering machine. Why do you think they behave in this manner? What would you suggest to convince them to use a speech recognition system?

9. Compare the concept of phoneme with that of morpheme (Chapter 8).

References and Bibliography

1. Derfler, F.J. "Voice E-Mail." *PC Magazine* (July 1990).
2. Doddington, G.D., and T.B. Schalk. "Speech Recognition: Turning Theory to Practice." *IEEE Spectrum* (September 1981).
3. Fink, D.F., and R. Holen. "Speech Input/Output Increases Industrial Quality Control Standards." *Speech Technology* (March/April 1986).
4. Gottesman, K. "The Reality of Voice Processing: Applications Span Range of Industries." *Journal of Information Systems Management* (Winter 1989).
5. Hixson, J.R. "His Master's Voice: Medspeak Arrives." *Medical Tribune* (December 14, 1989).
6. Hogan, R. "Voice Recognition." *Journal of the American Medical Association* 263 (March 2, 1990).
7. Joost, M.G., et al. "Voice Communication with Computers: A Primer." *Computers and Industrial Engineering* 7 (no. 2, 1983).
8. Lee, K. *Automatic Speech Recognition: The Development of the SPHINX System.* Norwell, Mass.: Kluwer Academic, 1989.
9. Lee, S.M., et al. "Voice Recognition: An Examination of an Evolving Technology and Its Use in Organizations." *Computers and Operations Research* 14 (no. 6, 1987).
10. Lennig, M. "Putting Speech Recognition to Work in the Telephone Network." *Computer* 23 (August 1990).
11. Nakatsu, R. "ANSER, An Application of Speech Technology to the Japanese Banking Industry." *Computer* 23 (August 1990).
12. Peacoke, R.D., and D.H. Graf. "An Introduction to Speech and Speaker Recognition." *Computer* 23 (August 1990).
13. Robbins, A.H., et al. "Radiology Reports: Assessment of a 5000-Word Speech Recognizer." *Radiology* 167 (1988):853–855.
14. Shiffman, S., et al. "Building a Speech Interface to a Medical Diagnostic System." *IEEE Expert* (February 1991).
15. Strathmeyer, C.R. "Voice in Computing: An Overview of Available Technologies." *Computer* 23 (August 1990).
16. Zue, V. "Automatic Speech Recognition and Understanding." In *AI in the 1980s and Beyond,* W.E.L. Grimson and R.S. Patial, eds. Cambridge, Mass.: MIT Press, 1987.

Chapter 10

Computer Vision

In the previous chapters, you have seen how various AI techniques are used to simulate the thinking and reasoning process. But as you know, the human brain does more than just pure thinking and reasoning. It is the central interpreter for all of our senses. The brain must have inputs about its surroundings to control the body. Our senses provide those inputs.

Of our five basic senses—sight, hearing, smell, taste, and touch—sight is probably the most valuable. Hearing is our second most important sense. Chapter 9 showed how computer hearing is implemented. In this chapter, we discuss artificial sight: the computer becomes a seeing machine. Today's computer vision systems are crude compared to real human sight, but they are performing many useful functions. The basics of computer vision involve the following topics:

10.1   Computer Vision Process

A computer mimics human sight in four basic steps: image acquisition, image processing, image analysis, and image understanding. Let's consider each of these steps in more detail.

Image Acquisition

Image acquisition in humans, which begins with the eye, translates visual information into a format that can be further manipulated by the brain. Similarly, a computer vision system needs an eye to take in the sights. In most computer vision systems that eye is a video camera. The camera translates a scene or image into electrical signals. These signals are translated into binary numbers so the "intelligent" computer can work with them.

The output of the camera is an analog signal whose frequency and amplitude represent the brightness detail in a scene. The camera observes a scene, a line at a time, scans it, and divides it into hundreds of fine horizontal lines. Each line creates an analog signal whose amplitude represents the brightness changes along that line.

Digital computers cannot deal with analog signals. For that reason, an **analog-to-digital converter** is required. It converts the analog signal representing one line of information into a stream of many binary numbers. The numbers are stored in a memory and become the raw data that the computer will process.

Image Processing

The next stage of computer vision involves some initial *manipulation* of the binary data. **Image processing** helps improve the quality of the image so it can be analyzed and comprehended more efficiently. Image processing improves the signal-to-noise ratio. The signal, of course, is the information representing objects in the image. Noise is any interference, flaw, or aberration that obscures the objects. Through various computational means, it is possible to improve the signal-to-noise ratio. For example, the contrast in a scene can be improved by removing flaws, such as unwanted reflections. The process is somewhat akin to retouching a photograph to improve its quality. Once the image has been cleaned up and enhanced, it is ready for analysis.

Image Analysis

Image analysis explores the scene to determine major characteristics of the object under investigation. A computer program begins looking through the numbers that represent the visual information to identify specific features and characteristics. More specifically, the image analysis program looks for edges and boundaries. An edge is formed between an object and its background or between two specific objects. These edges are identifiable because of different brightness levels on either side of the boundary. The computer produces a simple line drawing of all of the objects in the scene, just as an artist would draw outlines of all the objects. Image analysis also looks for textures and shadings between lines. Both are useful in helping to identify the scene.

At this point, a considerable amount of computer processing has taken place. Yet, objects still have not been identified and the scene is not yet understood. The processing, however, has prepared the image for the next step.

Image Understanding

The final step in the computer vision process is **image understanding,** by which specific objects and their relationship are identified. This portion of the computer vision process employs artificial intelligence techniques. The previous steps of image processing and analysis were done with algorithms. Now, symbolic processing is used to interpret the scene.

Understanding what is in a scene requires **template matching.** The computer is preprogrammed with prestored binary images or templates that represent specific objects. Using a search program and pattern-matching techniques, the computer looks through the binary information representing the scene and compares it to the various templates. When a match occurs, an object is identified. This template-matching process continues until all of the information in the scene has been analyzed and all of the objects have been identified. The computer then knows what is being viewed. Image understanding can be enhanced by neural computing.

Now that we have reviewed generally the process involved in computer vision, let's expand on each of the four major steps.

10.2   Image Acquisition

As mentioned earlier, a video camera translates the scene to be analyzed into signals. These analog signals are then translated into binary form by an analog-to-digital converter. The binary numbers are stored in random-access memory, then processed by the computer. Figure 10.1 illustrates the concept.

Video Cameras

The two devices most commonly used in computer vision cameras to convert light into an electrical signal are the **vidicon tube** and a **charged coupled device** (CCD) array. The vidicon tube has been around for many years, and it remains the primary device used in commercial television cameras. However, for computer vision systems, CCDs are far more common. These semiconductor

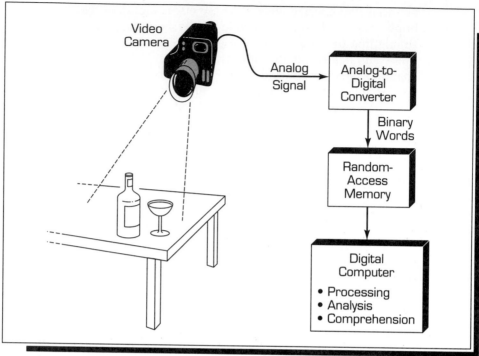

FIGURE 10.1 Image Acquisition

devices offer smaller size, greater light sensitivity, and lower power operation than vidicons. Nevertheless, both the vidicon and the CCD are still used.

Vidicon Tubes. Figure 10.2 is a simplified drawing of a vidicon tube. The key component is the photoconductive target on the left. The lens focuses the scene to be viewed on the target, and the target stores the scene in the form of an electrical charge. The electrical conductivity of the target varies with the amount of light absorbed. Where there is minimal light, the material has a high electrical resistance. The points on the target with considerable light have a lower resistance.

The remainder of the tube consists of an electron gun with surrounding magnetic coils. The cathode of the electron gun generates a stream of electrons focused into a narrow beam to strike the inside of the target. Other magnetic coils surround the vidicon tube to produce horizontal and vertical deflection of the electron beam. Signals applied to these coils cause the electron beam to scan from left to right and top to bottom across the inside of the target. This causes an electrical current to flow between the target and the transparent signal electrode. The current is proportional to the light amplitude. The result is the video output signal.

Numerous methods are available for scanning the target, but many systems use a standard pattern of 525 total scanning lines (called NTSC). Figure 10.3

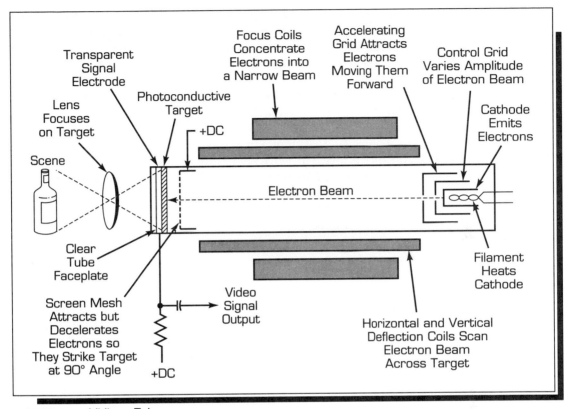

FIGURE 10.2 Vidicon Tube

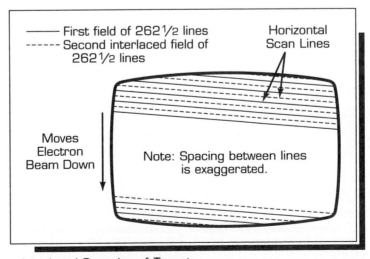

FIGURE 10.3 Interlaced Scanning of Target

illustrates the concept. As the electron beam scans the target, an electrical signal is generated. The varying amplitude in the signal represents brightness variation along one of the scan lines. As soon as one line is scanned, the vertical deflection signals move the electron beam a small distance farther down, and another horizontal scan line is developed. Special synchronization pulses designate the beginning and end of each horizontally scanned line. The signal thus developed appears as shown in Figure 10.4. The horizontal sync pulse is approximately 5 microseconds (μs) wide and occurs at a frequency of 15,750 Hz.

The electrical output signal shown in Figure 10.4 has an approximate voltage range of 0.7 volt (black level) to 1.5 volts (white level). Voltage levels between these two values, of course, represent varying shades of gray. The analog video signal between the sync pulses represents the light intensity variations of one scan line. It is this voltage that will be fed to the analog-to-digital converter for translation into binary numbers.

Charged Coupled Devices. A CCD is a light-sensitive integrated circuit designed to convert a rectangular visual image into a video electrical signal. A lens system focuses the scene onto a photoconductive substrate such as silicon. This device absorbs the light and stores it as an electrical charge on thousands of tiny square or rectangular capacitors (Figure 10.5). The silicon forms a single common plate for all of these capacitors. The other plates are individual tiny metal electrodes separated from the silicon photoconductor by a thin layer of silicon dioxide insulator. Light falling on the substrate causes the capacitors to charge and discharge to a level depending on the intensity of the light striking the substrate directly below the tiny capacitive plates.

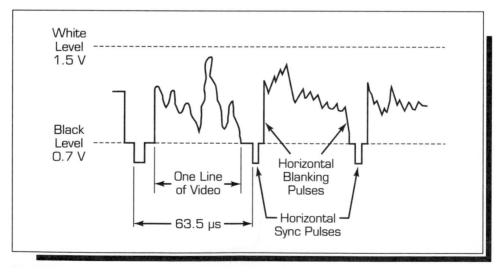

FIGURE 10.4 Video Signal with Sync Pulses

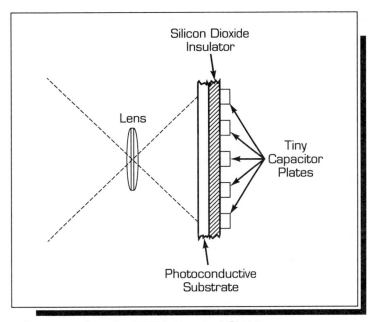

FIGURE 10.5 Cross-section of a CCD Integrated Circuit

To "read" the scene, voltages are applied to the capacitor electrodes in sequence from right to left. As the control voltage is applied, the capacitor is discharged and an analog signal is transferred to the common silicon substrate.

The tiny capacitive cells in the CCD are arranged in a rectangular or square array. Typical array sizes are 64 × 64, 244 × 190, 488 × 380, and 512 × 512. Figure 10.6 shows a segment of a CCD array. The larger the number of capacitive

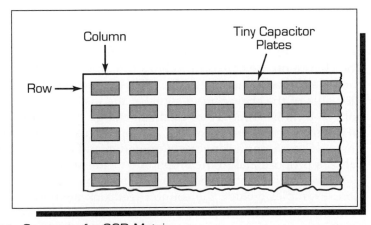

FIGURE 10.6 Segment of a CCD Matrix

storage cells, the greater the resolution. High resolution means good definition of detail.

The output signal from the CCD varies from approximately 0 to 1 volt, with the two extremes representing black and white respectively. Interlace scanning is not used. Instead, each row of the CCD matrix is scanned in turn. Each row in the matrix represents one scan line of the scene focused on the light-sensitive array.

CCD video cameras are preferred for computer vision. They are small, highly sensitive, and very reliable. They are also more rugged than the delicate vidicon tubes, and they do not require a filament voltage or the high voltage required by the vidicon. CCD units are also less expensive than vidicon cameras. One final important point should be made. Both vidicon and CCD cameras produce output that is a black and white analog video signal. These cameras do not recognize color; instead, they generate an output signal that represents gray levels between black and white. All computer vision systems are black and white. Color systems can be created, but they are far more complex and expensive. Yet color adds information that makes it easier for a computer to recognize shapes, objects, background, and other characteristics of the scene. An example of a system using color is the NAVLAB system developed at Carnegie-Mellon University. This system attempts to construct an autonomous vehicle. In it, color vision is exploited to find and follow roads. Because they are so complex and rare, color computer vision systems will not be discussed here.

Analog-to-Digital Conversion

The video output signal from the camera is fed to an analog-to-digital converter (ADC). The ADC then periodically samples the analog signal and converts the amplitude into a parallel binary number. This sampling process is shown in Figure 10.7. The sampling is usually done by a circuit called a track/store or sample/hold (S/H) amplifier (Figure 10.8). As the analog signal is applied to the input of the S/H amplifier, a digital clock signal occurring at a fixed rate drives a switch called the FET in the S/H amplifier. During its sample state, the FET conducts, and the output of the S/H amplifier is the same as, the analog input. The charge on the capacitor follows the input voltage value. When the binary control signal switches states, the FET is cut off and the amplifier stores or holds the value of the analog input signal at the instant the FET cuts off. That analog voltage level is stored as an electrical charge on a capacitor. The output of the S/H amplifier is then a fixed DC voltage. This signal is then fed to the ADC. The ADC performs a conversion operation and outputs a binary number whose value is proportional to the amplitude of the analog signal.

Several different methods can be used to produce analog-to-digital conversion. Examples include the counter feedback method, the dual slope method, and the successive approximations method. None of these, however, are used in video ADC applications. Instead, special high-speed parallel or flash

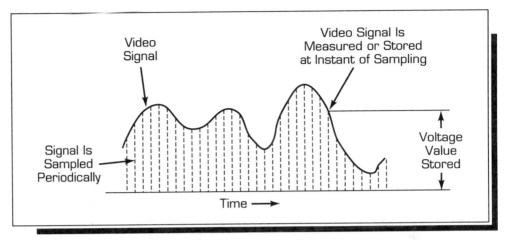

FIGURE 10.7 Sampling a Video Signal

converters are used. They are the only ADCs fast enough to digitize the high-frequency video signals.

Pixels. Each time the video signal is sampled by the ADC, we say that a pixel has been created. A **pixel** is the value of light intensity at one particular point on a scan line. A pixel, therefore, is a small element into which each scan line is broken. Each scan line contains approximately 200 to 500 pixels. These samples, then, give a fairly accurate representation of light intensity variation across the scan line. Naturally, the more pixels per line, the higher the definition. In any case, the pixel is a point of light that is, in effect, some shade of gray. That shade of gray is designated by a particular binary number.

The number of output bits in the ADC determines the total number of gray levels to be represented. In some low-definition systems, a 4-bit output is

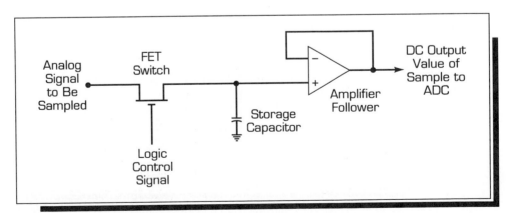

FIGURE 10.8 Sample/Hold Amplifier

satisfactory. With 4 bits, sixteen possible gray levels can be represented, ranging from 0000 for black to 1111 for white. For higher definition systems, more bits are used. Eight-bit ADCs are popular today because they provide 256 individual gray levels, which gives extremely fine detail.

By sampling the video signal, we are converting each scan line into dots of light of varying gray levels. The effect is representing the entire scene by a matrix of pixels as shown in Figure 10.9. Each pixel represents a light value occurring during the sampling process.

RAM

Each pixel is usually represented by an 8-bit binary number that is stored in a special large random-access memory (RAM). Semiconductor RAM chips are used in these memories. Their storage access time must be extremely fast to accept the high-speed output from the ADC. The memory must be very large to store the many pixel bytes that make up a scene. For example, if a 512 × 512 CCD is used, the scene will contain 512 × 512 = 262,144 pixels. This means that a RAM capable of storing at least 262,144 bytes must be used. (Note: 1K = 1,024; 256K = 262,114.)

In most computer vision systems, the special vision RAM is separate from the regular RAM used in the computer. It is usually called a buffer RAM, or

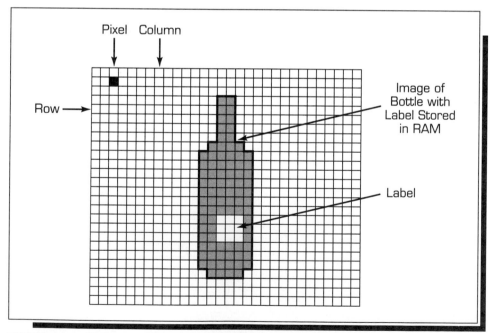

FIGURE 10.9 All Scenes Represented as Rows and Columns of Pixels of Varying Gray Shades

frame buffer, where frame refers to the digitized scene. Image storage requirements are demanding, and therefore this burden is not put on the regular RAM.

At this point, the computer has stored in its memory a digital representation of a scene to be analyzed and understood. Once this binary image of the scene is in memory, the computer can take over and perform many different operations on the scene to enhance it, analyze it, translate it into different forms, and to ultimately interpret what is there.

Monitors

Most computer vision systems also include a video monitor, a TV set without the channel tuning mechanism, for viewing the scene the camera sees. Its main component is a cathode ray tube whose electron beam scans across the phosphorous face, converting electron beam intensity into light variations. It is useful for the operator of a computer vision system to know exactly what the camera sees and what the computer has stored in its memory. One easy way to do this is to feed the video signal from the output of the camera directly into the video monitor. This lets the operator point the camera, focus it, or otherwise make adjustments so it will show exactly what is wanted.

If the sampling rate is very high, the scene displayed on the monitor will be a fairly accurate re-creation of the original input. If the sampling rate is low, the picture quality and definition will not be as good. The conversion process distorts the scene, but depending on the application, it is usually acceptable. Figure 10.10 is a complete diagram of the vision system hardware.

3-D to 2-D

Video cameras do not see in 3-D. They show us a two-dimensional representation of anything they look at. We see the accurate height and width of our subjects, but not the dimension of depth, or perspective. Without depth information, it is difficult to determine the distance between the camera and the objects being viewed. Furthermore, it is difficult to determine the distances between different objects in the scene. All of this missing information would lead to a better understanding of the total scene.

A direct approach to overcoming this problem is to more accurately emulate the human vision system. We are able to perceive depth for one reason: we have two eyes. The brain gets two similar but slightly different images of a scene because of the spacing between the eyes. These differences in the scene allow the brain to perform a type of "triangularization," thereby giving us the ability to sense depth and mentally measure distances from ourselves to objects and distances between objects.

To sense depth in a computer vision system, the usual procedure is to use two cameras. This produces binocular, or stereo, vision which permits depth to be determined. In 3-D vision systems, the same scene is viewed by two cameras as shown in Figure 10.11. Cameras are usually located at fixed and known

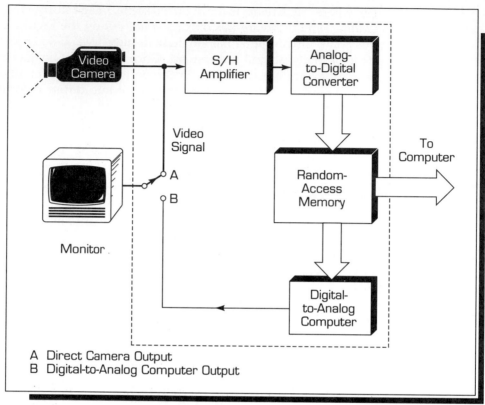

A Direct Camera Output
B Digital-to-Analog Computer Output

FIGURE 10.10 Computer Vision System

distances apart. The scenes from the two cameras are then digitized and stored in memory. Once objects in the scene have been identified, the computer can perform various mathematical operations to help compute the distances to objects and between objects.

Because extra camera equipment and conversion equipment are needed, as well as a significant amount of additional memory, 3-D computer vision systems are incredibly complex and expensive. The additional software to process the data is also an expense. As a result, few 3-D vision systems are used. Only in extremely critical situations can the 3-D cost be justified. Most computer vision systems accept the two-dimensional representation and learn to work with it or around it. Typical applications in which 3-D vision is necessary and has been shown to contribute significantly include the general (experimental) area of mobile robots (e.g., the NAVLAB at Carnegie-Mellon University) and execution of complex 3-D operations. For instance, Ford Motor Company's manufacturing system for crankshaft deburring requires precise determination of hole location and orientation. (Burrs can block the oil passage exit holes on a car engine's crankshaft line, so they must be removed.) Another important application is the 3-D reconstruction and analysis of aerial photographs (usually of a relatively

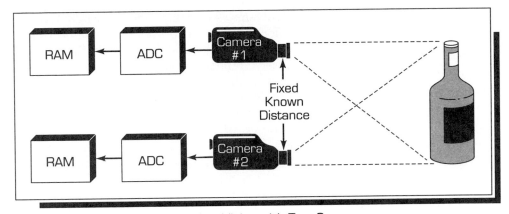

FIGURE 10.11   Stereo, or Binocular, Vision with Two Cameras

uniform urban scene), for example, by Carnegie-Mellon's MOSAIC system. For more information about the practical use of 3-D scenes, see Freeman [12].

Alternative techniques have been developed to detect depth differences. One analyzes distortions in stripes of light cast over the object, variable shadings, and other cues. An especially interesting, relatively recent method is the photometric stereo method employed at MIT for a robot system designed to pick up an object from an object pile. In this method, multiple images of the same scene are taken from the same position with different illumination conditions. Several brightness values result for each point of the image. There is no disparity between the images and therefore no need for matching them. However, surface orientation can be determined from the different brightness values.

In reality, the result of most of these techniques is a "2.5-D" sketch of the scene that includes various edge, depth, and orientation information on a 2-D image.

10.3   Image Processing

With the binary version of the scene stored in memory, image processing can now begin. Image processing, also known as **image enhancement,** is the process of improving the quality of the image. Anything that can be done to make the image clearer will simplify analysis and lead to improved understanding.

From the very instant the light reflected from a scene enters a computer vision system, it is distorted and misrepresented by system imperfections. For instance, the camera lens produces some distortion; also, inconsistencies in the target area of the vidicon or CCD produce uneven light intensities. Finally, the imperfect process of analog-to-digital conversion introduces further misrepresentations.

There can be other problems as well. Extremely low light levels can produce a scene that is difficult for the camera to see. The camera itself may not be sensitive enough to clearly capture the fine definition in the scene. The same is true for scenes with excessive brilliance; the camera may produce distortions.

Another problem is noise. In an electrical sense, noise consists of unwanted additions that obscure the desired signal. Noise shows up as "snow" or a "salt-and-pepper" background that obscures features in the scene.

Regardless of the source of the degradation of the signal, processing techniques can be used to eliminate or minimize these problems. These techniques, which use a process known as image enhancement, will be discussed in turn.

Preprocessing

Before image enhancement occurs, preprocessing takes place to improve the scene. First, filters may be attached to the lens to control the amount of light, its color, and the contrast of the various objects in the scene. Second, many computer vision systems operate in a controlled environment where it is possible not only to control illumination level, but also to position light sources or the objects to be viewed for maximum visibility and comprehension.

Now let's take a look at some of the ways that the computer can process the binary image stored in memory.

Noise Reduction

Image averaging helps to eliminate noise and distortion. In this process, the vision system captures sequential views of the scene and then averages them. Minor variations may occur in the scene. For example, if the light position changes or if the object moves, the reflections from the various objects in the scene will change. As the light source moves, shadows and reflections from the surfaces change. Since such noise is random, averaging it reduces it to a very low level.

In any case, the averaging process takes several views of the scene and stores them in memory. Naturally, the memory must be extremely large to accomplish this. Corresponding pixels in the various binary images are averaged by adding them and dividing by the number of pixels averaged. The result is a composite scene that usually has better clarity.

Gray Scale Modification

Another processing technique is to lighten or darken the scene; this is called **gray scale modification.** Suppose the brightness level of a pixel is represented by an 8-bit binary number where 0 (00000000) represents black and 255 (11111111) represents maximum white. All numeric values in between represent intermediate shades of gray.

If the scene is very dark, all of the pixels will have low values. One way to process the image is to lighten it up by adding a fixed value to each pixel. The relationship between adjacent pixels is not changed, but the effect is lightening of the whole scene.

Contrast improvement is one type of gray scale modification. Contrast is the range between the darkest and lightest points in an image. Fine detail shows up best when there is high contrast between adjacent pixels. However, the colors of adjacent objects, the intensity or position of the light, and system distortions can obscure edges and boundaries because there is insufficient contrast. In such cases, contrast can be improved by processing.

Depending on the kind of enhancement needed, modification is done by adding, subtracting, multiplying, or dividing pixel values by a constant. The effect is lightening of some pixels and darkening of others. This stretches or improves the contrast so that the fine detail in the scene is apparent.

Histogram Flattening

Another technique that helps improve some images is known as **histogram flattening.** A histogram is a vertical bar chart used to plot statistical information. A histogram can be constructed of the binary image by counting the number of times that each distinct gray level occurs. The result might look like the chart shown in Figure 10.12a. With this histogram constructed in memory, a program can determine if there are excessive high or low values. For example, one analysis may discover an unusually high number of very bright or very dark levels. If certain intensity values occur widely throughout the scene, histogram flattening can reduce them. Brightness values that occur only occasionally can be increased.

This process is done by setting threshold levels, thereby dividing the total pixel brightness range into blocks of brightness values. Pixel values within the various ranges are then identified and each pixel within that range is assigned a new common intensity value. The result, of course, is that the range of intensity values (number of pixels) in the scene is greatly reduced (Figure 10.12b).

Applications of Image Processing

As you can imagine, the processing of a binary image can take many forms. Because the computer can perform virtually any mathematical operation, the pixels in a scene can be manipulated in a variety of ways. Besides addition, subtraction, multiplication, and division, pixel processing techniques include calculus functions like differentiation.

Image enhancement is a subfield specialty of computer science. Perhaps you have seen real-life examples of image enhancement. Pictures of the planets received from the spacecraft Voyager have been processed and enhanced in a

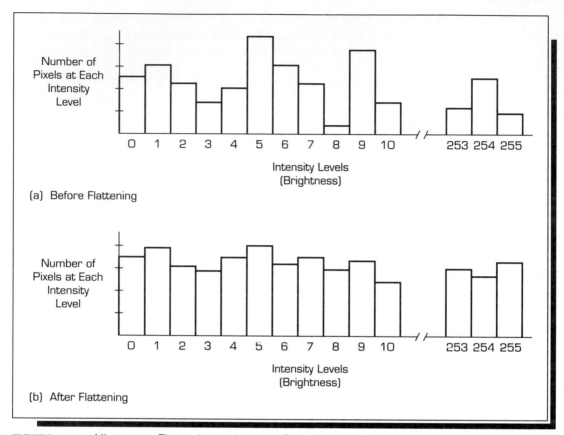

(a) Before Flattening

(b) After Flattening

FIGURE 10.12 Histogram Flattening to Improve Detail

variety of ways to improve contrast and clarity. The result has been astonishingly good detail.

Picture processing is also common in medicine. For example, the CAT scan uses image processing. (CAT stands for computer-assisted tomography.) A series of X-ray images of cross-sections of the human body are taken sequentially as the body is passed through the system. The X-ray images are then converted to binary format and processed mathematically to give an incredibly detailed, three-dimensional view of the body and its organs.

Image processing is also used in radar and sonar devices. Radio signals reflected from a target are received and converted into binary numbers. These are subjected to mathematical processing to improve clarity, definition, and identification of the target. Sonar signals—sound reflections from an underwater target—are digitized and processed to identify the target.

Once we have processed and enhanced our scene, we have a new binary image of it stored in memory. The scene is now ready for image analysis.

10.4   Image Analysis

Up to this point, we have been generally vague in describing the scene. It could be an outdoor landscape, an aerial photograph, a human face, or a toy block. Image analysis begins the process of locating and defining the various objects in the scene. Artificial intelligence then attempts to determine what the objects are.

Image analysis is accomplished by identifying regions and boundaries, or edges. Edges represent boundaries where two surfaces come together. They also identify the interface between two different surfaces or between an object and a background. An edge is also formed between two objects when one is in front or back of another. The line between an object and its shadow, and the outline of the shadow itself, form edges. Examples of these are given in Figure 10.13. The first step, therefore, in image analysis is to locate all of these edges and boundaries.

Edges and regions, or surfaces, completely define the scene. Regions are large, flat areas of an object or scene that have the same intensity value and occur between the various edges and boundary lines. Various mathematical techniques have been developed for detecting edges and surfaces, and these form the core of image analysis.

Surface Smoothing

Surfaces are easy to identify because they are relatively uniform in light intensity. Adjacent pixels within the surface have equal values or values very close to one another. Values may change gradually over the surface due to shadows or shading caused by the positioning of the light source.

Often, surfaces are smoothed out to remove irregularities or shading before edge detection is done. The averaging process routinely involves the use of a bit-map mask with predetermined weights for each pixel and its neighbors. The

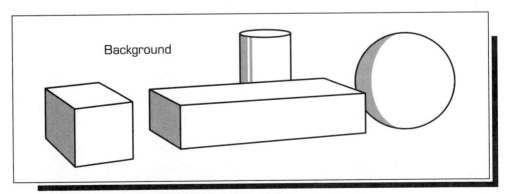

FIGURE 10.13 Examples of Edges and Boundaries

process of applying the mask is called convolution. The mask is usually a variation of a normal (Gaussian) curve; the "width" of the mask (actually the standard deviation of the Gaussian curve used) is an important parameter in the convolution process. The width of the mask determines the degree of "smoothing out" of the image, which is a trade-off between reducing noise on one hand and losing some information on the other.

Edge Detection

After surface smoothing, the computer begins looking for edges. A program in the computer scans through all of the binary numbers representing pixels to determine which of those pixels fall on the boundary between two surfaces. The program does this by comparing the intensity of adjacent pixels. For example, the value of one pixel is subtracted from the value of an adjacent pixel and the numeric value is noted. If the difference is very small, the two pixels are probably part of a large surface area. A large difference, on the other hand, indicates an edge, or boundary.

The edge detection program has to know in advance just how large a difference is going to be considered edge recognition. Therefore, some threshold value is usually established beforehand.

Edge detection generally takes place by having the computer program look at a small group of adjacent pixels in both the horizontal and vertical directions. In other words, it "looks" through a "window" at a small square of pixels. The size of this window may be anything from approximately 2 × 2 to 15 × 15 pixels. More than two adjacent pixels are examined to get a better fix on the size and location of an edge. Various *operators* can be used for detecting edges in different directions; that is, various computations can be carried out on the pixels seen through the window.

The window also allows the computer program to look in several directions rather than in a single horizontal or vertical direction. Comparing two adjacent pixels may produce no variation in the horizontal direction, but a significant difference in the vertical direction. The windowing process produces less ambiguity in edge detection. The size of the window is a trade-off between good noise immunity obtained with a large window and good sensitivity to definition obtained with a small window.

The output of this "windowing" (or application of operators in a mask-like fashion) stage is a series of microedges, or "edgelets." These can (though that is not necessarily the case) be connected to form *contours*, thus producing a description of the actual boundaries. Other local image processing techniques applied at this stage are edge refinement ("thinning" fuzzy edges) and connection of discontinuous line segments.

In actual systems the smoothing and edge detection phases are often conveniently combined into a single operator applied to the image; sometimes they are even hard-wired into the hardware. The image is therefore convoluted and edges are detected at the same time.

Another major local image processing technique—region growing—is the inverse to edge detection. Regions (surfaces or "blobs" as they are sometimes called) are gradually identified and merged by various thresholding techniques in which similar brightness values are relevant. Under favorable lighting conditions that might result in binary ("black and white") images, the background is suppressed and the objects are outlined. This is especially appropriate in industrial applications where lighting conditions can be controlled.

When the boundaries of all the objects in the scene have been identified, a line drawing of the scene can be made. A new version of the scene is created showing just the black outlines of all of the objects on a white background. This line drawing is referred to as a primal sketch. It is this primal sketch that completes the image analysis process. The comprehension part of the computer vision program will use the outline drawing to make a final identification of the various objects.

10.5   Image Understanding

Up to this point in the computer vision process, a lot of algorithmic computation has taken place. Yet, none of it is really AI. Even though an image has been acquired, enhanced, and analyzed, the computer still does not know what the scene means. The computer is not aware of the contents of the scene, what objects are represented, and how they are related to one another. The final stage of computer vision then is for the computer to have some knowledge about the things it may see in a scene. Object shapes and some kind of AI search and pattern-matching program enable the computer to examine the incoming scene and compare it to those objects in the knowledge base. The computer should be able to identify the objects there and thus understand what it sees. Unlike image analysis that essentially concerns local features, now extraction of *global* features takes place. In general, there are four comprehension paradigms in this phase:

1. *Hierarchical bottom-up processing:* Such processing is suitable for simple schemes and a limited number of objects known in advance.
2. *Hierarchical top-down processing,* or *hypothesize and test:* This processing method involves a goal (object-model)-directed search for a hypothesized object.
3. *Heterarchical approach:* In this method distributed control (with some "monitor") of the various system parts is used to modify their operation as necessary.
4. *Blackboard approach:* Various components interact via a common database (the "blackboard") that is accessible by all the others. This approach is especially useful when several hypotheses should be kept and tracked at several levels.

Sophisticated industrial systems commonly use both a bottom-up and a top-down approach. Usually a binary (black and white) image is formed, but the trend is toward the more flexible general gray scale representation.

As you might suspect, a considerable amount of research has gone into the comprehension process of computer vision. It is not an easy process. It is complicated by the fact that a three-dimensional scene is converted into two-dimensional format. From this two-dimensional view the computer must ascertain the existence of three-dimensional objects. However, some computer vision applications do involve what could be called two-dimensional scene analysis. In such cases, a simple template-matching technique is used to pick out specific object shapes. The template, which is stored in memory, is an outline or silhouette of an object that the computer knows. Thus, the comparison process that takes place during search and pattern matching can produce identification.

Template Matching

Template matching compares a model of a known object stored as a binary image in the computer to the binary image of the scene being viewed. The basis of comparison is the primal sketch (described earlier). Both the scene and the template are stored as primal sketches. The comparison is usually done on a pixel-by-pixel basis. Corresponding pixels in the two images are, for example, subtracted from one another to obtain a difference value. If the difference is zero, a match occurs; they are the same. Very small difference numbers produce a reasonably close match. High difference figures, of course, indicate wide disparity. Various statistical calculations can be made to determine just how close the match is between the template and the input scene.

It is difficult to match a known shape to a viewed shape because the template stored in memory is fixed in size and orientation. Chances are the template has a different size and position than the object in the scene. Therefore, to cause a match or near match to occur, the template object must be manipulated. Various processing techniques can be used to scale or increase or decrease the size of the template to more closely match the size of the object in the scene. In addition, other mathematical routines can be used to rotate or tilt the template to better approximate the orientation of the object in the scene.

Many of these calculations may have to be performed before obtaining a good approximation. *After each reorientation or scaling of the template, a new comparison is made.* If the object bears any resemblance to the template, a reasonable match will be found eventually. *It is at that point that the system "understands."* It can then state with reasonable certainty that it has viewed a particular shape or object.

On the other hand, the template-matching process may not produce a match, and the image comprehension program may simply move on to another template shape. In fact, the knowledge base for a computer vision system may be an entire set of templates of various shapes. The process is continued until an object is identified or no match occurs.

If no match occurs, the computer cannot understand the scene. The computer cannot recognize things it does not know about. If the template is not in the computer, that object can never be identified. Of course, that is one of the main limitations of computer vision systems.

Although template matching is a simple and crude process, it is a useful one. It is, in fact, the basis of most industrial and military machine vision systems. In such systems the scene can be tightly controlled and the objects to be identified can be defined very clearly. Under such circumstances, computer vision systems can view and identify objects with nearly 100 percent accuracy.

Other Techniques

Even though template matching is a widely used and highly successful technique, there are other methods of image understanding. The process still involves search and pattern matching, but at a different level. For example, instead of storing entire objects or shapes as templates, the computer can store bits and pieces of objects in its knowledge base. At the lowest level, the computer may store a line segment which it then manipulates and attempts to match against lines in the primal sketch. It could do the same with squares and rectangles or circles and ellipses. Another alternative is *feature matching*, in which key features (e.g., diameter, area) are stored, rather than the actual image.

A considerable amount of research in computer vision has dealt with what is generally called the *blocks world*. A blocks world is a contrived environment in which multiple blocks of different geometric shapes are used as objects to form a scene to be identified. Colored cubes, rectangles, cylinders, pyramids, triangles, and other blocks are stacked or placed adjacent to one another to form a limited controlled environment. The camera of a computer vision system is then focused on this assembly of blocks to acquire, process, and analyze the scene. The primal sketch is used as the basis for attempting to understand what is in the blocks world. But instead of looking for complete patterns or objects, the computer begins to look for identifying pieces. In a blocks world where all of the blocks are made of straight lines, it is easy to determine that all of these lines will come together in a few easily recognized formats. A line is formed between the edge of an object and the background, and between adjoining surfaces of an object. A line also is formed where two separate objects touch, overlap, or appear one behind another.

In addition, these lines form vertexes; that is, many of the lines come together to form a point. Lines form an L, a fork (Y), an arrowhead, or a T; these various vertex possibilities are illustrated in Figure 10.14. Each of these is represented in the knowledge base of the computer. Several other types are shown in Figure 10.15. The illustrations in Figure 10.15 show how a computer, knowing the types of vertexes, can misjudge a scene. The arrowhead or peak of the pyramid shown in Figure 10.15b could be mistaken for the corner of a square.

In Figure 10.15c, the computer could have a difficult time determining if this is (1) the picture of a cube with a small cube cut out of one corner or (2) a

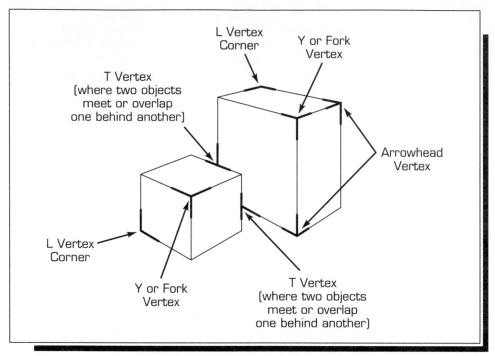

FIGURE 10.14 Types of Vertexes That Form Functions Between Objects in a Scene

small cube sitting in the corner where three larger planes form a corner of two walls and a floor. The computer must be given additional knowledge to help it discriminate. For example, in Figure 10.15c, the Y vertex will determine which of the two representations just described is correct. If the vertex is concave, or indented inward, the first description is correct. If that vertex is convex, or pointing outward, the second description is correct. Systems have been invented to determine whether a line or vertex is concave or convex.

Vertexes are not independent, of course. For instance, the *Waltz labeling algorithm* operates on the assumption that certain vertex types impose constraints on possible adjacent vertexes. Waltz [18] defined eleven line types (including, for instance, shadow edges) and created a vertex catalog with thousands of entries. However, by local elimination of impossible interpretations, the possible matches are filtered very quickly. Often, no further search is necessary.

The search process attempts to locate vertexes in the primal sketch and match them with the various vertex models stored in memory. When a match occurs, the computer knows that it has identified a particular type of vertex and that certain surfaces and shapes are associated with it.

The computer goes about looking for all of the various vertexes and junctions and slowly but surely builds up a complete picture of what is being represented. At some point, sufficient information becomes available so the computer can say that it has identified a cube, a rectangle, a pyramid, or whatever. Rules

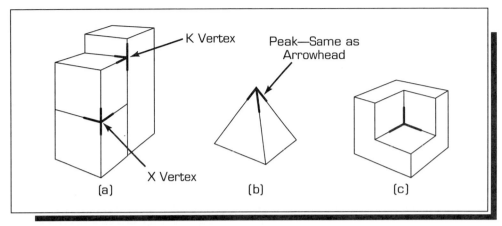

FIGURE 10.15 Other Types of Vertexes

stored in the knowledge base state facts about the vertexes and what they mean. In this way, the computer can decide what it has "seen."

Limitations and Improvements

Identifying objects in a simple blocks world is relatively easy. Identification is usually 100 percent. However, when we move out into the real world and attempt to identify outdoor scenes or even indoor scenes, the comprehension problem becomes incredibly difficult. In fact, few computer vision systems have been built that are capable of such scene understanding. The reason for this is that most scenes, whether they be outdoors or indoors, contain an incredible number of different objects. In a room, for example, there may be a personal computer on a desk. There may be a printer, a typewriter, a telephone, books, and many other objects. There may be pictures on the wall, hanging plants, chairs, and even people. The primal sketch is very complex. Picking out the various objects in the scene is difficult.

Moving outside further complicates the process. Some things like buildings, cars, trucks, and airplanes are relatively easy to identify. People are somewhat more difficult, and objects such as trees, bushes, and animals are very difficult. Anything with a curved or irregular surface is difficult to pick out.

For these reasons, computer vision systems have limited applications. They work best in controlled environments where the scenes they view are relatively simple and contain only a few objects. An exception is military applications where there is less pressure to justify the cost. As research continues in this field, more sophisticated techniques will be developed to deal economically with more complex scenes.

There are several ways to improve image understanding. One way is to use information from different sensor types (e.g., vision and touch) and *fuse* them to achieve a better understanding than with either alone. Another way is to use some aspect of the image surfaces, for example, light reflectance. Special filters can be added to the camera, such as Polaroid light filters, that enhance the contrast between different material types (e.g., metal and plastic). This is quite useful when inspecting an electronic circuit board where wires can be highlighted.

Another trend that might well be a predominant one in future computer vision is *parallel processing* (Chapter 19) of the input image. Vision lends itself well to parallel processing techniques at various phases of the processing, analysis, and comprehension levels. It is the common view nowadays that the human brain is capable of analyzing the huge amount of information it acquires only because of its parallel processing architecture.

Even more ambitious is the hope that *neural nets* (Chapter 18) might combine several stages of image processing and understanding and, in particular, learn to recognize objects from the original acquired or the processed image.

Detecting Motion. Most of the preceding discussion pertains to static images. However, vision is especially important when the object, the camera, or both are moving (as in the case of a mobile robot). In such situations *motion detection* is needed. Detecting motion is a complex process that is mostly experimental at the present time. It usually relies on several continuity constraints common to consecutive frames taken at close temporal intervals. The successive frames are compared and the motion flow (direction) vectors of each point are determined. Several military applications are available, but industrial applications are rare.

10.6   Applications of Computer Vision

Examples of the most common computer vision applications follow.

Machine Vision

The biggest nonmilitary application of computer vision is machine vision. Machine vision refers to the use of computer vision equipment and techniques with manufacturing processes usually carried out by some type of machine.

The purpose of machine vision in manufacturing applications is to replace people in some tasks and to help speed up or simplify the manufacturing process in others. Replacing people is a common objective, not because people are incapable or incompetent, but because in some applications, particularly highly repetitive and boring tasks, a machine does a better job. Once people get bored, they tend to miss details or otherwise botch the manufacturing process. Human beings get tired and make mistakes, machines don't. Also, machine vision can replace people who work in hazardous environments. Two examples of human tasks that can be greatly assisted by image understanding are recognizing blood vessel abnormalities in X-ray images and chromosome classification and analysis in microphotography. A lot of the research and development effort is invested in these types of tasks.

In industry, machine vision is mainly used for two types of tasks: guidance and inspection (or quality control). Giving vision to a machine can automate the manufacturing process. If a machine has some information about the materials it is handling or the component it is making, it can perform completely unattended or do most of its work with little or no human intervention. Machine vision systems greatly improve productivity, quality, and the cost and time of manufacturing. They also increase manufacturing precision and reduce operator injuries, as demonstrated, for instance, in the Ford guided crankshaft deburring experience mentioned earlier in the chapter.

Machine vision systems operate in a controlled environment. The objects to be viewed are generally well known, and highly accurate descriptions of them can be programmed into the knowledge base. The conditions under which the objects are viewed can be carefully controlled. Camera positioning and lighting can be optimized to ensure positive identification of objects. One way to make a template for such computer vision systems is to take the object to be identified, point the camera at it, and capture one complete frame. This frame then becomes the template. Because the template is prepared under the exact conditions in which the objects must be identified, highly accurate matching can be obtained.

Machine vision systems can identify and inspect physical objects. A system may look at a collection of various parts and identify each by its shape. Once the parts are identified, they may be sorted, moved to another location, discarded, or otherwise used. In a typical application, stacks of paper cups are counted quickly and accurately by a machine vision system, reducing the costs incurred formerly by overstacking to ensure the minimum number.

Computer vision systems are becoming very popular in quality control applications. Here, the camera looks at a particular object to determine if it has been made correctly. Such systems are good at correcting assembly errors or faults. For example, they are widely used for inspection of printed circuit boards. Initially, a correctly manufactured board is viewed and an image is captured for use as the template. The template is then compared to other boards to determine if components are in the right place, if solder joints have been made, or if any shorts, scratches, or breaks have occurred.

In some cases, such as in very-high-density semiconductor chips, machine vision is simply essential due to the multiple number of tiny features. Indeed, the electronics industry is currently the largest market segment for machine vision (see Box 10.1).

In other cases, machine vision is indispensable simply because in some instances humans cannot look at the real object or cannot perform the necessary job. For instance, the work done by the Jet Propulsion Lab for NASA (like the Mars Project or the Space Stations Project) assumes machine vision as essential. Another example is the X-ray process used by the food industry to inspect the contents of sealed packages. The packages are analyzed by machine vision for quality control purposes.

Box 10.1: Accuracy at High Speeds

Texas Instruments has developed a machine vision unit to perform vital quality tasks in high-speed production facilities. The tasks involve assembly of microchips and up to thirty-two other components onto printed circuit boards for personal computers. The job requires high precision (0.003 inch). A sensor system inspects each part (1,500 per hour!) and a robot's arm aligns it for placement, based on its picture of the circuit board.

By 1990 the corporate unit of Texas Instruments, called the Sensor System Branch, had completed more than 3,000 vision installations like the one described here. Some visual inspection is done at a speed close to 10,000 parts per hour. The systems combine vision, robotics, and expert systems. In their application niches, the Texas Instruments systems outperformed the human eye-brain combination.

(*Source: Information Technology Newsletter*, Texas Instruments, November 1990.)

Robot Vision

Another of the major applications of computer vision involves robots. Robots, as you will see in the next chapter, are machines that have been programmed to perform some physical manipulation. They are not smart because they cannot think for themselves. However, when attached to a computer with an artificial intelligence program, they do take on more intelligent characteristics. To be truly intelligent, a robot must also have sight. Sight provides feedback that allows it to adjust its operation to fit varying conditions. Vision is absolutely essential for a mobile robot and highly desirable for a static one.

Chapter Highlights

- □ Computer vision is that field of artificial intelligence devoted to mimicking human sight and visual understanding with hardware and software.
- □ The computer vision process involves four steps: image acquisition, image processing, image analysis, and image understanding.
- □ Image acquisition is the process of capturing a scene or picture electronically and converting it into a format compatible with the computer.
- □ A video camera is the main tool used for image acquisition. Cameras use either vidicon tubes or charged coupled devices, which are the most popular, to translate light into electrical (video) signals. Black and white cameras are used almost exclusively.

□ A charged coupled device is a semiconductor array that translates light into electrical charges. CCDs are smaller, lighter, more rugged, and more reliable than vidicon tubes.

□ An analog-to-digital converter changes the analog video signal into a sequence of binary numbers whose values represent light intensity levels. These are stored in a memory. An 8-bit ADC that can represent 256 gray levels between white and black is the most common. Each binary number is called a pixel.

□ The number of pixels in the converted scene determines the resolution of the image. The greater the number of pixels, the finer the representation of detail. A typical resolution is 512×512 pixels.

□ Very large RAMs are needed to store high-resolution scenes; they are referred to as frame buffers.

□ The stored binary image is a two-dimensional representation of a three-dimensional scene.

□ Sometimes a "2.5-D" sketch is used to add some 3-D information on top of a 2-D image.

□ Image processing refers to the enhancement of the stored image to improve quality and help ensure proper analysis and interpretation.

□ Image processing includes correcting distortions, improving contrast, changing the gray scale, and reducing noise.

□ Some image processing can be done optically with lenses, filters, and proper illumination prior to scene acquisition.

□ Most image processing is done by the computer by performing various calculations on each pixel in the scene.

□ Image analysis is the computer's process of determining the content of the scene by defining and locating objects and areas.

□ Computer image analysis is done by detecting edges, or recognizing boundaries, between objects and their background or other objects. This is done by comparing the values of adjacent pixels. Solid areas, or regions, are also identified.

□ During image analysis, the computer develops a primal sketch—a high-contrast outline drawing of all the objects and regions.

□ Image acquisition, processing, and analysis are not AI-based activities. However, the fourth and final step in computer vision, image understanding, is.

□ Image understanding, or comprehension, involves search and pattern-matching techniques to identify objects in the scene and their relationship to one another.

□ The main approaches to extraction of global features are bottom-up, or top-down processing, or a combination of both.

□ Picking out objects is done by template matching, that is, comparing a known template or silhouette of an object stored in the computer with objects in the scene.

□ Ultimately, parallel processing seems essential for efficient computer vision.

□ Motion detection techniques are growing in importance, though most applications are currently experimental.

□ Computer vision is most widely used in manufacturing operations. Systems used in this way are called machine vision systems.

□ Other application for computer vision involves robots.

Key Terms

analog-to-digital converter

charged coupled device

gray scale modification

histogram flattening

image acquisition

image analysis

image averaging

image enhancement

image processing

image understanding

pixel

primal sketch

template matching

vidicon tube

Questions for Review

1. What are the four basic steps in computer vision?
2. Define image acquisition and describe its process.
3. Explain image processing.
4. What is image analysis?
5. Define image understanding.
6. What is a pixel? How is it measured?
7. Describe the major methods of image enhancement.
8. Explain the major methods of image analysis.
9. Which of the basic steps of computer vision employs AI technology and why?
10. List and briefly describe the various paradigms used in image understanding.
11. What is template matching? How is it used in machine vision?
12. List the major benefits of computer vision.
13. List the major limitations of computer vision.
14. Describe how machine vision can be used to enhance quality control.
15. Why is computer vision so important in robotics?

Questions for Discussion

1. Explain the main differences between vidicon tubes and charged coupled devices.
2. Why do computer vision systems need a large random-access memory to process images? What about storing images for future use? Can you suggest space-saving alternatives?
3. Explain the advantages of smoothing out surfaces. Give a formal definition of the averaging process in a finite one-dimensional case (say, along the x-axis). Can you generalize it to a two-dimensional matrix of pixels?
4. How can edges be detected mechanically? Explain how different computers in the same window can be sensitive to different edge directions.

5. Discuss possible advantages and disadvantages of hierarchical bottom-up versus hierarchical top-down processing of global features.
6. What are the various advantages of machine vision? Think of examples where it would be highly useful.

References and Bibliography

1. Arbib, M.A. *Vision, Brain, and Cooperative Computation*. Cambridge, Mass.: MIT Press, 1987.
2. Ballard, D.H., and C. Brown. *Computer Vision*. Englewood Cliffs, N.J.: Prentice-Hall, 1982.
3. Barrow, H.G., and J.M. Teherbaum. "Computational Vision." *Proceedings of IEEE* 69(May 1981).
4. Blake, A., and A. Zisserman. *Visual Reconstruction*. Cambridge, Mass.: MIT Press, 1987.
5. Cappellini, V., and R. Marconi, eds. *Advances in Image Processing and Pattern Recognition*. Amsterdam: North Holland, 1986.
6. Cuadrado, J., and C. Cuadrado. "AI in Computer Vision." *Byte* 11(January 1986):237–258.
7. Deal, W.F., et al. "Machine Vision Giving Eyes to Robots." *Technology Teacher* 45 (no. 6, 1990).
8. Dornan, S.L. "Robotics and Vision: A Quality Idea at Ford." *Manufacturing Systems* (July 1989).
9. Dunbar, P. "Machine Vision." *Byte* 11(January 1986):161–173.
10. Foster, J.W., et al. "Automated Visual Inspection: A Tutorial." *Computers and Industrial Engineering* 18 (no. 4, 1990).
11. Freeman, H. *Machine Vision*. New York: Academic Press, 1988.
12. Freeman, H. *Machine Vision for Three-Dimensional Scenes*. New York: Academic Press, 1990.
13. Horn, B.K.P. *Robot Vision*. Cambridge, Mass.: MIT Press, 1989.
14. Iueuchii, K., K.H. Nishihara, B.K.P. Horn, P.S. Sobalvaro, and S. Nagata. "Determining Group Configurations Using Photometric Stereo and the PRISM Binocular Stereo System." *International Journal of Robotics Research*, 5 (Spring 1986).
15. Kanade, T., C. Thorpe, and W. Whitaker. "Autonomous Land Vehicle Project at CMU." In *Proceedings of ACM Computer Conference*. Cincinnati, February 1986.
16. Pope, Gregory. "Machine Vision Focuses on Profit." *High Technology Business* (January 1989).
17. Vinnucah, P. "Machines That See." *High Technology* (April 1983).
18. Waltz, D.L. "Generating Semantic Descriptions from Drawings of Scenes with Shadows." Technical Report AI-TR-271, MIT, Cambridge, Mass.
19. Watt, R. *Understanding Vision*. New York: Academic Press, 1990.
20. Wechsler, H. *Computational Vision*. New York: Academic Press, 1990.

Chapter 11

Robotics and AI

For centuries people have been enchanted with the idea of bringing images to life. Stories about robotlike creatures date back thousands of years ago. One story from the first century B.C. is about Virgril, the legendary magician of Naples, who supposedly drove away flies and gnats with bronze figures of a fly and a gnat. Enchantment with robots continues today as demonstrated by such robots as R2D2 of *Star Wars* fame. This chapter describes what robots are, what they can and cannot do, and how they function. The following topics are covered:

11.1 Introduction

From the beginning of time, we have been inventing machines that help us do our work faster and easier. As our knowledge of science, mathematics, and related technologies grew, we invented increasingly complex machines. The machines not only sped up and simplified our work, but they also allowed us to mass produce items with great precision.

For the most part, we worked in conjunction with a machine to perform many tasks. Machines were just devices that helped to multiply our capabilities. At some point, however, we decided that it was possible to produce machines that could totally replace us, at least in some jobs. In fact, it did become possible to create a machine that turned raw materials into the finished product without human intervention. This process is called automation.

The principles of automation eventually led to the idea of a more flexible or universal machine. Instead of creating a special machine designed to do only a few operations well, why not create a general-purpose machine that could perform many of the physical functions of human beings? Thus the idea of a robot was conceived.

A **robot** is a machine that attempts to duplicate one or more of the physical capabilities of a person. Just as AI attempts to mimic the human brain, a robot attempts to mimic human manipulative capability. The two ideas go hand in hand.

A robot, regardless of its sophistication and capabilities, is still basically a dumb machine. It cannot think, reason, solve problems, or make decisions. If it is to perform some function, it must be told specifically what to do. Electromechanical control systems put the robot through its physical paces according to a predetermined program of operations.

Such preprogrammed robots are useful, but they are greatly limited in the kinds of things they can do. They can replace us for only limited tasks that are repeated again and again. In addition, the robot cannot adjust to its environment. It cannot deal with changes or deviations. It will blindly go about what it has been programmed to do regardless of problems or varying conditions.

Even intelligent robots are still operated by simple electromechanical control systems. However, they are controlled by computers, so they have been given a "brain."

Some robots can be reprogrammed to meet changing conditions or new applications. Special robotics programming languages have been developed for these computers. With computer control, a robot becomes far more useful. Its operation can be changed to fit new jobs by simply creating a new program.

If a robot is to be able to adapt to changes in its work, it must be able to sense those changes. **Sensors** must be used with the work process to provide feedback signals to the computer. These feedback signals tell the computer what's going on. Once interpreted, they allow the robot to adapt to its situation.

Computer vision systems are the primary sensory input for advanced robots. Giving a robot the sense of sight lets it do more complicated jobs as well as increase quality and help in detecting malfunctions. Other kinds of sensors, such as pressure sensors, are also used to provide additional inputs to the control computer.

In this chapter you will see how AI techniques and feedback sensors make robots smarter and more useful. After a brief review of the field of robotics, we will consider how AI techniques based on sensory input can give robots the capability of operating on their own in a variety of environments.

11.2 Definitions and History

What Is a Robot?

Just what is it that you think of when you hear the word *robot*? If you are like most of us, you probably think of an electromechanical machine designed to mimic as closely as possible both the physical and mental attributes of a human being. The robot you imagine probably looks like a machine but is shaped to resemble a person. Most likely you have seen variations of such creations in TV programs and movies and may have read about them in science fiction stories. Robots of this type are referred to as androids.

Androids and Cyborgs. **Androids** are synthetic human beings with mechanical limbs and electronic brains. You will also hear this type of robot called a humanoid. Good examples of androids are R2D2 of the movie *Star Wars* and HAL 9000 from the movie *2001*.

Another term that you will often hear associated with robotics is *cyborg*. A **cyborg** is a human being who has been supplemented by some type of electromechanical device. A cyborg uses robotlike parts to correct a physical deficiency or to enhance mental or physical capabilities. Such human beings are partially robotic.

Despite continuing advances in the field of robotics, we are still far from capable of producing an android that accurately duplicates a human being. It is certainly not likely that we will do so in our lifetime and maybe not even within another century. Many expect that we will never be able to produce a fully electromechanical duplicate of ourselves.

Nevertheless, the future will bring us closer to producing a truly useful android. When we do, we will have an incredibly flexible tool to do much of our work. Daydreams about robots that clean the house, cook, and wash the dishes, or act like Robocop may become reality.

Definition. Many attempts have been made to define the term *robot*. The best definition is probably the one that has emerged from the manufacturers and users of industrial robots. The Robotic Institute of America defines an industrial robot this way: A robot is "a reprogrammable, multifunctional manipulator designed to move material, parts, tools, or other specialized devices through various programmed motions for the performance of a variety of tasks."

Brief History[1]

The word *robot* comes from a Czech word that means "forced labor." The term was invented by Karel Capek in his 1921 play *R.U.R.* (Rossum's Universal Robots). The play was about a man and his son constructing humanlike creatures that would perform obediently. Capek's play gave us the earliest definition of robot. "A robot is a mechanical version of human, to be used as a slave." That definition fits some of the early inventions built by skilled craftsmen in the seventeenth and eighteenth centuries.

Baron Wolfgang von Kempalen of Pressburg, Hungary, built a chess-playing robot that resembled a Turk with a long pipe and white turban. For years the Turk defeated all comers, including Frederick the Great and Napoleon (who tried to cheat). Actually, a midget hid inside the robot case which was engineered so that only one of its two doors would open at a time. The midget went undetected for years.

Other examples were "The Scribe" which wrote messages up to forty characters long; "Henri, the Draftsman" which could draw four different pencil sketches; and "Marianne, the Musician," which played an organ with all ten fingers. These robots were made by Pierre Jacquest-Droz, a Swiss, starting in 1768. Some of them took up to four years to complete.

People continued to invent creatures and to write about them. In most stories about robots, the plot was sinister and the robots were evil. This continued until the 1940s when Isaac Asimov began to write stories about robots that were benevolent. The main theme of his stories was robotics and he gave the science its name. Asimov also originated the three laws of robotics which have inspired many science fiction stories and movies about robots (see Box 11.1).

Robots remained in fiction until the 1950s when university-sponsored research led to new types of robots. The age of robots was ushered in with Shakey, a robot that had no resemblance to humans. (Shakey was developed at the Stanford Research Institute in Palo Alto, Calif., in 1958.) It made rudimentary decisions and used radar pulses, television eyes, and bump detectors to sense its surroundings.

Prior to this, during World War II and after, remote manipulators, or teleoperators, were used to handle radioactive substances. These manipulators, like prostheses, exoskeletons, and locomotive devices, are related technologies that do not qualify as robots.

George C. Devol was one of the leading proponents of modern robots. He patented a concept (in 1954) called Universal Automation. In 1961 he obtained a patent for the first robot, labeled Programmed Article Transfer (U.S. Patent 2,988,237). Devol went on to obtain thirty-nine other patents in robotics over the years. The first industrial robot was installed by Unimation Inc. Unimation

---

[1] Based, in part, on Logsdon [19].

Box 11.1: Laws of Robotics

If we are ever able to produce androids, we should make sure they are positive influences in our society. Isaac Asimov, in *I Robot* [3], wrote that all androids should follow the three laws of robotics:

1. A robot may not injure a human being or, through inaction, allow a human to be harmed.
2. A robot must obey orders given by humans except when that conflicts with the first law.
3. A robot must protect its own existence unless that conflicts with the first or second laws.

These laws could certainly put our minds at ease. However, human nature being what it is, some robots will be constructed for all the wrong reasons. Many books, movies, and TV shows are based on such incidences.

But right now, we really don't have to worry. Robots as they exist in our real world are nothing more than simple mechanical manipulators. They only simulate a fraction of total human capabilities, yet they are incredibly useful. For many years in the future, these are the robots we will develop and increasingly put to use improving our productivity and replacing humans in critical or dangerous environments.

was formed by Joseph Engelberger after he acquired some of Devol's patents. Engelberger convinced Devol to join him at Unimation and together they developed and installed robots for many years. (Engelberger is credited with being the Father of Robotics even though Devol invented and patented the robot.) Industrial robots that have evolved from their work are *not* very intelligent or responsive to their environment.

11.3   Types of Industrial Robots

Two basic types of robots are common in industry. The first type is the fixed but moveable arm. The second type is generally referred to as a mobile robot. Let's consider these types in more detail.

Fixed Robot

The most predominant type of industrial robot is the fixed robot with a moveable arm. An example is shown in Figure 11.1. These robots are mounted on a base in a single location close to the place where the work is to be performed. The

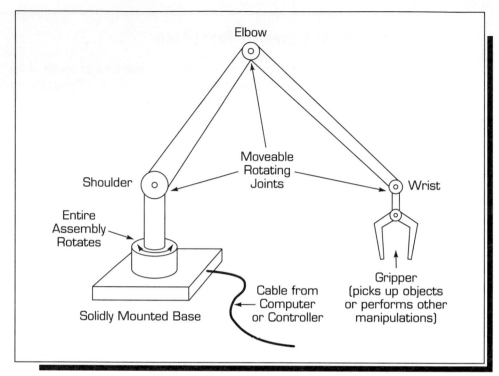

FIGURE 11.1 Typical Industrial Robotic Arm

robot is generally secured to a cement floor with heavy bolts or is mounted on a table or other work surface so that it cannot move. From there, the robot arm moves up and down, back and forth, in and out, and in whatever way it is programmed.

In some special applications, the entire arm can be moveable. For example, it may be mounted on rails so that it can slide along a production line. Even in such cases, the amount of movement is limited.

Mobile Robots

A mobile robot—**automated guided vehicle** (AGV)—is capable of moving around. Such robots are generally manipulator arms mounted on a small vehiclelike structure with wheels or bulldozerlike tracks. Other methods of propulsion may also be used in special circumstances. For example, robots with legs have been invented to provide greater mobility in difficult terrain. Underwater robots require a propulsion motor and control fins for exploration and retrieval work under water. Regardless of the type of movement implemented, mobile robots must have a propulsion system. Usually, this propulsion system is one or more electrical motors that run on battery power.

A mobile robot can go where the work is and position itself to get the job done. Mobile robots are excellent for replacing humans in hazardous environments. The robot can be sent instead of the human into nuclear power plants, polluted mines, beneath the sea, and into outer space. Mobile robots can be used in fire fighting and bomb disposal. An example of such a robot is shown in Figure 11.2. This robot is used for fire fighting and underwater repair of ships.

Most mobile robots are operator controlled by means of a long cable. In some cases, they are radio controlled. The operator usually can see the robot performing the task but is located remotely for safety purposes. Sensors on the robot can also provide some feedback.

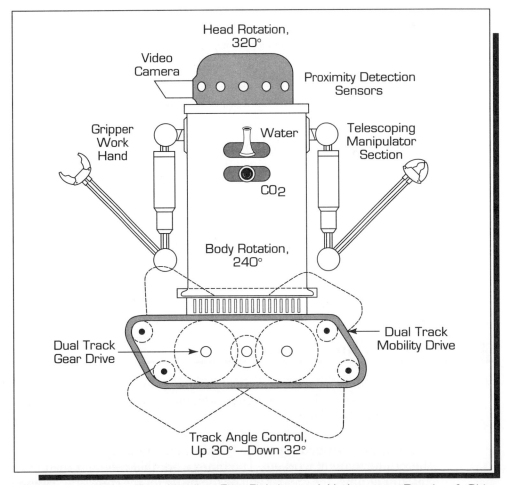

FIGURE 11.2 Robot That Handles Fire Fighting and Underwater Repair of Ships (*Source:* J. A. Gupton, *Computer-Controlled Industrial Machine Processes and Robots* [Englewood Cliffs, N.J.: Prentice-Hall, 1986].)

Box 11.2: Robot Fred Keeps His Guard Up

He can "see" through walls, detect body heat and motion 150 feet in any direction, and can warn of fire or flood. But Fred the robot was having more than a little difficulty navigating over the cracks in the sidewalks of New York as he took a promotional stroll through Wall Street. Marketed by Denning Mobile Robotics of Woburn, Mass., Fred is designed to replace human guards on patrol in warehouses, shopping malls, prisons, and other places where a mute guard might be needed. Denning President Warren George, who guided the four-foot-tall, 485-pound, black robot with a joystick as he staggered over the pavement to the amusement of tourists and other passers-by, said: "We should have put on its soft tires. It's too bumpy out here." A robot like Fred is already patrolling the World Trade Center in Boston and is being marketed nationwide at a cost of $69,000. John Parker, a human security guard at Morgan Guaranty, was skeptical that the electronic upstart could do his job. "It won't be any good if it can't shoot," he said.

In environments where the operator cannot see the work, the robot itself must send back signals which tell its location, position, and status. Video cameras are normally used for such feedback. With the visual information provided, an operator using radio control can operate the robot as required.

Some mobile robots are capable of performing on their own. An example is a security robot that roams around a building at night looking for intruders or sensing undesirable conditions such as fire (see Box 11.2). An example of a mobile robot is Heathkit's HERO I which can be programmed for security and other applications, although its primary application is education and entertainment.

11.4 Why Use Robots?

There are three main justifications for using robots: to improve productivity, to replace humans in hazardous environments, and to improve economic situations and the quality of life.

Productivity Improvement. Business and industry are very concerned about the productivity of workers. The more work that can be turned out in the least amount of time, the greater will be the profit for the company. High productivity is, however, hard to maintain. It can be achieved in short spurts, but sustaining it over a long period of time is difficult. Humans get tired, bored, or sick. We

TABLE 11.1 Advantages of Robots over Humans

More reliable work:	More consistent, accurate work:
Ninety-five percent uptime	Improved quality
Three shifts	Reduced scrap
No vacations	Production predictable
No coffee breaks	Efficient use of capital
Lower cost work:	Self-diagnosis of errors
No employee compensation	Improved work methods
No retirement benefits	Exclusively organization's work:
No insurance plans	No moonlighting
Environmentally insensitive work:	No espionage for competition
In poor climatic conditions	No sabotage
In high-noise environments	No theft
In hazardous locations	No featherbedding

Source: Adapted from *AI Scan Report*, U.S. Department of the Treasury, IRS, 1983.

take vacations and coffee breaks. We get angry, talk to our coworkers, and otherwise slow down the work.

Robots simply do not exhibit any of these deficiencies. Robots work tirelessly, never having to take breaks or time off the job. They are not affected by emotional work situations or demotivational actions. They simply grind away day after day doing their job. For these reasons, robots are particularly good in assembly line jobs where the same tasks are performed time and time again.

Replacing Humans in Hazardous Jobs. Many jobs in industry are dangerous for human beings. Workers are exposed to hazardous materials including sharp, heavy metal pieces, elevated temperatures, toxic chemicals, and high noise levels. Even when safety precautions are taken in such hazardous environments, accidents occur and humans are injured or killed. Such environments are suitable for robots—they can help eliminate human injuries and all the attendant suffering, expense, and waste.

Improving Economic Situations and Quality of Life. Robots also save money. Although there are major capital costs in purchasing robots and integrating them into the workplace, that high cost is eventually repaid. Over the long term, the work simply costs less than paying a human to do it. For a list of the advantages of robots over humans, see Table 11.1. Robots can also increase the quality of life by performing services that allow people more leisure time.

11.5 Components and Operation

To understand the importance of AI in robots of the future, you need to know how current industrial robots operate. This section gives you a brief overview of the main components of a robot and explains how they work together. The typical industrial robot consists of four major components: the manipulator arm, the end effector, the actuator, and the controller. Robots can be configured in many different ways by using variations and combinations of these basic components. Let's discuss each in detail.

Manipulator Arm

The **manipulator arm** is generally made to resemble or work like the arm of a human. It often has a shoulder joint, an elbow, and a wrist. The arm may rotate or slide for further flexibility. There are a variety of ways that manipulator arms can be made. Five basic types are used in industry. Their names reflect the method in which they access any given point within the space defined by their reach.

The simplest arm, shown in Figure 11.3a, is based on Cartesian, or rectangular, coordinates. The idea is to move the end effector of the arm to a given location in space to perform some function. This point in space is defined by the x-, y-, and z-axes of a rectangular coordinate system. The robot arm may move from right to left, up and down, and forward or backward. As the arm moves in the three possible directions within its limits in each direction, it traces out a cube-shaped work space. The end effector, of course, can be positioned anywhere inside the cube.

Another variation of the manipulator arm uses cylindrical rather than Cartesian coordinates. Instead of simply moving back and forth from left to right, the entire arm assembly can rotate 360 degrees.

The spherical, or polar, coordinates system is the third variation. It is illustrated in Figure 11.3b. The vertical, or y, component is replaced by another joint referred to as a shoulder joint. Vertical motion is achieved by rotation in this joint. Again, the entire arm can turn 360 degrees and the arm itself can move in and out (the z-axis). This arrangement traces out a work space that is a portion of a sphere.

A fourth type of arm is known as the articulated, or jointed, spherical coordinate. This was illustrated in Figure 11.1. Like the spherical or polar coordinate system, it can rotate 360 degrees. However, in addition to having a shoulder joint, it also has elbow and wrist joints. Thus the arm has greater flexibility of movement and, as a result, it can trace out a larger portion of a sphere. This type of arm is probably the most widely used in industry because of its great flexibility.

A fifth type of arm is illustrated in Figure 11.3c. It is known as the selective compliance assembly robot arm (SCARA). Its basic work space is a cylinder, which is derived in an unusual manner. Like most of the other arms, it can rotate 360 degrees. However, it has an elbow joint that moves horizontally rather than vertically. This permits it to fold in on itself in either direction. Arms of this type are sometimes used in high-speed assembly work, such as putting together electronic equipment.

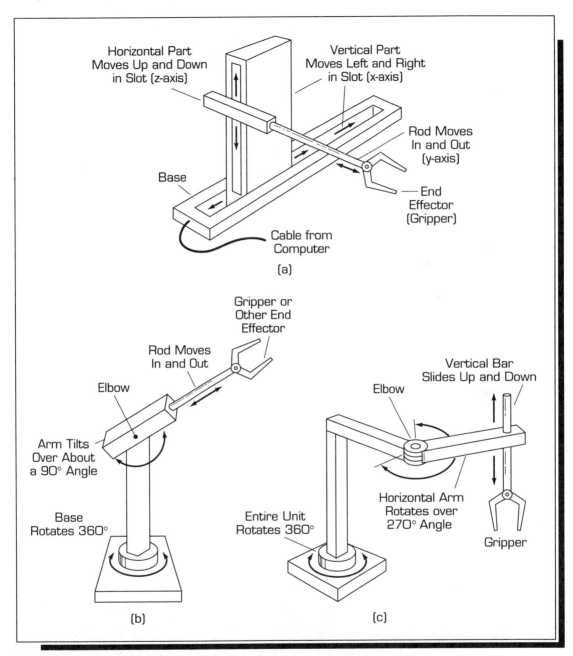

FIGURE 11.3 (a) Rectangular, or Cartesian, Coordinates Arm (b) Spherical, or Polar, Coordinates Arm (c) Selective Compliance Assembly Robot Arm

End Effector

The **end effector,** which attaches to the end of the arm, is the device that performs the specific tasks (e.g., welding, inserting a screw). An almost unlimited number of variations are possible. Most end effectors are specially designed for the job to be done. They are attached to the arm and frequently are interchangeable.

One of the most popular types of end effectors is a **gripper.** In its simplest form (see Figure 11.1) the gripper is a pinchertype assembly that simulates a thumb and one finger. This makes the robot capable of picking up objects within a certain size limitation. More sophisticated assemblies use three or more "fingers" for added flexibility.

Other methods also permit end effectors to pick up objects. For example, some use a sticky substance so they can adhere to an object and lift it. Others use a suction hose arrangement for picking up light objects.

The effector is usually mounted at the wrist of the arm and provides several additional movements referred to as wrist articulation (Figure 11.4). The wrist can rotate and swivel up and down and back and forth. Once the arm has been positioned, these additional wrist movements provide more flexibility in positioning the end effector for its work.

All of the methods of moving the arm and the wrist are classified by the degrees of freedom axes they possess. The term *degrees of freedom* refers to the number of axes about which parts of the robot arm can move. As you saw in Figure 11.3, the arms have three degrees of freedom (follow the arrows). With wrist articulation, three additional axes are achieved. This provides six degrees

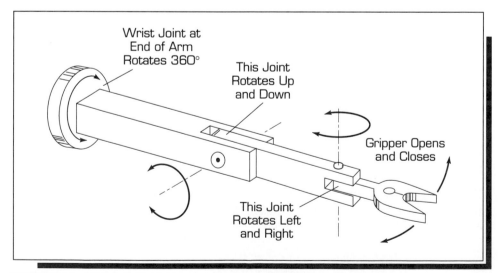

FIGURE 11.4 Wrist Articulation for Flexible End Effector Movement

of freedom, which permits excellent positioning flexibility. Modern robots may have twenty or even more degrees of freedom.

Actuator

The **actuator,** also referred to as the power source, is the basic source of energy for moving the arm, controlling the joints, and operating the end effector. Three basic types of power sources are used: electrical, hydraulic, and pneumatic.

Electrical actuators are AC or DC motors that provide rotation or joint movement. These are used in combination with mechanical assemblies such as gears or pulleys to make the basic movements. Usually there is one motor per joint. A high percentage of robotic arms are driven by electrical motors. Silent and powerful, motors can be conveniently controlled by electronic circuits.

Another commonly used power source is a hydraulic system consisting of a pump that puts a liquid such as oil under pressure. By use of valves and other mechanisms, this pressurized liquid can control all of the arm motion. Hydraulic systems are extremely powerful. They are capable of lifting far greater weights than electrical systems and are, therefore, used in applications requiring maximum strength and durability. Sometimes you will find electrical and hydraulic elements combined in an arm.

A few robotic arms use a pneumatic system for power. Compressed air is forced through lines to cause movement. Pneumatic systems are weak and are used only for work of very light duty. Currently, other sources of energy such as solar energy are used only limitedly, but they could be more prevalent in the future.

Controller

The fourth major component in a robotic system is the **controller.** This is the instrumentation that sends signals to the power source to move the robotic arm to a specific position and to actuate the end effector.

Controllers are electronic circuits. They can be special-purpose programmable controllers that give the robotic arm a sequence of movement instructions and actions. However, the most flexible kind of controller is a general-purpose digital computer, which allows the arm to be reprogrammed for a wide variety of applications.

The simplest form of control system is an open-loop controller. Open loop means that no feedback from the arm itself is used to determine its position. Instead, the controller moves the arm until it hits mechanical stops at selected points.

The most sophisticated kind of controllers are **servomechanisms.** These closed-loop control systems provide greater control over the robotic arm and its positioning. The servo-controlled arms use feedback sensors to send signals back to the controller giving information on the position of the joints. The servomechanism in the controller uses such feedback signals to determine where the arm is and when it reaches the desired position.

Programming

Getting the arm to do what you want it to do requires programming. In programming, the controller is given two sets of coordinates, the beginning coordinates and the ending coordinates. This provides point-to-point operation with no intermediate control. If a particular path must be used in moving from the beginning to the ending coordinates, intermediate points can also be programmed.

As an alternative to direct programming, a robot arm can be "taught" how to move by simply stepping it through the actions it is supposed to take. Many robotic arms have a handheld control box as part of the controller which allows manual positioning and actuation of the arm. An operator uses push buttons or levers on the control box to put the robot through the desired motions. The feedback sensors on the robot joints provide electronic signals that can be captured and stored in memory. In other words, the controller memorizes the movements it has to make as it is manually moved. From that point on, the stored sequence can be played back and the arm will make the desired movements. Such manual control greatly simplifies the task of controlling the robot and eliminates the need for complex programming.

Most modern robots use computers as controllers. Special robotic control programming languages have been developed to help speed up and simplify the process of telling a robot what to do, how, and when.

11.6   Robot Senses and Information Collection

Now let's take a more detailed look at the senses that robots can be given to perceive their environment. They are the same senses that we have, namely, vision, touch, hearing, and smell. (Taste is not included; it is doubtful that robots will need the sense of taste to be useful.) These senses collect information that is interpreted and then used as an input to guide the robots. Information can be provided by communication networks and by measuring instruments (e.g., instruments that measure temperature or infrared wavelengths).

Vision

More information about the work environment can be obtained by vision than by any other means. Machine vision systems are widely available and readily adaptable to robot systems. (Vision systems were covered in Chapter 10.)

Touch

The second most useful sense for a robot is touch. This sense enables the robot to know when it has come into contact with the workpiece or with some environmental object. Better still, touch is the sense of knowing how much pressure is being applied to a workpiece by the arm or end effector. A gripper applies a fixed amount of pressure as it picks up an item. If the pressure is not great enough, the workpiece will fall from the grip of the robot. Worse still, the pressure applied to the workpiece might be too great and cause damage.

Such problems can be overcome by applying pressure transducers to the gripper to tell the control computer exactly how much force is being used. Then it will be able to adjust that force to just the right amount to accomplish the desired objective.

Strain gauges are used on robot grippers to provide pressure feedback. They are a type of transducer whose electrical resistance varies with the pressure or stress applied to it. When connected into an electrical circuit, the strain gauge produces an analog signal proportional to the pressure.

Another kind of sensor used in robot systems is the *proximity detector*. Even though the proximity detector has nothing to do with touch, it does provide feedback on the position of an item relative to the arm.

Hearing

Hearing is currently not as important as vision and touch in robot systems. Nevertheless, there are some situations where the ability to hear can be useful. If sounds are associated with parts of the work, it may be desirable to detect them as a way of providing additional inputs to the robot. Such feedback could come from nothing more than a simple microphone and amplifier set up to detect some noise. In simple situations, the nature of the noise may not be important. It may be important to know that the noise occurs and at what time.

The ultimate in hearing perception, of course, is speech understanding, which we discussed in Chapter 9. There is absolutely no reason why a robot cannot be given a full voice recognition system. In this way, the robot could be controlled by a human giving it instructions. A robot that can recognize human speech and then carry out actions given by the human is certainly intelligent.

The human operator might say, for instance, "Find the bolt and pick it up by the head." Using its vision, the robot would spot the bolt and its arm would move to pick up the bolt. The vision system would be able to identify the head of the bolt, and the grippers would pick it up. At this point, the robot may stop and wait for additional directions. Next, the human operator might say, "Insert the bolt in the workpiece when it comes by." The robot could then rely on its proximity detector to determine when the workpiece is in position. At that point it would begin moving to orient itself to the proper position. The vision system would focus on the workpiece and when it was oriented correctly, the arm would move and insert the bolt. Vision feedback would ensure that the bolt goes into the right position.

In most cases, we want our intelligent robot to be an **autonomous robot,** that is, to carry out the work function without the intervention of a human. That is why we give the robot a control program and then provide feedback so that it can do the job automatically. On the other hand, there may be some situations in which human control of the robot may be desirable. Many robot arms are provided with a control box with appropriate buttons and levers that allow a human to operate it from some remote location. In most cases, the control box is on the end of a long cable; however, voice control systems can also be used.

Smell and Taste

Taste is a sense that probably will never be a major factor in robots, but smell might be an important consideration. Some industrial operations produce odors that may provide the feedback the robot needs to take intelligent action.

Nonhuman Sensing

A variety of electronic transducers are available to provide additional information about the work environment. For example, temperature sensors allow hot or cold conditions to be readily detected and fed back to the computer. Other sensors can monitor the pressure in a tank, the rate of liquid flow in a pipe, the level of liquid in a container, the degree of moisture in the air, and whether an item is accelerating or decelerating. Depending on the work environment and the job to be done, one or more of these sensors could be used to provide additional input to the smart robot.

11.7   Intelligent Robots

Most robots we use today are "dumb" because they cannot "think" or adapt to their surroundings. They simply carry out preprogrammed actions. Such robots are useful, but application of them is limited to situations where intelligence and adaptability are not required.

By "intelligence" in relation to robots we mean the use of information to modify actions. In this respect, **intelligent robots** attempt to mimic humans' sensing and decision-making capabilities so that they can adapt themselves to uncertain conditions and modify their actions. An intelligent robotic system should be able to interact with its environment and adapt the robot's behavior to changing conditions. Another area where intelligence can be developed is in expanding the capabilities of robots in executing more complex tasks. This area is being researched extensively (Alexsander [1], Maus and Allsop [20], Staugard [31]) but little commercialization has been reported. Therefore, the topic will not be discussed here.

Intelligent robotic systems offer potential benefits to a manufacturing operation beyond the performance of specific tasks. For example, they may, according to Powers [24],

☐ reduce the requirements for precise parts or special fixtures by adapting to variations and misalignments;

☐ permit the automation of a variety of custom-designed products; and

☐ perform a complex combination of tasks that would otherwise require multiple tools and operations.

Intelligent robots are perhaps the best example of how several AI technologies can be integrated into a comprehensive automated manufacturing system (Rajaram [25]). All of the branches of AI, especially expert systems and machine vision, can be applied to robotics. These techniques can come together to give the robot perception and thought. By doing so, the robot becomes far more useful. Let's see why and how this is done.

Need for Intelligence

The robot arm can be flexibly positioned, but its range of movement is sometimes limited. Therefore, work must be fed to the robot on a conveyor belt or some other mechanism. The workpiece, in many cases, must be positioned with high precision. As a result, the systems or mechanisms that bring the workpiece to the robot are often more complex and expensive than the robot itself.

The workpiece must be carefully positioned beforehand, so the end effector can be brought to the exact point before being told to do its job. The arm moves in a certain way to rest at a definite point in space. When that final point is reached, the end effector performs some operation, such as gripping, turning, welding, or spraying. If the piece to be worked on does not appear at the right location, the robot will fail in its task. A considerable amount of effort and dollars are expended in ensuring that the robot links up with the item to be processed.

We live in a random, variable, and imperfect environment. To be useful in a work situation, a robot must be able to deal with tolerance variations, disorder, errors, breakage, and other unplanned conditions. It must be able to sense and compensate for such problems. If we give the robot senses, and then give it the power to think, a robot will be able to take some appropriate action even under unpredictable circumstances.

A simple example will illustrate how "smart" robots can cope with a changing environment. Assume that the function of the robot is to pick up a bolt and insert it through a hole in a metal workpiece. The bolts are in a bin next to the robot. The arm picks up one of the bolts by its head and moves the bolt toward the workpiece. The workpiece is moved to the robot on a conveyor belt. The robot arm inserts the bolt in the workpiece, lets go of the bolt, and moves away. The workpiece is then moved on to another location for further processing while the arm goes after the next bolt.

All this works satisfactorily if the bolt is positioned so that the gripper can pick it up with the proper orientation. Also, the bolt is successfully inserted into the hole if the workpiece is properly positioned on the conveyor belt. But

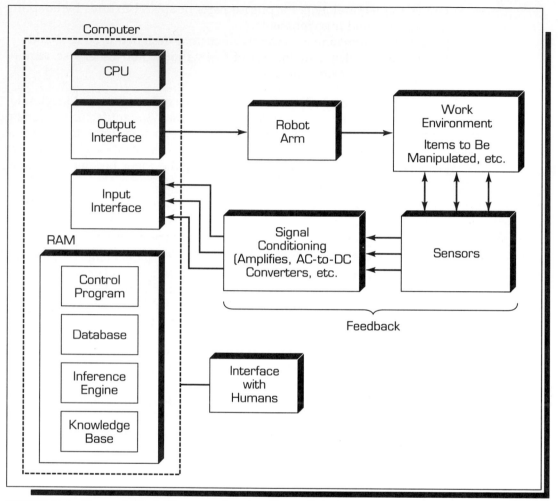

FIGURE 11.5 General Block Diagram of an Intelligent Robot

what happens if the bolts or the workpiece is not properly oriented? The answer is fairly simple. If the bolt is picked up incorrectly, it cannot be inserted into the workpiece. The operation fails. Even if the bolt is picked up successfully, the workpiece may be out of position, in which case the bolt will not be placed where it is supposed to be. Again the operation fails.

If a robot has the ability to *see* the items it is working with, it can certainly do a better job. The robot arm would first look for the head of the bolt to grip rather than some other portion. Furthermore, if the workpiece were slightly out of alignment with the position of the bolt, the robot would see this and move its arm to adjust the variation. When the robot gets some feedback, it can reason about variations that occur and take action to correct its own control program to get the job done. Those activities are part of the error recovery capabilities of intelligent robots (see section 11.8).

How Intelligence Is Provided

Figure 11.5 is a block diagram illustrating the main components of an intelligent robot. The work environment represents the objects to be manipulated. The robot arm block is self-explanatory and includes the end effector and the actuation system. The arm is driven by the computer from an output interface.

The sensors, or transducers, monitor various conditions in the work environment. The electrical signals they generate are conditioned by amplifiers, AC-to-DC converters, or other circuits to make them compatible with the computer input interface. This part of the system is the feedback mechanism.

Operation begins with sensors that monitor the environment and generate electrical signals and binary data compatible with the computer. The binary information is stored in the computer's memory (RAM). These data represent feedback signals that tell the computer what's going on.

As feedback data are analyzed, the knowledge base is referenced to make decisions. The outputs of the inferencing mechanism modify the control program, and the control program sends signals to the robot arm via the output interface. The sensors may then perceive changes that modify the database. With new facts to consider, the inference engine uses the knowledge base to make decisions about what changes to make in the control program to correct for any deviations in the work environment.

11.8   The Robot's Decision-making Framework[2]

The intelligence of robots is provided not by the sensory devices but by the interpretation of information and by the decision-making capabilities of an expert system in the robots. These capabilities as they relate to the concept of error recovery are discussed in this section.

Error Recovery Process

Errors may develop in the robots themselves or in their operating environment. For example, at IBM's automated assembly plant for personal computers in Austin, Tex. (see Saporito [28]), a major problem developed. Feeders that delivered the screws to the assembly robot frequently provided the screws at an incorrect angle. As a result, parts were cracked, jammed, or assembled incorrectly. In such situations the resulting products may be of poor quality and extensive reworking might be required. The handling of such situations by a robot is a good example of **error recovery**. It involves the detection of errors and the execution of corrective actions.

In this section we will briefly describe the error recovery process and how several experimental expert systems support the various steps of the process.

---

[2]This section is based on Turban [32].

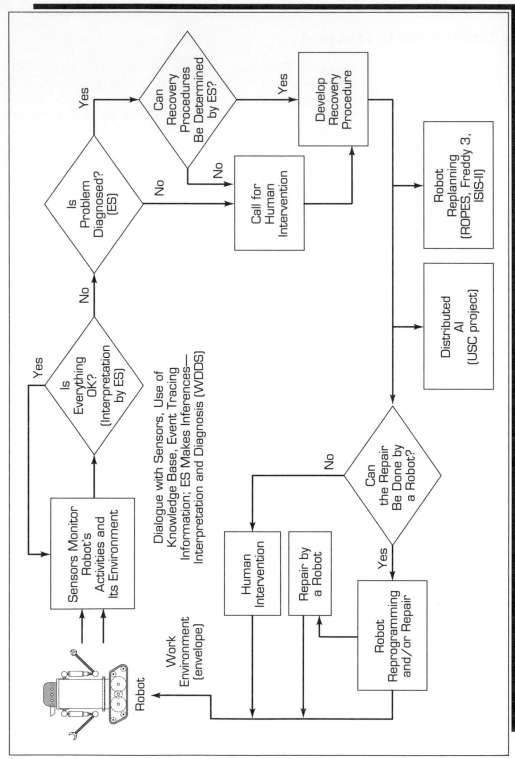

FIGURE 11.6 Error Recovery Process

Figure 11.6 presents a schematic view of the error recovery process together with the names of the robots (or expert systems) that are described here.

An intelligent robot is connected to a system of sensors (or other devices) that collect information (signals) from the environment. These sensors can be implanted in the robot or in its work environment. Signals can also be provided by other robots, a human voice, light, or other means of communication.

Once the signals are received they need to be interpreted. This is where expert systems can be extremely useful.

Interpretation and Diagnosis

The problem in using interpretation and **fault diagnosis** in robotics is that in some cases the initial symptoms of a malfunction may be insufficient to reach a conclusion. Thus, the expert system may require additional information which must be provided by sensors, by the robots' control system, or by a human. The signals that are delivered to the ES initially or at a request may be rather complex, for example, visual information collected by a camera. (For an extensive description of the use of ES in robot vision see Chin and Dyer [8] and Maus and Allsop [20].) Once such technical difficulties are overcome, an ES can perform the diagnosis phase fairly easily. (This is done usually with a rule-based system where the number of rules is only a few hundred.) For example, the robotic machines at Ford Motor Co.'s automotive assembly lines are maintained with expert systems. Another example of an expert system of this nature is WDDS (Weld Defect Diagnosis System, manufactured by Stone and Webster Engineering, Inc.). This system checks the work that is executed by robots and determines the cause of welding defects.

Once the ES determines what went wrong, it can infer the likely consequences of the situation, and then it can prescribe remedies. This capability is available, for example, in the IBM system described by Saporito [28]. More advanced robots will be able, with the help of additional expert systems, to reprogram themselves and even to repair malfunctions in areas controlled by the robot.

Robot Replanning

Robot replanning refers to the decision-making and planning activities that result from some changes. Robot replanning can be done at various levels. The most obvious level is where an ES might have to *plan* a sequence of activities to adjust to changes. At a more complex level, automated planning may be required to schedule the entire work cycle of a plant that includes several robots as well as other types of automated machinery.

Robot replanning activities are fairly complex; therefore they require expert engineers and take a considerable amount of time (see Box 11.3). Several attempts to automate the process with technologies such as general-purpose search heuristics, semantic networks, and first-order predicate calculus have

Box 11.3: Learning by Trial and Error

Professor T. Miller of the University of New Hampshire (Robotics Laboratory) has developed a 500-pound robot arm that can teach itself how to improve its own operation by using *adaptive learning*. (For discussion see R.D. Beer, *Intelligence as Adaptive Behavior* [New York: Academic Press, 1990].) The system includes a computerized network that allows the robot arm to learn via trial and error. Using a feedback mechanism, the computer processes information provided by sensors. As a result, the arm can adjust its own operations.

In the near future this research will probably result in commercial self-calibrating robots. Eventually such robots will be developed into fairly autonomous robots—almost like those we see in the movies.

resulted in limited success. For example, an ES called PULP-1, which uses analogy as an approach to introduce learning capabilities, is still very slow (Chi and Fu [7]). Other programs are effective only for small robotic systems with few independent tasks.

We have seen some encouraging results; an example of such an experimental system is reported by Chi and Fu [7]. Their system, titled ROPES, was successful in improving the planning performance and in increasing planning speed. Furthermore, ROPES can generate multiple possible solutions for a task and assist in evaluating them. The basic AI control strategies for ROPES are searching, matching, and backtracking.

Freddy 3 is an AI-based robot that contains robot replanning capabilities. Its inventors (Mowforth and Bratko [22]) attempted to create a flexible and efficient robot programming environment featuring

- automatic robot planning;
- inductive programming capabilities for the expert system;
- AI-based processing of sensory information;
- flexible use and transformation between different representations of the robot's world, tasks, and knowledge; and
- human transparent communication between robots.

Freddy 3 is one of the most sophisticated ES-based robotic systems ever constructed. It includes several robots, minicomputers, a local area network, and sensors. It was constructed with several ES building tools including Rule Master, an ES shell that provides inductive learning capability.

An example of an ES that helps in robot replanning as a part of an automated plant is ISIS-II. The system, for example, reschedules work in case of malfunctions. For details see Fox and Smith [12].

Control

A considerable amount of effort has been invested in attempts to make the robot's control devices more intelligent. One attempt in this direction involves the construction of an ES whose knowledge base contains information regarding the system to be controlled. For example, if the robot operates on an assembly line, the knowledge base contains information relating to the parts to be assembled, the tools to be used, the potential problem areas, and possible emergency actions. The ES determines the control signals required to obtain the desired response from the robots and their environments.

Teams of Robots

Most of today's robots are individually programmed for each particular task. However, in computer-integrated manufacturing, robots may be organized in a team and may be required to perform any number of tasks. For example, IBM's laptop computer is assembled by a team of three robots, each of which performs some assembly operations. In addition, there is a robot that provides material handling and one that performs tests.

Expert systems could direct robots to "communicate" and "reason" with each other. Work is currently being done at the Institute for Robotics and Intelligent Systems at the University of Southern California (USC) in an attempt to equip teams of robots at work on an assembly line with high-order decision-making capabilities. For example, the ES in the robots would be able to decide among themselves how best to accomplish a particular task. Thus, if a supply of parts arrives late, several robots (rather than one) could be assigned to the task of inspecting and preparing the parts so that the work team can catch up with the schedule.

The topic of robotic teamwork has spawned a new field of research which is part of distributed artificial intelligence. Commercial implementation of an intelligent robotics team, however, will not occur in the near future.

Maintenance by an Expert System

According to Ayres and Miller [4], an ultimate goal is for robots to complete the error recovery process by repairing themselves. This capability exists today only in a few research laboratories, some military devices, movies, and science fiction stories. As a preliminary step, though, expert systems and robots are combining their capabilities in the maintenance of nonrobotic mechanical systems.

The maintenance and repair of many mechanical systems is labor intensive and requires a high level of expertise. There are indications that the automotive industry may lead the way in using robots to perform this type of maintenance. For example, several years ago Volkswagen Corp. introduced a diagnostic system for some of its models in which an automatic electronic diagnostician was plugged into a specially designed connector built into the car. With expert system capability, an automated diagnostician could guide a human, or even a robot, through the needed repairs and adjustments, step by step, reducing the need for skilled human labor.

Considering the number of automobile parts that are commonly rebuilt, can you foresee ambitious robotic applications in automotive maintenance? Applications may range from carburetors and alternators up to automatic transmissions. In the future, robotic systems will combine the precision and dexterity developed for assembly operations with inspection capability. With the addition of an ES that can recognize parts needing replacement, a robot could perform the entire repair task; all it would require would be the old unit and a kit of replacement parts. Perhaps, in the future, this capability could be expanded to self-repair of robots.

Improved Safety

Accidents involving robots can result in severe damage, including the loss of human life (as has happened in both Japan and the United States). Accidents occur for several reasons. For example, one safety regulation for working with robots is that human employees must not enter the robot's working environment (called work envelope). Some employees do enter the work envelope; they are either unaware of safety regulations or ignore them. By integrating an expert system with robots and sensor devices such accidents can be prevented or their consequences can be minimized.

An example of ES application in safety is the Robotic Intelligence Safety System (RISS). RISS is built with rules like the following:

IF: The robot was commanded to be deactivated, and a person is
          inside the work envelope, and the robot remains active,
THEN: Cut off the main power circuit breaker.

RISS (see Ramirez [26]) constantly monitors the robots' environment for failures or abnormalities. If any are detected, they are diagnosed and corrective actions are executed. Information is gathered from several sources in the environment, including the robot's components (e.g., the end effector and the controller), sensors, other computers and machines, and human operators. Corrective actions for possibly dangerous situations are outputted to the robot's controller, the controllers of other machines, or to a display. Corrective actions may also be outputted to relays or alarms. The robot's next-scheduled actions can then be modified or halted.

Learning

For robots to exhibit a high level of intelligence, they must be able to learn. This capability will be provided by expert systems. For example, experiments at the Oak Ridge National Laboratory (see Spelt et al. [30]) attempted to teach a mobile robot to take advantage of its capability for (1) manipulating objects with its manipulator arms, (2) successfully docking in front of the control panel, and (3) diagnosing problems autonomously in various similar (but not identical) plant components (e.g., valves) and then repair them. The approach is one of trial and error and it is based on theories in machine learning.

11.9 What Robots Do

As you can imagine, robots perform a variety of tasks. Let's take a look at some of their more common functions.

General Applications

Currently, robots handle four manufacturing tasks: welding, materials handling, assembly, and painting.

Welding. A most frequent application of robotic arms in manufacturing is welding. The arms are set up along a production line conveyor. As various components are put into place, robotic arms move in and make spot welds at predetermined locations. Today, most auto bodies and frames are made using robot welders. The robot arm can position itself precisely and make the weld at the designated spot. It also can do it faster and more consistently than people. Limited continuous welding can be executed by robots as well.

For several reasons, welding is better done by robots than by humans. Welding is a dangerous activity that requires intense concentration and skill over a long period of time. Furthermore, the locations of many welds require humans to physically maneuver into difficult positions. Finally, fumes and gases present in welding are dangerous to human health.

Materials Handling. Another application is transfer of materials, components, and assemblies from one place to another using a robot arm. Such arms are generally referred to as "pick and place" robots. The robot arm is used for loading or unloading. Parts on a vehicle or conveyor may be transferred to another location. Manufactured goods may be loaded on a vehicle for transportation elsewhere. The robot arm is also handy for moving components from a work surface to a conveyor belt or vice versa. Some robot arms can look through an assembly of parts, select a specific part, pick it up, and move it to another place.

Assembly. In many manufacturing applications, robots actually perform the assembly of some machine or device. Individual components are picked up by the arm and put together in a proper sequence to form the device. A common application is "stuffing" printed circuit boards. Special robots pick up the integrated circuits, transistors, resistors, capacitors, and other components, bend the leads, and insert them into printed circuit boards. The boards are then automatically transferred to a flow soldering machine where the final assembly operation takes place. More complicated applications are assembly of laptop computers (IBM) and dishwashers (General Electric).

Spraying and Painting. Another widely used application is spraying. At the end of the robot arm, a special nozzle connected to a hose and a source of liquid is used to spray components during the manufacturing process. The most common form of spraying, of course, is painting. The robot arm can be programmed to move precisely to provide an even coat of paint to the most unusually shaped objects in a short period of time. The amount of paint can be controlled precisely. The automobile industry uses robots extensively in painting cars. Robots also can spray chemicals, for example, to prevent rust or corrosion. Oil might be sprayed for lubrication purposes.

In most spraying applications, the environment is extremely hazardous. Humans must be physically protected so their bodies do not become coated with the paint or other liquid. Goggles and breathing filters are particularly important. It is senseless to use humans in these applications when robots can perform the job faster, better, and more consistently without risk to people.

Other Operations. Other applications in manufacturing, and lately in services, are being developed. For example, with a proper attachment at the end of the robotic arm, an incredible variety of operations can be performed; screwing or tightening functions are an example. Riveting is another example. Other types of robot arms are used for pouring operations (e.g., in a foundry). In most cases, special tools are attached to the end of the robot arm to perform particular operations.

Specific Applications

It makes sense that expert systems could provide the technology for intelligent robots that will be able to cope with unstructured environments. Although extensive experiments are being conducted in research institutions, there are few commercial intelligent robots currently in use. As you'll see from the examples summarized below, however, there is a tremendous potential for such systems.

Assembly. IBM's laptop personal computer is the first computer to be assembled entirely by intelligent robots. The factory uses a process called flexible automation, which makes use of modular workstations that are programmed to perform a variety of tasks. From the receiving dock to the shipping dock, the computer is assembled, tested, packaged, and shipped by robots. The robots use extensive sensory systems (such as computer vision) to execute tasks as well as to detect errors. Once errors or malfunctions are detected, the information is transmitted to an expert system, which diagnoses the situation and reports the results to a human supervisor (there is only one such person in the entire plant). At the present time, the corrective actions suggested by the expert system are executed by humans.

The plant assembles over 100,000 computers a year and is being upgraded for increased output and reduced costs. For further details, see Saporito [28].

Expert Welding. Adaptiweld Systems (Adaptive Technologies, Inc.) is one of the first commercially available intelligent robot welding systems. It incorporates the knowledge of skilled welders. This knowledge is used for robot planning once the characteristics of a stream to be welded are collected by a 3-D vision system. Based on these characteristics, the expert system plans the welding task to be performed without direct human supervision. The rules in the knowledge base allow the system to best respond to particular welding conditions. For further information see Kerth [18].

Automated Materials Handling System. DEC has implemented a materials handling system in two of its manufacturing facilities. These systems control factory inventory and generate timely, accurate reports on work progress and quality. Key elements of each system are a pair of robots that transport assembly items and two expert systems that determine when and to where items should be dispatched.

The expert systems, named Dispatcher and Mover, are the controlling software for the entire materials handling system. Dispatcher determines the order in which work-in-progress (WIP) items are dispatched and to which workstations they will be sent. Mover coordinates and drives WIP items via the robots' carousels and conveyors.

Dispatcher uses information in its knowledge base to select the best work item(s) to dispatch to a workstation, depending on the current work status and demand on the factory floor. The knowledge base was created initially with interactive utilities that are part of the system. New work is entered into the system either by automatic utilities or iterative routines. Dispatcher performs updates automatically, but any exceptions that arise can be handled manually with interactive utilities.

Dispatcher's knowledge base contains information about four components that enable it to make decisions: workstations, route list, unit load, and WIP. These elements, along with the validation table that verifies valid workstations, operations, parts, and classes, represent the state of the factory floor. Since its implementation at DEC's Marlborough, Mass., facility in 1985, the materials handling system has been in operation six days a week for three shifts per day. During the first month, it reduced inventory by 50 percent, and inventory accounts increased in accuracy to 99.9 percent. DEC estimates that this system saves $25 million annually.

Automotive Diagnosis. Robots play a major role in the automotive industry, yet we sometimes hear about robots going askew—painting windshields or one another. Today's state-of-the-art technology involves human expert intervention in such cases. However, the human expert may not always be available when things go wrong. Ford Motor Co. developed an expert system that is used by inexperienced technicians via a personal computer. The technician responds to a series of questions generated by the ES. The system makes a diagnosis and suggests a corrective action. (For further details consult [2].)

Other Applications. A prototype ES-based error recovery system for off-line programming systems has been developed at the University of Minnesota. This rule-based system is still fairly limited in its capabilities, but a stronger inference mechanism is planned (e.g., by using the ES frame's representation and object-oriented programming).

One of the most interesting applications of error recovery is in mobile robots. For example, Hermies III (from Oak Ridge National Laboratory) is an automated guided vehicle that carries and retrieves materials in hazardous environments. It can also navigate and dodge obstacles and still figure out how to reach its goals. (For further information see [17]. For information about other fault diagnostic expert systems see [27].)

Chapter Highlights

- □ AI attempts to mimic or duplicate human thought, while robots attempt to emulate human physical activity.
- □ A robot is an electromechanical device that duplicates one or more physical functions of a human. Robots most often simulate an arm and hand.
- □ Robots are just dumb machines, but because some of them are computer controlled, they may be given "intelligence" with AI techniques.
- □ Androids are synthetic humans with a human shape and mechanical limbs.
- □ Cyborgs are humans with some robotic limb or prosthetic device.
- □ Industrial robots are defined as reprogrammable multifunctional manipulators.
- □ Most robots are fixed manipulator arms; they take the place of humans in manufacturing processes.
- □ Mobile robots provide a wider range of capabilities than fixed robots; they can propel themselves to the work.
- □ Robots are better at repetitive, boring, manual tasks than humans. They can work longer periods without relief and make fewer errors.
- □ Robots are ideal for taking the place of humans on dangerous jobs or in hazardous environments.
- □ Often robots do a job not only faster and more reliably but also cheaper than humans; this makes them economically justifiable.
- □ Robotic arms rotate and have moveable joints (shoulder, elbow, wrists) so they can move to any position within a given range. Various coordinate

systems are used to describe their position and define the scope of the work area.

□ The work of a robotic arm is done by the "hand," or end effector. The end effector is a tool that grasps, welds, sprays, or manipulates. Many end effectors are custom designed for a job and are interchangeable.

□ The robotic arm is moved by electrical motors or by hydraulic or pneumatic actuating mechanisms.

□ Robotic arms are controlled by feedback servomechanisms.

□ The trend is to operate robots from computers so their operations can be "tweaked" to optimize performance or changed completely to meet a different need.

□ Special robot programming languages have been created to help simplify the programming process.

□ Intelligent robots that think for themselves, reason, and make decisions are becoming practical and more widely used.

□ Robots are more powerful, productive, flexible, and useful if they can reason for themselves.

□ To be intelligent, a robot must have senses such as sight, hearing, feel, or smell. Transducers that detect pressure, light, temperature, liquid level, and other physical characteristics give robots inputs about their work and environment. These sensors let robots adapt to random, unpredictable, and imperfect surroundings and deal with unexpected events.

□ Computers controlling the robot use AI programs with a knowledge base and an inferencing system that give them the intelligence to operate independently and deal with widely varying situations successfully.

□ Robotic intelligence is expressed in the robot's ability to execute complex tasks and in its error recovery capabilities.

□ Intelligence is provided by expert systems and could be supported by voice recognition.

□ Sensing capabilities are necessary but not sufficient for error recovery.

□ The error recovery process involves fault diagnosis (what is wrong), recovery procedures, replanning of the robot, and physical repair (if needed).

□ An expert system that learns from experience will be able to function within an autonomous robot.

□ A most common robot function is welding. Other popular robot applications are materials handling, assembly, and spraying.

Key Terms

actuator	cyborg	intelligent robot
android	end effector	manipulator arm
automated guided	error recovery	robot
vehicle	fault diagnosis	sensor
autonomous robot	gripper	servomechanism
controller		

Questions for Review

1. Distinguish robotics from automation.
2. Why are robots described as "dumb"?
3. What is the role of computers in robotics?
4. Explain androids and cyborgs.
5. Define a robot.
6. What is an automated guided vehicle?
7. Give an example of productivity improvement created by a robot.
8. What is the purpose of an end effector? How can it add degrees of freedom to the robotic arm?
9. What types of power supply are common in today's robots?
10. What is the function of the controller?
11. Differentiate between open-loop and closed-loop controllers.
12. What is a servomechanism? How can it be used in robotics?
13. Explain how a robot can be programmed to move an object between two points.
14. List the types of senses used in robotics and their major functions.
15. Briefly describe the types of devices that can be used to provide a touching sense.
16. Describe the various steps of the error recovery process.
17. Define error recovery and discuss its importance in robotics.
18. Review the error recovery process shown in Figure 11.6 and identify all decision-making points.
19. What are the advantages of organizing a team of robots? What difficulties may arise in such a configuration? What can we do (at least in theory) about these difficulties?

Questions for Discussion

1. Review the advantages of a robot over a human. What are the advantages of a human over a robot?
2. If robots are so wonderful, why don't we see more of them around us?
3. Present two sides to Asimov's laws of robotics. Discuss why Asimov's laws are important, when they should/should not be adhered to, and whether they are practical in today's business environment.
4. It is said that robots are programmed in special computer languages and not in regular languages such as COBOL. Why?
5. Instead of being programmed, a robotic arm is "taught" how to work. What do we mean by *taught*, and why is it done this way?
6. How is speech recognition related to robotics? Would you recommend the integration of the two? Why?
7. Review the various expert systems mentioned in Figure 11.6. Discuss the tasks that each of them provides.

8. One of the main features of human intelligence is the ability to learn from experience (trial and error). Why is this capability difficult to duplicate in robotics? Find articles on this topic and summarize them.

References and Bibliography

1. Alexsander, I. "Artificial Intelligence for Production Engineering: A Historical Approach." *Robotica* 5 (1987).
2. *American Metal Market* (April 21, 1986).
3. Asimov, I. *I, Robot.* Garden City, N.Y.: Doubleday & Co., 1950.
4. Ayres, R.U., and S.M. Miller. *Robotics and Flexible Manufacturing Technology.* Noyer Publishing Co., 1985.
5. Barb, J.F. "An Assessment of Industrial Robots: Capabilities, Economics, and Impacts." *Journal of Operations Management* (February 1987).
6. Burks, B.L., et al. "Autonomous Navigation, Exploration and Recognition Using HERMIES-IIB Robot." *IEEE Expert* (Winter 1987): 18–27.
7. Chi, Z., and K.S. Fu. "Robot Planning Expert Systems." In *Proceedings, IEEE International Conference on Robotics and Automation.* San Francisco, April 1986.
8. Chin, R.T., and C.R. Dyer. "Model-based Recognition in Robot Vision." *ACM Computing Review* (March 1986).
9. Donald, B.R. *Error Detection and Recovery in Robotics.* New York: Springer-Verlag, 1989.
10. Engelberger, J.F. *Robotics in Service.* Cambridge, Mass.: MIT Press, 1989.
11. Flynn, A.M. "Gnat Robots." *AI Expert* (December 1987).
12. Fox, H.S., and S.F. Smith. "ISIS—A Knowledge-Based System for Factory Scheduling." *Expert Systems* 1 (no. 1, 1984).
13. Freedom, P., and A. Malowany. "SAGE: A DSS for Sequencing of Operations within a Robotic." *Decision Support Systems* (October 1988).
14. Gupton, J.A. *Computer-Controlled Industrial Machine Processes and Robots.* Englewood Cliffs, N.J.: Prentice-Hall, 1986.
15. Ho, C.Y., and G.W. Zobrist, eds. *Progress in Robotics and Intelligent Systems.* Norwood, N.J.: Ablex Publishing Corp., 1990.
16. Hunt, V.D. *The Robotics Sourcebook.* New York: Elsevier, 1988.
17. *IEEE Expert* (Winter 1987).
18. Kerth, W.J., Jr. "Knowledge-Based Expert Welding." *Robots* 9. June 1985.
19. Logsdon, T. *The Robot Revolution.* New York: Simon & Schuster, 1984.
20. Maus, R., and R. Allsop. *Robotics: A Manager's Guide.* New York: John Wiley & Sons, 1986.
21. Moravec, H. *Mind Children—The Future of Robot and Human Intelligence.* Cambridge, Mass.: Harvard Univ. Press, 1988.
22. Mowforth, P., and I. Bratko. "AI Robotics: Flexibility and Integration." *Robotica* 5 (1987).
23. Pollock, J. *How to Build a Person: A Prolegomenon.* Cambridge, Mass.: MIT Press, 1989.

24. Powers, J.H., Jr. *Computer Automated Manufacturing*. New York: McGraw-Hill, 1987.
25. Rajaram, N.S. "Artificial Intelligence—The Achilles Heel of Robotics and Manufacturing." *Robotics Engineering* (January 1986).
26. Ramirez, C.A. "Artificial Intelligence Applied to Robot Fail Safe Operations." *Robots* 9 (June 1985).
27. *Robots*. Special Issue (October 1985).
28. Saporito, B. "IBM's No-hands Assembly Line." *Fortune* 15 (September 1986).
29. Song, S., and K.J. Waldron. *Machines That Think*. Cambridge, Mass.: MIT Press, 1988.
30. Spelt, P.F., et al. "Learning by an Autonomous Robot at a Process Control Panel." *IEEE Expert* (Winter 1989).
31. Staugard, A.C., Jr. *Robotics and Artificial Intelligence*. Englewood Cliffs, N.J.: Prentice-Hall, 1987.
32. Turban, E. "Expert Systems-Based Robot Technology." *Expert Systems* (May 1990).
33. Vukobratovic, M., ed. *Introduction to Robotics*. New York: Springer-Verlag, 1989.

Part 4

Building Knowledge-based Systems

Part 4 concentrates on the construction of knowledge-based (or expert) systems; building other AI technologies is outside the scope of this book. Several topics are generic enough, however, to be used in the construction of a natural language processor or a machine vision system. In Chapter 12 the development process is described and its various steps are outlined. Expert systems can be constructed with many tools, and these are described in detail in Chapter 13. Of special interest are shells and hybrid environments. We also consider how to select among the many tools on the market. In Chapter 14 special design issues are presented. In the discussion of the user-computer interface in AI, the dialogue process and explanations are stressed. Then, several special architectures are reviewed: blackboard, distributed and parallel AI, and real-time systems. The chapter includes a presentation of an integrated design (interactive multimedia)—a preview of the integration issue that begins Part 5.

Chapter 12

Building Expert Systems

This chapter provides an overview of the process of building expert systems. The process, which consists of six major phases and several dozen activities, is executed differently depending on the nature of the system being constructed, the development strategy, and the supporting tools. The following topics form the framework for analyzing the building process:

(Continued)

12.1   Introduction

Building AI applications can be a very complex process, especially when robotics, natural language processors, and/or voice technologies are integrated with a computer-based information system. On the other hand, small expert systems applications can be built with relative ease. In either case, three basic questions must be answered (Figure 12.1):

1. What is the application to be built? (problem selection)
2. Who is going to build the application? (development strategy)
3. How is the application going to be built? (development process)

The answers to these questions are interrelated. In addition, several other questions, such as when to build and where to build, need to be addressed.

Our focus in this chapter is expert systems. It is impossible to describe the construction of all AI technologies or even expert systems in one chapter. All we can do is provide a general framework. If you are interested in details, refer to one of these books: Carrico et al. [11], Harmon and Sawyer [21], Prerau [42], and Walters and Nielsen [58].

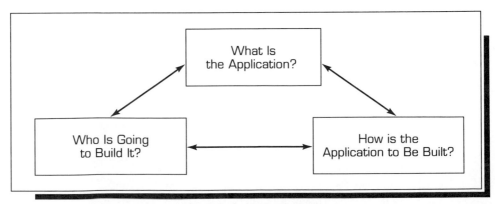

FIGURE 12.1   Basic Questions Regarding AI Applications

12.2 Development Life Cycle

An expert system is basically computer software and as such its development follows a software development process. The goal of such a process is to maximize the probability of developing viable, sustainable software within cost limitations and according to schedule. The main functions of a model of this process are to determine the order of the steps (or tasks) involved in the software development and to establish the transition criteria for progressing from one stage to another. Many such models have been proposed; notable is the waterfall model (see Boehm [9]) for a **system development life cycle**.

When expert systems are constructed, some or all of the software development tasks are being performed. The nature of the specific application determines which tasks are going to be performed, in which order, and to what depth. For example, a large-scale ES will be developed according to a complex life-cycle process (see Appendix A at the end of this chapter), whereas a small-scale system for end-users will include only a few of the tasks (see Appendix B at the end of this chapter).

The various tasks that are encountered in building expert systems are organized in six phases, as shown in Figure 12.2. Specific explanations of these phases and some of the tasks involved are provided in the remaining sections of this chapter.

Be aware, however, that the process is *not linear*; rather, some tasks are performed together, and as will be shown, a return to previous tasks or even phases happens frequently.

12.3 Phase I: Project Initialization

Finding an appropriate project for AI/ES is not an easy task. Dozens of factors must be considered, and many ES projects fail because of poor front-end analysis. Experts have developed methodologies and checklists for executing the tasks in this phase (e.g., Beckman [6], Carrico et al. [11], Harmon and Sawyer [21], Jain and Chaturvedi [24], Laufman et al. [30], Prerau [42], and Samuell and Jones [46]). In a large-scale project, several participants will probably be involved.

The typical tasks of this phase are shown in Table 12.1. The tasks are interrelated and may not follow any specific sequence (see Harmon and Sawyer [21] for a proposed flow of tasks). The details of the major tasks are discussed next.

12.4 Problem Definition and Needs Assessment

A clear definition of the problem simplifies the remaining tasks significantly and helps generate a productive program. Defining the problem is a matter of

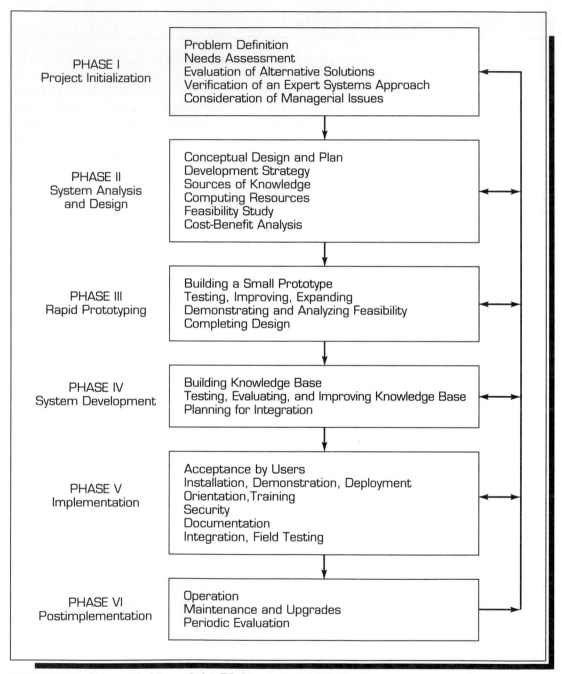

FIGURE 12.2   Schematic View of the ES Development Life Cycle

TABLE 12.1 Tasks in Project Initialization

Problem definition

Needs assessment

Evaluation of alternative solutions
(availability of experts, education and training, packaged knowledge, conventional software)

Verification of an expert systems approach
(requirements, justification, appropriateness)

Consideration of managerial issues
(project initiator, financing, resources, legal and other constraints, selling the project, identifying a champion)

Ending milestone: Approval of the project in principle

answering some basic questions. Just what is the problem? What are the real needs? Typical business problems could be low productivity, lack of sufficient expert knowledge to go around, information overload, time problems, or people problems. Whatever the problem or need, write a clear statement of it and provide as much supporting information as possible. Such a statement will serve as the guideline and specification for your development program.

Expert system technology is relatively new and many people are still discovering it. For that reason, people are inclined to seek problems that an expert system can solve just so they can get involved with the technology. Although there is nothing wrong with this approach, keep in mind that the real issue is to solve a problem in the best way; an expert system may or may not be the correct solution.

Most expert systems are being used to improve an aspect of poor job performance. For example, an employee may not be achieving a desired quantity or quality of work within time or cost constraints. Problems like this can often be traced to a lack of knowledge. The employee must either possess the knowledge or have access to it, whether in the form of an expert person or an expert system. The best way to understand the problem or need is to conduct a kind of formal study called **needs assessment**. In this study the suspected job performance problem is revealed and analyzed.

As we have seen, knowledge is at the heart of those problems that best fit expert system solutions. What does the employee know? What are his or her educational background, training, and experience? Are experts accessible? Of course, not all problems are going to be related to poor employee performance. Whatever the type of problem, collecting relevant background information is important because it gives you the data you need to make a decision about a computerized program. If knowledge is at the root of the problem, most likely you have a candidate for an expert system.

12.5   Evaluation of Alternative Solutions

Before you start a major ES development program, consider alternative solutions to the problem. Lack of knowledge is a problem that could be solved in ways other than with expert systems. Let's consider some examples.

Availability of Experts. If the problem is knowledge related, then someone must have the desired knowledge. One approach may simply be to make the expert more accessible to those needing the expertise. Perhaps the solution is as simple as making the expert's telephone number available to the person who needs it. Another solution might be to identify additional experts who can help. Hiring or creating new experts is another option.

Education and Training. People acquire knowledge through study and experience. One solution to a problem involving lack of knowledge is to provide additional education and training in the desired subject matter for those who need it. Appropriate courses or seminars may be available. If not, the experts could create and teach them. Employees could work with experts to acquire the knowledge and experience through on-the-job training. This solution creates new experts through education. Computer-aided instruction may be appropriate. Courses, seminars, and related materials are normally much less expensive to develop than an expert system.

Training and education are excellent long-term solutions because, having acquired them, the employee usually retains their benefits. Remember, though, that should the employee leave the job, the knowledge would be lost. Creating an expert system containing the knowledge is a superior permanent solution, but it can be far more time-consuming and expensive than training. The more people need to be trained, the less attractive is training in comparison with an expert system.

Packaged Knowledge. An alternative to additional education and training is to package the knowledge and related information into printed (or electronic) documentation. The expert may be able to create or help create a manual or job aid containing all the facts, figures, procedures, and other knowledge needed to do the job. In this form, an employee can readily access the knowledge. Many times this simple solution is all that is required.

Of course, it takes time to generate manuals and job aids. However, they are often less expensive than expert systems and a great deal faster and easier to create.

Conventional Software. A computer solution may still be best for a problem, but an expert system may not be completely appropriate. Once you've defined a problem, examine the possibility of using standard software packages. For example, a popular spreadsheet or database management system may work. If you have the ability to develop traditional software, evaluate this option. It may be a faster and simpler solution than an expert system. This is particularly true if expert systems are new to you and your organization; large overhead costs are associated with creating the first expert system because it is a learning process. However, if an expert system is a good fit for the solution, and there is general agreement to make the investment, then by all means do it.

12.6   Verification of an Expert System Approach

The fact that other alternatives are not appropriate for solving a problem does not mean that an expert system is necessary. A framework for determining a fit with an ES approach was proposed by Waterman [60]. According to this framework (which has been modified in this text), a three-part study should be conducted: requirements, justification, and appropriateness.

Requirements for ES Development. The following twelve requirements are *all* necessary to make ES development successful:

1. The task does not require common sense.
2. The task requires only cognitive, not physical, skills.
3. At least one genuine expert, who is willing to cooperate, exists.
4. Experts involved can articulate their methods of problem solving.
5. Experts involved can agree on the knowledge and the solution approach to the problem.
6. The task is not too difficult.
7. The task is well understood and is defined clearly.
8. The task definition is fairly stable.
9. Conventional (algorithmic) computer solution techniques are not satisfactory.
10. Incorrect or nonoptimal results can be tolerated.
11. Data and test cases are available.
12. The task's vocabulary has no more than a couple of hundred concepts.

Justification for ES Development. Like any other information system, an expert system needs to be justified. Of the following eight factors, at least one must be present to justify an ES:

1. The solution to the problem has a high payoff.
2. The ES can preserve scarce human expertise so it will not be lost.
3. Expertise is needed in many locations.
4. Expertise is needed in hostile or hazardous environments.
5. The expertise improves performance and/or quality.
6. The system can be used for training.

7. The ES solution can be derived faster than that which a human can provide.
8. The ES is more consistent and/or accurate than a human.

The derived benefits in one or more of these areas must be compared against the costs of developing the system. A preliminary justification is conducted in this phase, whereas a detailed analysis is performed in phase II.

Appropriateness of the ES. Waterman [60] suggests that the following three factors be considered in determining when it is appropriate to develop an ES:

1. Nature of the problem: The problem should have a symbolic structure, and heuristics should be available for its solution. In addition, it is desirable that the task be decomposable.
2. Complexity of the task: The task should be neither too easy nor too difficult for a human expert.
3. Scope of the problem: The problem should be of a manageable size; it also should have some practical value.

Checklists. Several checklists have been developed to assist in finding applications suitable for expert system development:

☐ An elaborate method with four separate checklists has been suggested by Slagle and Wick [49], who use a weighing point system.
☐ A simple two-page checklist has been published (see Appendix C).
☐ A computerized checklist built into a software program called Expert Ease is shown in Table 12.2. This simple checklist helps the user decide whether the task is appropriate for an ES. For instance, if the answer to A is yes, then an ES is not appropriate. A good ES candidate will be one with an answer such as: A-2, B-3, C-1, and D-1. Based on the user's answers, the program tells the user if the task selected is appropriate for ES development.
☐ A checklist approach that attempts to assess the strategic value of an ES has been suggested by Samuell and Jones [46].
☐ Detailed checklists have been proposed by Prerau [42].

The choice of problem should also take into consideration the generic areas discussed in Chapter 3 where ES have proved to be successful.

12.7 Consideration of Managerial Issues

Expert systems projects do not start by themselves (Figure 12.3). Sometimes they start because there is an acute need. But in many cases, they start because someone in the organization believes in AI technologies and is willing to support an ES project. A project may start as soon as a decision is made to look for an

TABLE 12.2 Checklist for Task Selection

A. Are the answers to your problem or your decisions determined at random?
   1. Yes
   2. No
B. How important is accuracy in the answers or decisions? What is the consequence of a wrong answer or decision?
   1. I need total accuracy. The consequences of a wrong answer or decision are catastrophic.
   2. Accuracy is important. I can tolerate occasional wrong answers, but I need the right answers most of the time.
   3. Although accuracy is still important, I can tolerate initial errors as long as I can adapt the system to new or changing circumstances.
C. How complete is the set of examples describing your problem or decision?
   1. My set of examples is 100 percent complete and covers every possible case that could arise.
   2. My set of examples is almost complete. I think it covers most cases that will arise.
   3. My set of examples covers only a small number of the possible situations that could occur.
   4. My set of examples covers very few of the possible situations that could occur.
D. How well will the people who will use the system be able to detect wrong answers?
   1. The people who will use the system are capable of spotting wrong answers. They can compensate for flaws or gaps in the set of examples.
   2. The people who will use the system will not be able to detect wrong answers.

Source: Expert Ease (now called Expert One), a software program from Human Edge, Palo Alto, Calif.

appropriate project. A project may start because the company has decided to follow a competitor's lead or because one of the company's employees did an ES project as a student. Who starts a project is obviously an important issue but there are several other managerial issues that need to be considered when an ES (or any other AI project) is launched:

- Availability of financing: Even if the project is potentially very profitable, it may take two years before the cash flow will be positive. Someone will have to pay the bill.
- Availability of other resources: An ES may require other resources, ranging from the attention of the information systems people to availability of certain equipment.
- Legal and other potential constraints: Such constraints can "kill" a project. They need to be identified as early as possible. Detailed attention is given to these topics in the feasibility study.
- Selling the project: All interested parties and especially top management must be convinced of the project's value. (See McCullough [35].)
- Identifying a champion: Someone in top management needs to sponsor the project strongly.

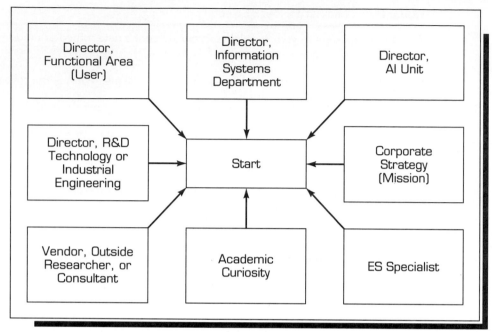

FIGURE 12.3 Potential Initiators of AI Projects

12.8   Phase II: System Analysis and Design

Once the idea of the project has been blessed, a detailed system analysis must be conducted to obtain some idea of how the system is going to look. Many tasks are performed in this phase, which may be supported by an initial prototype. These tasks are listed in Table 12.3.

TABLE 12.3 Tasks in Project Conceptualization and System Analysis

Tasks
Conceptual design and plan
Development strategy
Sources of knowledge
Computing resources
Feasibility study
Cost-benefit analysis
Ending milestone: approved complete project plan

12.9   Conceptual Design

A conceptual design of an ES is similar to an architectural sketch of a house. It gives you a general idea of what the system will look like and how it is going to solve the problem. The design shows the general capabilities of the system, the interfaces with other computer-based information systems, the areas of risk, the required resources, anticipated cash flow, the composition of the team, and any other information that is necessary for detailed design later. Vendors and consultants may play a major role in this phase because of their experience. The development team is being initiated and the participants start to assume their roles. Once the conceptual design is completed, it is necessary to decide who is going to do the project, which is discussed next.

12.10   Development Strategy

According to Vedder and Turban [57], there are several general classes of AI **development strategies:** do it yourself, hire an outside developer, enter into a joint venture, merge, and attack on all fronts. While some organizations use a single strategy, others use several. Thus, whenever a new application is developed it can be matched with any of the strategies.

Do It Yourself. This course of action is attractive for organizations that already possess the skills and resources needed for developing AI projects. It is also a strong candidate for companies that want to develop AI applications containing significant amounts of proprietary or sensitive knowledge (Odette [38]). Various options are available in this general class.

First, AI development can be *part of end-user computing*. The principal attraction of this strategy is that it provides a low-cost, low-risk entry into AI technology. It is an attractive option for organizations that are highly decentralized. A typical advocate of this approach is Du Pont, Inc. (Feigenbaum et al. [15]). It views ES development as an important component of end-user computing. By July 1988, Du Pont had more than 200 ES applications in regular use. In 1991, over 1,000 ES were in use for an annual savings of about $30 million.

Second, AI projects can be *completely centralized*. According to this strategy, all AI projects are centralized in a special unit or department. It is a typical strategy in very large organizations that are heavily involved with AI.

Third, AI development can be *decentralized*, but control can be centralized. Systems are developed using the Du Pont strategy but they are registered in a central unit. This unit assures appropriate maintenance, security, documentation, standardization of technologies, and interfaces with other computer-based information systems.

High technology islands are the fourth option. Some companies are using several specialized units for AI; this is the concept of the "technology island."

Each unit conducts a different task, for example, AI research, AI training, development of small systems, development of systems for service industries, and so on.

The fifth option involves utilizing *information centers*. According to this approach, an organization uses the existing information (or help) centers as the vehicles for disseminating ES.

Hire an Outside Developer. This class of strategies is appropriate for companies that have neither the desire nor the resources for pursuing an in-house development strategy, and whose knowledge base content includes little or no proprietary or sensitive knowledge. The first variation of this strategy is to hire a consulting firm. This is an attractive option for the many firms that do not have (or cannot afford) knowledge engineers in-house. Instead, they retain the knowledge engineering services of a consulting firm specializing in AI development. A second variation is to belong to a consortium of clients. An example of this strategy is the development of an ES called Underwriting Advisor (Harmon et al. [20]). Three insurance companies, American International Group, Inc. (AIG), Saint Paul Companies, Inc., and Fireman's Insurance Companies, hired a vendor (Syntelligence, Inc.) to develop an ES to help underwriters better assess and price risks (i.e., write complex insurance policies).

Enter into a Joint Venture. This is an attractive option for organizations seeking to acquire AI development expertise but unwilling to absorb all of the development risk or the cost. A joint development venture can be done with an AI tool kit vendor, a university, an ES consulting firm, or a research institute. The first variation of this strategy is to form a joint venture with a vendor. In such a strategy, the vendor develops a system for the client while testing its own products and services. A second variation is to sponsor university research and learn from the results. This is how Digital Equipment Corp. built the XCON system. XCON began in 1978 as a joint research effort between DEC and Carnegie-Mellon University. With the skills and experience gained from the XCON project, DEC initiated an aggressive program of developing many other AI applications in-house.

Merge, Acquire, or Become a Major Stockholder in an AI Company. An old adage applies to this strategy, according to DeSalvo and Liebowitz [14]: If you can't beat them, join them. A company might develop an expert systems capability by merging with or acquiring an AI company or by becoming a major stockholder.

12.11 Source(s) of Knowledge

The many sources of knowledge can be categorized into two basic groups: documented knowledge and undocumented (experts') knowledge.

Documented Knowledge. Documented knowledge contributes a major part of the knowledge base in many existing ES, particularly in small systems. Documented knowledge comes from the following sources:

- Textbooks: general and specific facts and rules
- Databases: empirical data, real-time information, case studies, facts, and rules
- Other sources: manuals, memos, reports, films, pictures, and audio and video sources

Undocumented (Experts') Knowledge. Undocumented knowledge is found in the minds of human experts. Table 12.4 lists some characteristics of human experts. Human experts possess knowledge that is much more complex than

TABLE 12.4 Attributes of an Expert

1. Highly developed *perceptual attention* ability—experts can "see" what others cannot.
2. Awareness of the difference between *relevant* and *irrelevant* information—experts know how to concentrate on what's important.
3. Ability to *simplify* complexities—experts can "make sense out of chaos."
4. A strong set of *communication skills*—experts know how to demonstrate their expertise to others.
5. Knowledge of when to make *exceptions*—experts know when and when *not* to follow decision rules.
6. A strong sense of *responsibility* for their choices—experts are not afraid to stand behind their decisions.
7. *Selectivity* about which problems to solve—experts know which problems are significant and which are not.
8. Outward *confidence* in their decisions—experts believe in themselves and their abilities.
9. Ability to *adapt* to changing task conditions—experts avoid rigidity in decision strategies.
10. Highly developed *content knowledge* about their area—experts know a lot and keep up with the latest developments.
11. Greater *automaticity* of cognitive processes—experts can do habitually what others have to work at.
12. Ability to *tolerate* stress—experts can work effectively under adverse conditions.
13. Capability to be more *creative*—experts are better able to find novel solutions to problems.
14. Inability to *articulate* their decision processes—experts make decisions "on experience."
15. Thorough *familiarity* with the domain, including task expertise built up over a long period of task performance, knowledge of the organizations that will be developing and using the ES, knowledge of the user community, and knowledge of technical and technological alternatives.
16. Knowledge and *reputation* such that if the ES is able to capture a portion of the expert's expertise, the system's output will have credibility and authority.
17. Commitment of a substantial amount of *time* to the development of the system, including temporary relocation to the development site if necessary.
18. Capability of *communicating* his or her knowledge, judgment, and experience.
19. *Cooperative, easy to work with*, and *eager* to work on the project.
20. *Interest in computer systems*, even if he or she is not a computer specialist.

Source: Items 1–14 from S. K. Goyal, et al. "COMPASS: An Expert System for Telephone Switch Maintenance," *Expert Systems* (July 1985). Items 15–20 adapted from J. Shanteau, "Psychological Characteristics of Expert Decision Makers," in *Proceedings, Symposium on Expert Systems and Audit Judgment*, Univ. of Southern California, Los Angeles, February 17–18, 1986.

what we find in documented sources. It is based on experience, and in many cases it can be expressed in terms of heuristics.

Selection. Expert systems use both documented sources and human experts as sources of knowledge. The more human expertise that is needed, the longer and more complicated the acquisition process will be. Several issues may surface in selecting sources of knowledge:

- Who selects the expert(s)
- How to identify an expert (what characteristics an expert should exhibit)
- What to do if several experts are needed
- How to motivate the expert to cooperate

The latter issue is briefly discussed next.

Many expert systems that are now functioning had little trouble with expert cooperation. Their experts were researchers, professors, or maintenance experts due to retire soon. The whole idea of ES was challenging, new, and innovative, so experts tended to cooperate. In some systems several experts were engaged, each of whom contributed a small portion of a large knowledge base.

This cooperative situation may change when different types of experts are involved. Experts are starting to ask questions such as, "What's in it for me?" "Why should I contribute my wisdom and risk my job?," and so on. For these reasons, before building an AI system that requires the cooperation of experts, management should ask questions such as these:

- Should experts be compensated for their contributions (e.g., in the form of royalties, a special reward, or payment)?
- How can one tell if the experts are telling the truth about the way they solve problems?
- How can experts be assured that they will not lose their jobs, or that their jobs will not be deemphasized, once the ES is fully operational?
- Are the experts concerned about other people in the organization whose jobs may suffer because of the introduction of ES, and what can management do in such a case?

In general, management should use some incentives to influence experts so that they will cooperate fully with the knowledge engineer.

12.12 Selection of Computing Resources

This step in phase II of the development life cycle involves decisions about software and hardware. The alternatives are many, and the selection of software depends on that of hardware. Three basic issues need to be explored: shells (or environments) versus languages (see Chapter 13); LISP machines versus standard hardware, and mainframe versus non-mainframe computing.

Shells Versus Languages. Choosing which software tool to use is a major decision in the development process. Your choice will depend on several important factors. For example, is programming capability available in-house and, if so, which languages are used? What type of computer system will be used to develop the software and what is the user's host computer? The selection of a tool will also be affected by the time and funds available to create the software. Will you use a **shell**, an AI language, or a conventional programming language? (The concept of a shell was discussed briefly in Chapter 3 and it is going to be revisited in the next chapter.)

Analyze your in-house software development capability. If you have a programming staff, identify workable languages and try to match those languages with tools that can run on your computers. Programmers should be able to write code quickly if they are familiar with the language. Remember, though, that programming an expert system from scratch is an enormous undertaking.

Another option is to consider adding AI programming language capability. If the project has sufficient funding, and if other systems are to be designed and built, it may be worthwhile to have programmers learn LISP or PROLOG. These languages give a general AI capability. But again, keep in mind that it takes time to learn the languages well enough to create an expert system with them.

The fastest and easiest approach is to use a shell. But is there a shell made for your computer? Does the shell format fit the domain of interest? Is the shell large enough and capable enough to handle the project you have in mind?

If this is your first expert system development project, you should strive for a shell. Start by identifying the shells available for your kind of computer. Most shells run on only a few target machines. Dozens of packages are available for IBM personal computers and various compatibles; fewer programs are available for the Apple Macintosh series. Several shells run extremely well on workstations such as Sun Microsystem's products. For minicomputers and mainframes, the choices are generally limited to IBM mainframes and DEC VAX minis.

If a shell is available for your computers and within budget, you need to determine if its capabilities fit your problem. You may have to do some initial knowledge engineering to see if the domain can be expressed properly in rule format. Match the specifications of the tool to other aspects of the problem, and if there is a fit, by all means make the investment. If a shell does not fit your machine, or if you need extensive interfaces with a conventional software, you should use conventional programming. Expert systems are programmed in COBOL, Pascal, and especially in C.

Another option already mentioned is to use the AI languages of PROLOG or LISP. LISP and PROLOG interpreters are available for almost any machine. PROLOG may seem the better choice because, in general, it is easier to create an expert system in PROLOG than it is in LISP. PROLOG has a built-in inference engine and all you need to do is properly format the knowledge in terms of facts and rules. LISP also has an inference engine, but with LISP you have to implement search, pattern-matching, and other system features from scratch. For selection guidelines for a specific software package, see Chapter 13. Also see Harmon et al. [20].

LISP Machine Versus Standard Computers. At the present time there is a trend to use standard computers rather than **LISP machines**. With the exception of very large systems and some research institutions, there is less and less tendency to use specialized, dedicated AI machines.

AI in the Mainframe Environment. Most ES work in the past was done on workstations and on micros rather than on mainframes. Four reasons account for this situation:

1. There are many more personal computers and users.
2. ES development tools for the personal computer are usually superior.
3. It is easy to buy a low-cost shell and experiment with the technology.
4. An MIS backlog plagues almost every mainframe operation.

Lately, however, a trend has also developed to build ES on the mainframe to exploit the advantages of integrated systems.

Any movement toward mainframe intelligence must be accomplished by a careful understanding, nurturing, and support. ES technology can greatly improve the operation of many mainframe-based information systems. One of the major issues in developing a mainframe ES is where the computerized corporate knowledge base should reside. Such knowledge provides, in many cases, the competitive edge of the corporation and it originates in the heads of experts who usually use microcomputers not a mainframe. Moreover, there is a considerable amount of information in the corporate database, residing on the mainframe. Experts need to access this information. Therefore, it makes sense to *connect* the personal computers with the mainframe. Users must be able to use ES on mainframes via their personal computers; that is, it is necessary to develop *distributed ES*.

About a dozen companies develop software for the mainframe, usually with the possibility of accessing it from personal computers. Representative examples are listed in Table 12.5. For information about these products see [3] and Schwartz [47].

Large, complex ES should be considered an organizational project. Systems like the one mentioned earlier for writing insurance policies, and one used by American Express to authorize credit (see Chapter 22), cost millions of dollars to develop and can significantly change the competitive capabilities of corporations. Obviously, such a project is of concern to top management and requires its involvement. Furthermore, in such a case vendor participation might be a necessity. An ES group needs to be established that will assume complete responsibility and control over the project. The director of the ES group selects the experts, deals with their motivation (e.g., by giving them rewards), and centralizes the entire operation.

TABLE 12.5 Examples of ES
Development Software for
the Mainframe

Product	Vendor
ADS	Aion Corp., Palo Alto, Calif.
Application Expert	Cullinet, Westwood, Mass.
ESE, KT, TIRS	IBM Corp., White Plains, N.Y.
ART, ART-IM	Inference Corp., Los Angeles, Calif.
KBMS	AI Corp.
KEE, KEE/370	IntelliCorp., Mountain View, Calif.
Nexpert	Neuron Data, Inc. Palo Alto, Calif.
KES	Software A&E, Arlington, Va.
S.1	Teknowledge Corp., Palo Alto, Calif.

12.13 Feasibility Study

The **feasibility study** for an ES is similar in structure to a feasibility study for
any information system. A proposed outline is shown in Table 12.6 (for details
consult books on system analysis and design). The larger the system the more
formal the steps must be, since approval by top management is required. (For
details see Walters and Nielsen [58].)

TABLE 12.6 Elements of a Feasibility Study

Economic (financial) feasibility	Cost of system development (itemized) Cost of maintenance Anticipated payoff Cash flow analysis Risk analysis
Technical feasibility	Interface requirements Networking issues Availability of knowledge and data Security of confidential knowledge Knowledge representation scheme Hardware/software availability/compatibility
Operational feasibility and impacts	Availability of human and other resources Priority as compared to other projects Needs assessment Organizational and implementation issues Management and user support Availability of expert(s) and knowledge engineer(s) Legal and other constraints Corporate culture User environment

12.14 Cost-Benefit Analysis

An expert system proposal can be viewed as an alternative investment. As such, it should show an advantage over other investment alternatives—including the option of "do nothing." Effective implementation may depend on the ability to show such advantage.

Each ES project requires an investment of resources (including money), which can be viewed as the cost of the system, in exchange for some expected benefit(s). The viability of a project is determined by comparing the costs with anticipated benefits. This comparison is termed a **cost-benefit analysis**, or cost-effectiveness analysis. In practice, such an analysis may become rather complicated. The iterative nature of ES makes it difficult to predict costs and benefits, because the systems are changed constantly. In addition, there are several factors, which we will now discuss, that complicate the analysis.

Getting a Handle on Development Costs. Expert systems may be expensive to develop and/or maintain. Like most other software projects, you'll make a major investment of time and money in creating a workable program. Knowing some of the costs involved helps you estimate the payoff.

First, factor in the cost of all development tools, such as languages and shells. Next, consider what additional hardware you might need. Include the cost of the expert, especially if that expert is not on your payroll. Usually you'll need a knowledge engineer and a programmer, although for a simple expert system you may not need the knowledge engineer, and if a shell is to be used, you may not need the programmer. Don't forget to include the time needed for employees to test, debug, and maintain the program. Finally, add in costs for outside consultants.

The secret to making a *realistic* estimate lies in determining the amount of time each of the participants will need. Software developers invariably are optimistic about the amount of time they will need to complete a project. Unless an individual has considerable software development experience and a good track record, it is almost inevitable that he or she will assume that the project can be done a lot faster than it will actually take. This is especially true if the expert system is the first one for the developer.

It is practically impossible to make a perfect estimate, but it is essential that an estimate of development costs be made. Even an educated guess is better than none at all.

A small system with fewer than a hundred rules may take only several months and require two or three people at most. Still, developing such a project could cost from $10,000 to $50,000. If you use an inexpensive shell on a personal computer and create a small expert system, you may be able to do it for several thousand dollars, assuming that your expert will also do the knowledge engineering and program the knowledge into the shell.

If you are planning a large expert system for a minicomputer or a mainframe, your costs will be more than $100,000. Even shells for larger computers are expensive; the smaller shells sell for about $10,000, but most are priced in the $20,000 to $60,000 range. The addition of knowledge engineering puts the costs above $100,000. To justify such costs, the proposed system has to be extremely beneficial.

At first sight, the cost of a project seems easy to identify and quantify. In practice, it is often difficult to relate costs to projects in a precise manner. Allocation of overhead costs is an example. Should they be allocated by volume, activity level, or value? What about future maintenance costs? A well-known "game" is to show the advantages of a certain alternative while neglecting future costs. There are additional accounting complications such as the impact of taxation and the selection of a proper interest rate for present-value analysis.

Evaluating the Benefits. The assessment of costs is not easy, but the assessment of benefits is more difficult for the following reasons: First, some benefits are intangible. Second, frequently a benefit cannot be precisely related to a single cause. Third, results of a certain action may occur over a long period of time. Fourth, a valuation of benefits includes the assessment of both quantity and quality. The latter is difficult to measure, especially when service industries are involved. Fifth, the multiplicity of consequences can pose a major problem for quantification. Some consequences like goodwill, inconvenience, waiting time, and pain are also extremely difficult to measure and evaluate.

The key is to identify the appropriate benefits. If the expert system can solve a problem whose losses are currently known, you have a starting point. Otherwise, you have to try to calculate a dollar value for the benefits.

An expert system will generate income for you or prevent the loss of income. For example, having an expert system may allow you to do more work in less time, thus bringing in more revenue. You gain through improved productivity. Many expert systems seem to eliminate losses rather than to generate new income. The expert system may minimize wasted time or wasted materials. Poor service due to lack of knowledge may be causing the loss of sales and poor quality may be ruining the business.

When to Justify. Cost justification should be done any time a go-no-go decision is to be made; that is, the justification process occurs throughout the life of the ES. Specifically, cost justification needs to be done (or reexamined) during every phase of the process:

- ☐ At the end of phase I, that is, when the project is initially blessed
- ☐ At the end of phase II, when the complete design is ready
- ☐ After the initial prototype is completed
- ☐ Once the full prototype is in operation
- ☐ Once field testing is completed (prior to deployment)
- ☐ Periodically after the system is in operation (e.g., every six or twelve months)

TABLE 12.7 Commonly Used Methods of Evaluating ES Proposals

Indicator	Advantages	Disadvantages
Internal rate of return (IRR)	Brings all projects to common footing. Conceptually familiar. No assumed discount rate.	Assumes reinvestment at same rate. Can have multiple roots.
Net present value or net worth (NPV or NW)	Very common. Maximizes value for unconstrained project selection.	Difficult to compare projects of unequal lives or sizes.
Equivalent annuity (EA)	Brings all project NPVs to common footing. Convenient annual figure.	Assumes projects repeat to least common multiple of lives, or imputes salvage value.
Payback period	May be discounted or nondiscounted. Measure of exposure.	Ignores flows after payback is reached. Assumes standard project cash-flow profile.
Benefit-to-cost ratio	Conceptually familiar. Brings all projects to common footing.	May be difficult to classify outlays between expense and investment.

Source: A. Smith and C. Dagli, "An Analysis of Worth: Justifying Funding for Development and Implementation," in *Managing Expert Systems*, E. Turban and J. Liebowitz, eds. (Harrisburg, Pa.: Idea Group Publishers, 1992).

How to Justify. Justification can be a lengthy, complex process (e.g., see Thompson and Feinstein [54] and Smith and Dagli [50]). Furthermore, several methods are available to compare the costs and the benefits. Be very careful. One method may yield a different go-no-go recommendation than another method.

Several methods can be used to evaluate ES proposals and none of them is perfect. Table 12.7 shows five common methods with the advantages and disadvantages of each. Smith and Dagli [50] proposed what they call holistic methods of justification. Such methods can better deal with fuzzy environments and multidimensional attributes. Table 12.8 lists some representative holistic methods. Table 12.9 is an example of a cost-benefit analysis of a small project.

12.15   Phase III: Rapid Prototyping and a Demonstration Prototype

Prototyping has been crucial to the development of many ES. A prototype in ES refers to a small-scale system. It includes representation of the knowledge captured in a manner that enables quick inference and the creation of the major

TABLE 12.8 Holistic Methods of Justification

Method	Procedure
Profile chart	Visual scorecard of how an alternative fulfills criteria. Non-numeric with uncertainty shown by shading more than one score for a given attribute. Good for a beginning project where not many details are known.
Symbolic scorecard	Similar to above but numbers are used to ascertain scores for each alternative's fulfillment of each selection criterion.
Linear additive models	Scoring by weighting each criterion by importance and each alternative's fulfillment of each criterion. Fulfillment scores are multiplied by weights and added together to arrive at a final tally. This method requires more detail be known than the above two, but does provide a final number with which projects can be ranked. Criteria can be added easily, as can scoring modifications.
Analytic hierarchy process (AHP)	Scores by developing ratio weighting of each selection criterion then comparing each alternative against each other. Each alternative is assigned a ratio rating on each criterion; ratings are normalized and summed to arrive at a final rank. This method does not require use of an absolute scale, only a comparative ratio scale. A measure of inconsistency is calculated as well.
Expert systems	A few project justification systems have been developed to synthesize judgment based on both monetary and nonmonetary factors. These systems attempt to tie together traditional and holistic evaluation methods to form a composite analysis. Currently this approach would require some customizing of available software.

Source: A. Smith and C. Dagli, "An Analysis of Worth: Justifying Funding for Development and Implementation," in *Managing Expert Systems*, E. Turban and J. Liebowitz, eds. (Harrisbury, Pa.: Idea Group Publishers, 1992).

components of an ES on a rudimentary basis. For example, in a rule-based system the prototype may include only fifty rules and it may be built with a shell. This small number of rules is sufficient to produce consultations of a limited nature.

The prototype helps the builder to decide on the structure of the knowledge base before spending a great amount of time on building more rules. Developing the prototype has other advantages, as shown in Table 12.10. Rapid prototyping is essential in large systems because the cost of a poorly structured, and then not used, ES can be very high.

TABLE 12.9 Cost-Benefit
Analysis of a Small Project

Cost-Benefit Analysis for a Spouse Survivor Benefit Plan

Development costs
1 knowledge engineer
   (4 months half time).. $ 7,230
1 domain expert
   (4 months half time).. $ 5,453
1 site license for the expert system shell..................... $ 5,000

Total costs (excluding maintenance).......................... $17,683

Benefits: (annual)
Reduction in need for overtime................................ $ 2,800
Elimination of need to hire two military pay specialists $56,086

Total... $58,886

Savings
Year 1 ($58,886 − $17,683)...................................... $41,203

Continuing annual savings (before maintenance)......... $58,886

Tangible benefits
1. Reduction of backlog from 380 cases to fewer than 40 cases.
2. Improvement in turnaround time from over 4 months to 2 weeks or less.
3. Audit trail, due to printout of consultation.

Intangible benefits
1. Risk reduction. If the only expert becomes unavailable, processing can continue.
2. Consistent application of former Spouse Survivor Benefit Plan laws.
3. Improved job satisfaction for both the military pay specialist and adjudicators.
4. More timely management information on backlogs.
5. Additional information—case status.
6. Legal requirements standardized.
7. Processing standardized.
8. Image improved with customers.

Note: The savings for the first year would be higher if the cost of the expert system shell software were amortized over many projects, rather than included in the cost of this project.

Source: T. Tubalkain and J. W. Griesser, "Expert Systems Catching on at the Navy Finance Center," in *Managing Expert Systems*, E. Turban and J. Liebowitz, eds. (Harrisburg, Pa.: Idea Group Publishers, 1992).

     The process of rapid prototyping is shown in Figure 12.4. We start with the *design* of a small system. The designer determines what aspect (or segment) to prototype, how many rules to use in the first cut, and so on. Then the knowledge is acquired for the first cut and represented in the ES. Next, a test

TABLE 12.10 Advantages of the Rapid Prototype

It allows project developers to get a good idea of whether it is feasible to attempt to tackle the full application using expert system technology.

It provides a vehicle through which to study the effectiveness of the knowledge representation.

It provides a vehicle through which to study the effectiveness of the knowledge implementation.

It may disclose important gaps or important problems in the proposed final system.

It yields a tangible product of the project at an early stage.

It gives an opportunity to impress management or system funders with a flashy system demonstration, helping to retain or increase support of the project.

It gives an idea of what the final system will do and will look like to outside experts and potential users.

It allows the possibility of an early midcourse correction of the project direction based on feedback from management, consulting experts, and potential users.

It provides a first system that can be field tested—yielding experience in using and testing the system and, if the tests are successful, credibility that the eventual final system will perform its desired function well.

It might provide a system with enough utility that, although not a final product, may be put in the field on an extended basis. This early deployment of a limited system yields some domain benefits, gives experience to system deployers, system operators, and system maintainers, and might identify potential problems in those areas.

It provides an accelerated process of knowledge acquisition.

It makes it easier for experts to criticize existing programs or provide exceptions to the rules.

It makes selling the system to skeptics easier.

It helps sustain the expert's interest.

It provides an idea of the value of the software and the hardware.

It provides an idea of the degree of the expert's cooperation.

It provides information about the initial definition of the problem domain, the need for the ES, and the like.

It demonstrates the capabilities of the ES.

Source: Based, in part, on D. S. Prerau, *Developing and Managing Expert Systems,* © 1990 by Addison-Wesley Publishing Company. p. 39. Reprinted with permission of the publisher

is conducted. The test can be done using historical or hypothetical cases. The expert is asked to judge the results. The knowledge representation methods and the software and hardware effectiveness are also checked. A potential user may be invited to test the system. The results are then analyzed by the knowledge engineer, and if improvement is needed the system is redesigned. Usually the system goes through several iterations with appropriate refinements. The process continues until the system is ready for a formal demonstration. Once the system is demonstrated, it is tested again and improved. This process continues until the final (complete) prototype is ready. For details on the prototyping process see Redin [44] and Cholawski [12].

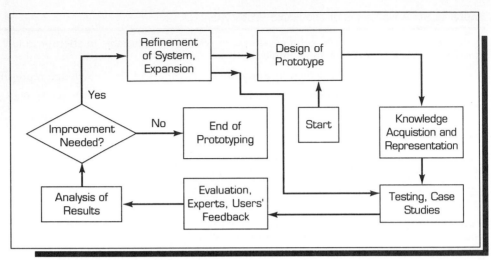

FIGURE 12.4 Rapid Prototyping

A prototype is also a good way to prove your concept before investing in a major program. If you use a shell, you can rapidly assemble a small prototype that will tell you if you're on the right track. A demonstration of the prototype can also be a valuable aid in acquiring approval and funding for your project.

One advantage of rule-based systems is that they are modular. Thus you can construct small subdivisions of larger systems and test them one step at a time. You can add to the system in a piecemeal fashion and build to the final system gradually. If each subsection is tested and approved separately, the final system should work the first time.

Large expert systems usually go through a series of development stages. The first stage is the demonstration prototype that shows that the system is viable. The system is put through several additional levels of development until it is considered a finished product. (See Appendix A of this chapter.)

The prototyping phase can be short and simple or it can take several months and be fairly complex. Figure 12.5 shows the possible tasks and participants in the process. The lessons learned during rapid prototyping are incorporated into the final design. Also, this is the time when another go-no-go decision is made. If the decision is "go," system development begins.

12.16 Phase IV: System Development

Once the initial prototype is ready and management is satisfied, system development begins. Obviously, a plan must be made about how to continue. At this stage, the development strategy may be changed (e.g., a consultant may be hired). The detailed design is also likely to be changed and so are other elements of the plan.

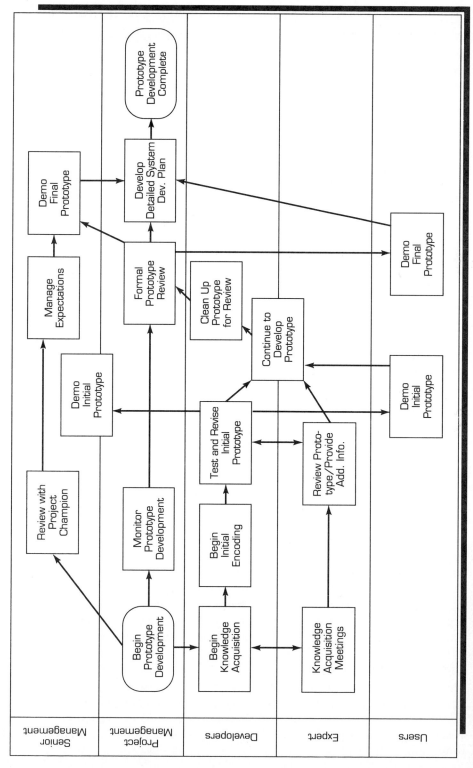

FIGURE 12.5 Prototype Development Effort (*Source:* P. Harmon and B. Sawyer, *Creating Expert Systems* [New York: John Wiley & Sons, 1990], p. 275.)

Depending on the nature of the system—its size, the amount of interface with other systems, the dynamics of the knowledge, and the development strategy—one of the following approaches for system development will be utilized:

- Continue with prototyping (evolutionary model)
- Use structured life-cycle approach
- Do both

The concept of prototyping in information systems allows two major options. One is called the *evolutionary model*. According to this option, the complete prototype from phase III becomes the interim working version, which is tested and improved in several iterations until the system is complete. According to the other option, which is called the *throwaway model* (see Bernstein [7]), the initial prototype is thrown away, a new design is made, and the system is built more or less according to the structured life-cycle approach. For example, prototyping may have been done with a shell, but actual system development is done with a language. The prototype may have been done on personal computers, but the system is developed on an AI workstation.

System development can be a lengthy and complex process. In this phase, the knowledge base is built and continuous testing, reviews, and improvements are carried out. Other activities include creation of interfaces (e.g., to databases), creating and testing the user's interface, and so on. For a list of tasks and participants, see Figure 12.6.

12.17   Building the Knowledge Base

Building the knowledge base means acquiring knowledge from experts and/or documented sources (as described in Chapter 4) and representing this knowledge in an appropriate form in the computer (Chapter 5). The following discussion supplements the material in Chapters 4 and 5; it is especially relevant to rule-based systems constructed with a shell.

Once the knowledge has been acquired from the expert, it has to be formatted into a knowledge base. Here we want to describe the process of organizing that knowledge in such a way that it can be understood and then translated into rules or another form of knowledge representation.

Define the Potential Solutions. The first step in organizing your domain knowledge is to list all of the possible solutions, outcomes, answers, choices, or recommendations. You must identify the exact outputs that will be presented on the computer screen to the user. Expert systems don't suddenly create advice based on a flash of genius; they have to know every possible answer ahead of time.

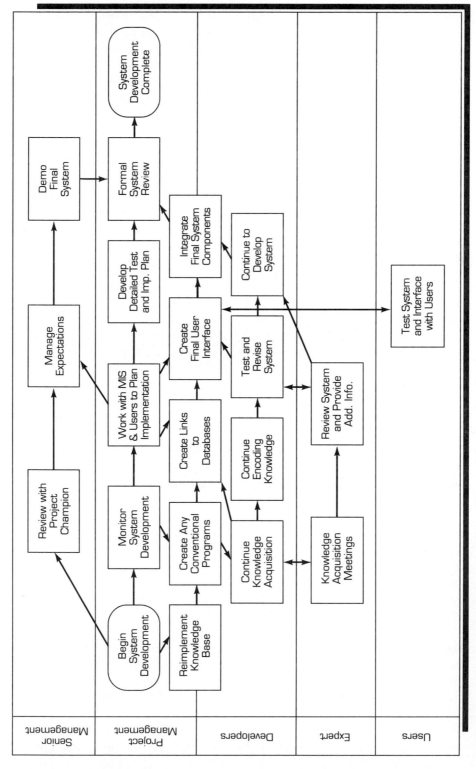

FIGURE 12.6 System Development Effort (Phase IV) (*Source:* P. Harmon and B. Sawyer, *Creating Expert Systems* [New York: John Wiley & Sons, 1990], p. 270.)

Your interview sessions with your expert should have covered a sufficient range of different problem-solving examples so that all the possible outcomes are defined. Annotate each of these possible outcomes. The reason for this is that most expert systems are capable of explaining their output. Expert system shells usually provide a means of entering comments that will supplement or explain each output conclusion.

If you're using a rule-based system, each conclusion will be in the THEN portion of a rule. At this point, you can begin creating the rules for each outcome. Some simple expert systems have a set of rules that defines each outcome and that's it. Decisions are not reached through a complex search or a decision tree. Instead, the expert system simply asks questions to gather the necessary data for the IF statements that will fire one of the rules leading to a conclusion.

Define the Input Facts. The next step is to identify and list all of the data that will be required by the system. These are the facts (e.g., symptoms) that the user will enter into the system. The expert system will actually ask questions to obtain these inputs. For example, the system may ask you how old you are if there is a rule that says that if you are 18 or older you can vote in the federal election. Data provided by the user will be compared to IF statements in the rules to begin or continue the search process.

Develop an Outline. Even though you may know the outcomes and needed input data, you may have difficulty writing the rules. Large, complex knowledge domains usually require some additional organization. One technique that may be useful is to develop an outline. Most domains lend themselves to some sort of taxonomy that will allow you to subdivide and classify the knowledge. An outline is nothing more than a hierarchy of these subdivisions. A way to better picture the knowledge is to convert your outline into a block diagram, which will look somewhat like a company's organizational chart.

Draw a Decision Tree. The elements of knowledge may be such that they organize themselves quickly into a tree format. If so, you may be able to proceed directly to the construction of a decision or search tree. Some knowledge bases are so large that you may not be able to create a decision tree for the entire domain. Don't worry about this; just create decision trees for subsets of the domain.

Map a Matrix. Some knowledge organizes itself neatly into a matrix showing the various attributes that produce a particular conclusion. Induction shells use this knowledge-formatting technique. If you have selected such a shell, you can proceed immediately to organizing your knowledge as examples.

Develop the Software. Once your rules are written, you can enter them immediately into a shell. Your first objective should be to build a small prototype.

Select one small subset of the knowledge base and enter its rules into the shell. You should be able to do this quickly. The result will be a prototype you can test to check your ideas and verify their implementation quickly. If your prototype works, you can proceed with confidence to enter the remainder of the rules.

12.18 Testing, Validating and Verifying, and Improving

The prototype, and later improved versions of the system, are tested and evaluated for performance both in the lab and in the field. Initially, evaluation is done in a simulated environment. The system is exposed to test problems (e.g., historical cases or sample cases provided by users). A close link exists between the evaluation and the refinements (improvements) of the ES. The evaluation may reveal cases not handled by the system's rules. As a result, new rules are added or old ones are modified. Such changes may have unexpected negative effects on parts of the system. For example, conflict could arise because of inconsistency in rules. A good development tool provides a rapid consistency check for the rules in the knowledge base.

Evaluation also deals with the issue of the quality of the advice rendered. Determining quality can be a very difficult activity if we lack standards for comparison (see Box 12.1). Expert systems often give advice in areas where there is no "gold standard," so a simple comparison is impossible.

As a result of these evaluation difficulties, expert systems are being evaluated in less formal and more experimental ways. The principal judge of the system's quality is the domain expert who can tell if the results are satisfactory. Potential users can also serve as judges in regard to ease of use, comfortable interface, and clarity of explanations.

A common method used to evaluate an ES is to compare its performance to an accepted criterion, such as a human expert's decision. In this approach, called the **Modified Turing Test**, managers are shown two solutions to a problem. One is the result of human judgment and the other of an ES. Without knowing which is which, managers are asked to compare the solutions. There are several problems with this approach. First, the open-endedness of many management problems may make it difficult to describe them to an independent evaluator. The problems may be so complex that even experienced managers may disagree on their proper interpretation and solution. Second, expert systems used by teams of managers should probably be evaluated by teams of managers; hence they may be more difficult to evaluate (because of possible disagreements). Despite such difficulties, an ES might be useful even if its only accomplishment is the reduction of the time needed to perform existing tasks without reduction in quality. Time reduction may be a good initial criterion for evaluation of an ES.

Box 12.1: Difficulties in Evaluating an Expert System

The following questions indicate the difficulties that stand in the way of evaluation studies:

1. What characteristics should be evaluated? The performance of the system has been the main characteristic of interest. However, the system's discourse or ease of use may also be key to its acceptance.

2. How should performance be evaluated? Owing to the nature of expert system applications, it is sometimes hard to define a "gold standard" against which to compare the system's performance. For example, a match between the conclusions of the system and the expert may be hard to obtain. Indeed, different experts may disagree on certain details or both the problem and the expert may be wrong. In evaluating performance, should one look only at the conclusion or should the program's line of reasoning be evaluated as well? What form should the evaluation take when the system provides multiple (as opposed to unique) answers?

3. How should the test problems be selected? The fact that the realism of real-world exceptions and irrelevancies can seriously affect the performance of an expert system is well known. However, in certain areas, the supply of realistic studies may be very limited. In the case of PROSPECTOR, for instance, there is only a small number of known ore deposits to draw on, and the time between initial and final characterizations of the deposit could be long. Similar problems occur with rare diseases and other cases when sampling costs are high.

4. How should one evaluate the program's mistakes? In judgmental areas, it is interesting to observe the type of mistakes an expert system may make. One is reminded that the work of Piaget on developmental psychology was prompted by the patterns of mistakes (not the correct responses) in IQ tests taken by children. The same search for error patterns occurs in intelligent tutoring systems, but the implications for evaluation studies appear to be unexplored. Clearly, this issue also relates to the requirement that expert systems "degrade gracefully."

(*Source*: A. A. Assad and B. L. Golden, "Expert Systems, Microcomputers, and Operations Research," *Computers and Operations Research* 13 [1986].)

In business settings ES can often be evaluated by experimentation. Say, for example, preventive maintenance is to be performed on several identical machines. An expert system's advice about frequencies of maintenance could be implemented in some of the machines while the rest are scheduled according to the vendor's recommendations. The relative breakdown rates and repair and maintenance costs under the two methods can then be compared to find which one is superior.

An Iterative Process of Evaluation. Each time the system is exposed to a new case, or whenever there are changes in the environment, the system needs a refinement. In a rule-based system, such a refinement is likely to produce more rules. XCON, for example, grew from a couple of hundred to about 20,000 rules in about ten years. Each time a substantial refinement is made, an evaluation should follow.

Evaluation occurs during and after each iteration. Performance is recorded as the system improves its use in either a simulated or real-life environment. Development and evaluation continue as long as improvements are achieved. For further details see Berry and Hart [8], Geissman and Schultz [17], Liebowitz [32], Preece [41], and Suen et al. [53].

Box 12.2: Some Requirements of a Good Expert System

1. The ES should be developed to fulfill a recognized and important need.
2. The processing speed of the system should be very high.
3. The ES should be able to increase the expertise of the user.
4. Error correction should be easy to perform.
5. The program should be able to respond to simple questions.
6. The system should be capable of asking questions to gain additional information.
7. Program knowledge should be easily modified (i.e., add, delete, and modify rules).
8. The user should feel that he or she is in control.
9. The degree of effort (both physical and mental) used by the novice should be reasonable.
10. Input requirements (in terms of data) should be clear and simple to obtain.

(*Source:* Based, in part, on D. C. Berry and A. E. Hart, "Evaluating Expert Systems," *Expert Systems* [November 1990].)

The evaluation involves both validation and verification. **Validation** refers to the determination of whether the right system was built; that is, whether the system does what it was meant to do and at an acceptable level of accuracy. **Verification** confirms that the ES has been built correctly (according to the specifications).

12.19   Phase V: Implementation

The process of implementing an ES can be long and complex—similar to the implementation of any software project. Here we will briefly touch on several issues; in Chapter 16 implementation problems and strategies will be revisited.

Acceptance by the User. Even if an ES is more accurate than a human expert, it does not necessarily mean that the system will be accepted by the user. Acceptance depends on behavioral and psychological considerations. It is important that the development of specific ES be communicated as widely as possible to foster a climate of acceptance among the people who will use the system.

Installation Approaches. The expert system is ready to be field tested when it reaches an acceptable level of stability and quality. In rule-based systems, this may occur when the system can handle 75 percent of the cases and exhibit less than a 5 percent error rate. The installation approach depends on the situation. For example, an ES may be used in parallel with a human expert for six months.

Demonstration. Demonstrating the fully operational system to the user community is important. Viewers can become believers. Proper demonstration can increase acceptance by users.

Mode of Deployment. Several deployment modes for ES may be considered. The final system could be delivered to users as a turnkey, stand-alone system; it could be operated as a separate entity but integrated into the users' environment; it could be embedded into another system; or it could be run as a service, with the users' requests and data accessed remotely and results delivered to the users.

The users of the expert system may be responsible for operating it, maintaining it, or neither. The system could be available on a demand, scheduled, or continual basis. It could be available twenty-four hours a day or during selected hours, and it could be run interactively or in batch mode. A single system could service one user, many users in one site, or many users in many sites. There may be one level of service provided or a set of service levels, depending on the user or the price.

Orientation and Training. Depending on the mode of deployment, the builders must plan appropriate orientation and training. If the users are assigned maintenance responsibilities, the training may be fairly extensive.

Security. Security is a heightened concern in ES. Such systems are no longer akin to computer software templates that have only the capacity to manipulate numbers. Instead, expert systems may contain the accumulated proprietary knowledge of a firm. Communicating and distributing the end product, protecting the software, and at the same time providing an environment that does not constrain authorized users in its application form a substantial practical problem. Although the value of a system may diminish over time if it is not continuously updated and maintained, the implications of misappropriation or unauthorized use or transfer of the system are more significant than with many other software products. Accordingly, organizational and hardware and/or software controls assume increased importance in the design and distribution of expert systems. Special care must be taken to control the maintainers of the knowledge.

Documentation. Implementation of ES must include appropriate documentation. Prerau [42] has said:

> There is a tendency to skimp on documentation during system development and then to complete it quickly and sometimes haphazardly at the end of a project. Clearly expert system project leaders should try to avoid this situation.
>
> Standard techniques of documentation can be used where applicable for documenting expert system programs. For example, reports can be written describing for each program module its purpose, inputs, outputs, and so on. But beyond such standard techniques, there are some aspects of expert system implementations that may allow additional types of documentation.
>
> If a knowledge documentation is compiled and kept updated as part of knowledge acquisition, it becomes a significant piece of program documentation. It is a program specification that is constantly up to date and relevant. If the documented knowledge has clear parallels to the implementation (by rule correspondences, naming conventions, specific references, and other means), it can act as a pointer to the program code. (p. 280)

The documentation that will accompany the system might consist of printed manuals, online documentation, or both. There may be levels of documentation for system maintainers, system operators, and system users.

Integration and Field Testing. If the expert system stands alone, it can now be field tested. A system that needs to be integrated (see Chapter 15) is physically added to the existing computer-based information system before testing in the field is conducted. Field testing is extremely important because conditions in the field may differ from those that exist at the developer's lab. The following five factors may influence the system's performance:

1. *Hardware:* The hardware in the field may be different from that in the lab. Storage, processing time, and the fit between the hardware and software can affect performance.
2. *People:* The characteristics of the people in the field may differ from the characteristics of the people in the lab who served as potential users.
3. *Networks:* If the system needs to be networked, the equipment and protocols of the field could be different from those in the lab.
4. *Test cases:* These are almost never the same as real-world situations. Reality may bring some surprises, and they are not always pleasant.
5. *Response time:* A response time need in the field is not always provided by a system fresh from the lab.

Field tests need to be planned and coordinated. In many cases they last longer than people think. For example, the expert may be needed for some refinements, but he or she may be busy. Often, field tests may take many months.

12.20   Phase VI: Postimplementation

Several activities are performed once the system is distributed to users. The most important of the activities are system operation, system maintenance, system upgrading and expansion, and system evaluation.

Operations. According to Prerau [42],

> if the expert system is to be delivered as a service, a system operations group (or several groups if there are several sites) should be formed and trained. If the system is to be a product run by users, an operator training group may need to be formed, and consideration should be given to providing help for user-operators with problems. Complete operator documentation should be provided. If the system is embedded into another system, the operators of the other system should be trained in any new operating procedures required.

Maintenance. Prerau [42] has also said:

> A long-term maintenance group (or groups) should be designated or formed and, if necessary, trained. Maintenance encompasses not only fixing problems found during system operation but also revising internal data and knowledge that has changed over time. Since maintenance will surely require not just changes to the implementation of knowledge' but also changes to the knowledge itself, it is almost mandatory that a domain expert be involved in the maintenance process—at least on a consulting basis. A decision must

be made whether to have centralized maintenance, with program patches and new releases coming from a single source, or a more distributed maintenance. The latter results in many non-standard versions of the system and thus may not be preferred; however, it does allow complete customization of the system to the different circumstances of each site (a major advantage if such differences are important).

If the expert system is embedded in another system, some thought should be given to whether one maintenance group will serve the overall system or whether the expert system will be maintained separately. If separate maintenance is chosen, procedures for coordinating the two maintenance groups should be formed. For further discussion of maintenance and upgrading see Agarwal et al. [1] and McCaffrey [34].

Expansion (Upgrading). Expert systems are continuously expanded. All new knowledge needs to be added, and new features and capabilities need to be added as they become available. Also, the ES may be integrated with other systems. An example is the XCON system that was described in Chapter 3; expansions include new products, marketing decision making (in addition to manufacturing), and engineering and design advice. Expansion can be carried on by the maintainer, the original builder, or a vendor.

Evaluation. Expert systems need evaluation periodically (e.g., every six or twelve months). In such an evaluation, questions such as these should be answered:

☐ What is the actual cost of maintaining the system as compared to the actual benefits?
☐ Is the maintenance provided sufficient to keep the knowledge up-to-date so that system accuracy remains high?
☐ Is the system accessible to all users?
☐ Is acceptance by users increasing?

12.21   Organizing the Development Team

Many expert systems are developed by a team—a team that needs to be organized. Some members of the team (the core) participate in the initial steps (phases I–V); others are added only after the development strategy has been finalized (phase VI).

A typical development team consists of an expert, a knowledge engineer, and a programmer (see Figure 12.7). However, a vendor, a user, or information system specialist may also be included. The knowledge engineer extracts the expert's knowledge and puts it into a suitable form. The programmer writes the codes for putting the knowledge into memory and creates the inference engine and other components as required.

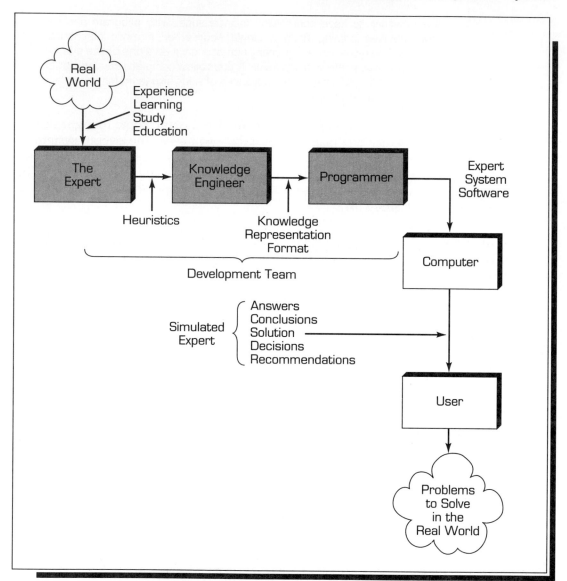

FIGURE 12.7 Expert System Development Team

Although the team approach is probably the best development arrangement, it does require a great deal of cooperation and communication among the team members. A large system may require more members. The larger the team, then, the better the organization and management needed to create a workable system. The size of the team and its composition depend on a specific application. Table 12.11 lists many of the possible functions and roles that may be found in an ES team. An end-user ES may include only *one* participant who is helped, on a part-time basis, by other people.

TABLE 12.11 Functions and Roles in an Expert System Team

Knowledge engineer	Knowledge acquirer	Technical leader
Expert	Knowledge representor	System engineer
System analyst	Knowledge implementer	Integration specialist
Programmer	Tool developer	Technical demonstrator
Vendor	System tester (evaluator)	Security specialist
End-user	Trainer	Documentation writer
Project champion	System developer	System operator
Project manager	Hardware (software) specialist	
Consultant	Network expert	

Source: Based on D. S. Prerau, *Developing and Managing Expert Systems,* © 1990 by Addison-Wesley Publishing Company. p. 57. Reprinted with permission of the publisher.

Many teams include two additional important players: the project champion and the project leader. The *project champion* is a person with power and influence and a major interest in facilitating the project's successful completion. The project champion provides the authority and the resources. He or she may be a senior vice president of a functional area (e.g., finance, manufacturing) or a corporate generalist. The *project leader* is a specialist who manages the project on a day-to-day basis. The leader is familiar with the application, is user oriented, and understands the technology. This individual manages, coordinates, and runs the project using a particular project management approach.

12.22 Project Management

Building an expert system or other large-scale AI applications can be lengthy, expensive, and complex. For this reason, the project should be managed by the development team just like any other large-scale software development project. Of the many issues that are involved in project management, only a few are considered here:

- □ *Function:* The major purpose of project management is to keep the project on target (minimum delays and cost overruns). To do so, project management must address the next two issues.
- □ *Methodology:* Project management is a process that involves the nine steps shown in Figure 12.8. Although the process is shown as linear, it is really cyclical; that is, at the conclusion of any step, adjustments may be made in previous steps. For details about these steps see any project management text and Khan and Martin [26], Lackman [29], and Stanley [52].
- □ *Methods and Software:* Project management can be supported by tools such as Gantt charts, dependency networks, CPM, and PERT (the most widely used tools). Several dozen software products for all types of computers are available. For details see Wasil and Assad [59].

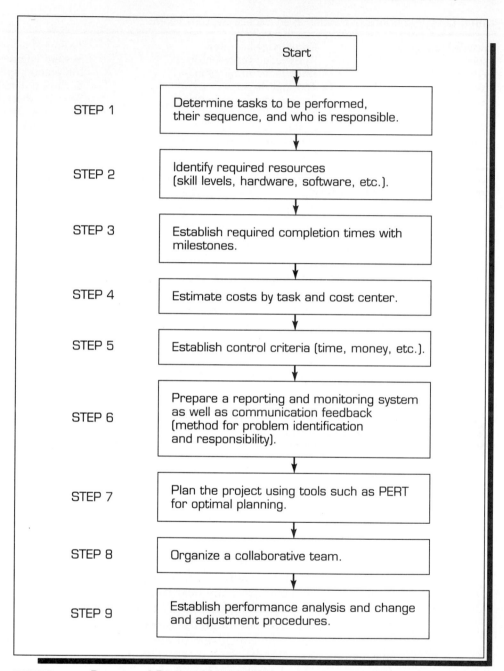

FIGURE 12.8 Process of Project Management

Chapter Highlights

- □ Building an expert system is a complex process with six major phases: system initialization, system analysis and design, rapid prototyping, system development, implementation, and postimplementation.
- □ Project initialization is done to determine the problem and its suitability for solution by an expert system.
- □ Defining the problem properly will simplify the remaining development tasks.
- □ Sometimes conventional technologies do a better job than expert systems.
- □ Knowledge can be increased by providing training; this classical method is valid in many, many cases.
- □ Many requirements are essential to the success of ES.
- □ Like any other project, an ES must be justified.
- □ Without the commitment of resources, the ES will fail.
- □ Top management support is essential from the inception of the project.
- □ A large ES needs a champion as a sponsor.
- □ Expert systems can be developed in-house (internally) or can be subcontracted; there are several variations to each option.
- □ Expert systems developed by end-users can be successful. One system may save little in costs, but many little savings accumulate.
- □ Selecting experts can be difficult; candidates need to exhibit many different attributes.
- □ Although ES can be developed with many tools, the trend is to develop the initial prototype with simple (and inexpensive) integrated tools (either shells or hybrid environments).
- □ Currently, most ES are being developed and run on standard computers (personal computers, workstations, mainframes).
- □ A feasibility study is essential for the success of any medium- to large-sized ES.
- □ Expert systems are difficult to justify because of the many intangible factors.
- □ Justification is done several times during the development process, and so is the go-no-go decision.
- □ There are many methods for justification and the selection of the appropriate method is very important.
- □ Many ES are being built by creating a small-scale prototype, testing it, and improving and expanding. The process, which can be repeated many times, has many advantages.
- □ The initial prototype can lead to either system development by further prototyping or to a conventional structured life-cycle approach.
- □ The major aspects of system development are building the knowledge base and evaluating and improving the system.

□ Evaluation of expert systems is difficult because of the many attributes that need to be considered and the difficulties in measuring some of them.

□ Implementing an ES is similar to implementing any other computer-based information system. However, integration may be difficult to accomplish.

□ Once the system is distributed to users, it is necessary to perform several tasks: operation, maintenance, upgrade, and postimplementation evaluation.

□ Developing the proper team for ES development can be challenging; size, composition, and leadership are only some of the important factors.

□ Large-scale ES development must be managed like any other large-scale software project; appropriate project management techniques are necessary.

Key Terms

cost-benefit analysis
development life cycle
development strategy
documented
   knowledge

feasibility study
LISP machines
Modified Turing Test
needs assessment
shell

validation
verification

Questions for Review

1. List the phases in the ES development life cycle.
2. Describe the criteria that can be used to justify ES.
3. Give some guidelines for selecting a task suitable for an ES.
4. Describe the activities of project initialization.
5. What is included in a conceptual design of ES?
6. Explain documented knowledge.
7. Describe the difficulties in finding a good expert.
8. What are the major guidelines for selecting experts?
9. How do shells relate to expert system development?
10. What is a feasibility study? Why is it done?
11. What is the purpose of rapid prototyping?
12. What is meant by a champion?
13. Define postimplementation.
14. List all the activities conducted in implementation.

Questions for Discussion

1. Compare a conceptual design with a final design.
2. Discuss the general classes of AI development strategies.
3. The selection of an *appropriate* ES project is considered most important. Why? Why is it difficult to do it?

4. Review the elements that go into a feasibility study. Why is it difficult to conduct one?
5. Describe some intangible benefits of expert systems.
6. Why is it necessary to conduct cost-benefit analyses several times during the development process?
7. Why is it hard to evaluate expert systems?
8. Distinguish between acceptance by a user and acceptance by a designer.
9. Why is the security issue so important to expert systems?
10. Training is an alternative to an expert system. Under what circumstances would you train rather than use an ES (and vice versa)?
11. Two major development strategies are to do it yourself or to subcontract. Compare and contrast the two approaches.
12. Review the attributes of experts listed in Table 12.4. Which of them, in your opinion, are the five most important ones and why?
13. A shell a versus a language is an ongoing debate. Find some material on the topic and prepare a table showing the advantages and disadvantages of each.
14. There are many benefits to prototyping (Table 12.10). Can you think of some disadvantages?
15. Review the elements that go into a knowledge base. If you are using a shell, relate these elements to the components of the shells. Report differences in terminology.

Exercises

1. **Feasibility study for expert systems:** Assume that the president of a company or the commander of a military base asks you to prepare a feasibility study for the introduction of an expert system in the organization. Prepare a report that includes the following information:
   a. Identification of a problem area—go through the process in this chapter
   b. Description of the expert(s) to be involved—their capabilities and willingness to participate
   c. Software and hardware to be used in this project and why you chose them
   d. Development team and why each member is necessary
   e. Timetable for development and implementation
   f. List of the potential difficulties during the construction period
   g. List of managerial problems (related to the *use* of the system) that could appear if the expert system is introduced
   h. Construction and operating budgets
   i. List of the interfaces (if needed) with other computer-based information systems
2. **Starting an ES project:**
   a. Think of a specific problem that could be aided by (or even replaced with) an expert system. Preferably, the problem should be one about which you

can obtain the required knowledge from an expert; however, if this is not possible, you may choose a problem in which the knowledge is obtained from published materials. Problems in which you are the expert should be selected only as a last resort. Describe the problem task in general terms.

b. How is this task normally performed without the aid of an expert system? Who is responsible for the final judgment? What sort of training and/or experience does this person normally have?

c. Identify the generic category that best describes your problem task and explain why.

Case 1: Development of an Expert System at a Major Oil Refinery[1]

Background

This case study describes the development of an expert system at a major West Coast oil refinery. The intent is not to describe the actual programming steps and development hurdles. Rather, it is to describe the reasoning that went into deciding why and how the system should be developed.

Management Support

By far the single biggest reason that development began on the expert system was that corporate management was convinced of the long-term applicability of such systems. Although the oil industry has been undergoing considerable restructuring (including cutbacks in personnel and capital expenses), management at this company has been approving funding for applied research in artificial intelligence. In this specific case, funding was approved before any specific expert system applications were even considered.

On a local level, considerable enthusiasm was generated for expert systems largely through simple personal-computer-based systems that belonged to refinery engineers. In particular, a "wine-taster" PC-based expert system, which recommends wines based on meal selection and cost constraints, convinced a number of superintendents that a computerized expert system could improve operating decisions.

---

[1]This case was developed by Ted Oakes, an MBA student, Graduate School of Business Administration, University of Southern California, 1985.

Selection of an Application

Selection of an application was based on a few key concepts. First, the system should be applied to a process where there is a strong economic incentive for improved knowledge propagation. Second, the process should lend itself to improvement through descriptive instructions rather than mathematically precise solutions. Third, corporate experts should be available who could be "tapped" for decision rules. Finally, the potential should exist to extend the application to a sensor-integrated expert system in the future.

The refinery process selected as the object of a computer-based expert system was the catalytic reforming process. In this process, low-octane gasoline components are converted under pressure to high-octane components and hydrogen. Because high lead levels are no longer an environmentally acceptable method for improving gasoline octane, the reforming process is rapidly becoming more critical in the refining industry. This process is having a growing impact on refinery profitability.

The process is conceptually simple. What generally leads to operating success is *not* the implementation of sophisticated operating strategies. Rather, it is reacting to and correcting occasional abnormalities. Many of the abnormalities tend to resurface, but only after months or years. For this reason, an expert system is a more appropriate tool than a computerized plant model.

This oil company is an industry leader in catalytic reforming technology. It markets and licenses this technology to other refineries throughout the world. As an industry leader, it employs a number of experts in this process who have decades of experience in troubleshooting problems with the catalytic reforming process. In addition, a number of these experts are within five years of mandatory retirement. An expert system is seen as a means by which their expertise can be preserved.

Finally, this particular process plant is operated with the assistance of a sophisticated, direct, digital control computer system. Therefore, it may be possible to take advantage of the many process sensor signals already being transmitted into computer signals.

Selection of Software

Software selection was based primarily on the grounds of previous corporate experience, a desire to quickly develop a working prototype, and hardware considerations.

Although this company has never before explicitly embarked on an expert system development project, many research staff members have experimented with expert systems in the course of their everyday work. In particular, a number of "mini" expert systems have been developed on personal computers.

Several advantages were seen to developing a PC-based system. First, because of the accessibility of personal computers throughout the corporation, a PC-based system would be easy to implement corporatewide. Not only is the equipment available in most of the company's refineries, but generally knowledgeable PC users are available as well. By using PCs it would be possible to easily "customize" the software for each individual refinery. PCs are considered highly reliable. They are not subject to communication problems or system downtime. If a PC breaks, a substitute can be readily found.

The expert system shell EXSYS was adopted for this application. It was selected primarily because research members had already used it on a periodic basis. It was viewed as a user-friendly and developer-friendly tool that could be used by a novice engineer with minimal training. Its cost is relatively low and it is a fairly powerful shell. It includes a built-in rule editor and it can construct systems of up to 5,000 rules.

Progress

In four months, a prototype system has been developed. The system embodies decision rules from a catalytic reforming expert in the research department. It was submitted to plant engineers who assessed the usefulness of the system and attempted to customize it for site-specific applications. After approximately two months of on-site evaluation, the system was modified to incorporate actual day-to-day problem decision rules. The system was made available for corporatewide use about six months later.

Questions

1. Review the manner in which the ES started and comment on it.
2. Review the initial development process in light of the steps suggested in this chapter and comment.
3. Discuss the importance of a personal computer as a delivery vehicle for the system.
4. How will the expert system be related in the future to other existing computer-based systems?
5. Review the criteria used for selecting the domain. Comment.
6. Review the shell selection criteria and comment.

References and Bibliography

1. Agarwal, R., et al. "Knowledge Base Maintenance." *Expert Systems: Planning, Implementation, Integration* (Summer 1991).
2. Alpar, P. "Toward Structured Expert Systems Development." *Expert Systems with Applications* 1 (no. 1, 1990).
3. *Artificial Intelligence Research*, July 3, 1989 (New Science Associates).
4. Assad, A.A., and B.L. Golden. "Expert Systems, Microcomputers, and Operations Research." *Computers and Operations Research* 13 (no. 2, 1986).
5. Bauer, R.J., and M.D. Griffiths. "Evaluating Expert System Investment: An Introduction to the Economics of Knowledge." *Journal of Business Research* 17 (1988): 223–233.

6. Beckman, T.J. "Selecting Expert Systems Applications." *AI Expert* (February 1991).

7. Bernstein, A. "Short Cut to System Design." *Business Computer Systems* (June 1985).

8. Berry, D.C., and A.E. Hart. "Evaluating Expert Systems." *Expert Systems* (November 1990).

9. Boehm, B.W. *Software Engineering Economics*. Englewood Cliffs, N.J.: Prentice-Hall, 1981.

10. Bramer, M., ed. *Practical Experience in Building Expert Systems*. New York: John Wiley & Sons, 1990.

11. Carrico, M.A., et al. *Building Knowledge Systems*. New York: McGraw-Hill, 1989.

12. Cholawski, E.M. "Beating the Prototype Blues." *AI Expert* (December 1988).

13. Cupello, J.M., and D.J. Mishelevich. "Managing Prototype Knowledge/Expert Systems Projects." *Communications of ACM* (May 1988).

14. DeSalvo, D.A., and J. Liebowitz, eds. *Managing AI and Expert Systems*. Englewood Cliffs, N.J.: Yourdon Press/Prentice-Hall, 1990.

15. Feigenbaum, E., et al. *The Rise of the Expert Company*. New York: Random House, 1988.

16. Gal, G. "Expertise, Experts, and Expert Systems Development." *Expert Systems: Planning, Implementation, Integration* (Summer 1990).

17. Geissman, J.R., and R.D. Schultz. "Verification and Validation of Expert Systems." *AI Expert* (February 1988).

18. Gevarter, W.B. "The Nature and Evaluation of Commercial Expert Systems Building Tools." *Computer* (May 1987).

19. Goyal, S.K., et al. "COMPASS: An Expert System for Telephone Switch Maintenance." *Expert Systems* (July 1985).

20. Harmon, P., et al. *Expert Systems Tools and Applications*. New York: John Wiley & Sons, 1988.

21. Harmon, P., and B. Sawyer. *Creating Expert Systems*. New York: John Wiley & Sons, 1990.

22. Holsapple, C.W., and A.B. Whinston. *Building Expert Systems (using GURU)*. Homewood, Ill.: Richard D. Irwin, 1987.

23. Irgon, A., et al. "Expert Systems Development—A Retrospective View of Five Systems." *IEEE Expert* (June 1990).

24. Jain, H., and A.R. Chaturvedi. "Expert Systems Problem Selection: A Domain Characteristic Approach." *Information and Management* 17 (no. 4, 1989).

25. Kenney, T.P. "Search and Solve." *AI Expert* (March 1991).

26. Khan, M.B., and M.P. Martin. "Managing the Systems Project." *Journal of Systems Management* (January 1989).

27. Khan, U.A.F. "Managing KBS Development Using Standard Life-Cycle Techniques." In *Managing Expert Systems*, E. Turban and J. Liebowitz, eds. Harrisburg, Pa.: Idea Group Publishers, 1992.

28. Kline, P., and S. Dolins. *Designing Expert Systems*. New York: John Wiley & Sons, 1990.

29. Lackman, M. "Controlling the Project Development Life Cycle." *Journal of Systems Management* (February 1987).

30. Laufman, S., et al. "A Methodology for Evaluating Potential KBS Applications." *IEEE Expert* (December 1990).

31. Lenat, D.B., and R.V. Guha. *Building Large Knowledge-Base Systems*. Reading, Mass.: Addison-Wesley, 1990.

32. Liebowitz, J. "Useful Approach for Evaluating Expert Systems." *Expert Systems* (April 1986).

33. Liebowitz, J. "When Is a Prototype an Expert System?" *Expert Systems: Planning, Implementation, Integration* (Spring 1991).

34. McCaffrey, M.J. "Maintenance of Expert Systems—The Upcoming Challenge." In *Managing Expert Systems*, E. Turban and J. Liebowitz, eds. Harrisburg, Pa.: Idea Group Publishers, 1992.

35. McCullough, T. "Six Steps to Selling AI." *AI Expert* (December 1987).

36. Mettrey, W. "An Assessment of Tools for Building Large Knowledge-Based Systems." *AI Magazine* (Winter 1987).

37. Murdoch, H. "Choosing a Problem—When Is AI Appropriate for the Retail Industry?" *Expert Systems* (February 1990).

38. Odette, L. "Expert Systems: When to Make Them, When to Buy Them." In *Proceedings of the 1987 Expert Systems in Business Conference*, J. Feinstein, J. Liebowitz, H. Look, and B. Sullivan, eds. Medford, N.J.: Learned Information, 1987.

39. O'Neill, M., and A. Morris. "Expert Systems in the United Kingdom: An Evaluation of Development Methodologies." *Expert Systems* 6 (1990): 90–99.

40. Payne, E., and R. McArthur. *Developing Expert Systems: A Knowledge Engineer's Handbook for Rules and Objects*. New York: John Wiley & Sons, 1990.

41. Preece, A.D. "Towards a Methodology for Evaluating Expert Systems." *Expert Systems* (November 1990).

42. Prerau, D.S. *Developing and Managing Expert Systems*. Reading, Mass.: Addison-Wesley, 1990.

43. Rauch-Hindin, W.B. *A Guide to Commercial AI*. Englewood Cliffs, N.J.: Prentice-Hall, 1988.

44. Redin, P. "Developing ES on PC's—A Methodology." *AI Expert* (October 1987).

45. Sacerdoti, E.D. "Managing Expert System Development." *AI Expert* (May 1991).

46. Samuell, R. III, and W.T. Jones. "A Method for the Strategic Assessment of Expert Systems Applications." *Expert Systems with Applications* (Fall 1990).

47. Schwartz, T. *Expert Systems in a Mainframe Environment*. Special Report. New York: Intelligent Systems and Analyst, 1988.

48. Shanteau, J. "Psychological Characteristics of Expert Decision Makers." In *Proceedings, Symposium on Expert Systems and Audit Judgment*. Univ. of Southern California, Los Angeles, February 17–18, 1986.

49. Slagle, J., and M. Wick. "A Method for Evaluating Candidate Expert Systems Applications." *AI Magazine* (Winter 1988).

50. Smith, A., and C. Dagli. "An Analysis of Worth: Justifying Funding for

Development and Implementation." In *Managing Expert Systems*, E. Turban and J. Liebowitz, eds. Harrisburg, Pa.: Idea Group Publishers, 1992.

51. Sprague, K.G. "Cultivating a Prototyping Approach to Expert Systems Development." *Expert Systems: Planning, Implementation, Integration* (Fall 1990).

52. Stanley, F.J. "Establishing a Project Management Methodology." *Journal of Information Systems Management* (Fall 1988).

53. Suen, C.Y., et al. "Verifying, Validating and Measuring the Performance of Expert Systems." *Expert Systems with Applications* (June 1990).

54. Thompson, D.M., and J.L. Feinstein. "Cost-Justifying Expert Systems." In *Managing AI and Expert Systems*, D.A. DeSalvo and J. Liebowitz, eds. Englewood Cliffs, N.J.: Yourdon Press/Prentice-Hall, 1990.

55. Tubalkain, T., and J.W. Griesser. "Expert Systems Catching on at the Navy Finance Center." In *Managing Expert Systems*, E. Turban and J. Liebowitz, eds. Harrisburg, Pa.: Idea Group Publishers, 1992.

56. Turban, E., and Liebowitz, J. *Managing Expert Systems*. Harrisburg, Pa.: Idea Group Publishers, 1992.

57. Vedder, R., and E. Turban. "Strategies for Managing Expert Systems Development." In *Managing Expert Systems*, E. Turban and J. Liebowitz, eds. Harrisburg, Pa.: Idea Group Publishers, 1992.

58. Walters, J., and N.R. Nielsen. *Crafting Knowledge-based Systems*. New York: John Wiley & Sons, 1989.

59. Wasil, E.A., and A.A. Assad. "Project Management on the PC: Software, Applications and Trends." *Interfaces* (March/April 1988).

60. Waterman, D.A. *A Guide to Expert Systems*. Reading, Mass.: Addison-Wesley, 1985.

61. Weitzel, J.R., and L. Kerschberg. "Developing Knowledge-based Systems: Reorganizing the System Development Life Cycle." *Communications of ACM* (April 1989).

62. Wetz, R.R., and A. DeMeyer. "Managing Expert Systems: A Framework and Case Study." *Information and Management* (September 1990).

Appendix A: Developing Large Expert Systems[1]

Building a large expert system is a complex task. The following six-phase process has been suggested by Kameny et al. The main characteristic of this approach is the reduction of risk by developing an ever-increasing understanding of the problem, user needs, and requirements through demonstration and use. Major application issues such as user interface, integration, and security are addressed in every phase. All stages of development emphasize the need for a team support effort of ES developers, users and experts, maintenance people, security

---

[1] Condensed from I. Kameny, U. Kahn, J. Paul, and D. Taylor, Guide for the Management of Expert Systems Development, Report R-3766-P&L (Santa Monica, Calif.: The RAND Corp.), pp. 11–13. This research was sponsored by the U.S. Dept. of Defense and it is not copyrighted.

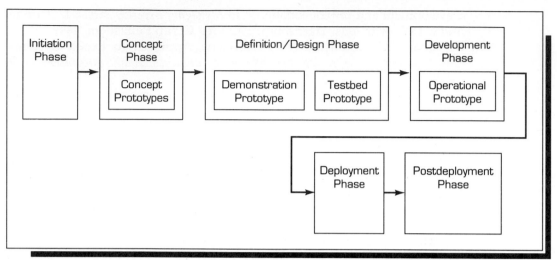

FIGURE 12A.1 Development Life Cycle of an Expert System (*Source:* I. Kameny, et al. *Guide for the Management of Expert Systems Development* [Santa Monica, Calif.: RAND Corp., 1989].)

and systems people, and management. The proposed process is composed of six phases, as shown in Figure 12A.1.

The *initiation phase* is concerned with deciding what is wanted. It asks what the problem is, whether ES technology can be feasibly applied to the problem, how to begin exploring the problem, and whether the problem solution satisfies the users' mission needs. The culmination of this phase is a review which, if successful, brings the project to the next phase.

The *concept phase* involves further exploration of the problem and deciding how best to solve it. In-house ES building tools and other support tools are used to develop rapid prototypes of parts of the problem solution. These *concept prototypes* focus on those items identified as high risk. The result of this activity is not a single, integrated concept prototype but rather many small prototypes. Such prototypes may demonstrate how the general problem solution will work, how parts of the problem solution that strain ES capabilities might be handled, how the user interface may be structured, how integration with other computer-based information devices will be handled, and how security may be handled.

The *definition/design phase* is concerned with the development of the final design for the problem solution. This design is embodied in a working prototype and associated documentation. The phase is divided into two stages corresponding to the two prototypes used for design development: the demonstration prototype and the testbed prototype.

The *demonstration prototype* focuses on rapid design and prototyping of the problem solution in a stand-alone mode by the knowledge engineer through extensive interaction with the expert(s) and to a lesser degree with end-users. The ES tool used in this stage is primarily selected for its ability to support the design effort and should offer extensive support for debugging, graphics, knowledge acquisition, multiple modes of reasoning, and knowledge representation. The major goal of this stage is to correctly demonstrate the problem solution with an adequate user interface. The demonstration prototype is not directly concerned with fast execution (tool choice may be the result of selecting development functionality and speed over fast operational execution). The interfaces with other systems should at least be conceptually designed and the data exchanges simulated. Security may be planned for, but the underlying support (e.g., from the operating system) may be lacking in the demonstration prototype software base.

The *testbed prototype* is a redesign and a reimplementation of the functions defined and demonstrated in the demonstration prototype, possibly with enhancements. This prototype may be implemented using the ES tool that will be used in the deployed system, or it may be coded directly in a programming language. Correctness is required of the testbed prototype, and formal test and evaluation procedures should validate that it meets its requirements as specified. Again, integration interfaces should be implemented but they will not be directly linked into an AI system. Security aspects of the workstation environment should be implemented and tested.

The *development phase* produces the *operational prototype*. It is the result of integrating the testbed prototype into an example operational environment using the actual deployed tool and other computer-based information systems. Correctness and performance should be validated as should requirements for integration and security. With the completion of the operational prototype, the ES is ready for deployment.

In the *deployment phase*, the fully integrated system is delivered to the field. This phase culminates in a review; if the review is successful, the system is turned over to the support organization that will maintain it.

The *postdeployment phase* is concerned with maintenance of the system, evaluation of the use of the system to determine lessons learned, and planning of enhancements to be implemented in system upgrades.

Appendix B: Developing Small Expert Systems

Small expert systems, like small decision support systems, go through an abbreviated development process. They are usually developed with ES shells, and they are usually rule based. Several suggestions have been made for the short process. For example, Harmon [2] advocates the following seven-step process:

□ Phase 1: Identify problem characteristics, analyze cost-effectiveness, and arrange for management support.
□ Phase 2: Identify task and knowledge.
□ Phase 3: Develop small prototype.
□ Phase 4: Develop system (add knowledge as needed).
□ Phase 5: Test with actual users.
□ Phase 6: Transport to field and train users.
□ Phase 7: Update and maintain system.

Another process suggested by Harmon et al. [3] has six phases:

1. Select a tool and implicitly commit yourself to a particular consultation paradigm.
2. Identify a problem and then analyze the knowledge to be included in the system.
3. Design the system on paper with flow diagrams, matrices, and a few rules.
4. Develop a prototype of the system using a tool. This includes creating a knowledge base and testing it by running a number of consultations.
5. Expand, test, and revise the system until it does what you want it to do.
6. Maintain and update as needed.

The relatively low cost that is involved in small systems enables shortcuts that can save development time.

Small expert systems are being developed by end-users. An example is given in Chapter 21 (the EXTELCSYS example). A detailed example is provided by Frenzel [1]. Small expert systems may be subject to the dangers involved in end-user computing. For example, the developers do not have the expertise in developing systems and as a result the systems may have poor (or no) documentation, bad interfaces, an unacceptable security system, and so forth. Despite these dangers, which can be controlled and managed, developing small systems can, at the least, be a good training exercise for the builder; it also could result in significant benefits.

References

1. Frenzel, L.E. *Understanding Expert Systems*. Indianapolis: W.W. Sams, 1987, pp. 171–181.
2. Harmon, P. *Expert Systems Strategies* (January 1986).
3. Harmon, P., et al. *Expert Systems Tools and Applications*. New York: John Wiley & Sons, 1988.

Appendix C: The One-Minute Knowledge Engineer[2]

(The One-Minute Knowledge Engineer is from: *IS Analyzer* (formerly EDP Analyzer), March, 1987, p. 61–62. Currently © United Communications Group, 4550 Montgomery Ave., Bethesda, MD 20814.)

Justification: To determine if there is economic justification.

_____Is there a need to make the knowledge of a specially trained or talented individual more widely available?

Definitely—6 Probably—4 Maybe—2 No—0 Not applicable—0

---

[2] Reprinted with permission from "Commentary," *IS Analyzer* (March 1987): 61–62.

_____Will the expertise be lost if not captured by an expert system?
Definitely—6 Probably—4 Maybe—2 No—0 Not applicable—0

_____Will there be significant savings or payoffs from an expert system?
Definitely—6 Probably—4 Maybe—2 No—0 Not applicable—0

_____Is there a need to increase the efficiency of the decision-making process through improved consistency and timeliness?
Definitely—5 Probably—3 Maybe—1 No—0 Not applicable—0

_____Is it expensive to train individuals to deal with the problem area?
Definitely—5 Probably—3 Maybe—1 No—0 Not applicable—0

_____Will building an expert system help future development?
Definitely—4 Probably—2 Maybe—1 No—0 Not applicable—0

_____Can the proposed expert system be integrated into existing service or product lines to increase their value?
Definitely—5 Probably—3 Maybe—1 No—0 Not applicable—0

_____Will an improved understanding of the problem, gained through expert system development, be valuable to the organization?
Definitely—4 Probably—2 Maybe—1 No—0 Not applicable—0

Scoring: Add up the points. If they are (1) greater than 30 points, this is an excellent expert system opportunity, (2) from 20 to 29 points, this may be a good opportunity if the cost is not too great, or (3) less than 20 points, it may not provide sufficient payback.

Expertise: To determine if the expertise in the problem area is adequate.

_____Is there an expert(s) available who solves problems significantly better than the majority of the intended users of the expert system?
Definitely—6 Probably—4 Maybe—2 No—0 Not applicable—0

_____Is the expertise to be used accurate and correct?
Definitely—5 Probably—4 Maybe—1 No—0 Not applicable—0

_____Are there a few key people with specialized knowledge or expertise spending excessive time helping many others?
Definitely—5 Probably—3 Maybe—1 No—0 Not applicable—0

_____Are the experts articulate enough to explain their methodology?
Definitely—5 Probably—3 Maybe—1 No—1 Not applicable—0

_____Are the experts willing to work with a knowledge engineer?
Definitely—5 Probably—3 Maybe—1 No—0 Not applicable—0

_____Will the expert(s) have time to complete the development process?
Definitely—5 Probably—3 Maybe—1 No—0 Not applicable—0

_____If multiple experts contribute, is one the final authority?
Definitely—4 Probably—2 Maybe—1 No—0 Not applicable—0

Scoring: Add up the points. If they are (1) greater than 20 points, expertise should be very adequate to support the project, (2) from 15 to 19 points, expertise may not be adequate for expert level performance, or (3) less than 15 points, insufficient expertise will probably handicap the project.

Problem characteristics: To determine if the problem domain lends itself to expert system development.

_____Does the problem require mainly experience-based reasoning?
          Definitely—5 Probably—3 Maybe—1 No—0 Not applicable—0

_____Is the problem solution dependent on commonsense reasoning?
          Definitely—0 Probably—1 Maybe—2 No—5 Not applicable—0

_____Does the problem require small amounts of time for the expert to solve or explain (less than two hours), or can it be subdivided?
          Definitely—5 Probably—3 Maybe—1 No—0 Not applicable—0

_____Do the users require all possibilities known in advance?
          Definitely—0 Probably—1 Maybe—2 No—5 Not applicable—0

Scoring: Add up the points. If they are (1) greater than 15 points, the problem area can be supported by an expert system, (2) from 10 to 14 points, some aspects of the problem may be difficult to capture, or (3) less than 10 points, it may be difficult to support the problem with an expert system.

Organizational and political characteristics: To determine whether the people involved are prepared to support and use the final product.

_____Is there adequate managerial commitment for the effort?
          Definitely—5 Probably—3 Maybe—1 No—0 Not applicable—0

_____Are the users committed to using the expert system?
          Definitely—5 Probably—3 Maybe—1 No—0 Not applicable—0

_____Will the introduction of an expert system cause political or control repercussions either from its use, contents, or recommendations?
          Definitely—0 Probably—1 Maybe—2 No—5 Not applicable—0

_____Will the system handle a real and necessary business need?
          Definitely—5 Probably—3 Maybe—1 No—0 Not applicable—0

_____Is it acceptable to complete the system in phases?
          Definitely—5 Probably—3 Maybe—1 No—0 Not applicable—0

Scoring: Add up the points. If they are (1) greater than 20 points, the organization will support the project, (2) from 15 to 19 points, full success may be difficult, or (3) less than 15 points, obstacles may hinder the project.

Chapter 13

Tools for Expert Systems

This chapter presents an overview of the various software tools that can be used in constructing an expert system. In addition, it raises the issue of hardware support. The following topics are covered:

13.1 Introduction

AI systems can be constructed with the aid of a large number of tools (or tool kits). The tools appear under different names and range from programming languages to comprehensive integrated development packages known as environments. Our attention in this chapter is directed toward expert systems software packages, although several of these packages can be used to construct other AI applications. In building AI applications, a single package or several packages may be used. We begin by classifying the various packages; then we survey each of the major classes. Next we discuss software selection. Lastly, we describe issues of hardware support.

13.2   Software Classification

The many AI software tools can be classified in several ways (e.g., by the size or complexity of the system they are being used to construct). We have found it helpful to classify software into five **technology levels:** languages, support tools, shells, hybrid systems, and ES applications (specific ES). The boundaries between the levels are fairly fuzzy, and our classification approach is used mainly for providing an initial understanding of ES software. Figure 13.1 illustrates the levels.

Roughly speaking, the specific application (top of figure) can be constructed with shells, and/or support tools, and/or hybrid systems, and/or languages.

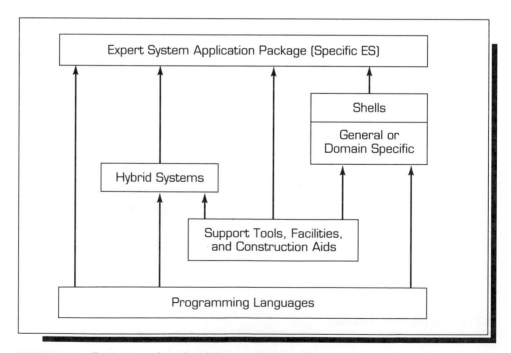

FIGURE 13.1 Technology Levels of Expert System Software

Shells and hybrid systems can be constructed with languages and/or support tools, and support tools are constructed with languages.

The higher the level of the software in Figure 13.1, the *less programming* is required. The trade-off is that the higher the level, the *less flexible* is the software. Generally speaking, the use of higher levels of software enables quicker programming (even by end-users). On the other hand, complex and nonstandard applications must be built with lower levels of software.

Description of Levels

Specific Expert Systems. Specific ES are the application products that advise a specific user on a specific issue, for example, a consultation system that diagnoses a malfunction in a locomotive and systems that advise on tax shelters or on buying software. Most specific ES are custom-made, but some are ready-made. Ready-made ES can be used by any end-user with a specific problem (e.g., any taxpayer looking for a tax shelter). Such systems are available for sale from several vendors or even off the shelf in computer stores. Specific ES can be used in a very restricted application area in one company, or one segment of a company, or even as a part of a piece of equipment (e.g., a diagnostic system for finding malfunctions in the electrical system of GE's model D-1 locomotives). They can also be used by an entire industry (e.g., airlines or telephone companies).

Shell (Skeletal) Systems. Instead of building an ES from scratch, it is often possible to borrow extensively from a previously built specific ES. This strategy has resulted in several integrated software tools that are described as **shell (skeletal) systems.** The expert systems are stripped of their knowledge component, which leaves only a shell—the explanation and inference mechanisms.

Shells are integrated packages in which the major components of the expert systems (except for the knowledge base) are preprogrammed. The programmer needs only to insert the knowledge in order to build a system.

Support Tools. With shells, the system builder needs to construct only the knowledge base. In contrast, many other types of tools help build the various parts of the system. They are aids for knowledge acquisition, knowledge validation and verification, and construction of interfaces to other software packages.

Hybrid Systems (Environments). **Hybrid systems** are composed of several support tools and programming languages. They enable systems to be built faster than they would be built if only programming languages were used. Hybrid systems provide skilled programmers with a rapid prototyping environment in which they can build shells or specific ES. ART, for example, contains modules from which an inference engine can be assembled. One module provides a procedure for handling measures of uncertainty, while another module provides a Bayesian procedure for handling probabilities. The knowledge engineer builds an inference engine and then proceeds to use that engine in conjunction with a knowledge base to build an expert system.

Shells and tools (or environments) differ in their degree of focus. Tools (environments) are more flexible but less focused. They place more responsibility on the knowledge engineer. Shells address a narrower application area and provide a more focused approach. Shells and tools can be general or they can aim at specific industries, domains, or even applications. For example, ARBIE and IN-ATE are designed for building ES for electronic equipment diagnosis; REVEAL is aimed at financial applications. Several tools (and shells) are available for diagnostic ES, for real-time ES, and so forth. (See Knaus and Blecker [18] for examples.)

Programming Languages. Expert systems can be constructed with one of many programming languages—ranging from AI languages to standard procedural languages (such as COBOL). They can even be programmed with fourth-generation languages such as Lotus 1-2-3.

Discussion of Levels

To illustrate the concept of software levels, let us examine the history of the development of the MYCIN family. The MYCIN family (Figure 13.2) originated with a rule-based ES for the diagnosis and treatment of infectious blood diseases. Its general methodology gave rise to a shell called EMYCIN and a related programming aid, TEIRESIAS that could assist in the knowledge acquisition process. PUFF, an expert system for interpreting respiratory data and diagnosing pulmonary diseases, was the first actual application built with EMYCIN. KS 300 combined many of the best features of EMYCIN and TEIRESIAS and has supported numerous commercial specific ES. Two of these—WAVES and Drilling Advisor—illustrate the breadth of systems that can be built with it. WAVES is an ES that assesses a data analysis problem for a geophysicist and prescribes the best way to process the data using selected modules from a million-line FORTRAN analysis package. The Drilling Advisor, on the other hand, determines the most likely cause for a stuck oil drill bit and prescribes expert corrective and preventive measures. KS 300 was further developed to S.1, an enhanced commercial domain independent shell. Another subset of EMYCIN is called Personal Consultant.

13.3 Programming Languages

Numerous programming languages are oriented toward artificial intelligence. Commercial versions of these languages and their variants are available for a wide range of computers, from micros to large computers. The programming

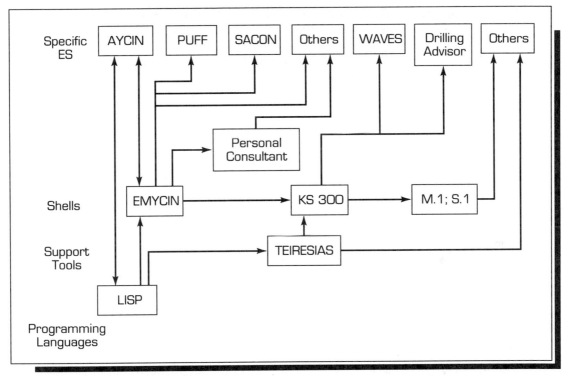

FIGURE 13.2 MYCIN Family of Software

languages can be classified into five categories: non-AI languages, AI languages, object-oriented languages, higher-level AI languages, and general-purpose knowledge engineering languages.

Non-AI Languages

Some ES development tools are written in non-AI languages; for example, TIMM is written in FORTRAN 77, INSIGHT 2 (now Level5) in Turbo Pascal, and EXSYS in C. Some specific ES have also been completely programmed in such languages. Why? A most likely reason is that no other language is available for the hardware on which the ES is to run. Another likely reason is that some ES must run on personal computers. Implementation of AI languages *may* require more memory and may not give programmers the fine control they need to conserve memory. Therefore, the AI language may be too restrictive. Expert systems written in non-AI languages may run much faster on micros than if they were written in an AI language. Finally, the interface of an ES with databases, or with any computer-based information system, can be much easier if the ES is written in a conventional language.

There are ways to circumvent the aforementioned problems. Programmers, for example, can recode from one language to another. First they design their

ES with AI languages like PROLOG or LISP. Once they are satisfied that the system works, they translate the code into Pascal, FORTRAN, or C. (Automatic translation is available for several codes.)

Languages like FORTRAN suffer from a disadvantage in that they can manipulate effectively only a small range of AI data types (e.g., numbers, logical values). In writing AI, the programmer may need to handle objects like rules, semantic nets, and explanations. Although the latter can be conveniently programmed with Pascal (or its variants), Pascal is inefficient for the following reason: In programming AI, it is sometimes necessary to build and split rules or construct nets continuously. In the course of such operations the computer's memory is filled, temporarily, with a large quantity of intermediate results. To avoid running out of memory, these results must be removed. In Pascal, the programmer must write instructions to do so. In AI languages, the memory is cleaned automatically by a process called garbage collection.

AI (Symbolic) Languages

The AI, or symbolic manipulation, languages provide an effective way to present AI-type objects. The two major languages are LISP and PROLOG. With these languages, the programming and debugging procedures can frequently be done much faster. The major characteristics of the two languages are described next.

LISP. LISP (for list processor, see Winston and Horn [33]) is one of the oldest general-purpose languages. Developed at MIT by McCarthy in 1958, it is still in active use. LISP's applications include expert systems, natural language processing, robotics, and educational and psychological programming. Its unique features give the programmer the power to develop software that goes far beyond the limitations of other general-purpose languages such as COBOL and Pascal.

Specifically, LISP is oriented toward symbolic computation; the programmer can assign values to terms like *financial* and *liquidity*. Although the values have no direct meaning in LISP, the LISP program can conveniently manipulate such symbols and their relationships. LISP programs also have the ability to modify themselves. In a limited sense, this means that a computer can be programmed to "learn" from its past experiences.

LISP allows programmers to represent objects like rules and nets as "lists"— sequences of numbers, character strings, or other lists. It provides them with operations for splitting lists apart and for making new lists by joining old ones. Conventionally, LISP programmers write lists as bracketed sequences of elements. They often draw them as box-and-arrow diagrams. The accompanying illustration shows a list that represents the sentence "PC is a computer."

In most programming situations, lists contain other lists or sublists as elements. Here is a simple example of list code, a recursive definition of a function that sums two integers:

```
(defun sum (A B)
  (cond ((eq A O) B)
    (t (sum (minus 1 A) (plus 1 B))))
```

This definition says: "If you have two numbers and the first [A] is 0, then the other [B] is their total. If the first is not 0, then try for the sum $(A - 1, B + 1)$." In this example, *sum* is a newly defined function, whereas the remaining functions (e.g., defun, cond, minus 1, t) are predefined. LISP programs consist of many such functions.

LISP code is usually executed directly by a LISP interpreter. In some versions the source program is compiled to increase efficiency.

There are numerous variations of LISP. Some include built-in features for special applications. Most notable are COMMON LISP, IQLISP, INTERLISP, MACLISP, ZETALISP, GOLDEN COMMON LISP, and FRANZLISP (UNIX based). Each of these may have several subvariants.

PROLOG. Although LISP is the most popular AI language in the United States, **PROLOG** (for programming in logic) is the most popular AI language in Japan and probably in Europe (see Clocksin and Mellish [7]). Its basic idea is to express statements of logic as statements in programming language. The proof of a theorem using these statements could be thought of as a way of executing those statements. Thus logic itself could be used directly as a programming language. For example, the statements "all dogs are animals" and "Lassie is a dog," and the theorem "Lassie is an animal," could be expressed formally in PROLOG as follows:

PROLOG	Meaning
animal (X):-dog(X)	(X is an animal if X is a dog)
dog (Lassie)	(Lassie is a dog)
?-animal (Lassie)	(Is Lassie an animal?)

PROLOG can then be run to try to prove the theorem, given the two statements. Clearly, it will come to the conclusion that the theorem is true.

There are three basic types of statements in PROLOG:

:-P	means P is a goal (or predicate) to be proven
P.	means P is an assertion or a fact
P:-Q,R,S	means Q, R, and S imply P

To define a goal, several clauses may be required. One of the techniques of knowledge representation is first-order logic. Because PROLOG is based on a subset of first-order logic (predicate calculus), it can use this format of knowledge representation. PROLOG has the additional advantage of having a very powerful inference engine in place. Therefore, the algorithm used in PROLOG is more powerful than the simple pattern-matching algorithms commonly used with LISP in production-rule representations of knowledge.

PROLOG's basis in logic provides its distinctive flavor. Because a PROLOG program is a series of statements in logic, it can be understood declaratively; that is, it can be understood quite separately from considerations of how it will be executed. Traditional languages can be understood only procedurally, that is, by considering what happens when the program is executed on a computer. Representative variants of PROLOG include MPROLOG, ARITY PROLOG, QUINTUS PROLOG, and Turbo PROLOG.

LISP has been and still is the favorite AI language in the United States. To a large extent this is due to the existence of sophisticated programming environments and specialized **AI workstations.** The situation is changing, however, as more sophisticated implementations of PROLOG supported by improved environments are appearing in the market.

PROLOG allows a program to be formulated in smaller units, each with a natural declarative reading; by contrast, the size and multiple nesting of function definitions in LISP are barriers to readability. In addition, PROLOG's built-in pattern-matching capability is an extremely useful device. PROLOG does, however, have certain deficiencies. For example, the use of built-in input/output predicates creates symbols that have no meaning in logic.

The arguments for (and against) LISP and PROLOG are likely to go on for some time. In the meantime, some attempts are being made to combine the two. One such example is a product called **POPLOG**—a programming environment that combines PROLOG, LISP, and POP-11 (POP-11 is an extension of PROLOG) into a single package. The package is friendlier than its components, and when compiled it runs faster than PROLOG, LISP, or POP-11.

Object-oriented Languages

Object-oriented languages such as C++ and Smalltalk-80 (see Chapter 5) are becoming popular in AI. Usually they are employed with other programming languages.

Higher-level AI Languages

The ease of creating new functions in LISP is very important for ES design. It makes LISP an excellent base for **higher-level languages** that address problems specific to the domain being modeled. For example, XPLAIN is programmed in a powerful higher-level language called XLMS (for experimental linguistic memory system), which is an extension of LISP. XLMS helps generate clear, nonredundant explanations from the program, which was one of the major goals of the XPLAIN system. The XPLAIN system itself is used for constructing the explanation subsystem in a shell or in a specific ES. Incidentally, this example demonstrates that there can be several layers of tools within a system classified at one level. Another example of such a higher-level language is LOOPS.

General-purpose Knowledge Engineering Languages

Several general-purpose languages have been developed specifically for knowledge engineering. Generally, they are more flexible and less constrained than shell systems. On the other hand, they may lack sophisticated facilities for input and/or output processes, for knowledge-base construction, and for explanation. Therefore, their programming environment is not as comprehensive as those provided by shell programs. Unlike the shell programs, which are restricted to generic applications (e.g., diagnosis), these programs are unrestricted. Because they are not as closely tied to particular frameworks, they allow for a wider variety of control structures. They can thus be applied to a broader range of tasks, although the process of applying them may be more difficult than it is with shell systems.

Four pioneering languages are part of this category: HEARSAY-III, ROSIE, OPS5, and RLL. For further discussion, information, and references see Hayes-Roth et al. [15]. These languages are the predecessors of hybrid systems (section 13.6).

13.4 Support Aids and Facilities

Large numbers of aids and facilities are available to support AI construction. These tools support knowledge acquisition, programming, editing, representation, and explanation. Hundreds of software packages on the market fall into this category.

System-building Aids. System-building aids consist of programs that help acquire and represent the domain expert's knowledge and programs that help the design and construction of specific ES. The two major categories are design aids and knowledge acquisition aids. Representative design aids are AGE and TIMM. Some knowledge acquisition aids are TEIRESIAS, ROGET, and SEEK. For further details see Hayes-Roth et al. [15] and Waterman [32].

Support Facilities. Support facilities are tools used by programmers to increase productivity. Four typical categories have been identified by Waterman [32]: debugging aids (e.g., for tracing rules used), knowledge-base editors (e.g., for checking the consistency of added rules, for knowledge extraction, and for syntax checking), input/output facilities (e.g., menus and natural language processors), and explanation facilities.

Natural Language Processors. Expert systems can be integrated with natural language tools to provide a friendlier interface. (See Chapter 8 for details.)

Explanation Facilities. Users should be able to ask for information on how a system is solving their problem. For example, a *why* question by users causes the system to explain why it has requested certain information from the users. This may include printing out the rule that the system is currently considering. A *how* question causes the system to explain how a particular conclusion was obtained. For example, it specifies which rules were used to make the conclusion (i.e., it displays reasoning that leads to the conclusion).

The combination of *why* and *how* questions provides users with an explanation facility and a great deal of insight into how the system reaches its conclusions. Then users can fully accept (or have a valid reason to reject) the system's conclusions. Such explanation capabilities can also provide excellent tutorial sessions to the user during the consultation.

13.5   Shells (Skeletal Systems)

Expert systems, as described earlier, are composed of six basic components: knowledge acquisition subsystems, inference engine, explanation facility, interface subsystem (for conducting consultation), knowledge base management facility, and knowledge base. The first five subsystems constitute what is called an expert system shell. The knowledge base is the *content*, or the "inside," of the shell. Experience has shown that there is no need to program the first five subsystems of the shell for every application. On the contrary, once a shell is constructed it can be used for many applications; all one has to do is insert the necessary knowledge. By using the shell approach, expert systems can be built much faster. Furthermore, the programming skill required is much lower. All factors together contribute to a cost reduction. The shell concept, which is illustrated in Figure 13.3, is especially useful in rule-based systems.

Here are some examples of rule-based shells:

- □ Small size: EXSYS, Personal Consultant Easy, VP Expert, Level5
- □ Medium size: EXSYS Professional, Guru, KES 2.2, Nexpert, Personal Consultant Plus
- □ Large size: ESE, S.1, AES, IMPACT, SYNTEL, ADS
- □ Induction: 1st-CLASS, TIMM

For additional information on all types of shells see Gevarter [10], Harmon et al. [13], and Rosenthal [26].

A shell can be extremely useful in developing expert systems for a specific application, provided it is well chosen. Two types of shells exist: general and domain specific. When you select a shell, make sure it can handle the specifics

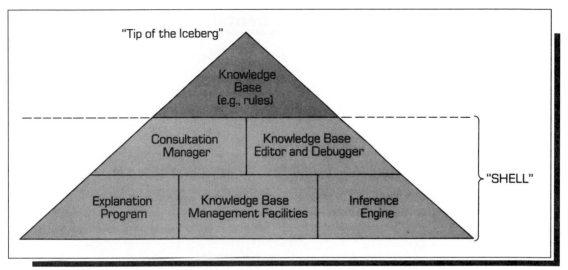

FIGURE 13.3 Shell Concept for Building Expert Systems (*Source:* B. G. Buchanan in Texas Instruments First Satellite Program)

of the application properly (including explanation and interface with databases and other computerized systems).

Shells do have limitations and disadvantages. Because they are inflexible, it may be difficult to fit them to nonstandard problems and tasks. As a result, a builder may use several shells, as well as environments and other tools, even in one application. Such proliferation may cause problems in training and maintenance. Shells also add an interface layer that requires its own resident interpreter. Shells are end-user tools (similar to fourth-generation languages), and their use is subject to the problems of end-user computing (poor documentation, weak security, improper maintenance). Expert system shells can be considered as limited programming environments. For example, they may use only rule representation and only backward chaining.

Despite their limitations, shells are being used extensively by many organizations, small and large. In some cases they are used primarily for training or as the starting tool in the prototyping cycle.

Domain-specific tools are designed to be used *only* in the development of a specific area. For example, there are shells for diagnostic systems, shells for configuration, and shells for scheduling. A domain-specific tool may include some rule-based tools, an inductive mechanism, or a knowledge verification component. Domain-specific tools enhance the use of more standard tools by providing special development support and users' interface. Such features permit a much faster construction of applications. Presently, there are only a few commercial domain-specific shells and tools available. They cost much more than general-purpose software. For further discussion see Knaus and Blecker [18] and Price [25].

13.6 Hybrid Systems (Environments)

Development environments are defined by Harmon et al. [13] as development systems that support *several* different ways of representing knowledge and handling inferences. They may use frames, object-oriented programming, semantic networks, rules and metarules, different types of chaining (forward, backward, and bidirectional), nonmonotonic reasoning, a rich variety of inheritance techniques, and more (see Table 13.1). Hybrid systems permit a programming environment that allows for building complex specific systems or complex tools. Initially, hybrid tools were developed for large computers and AI workstations. Now they are available on personal computers. The following are representative packages:

- Large systems: ART, KEE, Knowledge Craft, Aion Development System, KBMS
- PC systems: GoldWorks II, Nexpert Object, ART-IM, Keystone, KEE/PC, Personal Consultant Plus, DAI-SOGEN, Level5 Object, and Kappa PC.

Environments are more specialized than languages. Therefore they can increase the productivity of system builders. Although environments require more programming skills than shells, they are more flexible. Hybrid systems are based on two basic tools: Smalltalk and OPS.

Smalltalk was developed initially as an object-oriented programming language. It was expanded to include facilities for data abstraction, message sending, object classification, and interactive development. Now it is a complete development tool kit used for rapid prototyping of AI systems. Smalltalk has many built-in graphic interfaces (e.g., icons). One interesting feature is that the

TABLE 13.1 Features of Hybrid Systems

Backward, forward, and bidirectional chaining
Object-oriented programming, frames
Metarules
Hypothetical reasoning
Complete pattern matching or variable rules
Nonmonotonic reasoning or truth maintenance
Dynamic graphics, icons, visual interactive simulations
High-quality browsing utilities
CASE library facilities
Ability to set breakpoints or interrupt a consultation
Semantic networks
Interfaces to databases, spreadsheets and hypermedia, neural networks
Real-time capabilities

Source: Based on Expert Systems Strategies 4 (no. 2, 1988). Published by Harmon Associates.

code of Smalltalk is similar to that of Pascal. Smalltalk and its derivatives (e.g., Smalltalk-80) are used extensively in developing user-friendly interfaces (e.g., Windows from Microsoft).

OPS is a production system programming. Production system techniques are useful when the knowledge related to a programming problem occurs (or can be expressed) in a natural rule structure. The OPS family was used in developing the XCON system. It combines a rule-based language with a conventional procedural programming technique. Two commercial products were developed from the initial research tool: OPS5 (implemented in LISP) and OPS83 (incorporates an imperative sublanguage that resembles Pascal or C). It is now being used in a comprehensive commercial environment known as Knowledge Craft.

Hybrid systems are gaining popularity; therefore we decided to support this book with Level5 Object. Several other packages are briefly described next.

ART is a comprehensive LISP-based environment; it is a forward-chaining rule-based system. It is based on OPS5, but many features have been added. ART has four main components: rules (mainly for procedural knowledge), facts, schemata, and viewpoints (for declarative knowledge). A related product, ART-IM, is written in C and runs on workstations and personal computers.

KEE is basically an object-oriented-based environment. Thus, the primary knowledge representation method is a frame. In contrast with ART, which approaches problems from a rule-based perspective, KEE begins by conceptualizing a problem in terms of objects and the relationships among them. KEE uses extensive graphics, icons, and windows and can be used on a variety of computers (including advanced personal computers). Related products are KEE/370 (for IBM machines) and KEE/PC.

Nexpert Object can run on IBM's PC-AT or larger personal computers (386's). Nexpert Object is known for its extensive built-in interfaces (Figure 13.4).

13.7 Commercial Knowledge Engineering Tools

Building aids, shells, and other software are frequently referred to as knowledge engineering tools, or tool kits. Such tools are now responsible for about 90 percent of the expert systems in use, and the percentage is likely to increase. By the end of 1992, small shells such as EXSYS and Level5 will have been sold to thousands of customers.

Working with knowledge engineering tools makes ES more economically justifiable, especially when they are being developed on personal computers. Furthermore, the cost of throwing away unsuccessful systems is low. Several commercial knowledge engineering development tools for mainframes and minis appeared on the market in the early 1980s. They were followed by a host of microbased packages starting in 1984. Some of these systems can be used to construct simple ES, sometimes even without the services of knowledge

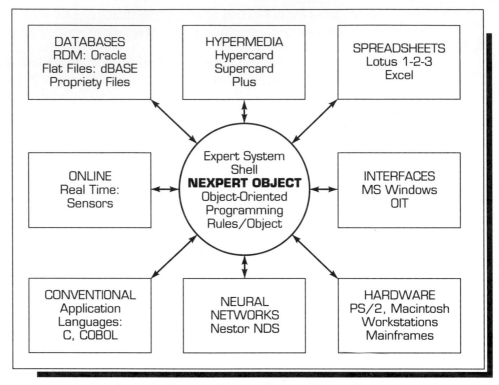

FIGURE 13.4 Interfaces of Nexpert Object (*Source:* Neuron Data, Inc.)

engineers. Many commercial systems have evolved from shell systems through enhancements aimed at increasing usability and generality. This latest development could have a significant effect on the use of ES. Let us examine a similar phenomenon: the widespread use of end-user computing and spreadsheets.

Desktop computers did not become widely accepted until it was no longer necessary for the user to "program" them or until the programming task became fairly easy. The emergence of user-friendly software like electronic spreadsheets, word processing packages, relational databases, DBMS, and fourth-generation decision support system generators stimulated the rapid expansion of the desktop computer industry. The movement of knowledge engineering tools into practical applications is analogous to the development of end-user computing. Until now, most ES have required well-trained engineers to be in the loop between the machine and the application. As long as this is the case, the diffusion of ES will be slow. Only when user-friendly application software is available to bridge the gap between the user and the application will the use of ES software become widespread, especially in the personal computing market.

Representative commercial shells and other tools are listed in Appendix A at the end of the chapter. For further details see Harmon et al. [13], Waterman [32], Lehner and Barth [20], and Assad and Golden [3].

Problems with Commercial Tools

The increased availability of development tools (including shells) does not mean that all ES will be constructed according to this approach. There are several problems with some of the development tools that make their use inappropriate in some cases. One problem is that applying a particular tool to someone else's problem really means looking for someone with a problem that matches the software. Such a match may not exist. Other difficulties arise when the ES is being integrated with other computer systems. For example, Archibald et al. [2] report that Shell Research Ltd. had to reprogram an ES with PROLOG after the system was initially programmed with the SAGE shell. The reason in this case was that a need had developed to incorporate conventional system tools into the knowledge base to perform such tasks as database management, screen handling, and substantial numeric calculation. Furthermore, SAGE's inference system was strictly backward chaining. This meant that it was not possible to volunteer information and allow the consequences of the new data to propagate through the inference networks. Another problem is that the ES constructed with shells may not be as user-friendly as needed; for example, it might provide only limited graphic representation.

Indeed, Arthur D. Little, Inc.—a major management consulting company using the powerful KEE package—finds KEE applicable in only about 50 percent of its large ES. In the other 50 percent, the company either supplements KEE with additional programming or programs from scratch. The better commercial packages are aiming for about 90 percent tool-based design and development. In other words, 90 percent of the cases will not require any additional programming. Tool vendors are adding interfaces (e.g., KEE Connection) and other software products that make the use of shells, and especially environments (see Figure 13.4), much more desirable.

13.8   Building Expert Systems with Tools

Several software tool kits may simplify the construction of ES.[1] In fact, most knowledge engineers build ES by using some commercial knowledge engineering development software; they add only a problem-specific knowledge base. Over the past twenty years, these tools have evolved from low-level languages to high-level knowledge engineering aids. Now, commercial-quality software tools are becoming available.

A knowledge engineering tool reflects a certain knowledge engineering viewpoint and a specific methodology for building ES. It includes a problem-solving paradigm. It may, for example, reflect a preference for building diagnostic

---

[1] This section is based on Hayes-Roth et al. [15].

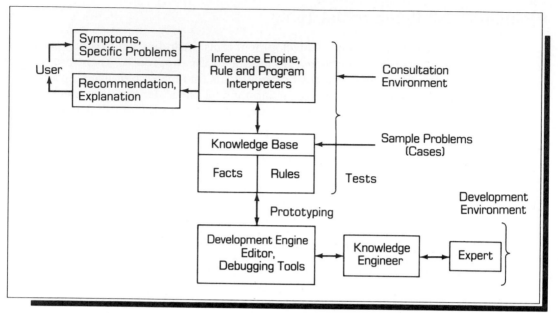

FIGURE 13.5   Building Specific Expert Systems within a Shell (*Source:* Adapted from P. Kinnucan, "Software Tools Speed Expert Systems Development," *High Technology* [March 1985].)

ES by capturing an expert's empirical symptom-problem associations. A specific paradigm constitutes a strategy for using knowledge to solve a class of problems.

Each paradigm implies certain design properties for the knowledge system architecture, and a knowledge engineering tool generally builds these properties directly into its knowledge base structure and inference engine. A shell such as EXSYS supports the construction of ES with rule-based, backward-chaining architecture. This may appear restrictive because the design constrains what a knowledge engineer can do and what the specific ES can do. On the other hand, EXSYS exploits its knowledge-system-designed constraints to improve the quality and power of the assistance it gives. Because the knowledge engineering tool "knows" how knowledge is stored within the knowledge base, the detailed operation of the inference engine, and the organization and control of problem-solving activities, it can simplify development tasks considerably. There is an analogy here to any focused software. A spreadsheet, for example, constrains the user to rows and columns, which makes programming a natural and easy process; that is, constraints may be very useful.

Building an ES with knowledge engineering tools involves the following four steps:

1. The builder employs the tool's development engine (Figure 13.5) to load the knowledge base.

2. The knowledge base is tested on sample problems using the inference engine. The test may suggest additions and changes that could result in an improved knowledge base. This is basically a prototyping step done with the aid of the editor and debugging tools.
3. The process is repeated until the system is operational.
4. The development engine is removed and the specific expert system is ready for its users (using a *runtime* component of the tool).

13.9 Software Selection

Software packages of languages, aids, environments, and shells are plentiful. You can choose from several hundred commercial packages for knowledge acquisition, representation, browsing, debugging, editing, explaining, and so on. The ES builder is frequently puzzled by what is described as an "ES software jungle." Selecting software, in general, is a complicated matter because of frequent changes in technology and the many criteria against which the alternative packages are compared. In this section we will discuss mainly issues related to ES software. Remember, however, that generic issues of software selection (such as vendor's reliability, ease of use, and cost) must also be considered (see Anderson [1]).

In principle, the selection of a tool is based on a match between the varieties of knowledge to be represented and the built-in features of the tool. In practice, this selection process is complex for several reasons:

□ It is difficult to make the transition from problems to tools. At issue is the difference between the problem and the problem-solving strategy. The same problem can be approached differently by different experts. Often, it is hard at the outset to know what methods the expert will use to solve the problem.

□ Tool selection is affected by whatever tool one may already own and the degree of familiarity with ES tools. Stretching a known piece of software to its limit may be more practical than acquiring and learning the ins and outs of a new, more powerful tool. (By analogy, in the world of statistical packages, BMD is well known for its flexibility in handling analysis of variance. However, if your data set is embedded in SPSS, you might choose to remain in SPSS rather than pay the cost of transferring the data, learning about BMD, and so on.)

□ Currently, tools on the market are more similar than they are different. Among commercially available software are many rule-based knowledge engineering tools. Lately, there have appeared several tools for frames and hybrid representations, most of which run on standard workstations and personal computers.

The major issues involved in the *selection* of ES development software are summarized in Table 13.2.

TABLE 13.2 Representative Issues in Software Selection for Expert System Development

Can the tool be easily obtained and installed? (This includes cost factors, legal arrangements, and compatibility with existing hardware.)

How well is the tool supported by the vendor? Is the current version of the system fairly stable?

How difficult will it be to expand, modify, or add a front-end or a back-end to the tool? Is a source code available or is the system sold only as a black box?

Is it simple to incorporate LISP (or other language) functions to compensate for necessary features that are not built in?

What kind of knowledge representation schemes does the tool provide? (rules? networks? frames? others?) How well do these match the intended application?

Can the tool handle the expected form of the application data? (continuous, error filled, inconsistent, uncertain, time varying, etc.)

Do the inference mechanisms provided match the problem?

Does the allowable granularity of knowledge match what is needed by the problem?

Does the expected speed of the developed system match the problem if real-time use is required?

Is there a delivery (consultation) vehicle available if many copies of the application will be needed?

What is the track record of success of the package?

What are the in-house software capabilities? (Are programmers available and qualified?)

What are the existing programming languages in systems that are likely to interface with the proposed application?

What are the future plans and strategy regarding AI dissemination and the use of languages and tools?

What hardware and networks are present in the organization?

Is this the organization's first ES application? Or have systems been developed before? What software was used in the past?

What is the anticipated maintenance plan? Who is going to do it?

Where is the product going to be used and by whom?

How easy is it to port applications to different hardware environments?

What training is necessary for the builder and for the users?

Source: Modified from S. K. Goyal et al., "COMPASS: An Expert System for Telephone Switch Maintenance," *Expert Systems* (July 1985).

The selection of hardware is a problem only when large systems are being constructed. Small systems are routinely developed and implemented on personal computers. Even large systems can be developed on existing workstations. For complex systems a builder may use several software development packages.

Evaluation Procedures

Several methodologies have been proposed for evaluation of ES software. Generally speaking, these methods develop a set of attributes against which existing packages are compared. In addition, in-depth evaluations of popular packages appear periodically in magazines. One problem is that most of these evaluations are subjective. Also, the capabilities of the packages change rapidly as new versions appear. The following references can be reviewed for both proposed methodologies and actual evaluations: Gevarter [10], Harmon et al. [13], Holsapple and Whinston [16], Mettrey [23], and Rosenthal [26]. Figure 13.6 shows the various attributes and capabilities that could be used to assess the various packages. All other things being equal, cost-effectiveness can be the determining factor in software selection.

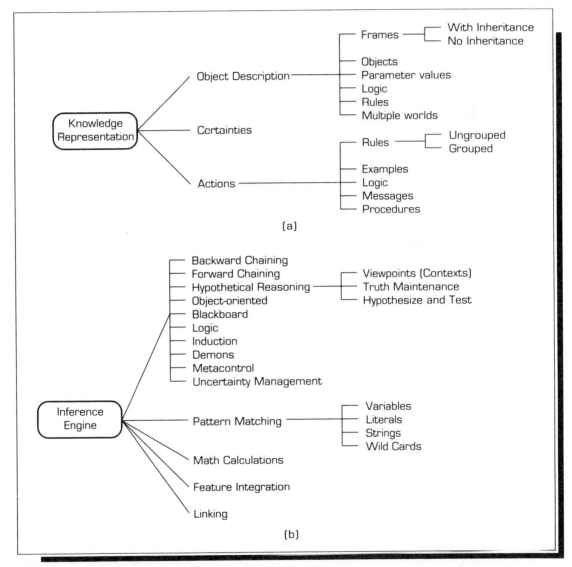

(a)

(b)

FIGURE 13.6 Attributes and Capabilities of Expert System Software (*Source:* W. B. Gevarter, "The Nature and Evaluation of Commercial Expert Systems Building Tools," *Computer* [May 1987].)

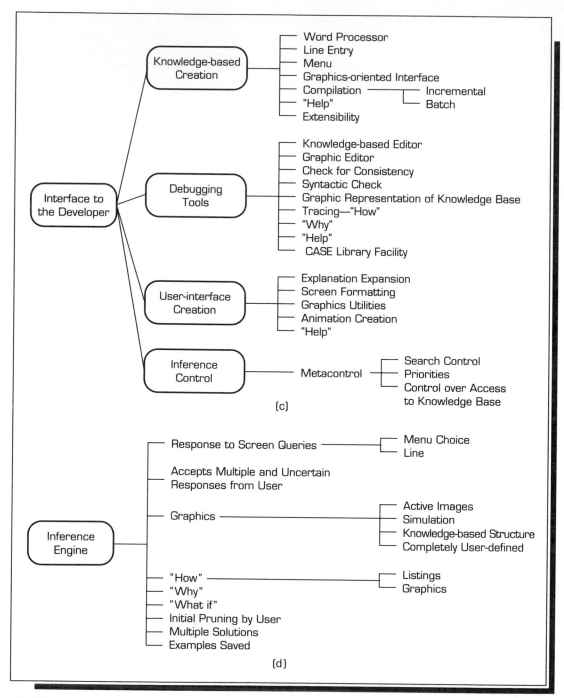

FIGURE 13.6 (continued)

13.10 Hardware Support

The choice of software packages is frequently determined by the hardware used and its processing and memory power, which could be a significant constraint on many ES developments. Efficient LISP execution, for example, may require very specialized hardware architectures. Such architectures have been commercially available for only the past few years under the name **LISP machines.** Although LISP implementations exist for a wide variety of conventional computers (including micros), performance could be marginal for many large-scale or complex commercial applications. However, the development of dedicated AI workstations, such as LISP machines, together with progress in semiconductor devices and new computer architectures, has set the stage for rapid movement of AI workstations into the real world.

Dedicated AI machines have processors whose machine code is especially designed to obey instructions useful to LISP (e.g., "check that this is a number" and "split this list here"). These machines support a single user, or a small number of users, with a complete programming environment, including editors, LISP debuggers, and a network interface. AI workstations have also been found to be useful in facilitating the development of software that is not related to AI.

There are seven major features of AI workstations:

1. Single-user or a small number of users (versus time sharing in a regular computer)
2. Maximum efficiency of symbolic processing
3. Very high-speed processing (allows more search in a limited time) when LISP programs are used
4. Large memory (AI programs usually require more RAM and more storage space on the disk drive than other programs do. These are provided by the AI workstation. For example, Symbolics 3670 provides 30 megabytes of RAM and 474 megabytes on its disk drive [external memory].)
5. High resolution that permits display of more text at one time
6. Specialized keyboard (About two dozen extra keys are provided to improve programmers' productivity and increase the speed of use.)
7. Mouse device (for faster communication without a keyboard)

Special software available for these machines includes programming languages, ES development tools, editors, debuggers, and screen windows.

For ES to be more cost-effective, the cost of hardware must be reduced. This could be done, for instance, with a bus-centered architectural design that allows for resource sharing. In addition, it provides an efficient means to augment existing non-AI application software with powerful AI tools. For example, a LISP machine equipped with both LISP and UNIX processors (with full-communication, bus-centered systems) can also furnish an environment for PROLOG and/or UNIX-based software. This will enable dedicated AI workstations to be used for general-purpose computing—a considerable cost reduction to the user.

Some commercial vendors are moving away from LISP or PROLOG and toward conventional languages like C. Another approach is to develop the ES on special hardware, using LISP or PROLOG, then run the ES consultation on a less powerful AI computer or on a standard computer. Many ES can run on regular computers. In general, mainframes or large minicomputers are usually adequate for both AI and other languages, provided that enough memory is available. The typical situation where such machines show their limits is one in which many users are running the same program at the same time. Usually there is not enough memory to hold more than five or ten copies of a LISP or PROLOG program.

The LISP machines are designed for running much faster than conventional machines. If properly used, LISP machines can have many advantages. Furthermore, data input, data-type checking, and other programming duties can be improved dramatically (for a complete description see Graham [12]). Indeed, Symbolic's top machines (now using the Ivory chip) and EXPLORER II (Texas Instruments) with its superb graphics and color capabilities can help in both building and running ES. Nevertheless, the latest technological developments may change the role of the dedicated AI workstations in favor of conventional machines that are enhanced with innovations. Here are some examples of such developments:

□ Reduced instruction set computers (RISC), which are still in their infancy, show a tremendous suitability for LISP development and delivery. According to Somel [29], the Sun 4 may excel in LISP performance.
□ Both Symbolic and Texas Instruments are combining their CPUs with Mac II. For example, MicroExplorer (from TI) is a combination of Mac II and EXPLORER; TI's LISP chip is integrated with Mac II. Thus, it is possible to run programs concurrently on the two processors and enjoy the best of both machines (e.g., Mac's superb user interface and EXPLORER's symbolic processing power). Furthermore, the merger permits sharing resources (such as memory, display, and hard disks), which reduces costs.

Chapter Highlights

□ Development of expert systems can be greatly expedited with a set of programming tools.
□ ES software development tools can be classified into five technology levels: languages, support aids, shells, environments, and ES applications.
□ Lower-level tools (e.g., languages) are flexible but require more programming skills.
□ A shell is constructed from an existing expert system by emptying the knowledge base.
□ Developing a specific ES involves entering knowledge into the shell or writing a program in a selected language.

□ Shells, the highest level software product, are inflexible. Their major advantages are that they can be used to build systems quickly and that they require few programming skills.

□ Shells are intended to be used by end-users. They are very easy to work with and are especially useful in rule-based systems.

□ ES tools and shells can be used for a wide range of applications, or they can be limited to a narrow domain (domain-specific tools and shells).

□ A developer may use several tools to build one system.

□ Selecting software for ES construction is difficult. Many packages are available and dozens of criteria may be considered.

□ The trend is to use shells and environments in building ES.

Key Terms

AI workstation	hybrid system	POPLOG
development	higher-level language	PROLOG
environment	LISP	shell (skeletal) system
domain-specific tool	LISP machine	technology level
explanation facility		

Questions for Review

1. Describe the classification of ES development tools used in this chapter.
2. What is the difference between a shell and a tool?
3. What is the difference between a shell and a programming environment?
4. Explain how the software packages EMYCIN and MYCIN are related.
5. Discuss some of the characteristics of LISP.
6. Why is LISP called a symbolic language?
7. Discuss some of the characteristics of PROLOG.
8. Define a general-purpose language and give two examples.
9. What are the major components of a shell?
10. Describe the major advantages of a shell; also list the major limitations.
11. What are the differences between domain-specific tools and general-purpose tools?
12. Define environments and discuss their use.
13. Explain the difficulties in selecting ES software packages.
14. List five issues related to software selection.
15. Describe the major types of hardware available for expert systems.
16. Name five advantages of dedicated AI workstations.

Questions for Discussion

1. Describe some of the difficulties in using development tools for solving real-life problems.

2. Most ES shells are geared to deal with diagnosis and prescription of a treatment. Why is this so?
3. Compare the major characteristics of LISP and PROLOG. How do they differ from each other?
4. Comment on the following statement: "Constraints in software development tools may be very helpful."
5. Review the process of building a specific ES with knowledge engineering tools. Compare it with building any information system with tools (for example, a spreadsheet).
6. Discuss the advantages and disadvantages of AI workstations as compared with standard computers. Distinguish between micros and larger computers.
7. Why is it so difficult to select ES software?
8. Compare ART with KEE.
9. Compare a shell with a fourth-generation tool such as Lotus 1-2-3 or dBASE.
10. Some say it is much easier to program with a simple ES shell (e.g., EXSYS or VP Expert) than to program with Lotus 1-2-3. Why?
11. Explain the difference between a domain-specific shell and a general shell. Why is the former more expensive?
12. Describe the advantages and disadvantages of various types of hardware and explain how they are fitted with software for specific applications.
13. Why is it difficult to match a problem and ES development tools?
14. Which should be selected first, software or hardware? Why?

Exercises

1. What types of hardware would you suggest for each of the following situations and why?
   a. Advising on admissions for a medium-sized college
   b. Scheduling maintenance for a major airline
   c. Diagnosing complex problems in a large machine
   d. Advising students on what classes to take
2. Many software and computer magazines conduct frequent evaluations of ES development tools. Find a recent evaluation and identify all the criteria against which the software is being judged.
3. Obtain a demonstration copy of an ES development tool (or get one from your instructor). What type of software is it? What is its level of classification? What do you like and dislike about it?
4. The future of symbolic languages (such as LISP) is being challenged by many who believe that the role of these languages will be limited to that of building ES tools or supporting special situations. Others believe that symbolic languages will prosper. Search the current literature for supporting documents and be ready to debate the issue.
5. Search for current supportive material on LISP and PROLOG and be prepared to defend each in a debate.

References and Bibliography

1. Anderson, E.E. "Choice Models for the Evaluation and Selection of Software Packages." *Journal of MIS* (Spring 1990).
2. Archibald, I.G., et al. "Bridging the Generation Gap: Expert Systems." *R & D Management* (February 1985).
3. Assad, A.A., and B.L. Golden. "Expert Systems, Microcomputers, and Operations Research." *Computers and Operations Research* 13 (no. 2, 1986).
4. Bochenski, B. "Declaring the Facts of the Inference Difference." *Software Magazine* (May 1989).
5. Bryant, N. *Managing Expert Systems*. New York: John Wiley & Sons, 1988.
6. Cholawski, E.M. "Beating the Prototype Blues." AI Expert (December 1988).
7. Clocksin, W.F., and C.S. Mellish. *Programming in PROLOG*. 3rd ed. New York: Springer-Verlag, 1987.
8. Fields, S. "Survey of AI Languages." *PC AI* (Spring 1987).
9. Fontana, M., and J. Zeimetz. "Elements of Expert System Shells." *PC Tech Journal* (May 1988).
10. Gevarter, W.B. "The Nature and Evaluation of Commercial Expert Systems Building Tools." *Computer* (May 1987).
11. Goyal, S.K., et al. "COMPASS: An Expert System for Telephone Switch Maintenance." *Expert Systems* (July 1985).
12. Graham, P. "Anatomy of a Lisp Machine." *AI Expert* (December 1988).
13. Harmon, P., et al. *Expert Systems Tools and Applications*. New York: John Wiley & Sons, 1988.
14. Harrison, P.R. *Common Lisp and Artificial Intelligence*. Englewood Cliffs, N.J.: Prentice-Hall, 1990.
15. Hayes-Roth, F., et al. *Building Expert Systems*. Reading, Mass.: Addison-Wesley, 1983.
16. Holsapple, C.W., and A.B. Whinston. *Building Expert Systems (using GURU)*. Homewood, Ill.: Richard D. Irwin, 1987.
17. Kinnucan, P. "Software Tools Speed Expert System Development." *High Technology* (March 1985).
18. Knaus, R., and H. Blecker. "Domain-specific Shells for Experts in PROLOG." *AI Expert* (January 1990).
19. Kulikowski, C., and S. Weiss. *A Practical Guide to Designing Expert Systems*. Totowa, N.J.: Rowman and Allanheld, 1985.
20. Lehner, P.E., and S.W. Barth. "Expert Systems on Microcomputers." *Expert Systems* (October 1985).
21. Liebowitz, J. "Useful Approach for Evaluating Expert Systems." *Expert Systems* (April 1986).
22. Marcellus, D.H. *Expert System Programming in Turbo PROLOG*. Englewood Cliffs, N.J.: Prentice-Hall, 1990.
23. Mettrey, W. "An Assessment of Tools for Building Large Knowledge-Based Systems." *AI Magazine* (Winter 1987).

24. New Science Associates. "Mainframe Tools: The Battle for Market Share." *Artificial Intelligence Research* (July 3, 1989).

25. Price, C.J. *Knowledge Engineering Tool Kits.* Englewood Cliffs, N.J.: Prentice-Hall, 1990.

26. Rosenthal, S. "You Don't Have to Be an Expert to Use Expert Systems." *PC Week* (December 19, 1988).

27. Schwartz, T. *Expert Systems in a Mainframe Environment.* Special Report. New York: Intelligent Systems and Analyst, 1988.

28. Sherman, D.S. "Problem-solving—Expert Systems Style." *System Builder* (February/March, 1989).

29. Somel, J. "AI on Your Personal Computer." *AI Expert* (December 1988).

30. Teft, L. *Programming in Turbo PROLOG with an Introduction to Knowledge-based Systems.* Englewood Cliffs, N.J.: Prentice-Hall, 1990.

31. Tello, R. *Mastering AI Tools and Techniques.* Indianapolis: H. W. Sams, 1988.

32. Waterman, D.A. *A Guide to Expert Systems.* Reading, Mass.: Addison-Wesley, 1985.

33. Winston, P.H., and B.K. Horn. *LISP,* 2nd ed. Reading, Mass.: Addison-Wesley, 1985.

APPENDIX A: Software Sampler

Several hundred software products are available, and they change rapidly. *PC AI*, for example, has an annual product guide (in its July/August issue). In 1990, the list included about 300 items. This appendix is a representative list of well-known products. It is based on a list that appeared in the May 1991 issue of *AI Expert* and is organized by vendor.

Vendor	Products
AI Technologies	Mercury KBE, ISIU
Aion Corp.	ADS, KBMS, 1st-CLASS, Fusion HT
ARITY Corp.	The Arity/Expert Development Package
ATTAR Software	Xpert Rule
Bell Atlantic Software Systems	Laser
Cullinet Software	Enterprise Expert, Application Expert
Carnegie Group	Test Bench, Knowledge Craft, IMKA Technology
Cogent Software	Personal Hyperbase, Hyperbase Developer

Vendor	Products
Computer Associates	CA-DB: Expert/VAX, CA-DB Expert/Voice
Computer-Aided KE Systems	Knowledge Analysis Tool Knowledge Quest
Emerald Intelligence	Diagnostic Advisor, Mahogany Helpdesk, Magellan
Expert Systems International	ESP Frame Engine
Experteligence	Action!
Exsys, Inc.	EXSYS EL, EXSYS Professional
Firstmark Technologies	Knowledge Seeker
Gensym Corp.	G2
Ginesys Corp.	K-Base Corporate, K-Base Builder, K-Induction
Gold Hill, Inc.	GoldWorks II
The Haley Enterprise	Eclipse DOS Developer's Edition, Eclipse Toolkits
IBM Corp.	TIRS, ESE, AD/Cycle
Inference Engine Technologies	Sienna OPS5
Inference Corp.	ART, ART-IM, CBR Express, Xi Plus
Information Engineering Systems	USER: Expert System, IE-Expert
Information Builders	Level5, Level5 Object
Integrated Systems	RT/Expert
IntelliCorp.	KEE, ProKappa, Kappa PC
Intelligence Ware, Inc.	IXL, Auto-Intelligence
Intelligent Environments, Inc.	CRYSTAL, CRYSTAL Induction
Intellipro, Inc.	OPS-2000
Jordan-Webb Info Systems	EXSYS
KDS Corp.	KDS, KDS/VOX
Knowledge Garden	KnowledgePro
Logicware, Inc.	Twaice
M.I.S. International	Consult-I
Micro Data Base Systems	Guru, Guru Solver
Mystech Assoc.	AURORA
Neuron Data	Nexpert Object, NEXTRA
Norrad	NetLink+
Oxko	Inducprl, Maingen
Paperback Software	VP Expert
Park Row Software, Inc.	Easy Expert
Perceptics, Inc.	Knowledge Shaper
Production Systems Technology	OPS83, RAL
Rosh Intelligent Systems	Knowledge-CAIS, Brief-CAIS, Hyper-CAIS

480

Vendor	Products
Softsync, Inc.	SUPEREXPERT
Software Plus	Cxpert
Software A&E	Knowledge Engineering System (KES)
Software Artistry	PC Expert Professional, Knowledge Engine
Symbologic Corp.	Symbologic Adept
Transform Logic	Transform Expert
Wang Laboratories	CommonKnowledge

Chapter 14

User Interfaces and
Design Issues

AI applications are most beneficial if they are designed properly. In earlier chapters we concentrated on knowledge engineering issues. Specifically, we dealt with knowledge acquisition and representation and with inferencing. Now we need to consider the design of an appropriate user-machine interface and to fit the knowledge bases into organizational information systems.

Since it is impossible to cover all design topics in a survey-type book, we selected the topics that we think are most important. Specifically, the following design issues will be discussed:

14.1   User Interfaces: An Overview

Most AI users have limited computer experience.[1] They are not prepared to learn the computer-oriented details typically required of experienced users. Often, they expect to walk up and use an AI application as easily as they use the telephone or drive a car. But the operating systems and other software supporting AI applications were developed for users accustomed to carrying out complicated tasks. The desire to meet the needs of users who demand power without complication has made the AI industry increasingly sensitive to the design of the user interface.

The user **interface** may be thought of as a surface through which data is passed back and forth between user and computer. Physical aspects of the user interface (Figure 14.1) include display devices, audio devices, and input devices such as tablet, joystick, mouse, microphone, or keyboard.

Data displayed on the workstation provides a context for interaction and it gives cues for action by the user (we assume the user knows how to interpret what is displayed). The user formulates a response and takes an action. Data then passes back to the computer through the interface. In this concept of an interface, all aspects of the system that are known to the user are defined at the interface. The quality of the interface, from the user's perspective, depends on what the user sees (or senses), what the user must know to understand what is sensed, and what actions the user can (or must) take to obtain needed results. The cyclical process shown in Figure 14.1 consists of these elements:

1. **Presentation language:** This is the information displayed to the user. It can be shown as display menus, windows, or text. It can be static or dynamic, numeric or symbolic. It can appear on the CRT, as voice, or as print.
2. User's reaction: The user interprets the display, processes the content, and plans an action.
3. **Action language:** The user's action can take various shapes. He or she can select an item from the menu, answer a question, move a display window, or type in a command. He or she can use one or more input devices.
4. Computer: The computer interprets the user's action (input), executes a task (e.g., computation), and generates a display that is basically the presentation language, or the output of the computer.

These elements can be designed and executed in different manners. The combination of presentation and action languages is referred to as an interactive (or dialogue) style.

---

[1]This section has been condensed from Bennett [2].

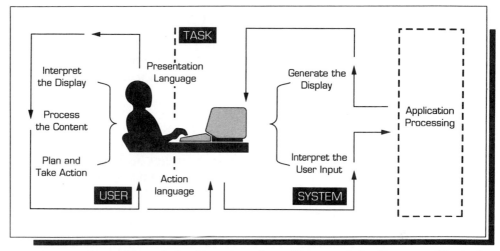

FIGURE 14.1 Two Sides of the User Interface (*Source:* J. L. Bennett, "Tools for Building Advanced User Interfaces," *IBM Systems Journal* [no. 3/4, 1986].)

14.2 Interface Modes (Styles)

Interface modes refer to the interactive communication between the user and a computer. The interface mode determines how information is displayed on the monitor and how information is entered into the computer, as well as the ease and simplicity of learning the system and using it. The topic appears under several names, for example, dialogue styles, dialogue modes, and conversational formats. In this section we look at the following styles: menu interaction, command language, question and answer, form interaction, natural language, and object manipulation.

Menu Interaction. With the **menu interaction** interface, the user selects from a list of possible choices (the menu) the one he or she wants to perform, for example, what report to produce or what analysis to run. The choice is made by use of input devices ranging from a remote control infrared device to a keyboard. Menus appear in a logical order, starting with a main menu and going on to submenus. Menu items can include commands that appear in separate submenus or in the menus with noncommand items. Development tools such as EXSYS, VP Expert, ART, and Level5, as well as most AI applications, involve extensive use of commands that are a part of a menu. Menus can become tedious and time consuming when complex situations are being analyzed, since it may take several menus to build or use a system and the user must shift back and forth among the menus.

Command Language. In the **command language** style, the user enters a command such as "run" or "plot." Many commands are composed of a verb-noun combination (e.g., "plot sales"). Some commands can be executed with the function keys (F1 through F10) on the keyboard. Another way to simplify commands (or even a series of commands) is to use macros.

Question and Answer. The **question and answer** interface mode in ES begins with the computer asking the user a question. The user answers the question with a phrase or a sentence (or by selecting an item from a menu). The computer may prompt the user for clarification and/or additional input. Their dialogue may involve a large number of questions, some of which result from previous answers. A question may involve the presentation of a menu from which the answer is to be selected. In certain AI applications, the sequence of questioning may be reversed: the user asks a question and the computer gives an answer.

Form Interaction. In the interface style called **form interaction,** the user enters data or commands into designated spaces (fields) in forms. The headings of the form (or the report or the table) serve as a prompt for the input. The computer may produce some output as a result, and the user may be requested to continue the form interaction process. In some expert systems, instead of being asked to answer one question at a time, the user is asked to answer several questions at one time. The dialogue may involve a table or a form to fill in.

Natural Language. A human-computer dialogue that is similar to a human-human dialogue is referred to as **natural language.** Such a dialogue will be conducted, in the future, using voice as input and output. Today, natural language dialogue is done with the keyboard. The problem of using natural language is essentially the inability of the computer to *understand* natural language (such as English or Japanese). However, as discussed in Chapter 8, advances in AI enable limited natural language dialogue. For example, natural language processors are being used to access databases.

Object Manipulation. In the **object manipulation** style, objects, usually represented as icons (or symbols), are directly manipulated by the user. For example, the user can point the mouse or the cursor at an icon and use a command to move it, enlarge it, or show the details behind it.

Several studies have been conducted to determine the efficiency and accuracy of the various interface styles. Majchrzak et al. [22] have summarized the research in this area and have evaluated the usability of four of the styles along four dimensions. Table 14.1 presents their research with the addition of the last three dimensions and the last column.

Several other interface modes are being developed (see Box 14.1). Natural language processing complemented with voice recognition will probably be the style preferred by AI users of the future.

TABLE 14.1 Comparison of Interface Modes

Dimensions	Menu Interaction	Fill in the Blanks (Forms)	Command Languages	Object Manipulation	Questions and Answers
Speed	Slow at times	Moderate	Fast	Could be slow	Slow at times
Accuracy	Error free	Moderate	Many errors	Error free	Moderate
Training time	Short	Moderate	Long	Short	Short
Users' preference	Very high	Low	Prefer, if trained (only)	High	High
Power	Low	Low	Very high	Moderate-high	Moderate
Flexibility	Limited	Very limited	Very high	Moderate-high	High (if open ended)
Control	The system	The system	The user	The system and the user	The system

Source: Based, in part, on A. Majchrzak et al., *Human Aspects of Computer-Aided Design* (Philadelphia: Taylor and Francis, 1987).

14.3 Interfaces and Knowledge-based Systems

Human-machine interaction in knowledge-based systems differs from that of most conventional systems because the dialogue is much more two way; that is, the question and answer mode is used. Often, questions and answers are combined with menus and/or object manipulation. The interaction can be

Box 14.1: Paperlike Interface

Researchers at IBM, Bell Labs, Texas Instruments, and other research institutions are exploring a way to use computers in which people simply write on a flat surface. The user writes with a kind of "electronic ink." Then, handwriting-recognition software instantly translates the writing and other hand-drawn marks, mathematical symbols, and even musical notes into words, numbers, and commands for the computer. Commercial versions of a simplified version are available on the market (e.g., from GRID Corp. and from NCR).

conducted via voice, and it can be supported by a natural language processor. Several issues related to the interface with expert systems are discussed next.

Interface Issues

Explanation. Human-machine dialogue in knowledge-based systems involves not only questions and answers but also **explanations.** The user of such a system needs to be able to understand and trace the reasoning involved. This feature may be provided by anything from a sophisticated explanation facility (capable of answering many questions) to a simple facility that traces rule firings (showing the rules and possibly the path of logic used by the system in arriving at its conclusions). Since there is no standard reasoning mechanism embodied in AI applications, the reasoning for each situation needs to be explicated and justified. All things being equal, a conventional software system will function the same way each time it is being executed because it uses an algorithm that assures its consistency. An AI system addresses problems by employing heuristics rather than algorithms alone; so, users need to be *convinced* that the system's behavior is proper. Therefore, the ability of a KBS to explain itself to the end-user is directly tied to its acceptance and use.

Open-ended Questions and Answers. Many knowledge-based systems are inflexible. Their menus force the user to select an item. In many cases the user's true choice does not coincide with an offering on the menu. (It is like going to a restaurant that offers a very limited menu.) Users prefer an extremely large menu, where they can mix and match items, or use completely open-ended questions. Many ES shells provide limited menus, even when numeric values are involved.

Sequencing of Questions. Some people are irritated when you ask them too many questions or questions that seem to be irrelevant. In certain cases the inference engine uses an arbitrary sequencing of questions. Also, it can ask one question at a time (e.g., as a result of the search process) or it can ask several questions up front in a checklist. People have different preferences and we do not have sufficient knowledge about their preferences.

User's Mental Properties. The user's understanding or misunderstanding of the questions is an important issue. Remember that the questions were developed by experts in the domain of interest, but the user is not an expert.

Display. Most of the discussion in this chapter is related to the input of information and the user-machine dialogue during data entry. The **display** of information can be equally important. For example, several knowledge-based tools provide a multiwindow display, which experienced users may favor. The inexperienced user, however, may become frustrated with such a display.

Multimedia Support. To add a more realistic environment to a consultation with a knowledge-based system, video and audio support are sometimes added. For example, some banks support their interactive sessions by a picture of a person on a TV screen. If they add voice, the situation becomes more useful. The prevalence of multimedia as front-ends to expert systems will greatly help the acceptance of such systems (see section 14.6).

Intelligent Front-ends

To overcome some of the problems just outlined, it makes sense to provide the system with a natural language **front-end interface.** Users who are used to communicating with human experts would prefer to communicate with an "expert machine" in a similar manner, namely, by using a natural language.

Although this solution sounds logical, it is not easy to implement. First, a knowledge-based system does not have the same breadth of knowledge as its human counterpart; it is usually confined to a narrow domain. Extra knowledge (and common sense) may be needed for a true natural dialogue. Second, the vocabulary of natural language processing is limited. The larger we make it, the more expensive the front-end is going to be. Third, users overlook the limitations of the machine. They may assign too high a level of intelligence to the system and as a result, the system may give them unreliable answers.

Despite difficulties and current high costs and limitations, natural language processing will probably be the front-end for knowledge-based systems in the future. Possibly it will be accompanied by voice technologies.

14.4   Blackboard Architecture

The concept of a **blackboard** can best be understood by visualizing a group of experts standing around a blackboard while they work on the same problem. The blackboard approach (see Englemore and Morgan [10] and Jagannathan et al. [17]) provides an organizational schema to assimilate a variety of expertise, goals, beliefs, and knowledge representations and means for reconciling differences among several experts.

Blackboard Approach

A blackboard is a working memory that maximizes independence among knowledge sources by appropriately dividing the problem domain. In this approach, expertise is divided among subdomains (one expert for each sub-domain) and the experts cooperate to solve the problem. Interaction, however, is kept to a minimum. Many expert systems have been developed using the blackboard system architecture. For example, ExperTax (see Shipilberg et al. [30]), and HEARSAY-III (see Englemore and Morgan [10] and Jagannathan et al. [17]) were developed with a blackboard approach.

Blackboard architecture is used to represent and control knowledge. It includes independent groups of rules, called **knowledge sources,** that communicate through a central structure, similar to a database, called a blackboard. The user of a blackboard may store or retrieve information from any of the knowledge sources. The blackboard provides a centralized way of recording and tabulating intermediate decisions about a problem.

Blackboards are generally used when a problem requires multiple experts or knowledge sources. They can be also used for complex problems that can be divided into smaller problems. This architecture can accept any type of knowledge.

As an example, consider a blackboard used to plan a ground assault on an enemy in the desert (Figure 14.2). The knowledge sources are the various specialists who are involved in the planning of the assault. The process is controlled by the chief commander (the control source). The specialists sit or stand around the blackboard. In a computerized system, the experts are replaced by knowledge bases.

Blackboards have two main purposes. First, they are used to share or inherit information that is already known between different components in a knowledge base. Blackboards of this type are called *data blackboards.* Second, blackboards are used in the problem-solving process as a control mechanism *(control blackboards).*

Control and Inferencing in Blackboards

The blackboard architecture is used for problem solving in the following manner.[2]

Structure. A blackboard architecture is usually described as a software package in an ES; it has three components:

1. Knowledge sources containing the knowledge required to solve the problem: These are modular, independent units that contain different types of knowledge.
2. Blackboard data structure: Here the problem-solving data is kept in a global data store or database referred to as the blackboard.
3. Control: This structure determines the mode of operation of the various knowledge sources. It contains the problem-solving knowledge.

The knowledge sources respond opportunistically to changes in the blackboard. They generate changes in the blackboard which lead, incrementally, to a solution to the problem. Communication and interaction among the sources take place only through the blackboard. For example, conclusions of different

---

[2]Most of the discussion in this section is based on the work of Raghupathi et al. [36].

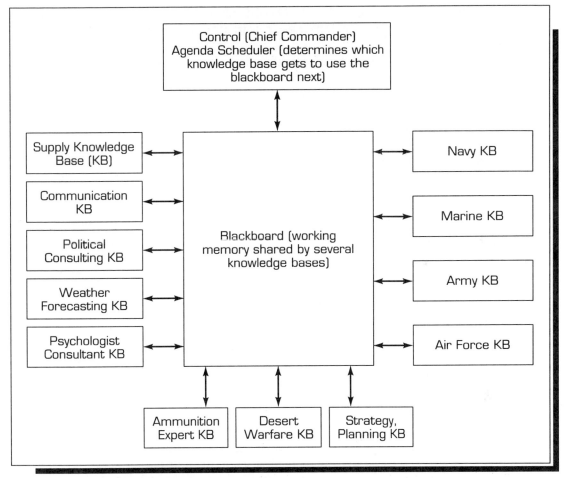

FIGURE 14.2 Blackboard Architecture for Military Planning

knowledge sources are posted on a blackboard and are available to all knowledge sources.

Knowledge sources are rules with condition and action parts. The condition component specifies the situations under which a particular knowledge source could contribute to an activity. A control component called the scheduler (or manager) controls the progress toward a solution by determining the knowledge source to schedule next or the problem subdomain on which to focus. Applications can be implemented with different combinations of knowledge representations, reasoning schemes, and control mechanisms, thereby offering flexibility in design. Computationally, the different knowledge sources represent the multiple experts, and the control component could be modeled after a primary expert who coordinates the interaction.

The solution space in a blackboard model is organized into one or more application-dependent hierarchies. Information at each level in the hierarchy represents partial solutions and is represented by a unique vocabulary that describes the information. The domain knowledge is partitioned into independent modules of knowledge that transform information from one level of hierarchy into other levels. The knowledge modules perform the transformation using algorithmic procedures or heuristic rules that generate actual or hypothetical transformations.

Opportunistic reasoning is applied within the overall organization of solution space and task-specific knowledge. In other words, the module of knowledge to apply is determined dynamically one step at a time and results in an incremental generation of partial solutions called *islands*. The islands merge to form a solution. The choice of a knowledge module is based on a solution state and on the existence of knowledge modules capable of improving the current state of the solution. At each step of the knowledge application, either the forward or backward reasoning approach may be applied. Actually, any of the many reasoning methods can be applied at each step in the problem-solving process, since each knowledge source can have its own reasoning mechanism. For example, one knowledge source can be rule based, another case based, and yet another model driven.

Generally, blackboards have been applied to two types of problems: (1) interpretation—working in a generally bottom-up manner with low-level inputs and producing high-level output as a desired result, and (2) generation—presenting highest-level representations and requiring generation of lowest-level representations. Blackboard models are also suitable for designing and planning problems in which the decision path is not defined a priori, but rather requires opportunistic and incremental problem solving.

Blackboards offer a holistic view of problems and solutions. They facilitate dynamic interaction and provide feedback among multiple sources of knowledge. No individual can solve the problem alone—problem solving depends on the combined contribution of different specialists.

Limitations. The blackboard approach makes several assumptions: (1) all of the agents (knowledge sources) can see all of the blackboard all of the time—what they see is the current state of the solution; (2) any agent can write conclusions on the blackboard at any time without getting into anyone else's way; and (3) the act of writing on the blackboard does not confuse any of the other agents as they work. In reality, each knowledge source can only see a small segment of the blackboard. In practice, experts are dependent on each other as opposed to not getting into each other's way. The general nature of the blackboard impedes specialization and power.

The trade-off between interpretive versus compiled knowledge is a relevant design issue. For this reason, the blackboard approach generally generates satisfying solutions because of the negotiation, cooperation, and conflict resolutions that take place among the knowledge sources.

Control[3]. The key to success in blackboard architecture is control. The focus of control is determining what is placed on the blackboard. Strategies for control include goal focus, model focus, and event focus.

A goal focus strategy adds elements to the blackboard that move toward the goal. Only "need-to-know" sources are included. Model focus strategy involves the establishment, adoption, or adaptation of a model for emulation. Models can establish sequences, priorities, and characterizations about the problem and knowledge sources. An event focus strategy is a reactive strategy to events as they occur. Overall strategy varies according to new conditions and alters its focus accordingly. Take the example of building a house; inspections, weather conditions, and materials sometimes cause unplanned changes in the work plan. Strategies may be driven by the blackboard objects, the knowledge source, or a combination of the two.

Software. Generic Blackboard (GBB) is a tool kit from Blackboard Technology Group for developing blackboard-based AI applications. GBB provides the blackboard database infrastructure, knowledge source languages, and control components needed by a blackboard application. These tools eliminate the need for building blackboard-based applications from the ground up; instead, they allow developers to immediately concentrate their efforts on application-specific details. GBB has been used in developing diverse applications in areas ranging from planning, scheduling, and process control to sensory interpretation, diagnosis, and knowledge-based simulation.

14.5 Distributed and Parallel AI

Some knowledge-based systems are complex, memory intensive, require intensive computations (mostly symbolic, but some numeric), and need to interface with other computer-based information systems. Most knowledge-based systems reside on a single machine, and as a result executions (computations) may be slow. Various attempts have been made to speed up execution time so that larger problems can be addressed. Two such approaches are parallel processing and distributed artificial intelligence. Use of these methods can result in many benefits, as shown in Table 14.2. The principal benefit is that the efforts of problem solving are distributed among several agents (e.g., ES processors). The essentials of the methods are described next.

Parallel Processing

In 1945, John von Neumann outlined a logical structure of processing information with a computer. He specified a theory of information processing that has

---

[3]This paragraph is based, in part, on Tuthill [34].

TABLE 14.2 Benefits of Distributing Problem Solving

Faster computations
More efficient computations
Improved reliability through redundancy
Increased modularity
Increased reconfigurability
Multiple perspectives (several experts, several sources)
Accommodation of open systems (no need to close the systems)
Adaptability (parallel systems are more adaptable than sequential systems)
Fit with problems that are distributed in nature
Better modeling and analysis of complex problems

Source: Based on L. Gasser, "Distributed AI," *AI Expert* (July 1989).

permeated the development of computers ever since. In fact, modern computers are sometimes called von Neumann machines because their information processing methods have descended directly from his theories. One important element of the von Neumann machine that has stood the test of time is the concept of sequential processing.

Computers, which may seem to be doing many things at once, actually perform actions one at a time, in sequence. One of the goals of advanced computer research is to increase computing speeds, and one method of increasing speed is to abandon the sequential processing model and have more than one computation executed at a time. This technique, called **parallel processing,** is shown schematically in Figure 14.3.

Parallel architectures are being considered for future AI machines. They are especially attractive for PROLOG (e.g., see Eadline [9]) because its structure facilitates parallel search. Parallel processing techniques provide a way for computers to solve large problems faster according to the premise that dividing a problem into smaller parts will yield results faster. The underlying concept behind all new parallel architectures is to have small blocks of tightly coupled memory elements divide the algorithm and process its parts concurrently. As a result, larger problems can be solved faster.

According to Gasser [13], it is possible to increase performance, efficiency, or modularity of AI computations by using parallel processing. Parallelism can be achieved in hardware, in distributed operating systems, in use of programming languages, and in integrated systems combining several levels or kinds of parallelism. Neural computing, which is discussed in Chapter 18, is a special type of parallel processing.

Distributed AI

While parallel processing can increase efficiency and performance and improve reliability, different goals can be achieved by the use of **distributed artificial**

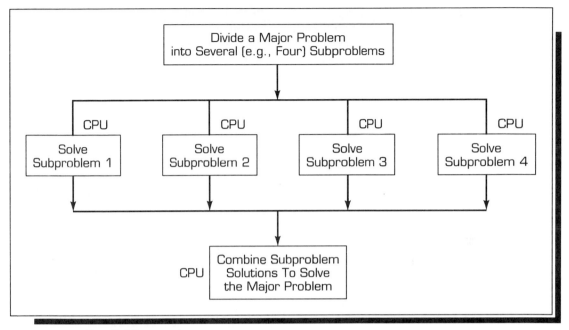

FIGURE 14.3   Parallel Processing

intelligence.[4] The basic idea of distributed AI (see Bond and Gasser [4]) is to distribute a problem over multiple expert systems that cooperate and communicate with each other toward a common goal. Such a goal can be finding an appropriate fit to a problem, handling uncertainty, modeling complex natural problems, or increasing efficiency. Distributed AI can be divided into two complementing subareas: distributed problem solving and multiagent systems.

Distributed problem solving considers how the work of solving a problem can be achieved by dividing the knowledge about the problem and the problem-solving strategies (the control). **Multiagent systems** assume the existence of autonomous, **intelligent "agents"** that can coordinate their knowledge, goals, skills, and plans to take an action or solve a problem. The agents may be working on an agreed upon single goal or on separate individual but interacting goals. A major problem in a multiagent system is coordination, especially where global control, globally consistent knowledge, or other agreed on global factors are not possible.

Software. Several distributed AI tools have been developed in universities and research institutions (e.g., see Gasser [13]). None of them is in commercial use. The tools include languages, editors, debuggers, modelers, and integrators. The

---

[4]This section is based, in part, on Gasser [13].

difficulty in building support software is that in distributed AI either knowledge, control (problem-solving procedures), or memory—or all—must be distributed, either by applications or by the system being transparent to the applications. Therefore, in building distributed AI tools, it is necessary to arrange for efficient knowledge (and data) distribution, intelligent ways for distributing the control, and appropriate distribution of memory. To achieve these objectives, the software must be driven by the specific application. Furthermore, the software must provide for communication between the AI systems (at the application level) and communication during processing.

Kannan and Dodrill [19] have developed software that attempts to achieve these goals. Their experimental system, which runs on a personal computer, is called DAIS (a distributed AI programming shell). The software can be used to develop small distributed AI systems. Its architecture is shown in Figure 14.4. As you can see in the figure, the system includes an expert system in the center (RB, IE, KB and KR). A message management system (DMMS) provides communication between agents; it functionally links the machine-dependent communication layer (MDCL) and the rest of the DAIS system. Information is distributed among agents and is extracted and examined by the server. There could be several knowledge bases, even at remote locations (not shown in the figure). A remote processor (RP) module enables agents to operate on remote knowledge bases.

Application Areas. Typical application areas for distributed AI are multiple robot control, distributed sensing and interpretation, air-traffic control, telecommunication management, and human-machine interaction. Let's look at a specific example—teams of robots. Most of today's robots are individually programmed for each particular task. However, in computer-integrated manufacturing, robots may be organized in a team and may be required to perform any number of tasks. For example, IBM's laptop computer is assembled by a team of three robots, each of which performs some assembly operations. In addition, there is a robot that handles materials and one that performs tests.

What if expert systems could direct the robots to "communicate" and "reason" with each other? Work is currently being done at the Institute for Robotics and Intelligent Systems at the University of Southern California in an attempt to equip teams of robots at work on an assembly line with high-order decision-making capabilities. For example, an expert system would enable the robots to decide among themselves how best to accomplish a particular task. Thus, if a supply of parts arrives late, several robots (rather than one) could be assigned to the task of inspecting and preparing the parts so that the work team can catch up with the schedule.

Implementation. Distributed AI can be implemented in several architectures and frameworks. One of these is the blackboard architecture described earlier in this chapter. Such an architecture can handle multiple agents (e.g., databases

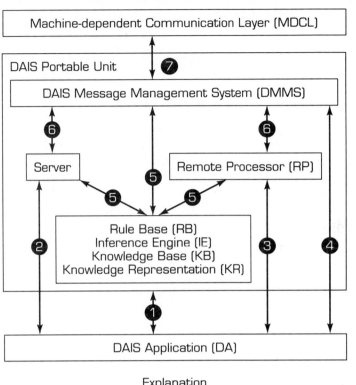

FIGURE 14.4 Architecture of DAIS—Distributed AI Programming Shell (*Source:* R. Kannan and W. H. Dodrill, "DAIS-A Distributed AI Programming Shell," *IEEE Expert* [© December 1990, IEEE].)

or knowledge sources) and can be adapted for use with distributed AI (see Gasser [13] for details).

14.6 Intelligent Interactive Multimedia

An unstated objective of AI is to increase the number of AI applications and the number of AI users. In previous sections we saw that by providing a better user interface and by developing special designs, this objective could be met. In this section, we demonstrate how AI technologies and especially expert systems can be merged with the state of the art of another new technology: multimedia (and related technologies such as hypermedia and hypertext). Such an integration may result in many innovative applications that could appeal to a large number of users. The merger may also induce users to utilize existing applications.

Multimedia

Multimedia refers to a pool of human-machine communication media, some of which can be combined in one application (Table 14.3). In information technol-

TABLE 14.3 Human-Machine Communication Media

Computer	Projected still visuals
CRT and terminals	Slide
CD-ROM	Overhead projector
Computer interactive	
videodisc	Graphic materials
Digital video interactive	Pictures
Compact disc interactive	Printed job aids
Computer simulation	Visual display
Teletext/videotext	
Intelligent tutoring system	Audio
Hypertext	Tape/cassette/record
Image digitizing	Teleconference/
Scanners	audioconference
Screen projection	Sound digitizing
Object-oriented programming	Microphone
	Compact disc
Motion image	Music
Video disc (cassette)	
Motion picture	Text
Broadcast television	
Teleconference/	
videoconference	
Animation	

Source: P. Chao, et al., "Using Expert Systems Approaches to Solve Media Selection Problem: Matrix Format," in *Proceedings of the Association of Computer Interface System,* © November 1990, IEEE.

ogy, the basic idea behind what is called an **interactive multimedia approach** is to use computers to improve human-machine communication by utilizing several items of the media pool with the computerized system as the center of the application. One new class in the multimedia collection is called hypermedia.

Hypermedia. **Hypermedia** is a term used to describe documents that could contain several types of media—text, graphics, audio and video elements— which allows information to be linked by association. Hypermedia may contain several layers of information; here are some examples:

- □ A *menu-based natural language interface* to provide a simple and transparent way for users to run the system and query it
- □ An *object-oriented database* that permits concurrent access to its data structures and operations
- □ A *relational query interface* that can efficiently support complex queries
- □ A *hypermedia abstract machine* that lets users link different types of information
- □ *Media editors* that provide ways to view and edit text, graphics, images, and voice
- □ A *change management virtual memory* to manage temporary versions, configurations, and transformations of design entities

By adding control structures on top of hypermedia systems, computer-aided instruction, computer-aided design, CASE, cooperative authoring, and groupware systems can be built.

Work being done at Texas Instruments with hypermedia is aimed at producing widely applicable software tools for dealing with "semistructured" information. A hypermedia system is considered an authoring tool and an information organizer.

Hypermedia[5] are characterized by (1) having linked, different information structures in which links are explicit, (2) being in effect multimedia (e.g., text, graphics, animation, voice), and (3) allowing information to be linked by association. They present an opportunity for delivering new services and products.

There are two classes of hypermedia. One is called presentation (or the *navigation* of the knowledge and of the data, and it is the common way of viewing hypermedia). The other is an active/generative component that records the process as it is going on. Hypermedia help capture the process and results— as you analyze data, interact with colleagues, and perform your tasks—and help to put the results into your presentation vehicle.

Figure 14.5 shows the typical view of hypermedia, that is, its use for knowledge navigation. Examples of commercial products include HyperCard and NoteCards. The idea here is that the context lengths are hard-wired into a

---

[5]This paragraph, and the next two, are condensed from Paul [24].

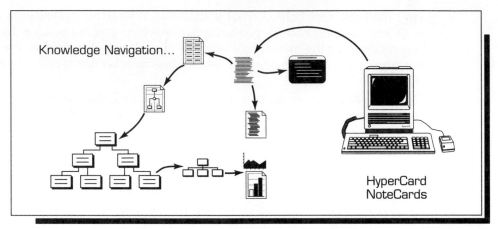

FIGURE 14.5 Hypermedia as a Presentation Tool (*Source:* J. Paul, "Toward a Strategy for Managing Computer-based Research," in *Proceedings, FAIM 90* [Alexandria, Va.: Defense Systems Management College, 1990]. RAND Corp.)

multimedia information base, and it's up to the user to choose which way to go. What does the user want to see next? All of the links are built in by the developer, but the order in which they are processed can be affected by the *navigator*, the consumer of the products.

Figure 14.6 shows the role for hypermedia as suggested by the RAND Corp., that is, active participation in research to help record, organize, and integrate information and processes. The essence of the role is support of intelligent research management and information synthesis. The components include an active knowledge base, multilevel annotation, and multimedia integration. Hypermedia are valuable for a fast search of specific information; they have an open architecture and can be used with relative ease by nonprogrammers to rapidly build computer applications.

Hypertext. One of the most recent ingredients to the multimedia pool is **hypertext.** Hypertext is an approach for handling text and graphic information that allows the users to jump from a given topic, whenever they wish, to related ideas. Reading or viewing of information thus becomes open ended and controlled by the user. Hypertext allows users to access information in a nonlinear fashion by following a train of thought. It lets the reader control the level of details and the type of information displayed. It allows a quick search according to the reader's interest. For example, as you started reading this section the first word was *multimedia.* Using the hypertext approach, you can highlight the word *multimedia*, then press a button; the computer would show you a passage of text related to this topic. When you are finished, you can return to the beginning of the section or jump to any other related topic.

Hypertext is still in its developmental stages (for an overview and products see *Byte* [5]). The concept may contribute to improved user interfaces in AI and especially in expert systems. Hypertext is a natural companion to ES development tools. Both technologies deal with the *transfer of knowledge*. In hypertext, however, the user controls the tools, and he or she may not do it in the most efficient way. Expert systems can lead and direct users. For further information, see Shafer [28]. Several products perform such an integration. For example, KnowledgePro integrates hypertext and expert systems. Such integration enables a powerful knowledge representation including easy access to colors, windows, and mouse control. It lets communication take place between expert and novice, teacher and pupil, consultant and manager. It lets each side react to what the other says. For more information see Shepard [29]. The VP Expert package includes hypertext capabilities. AI Corp. is also marketing several products in the 1st-CLASS family which offer ES and hypertext programs. Another example of a hypertext product that can be integrated with an ES is HyperCard.

HyperCard. HyperCard is a graphically based data management software program for the Macintosh (II, SE, and PLUS), from Apple Computer, Inc. HyperCard creates a visual and logical metaphor to the hierarchical structure of data files. It also employs the concept of hypertext in which texts, images, and data are linked to other text, images, and data by buttons. Click on a designated button and the linked items are brought onto the screen.

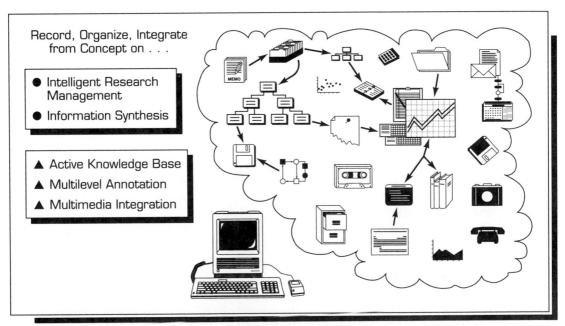

FIGURE 14.6 Active Role of Hypermedia (*Source:* J. Paul, "Toward a Strategy for Managing Computer-based Research," in *Proceedings, FAIM 90* [Alexandria, Va.: Defense Systems Management College, 1990]. RAND Corp.)

HyperCard's data structure illustrates the logical relationship between data elements in a simple manner. Instead of programs or databases, HyperCard uses stacks. Instead of files, it uses cards. This organization enables presentation of information and knowledge in a way that makes sense to the user. HyperCard is not simple to learn because of the abundance of creative tools. Once you learn it, however, it can provide you with almost unlimited opportunities. HyperCard extends the Macintosh user interface and makes everybody a programmer. It is supported by HyperTalk, a simple, object-oriented language whose syntax is similar to that of COBOL. It includes event-oriented scripts that are executed when a certain event occurs. These events go through HyperCard as messages. (For further details see Goodman [14].)

HyperCard can be used as an ES knowledge base source. A user can view information that resides in the stacks and cards during ES consultation. Since pictures can be stored in it, HyperCard can support regular rule-based systems very well. MacSMARTS, for example, permits the user of its ES to enter a HyperCard file, look up the answer to a question, and return to MacSMARTS. A similar approach is executed by Instant Expert Plus, a product tightly integrated with HyperCard. In addition, HyperCard can be used as an extremely user-friendly front-end to an expert system shell. This approach is used in an ES shell called Cognate. For further discussion on how HyperCard can make user interfaces friendlier, see Shafer [28].

Multimedia and Expert Systems

Multimedia technology has been used extensively in training by major computer manufacturers such as IBM, Intel, DEC, Philips, General Electric, Panasonic, and Motorola. An array of products have been developed to support multimedia training (e.g., see Szuprowicz [33]). Since 1989, increased numbers of multimedia applications include expert systems. Such a merger is called an *intelligent multimedia* system. It integrates information from several media for either *presentation* (Figure 14.5) or for *processing* (Figure 14.6). In either case, an expert system can be helpful.

The merger of ES and multimedia can provide, according to experts (e.g., see Veljkov [35] and Parsaye et al. [25]), an unparalleled impact on presentation of expertise either for training purposes or for rendering advice. One reason for the impact is that the interest and attention of the audience increase as well as their retention rate. Several specific benefits of the ES-multimedia merger are now apparent.

Guide for Navigation in Hypermedia. Hypermedia contain highly sophisticated textual, graphic, image, and other media of knowledge. Users of hypermedia do not have any systematic procedure to navigate through the accumulated knowledge (see Tuthill [34]). Users have complete freedom of navigation. The quality of the navigation depends on the objective of the system. If the objective is learning or exploration, the results can be excellent. If a user is looking for specific knowledge, he or she may inadvertently navigate around (and therefore miss) important points of information.

Expert systems explore knowledge bases by presenting a user with options or by evaluating user input. Based on the user's response, the system then branches to an appropriate portion of the knowledge base and presents other options to the user. The process continues until a conclusion is reached or a list of recommended options is presented. In this way, all the critical knowledge components are touched by prepathed, mapped, or guided navigation. The merging of ES and hypermedia allows the user to be guided in the navigation progress, thereby achieving complete use of the hypermedia system. One industry where such applications are useful is tourism. A prospective tourist can be guided through pictures, maps, text, and even sounds of a site he or she may choose to visit.

Media Selection. Another application of expert systems in multimedia technology is the selection of specific media items as proposed by Chao et al. [6].

Display of ES Results. One of the major objectives of ES is to provide advice, for example, to conduct troubleshooting and suggest repair procedures. When complex equipment is involved, the advice can be supported by the pictures or diagrams that hypermedia provide. This application can also be important in training.

Dialogue Enhancement. Multimedia can enhance dialogues with expert systems. This application is available in some banks. Instead of the common question and answer interface, some banks have a dialogue system in which a picture of a person is displayed on a TV screen and questions are asked (voice synthesis.) Currently, customers enter their answers via the keyboard, but sooner or later they too will use voice input.

Explanation. Explanation is essential in AI systems. Multimedia can support explanations and thus increase the chance of acceptance of AI applications by users.

Architecture. The integration of ES and multimedia can take several shapes depending on the purpose of the integration. A proposed structure is shown in Figure 14.7 (self-explanatory).

Examples of Integrated Systems. Several systems have been developed as prototypes in research institutions. In fact, some commercial systems have begun to appear on the market. Our first example is the Intelligent Image Management System for NASA (Ragusa and Orwig [26]). Several million color pictures (8 by 11 inches) are stored at the Kennedy Space Center. (About 100,000 pictures are taken for every space shuttle prelaunch.) These pictures are part of

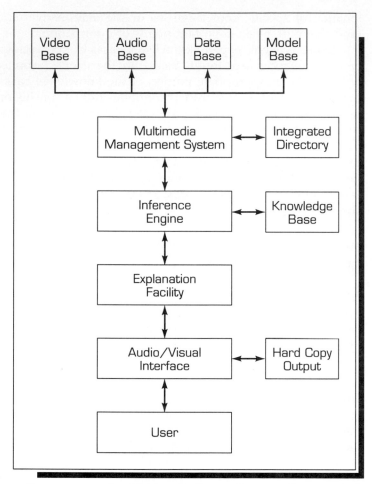

FIGURE 14.7 Components of a Multimedia Expert System (*Source:* J. C. Sipior and E. J. Garrity, "Merging Expert Systems with Multimedia Technology," in *Proceedings, ACM SIGBDP Conference on Expert Systems*, Florida, November 1990.)

studies by engineers from NASA and several dozen contracted companies to verify that essential installations, tests, or repair procedures have been completed and to help in designing improvements. Managing these pictures, including maintaining accessibility to them, is a complex task. The management system combines hypermedia software, image digitization, an analog laser disk (CD-ROM) database, a high-definition expert system, and a natural language processor. The system enables easy storage and retrieval of pictures from the database. It could be expanded to include hypertext and digital video interactive compact disk for storing motion video. The expert system's role is to assist in classification and retrieval of images.

Another example of an integrated system is an expert diagnostic system (Ford [12]) that helps technicians diagnose faults in electromechanical military equipment. In addition to the expert system, a multimedia support of hypertext, still graphics, and full-motion graphics is available for presenting the findings, recommendations, and explanations of the expert system.

A flow diagram of the system, which is called ACES (for Advanced Cooling Cart System), is shown in Figure 14.8. Once the system is loaded (step 1), the

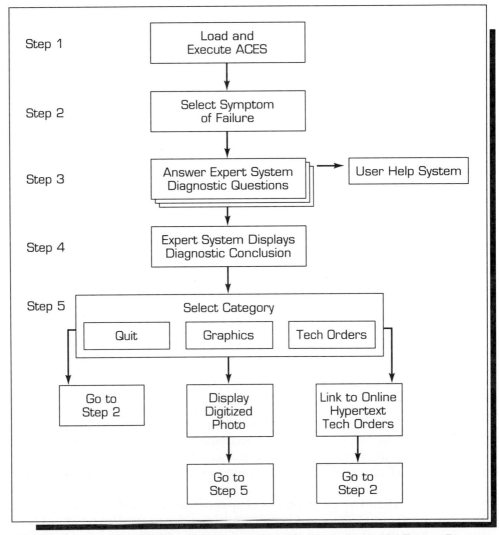

FIGURE 14.8   Sample ACES Diagnostic Session (*Source:* B. Ford, "An Expert Diagnostic System Using Multimedia," *Expert Systems: Planning, Implementation, Integration* [Fall 1990].)

TABLE 14.4 Representative Applications of Intelligent Interactive Multimedia

Company	Application	Media Involved
Electric Power-Research Institute (EPRI) with Honeywell Inc.	Troubleshooting and rapid diagnosis—provides advice and repair suggestions	Voice, text, video graphics, GRID Laptop, CD-ROM, ES
Competitive Solutions Inc.	"Walk" of a prospective home buyer around a property and through the interior of a house; analysis of mortgage	Images, voice, descriptions, relational DBMS, ES
Texas Instruments (research project)	Hand-held information delivery systems connected to a central database (e.g., for tourist guides, commodity trading)	Voice, text, graphics, CD-ROM
Texas Instruments (research project)	Interaction with corporate databases—a tool for users to build their own data-retrieval applications	Text, graphics, voice

Note: The March/April 1991 issue of *PC AI* is dedicated to expert systems in conjunction with hypertext and hypermedia.

user is questioned about the nature of the fault (step 2). After the technician identifies the fault, the system asks diagnostic questions (step 3) to verify the initial choice. The technician can receive explanations and guidance from the user help system. Based on this dialogue, a final diagnosis is made (step 4). Strong graphic support is available in step 4. Next, suggested repair activities are provided (step 5). The user has three options: quit, view graphics (digital photos), or go to an online hypertext of the maintenance manual. The technician may conduct an alternative analysis of suspected parts or subsystem if he or she is not happy with the diagnosis. The system runs on a microcomputer with the VP Expert shell. The system interfaces with dBASE III Plus, which manages maintenance records.

There are many potential applications of interactive intelligent multimedia. For example, the expert system laboratory at the University of Central Florida has developed several dozen prototype applications under the leadership of J.H. Ragusa. Other representative applications are shown in Table 14.4.

14.7 Real-time Expert Systems

Real-time computer systems are systems in which there is a strict time limit on the system's response time. The response time should be *fast enough* to control the process being computerized. In other words, the system should *always* produce a response by the time it is needed.

Real-time computer systems have become an integral part of our lives, and they are being used in a growing number of applications. The complexity of these systems is increasing along three dimensions: (1) the number of functions controlled, (2) the rate at which the functions must be controlled, and (3) the number of factors that must be considered before a decision can be made. For example, control rooms on oil platforms are being planned that will make available as many as 20,000 signals for just two or three operations. In such situations, it becomes difficult for people to interpret and act in a timely manner. So expert systems are being developed to assist the human operators by reducing the cognitive load or by enabling the operators to increase their productivity without an increase in the cognitive load. (Cognitive load refers to the manner in which people perceive and/or process information.)

Real-time ES, also known as online real-time systems, obtain information directly from the process they control. They take *complete control* over the process, in a real-time environment, without human interaction. Such systems are especially important in situations where data changes rapidly. Table 14.5 lists some applications for real-time expert systems, and specific examples follow.

A System for Managing Computer Operations

Large, computerized data processing systems and their assorted networks often involve multiple processors and a large number of peripherals—a multimillion dollar investment. Decisions in such systems center around job scheduling,

TABLE 14.5 Applications of Real-time Systems

Process control
Intelligent robotics
Quality control
Automated materials handling
Financial trading (stocks, commodities)
Energy management
System fault analysis and diagnosis
Adoptive controls
Process simulation for design and training
Data acquisition and recording

monitoring performance and delays, and making adjustments and maintenance decisions whenever needed.

Typically, planning and control of such systems rest largely in the hands of a few operators. In addition to routine activities like mounting tapes, these operators continually monitor the condition of the computer's operating system—the program that controls all the computer's activities—and initiate queries and/or commands to diagnose maintenance problems and other delays as they arise. These conditions require that decisions be made in a real-time environment.

Researchers at the IBM Thomas J. Watson Research Division (Yorktown Heights, N.Y.) have successfully applied ES techniques to problems in managing computer installations and operations with the MVS operating system as their subject. MVS is the most widely used operating system in large mainframe IBM computers.

Most existing ES applications are oriented toward consultation; that is, instead of acting on their own, they run through a session in a batch mode and deal with a static world. In contrast, a real-time ES must base its conclusions on facts obtained directly from the system being monitored. There is no time to review data observed and interpreted by humans.

YES/MVS II is a continuous, real-time ES that exerts interactive control over the computer's operating system as an aid to computer operators. It can summarize system conditions and respond instantly and automatically to needs. Its response is done in conjunction with a human who can override the ES. When a potential problem is detected, the operator may ask MVS for additional information and send one or more corrective commands. The system, which is written in a version of PROLOG called PSC PROLOG, is used on mainframe computers.

Figure 14.9 illustrates how the system works. (For further information, see Ennis et al. [11].) It shows how YES/MVS makes a "decision." The goal of YES/MVS in this example is to keep 50 percent of the computer's job queue space available at all times. The expert system will combine the facts it has about the system's condition with the rules it possesses to make an inference. It will use the inference about the system to get more data or to make a "decision" about what to do to achieve or maintain the goal. For example:

1. MVS says queue space is low (FACT)
2. . . . and a RULE says that when space is low, query the printer's state . . .
3. . . . which is an INFERENCE . . .
4. . . . which starts the program over again, by determining that . . .

1. (FACT) a. The printer has a few short jobs
          b. The printer is holding a long job
          c. The printer is limited to printing 30,000 lines
   . . . combining these FACTS with the
2. . . . RULE that is a, b, and c are true, the correct

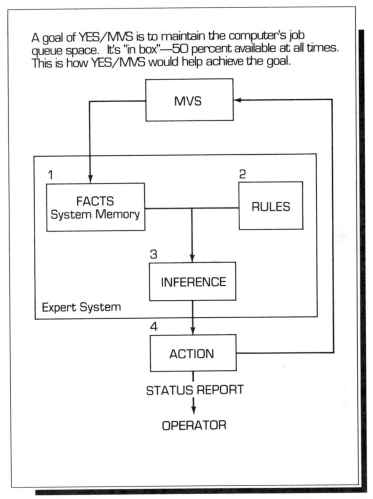

A goal of YES/MVS is to maintain the computer's job queue space. It's "in box"—50 percent available at all times. This is how YES/MVS would help achieve the goal.

FIGURE 14.9 Expert System YES/MVS II Makes a "Decision" (*Source: IBM Research Highlights* [no. 2, 1984].)

3. . . . INFERENCE is to raise the printer's line limit . . .
4. . . . an ACTION is initiated; raise the printer's line limit.

The action frees the computer's job queue space by releasing the large printing job on hold. This achieves the goal (i.e., the system's jobs queue space becomes at least 50 percent available). For further discussion see Chekaluk et al. [7].

An Automated Materials Handling System

DEC has implemented materials handling systems in two of its manufacturing facilities. These systems control factory inventory and generate timely, accurate reports on work progress and quality. Key elements of each system are a pair of robots that transport assembly items and two expert systems that determine when and to where items should be dispatched.

The expert systems, named Dispatcher and Mover, are the controlling software for the entire materials handling system. Dispatcher determines the order in which work-in-progress (WIP) items are dispatched and to which workstations they will be sent. Mover coordinates and drives WIP items via the robots' carousels and conveyors.

Dispatcher uses information in its knowledge base to select the best work item(s) to dispatch to a workstation, depending on the current work status and demand on the factory floor. The knowledge base was created initially with interactive utilities that are part of the system. New work is entered into the system either by automatic utilities or iterative routines. Dispatcher performs updates automatically, but any exceptions that arise can be handled manually with interactive utilities.

Dispatcher's knowledge base contains information about four components that enable it to make decisions: workstations, route list, unit load, and WIP. These elements, along with the validation table that verified valid workstations, operations, parts, and classes, represent the state of the factory floor. Since its implementation at DEC's Marlborough, Mass., facility in 1985, the materials handling system has been in operation six days a week for three shifts per day. During the first month, it reduced inventory by 50 percent, and inventory accounts increased in accuracy to 99.9 percent. DEC estimates that this system saves $25 million annually. For further details see Wynot [37]. For additional examples see Dunning and Switlik [8] and Kaemmerer et al. [18].

Development Packages

Several development packages for real-time systems are available, usually for simulations and system control. Representative examples are RT Expert, ISIM, RTES, and G2.

Chapter Highlights

□ An appropriate human-machine (user) interface is critical to the success of AI applications.
□ A user interface is composed of an action language (input) and a presentation language (output, or display).
□ The manner in which users interpret the display and the ease with which the action language can be used are very important for the acceptance of AI applications.
□ Several interface modes that can be used separately or in combination are menus, commands, questions and answers, form interaction, object manipulation, and natural language.

- Actual communication can be done via the keyboard, by using several input devices, by using voice, or by employing handwriting recognition software.
- Interface to ES (or knowledge-based systems) is complicated because of the need to provide explanation and the two-way dialogue.
- Blackboard architecture is used when a problem is complex (involving several sources of knowledge).
- A blackboard enables coordination of several knowledge bases. Coordination is exercised by a controlling component.
- To deal with complex systems, a problem can be segmented and its solution delegated to several intelligent agents (expert systems). Such an arrangement is called distributed artificial intelligence.
- Large, complex problems can also be solved with a parallel processing approach.
- Distributed artificial intelligence can be applied to complex problems (e.g., a team of intelligent robots in an automated factory).
- The term *multimedia* refers to a collection of communication media such as text, audio, and video.
- The use of several media together can increase learning and retention of material studied.
- Interactive multimedia are arrangements in which computers enable a builder (an author) to create complex systems for presentation and processing of information.
- Hypermedia allow information to be linked by association.
- Hypertext is an approach for handling text and graphic information that allows the user to jump from one topic (or place) to another.
- Expert systems can guide users in certain hypertext applications.
- When an expert system is added to multimedia, the system is considered intelligent interactive multimedia technology. Such a technology can be used to enhance many computerized applications.
- The several possible models of integrating ES and multimedia result in a variety of applications.
- An important merger is the use of multimedia to display the results of an expert system's work.
- If an expert system is the front-end of multimedia, the media can be used more wisely.
- Computerized systems that provide responses quickly enough to control processes while they are running are called real-time systems.
- Real-time ES are difficult to build because of the fast response time that is required.
- Real-time systems are extremely important in areas such as process control, quality control, robotics, materials handling, energy management, and certain financial transactions (e.g., stocks).

Key Terms

action language	front-end interface	multiagent systems
blackboard	HyperCard	multimedia
command language	hypermedia	natural language
display	hypertext	object manipulation
distributed artificial	intelligent agent	opportunistic
intelligence	interactive multimedia	reasoning
distributed problem	approach	parallel processing
solving	interface	presentation language
explanation	knowledge source	question and answer
form interaction	menu interaction	

Questions for Review

1. What is a user interface?
2. Why do some say that the interface is the most important component of a computerized system?
3. Describe the *process* of user-computer interaction.
4. Define presentation and action languages.
5. What is meant by form interaction?
6. Which interface style will probably be preferred by AI users in the future?
7. Why is explanation so important in knowledge-based systems?
8. In what situations may you prefer an open-ended dialogue with a computer?
9. What is an intelligent front-end?
10. Define blackboard architecture and describe its major purpose.
11. Define knowledge sources and describe their role in blackboard architecture.
12. What are the major components of blackboard architecture?
13. What is opportunistic reasoning? Provide an example and contrast it with nonopportunistic reasoning.
14. List some of the limitations of the blackboard architecture.
15. Define parallel processing and contrast it with sequential processing.
16. Why is parallel processing of interest to the AI community?
17. What is the logic of using a distributed problem-solving approach?
18. Define distributed problem solving and multiagent systems, and describe the relationships between them.
19. Define multimedia. Why is a multimedia approach considered to be important in training?
20. How are hypermedia and multimedia related?
21. What is meant by navigation?
22. Describe how hypertext works. What is its major advantage?
23. How can multimedia help expert systems and how can expert systems help multimedia?
24. Define a real-time system.
25. Describe a real-time expert system.

Questions for Discussion

1. Why is menu interaction probably the most liked interface style?
2. Why is a command language the preferred style of experienced users?
3. Describe a combination of menus and commands from your own experience.
4. Search for a recent article or vendor's publicity on a handwriting recognition computer (pen computers). What are the advantages of such a machine?
5. Why is blackboard architecture appropriate for distributed artificial intelligence?
6. Explain how distributed artificial intelligence can help a team of robots in distress.
7. Review the literature for a recent application of intelligent interactive multimedia. Analyze it in light of the material in this chapter.

References and Bibliography

1. Botton, N., and T. Raz. "Using Hypertext to Enhance a Legal Expert System." *PC AI* (February 1989).
2. Bennett, J.L. "Tools for Building Advanced User Interfaces." *IBM Systems Journal* (no. 3/4, 1986).
3. Bielawski, L., and R. Lewant. *Intelligent Systems Design: Integrating Hypermedia and Expert Systems Technologies.* New York: John Wiley & Sons, 1990.
4. Bond, A.H., and L. Gasser, eds. *Reading in Distributed AI.* San Mateo, Calif.: Morgan Kaufman, 1988.
5. *Byte* (October 1988).
6. Chao, P., et al. "Using Expert Systems Approaches to Solve Media Selection Problem: Matrix Format." In *Proceedings of the Association of Computer Interface System*, November 1990.
7. Chekaluk, R.A., et al. "Expert Operator: Deploying YES/MVS II." In *Innovative Applications of AI.* H. Schorr and A. Rappaport, eds. Cambridge, Mass.: AAAI/MIT Press, 1989.
8. Dunning, B.B., and J. Switlik. "A Real-time Expert System for Computer Network Monitor and Control." *Data Base* (Summer 1988).
9. Eadline, D. "Making Prolog Parallel." *AI Expert* (July 1989).
10. Englemore, R., and T. Morgan, eds. *Blackboard Systems.* Reading, Mass.: Addison-Wesley, 1989.
11. Ennis, R.L., et al. "A Continuous Real-Time Expert System for Computer Operations." *IBM Journal of Research and Development* (January 1986).
12. Ford, B. "An Expert Diagnostic System Using Multimedia." *Expert Systems: Planning, Implementation, Integration* (Fall 1990).
13. Gasser, L. "Distributed AI." *AI Expert* (July 1989).
14. Goodman, D. *The Complete HyperCard Handbook.* (New York: Bantam, 1987).
15. Hartson, R., and D. Hix. "Human-Computer Interface Development: Concepts and Systems for Its Management." *ACM Computing Surveys* (March 1989).

16. Huhns, M.N., ed. *Distributed Artificial Intelligence.* (Pittman Publishing, 1987).
17. Jagannathan, V.R., et al., eds. *Blackboard Architectures and Applications.* New York: Academic Press, 1989.
18. Kaemmerer, W.F., et al. "Integrating Expert Systems with Process Manufacturing." *Expert Systems: Planning Implementation, Integration* (Fall, 1990).
19. Kannan, R., and W.H. Dodrill. "DAIS-A Distributed AI Programming Shell." *IEEE Expert* (December 1990).
20. Lamberti, D.M., and W.A. Wallace. "Intelligent Interface Design: An Empirical Assessment of Knowledge Presentation in Expert Systems." *MIS Quarterly* (September 1990).
21. Long, J., and A. Whitefield, eds. *Cognitive Ergonomics and Human-Computer Interaction.* Cambridge: Cambridge Univ. Press, 1989.
22. Majchrzak, A., et al. *Human Aspects of Computer-Aided Design.* Philadelphia: Taylor and Francis, 1987.
23. Nielson, J. *Hypertext and Hypermedia.* New York: Academic Press, 1990.
24. Paul, J. "Toward a Strategy for Managing Computer-based Research." In *Proceedings, FAIM 90.* Alexandria, Va.: Defense Systems Management College, 1990.
25. Parsaye, K., et al. *Intelligent Databases: Object-oriented, Deductive Hypermedia Technologies.* New York: John Wiley & Sons, 1989.
26. Ragusa, J.H., and G.W. Orwig. "Expert Systems and Imaging: NASA's Start-up Work in Intelligent Image Management." *Expert Systems: Planning, Implementation, Integration* (Fall 1990).
27. Schneiderman, B. *Designing the User Interfaces: Strategies for Effective Human-Computer Interaction.* Reading, Mass.: Addison-Wesley, 1987.
28. Shafer, D. "Hypermedia and Expert Systems: A Marriage Made in Hyper Heaven." *Hyperage* (May-June 1988). Also see *PC AI* (July-August 1988 and March-April 1991).
29. Shepard, S.L. "AI Meets Hypertext—KnowledgePro and Knowledge Maker." *Language Technology* (November-December, 1987).
30. Shipilberg, D., et al. "ExperTax: An Expert System for Corporate Tax Planning." *Expert Systems* (July 1986).
31. Sipior, J.C., and E.J. Garrity. "Merging Expert Systems with Multimedia Technology." In *Proceedings, ACM SIGBDP Conference on Expert Systems.* Florida, November 1990.
32. Sutchliffe, A. *Human-Computer Interface Design.* New York: Springer-Verlag, 1989.
33. Szuprowicz, B.O. "The Multimedia Connection." *Expert Systems: Planning, Implementation, Integration* (Winter 1991).
34. Tuthill, G.S. *Knowledge Engineering.* Blue Ridge Summit, Pa.: TAB Books, 1990.
35. Veljkov, M.D. "Managing Multimedia." *Byte* (August 1990).
36. Raghupathi, W., et al. "Multiple Cooperative Expert Systems for Organizational Decision Support: Exploring the Blackboard Approach." Working paper, School of Business, Cal. State Univ., Chico, CA. 1991.
37. Wynot, M. "AI Provides Real-Time Control of DEC's Material Handling Process." *Industrial Engineering* (April 1986).

Part 5

Implementation

The systems constructed in Part 4 can be implemented as stand-alone systems, but they also can be integrated with other computer-based information systems. Certain integrations take place when the systems are in development, whereas others can occur only during implementation. Therefore Part 5, which deals with implementation issues, begins with the topic of integration (Chapter 15). The past few years have brought the recognition that the benefits of AI technologies integrated with other computer systems (such as databases or decision support systems) can be enormous. Several modes of integration are described as well as the difficulties and problems.

Since the introduction of AI technologies may create a significant change in an organization, the implementation process should be designed carefully. The process of implementing AI technologies is similar to that of other computer systems, but it is not identical. Both the generic and unique aspects of AI implementation are described in Chapter 16. In Chapter 17 we address potential organizational and societal impacts. Of special interest is the issue of AI's effect on employment—a highly debated topic. Again, generic implementation issues are discussed because AI is so frequently integrated with other technologies.

Chapter 15

Integrating AI Technologies

In previous chapters we introduced several AI technologies as being completely independent of each other, and indeed, many such systems are unrelated. However, there is increasing evidence that integrating among themselves, and/or with other computer-based information systems (CBISs), may enhance the quality and efficiency of computerized systems. This chapter examines the various issues of AI integration in the following sections:

15.1   What Is Systems Integration?

Integration of computer-based systems means that the systems are integrated into one facility rather than having separate hardware, software, and communications for each independent system. Integration can be at the development tools level or at the application system level. There are two general types of integration: functional and physical.

Functional integration implies that different support functions are provided as a single system. For example, working with electronic mail, using a spreadsheet, communicating with external databases, creating graphic representations, and storing and manipulating data can all be accomplished at the same workstation. A user can access the appropriate facilities through a single, consistent interface and can switch from one task to another and back again.

Physical integration refers to packaging of the hardware, software, and communication features required to accomplish functional integration. Software integration is determined to a large extent by the hardware integration. The major approaches to physical integration, according to Newman [42], are shown in Figure 15.1 and are summarized next.

Access Approaches

According to the access approach, AI development tools and/or application programs can *access* each other or access standard applications or development

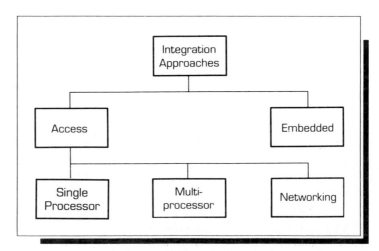

FIGURE 15.1   Major Approaches to Physical Integration

software. The access can be done based on one of three types of hardware configuration: single processor, multiprocessor, or networking.

Single Processor. This simple and most common approach relies on different software operating on the same processor. With this approach, traditional programs and databases are callable from computer memory or from some software package. An example of such an integration is the availability of LISP and/or PROLOG on a single processor with conventional languages. The Hewlett-Packard AI system is a good illustration. It integrates LISP, FORTRAN, C, Pascal, and HP-UX (a version of UNIX). As a result, programmers can edit, compile, test, and debug FORTRAN, C, and Pascal programs incrementally and interactively using either LISP or UNIX without ever leaving the LISP editor. The single-processor approach is not expensive, and the processor can be highly utilized, but it is *not as powerful* as the following two approaches.

Multiprocessors. According to this approach, different software operates on different processors within the same machine. For example, while UNIX is being used during data acquisition, LISP can be used for data representation and analysis. Texas Instruments is using such an approach by combining an EXPLORER processor with that of the Macintosh. The multiprocessor approach is much more expensive than the single-processor approach, but it is more flexible and it can assist in faster processing of complex jobs.

Networking. Integration requires some kind of networking if AI programs and/or conventional systems reside in completely different machines but can interface with each other. Networking permits an easy and quick interface among different software products. An example is General Motors' MAP (for manufacturing automation protocol), which is supported by powerful AI-dedicated workstations. These machines support Transport Control Protocol, Ethernet, Internet Protocol, and SNA, thus enabling a wide range of networking. Texas Instruments' EXPLORER is an example of a dedicated AI workstation that is networked with other systems. Apollo's Domain communication board, for example, is plugged into EXPLORER. The Domain's virtual-demand-paged capabilities allow any computer on the network to store, access, or execute information on any other Domain-network computer as if it were on its own.

Embedded Systems

In this approach to physical integration, the AI software is embedded in a conventional information system program, e.g., database. **Embedded systems** can be considered the "second generation" of integrating AI and conventional systems. Such systems embed value-added AI capabilities in conventional programs. Users see a single application with which they can work; there is no distinction between AI and conventional parts. An example of an embedded development tool is Guru, which embeds an ES shell and a natural language processor in an environment that supports integrated spreadsheets, text processing, relational DBMSs, graphics, report generation, communication, and business computing (for details see Rauch-Hindin [45]).

Embedded systems, which are usually more efficient than systems with access approaches, could be the most important information technologies of the future. Although embedded systems seem to be desirable, they are more difficult and more expensive to construct. On the other hand, there are many standard components on the market that can support the access approaches and can result in savings of time and/or money. Selection of an appropriate integration mode is outside the scope of this chapter; however, it certainly should be considered in the design phase of an integrated project. For further discussion see King [35].

Loose Versus Tight Integration

Another way to describe integration architectures is to distinguish between loose integration (or **loosely coupled** systems) and tight integration (**tightly coupled** systems). Loose integration refers to *two* (or more) *independent systems* that are connected via communication lines (networking). For example, an ES can be tied to a DBMS that serves a database or a decision support system via a communication link. The ES may be used to analyze the data generated by the decision support system. In such a case, the data produced by the decision support system can be stored in an external (text) file that is read by the ES application. A schematic view of such integration is shown in Figure 15.2b. Note that the user sees two systems. Access systems in general are loosely coupled.

Embedded systems, on the other hand, are considered to be tightly coupled. Figure 15.2a shows such an integration; it is basically what we call an embedded system. In such a case, the user sees one system (notice that there is only one user interface). Figure 15.2 is based on an ES shell named KES. Notice that there are no communication links or files in a tightly integrated system.

Expert Systems on a Chip

Computer hardware advances have made possible an expert system embedded in a microprocessor chip to form an integrated package of hardware and software. Such an integrated ES can be embedded in a piece of equipment (e.g., a complex electronic gear or robot) to form an intelligent system. One specific example is the EEG Analysis System—an ES embedded in a Motorola MC6801 single-chip, 8-bit microcomputer designed to interpret electroencephalograms recorded from patients with renal diseases.

Computer hardware size and price reductions have made it feasible for complex equipment to contain a dedicated computer and to run an ES that takes

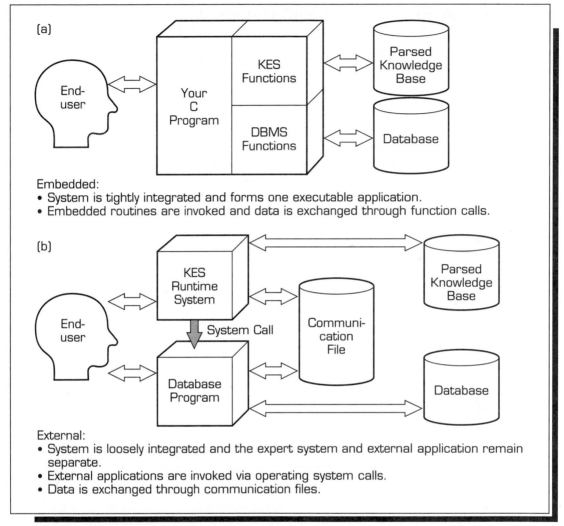

FIGURE 15.2 Embedded Versus External (Access) Integration (*Source:* Courtesy of Software A&E Inc.)

care of the equipment in some way. The integrated ES handles tasks such as monitoring and controlling equipment operation, detecting and diagnosing equipment faults, assisting in correcting the faults, and planning ways to work around the faults until they are corrected. The integrated ES is hard-wired into the equipment with direct connections to sensors and switches that allow the ES to monitor and, in some cases, control the equipment. For applications in which dangerous or unexpected situations are likely to arise, the operator could be taken out of the loop completely.

15.2   Integrating the DSS and the ES: An Overview

A decision support system (DSS) is composed of three components: a database and its management, a model base and its management, and a human-machine interface. In the next three sections, we will discuss integration with each of these components. Such integrated systems can be used, of course, with other computer-based information systems.

In certain problem domains, both the ES and the DSS may have distinct advantages that, when combined, yield synergetic results. A DSS typically gives full control to the decision maker about information acquisition, information analysis (quantitatively), and the final decision. As research has shown, human judgmental biases may be present in complex decisions that are supported by a DSS. An ES, on the other hand, is free from acquisition, evaluation, and judgmental biases, at least in the human sense (*if* the knowledge of the expert is properly represented in the ES and *if* the ES is properly designed). The ES can provide intelligence for a particular domain and make a tentative decision. The decision maker can also utilize the DSS in the traditional sense and arrive at a tentative decision. If the results of the ES and DSS could be reconciled and evaluated, the joint effort would probably produce better results than either approach independently. The joint approach is not necessarily constrained by the narrowness of the domain of the ES, because an operational DSS can also be domain specific (e.g., a DSS for routing vehicles in a textile company, or a DSS for determining the allocation of customer engineers to geographic territories). Although typical decision support systems focus on quantitative mathematical and computational reasoning, they should also support qualitative analysis.

15.3   Intelligent Databases and Their Management

Tying expert systems and natural language processors to databases, especially large ones, is one of the most critical and rewarding areas of AI integration. There are several goals and several physical modes of such integration into **intelligent databases**.

Goals and Modes

Organizations, private and public, are continuously collecting data, information, and knowledge (all are referred to here as information) and storing it in computerized systems. Updating, retrieving, use, and removal of this information become more complicated as the amount increases. At the same time, the number of individuals who are interacting with this information increases due to networking, end-user computing, and reduced costs of information processing. Working with large databases is becoming a difficult task that requires considerable expertise.

Developing AI applications requires access to databases. For example, without database access it would be difficult to use ES in large MIS applications such as factory automation and credit card authorization.

Expert systems can make the use as well as the management (e.g., updating, deleting, adding, or combining) of databases simpler. One way to do so is to *enhance* the database management system by providing it with an inference capability. Al-Zobaidie and Grimson [4] provide three possible architectures for such a coupling. They also explain how the efficiency and functionality of the DBMS can be enhanced. The contribution of an ES in such a case can be further increased if it is coupled with a natural language processor. For a description of integration of a database, DBMS, ES, and natural language processor, see Harris [22].

Another purpose of ES and DBMS integration is to improve the *management* of the ES's knowledge base **(intelligent knowledge management).** As ES become increasingly complex and diverse, the need for efficient and effective management of their growing knowledge base is apparent. Al-Zobaidie and Grimson [4] proposed an enhanced ES to deal with such situations: this ES will have a special DBMS that can be used to manage its own knowledge base.

A different way of looking at ES and database integration is shown in Figure 15.3. In this case the integration is tight; there is only one user interface. The application program can be driven by data generated by the database directly and/or by data generated by the database and then processed (e.g., interpreted) by the ES.

In addition to the enhanced DBMS and the enhanced ES, it is possible to integrate the ES and the DBMS via a network. Such an integration is discussed by Al-Zobaidie and Grimson [4].

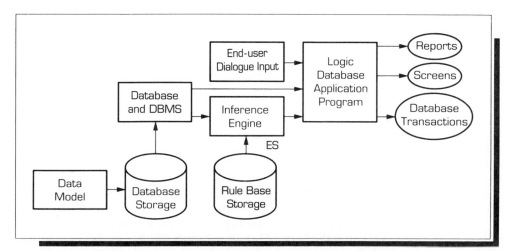

FIGURE 15.3 Intelligent Database Showing One Way of ES and Database Integration (*Source:* Based on B. Cohen, "Merging Expert Systems and Databases," *AI Expert* [February 1989].)

Difficulties in tying ES to large databases have been a major problem, even for large corporations (e.g., Boeing Co., American Express). Several vendors have recognized the importance of such integration and have developed software products to support it. An example of a product is the Oracle relational DBMS (Oracle Corp.), which incorporates some ES functionality in the form of a *query optimizer* that selects the most efficient path for database queries to travel. In a distributed database, for example, a query optimizer would recognize that it is more efficient to transfer two records to a machine that holds 10,000 records than vice versa. (The optimization is important to users because with such a capability they need to know only a few rules and commands to use the database.) This product includes a knowledge base that can incorporate, for example, rules for selecting which indexes to create or delete.

One of IBM's current main thrusts in commercial AI is providing a knowledge processing subsystem to work with a database and enable users to extract information from the database and pass it to an expert system's knowledge base in several different knowledge representation structures. Another IBM project is easy transferability of data from a typical database format (e.g., COBOL) to an ES format (e.g., LISP) and vice versa.

Another product is the KEE Connection (IntelliCorp.), which translates KEE commands into database queries and automatically keeps track of data passed back and forth between KEE's knowledge base and a relational database using SQL. Other benefits of such integration are the ability to use symbolic representation of data; improvements in the construction, operation, and maintenance of the DBMS (see Jarke and Vassiliou [29]); and the benefit for the ES itself, which is derived from accessibility to a database.

A current issue in database technology is the introduction of the object-oriented approach. In addition, databases now store pictures and sophisticated graphics. Therefore, the management of databases is becoming more difficult and so are the accessibility and retrieval of information. For a discussion of intelligent object-oriented databases see Parsaye et al. [43] and the discussion on hypermedia in Chapter 14.

The integration of ES and databases has been the topic of several international and national conferences, books, and dozens of papers. For further information see Brodie and Mylpoulos [8], Cohen [9], Hsu and Skevington [27], Kerschberg [33], Kennedy and Yen [32], Risch et al. [47], and Schur [49].

Online Databases

Commercial online databases are developed independently of each other, with different command languages, file structures, and access protocols. If we add to this the complexity of searching, the proliferation of online databases (several thousand), and the lack of standardization, it is not difficult to see why there is a need for extensive knowledge to use these databases efficiently. Expert systems are being utilized (usually combined with a natural language processor) as interfaces to such databases. The knowledge base of the ES includes knowledge about search strategy. For example, such a system can advise a casual user on how to conduct a simple search or it can guide the more experienced user in accessing databases with complex organizations. In all, the ES can make an online system transparent to the user. Such an integration is extremely important for information systems that use external databases frequently (e.g., executive information systems). For details see Kehoe [31] and Hawkins [23].

15.4   Intelligent Modeling and Model Management

Model management software packages include quantitative models (such as statistical, financial, or management science) and/or an appropriate computer program to manage these (and other) models. Managing a model means the ability to perform such tasks as adding models, deleting models, updating models, connecting models with databases, inspecting models, combining models, selecting appropriate models, and invoking and running models. Adding intelligence to the process of modeling (building models or using existing models) and to their management makes lots of sense because some of the tasks involved (e.g., modeling and selecting models) require considerable expertise. The topics of intelligent modeling and **intelligent model management** have attracted significant academic attention in recent years (e.g., see Blanning [7], Fedorowicz and Williams [14], Elam and Konsynski [13], Liang [39], and Vasant and Croker [63]) because the potential benefits could be substantial. It seems, however, that the implementation of such integration is fairly difficult and slow.

Issues in Model Management

Four interrelated subtopics of model management will be investigated: problem diagnosis and selection of models, construction of models (formulation), use of models (analysis), and interpretation of output of models.

Problem Diagnosis and Selection of Models. Several commercial ES are now helping in the selection of appropriate statistical models (e.g., Statistical Navigator). Goul et al. [20] have developed a selection ES for mathematical programming and Courtney et al. [10] have developed an expert system for problem diagnosis. Zahedi [65] has developed a system for model selection. By way of examples, Elam and Konsynski [13] show how future model management systems will work when supported by ES.

Construction of Models. The construction of models for decision making involves the simplification of a real-world situation so that a simplified representation of reality can be made. Models can be normative or descriptive and they are being used in various types of computer-based information systems (especially the DSS). Finding an appropriate balance between simplification and representation in modeling requires expertise. The definition of the problem to be modeled, the attempt to *select* a prototype model (e.g., linear programming), the data collection, the model validation, and the estimation of certain parameters and relationships are not simple tasks either. For instance, data may be tested for suitability to a certain statistical distribution (e.g., "Does the arrival rate in queuing follow a Poisson distribution?"). The ES could guide the user in selecting an appropriate test and interpreting its results, which in turn can help in appropriate modeling of the situation.

Use of Models. Once models are constructed they can be put to use. The application of models may require some judgmental values (e.g., setting an alpha value in exponential smoothing). Experience is also needed to conduct a sensitivity analysis as well as to determine what constitutes a significant difference ("Is project A really superior to B?"). Expert systems can be used to provide the user with the necessary guidelines for use of models. In addition, the ES can conduct a cause-effect analysis.

Interpretation of Results. Expert systems are able to provide explanation and interpretation of the models used and the derived results. For example, an ES can trace anomalies of data. Furthermore, sensitivity analysis may be needed, or translation of information to a certain format may be the desired implementation.

Quantitative Models

Most experimental ES are *not* being developed according to the four model management issues just discussed. Instead, they are being developed according to the type of quantitative model used. Then, some portion of one or more of the four issues may be considered. A representative list of quantitative models is given in Table 15.1 with appropriate references.

For a proposed architecture for a quantitative intelligent model management, see Figure 15.4.

Human experts often use quantitative models to support their experience and expertise. For example, an expert may need to forecast the sales of a certain product or to estimate future cash flow using a corporate planning model. Similarly, many models are used by experts in almost all aspects of engineering. Such a model stands alone (meaning the expert can run the model on a computer as needed), or it can be part of a computer-based information system used by several decision makers and experts.

ES contributions in the area of quantitative models and model management can be demonstrated by examining the work of a consultant. A consultant is involved in the following steps:

	Topic	References
TABLE 15.1 Quantitative Models and Sources for More Information	Financial models	Turner and Obilichetti [61]
	Forecasting	Feng-Yang [15], Kumar and Cheng [36]
	Mathematical programming	Goul et al. [20], Murphy and Stohr [41]
	Project management	Hosley [25], Sathi et al. [48]
	Queuing	Hossein et al. [26]
	Simulation	Doukidis [11], Ford and Schroer [16]
	Statistics	Hand [21], Gale [18]
	Strategic planning	Goul et al. [20], Lee and Lee [38]
	System dynamics	Wu [64]

1. Discussing the nature of the problem with the user
2. Identifying and classifying the problem
3. Constructing a mathematical model of the problem
4. Solving the model
5. Conducting sensitivity analyses with the model
6. Recommending a specific solution
7. Assisting in implementing the solution

The system involves a decision maker (user), a consultant, and a computer.

If we can codify the knowledge of the consultant in an ES, we can build an intelligent computer-based information system capable of the same process. Unfortunately, at this time relatively little is known about the nature of the cognitive skills that consultants use. However, interesting work has been done by Goul et al. [20] who have developed a system that attempts to replicate a manager-consultant-computer combination. In their system the computer queries the manager to determine the general category of the managerial problem (e.g., an allocation problem versus inventory management). Next the computer queries the manager to determine the *exact nature* of the problem (e.g., what kind of allocation problem). Then the computer suggests which quantitative model to use (e.g., dynamic programming versus linear programming). The manager can ask the system to define terminology to justify the recommendation made by the machine, and to explain the model used. The decision maker then can formulate the problem using the model, conduct what-if analysis, or use an alternative model. The ES, in this case, helps in identifying and classifying the managerial problem, acts as a tutor, provides illustrative examples, and selects the model(s) to be used.

Expert systems can be used as an **intelligent interface** between the user and quantitative models. Such an integration is demonstrated by BUMP, a

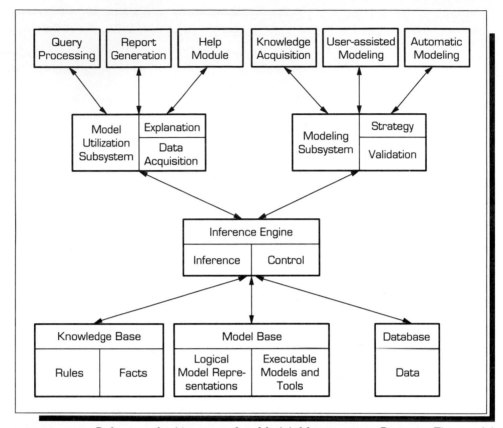

FIGURE 15.4 Software Architecture for Model Management System. The model utilization subsystem (left) directs the effective use of the model. The modeling subsystem (right) helps in increasing the productivity of model building. The inference engine drives the model selection and integration, and the integration of the model base, database, and knowledge base. (*Source:* T. Liang, "Development of a Knowledge-based Model Management System," Reprinted with permission from *Operations Research*, No. 6, 1988, Operations Research Society of America. No further reproduction permitted without the consent of the copyright owner.)

statistical ES (Hand [21]). Large numbers of statistical packages available on the market are being used in industry and in educational institutions to support managerial decision making and research. They contain statistical tests and models that may be included in the model base of a DSS. A major dilemma faced by a nonexpert user is to determine which statistical models to use for what purposes. This is where BUMP is brought into action. This ES selects the appropriate statistical procedure and guides the novice user in using the not-so-friendly statistical packages that usually require a trained statistician for operation.

Several commercial systems are available on the market to assist with statistical analysis. Statistical Navigator (Idea Works, Inc.) is an expert system that helps the user select an appropriate statistical analysis from a pool of over 130 routines available in packages such as SPSS, SAS, and SYSTAT. The program does not execute the analysis, but it supplements existing statistical packages. If several routines can do the job, Statistical Navigator ranks them by suitability. The program is built with the EXSYS shell.

15.5   Intelligent Human-Machine Interfaces

If expert systems and natural language processors are integrated with the human-machine interface subsystem, the human-machine dialogue is conducted faster and better. Currently, expert systems are being used as front-ends to many application and development software packages. For example, Conversational Advisory System serves as a front-end to several DBMS products, and CLOUT is used as a front-end to R:BASE 5000. For details on this role of ES see Harris [22], Isshikawa [28], Shafer [51], and Chapters 8 and 14 of this book.

In previous sections we discussed the benefits of integrating ES with the three components of a DSS. These benefits are summarized in Table 15.2, together with the benefits from an overall system integration. In the forthcoming section, we will introduce several models of ES and DSS integration.

15.6   Models of ES and DSS Integration

Several researchers and practitioners have proposed models for integrating expert systems and decision support systems. The following models are described in this chapter: expert systems attached to DSS components, ES as a separate DSS component, ES generating alternative solutions for DSSs, and a unified approach.

Expert Systems Attached to DSS Components

Expert systems can be integrated into all DSS components. This arrangement (according to Turban and Watkins [59]) is shown in Figure 15.5. It includes five expert systems:

- □ ES #1: Database intelligent component
- □ ES #2: Intelligent agent for the model base and its management
- □ ES #3: System for improving the user interface
- □ ES #4: Consultant to DSS builders. In addition to giving advice on constructing the various components of the DSS, this ES gives advice on how to structure a DSS, how to glue the various parts together, how to conduct a feasibility study, and how to execute the many activities that are involved in the construction of a DSS.

TABLE 15.2 Benefits of Integrating Expert Systems and Decision Support Systems

DSS Component	ES Contribution
Database and database management systems	Improves construction, operation, and maintenance of DBMS [29] Improves accessibility to large databases Improves DBMS capabilities [29] Permits symbolic representation of data
Models and model base management systems	Improves model management [12] Helps in selecting models [20, 21] Provides judgmental elements to models Improves sensitivity analysis [20] Generates alternative solutions [46] Provides heuristics [24] Simplifies building simulation models Makes the problem structure incrementally modifiable
Interface	Enables friendlier interface [22, 29] Provides terms familiar to user [24] Acts as a tutor [20] Provides interactive, dynamic, visual problem-solving capability [5]
System capabilities (synergy)	Provides intelligent advice (faster and cheaper than human) to the DSS or its user Adds explanation capability [24] Expands computerization of the decision-making process [20]

☐ ES #5: Consultant to users. The user of a DSS may need the advice of an expert for complex issues such as the nature of the problem, the environmental conditions, or possible implementation problems. A user also may want an ES that will guide him or her in how to use the DSS and its output.

In many cases, not all five systems are operational. Frequently it is beneficial to attach only one or two expert systems.

ES as a Separate DSS Component

According to this proposal (Turban and Watkins [59]), an ES is added as a separate component. In Figure 15.6 notice that the systems share the interface as well as other resources. However, as indicated by King [35], such an

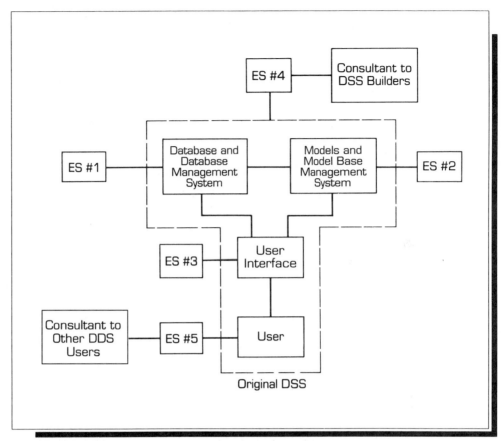

FIGURE 15.5 Integration of ES into All DSS Components

integration is also available via a communication link (networking, as discussed in section 15.1). There are three possibilities for such an integration.

ES Output as Input to a DSS. DSS users may direct the ES output to the DSS. For example, the ES is used during the initial phase of problem solving to determine the importance of the problem or to identify the problem. Then the problem is transferred to a DSS for possible solution. For an example see Courtney et al. [10].

DSS Output as Input to ES. In many cases, the results of computerized quantitative analysis provided by a DSS are forwarded to an individual or a group of experts for the purpose of interpretation. Therefore, it would make sense to direct the output of a DSS into an ES that would perform the same function as an expert, whenever it is cheaper and/or faster to do so (especially if the quality of the advice is also superior). An example is a postoptimality analysis of results provided by optimization models (see Lee and Lee [38]).

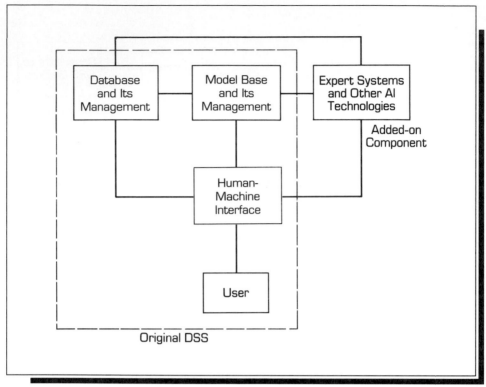

FIGURE 15.6 ES as a Separate Component of a DSS

Feedback. According to this configuration, the output from the ES goes to a DSS, and then the output from the DSS goes back to the original ES (or to another ES).

The three possibilities are illustrated in Figure 15.7.

Generating Alternative Solutions

Reitman [46] points out that most current decision support systems help users evaluate and choose among potential courses of action. Unlike a staff assistant, however, these systems cannot suggest the alternative courses of action that should be considered. He contends that this deficiency might be met by applying concepts and techniques taken from artificial intelligence.

Reitman describes an AI system that plays a game called *Go*. This system is able to work with nonnumeric data to develop alternative game strategies, evaluate them, and select the best alternative. He provides a detailed description of the strategies employed by the system to find or develop courses of action:

  ▫ Use of a network of experts at various levels of complexity of the game
  ▫ Successful refinement of problems from general to specific

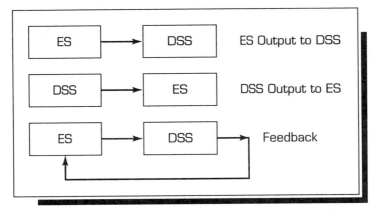

FIGURE 15.7 Interface Possibilities between Expert Systems and Decision Support Systems

□ Assignment of priorities to situations
□ Use of an "expert and critic" structure

Reitman demonstrates how the system tests alternatives and how it limits a search to keep the solution to a manageable task.

After describing the *Go* system, Reitman considers how AI-based DSSs might be transferred to systems in a business context. For example, decisions regarding trading futures of commodities appear to be roughly of the same order of complexity as existing AI applications; therefore, they appear to be a promising place to begin exploring the practical use of AI-based DSSs.

A Unified Approach

Teng et al. [57] have proposed a unified architecture for ES and DSS integration. The proposal is shown in Figure 15.8. According to this proposal, the ES is placed between the data and the models. Its basic function is to integrate the two components in an intelligent manner.

15.7 Integrating Management Support Technologies

Expert systems and natural language processors are used extensively in support of managerial decision making. In fact, expert systems are frequently referred to as expert support systems. Therefore, it is logical to configure AI technologies, and especially ES, with other managerial support systems such as a decision support system and executive information system.

Integration of the various management support tools can be explored best by viewing the support given by such a system. The major aim of integrated

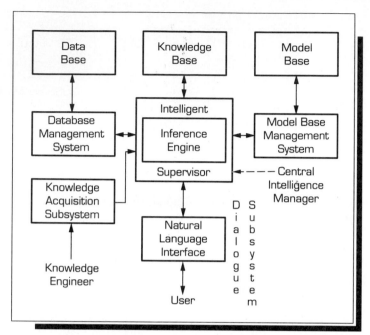

FIGURE 15.8   Unified Architecture for an Intelligent Decision Support System (*Source:* J. T. C. Cheng, et al., "A Unified Architecture for Intelligent DSS," in *Proceedings, 21st HICSS*, Hawaii, January 1988.)

management support is provision of intelligent capabilities by using expert systems.

Figure 15.9 shows the integration of ES in supporting a typical managerial process. It presents the potential use of seven different expert systems; their areas of application are marked from ES 1 to ES 7.

ES 1. The system can help in the design of the flow of information to managers (e.g., what data to monitor and when) and in the *interpretation* of the collected information. Because some of the information is fuzzy, a combination of ES, fuzzy logic, and neural computing can be very helpful. The entire area of scanning, monitoring, forecasting (e.g., trends), and assessment (or interpretation) can be helped considerably by automation in general (e.g., electronic mail) and by ES in particular. The use of ES with external databases was discussed in section 15.3. The expert system can be supported by several natural language processing devices such as summarization of news, understanding of messages, and translation of foreign languages.

ES 2. Based on the information collected, a problem (opportunity) is identified. Expert systems can play an important role in this step in supporting the manager (e.g., see King [35]) and in helping with a precise definition of the problem (e.g., see Courtney et al. [10]).

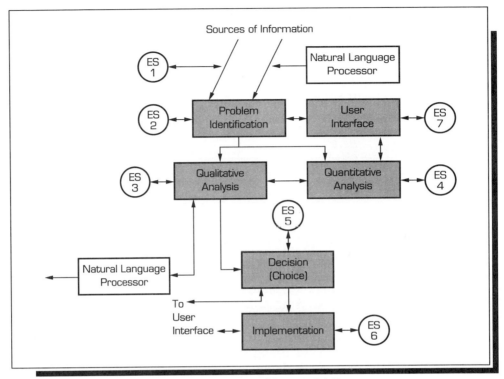

FIGURE 15.9 Expert System Support of the Managerial Process

ES 3. Qualitative analysis is based on the use of expertise. Here, experts can be replaced with expert systems (with a substantial saving of time and money). For example, an ES can give advice on legal or tax issues that relate to the problem. Another possible use of ES at this time is for supporting qualitative forecasting methods.

ES 4. The support of ES for quantitative analysis was discussed in detail in section 15.4. Of special importance is the capability of explaining the results of the analysis. The analysis may be executed by staff analysts.

ES 5. A final choice of an alternative can be made by an individual or by a group. Both may need interpretation of information generated during the analysis and execution of additional predictions. These are two typical generic categories of ES. However, the decision makers can also use the ES to help in developing the final design and planning (including an implementation plan) of the proposed action. The role of ES in decisions made by groups (e.g., in a group decision support system, or GDSS) can be extremely important; at present, we have little information about this topic (see discussion by Agarwal and Prasad [1]).

ES 6. Expert systems have been found to be very helpful in increasing the chances of successful implementation. Major benefits could be in the areas of explanation and training.

ES 7. A superb user interface is a key to successful implementation of any management support system. Expert systems can improve the interface, especially when they are combined with natural language processors.

15.8   Links with Other Computer-based Information Systems

AI applications may be linked with others of the same kind. Expert systems may "talk" to each other much like experts do. One ES may feed into another one or provide data to a powerful linear programming package that conducts optimization and returns the result to the ES for evaluation.

An important integration takes place under what is described as computer-integrated manufacturing (CIM). CIM is composed of several computer programs that are used to plan and control different machines, materials handling facilities, robots, and other components. An expert system, for example, can be used to execute production planning in conjunction with some DSS. The planning will attempt to coordinate all activities of the plant, to achieve efficiency in the use of resources, to maximize productivity, to meet delivery dates, and so forth.

Another application of ES is in the area of error recovery. An automated factory is monitored by several sensors and other detecting devices. Any interruption can be detected and interpreted (as was shown in Chapter 11 on robotics).

Various AI systems have been connected to computer-aided design/computer-aided manufacturing (CAD/CAM) systems, sensory systems, materials handling, maintenance, quality control, assembly, and several manufacturing applications software. For further information see Kusiak [37], Mellichamp [40], and Siegel [52]. A comprehensive CIM system is shown in Figure 15.10 and explained in Table 15.3.

15.9   Problems and Issues in Integration

Many factors should be considered when AI systems are integrated. This section describes some of the most important problems and issues.

Need for Integration. Integration may or may not be desirable. A comprehensive *feasibility* study is essential. Technological, economical, organizational, and behavioral aspects need to be analyzed.

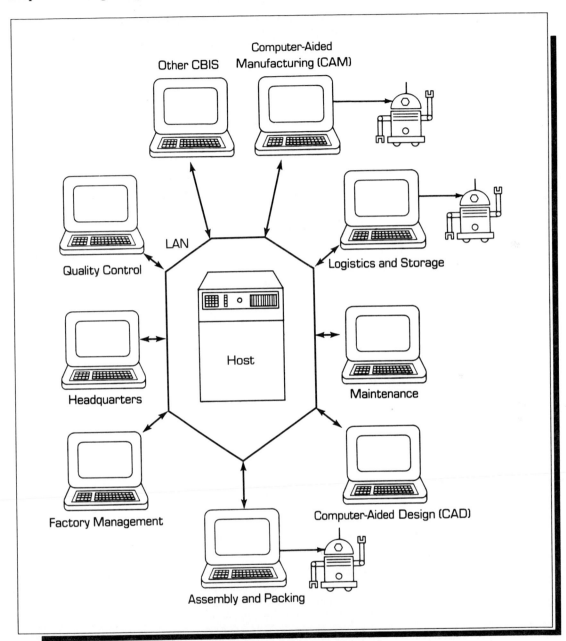

FIGURE 15.10   Computer-integrated Manufacturing in the Factory of the Future

TABLE 15.3 Role of Artificial Intelligence and Decision Support Systems in Computer-integrated Manufacturing—the Factory of the Future

Function Aided by Computers	Description	Supported by			
		ES	NLP	Robots	DSS
Assembly and packaging	Uses robots to put together parts fabricated on site and purchased from outside. Packages ready for shipment.	X	X	X	X
Design (CAD)	Creates a design for a product.	X			
Engineering	Designs the tools, molds, and other facilities needed for manufacturing.	X			
Factory management	Runs the entire production process, coordinates incoming orders, requests components and material, plans and schedules, oversees cost control, arranges deliveries.	X	X		X
Headquarters	Decides what products to make, when, and how much (based on market research, available resources, and strategic planning).	X	X		X
Logistics and storage	Purchases and distributes materials, handles inventory control, removes materials, manages supplies. Shuttles incoming materials and parts, work in process, and final products.	X		X	X
Maintenance	Monitors equipment and processes, makes adjustments when needed, takes care of emergency breakdowns, diagnoses faults, does preventive and corrective maintenance.	X	X	X	
Manufacturing (CAM)	Fabricates metals, plastics, and other materials by molding, machining, welding, etc.	X		X	
Quality control	Tests incoming materials and outgoing products, tests processes in progress, assures quality.	X	X	X	

Architecture of Integration. Several alternatives are available for executing the integration. Each of these options has some benefits as well as costs and limitations. A careful analysis should be undertaken before the integration.

Justification and Cost-Benefit Analysis. While integrated systems have many benefits, they also obviously have costs. Making a computer system more intelligent is a novel idea, but someone will have to pay the bill. This issue is very important today since many people are questioning the economics of computerized systems and their alignment with organizational goals.

Peoples' Problems. The integration of AI tools with conventional computerized systems brings together two different styles: the heuristic-judgmental and the algorithmic-analytical. This combination will certainly mean a change to many people. Builders and other users who are used to working with conventional tools and applications will be asked to be engaged with symbolic processing. How will these people be affected? How will the analytical-type individual react to a heuristic approach? And how will the AI people handle the "burden" of an added structured analysis? Combining the two approaches may not be simple. For example, what if there are preferences for different user-interface modes? These are just some of the questions that need to be answered.

Finding Appropriate Builders. Finding skilled programmers who can work with both AI technologies and conventional computer systems can be a major task, especially if complex systems are involved. Frequently, use of vendors and/or consultants is the only solution. Many companies subcontract most system integration jobs—a very expensive solution.

Attitudes of Information Systems People. Some information systems professionals have not taken AI seriously, just like they did not take microcomputers seriously for a long time. They are reluctant to learn about these new technologies. They should understand, however, that AI is a valuable supplement to conventional tools and applications, *not* a substitute for them.

Part of the problem is cultural. The analysis, design, knowledge acquisition, testing, and debugging of AI are much more difficult and time consuming than the coding itself. The professionals can learn the coding rather fast, but they sometimes do not have the energy to learn all the other activities. Therefore, they depend on AI experts and may reject opportunities to use AI.

Development Process. The development process of many CBIS projects follows a sequential life-cycle approach. In contrast, expert systems are prototyped. When the two are combined, a problem of being "out of phase" may be created; that is, the CBIS project may not be ready for the AI for a long time, and then, when it is ready, the AI process may slow down the CBIS project due to the needed prototyping.

Organizational Impacts. One of the biggest impacts of AI could be on the director of information systems. This director needs AI to better manage conventional CBIS applications. AI could enhance the director's productivity. The manner in which the director will react to such an opportunity, and the implications on structure, job description, and power distribution within the information systems organization as well as within the entire corporation, need to be considered and researched.

Data Structure Issues. AI applications are centered around symbolic processing, whereas CBIS projects are built around numeric processing. When these systems are integrated, data will have to flow from one environment to a different one. Databases are structured quite differently from knowledge bases (e.g., see Rauch-Hindin [45]). In a knowledge base, procedural information and declarative information are separated, whereas in a database everything is combined. Another mismatch is that AI technologies use object-oriented programming in an accelerated rate. Object-oriented databases are just beginning to appear. It is easy to develop a conceptual system with a database and knowledge base and show that the two are interconnected. But somewhere a translation is needed. Who will do it and how?

Data Issues. Several AI applications, especially expert systems, can absorb heterogeneous, partially inconsistent, and incomplete data of different dimensions and accuracy. Traditional CBIS applications cannot operate with this kind of input data. When using, for example, an ES as a front-end to a database, the incomplete data must be organized and prepared according to the input requirement of the database. The same is true when the traditional CBIS output is inputted into an ES.

Connectivity. AI applications, as we have seen, may be programmed with LISP, PROLOG, ES shells, or special knowledge engineering tools, or with a combination of them. The shells may be written in C, FORTRAN, or Pascal, but not necessarily in the *same* language that was used to write the CBIS application that is being integrated with the AI part. Another problem is that although some AI tool vendors provide interfaces to DBMSs, spreadsheets, and so on, these interfaces may not be easy to work with. Furthermore, they may be expensive and will have to be updated constantly (see Pederson [44]).

It is also important to realize that most ES do not make CBIS techniques more "intelligent" or "smarter." They make them more efficient or effective. Systems are also integrated because the integration makes them more friendly.

Integrating ES in CBIS projects is a challenge and an opportunity. It is a challenge because to succeed we must overcome many of the difficulties we just discussed. It is an opportunity because if integration is implemented successfully, it can greatly increase the boundaries of a CBIS, thereby making it more widely applied, more respectable, and more profitable.

15.10 Examples of Integrated Systems

Manufacturing

Integrated Manufacturing System. A system called Logistics Management System (LMS) was developed by IBM for operations management (see Sullivan and Fordyce [54]). The system combines expert systems, simulation, and decision support systems. In addition, the system includes computer-aided manufacturing and distributed data processing subsystems. It provides plant manufacturing management a tool to assist it in resolving crises and help in planning. A similar system is used at IBM by financial analysts to simulate long-range financial planning; an ES provides judgmental information and other pertinent factors.

DSS/Decision Simulation (DSIM). DSIM (IBM) is the outcome of combining decision support systems, statistics, operations research, database management, query languages, and artificial intelligence (see Sullivan and Fordyce [54]). AI, especially natural language interfaces and expert systems, provides three things to DSIM:

1. Ease of communication of pertinent information to the computational algorithm or display unit
2. Assistance in finding the appropriate model, computational algorithm, or data set
3. A solution to a problem where the computational algorithm(s) alone is not sufficient to solve the problem, a computational algorithm is not appropriate or applicable, and/or the AI creates the computational algorithm.

Marketing

Promoter. This ES analyzes the effects of promotions and advertisements on sales in the packaged goods industry. It was developed by Management Decision Systems, Inc., and it must be used together with the company's mainframe DSS development tools.

TeleStream. This ES developed by Texas Instruments supports salespersons who work in distributed centers that are selling thousands of products. The system has two parts: Sales Advisor and Sales Assistant. The Sales Advisor tells the salesperson what to offer to the customer. It also describes accessories and supplies. The DSS part attempts to maximize management goals (such as profits and low inventories). The Sales Assistant is an interface that determines the content of the information to be presented to the user and the method of presentation. For details see [2].

Engineering

An integrated system was designed to boost engineers' productivity at Boeing. The DSS portion, called STRUDL (for structured design language), is essentially a passive tool whose effectiveness depends on the user's abilities. By supplying the proper data into the formula or the graphic modeling application, a design engineer can gain insight into the potential of his or her design prototype. Unfortunately, STRUDL cannot help the engineer decide what questions to ask or what data to key in, nor can it give any hints about further actions to take based on the results of analysis. However, an expert system that assumes the role of teacher/partner was added on to do all this.

Financial Services

A large financial services company (see Scott-Morton [50]) uses an integrated system to match its various services with individual customers' needs (e.g., placing a customer's assets into optimal investment packages). Similar applications are being actively developed by large international accounting firms for combining analytical methods and judgment in auditing, and by other business entities for credit evaluation, strategic planning, and related applications. General Dynamic Corp., for example, is using expert systems to support project management analysis.

FINEXPERT[1] is an intelligent system designed to produce financial reports and analyses of corporations. It was developed in France by EXPERTeam in cooperation with Texas Instruments. Linked to a company's standard accounting system, the ES can produce all the standard financial reports and fifty different charts. Then it performs a financial analysis that includes financial activity, ratio analysis, risk analysis, profitability, and financial equilibrium. Its report satisfies the U.S. Securities and Exchange Commission's requirements for publicly held corporations. The system can run simulations and forecasting models, and a sophisticated explanation facility is available. The system is marketed worldwide as a ready-made system. For further details see [2].

Retailing

Buyer's Workbench. In retailing, especially in the supermarket industry with its typically small profit margins, the ability to draw on the experience of senior buyers is a key factor in a company's success. Because of the thousands of items that must be tracked for pricing, inventory, and other reasons, buying is often a reactive process. The implementation of an expert system running in tandem with mainframe databases can be an effective tool in changing the process into a proactive one.

A system called Buyer's Workbench[1] was developed by Deloitte and Touche for Associated Grocers (a supermarket chain in the Northwest). A buyer interacts with the knowledge base via an SQL windows/Microsoft Windows interface. The interface is used to select items that are candidates for action; it also retrieves the data from mainframe databases and analyzes it using an expert system. The expert system contains a large rule base of expert knowledge (obtained from senior buyers) about consumer preferences, vendor characteristics, seasonality, and a variety of other factors (Figure 15.11). The expert system then communicates the results of the analysis to the user via a user interface window.

---

[1]Based on material provided by Neuron Data, Inc. and by [3].

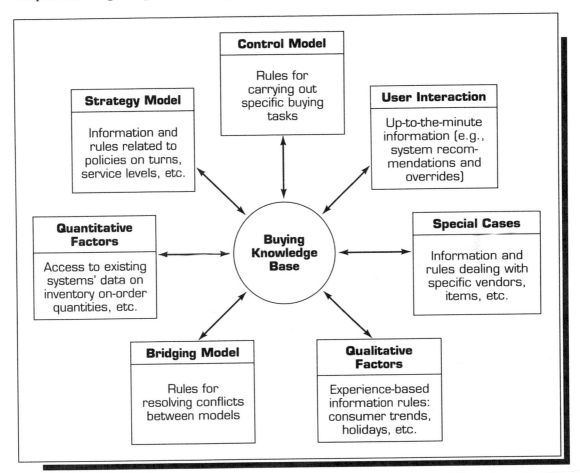

FIGURE 15.11 Categories of Knowledge in Expert System That Is Part of Buyer's Workbench (*Source: AI Topics*, August 1989 [Deloitte and Touche].)

The Buyer's Workbench takes advantage of the division of functionality inherent in a client-server architecture. The user interface runs on the client machine and the server contains the knowledge base, which is then linked to the mainframe database. Communication between the client and the server is handled via Microsoft Windows' DDE (dynamic data exchange). The technical architecture of the system, which is built around Nexpert Object, is shown in Figure 15.12. The client-server model allows flexibility on the client's side by permitting new applications to be integrated via the user interface. Also, the portable nature of the expert system allows the system to be scaled or redeployed to a remote server. In this way, the knowledge base can be expanded without sacrificing connectivity.

Expert systems working in tandem with *relational* databases can provide important capabilities for more efficient application of knowledge to other computer-based information systems.

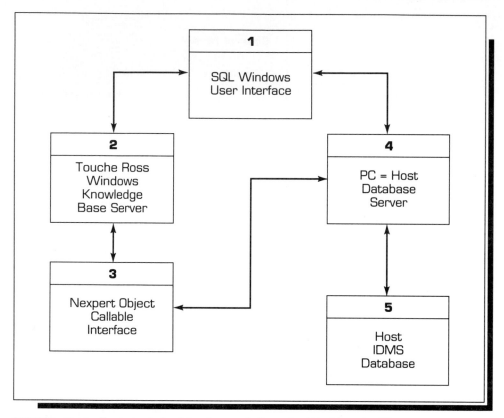

FIGURE 15.12 Technical Architecture of Buyer's Workbench (*Source: AI Topics*, August 1989 [Deloitte and Touche].)

Commodity Trading

Intelligent Commodities Trading System (ICTS), developed by Fusion Group, integrates the capabilities of expert systems, neural networks, and relational databases in a distributed environment. By examining a set of broad market indicators, the system can make trading recommendations, or optionally execute trades based on its own findings. The indicators watched include rising and falling volume, price movements, and market trends. The rule base applies analytics appropriate to the market situation as characterized by the computed parameters. The analytics employed include moving averages, regression analysis, and probabilities (risk analysis). The neural network is used to perform pattern recognition to forecast price velocity and direction.

ICTS uses Nexpert Object for rule-based processing, the Sybase package for database manipulations, and ANZA Plus as a neurocomputing coprocessor. It also uses Fusion's own Market Data Server to distribute real-time market data. ICTS is designed to run across a variety of UNIX workstations; the current

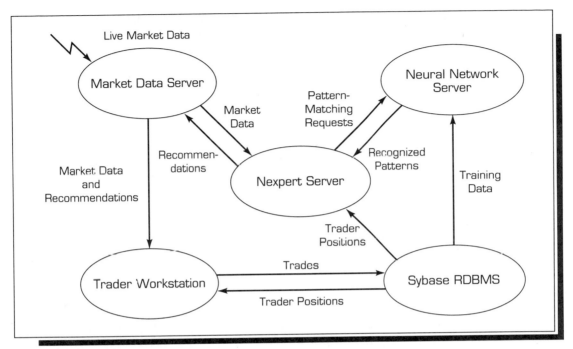

FIGURE 15.13 Data Flow for the Intelligent Commodities Trading System (ICTS) (*Source*: Courtesy of Neuron Data Inc.)

implementation employs hardware from Sun Microsystems Corp., Digital Equipment Corp., Pyramid Technology, and Sony—all connected via a local area network.

Fusion has also developed an interface library to allow the neurocomputing hardware to communicate with the powerful Sybase relational database manager. This interface uses the Sybase Open Server product, which allows an application to respond to the Sybase networking protocol. This allows Nexpert Object to communicate with the ANZA board without additional programming. The data flow diagram for this system is shown in Figure 15.13.

Maintenance

Pacific Gas and Electric (PG&E) has implemented an expert system titled RARE (for repair and replacement) as an aid to planning welding repairs for its Diablo Canyon nuclear reactor complex.[2] RARE is an engineering aid for plant personnel who must keep track of the multitude of piping systems that are at the heart of any nuclear facility.

---

[2]Based on material provided by Neuron Data, Inc.

Periodic examination of welds using nondestructive techniques generates a large volume of data stored in a database that must be accurately tracked to maintain the safety of the facility. The requirements mandated by a wide set of safety codes made the matter of assembling a knowledge base a critical task. The RARE system stores the knowledge from the safety codes and also knowledge from experts, and it allows expert system software to query the database for applicable knowledge and present it to the engineer-users. There are many different methods of welding and a correspondingly large bank of procedures that must be followed for examination and certification of the weld repairs after the job has been completed.

Before RARE was implemented, the procedure for weld requirements was that a site engineer determined what needed to be accomplished and then called experts in San Francisco who went through a manual process of selecting the repair methods and quality requirements. By computerizing this knowledge, PG&E leveraged the existing knowledge of experts and made it available online to site engineers.

Fifth-generation Project

The efforts of the **Fifth-generation Project** can be used as an example of the movement toward integrating AI with conventional computing. Figure 15.14 presents the conceptual diagram of the software system envisioned by the Japanese. The key elements of the system are the knowledge base and its management system, which would enhance the database, model base, and the DBMS of a conventional CBIS. The problem-solving inference system would be the ES aspect, and the intelligent interface system would encompass a natural language interface. In addition, intelligent systemization and utility systems would be developed. The basic application system would then interface with the rest of the components much like a current CBIS. (See Bishop [6].)

Table 15.4 shows some of the major constituents of a fifth-generation system. Central to the problem-solving and inference system is the core language (a PROLOG derivative). It is also used to write much of the software for the knowledge-based system and the intelligent interface system.

Expert systems are related to the Fifth-generation Project in two ways. First, expert systems are viewed as a major application of the new computers, which are intended to tackle a range of nonnumeric processing tasks presently untouched by computers. The new architecture and faster processing speeds will allow much more sophisticated expert systems to be built and will offer researchers ways of solving some of the more difficult problems inherent in the technology. (For further discussion see Johnson [30].)

The second aspect of the relationship between the Fifth-generation Project and expert systems is that expert systems will be an integral part of the new computers. The hardware will be so complicated that it will be impossible for ordinary users to make the best use of it. The users' interface with the computer will be guided by an expert system (or several expert systems), probably using a natural language interface.

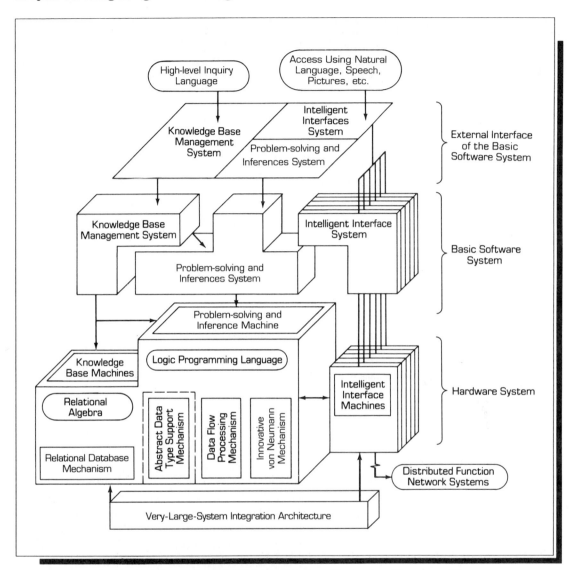

FIGURE 15.14 Basic Configuration of Fifth-generation Computer Systems (*Source:* Japan Information Processing Development Center)

15.11 Integration of Tools

Building an integrated, intelligent CBIS can be greatly facilitated by the use of integrated development tools, that is, tools that provide easy interfaces to other tools (such as databases, graphics, and spreadsheets). The hybrid tools discussed in Chapter 13 are typical examples. Many ES development tools offer interfaces

TABLE 15.4 Components of a Fifth-generation System

	Knowledge Base Management System	Problem-solving and Inference System	Intelligent Interface System
External interface to basic software	High-level inquiry language	Core language (PROLOG derivative)	Natural language, speech, pictures, etc.
Basic software	Knowledge representation language	Intelligent programming system	Intelligent parser and meaning analyzer
	Knowledge base support system	Meta-inference system	Continuous speech recognizer
	Knowledge acquisition system	Distributed problem solving	Picture processing system
	External knowledge bases		
Hardware	Relational database machine	Data flow machine	Image processing machine
	Parallel relational operations	Abstract data-type mechanism	Speech processing machine
		Parallel inference mechanism	

Source: M. Van Horn, *Understanding Expert Systems* (Toronto: Bantam, 1986).

to spreadsheets, databases, hypertext technology, graphics, word processing, and the like. Some of them have a natural language interface (e.g., Guru; for details see Rauch-Hindin [45]). Nexpert Object has extensive interfaces with many databases and decision support tools, for example, spreadsheets, communication networks, and database management systems. VP Expert and EXSYS also include a few interfaces. Finally, Level5 Object is fully integrated with a sophisticated DBMS (FOCUS), and it has many interfaces and capabilities (see Table 15.5).

Built-in interfaces allow the user operations such as the following (in a rule-based system):

- The premise of any rule can directly reference database fields, spreadsheet cells, statistical variables, and so forth.
- The conclusion of any rule can involve DBMS operations, SQL queries, spreadsheet operations, graphics, and so on.
- A rule set can consult other rule sets, examine databases, do statistical analysis, and execute procedural models.

TABLE 15.5 Capabilities of Level5 Object

Complete ES Development Environment

Visual programming environment to enhance knowledge engineering

Automatic code generators for ease of use

Hybrid knowledge representation and multiple inferencing strategies with forward, backward, and mixed chaining in the same knowledge base

SAA-compliant graphical user interface with windows, pull-down menus, dialogue boxes, radio buttons, check boxes, and more

Enhanced reporting tools in a symbolic debugging environment for easy trace and line-of-reasoning analysis (explanation)

Support for complex pattern matching, dynamic agendas, and other inferencing and interface methods

Connectivity

Direct data access and complete JOINing facility for major file types:

IBM Mainframe: FOCUS, DB2, SQL/DS, VSAM, IMS, flat files

DEC VAX: FOCUS, Rdb, RMS/CDD Plus, RS/1, Oracle, flat files

IBM PC: FOCUS, dBASE, Lotus, SQL Server, ASCII

UNIX: FOCUS, Oracle, flat files

Macintosh: Excel, Foxbase, dBASE/Mac, HyperCard, TDF

Portability

Flexible development and deployment options with application portability between environments today: IBM mainframe—MVS and VM; DEC/VAX—VMS; PC—PC-DOS, MS-DOS, OS/2; UNIX; Macintosh

FOCUS Integration

FOCUS is a 4GL/DBMS for application development and decision management across mainframe, mini, and microcomputer platforms.

Level5 for FOCUS is inference-based technology embedded directly in FOCUS.

Level5 provides added value to FOCUS in the form of intelligent query, data validation, and powerful inference-based logic processing and management.

Direct database interfaces to FOCUS give LEVEL5 users additional data access.

Total Object-oriented Environment

Object-oriented programming provides maximum flexibility and versatility.

Object-oriented database management simplifies handling of complex data structures.

Inheritance

Built-in System Classes facilitate rapid prototyping and application development—all new with Level5 Object.

Attributes of System Class instances can be edited to create custom instances quickly and easily.

Window-driven editor subsystem simplifies development of powerful data structures (objects, classes, instances, facets, and methods).

Ease of Use

Easy learning curve is provided through Rule Talk, the sophisticated knowledge-engineering toolbox.

Automatic facilities import standard PRL (Production Rule Language) code into object-oriented knowledge bases.

System Classes provide a rich array of built-in logic and object tools.

Customized support is provided for end users through system-wide help facilities and hyperregions.

Source: Adapted from brochure for Level5, Information Builders, Inc., New York.

□ Any spreadsheet cell can be defined in terms of ES consultation.
□ The conclusion of any rule can involve serial communication by dialing a remote database or by downloading data from data tables. Such transactions are invoked by very short commands.

Chapter Highlights

□ When AI technology is integrated with conventional computer-based information systems, the functionality of the latter is increased.
□ Functional integration differs from the physical integration that is required to accomplish it.
□ Integration can be achieved by three types of access methods: single processor, multiprocessor, and networking. Alternatively, integration can be embedded.
□ An embedded system appears to the user as a single application.
□ Another view of integration distinguishes between loosely coupled and tightly coupled systems, intelligent interfaces, and expert command languages.
□ The major area of integration is that of databases (and database management systems) with expert systems and natural language processors. The result is intelligent databases.
□ Expert systems can be used to simplify accessibility to databases, either corporate or commercial (online).
□ The second major area of integration is the use of expert systems to interpret results of data generated by models, particularly quantitative models.
□ Expert systems can be used to enhance knowledge management and model management.
□ Expert systems are being successfully integrated with decision support systems; the result is many useful applications.
□ Several conceptual models of integration are applicable to expert systems and decision support systems.
□ Natural language processors, expert systems, and neural computing can be integrated to improve the human-machine interface.
□ AI technologies are being integrated with many computer-based information systems, ranging from CAD/CAM to office automation.
□ Many problems exist with respect to the integration of AI technology. They include technical, behavioral, and managerial factors.
□ The fifth-generation computer system is the most publicized example of integrating AI technologies with conventional computer-based information systems.
□ Several development tools are available to support the construction of AI-integrated applications; well-publicized examples are Guru and Nexpert Object.

Key Terms

embedded system	intelligent knowledge	loose coupling
Fifth-generation Project	management	physical integration
functional integration	intelligent model	tight coupling
intelligent database	management	
intelligent interface		

Questions for Review

1. What is the difference between functional and physical integration?
2. Describe an embedded system.
3. What is the difference between embedded and access integration?
4. DSS and ES integration may result in benefits along what three dimensions?
5. It is said that an ES is an intelligent DSS. Describe their common characteristics. Do you agree with this statement? Why or why not?
6. How can synergy result when decision support systems and expert systems are integrated?
7. What are intelligent databases and why are they so popular?
8. Summarize the benefits a DSS can gain in its database when it is integrated with an ES.
9. How can expert systems enhance knowledge management?
10. Why is an ES needed as an interface to commercial databases?
11. How can the knowledge base of an ES help a DSS?
12. What is model management?
13. Summarize the benefits that an ES can provide to a DSS in the area of models and their management.
14. What is the major capability of BUMP?
15. Summarize the benefits that an ES can provide to a human-machine interface.
16. List various possibilities of integrating decision support systems and expert systems according to the model suggested in Figure 15.6.
17. Give an example of an ES output that can be used as an input to a DSS. Also give an example of the reverse relationship.
18. How can an ES assist in generating alternative courses of action?
19. List some technical issues of integration.
20. List some behavioral issues of integration.
21. List some design issues that may arise during integration.

Questions for Discussion

1. Why may it be difficult to integrate an expert system with an existing information system? Comment on data, people, hardware, and software.

2. Explain this statement and give an example of both cases: Integration of a DSS and an ES can result in benefits during the construction (development) of the systems and during their operation.

3. Compare embedded integration with access integration. What are the major advantages and disadvantages of each?

4. Intelligent databases are considered extremely important. Explain what makes them intelligent and why they are so important.

5. One expert system may be used to consult several decision support systems. What is the logic of such an arrangement? What problems may result when two or more decision support systems share an expert system?

6. Review the work of Goul and associates [20]. Assume they will be successful in developing an ES that will perform as well as a management scientist-consultant. What could be the major implications of such a system? Why is it difficult to build it?

7. Compare the work of Goul and associates with that of Hand [21]. Specifically, what is the major similarity between BUMP and Goul's system?

8. Why is visual problem solving (or visual modeling) considered an integration of decision support systems and expert systems?

9. Explain how the addition of an ES capability can improve the chance of successful implementation of a DSS.

10. Compare Figures 15.5 and 15.6. What are the major differences? What are the similarities? Can Figure 15.6 be viewed as a special case of Figure 15.5? Why or why not?

11. Review current journals and identify a system that you believe is an integration of ES with other AI technologies. Analyze the system according to the models suggested in this chapter.

12. Explain why the Fifth-generation Project is viewed as a DSS and ES integration.

13. There are many potential problems when AI is integrated with a CBIS. Find an example of such a problem in a real-life situation (check the journals if you cannot find one in a workplace) and report your findings.

14. In some of our models we suggested that several ES are included in one CBIS. What is the logic of such an arrangement?

15. Modeling involves three activities: construction, use, and interpretation. Give an example of modeling from an area that you are familiar with and explain how an ES can help the process.

16. How can model management be intelligent?

References and Bibliography

1. Agarwal, R., and Prasad, K. "Enhancing the Group Decision Making Process: An Intelligent Systems Architecture." In *Proceedings, 23rd HICSS*. Hawaii, January 1989.

2. *AI Letter* (June 1958 and April 1989), Texas Instruments.

3. *AI Topics* (August 1989), Deloitte and Touche.

4. Al-Zobaidie, A., and J.B. Grimson. "Expert Systems and Database Systems: How Can They Serve Each Other?" *Expert Systems* (February 1987).

5. Bell, P.C., D.C. Parker, and P. Kirkpatrick. "Visual Interactive Problem Solving—A New Look at Management Problems." *Business Quarterly* (Spring 1984).

6. Bishop, P. *Fifth Generation Computers: Concepts, Implementations, and Uses.* Chichester, England: Ellis Horwood, 1986.

7. Blanning, R.W. "The Application of Artificial Intelligence to Model Management." In *Proceedings, 21st HICSS.* Hawaii, January 1988.

8. Brodie, M.L., and J. Mylpoulos. *On Knowledge Base Management Systems: Integrating Artificial Intelligence and Database Techniques.* New York: Springer-Verlag, 1986.

9. Cohen, B. "Merging Expert Systems and Databases." *AI Expert* (February 1989).

10. Courtney, J.F., Jr., et al. "A Knowledge-based DSS for Managerial Problem Diagnosis." *Decision Sciences* (Summer 1987).

11. Doukidis, G.I. "An Analogy on the Homology of Simulation and Artificial Intelligence." *Journal of the Operational Research Society* (August 1987).

12. Dutta, A., and A. Basu. "AI-Based Model Management in DSS." *Computer* (September 1984).

13. Elam, J.J., and B. Konsynski. "Using AI Techniques to Enhance the Capabilities of Model Management System." *Decision Sciences* (Summer 1987).

14. Fedorowicz, J., and G. Williams. "Representing Modeling Knowledge in an Intelligent Decision Support System." *Decision Support Systems* 2 (no. 1, 1986).

15. Feng-Yang, K. "Combining Expert Systems and the Bayesian Approach to Support Forecasting." In *Proceedings, 21st HICSS.* Hawaii, January 1988.

16. Ford, D.R., and B.J. Schroer. "An Expert Manufacturing Simulation System." *Simulation* (May 1987).

17. Freundlich, Y. "Transfer Pricing—Integrating Expert System in MIS Environment." *IEEE Expert* (February 1990).

18. Gale, W.A. *Artificial Intelligence and Statistics.* Reading, Mass.: Addison-Wesley, 1986.

19. Gallagher, J.P. *Knowledge Systems for Business: Integrating Expert Systems and MIS.* Englewood Cliffs, N.J.: Prentice-Hall, 1988.

20. Goul, M., B. Shane, and F. Tonge. "Designing the Expert Component of a Decision Support System." Paper delivered at the ORSA/TIMS meeting. San Francisco, May 1984.

21. Hand, D.J. "Statistical Expert Systems: Design." *Statistician* 33 (October 1984):351–369.

22. Harris, L.R. "The Natural-language Connection; An AI Note." *Information Center* (April 1987).

23. Hawkins, D.T. "Applications of AI and Expert Systems for Online Searching." *Online* (January 1988).

24. Hayes-Roth, F., D. Waterman, and D. Lenat. *Building Expert Systems.* Reading, Mass.: Addison-Wesley, 1983.
25. Hosley, W.N. "The Application of Artificial Intelligence Software to Project Management." *Project Management Journal* (August 1987).
26. Hossein, J., et al. "Stochastic Queuing Systems, An AI Approach." In *1987 DSI Proceedings.*
27. Hsu, C., and C. Skevington. "Integration of Data and Knowledge in Manufacturing Enterprises; A Conceptual Framework." *Journal of Manufacturing Systems* 6 (April 1987).
28. Isshikawa, H. "KID, Knowledge-based Natural Language Interface for Accessing Database Systems." *IEEE Expert* (Summer 1987).
29. Jarke, M., and Y. Vassiliou. "Coupling Expert Systems with Database Management Systems." In *Artificial Intelligence Applications for Business,* W. Reitman, ed. Norwood, N.J.: Ablex Publishing Corp., 1984.
30. Johnson, R.C. "Japan's AI Computer: The Fifth Generation?" *PC AI* 3 (May/June 1989):54–55.
31. Kehoe, C.A. "Interfaces and Expert Systems for Online Retrieval." *Online Review* (December 1985).
32. Kennedy, A.J., and D.C. Yen. "Enhancing a DBMS Through the Use of Expert Systems." *Journal of Information Systems Management* (Spring 1990).
33. Kerschberg, L., ed. *Expert Database Systems.* Menlo Park, Calif.: Benjamin-Cummings, 1987.
34. Keyes, J. "Expert Systems and Corporate Databases." *AI Expert* (May 1989).
35. King, D. "Intelligent Decision Support: Strategies for Integrating Decision Support, Database Management, and Expert System Technologies." *Expert Systems with Applications* 1 (no. 1, 1990).
36. Kumar, S., and H. Cheng. "An Expert System Framework for Forecasting Method Selection." In *Proceedings, 21st HICSS.* Hawaii, January 1988.
37. Kusiak, A., ed. *Artificial Intelligence, Implication for CIM, IFS.* New York: Springer-Verlag, 1988.
38. Lee, L.K., and H.G. Lee. "Integration of Strategic Planning and Short-term Planning: An Intelligent DSS Approach by the Post Model Analysis Approach." *Decision Support Systems* (1988).
39. Liang, T. "Development of a Knowledge-based Model Management System." *Operations Research* (November-December 1988).
40. Mellichamp, J.H. "An Expert System for FMS Design." *Simulation* (May 1987).
41. Murphy, F., and E. Stohr. "An Intelligent Support for Formulating Linear Programming." *Decision Support Systems* 2 (no. 1, 1986).
42. Newman, W.M. *Designing Integrated Systems for the Office Environment.* New York: McGraw-Hill, 1987.
43. Parsaye, K., et al. *Intelligent Database: Object-Oriented Deductive Hypermedia Technologies.* New York: John Wiley & Sons, 1989.
44. Pederson, K. "Connecting Expert Systems and Conventional Programming." *AI Expert* (May 1988).

45. Rauch-Hindin, W. "Software Integrates AI, Standard Systems." *Mini-Micro Systems* (October 1986).

46. Reitman, W. "Applying Artificial Intelligence to Decision Support." In *Decision Support Systems*, M.J. Ginzberg, W. Reigman, and E. Stohr, eds. Amsterdam: North Holland, 1982.

47. Risch, T., et al. "A Functional Approach to Integrating Database and Expert-Systems." *Communications of ACM* 31 (1989).

48. Sathi, A., et al. "CALLISTO: An Intelligent Project Management System." *AI Magazine* (Winter 1986).

49. Schur, S. "Intelligent Databases." *Database Programming and Design* (June 1988).

50. Scott-Morton, M. "Expert Decision Support Systems." Paper presented in a special DSS conference, Planning Executive Institute and Information Technology Institute. New York, May 21–22, 1984.

51. Shafer, D. *Designing Intelligent Front Ends for Business Software.* New York: John Wiley & Sons, 1989. (Also see *PC AI*, July/August 1990.)

52. Siegel, D.L. "Integrating Expert Systems for Manufacturing." *AI Magazine* (Supplement, Summer 1990).

53. Simos, M.A. "Knowledge-based Systems and Software Engineering: Toward a More Perfect Union." *Expert Systems* (Fall 1989).

54. Sullivan, G., and K. Fordyce. *Decision Simulations, One Outcome of Combining AI and DSS.* Working paper no. 42-395. Poughkeepsie, N.Y.: IBM Corp. 1984.

55. Sullivan, G., and K. Fordyce. "The Role of Artificial Intelligence in Decision Support Systems." Paper delivered at the International Meeting of TIMS. Copenhagen, June 1985.

56. Tannenbaum, A. "Installing AI Tools into Corporate Environments." *AI Expert* (May 1990).

57. Teng, J.T.C., et al. "A Unified Architecture for Intelligent DSS." In *Proceedings, 21st HICSS.* Hawaii, January 1988.

58. Turban, E., and R. Trippi. "Integrating Expert Systems and Operations Research: A Conceptual Framework." *Expert Systems with Applications* (December 1990).

59. Turban, E., and P. Watkins. "Integrating Expert Systems and Decision Support Systems." *MIS Quarterly* (June 1986).

60. Turban, E., and H. Watson. "Integrating ES, EIS and DSS." In *DSS '89 Transactions.* San Diego, June 1989.

61. Turner, M., and B. Obilichetti. "Possible Directions in Knowledge-based Financial Modeling Systems." In *DSS '85 Transactions.* Providence, 1985.

62. Van Horn, M. *Understanding Expert Systems.* Toronto: Bantam, 1986.

63. Vasant, D., and A. Croker. "Knowledge-based Decision Support in Business: Issues and a Solution." *IEEE Expert* (Spring 1988).

64. Wu, W. "An Integrated System Based on the Synergy Between System Dynamics and Artificial Intelligence." In *Proceedings, 1988 International Conference of the Systems Dynamics Society.* La Jolla, Calif., July 1988.

65. Zahedi, F. "Qualitative Programming for Selection Decisions." *Computers and Operations Research* 14 (no. 5, 1987):395–407.

Chapter 16

Implementing AI

The successful implementation of any computer-based ir.formation depends on many social, behavioral, organizational, technical, economic, and environmental factors. AI technologies are no exception. They, too, depend on many factors, and they may fail as well. What determines the successful implementation of AI systems? What strategy can be used to increase the chance of successful implementation? This chapter explores these and other questions. Specifically, the following sections are presented:

16.1   Introduction

As with any other computer-based information system, implementation of an AI system is not always a success story. As a matter of fact, there is increasing evidence that AI technologies, and especially expert systems, fail at an extremely high rate (e.g., see Keyes [19] and Yorman [36]). Informal reports estimate the failure rate at over 80 percent. Implementation is an ongoing process of preparing an organization for the new system and introducing the system in such a way as to assure its success.

Implementation in regard to AI technologies is complex because these systems are not merely information systems that collect, manipulate, and distribute information. Rather, they are linked to tasks that require intelligence. Nevertheless, many of the implementation factors are common to any information system. Hence much of the discussion in this chapter is based on general experience gained in the implementation of information systems. For an overview see Swanson [33]. This chapter surveys major relevant factors, discusses their impact on implementation, and suggests implementation strategies.

16.2   Implementation: Success and Failure

What Is Implementation?

Machiavelli astutely noted over 400 years ago that there was "nothing more difficult to carry out, nor more doubtful of success, nor more dangerous to handle, than to initiate a new order of things." The implementation of AI is, in effect, the initiation of a new order of things, or in contemporary language—the introduction of change.

The definition of implementation is complicated because implementation is a long, involved process with vague boundaries. Implementation can be defined simplistically as getting a newly developed, or significantly changed, system to be used by those for whom it was intended.

According to Lucas (21), the implementation of a CBIS is an ongoing process that takes place during the entire development of the system—from the original suggestion through the feasibility study, systems analysis and design, programming, training, conversion, and installation of the system. Other authors refer to implementation as only the final stage in the system's life cycle. The definition of implementation for AI systems, and especially ES, is more complicated because of the iterative nature of their development.

If the AI system is intended for a repetitive use, then implementation means a commitment to routine and frequent use of the system, or *institutionalization*.

Measuring Implementation Success

The definition of implementation includes the concept of success. A number of possible indicators for a successful information system have been suggested in various implementation studies. Unless a set of success measures is agreed on, it will be difficult to evaluate the success of a system. Dickson and Powers (11) suggest four independent criteria for success:

1. Ratio of actual project execution time to the estimated time
2. Ratio of actual cost to develop the project to the budgeted cost for the project
3. Managerial attitudes toward the system and how well managers' information needs are satisfied
4. Impact of the project on the computer operations of the firm

Other measures for judging the success of a CBIS include the following:

☐ Use of the system as measured by the intended and/or the actual use (e.g., the number of inquiries made of an online system)
☐ User satisfaction (measured with a questionnaire or by an interview—see Swanson [33], Chapter 6)
☐ Favorable attitudes (either as an objective by itself or as a predictor of use of a system)
☐ Degree to which a system accomplishes its original objectives (i.e., whether it provides reasonable advice)
☐ Payoff to the organization (through cost reductions, increased sales, etc.)
☐ Benefits to cost ratios
☐ Degree of institutionalization of AI in the organization

In evaluating the success of expert systems in particular, additional measures of success might be used:

☐ Degree to which the system agrees with a human expert when both of them are presented with the same cases
☐ Adequacy of the explanations provided by the system
☐ Percentage of cases submitted to the system for which advice was not given
☐ Improvement of the ES on the learning curve, or how fast the system reaches maturity

Partial Implementation

Feasibility decisions are frequently made on the basis of the payoff shown if *total* implementation is achieved. In reality, a 90 percent, or even 70 percent, implementation is likely. One reason for less than 100 percent implementation is that a change introduced at one place in the system may precipitate compensatory and possibly negative impacts elsewhere. Management may then drop the parts of the project that created the negative impacts. Thus, less than 100 percent of the original project is implemented. Another reason for partial completion is a reduction in the budget.

Implementation Failures

The implementation of information systems involves several problems that have been subject to extensive research (see Lucas [21] and Meredith [23]). Very little evidence is available, however, to substantiate the true extent and magnitude of the problems. Actual information on implementation failures is a closely held secret in many organizations, especially when millions of dollars have been spent on unimplemented systems.

Frequently, the absence of conditions necessary for successful implementation result in what Dickson and Wetherbe [10] call "tactics of counterimplementation." Counterimplementation at managerial levels includes (1) diverting resources from the project, (2) deflecting the goals of the project, (3) dissipating the energies of the project, and (4) neglecting the project with the hope that it will go away. At an operating level, tactics of counterimplementation take the form of (1) making errors on purpose, (2) using the system for purposes other than those for which it was intended, (3) failing outright to use the system, and (4) relying on old manual procedures whenever possible.

Even an initial *attempt* to implement an information system can trigger a failure. Mohan and Bean [25] report:

> There is considerable evidence that firms . . . experience *severe internal disruptions and change as the new technology* is introduced. In some cases the reactions have been adverse enough to result in temporary rejection of the technology, and a period of three to five years has been necessary for reintroduction.

The initial failure not only postpones progress for a number of years, but it also makes later attempts more likely to fail.

Although there is not much formal data available on AI failures, there are many informal reports on unsuccessful implementation. Why such systems fail and the necessary conditions to minimize failures are dealt with in the following sections.

16.3   Models of Implementation

The importance of the implementation problem has led to extensive research about the determinants of successful implementation. Research began several decades ago with studies conducted by behavioral scientists to examine resistance to change. The management science movement has been occupied with this issue since the late 1950s, and MIS researchers have been studying implementation issues for more than a decade. Considerable numbers of ideas and theories have been accumulated and several models of implementation have been proposed for information systems (see Lucas [21], Swanson [33], and Meredith [23]). Recently, because of the large failure rate of ES, several papers have appeared that attempt to analyze the problems and prescribe remedies. For example, see Badiru (2) and Barsanti [3].

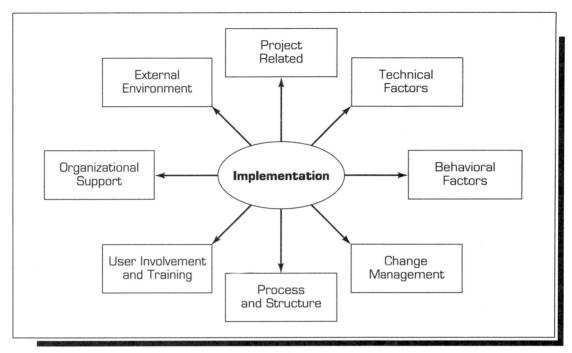

FIGURE 16.1 Determinants of Successful AI Implementation

Several dozen factors could determine the degree of success of any information system. The words *factor* or *success factor* refer to a condition present in the organization (such as the support of top management) or to the specific application (such as the use of appropriate software). Success factors can be divided into two categories: the generic factors that relate to any information system and those related specifically to AI technologies. A methodology for overcoming organizational and behavioral implementation barriers can be found in Dologite and Mockler (12).

The success factors of implementation discussed in this chapter are grouped in eight categories (Figure 16.1). These categories are frequently interrelated and some factors can be classified under two or more categories. Thus, regard this classification as a rough attempt to organize the many factors involved.

16.4   Technical Factors

Technical factors relate to the mechanics of the implementation procedure. Several are of major importance.

Level of Complexity

To maximize the likelihood of successful implementation, the basic rule is to keep the system as simple as possible. The advantages of simplicity for

TABLE 16.1 Technical
Implementation Issues

Lack of equipment
Lack of standardization
Problems with the networks
Mismatch of hardware/software
Low level of technical capacity of the project team

implementation success are many: fewer errors, greater integrity of design, simpler data requirements, easier user training, managerial transparency, ease of control, and speed of installation. Of course, simplicity must be tempered with another desirable system characteristic: completeness of critical aspects.

System Response Time and Reliability

Situations in which the system reacts too slowly, crashes, or is unavailable when needed have been known to create user dissatisfaction. Slow response time was typical in some expert systems when standard hardware was used (prior to 1987). Response time today is less than a major problem as a result of technological developments.

Inadequate Functions

Limited primary core memory, an imbalance between hardware and software capabilities, poor graphics, complex text manipulation, user-unfriendliness, and inability to deal quickly with changing situations are all examples of inadequate functions that tend to discourage users. In addition to the technical issues just pointed out, several other related issues are listed in Table 16.1.

Technical issues can be classified into two categories: (1) technical constraints, which are due mainly to the limitations of available technology, and (2) technical problems, which are not the result of the technology but are caused by other factors such as scarcity of resources. The first category may disappear when new technologies are developed. The second category can be solved by increasing available resources.

16.5   Behavioral Factors

The implementation of computer-based information systems in general, and AI in particular, is affected by the way people perceive these systems and by how people behave. The topics discussed in this section are decision styles, organizational climate, organizational expectations, and organizational politics. Another important behavioral topic, resistance to change, is presented in the next section.

Decision Styles

Individuals make decisions differently; they have different *decision styles*. They may use different approaches to making decisions, a different sequence of the same steps in the process, or the same sequence but with the steps emphasized differently.

A popular explanation as to why people make decisions differently is that they possess different cognitive styles. A classic distinction is the one between the analytical and heuristic styles. Managers with more analytical styles are usually predisposed to accept traditional computing that involves quantitative analysis. Those with more intuitive styles tend to reject traditional computing; however, they tend to accept AI, especially if the explanation component is effective. The analytical managers can learn to adapt to AI technology.

Organizational Climate (Culture)

Sometimes the **organizational climate** of a company is so hostile to innovation that it is difficult to introduce any changes. If the attitudes of organizational members are poor toward attempts to introduce computer-based systems, then introducing new AI technologies will be even more difficult. On the positive side, if there is an openness in the organization so that opinions and values are shared, change can be facilitated. Researchers studying organizational change have spoken of a climate that supports mutual trust between the potential users of the system and its developers (e.g., see Zmud and Cox [39]).

In most cases, the influence of senior management is vital in determining organizational climate. If the climate is poor, steps must be taken to improve matters before any attempt is made to introduce change. Typical cases such as the introduction of automation in the U.S. Post Office (see Dickson and Wetherbe [10]) have repeatedly shown that there is strong resistance to change in poor organizational climates.

Organizational Expectations

During the past several years, tremendous publicity has been given to artificial intelligence in general and to expert systems in particular. Now the general level of expectations both by top management and users may be too high. Overexpectations can be dangerous to the success of AI, especially for initial applications in which the strategy may be to sacrifice potential payoff and speed for effectiveness and quality. If people expect quick, large savings from ES but do not get it, they will not continue to support such ventures. Therefore, expectations must be maintained at realistic levels.

Organizational Politics

As an organization's growth slows, internal relationships tend to stabilize, division of authority and power is negotiated, and a sense of security and well-being sets in. Implementation of a large-scale AI project may threaten this equilibrium and arouse opposition toward the project. This is where "politics" frequently enters the picture. The prevalence of politics in organizations, especially large ones, is often underestimated or ignored. However, the successful implementation of a project may well depend on politics. The AI team leader may be well advised not to remain neutral but to become involved, learn the rules, and determine the power centers and cliques. For further discussion see Markus [22].

16.6   Resistance to Change and How to Manage It

Introducing new technologies into organizations will almost always result in some change. The application of AI means a change in the manner in which decisions are made, communications are transmitted, control is exercised, and power is distributed. It is only natural to assume that behavioral problems related to such changes will develop, together with some kinds of dysfunctions.

The changes that result from implementing AI can be social, technical, psychological, structural, or a combination of these factors (see Box 16.1). When managers (or other users) resist the logical arguments presented in defense of AI, they may not be resisting the technical aspects of the proposed change as much as the perceived social or psychological ramifications. Managers often feel threatened by modern techniques of analysis and sense that a computerized project may take over or jeopardize their job. This fear of change may originate from apprehension that their jobs will be eliminated, that previous performance will prove inefficient relative to the new technique, or that the new technique will result in a downgrading of the status or intrinsic satisfaction of their job. In addition, irrational fears relating to computers (computer phobia) still exist.

Of course, top management may think that such beliefs are absurd. The important point, however, is that what governs the user's behavior is not so much the real threat as the *perceived* threat. A good way for the system analyst, or whoever introduces the system, to cope with the fear of change is to eliminate the perceived threat. The problem is that some of the perceived threat is probably real (e.g., workers may be laid off and the importance of certain jobs may be reduced). In addition, some of the consequences of the change are uncertain or even unknown in advance.

Sometimes users are afraid of changes in their actual job responsibilities. If job content and meaning are changed, users may be unsure about how they will perform their jobs in the future. They may foresee more responsibility (which many like to avoid), more control, and more accountability. Although users may not want their job to become more challenging, on the other hand, they may not want it to become more routine.

The topic of dealing with resistance to change and its many dimensions (Box 16.1) is gaining momentum in many organizations. **Change management,** as it is frequently called, is emerging as an important discipline, especially for

Box 16.1: Dimensions of Change

AI implementation can cause change in an organization in many ways:

- *Rivalries and territorial threats:* The system can increase the power or influence of one department, an individual, or one group over another.
- *Fear of obsolescence:* The system can diminish job responsibilities or contribute to a feeling of loss of esteem.
- *Group cohesiveness leading to resistance to outsiders:* System specialists and/or consultants may be resisted because they are not part of the local group and do not "understand the business."
- *Cultural factors:* The system may be resisted because it does not fit in with present practice or goes against the experience of incumbent managers.
- *Job security:* Concerns arise that jobs will be eliminated or that job duties will be diminished.
- *Information possessiveness:* The system could make information that is presently closely held available to others. Of special concern is the fact that subordinate managers may lose decision autonomy or excuses for poor performance based on a lack of information. Furthermore, data and information are an element of power and must be protected if currently held or sought if not possessed.
- *Job pattern changes:* The system can change communication patterns with peers, present psychic rewards, and affect work group norms.
- *Invasion (or loss) of privacy:* Employees involved with personnel-type information systems anticipate problems with privacy of data.
- *Other:* Fear of the unknown, uncertainties, and disruption of stability are experienced by many employees.

(*Source:* This material is condensed from G. W. Dickson and J. C. Wetherbe, *The Management of Information Systems* [New York: McGraw-Hill, 1985].)

technologically oriented organizations. For more information about the various potential resistors (Box 16.2), the nature of the problem, and ways to manage the problem, refer to Ginzberg [15], Fallik [13], and Morino [26].

16.7 Process Factors

The way in which the process of developing and implementing AI is managed can greatly influence the success of implementation. Topics that are relevant to

Box 16.2: The Resistors

- Experts—some fear undue exposure or a reduction in uses for their skills
- Nonexperts—some fear further lack of recognition and even less opportunity to prove themselves
- The generally insecure—some in every organization are routinely insecure
- Technologists—some may fear that if the technology is outside their data processing department, they will lose power and control
- Users—some resist computerization in general and experience problems with the human-machine interface
- Training staff/management—some may fear that self-instruction by interacting with the expert system will diminish their role
- Troublemakers—some in every organization may be envious or just wish to exert power

(*Source:* A. C. Beerel, *Expert Systems: Strategic Implications and Applications* [New York: Ellis Horwood/John Wiley & Sons, 1987], p. 152.)

process factors are top management support, management and user commitment, institutionalization, and length of time users have been using computers. Each of these will be discussed in turn.

Top Management Support

Top management support has long been recognized as one of *the* most important ingredients necessary for the introduction of any organizational change. Meredith (23) cites nineteen references that support this phenomenon in computer-based information systems, and it has also been found to be true for expert systems (see DePree [9]).

If top management advocates and devotes full attention to a system, the chances of successful implementation are enhanced. Furthermore, if top management *initiates* the project, the likelihood of success increases markedly.

The support from top management must be meaningful. Top managers must know about the difficulties of the project and the amount of time and resources required to support it. Such support is more likely if the managers have had previous experience with similarly sophisticated projects. It is also helpful if top managers are familiar with the need to accept trade-offs in system designs and are willing to allow a sufficient time span to implement large-scale AI projects. An important aspect in AI systems is the need for *continuous* financial support to maintain the knowledge bases. Without a commitment for such support, projects are doomed. An example is the famous XCON ES whose maintenance costs became so large that management had to completely reprogram the system at a large one-time charge to reduce the costs and to avoid a failure.

There is danger in advocacy when the support comes primarily from one person. If he or she leaves or is transferred, the support disappears. Clearly, top management support must be broad based to be meaningful.

Obtaining support is easier said than done. In some cases, top management still views the computer as a tool solely intended for financial and accounting purposes. If the AI application is in any other functional area, it may not have top management's support.

Extensive research has focused on specific means to gain top management support. Essentially, top management had to be *sold* on the value of the project in terms of the benefits to be gained. This is not a simple task because of the difficulty in measuring intangible benefits and proving savings.

Although there are no specific studies in the literature dealing with methods to increase top management support for AI, there are several recommendations related to information systems in general. For example, Rockart and Crescenzi [29] have proposed a three-phase process to get senior managers more meaningfully involved in information systems projects: (1) linking management needs of the business to the proposed information system, (2) developing system priorities and gaining confidence in the recommended system, and (3) rapid development of low-risk, managerially useful systems. The third phase is easily attainable for expert systems by use of shells and rapid prototyping. Another model, proposed by Young [37], recommends five activities: (1) receiving executive guidance, (2) forming a steering committee, (3) educating senior management, (4) developing functional budgets and (5) explaining tactical information system processes to senior managers.

Management and User Commitment

Support, as already described, means understanding issues, participating and making contributions. It is significantly different, however, from commitment, as demonstrated in the case of the chicken and the pig in Box 16.3. Ginzberg [15] has shown that two kinds of commitment are required for successful implementation. The first is a commitment to the project itself. The second is a commitment to change. Commitment to the project means that during the stages of system development, installation, and use, management ensures that everyone understands the problem the system is being designed to deal with, and that the system developed solves the right problem. Both users and management must develop this commitment to increase the odds that appropriate actions will be taken at each stage of system development. Commitment to change means that management and users are willing to accommodate the change that is likely to be required to implement the system or will be the result of its introduction.

Box 16.3: The Case of the Chicken and the Pig (C&P)

A chicken and a pig grew together since childhood and became very friendly. One day they decided to embark on a new venture. The chicken, who was the quick thinker, suggested that they open a restaurant that serves breakfasts. "Can you imagine," the chicken said, "the comparative advantage that we possess having all the ingredients right here, and we can serve the freshest ham-and-egg meals in the country." The pig, who was a much slower thinker, was at first amazed at the clever idea. However, after some additional thinking the pig said: "My dear friend, what you are proposing does not seem to be a fair partnership. While you will make a *contribution* to the venture, you want me to make a *commitment*."

Institutionalization

Institutionalization is a process through which the AI system becomes incorporated as an ongoing part of organizational activities. It can occur in several ways: use of the system by successors to the original users, diffusion of the system to other users, change initiated in the work of employees, and change caused in the structure and processes of the organization. Finally, adding more AI applications throughout the organization is evidence of institutionalization. All these changes are expected to be permanent. Institutionalization clearly points to the successful implementation of AI; it also helps to create a supportive organizational culture for future, specific AI applications.

Length of Time Users Have Been Using Computers and AI

The length of time that a user has been using computers has been shown to be a critical factor contributing to satisfaction with a decision support system (see Sanders and Courtney [30]). In general, the longer people use a DSS, the more satisfied they become. We can assume that the same is true for AI, because both DSS and many AI applications support managerial processes.

16.8 User Involvement and Training

User involvement refers to participation in the system development process by users or representatives of the user group. It is almost an axiom in MIS literature that user involvement is a necessary condition for successful development of a CBIS (see Ives and Olson [18]).

In expert systems, user involvement is less important because the builder may not know who the users are going to be. It is only in the phases of testing and improving the systems that involvement of users becomes important. In building other AI projects, such as natural language processors and intelligent computer-aided instruction, user involvement could be extremely important.

Although most researchers agree that user involvement is important, the questions of when it should occur and how much is appropriate have not received adequate research attention. Another issue that needs to be clarified is the concept of *user* in expert systems. Is it the person who uses the system to seek advice (e.g., a loan officer or a maintenance technician) or is it the head of the department where the systems are going to be used by unidentified employees?

Generally speaking, the **training** required to use AI technologies is fairly minimal. In some large-scale integrated systems, however, the required training may be substantial. Training should describe the system and explain why it is being installed; it also must teach users how to ask for information and how to use the information they receive. Training is a continuous process: it must be conducted as new people enter the system, and it should take place whenever significant changes are made in the system.

Guidelines for successful AI training programs are similar to those for other CBIS training. Zmud [38] argues that for online systems, a training routine on the computer is preferred over a formal training program. In most instances, however, formal training is used.

16.9   Organizational Factors

Organizational factors may cause AI systems to fail. Several are particularly important for AI and are discussed briefly in this section.

Competence (Skills) and Organization of the AI Team

The skills of the participants, especially those of the AI builder and the technical support people, are critical for the success of the application.

The *organization of the building team* can affect implementation. Organization is reflected by team size and composition, team leadership, the department to which the team reports, the person who controls the team, and how much status the team possesses.

Relationship with the Information Systems Department

Many AI applications may be connected with the organization's database. The existing information system must be capable of providing current and historical data that can be used in the knowledge base. Distributed AI requires the use of the corporate networks, and some AI applications need minicomputers or mainframes. Therefore, the relationship with the information systems department may be crucial to the success of AI.

One aspect of this issue is to whom the AI unit (if it exists) reports. AI units do not always report to the information systems department; they may, for example, report to a technology or research and development department. In such a case, cooperation with the information systems department is vital.

Goals, Plans, and Communications

The mission of the project, the responsibilities, the constraints, and the plans must all be clear. Plans and schedules for the project must be available.

Sufficient information must be accessible to all participants. Formal lines of communication need to be established among all concerned parties.

Selection of Projects

The concept of **organizational validity** developed by Schultz and Slevin [31] implies that for a project to be implemented successfully, it must be compatible with, or "fit," the particular organization. This fit *must* occur at three levels: individual, small group, and organizational. If an AI project requires an extraordinary amount of change in individual attitudes, small-group dynamics, or organizational structure (i.e., there is no fit), then the probability of successful implementation is reduced. Schultz and Slevin have suggested several methods for measuring the fit. Such information, which should be acquired in the planning stage, can determine the strategy of AI development and implementation.

Values and Ethics

Management is responsible for considering the ethics and values involved in implementing an AI project. Three points are important:

1. *Goals of the project:* Because the process of implementation is based on an attempt to attain organizational or departmental goals, the AI team should decide whether the ultimate goals desired are ethical. The team should also determine whether the goals are ethical to those people who are crucial to the implementation process.
2. *Implementation process:* Another question the AI builders should ask is whether the implementation process is ethical, or even legal. Although the goals are ethical, the implementation process itself may not be; for example, consider an attempt to attain a sales goal through violation of a government antitrust law.
3. *Possible impact on other systems:* The goals and processes may both be ethical, but the impact of the implemented project on another system may not be.

Adequacy of Resources

The success of any AI project depends also on the degree to which organizational arrangements facilitate access to the required computerized system and other resources. Success depends on factors such as availability of terminals and microcomputers, quality of the local area network, accessibility to databases, and user fees. Other factors include support and help facilities (e.g., availability of a help center), maintenance of software (see Swanson [33]), and availability of hardware.

Other Organizational Factors

Other organizational factors important in AI implementation are the role of the **system advocate** (sponsor) who initiated the project and compatibility of the system with organizational and personal goals.

16.10   External Environment

AI implementation may be affected by factors outside the immediate environment of the development team. The external environment includes legal, social, economic, political, and other factors that could affect the implementation of an AI project either positively or negatively.

For example, government regulations regarding telecommunications across international borders may restrict the use of an otherwise successful ES to a single country. Legal considerations may limit the use of an ES because developers may be afraid of legal action if the advice rendered by the ES leads to damages. Vendors, research institutions, venture capital organizations, and universities can all play an important role in AI implementation. (Some legal issues are discussed in the next chapter.)

16.11   Project-related Factors

Most of the factors discussed in the previous sections can be considered elements in the implementation climate. Climate consists of the general conditions surrounding any application implementation; that is, climate is independent of any particular project. A favorable climate is helpful, but not sufficient. Each specific AI project (application) must be evaluated on its own merits, such as its relative importance to the organization and its members. It must also satisfy certain cost-benefit criteria. Evaluation of a project involves several dimensions and requires consideration of several factors. For information systems in general, these factors, according to Meredith [23], can be described as follows:

- □ An important or major problem that needs to be resolved
- □ A real opportunity that needs to be evaluated
- □ Urgency of solving the problem
- □ High-profit contribution of the problem area
- □ Contribution of the problem area to growth
- □ Substantial resources tied to the problem area
- □ Demonstrable payoff if problem is solved

Several of these factors will be highlighted in the discussion that follows.

Expectations from a Specific System

Expectations on the part of users as to how a system will contribute to their performance and the resultant rewards can greatly affect which system is utilized (see Robey [28]). Expectations are especially important in AI technologies, which sometimes are presented as magic.

Expectations about a system's value bear some relationship to how the need for a system is perceived. If users don't expect a system to enable them to do their jobs better and increase organizational efficiency, then they are not likely to perceive a great need for the system. Similarly, if users don't expect that the job tasks supported by the system will assist them in achieving their goals, they will be unlikely to use the system. Expectations can be affected by training, experience, and attitudes.

Cost-Benefit Analysis

Any AI application can be viewed as an alternative investment. As such, the application should show an advantage over other investment alternatives, including the option of "do nothing." Recently, the pressures to justify information systems (e.g., see Allen [1]), including AI systems, have increased. Effective implementation depends to a great extent on the ability to make such justifications.

Each AI project requires an investment of resources that can be viewed as the cost of the system in exchange for some expected benefit(s). The viability of a project is determined by comparing the costs with anticipated benefits. This comparison is termed a **cost-benefit analysis,** or cost-effective analysis. For a complete overview and methodologies see Turban and Liebowitz [34]. In practice, such an analysis may become rather complicated. The iterative nature of expert systems, for example, makes it difficult to predict costs and benefits; the systems are changed constantly. The analysis is complicated even more by the following factors: cost valuation and benefit valuation.

Cost Valuation. The costs of a project may seem, at least at first sight, easy to identify and quantify. In practice, it is often difficult to relate costs to projects in a precise manner. Allocation of overhead costs is an example. Should they be allocated by volume, activity level, or value? What about future costs? A well-known business "game" is to show the advantages of a certain alternative while neglecting future costs. In addition, there are additional accounting complications such as the impact of taxation and the selection of a proper interest rate for present-value analysis.

Benefit Valuation. While the assessment of costs is not easy, the assessment of benefits is even more difficult for several reasons. First, some benefits are intangible. Second, frequently a benefit cannot be related precisely to a single project. Third, results of a certain action may occur over a long period of time, or they may be realized in several portions. Fourth, a valuation of benefits includes the assessment of both quantity and quality. The latter is difficult to measure, especially when service industries are involved. Fifth, the multiplicity of consequences can pose a major problem for quantification. Some consequences like goodwill, inconvenience, waiting time, and pain are extremely difficult to measure and evaluate.

Project Management

Several practical **project management** questions should be answered before implementation of the AI project:

- □ Who will be responsible for executing each portion of the project?
- □ When must each part be completed?
- □ What resources (in addition to money) will be required?
- □ What information is needed?

In brief, a complete planning document for implementation should be prepared. With the answers to these questions, operating procedures, necessary training, and transitions can be planned beforehand so they do not become implementation problems later. Such planning is difficult to perform because of the iterative nature of system development. For further discussion of project management for ES development refer to Chapter 12 in this book and Turban and Liebowitz [34].

Availability of Financing

All required financing, cash flows, identification of sources, and assurances of funds should be planned in advance. Commitments should be secured so that money will be available when needed. Lack of appropriate financing is frequently cited as a major obstacle to implementation and/or continuous use of large-scale AI systems.

Timing and Priority

Two interrelated factors in project implementation are timing and priority. For example, an AI builder may find that an issue considered very important at the time of the feasibility study is not as important at implementation time. Usually, timing and priority are uncontrollable factors as far as the AI team is concerned.

16.12   Examples of AI Organizational Structures

The implementation strategies described in the previous sections may depend on the organization and structure of the AI unit. The AI units of several major corporations are presented next.

Digital Equipment Corp. (DEC)

DEC views AI as an integral part of its business success. DEC got involved in AI in 1978 because it had a critical business problem that could not be solved by any other means. Today, DEC uses AI to create and manage what it refers to as the company's "knowledge network." The majority of DEC's AI systems are large systems that combine AI techniques with conventional programming techniques, models, and databases.

The use of AI technologies to solve key strategic business problems is part of DEC's corporate philosophy. To ensure that this philosophy is communicated throughout the company, DEC has established an AI Board of Directors, chaired by a vice president, that reports directly to the senior vice president for commercial operations, and in turn, to DEC's CEO. This board supervises the Artificial Intelligence Technologies Center (AITC), which is composed of four departments (Figure 16.2).

The AITC provides central education and training services, system development, system validation, and technology transition functions. In addition, several formal and informal groups implement AI—most notably the Configuration Systems Development Group (CSDG). This group reports to DEC's corporate manufacturing operation and is responsible for the specific activities shown in Figure 16.3 for all of DEC's configuration management systems companywide (this is where the XCON project is managed).

DEC stresses that total corporate commitment to AI is essential and that individuals at all levels throughout the company must be educated and involved if the AI program is to be successful. Table 16.2 lists the key roles and functions that DEC believes various individuals should play in ensuring a successful implementation.

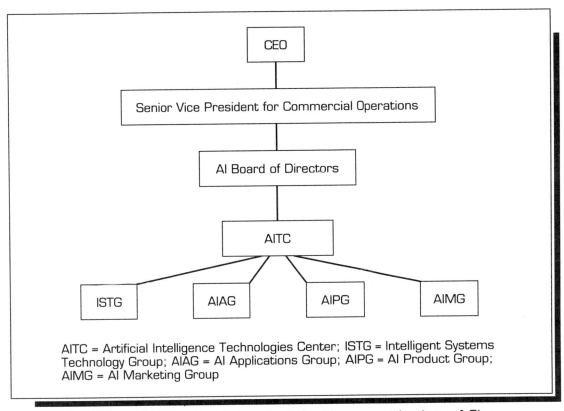

FIGURE 16.2 AI Organization of DEC (*Source:* Logistics Management Institute, *A Plan for the Application of AI to DOD Logistics,* Report PL816R1.)

TABLE 16.2 Key Personnel Role Models for Digital Equipment Corp.'s AI Program

Role	Function
Champion	Has strategic vision, believes in the technology
	Has political savvy and ability to provide support/enabling environment
Sponsor (advocate)	Has ownership of business problem, commitment to solve problem, organizational stature and support, and appropriate resources
Program manager	Manages the interface between players
Technical team: knowledge engineer	Develops and tests AI part of the system
Software systems integration engineer	Designs and develops traditional part of system, performs release management, and supports installed systems
Experts	Provide domain knowledge
Users	Provide knowledge of how system will fit into the current/future business process and relevant job satisfaction issues

Source: Logistics Management Institute, *A Plan for the Application of AI to DOD Logistics,* Report PL816R1.

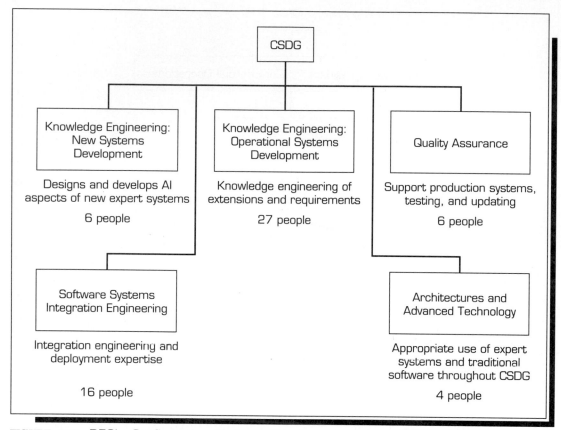

FIGURE 16.3 DEC's Configuration Systems Development Group—CSDG (*Source:* Logistics Management Institute, *A Plan for the Application of AI to DOD Logistics,* Report PL816R1.)

International Business Machines Corp. (IBM)

In 1985 IBM made a top-level management commitment by creating an AI Steering Committee adjacent to its Corporate Management Board (Figure 16.4). The major task of the senior-level committee is to provide policy guidance and direction for AI.

In 1985 IBM also established an AI Project Office (AIPO) as a temporary organization that was intended to solidify its project plan for expert systems, to develop an internal AI use program, and to develop marketing strategies and plans for external sales of IBM AI technology products such as its expert systems development software.

The AI Support Center (AISC) provides consulting services, education and training services, information services, and communications services throughout IBM.

Knowledge-based systems development activities within IBM are both centralized and decentralized. Nearly 1,000 IBM personnel are actively involved

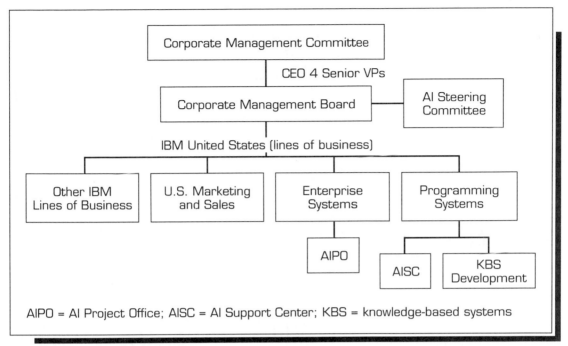

FIGURE 16.4 AI Structure of IBM (*Source:* Logistics Management Institute, *A Plan for the Application of AI to DOD Logistics,* Report PL816R1.)

in decentralized development of systems; however, IBM also has a central group of developers located at their KBS Development Laboratory.

Lockheed Corp.

Lockheed's organized involvement with AI started in 1985 when a corporate task force decided that the company needed to understand and use the technology and recommended that it establish the Artificial Intelligence Center (AIC). The AIC is part of Lockheed's Missiles and Space Systems Group and it reports to the Research and Development Division of that group. Figure 16.5 depicts the organizational structure of the AIC. It clearly shows the center's three major functions: technology development, technology transfer, and training and education. (About 50 permanent employees were part of the AIC in 1990.)

Lockheed also plays an active role in technology development. It maintains close ties with AI researchers at universities. In addition, it uses vendors' services when appropriate. Lockheed also invests heavily in applied AI research, including tool development and ownership of AI companies.

General Motors (GM)

GM started robotics work in the early 1970s, and by the late 1970s GM's manufacturing staff was using robotics and machine vision. Around 1985, GM's

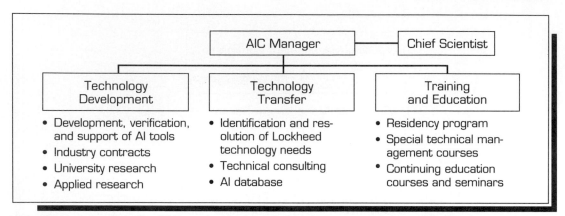

FIGURE 16.5 Lockheed's AI Organization: Artificial Intelligence Center—AIC (*Source:* Logistics Management Institute, *A Plan for the Application of AI to DOD Logistics,* Report PL816R1.)

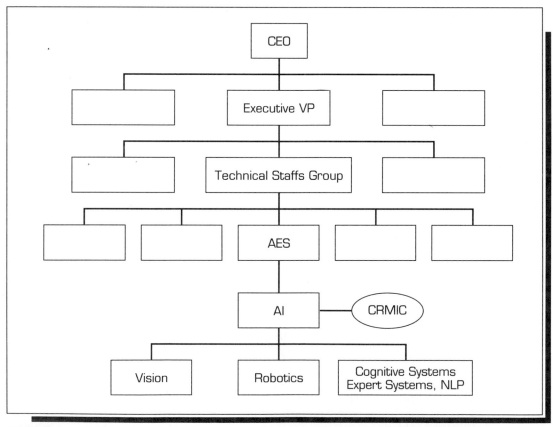

FIGURE 16.6 AI Group at GM—Part of the Advanced Engineering Staff (AES) Unit. CRMC = Corporate Robotics and Machine Intelligence Council (*Source:* Logistics Management Institute, *A Plan for the Application of AI to DOD Logistics,* Report PL816R1.)

advanced engineering staff (AES) added natural language processing and expert systems groups. As depicted in Figure 16.6, the AI group is part of the AES unit, which in turn reports to the Technical Staffs Group (TSG) and its group vice president.

The Corporate Robotics and Machine Intelligence Council (CRMIC), an adjunct to the AI group, is made up of divisional representatives and meets monthly to solve problems and share information and ideas.

The AES has three objectives in technology transfer: to discover and develop new technology, to deploy that new technology, and to transfer new technology to the divisions. Technology transfer proposes to impart an understanding for the purpose of proliferation and maintenance throughout GM. The AES may provide seed money, but the divisions have to pick up the costs of the application after that.

Chapter Highlights

- Many AI projects either fail or are not completed.
- Successful implementation of AI systems is determined by many factors.
- Implementation of AI is an ongoing process.
- Implementation means introducing change.
- Success of implementation can be partial, and it is usually measured by several criteria (e.g., user satisfaction, degree of use, and payoff to the organization).
- Technical success is related to the system's complexity, reliability, and responsiveness; hardware, network, and software compatibilities; and the technical skills of the builders.
- AI uses a symbolic qualitative approach that needs to fit users' decision-making styles.
- Organizational climate and politics can be detrimental to the success of AI applications.
- There are many dimensions to change and to its resistance; overcoming resistance is a complex process.
- The many individuals who may resist AI include experts, nonexperts, training staff, managers, and information system technologists.
- Managers in many organizations have as their goal to manage change and make it a positive experience for the organization.
- Top management support is crucial; it can be increased through guidance, education, participation, communication, and appropriate budget procedures.
- Institutionalization means that AI becomes an integral part of the organization.
- Involvement of users at the various stages of system development varies in its importance depending on the AI technology.
- Training to use AI applications is usually minimal, but online (computerized) training can be very helpful.

□ Several organizational factors are important to successful AI implementation; they range from the profile of the team (organization, size, composition, skill levels) to the relationship with the information systems department.

□ Lack of adequate resources means failure.

□ AI projects must go through a rigorous cost-benefit analysis. Assessing benefits may be very difficult because many of them are intangible.

□ AI applications are basically information systems and they should, therefore, be developed with appropriate project management techniques.

□ AI activities can be situated in various positions in an organization, ranging from high in the hierarchy to low. In most large, technically oriented organizations, AI is at the top and is separated from the information systems department.

Key Terms

cost-benefit analysis	organizational climate	system advocate
change management	(culture)	top management
counterimplementation	organizational validity	support
decision style	overexpectations	training
institutionalization	project management	user involvement

Questions for Review

1. Define implementation in a broad sense.
2. Define implementation in a narrow sense.
3. What is institutionalization?
4. Describe the various criteria for measuring the success of an implemented information system.
5. List several measures for evaluating success of expert systems.
6. Describe the technical factors related to successful implementation.
7. What is meant by system response time?
8. What is a decision style?
9. Explain the difference between analytical and heuristic decision styles.
10. List some of the dimensions of change related to AI implementation.
11. What is information possessiveness?
12. List some of the potential resistors to AI.
13. Why is the support of top management vital to system implementation?
14. List some of the ways to increase the support of top management.
15. Describe some of the organizational factors that can affect the success of implementation.
16. What are some of the difficulties in conducting cost-benefit analyses of AI technologies?
17. Compare the AI structures of DEC and IBM. Discuss the differences.

Questions for Discussion

1. Why is implementing AI technologies more complex than implementing MIS technologies?
2. How can an organizational climate influence AI implementation?
3. What actions can be taken by top management to support AI application?
4. What is the difference between user involvement and user commitment?
5. Why is the issue of expectation so important in ES implementation?
6. List and briefly describe the various AI development strategies.
7. The question of why so many expert systems fail is important. Find an article on this subject and discuss it. (For example, see Chapter 1 in Turban and Liebowitz [34].)
8. Review the XCON case in Chapter 3, Appendix C. Identify factors that could have contributed to the success of this system.
9. Visit a company that uses AI technologies. Study the structure of the AI unit and compare it to the structures described in section 16.12.

Case 1: Campbell Soup Puts Expert System to Work in Their Kitchens

The process of soup making is highly automated from beginning to end, but minor malfunctions do occur[1]. So the Campbell folks decided that expert system approaches could help their repair and maintenance people to anticipate and prevent malfunctions and to diagnose them faster when they occurred.

Campbell worked with Texas Instruments (TI) Corp. to select the first application for an expert system. The application they chose was the diagnosis of malfunctions that can occur in cooker systems (more formally called "hydrostatic sterilizers"). Cookers are the working heart of every Campbell canning plant. The cooker's vital job is to sterilize the food. Elaborate conveyor systems load and unload the cookers. Downtime is expensive and disrupts shipping schedules.

Campbell plant operators and maintenance people are well able to handle day-to-day operation of the cookers and to correct common malfunctions in their many plants worldwide. Occasionally, though, difficulties arise that demand diagnosis by an expert—someone thoroughly versed in the design, installation, and operation of the cookers. The Campbell people wanted to capture this expertise in an inexpensive computer system, so that even their smallest plant could have the expertise available immediately. That would also

---

[1]*Source:* Condensed from the *Artificial Intelligence Letter* 1 (no. 5, November 1985). Published by Texas Instruments, Data Systems Group, Austin, Tex.

free their experts to concentrate on design improvements and new processes. A secondary objective was to use the system as a training tool for new maintenance personnel.

The system was developed in 1985 on a microcomputer. The ES can be delivered on any IBM PC (or compatible) because PCs are inexpensive, familiar, and easy to use. The system was developed with the Personal Consultant shell.

The following extract is an example of an English translation of one of the rules in Campbell's expert system.

> IF the cooker's symptom is TEMPERATURE-DEVIATION, and the problem temperature is T30-INTERMEDIATE-COOLING-SPRAY, and the input and output air signals for TIC-30 are correct, and the valve on TCV-30 is not open,
>
> THEN the problem with the cooker is that TCV-30 is not working properly. Check the instrumentation and the air signal.

Development of Campbell's first expert system took about six months from initial contact with the human expert to field testing. The history of its development is instructive. On November 5, 1984, the Campbell cooker expert met with TI knowledge engineers for the first time. The expert was understandably skeptical, but completely cooperative. The first four days were devoted to teaching the TI people about the normal operation of the cookers, so they could discuss malfunctions intelligently.

On December 10, TI returned to Campbell with a first-draft system that used 32 rules. TI's development philosophy is to get a prototype system up and running as quickly as possible for early evaluation by the clients. It has proven to be the best strategy for eliciting further knowledge. Many people have difficulties in providing their knowledge directly, but can easily provide constructive criticism, which generates knowledge indirectly.

With the wealth of additional knowledge elicited in a three-day review of the prototype with Campbell management, TI enlarged the system to 66 rules and presented it to Campbell on January 22, 1985. This time, the review produced no great changes. Rather, some of the terms were refined and some detailed steps were added to certain diagnostic procedures.

Also at this point, the system was demonstrated to potential users—a shift supervisor at Campbell's Camden, N.J., plant, and several operations and maintenance people at Campbell's Napoleon, Ohio, plant. Their consensus was that the system would be useful to have at the plants. During these trips, Campbell also decided to expand the expert system to cover both startup and shutdown procedures.

On February 12, TI presented the next refinement of the system to Campbell. It had now grown to 85 rules, plus 12 startup and shutdown procedures. After a few minor flaws were corrected, Campbell declared this first phase of the system ready. A second phase covering rotary cookers had been added by Campbell after the hydrostatic sterilizer system appeared destined for success.

On March 19, an expert system covering hydrostatic cookers, their startup and shutdown procedures, and rotary cookers was presented by TI. The system had now grown to 125 rules. On this visit, the system was demonstrated to a wider circle of Campbell's management, and there was consensus that Campbell's first expert system was nearly ready for field testing. The next month was spent refining the rotary cooker rules and including rules covering a different type of hydrostatic cooker used at only one of Campbell's plants.

By November 1, 1985, the expert system contained 151 rules plus startup and shutdown procedures, and Campbell was fanning out the system to its plants.

Four of the key people in the project—Aldo Cimino and Reuben K. Tyson of Campbell and Richard Herrod and Michael D. Smith of TI—have summarized some of the practical lessons learned or reconfirmed:

- It's more important to put together a prototype fast than to make it complete.
- Extracting knowledge from the human expert is a difficult process for both the expert and the knowledge engineer, and they must guard against discouragement.
- The knowledge engineer must be prepared to accept frequent corrections—and the expert must be willing to give them.
- Because experts are seldom aware of all their thinking processes, each review of a developing system is helpful in uncovering additional needed knowledge.
- The expert must be fully cooperative, even if skeptical.
- Strong management commitment to a project of this type is absolutely essential to its success. An expert's time is in short supply and the project must have a high enough priority to assure adequate access to the expert.
- Early demonstration to potential users is important. Without their feedback about perceived deficiencies, and without their support, even a well-conceived system can end up in a closet collecting dust.
- An expert system must continue to grow to cover unforeseen situations and equipment modifications. Fortunately, it's fairly easy to add new knowledge to an expert system.

Questions

1. Trace the development process of this system. List all the measures that were taken to ensure successful implementation.
2. Compare the practical lessons listed at the end of this case with the theoretical approach to successful implementation proposed in this chapter. Discuss similarities and differences.
3. Discuss some of the potential benefits of this system.
4. Development of the system was done by an outside vendor working as a consultant. Discuss the advantages and disadvantages of such an approach from an implementation point of view.
5. User involvement in this case occurred about midway in the development cycle. This is fairly typical in expert systems. In conventional information

systems, on the other hand, users are involved much earlier. Explain the logic behind these two practical approaches. Do you agree with them? Why or why not?

6. A close relationship between the expert and the knowledge engineer is essential to successful implementation. Review the case and point out the incidents of interaction between the two and the lessons learned.

7. Why is it so important to complete the first prototype early? How can it enhance implementation?

References and Bibliography

1. Allen, B. "Make Information Services Pay Its Way." *Harvard Business Review* (January–February, 1987).

2. Badiru, A.B. "Successful Initiation of Expert Systems Projects." *IEEE Transactions on Engineering Management* (August 1988).

3. Barsanti, J.B. "Expert Systems: Critical Success Factors for Their Implementation." *Information Executive* (Winter 1990).

4. Beerel, A.C. *Expert Systems: Strategic Implications and Applications.* New York: Ellis Horwood/John Wiley & Sons, 1987.

5. Berry, D., and A. Hart, eds. *Expert Systems: Human Issues.* New York: Chapman and Hall, 1990.

6. Buchanan, B.G., and E.H. Shortliffe. *Rule-Based Expert Systems: The MYCIN Experiments of the Stanford Heuristic Programming Project.* Reading, Mass.: Addison-Wesley, 1984.

7. Buswick, T. "AI Training: Myths and Realities." *PC AI* (Spring 1988).

8. Cooper, R.B., and R.W. Zmud. "Information Technology Implementation Research: A Technological Diffusion Approach." *Management Science* (February 1990).

9. DePree, R. "Implementing Expert Systems." *Micro User's Guide* (Summer 1988).

10. Dickson, G.W., and J.C. Wetherbe. *The Management of Information Systems.* New York: McGraw-Hill, 1985.

11. Dickson, G., and R. Powers. "MIS Project Management: Myths, Opinions and Realities." In *Information Systems Administration*, W. McFarlin, et al., eds. New York: Holt, Rinehart & Winston, 1973.

12. Dologite, D.G., and R.J. Mockler. "Developing Effective Knowledge-Based Systems: Overcoming Organizational and Individual Behavioral Barriers." *Information Resource Management Journal* (Winter 1989).

13. Fallik, F. *Managing Organizational Change: Human Factors and Automation.* Philadelphia: Taylor and Francis, 1988.

14. Feigenbaum, E., P. McCorduck, and H.P. Nii. *The Rise of the Expert Company.* New York: Times Books, 1988.

15. Ginzberg, M.J. "Key Recurrent Issues in the MIS Implementation Process." *MIS Quarterly* 5 (no. 2, 1981).

16. Harmon, P., R. Maus, and W. Morrisey. *Expert Systems: Tools and Applications.* New York: John Wiley & Sons, 1988.

17. Helton, T. "AI Infusion: Getting Your Company Involved." *AI Expert* 5 (March 1990): 54–59.
18. Ives, B., and M.H. Olson. "User Involvement in Information System Development: A Review of Research." *Management Science* 30 (May 1984).
19. Keyes, J. "Why Expert Systems Fail." *AI Expert* (November 1989).
20. Liebowitz, J. *Institutionalizing Expert Systems: A Handbook for Managers.* Englewood Cliffs, N.J.: Prentice-Hall, 1991.
21. Lucas, H.C. *Implementation: The Key to Successful Information Systems.* New York: Columbia University Press, 1981.
22. Markus, M.L. "Power, Politics and MIS Interpretation." *Communications of ACM* (June 1983).
23. Meredith, J.R. "The Implementation of Computer-Based Systems." *Journal of Operational Management* (October 1981).
24. Meyer, M.H., and K.F. Curley. "Expert Systems Success Model." *Datamation* (September 1, 1989).
25. Mohan, L., and A.S. Bean. "Introducing OR/MS into Organizations: Normative Implications of Selected Indian Experience." *Decision Sciences* 10 (1979).
26. Morino, M.M. "Managing and Coping with Change: An IS Challenge." *Journal of Information Systems Management* (Winter 1988).
27. Odette, L. "Expert Systems: When to Make Them, When to Buy Them." In *Proceedings of the 1987 Expert Systems in Business Conference,* J. Feinstein, J. Liebowitz, H. Look, and B. Sullivan, eds. Medford, N.J.: Learned Information, 1987.
28. Robey, D. "User Attitudes and MIS Use." *Academy of Management Journal* 22, (September 1979).
29. Rockart, J.F., and A.D. Crescenzi. "Engaging Top Management in Information Technology." *Journal of Systems Management* (April 1986).
30. Sanders, G.L., and J.F. Courtney. "A Field Study of Organizational Factors Influencing DSS Success." *MIS Quarterly* (March 1985).
31. Schultz, R.L., and D.P. Slevin, eds. *Implementing Operations Research/Management Science.* New York: Elsevier, 1975.
32. Smith, D.L. "Implementing Real World Expert Systems." *AI Expert* (December 1988).
33. Swanson, E.B. *Information System Implementation.* Homewood, Ill.: Richard D. Irwin, 1988.
34. Turban, E., and Liebowitz, J., eds. *Managing Expert Systems.* Hershey, Pa.: Idea Group Publishers, 1992.
35. Van Horn, M. *Understanding Expert Systems.* Toronto: Bantam Books, 1986.
36. Yorman, D. "Success Factors for Expert Systems." *Capital PC Monitor* 7 (May 1988).
37. Young, J. "Ways to Win Top Brass Backing." *Computerworld* (November 4, 1987).
38. Zmud, R.W. "Individual Differences and MIS Success: A Review of the Empirical Literature." *Management Science* 25 (no. 10, 1979).
39. Zmud, R.W., and J.F. Cox. "The Implementation Process: A Change Process." *MIS Quarterly* (June 1979).

Chapter 17

Organizational and Societal Impacts of AI

In the course of this book we have introduced several applied AI technologies. If AI-based systems grow in importance in the information systems market, they could have a profound effect on organizations, people, and society. This chapter deals with some of the potential impacts of AI technologies in the following sections:

585

17.1 Introduction

AI systems are important participants in the Information Revolution, a cultural transformation that most people are only now coming to terms with. Unlike slower revolutions of the past, such as the Industrial Revolution, the Information Revolution is taking place very quickly and affecting every facet of our lives. Inherent in this rapid transformation is a host of managerial and social problems: impact on organizational structure, resistance to change, possible increased unemployment levels, and so on. The AI share of the computer industry could reach 20 percent by the year 2000, so its impact can be substantial.

Separating the impact of AI from that of other computerized systems is a difficult task, especially because of the trend to integrate AI with other computer-based information systems. Very little published information about the impact of AI technologies exists because the techniques are so new. Some of our discussion thus must relate to computer systems in general rather than to AI specifically. We recognize, however, that AI technologies do have some unique organizational, social, and cultural implications, and they will be highlighted throughout this chapter.

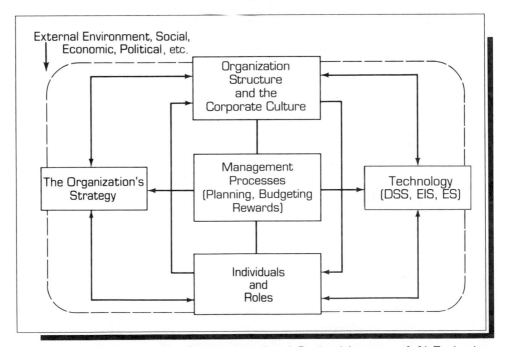

FIGURE 17.1 Framework for Organizational and Societal Impacts of AI Technology (*Source:* M. Scott-Morton, "DSS Revisited for the 1990s," paper presented at DSS 1986, Washington, D.C., April 1986.)

AI can have both micro- and macro-implications: it can affect particular individuals and jobs, the work structure of departments, and units within the organization (microeffects); it can also have significant long-term effects on total organizational structures, entire industries, communities, and society as a whole (macroeffects).

Figure 17.1 presents a framework for research that shows a complete management system. Such a system stays in equilibrium as long as all of its parts are unchanged. When there is a change in one of the components, the change will affect some of the other components. The major change stimuli are strategy and technology, especially computerized systems like a DSS or ES. For further discussion, see Benjamin and Scott-Morton [5] and Wijnhoven and Wassenarr [49].

The purpose of this chapter is to foster a basic understanding of the major organizational and societal impacts of widespread use of AI.

17.2   Overview of Impacts

The impacts of computers and AI technology can be divided into two general categories: organizational (microlevel) and societal (macrolevel). Computers have had an impact on organizations in many ways. We cannot discuss all of the ways in this chapter, so we selected those topics that we felt are most relevant to AI. They are designated in Table 17.1 along with the chapter section in which the topics are discussed.

Computer technology has already changed the world in which we live, and much more change is anticipated. Table 17.2 summarizes some of the major

TABLE 17.1 Organizational Impacts of Computer Technology

Area of Impact	Section in This Chapter
Structure	17.3
Span of control	17.3
Centralization versus decentralization	17.3
Authority, power, and status	17.3
AI special units	17.3
Job content and roles	17.4
Career ladder	17.4
Supervision	17.4
Individuals	17.5
Productivity and competitiveness	17.6
Decision making and the manager's job	17.7
Organizational intelligence	17.8
Legal implications	17.9

TABLE 17.2 Social Impacts of Computer Technology

Area of Impact	Section in This Chapter
Structure of the economy	17.10
General form of a business	17.10
Position of the national economy on a global scale	17.10
Employment levels	17.12, 17.13
Education and training	17.14
Work in hazardous environments	17.15
Opportunities for the disabled	17.15
Changing role of women	17.15
Telecommuting (working at home)	17.15
Consumers	17.15
Quality of life	17.15
Computer crime	17.15
Social responsibility	17.16

areas of social impact and designates the chapter sections in which they are discussed.

17.3   Organizational Structure and Related Areas

The organizational impacts of computer technology may be felt along several dimensions, ranging from structure and degree of centralization to distribution of power. Here we deal only with a few of the issues.

Structure

Computer-based systems have already created changes in organizational structures. AI could further enhance these changes in several ways.

Flatter Organizational Hierarchies. AI allows increased productivity of managers, an increased **span of control** (less need for supervision), and a decreased number of experts (because of expert systems). It is reasonable to assume, then, that *fewer* managerial levels will exist in many organizations; there will be fewer staff and line managers. This trend is already evidenced by the continuing phenomenon of the "shrinking size of middle management" (e.g., see Lucas [25] and [35]).

Flatter organizational hierarchies will also result from the reduction in the total number of employees as a result of increased productivity and from the ability of lower-level employees to perform higher-level jobs (e.g., by using ES). As one example consider the Bank of America's reorganization, announced in 1985; it resulted in a smaller corporation and a much flatter structure. The main cause for the changes was the increased use of computers.

Staff-to-Line Ratio. The ratio of staff to line workers in most organizations has increased with the replacement of clerical jobs by computers and with the increased need for information systems specialists. The expansion of AI, and especially ES, may reverse this trend. Specifically, the number of professionals and specialists could *decline* in relation to the total number of employees in the organization.

Centralization of Authority

The relationship between computerized systems and the degree of centralization of authority (and power) in the organizations that these systems serve has been debated extensively, especially since the introduction of microcomputers. It is still difficult, however, to establish a clear pattern. For example, the introduction of ES in General Electric's maintenance area increased the power of the decentralized units because they became less dependent on the company's headquarters. On the other hand, ES can be used as a means of increasing control and centralization.

Computer-based information systems can support either centralization or decentralization of electronic information processing within an organization. For a detailed discussion see Boxes 17.1 and 17.2 and Huber [16]. Although

Box 17.1: To Centralize or Decentralize

- □ *Centralization:* Large, central computer systems, where large AI systems are developed and used, allow upper management to centralize the decision making formerly done at lower levels of the organization.
- □ *Decentralization:* Personal computers, data communication networks, and distributed AI allow top management to delegate more responsibility to middle managers and to increase the number of branch offices (or other company units) while still providing it (top management) with the ability to control the organization.

Box 17.2: Huber's Propositions about Computers' Impacts on Organizations

The use of AI and other computer-assisted communication technologies leads to the following organizational changes:

1. A large number and variety of people participating as decision sources
2. A decrease in the number and variety of people participating in traditional face-to-face communication
3. Less time in meetings
4. Better chance that a particular organizational level will make a particular decision
5. Greater variation across the organization in the levels at which a particular type of decision is made
6. Fewer organizational levels involved in authorizing actions
7. Fewer intermediate information nodes within the organizational information processing network
8. Fewer levels involved in processing messages
9. More frequent development and use of databases
10. More rapid and more accurate identification of problems and opportunities
11. Organizational intelligence (e.g., scanning, monitoring) that is more accurate, comprehensive, timely, and available
12. Higher-quality decisions
13. Shorter time required to authorize actions
14. Shorter time required to make decisions

(*Source:* Condensed from G.P. Huber, "A Theory of the Effects of Advanced Information Technologies on Organizational Design, Intelligence, and Decision Making." *Academy of Management Review.* 15 (no. 1 1990).

information systems are usually established *after* an organizational structure is completed, it is quite possible that a new or modified information system will change the organizational structure and/or the degree of decentralization.

Because of the trend toward flatter organizations, centralization may become more popular. However, this trend could be offset by specialization. Whether extensive use of AI will result in more centralization or decentralization of business operations and management may depend on top management's philosophy. After all, people can control the direction in which computers take them.

Power and Status

Knowledge is power—this fact has been recognized for generations (e.g., see Buckland [7]). The latest developments in computerized systems are changing the power structure within organizations. The struggle over who will control the computers and information resources has become one of the most visible conflicts in many organizations, both private and public. Expert systems, for example, may reduce the power of certain professional groups because their knowledge will become public domain (see Ryan [37]). On the other hand, individuals who serve on AI application teams may gain considerable prestige, knowledge, power, and status. In contrast with a regular CBIS, the issues at stake in AI systems could be much more important and visible, because complex decision situations and upper management may be involved. An intelligent information system may control some of the major decisions in an organization, including long-range strategic ones. In addition, expert systems may shift power from professionals to administrators.

Special Units

Another change in organizational structure is the possibility of creating an AI department (or unit). Several large corporations have already created AI departments. For example, FMC Corp. created one of the earliest and largest AI departments (Box 17.3); Boeing Co. operates a large AI department. In both cases, the departments are involved in extensive training in addition to research, consulting, and application activities.

Box 17.3: Artificial Intelligence at FMC Corp.

FMC Corp. (Santa Clara, Calif.) has made a major commitment to AI. In the mid-1980s the company built a ninety-person AI center. Major applications started in the defense area and moved to the industrial machinery (manufacturing and maintenance) area. Initial expert systems operated in oil pumping operations, automotive engine design, and tool design. Applications now range from the operations of chemical plants to machinery manufacturing. Robotics and machine vision technology are being transferred from defense to the manufacturing plants.

To build up the necessary personnel, the company has designed an in-house training program equivalent to a master of science program for the AI specialists. With a rich application environment and strong corporate commitment, the company has become an industrial center of excellence in applied AI.

17.4   Personnel Management Issues

One of the major impacts of AI, and especially of ES, is on the content of many jobs in both private and public organizations. **Job content** is important not only because it is related to organizational structure, but also because it is interrelated with employee satisfaction, compensation, status, and productivity. The topics discussed next could be important considerations in any large-scale AI or ES applications.

Role of Employees and Managers

AI projects could cause major changes in the roles that managers and employees play. Many experts in organizations will stop providing routine advice; instead, they will conduct more research and development. For example, at General Electric, technicians using ES perform some tasks previously done by engineers. At Security Pacific Bank, junior financial analysts at low levels perform some tasks previously done by higher-level employees. Thus, many role definitions will be changed. New jobs such as knowledge engineers will also be created.

On the other hand, some jobs will disappear altogether. For example, an ES that can advise people about what immunizations are required when traveling abroad could eliminate the position of the person who currently gives out this information. Similarly so-called help desk ES have eliminated jobs of employees who provided routine information.

Box 17.4: Change in the Experts' Jobs— The XCON Experience

Before the expert system XCON was available, even experts had to do manual checking, undertake tedious jobs, and handle repetitive, boring tasks. They, too, made mistakes that had to be corrected, and their jobs were given low status.

After XCON became available, the experts' jobs changed. Here is what the experts do:

- □ They check what XCON does.
- □ They do the 2 percent that XCON cannot do.
- □ They update XCON's knowledge base with new information.

Now the experts are considered custodians of XCON's pool of configuration knowledge, and they are accorded high status.

The support staff for a manager will generally consist of information specialists (e.g., employees of the AI center), whereas today's typical manager has mainly specialists in functional areas (e.g., finance, law, accounting). The need for functional specialization will decrease mainly as a result of the introduction of ES. An interesting change could occur in the jobs of experts who are supported by ES (see Box 17.4). For further discussion on changes in roles and responsibilities see Sviokla [41].

Role Ambiguity and Conflict

Changes in the job content will result in opportunities for promotion and employee development. But these changes could create problems of role conflict and **role ambiguity**, especially in the short run (e.g., see Katz and Kahn [19]). In addition, there may be considerable resistance to changes in roles, primarily on the part of managers who favor a noncomputerized information system.

Employee Career Ladders

The increased use of AI in organizations could have a significant and somewhat unexpected impact on career ladders. Today, many highly skilled professionals have developed their abilities through years of experience. This experience is gained by holding a series of positions that expose the person to progressively more difficult and complex situations. The use of AI may "block out" a portion of this learning curve. Those tasks of low and medium difficulty that now are a part of a professional's experience may be performed in the future with considerable assistance from AI technologies. However, skilled professionals will still be required for highly complex activities. Several questions remain unaddressed: How will high-level human expertise be acquired with minimal experience in lower-level tasks? What will be the effect on compensation at all levels of employment? How will human resource development programs be structured? What career plans will be offered to employees?

Changes in Supervision

The fact that an employee's work is performed online and stored electronically introduces the possibility for greater electronic supervision, especially when enhanced by AI technologies. For professional employees whose work is often measured by completion of projects, "remote supervision" implies greater emphasis on completed work and less on personal contacts. This emphasis is especially true if employees work in geographically dispersed locations away from their supervisors. In general, the supervisory process may become more formalized, with greater reliance on procedures and measurable outputs than on informal processes.

For clerical work, and some other routine jobs, such formalization will mean short-term external pacing of work as well as close monitoring of any measurable work, such as number of keystrokes or number of lines typed. Many word processing systems, for example, already monitor work electronically and record the results at a supervisory workstation. The use of AI to support supervision could become a significant issue. Another potential issue is the required skill and training of supervisors who use AI technologies.

Other Considerations

Several other personnel-related issues could surface as a result of using AI. For example, what will be the impact of AI on office work?, on job qualifications?, on training requirements?, and on worker satisfaction? How can jobs involving the use of AI tools be designed so they present an acceptable level of challenge to users? How might AI be used to personalize or enrich jobs? What can be done to make sure that the introduction of AI does not demean jobs or have other negative impacts from the workers' point of view? What principles should be used to allocate functions to people and machines, especially those functions that can be performed equally well by either one? Should cost or efficiency be the sole or major criterion for such allocation? All these and even more issues could be encountered in any system implementation and should be the subject for research by the academic and business communities.

17.5   Individuals

AI systems may affect individuals in various ways. What is a benefit to one individual may be a curse to another. What is an added stress today can be a relief tomorrow. Some of the areas where AI systems may affect individuals, their perceptions and behaviors, are described next.

Job Satisfaction

Although many jobs may become substantially more "enriched" with AI, other jobs may become less satisfying in the new, more structured organizational environment. Because AI, like other technologies, can either help improve jobs or make them less satisfying, designers of AI systems should take into account the opportunity to improve the quality of work life rather than just focusing on technical quality.

Behavioral scientists (e.g., Argyris [2] predicted that computer-based information systems would reduce managerial discretion in decision making and thus create dissatisfied managers. Although such a prediction has not been realized to date, it should be reexamined in light of the introduction of AI.

Inflexibility and Dehumanization

A frequent criticism of traditional data processing systems is their negative effect on people's individuality. Such systems are criticized as being impersonal: they dehumanize and depersonalize activities that have been computerized, because they reduce or eliminate the human element that was present in the noncomputerized systems. Many people feel a loss of identity; they feel like "just another number."

One of the major objectives of AI is to create *flexible* systems that will allow individuals to input their opinion and knowledge. AI systems should be people oriented and user-friendly to make them more easily accepted. By having these qualities, AI can help promote greater personalization and attention to the individual than would otherwise be possible.

Cooperation of Experts

Human experts who are about to give their knowledge to an ES may have reservations. Consider these examples of thoughts that may enter an expert's mind:

- □ "The computer may replace me."
- □ "The computer may make me less important."
- □ "Why should I tell the computer my secrets? What will I gain?"
- □ "The computer may find out that I am not as great an expert as people think."

This kind of thinking may cause the expert not to cooperate, or even to give incorrect knowledge to the computer. To deal with such situations, management should motivate (and possibly compensate) experts so that they truly work with knowledge engineers to create a good ES.

Psychological Impacts

The widespread use of home terminals, for instance, threatens to have an even more isolating influence than television. If people are encouraged to work and shop from their living rooms, some unfortunate psychological effects such as stress and loneliness could develop. Some researchers predict that commercially available AI systems will be used not only in task-oriented ways but as surrogates for human contact as well.

17.6 Productivity and Competitiveness

In the previous chapters, we introduced various AI technologies and discussed their benefits. The major benefits, which can result in a competitive advantage, are summarized here:

□ *Increased productivity:* Productivity is increased when workers can accomplish their tasks faster or with fewer interruptions (e.g., see Liebowitz [24] and Sviokla [41]).

□ *Increase in quality:* Quality is increased by reduction of errors, by production of more consistent products and services, and by improvements in inspection and quality control (all at a reasonable cost).

Box 17.5: Competitive Analysis Framework for ES

1. Technology assessment
2. Establishment of industry-level focus
   a. Significant structural change + internal operations (example: XCON)
   b. Significant structural change + competitive marketplace (example: XSEL marketing system)
   c. Traditional products and services + internal operations (example: DELTA)
   d. Traditional products and services + competitive marketplace (example: Investment Analysis Systems)
3. Company-level analysis
   a. Gaining power over buyers and over suppliers
   b. Creating cost-effective product substitutes
   c. Setting up barriers to potential competitors
4. Strategy-level analysis
   a. Cost leadership within industry
   b. Product or service differentiation
   c. Concentration on market or product niche
5. Strength identification
   a. Sole development
   b. Joint venture or consortium
6. Portfolio selection

(*Source*: R.F. Monger, "AI Applications: What's Their Competitive Potential?," Reprinted from *Journal of Information Systems Management* [New York: Auerbach Publishers]. © Warren, Gorham, & Lamont Inc. Used with permission.)

□ *Cost reduction:* Producing a product or providing a service at a lower cost than competitors (yet with the same quality) provides a competitive edge. For examples, see Liebowitz [24] and Beerel [4].

□ *Timely production:* Producing products (and providing services) whenever needed results in a competitive advantage.

□ *Fast training of employees:* The costs of training can be very high, especially if turnover is high or in cases of rapid technical changes. Training time (and cost) can be reduced drastically with AI (e.g., see Senker [39]).

□ *Increased production (service) capacity:* Because they allow improved planning, ES can increase production or service capacity. For example, Jacobson and Klahr report on the successful increase of maintenance capabilities at American Airlines [18]. (Also see Chapter 22).

□ *Unique services:* Voice technology, for example, enables banks and telephone companies to offer new and unique services (e.g., see Chapter 9).

In addition to these benefits, ES can enhance other computer systems that contribute to increased productivity and competitiveness. For an overview on information technology as a competitive weapon see Wysocki and Young [50], Beerel [4], our discussion of the Fifth-generation Project (section 17.11), and Szewczak et al. [42]. Also refer to Box 17.5.

17.7   Decision Making and the Manager's Job

Computer-based information systems have had an impact on the manager's job for about two decades. However, this impact was felt mainly at the lower- and middle-managerial levels. Now AI systems could have an impact on the top manager's job as well.

The most important task of managers is making decisions (see Box 17.6). AI technologies can change the manner in which many decisions are being made and consequently change the managers' jobs. The impacts of AI on decision making can be many; the most probable areas are listed here:

□ Automation of routine decisions
□ Less expertise (experience) required for many decisions
□ Faster-made decisions
□ Less reliance on experts (staff) to provide support to top executives
□ Power redistribution among managers

Allowing an "intelligent" computer to take over routine decisions should not be viewed by managers as a threat but as an opportunity to engage in more creative activities with more "quality" time for the benefit of the organization. Many managers have reported that the computer has finally given them time to "get out of the office and into the field." They also have found that they can

Box 17.6: Ability to Make Decisions Rated First in Survey

In almost any survey of what constitutes good management, you are likely to find prominently mentioned the ability to make clear-cut decisions when needed.

It is not surprising, therefore, to hear that the ability to make crisp decisions was rated first in importance in a study of 6,500 managers in more than 100 companies, many of them large, blue-chip corporations.

As managers entered a training course at Harbridge House, a Boston-based firm, they were asked how important it was that managers employ certain management practices. They also were asked how well, in their estimation, managers performed these practices.

It was from a statistical distillation of these answers that Harbridge ranked "making clear-cut decisions when needed" as the most important of ten management practices.

And it was from these evaluations they concluded that only 20 percent of the managers performed "very well" on any given practice.

Ranked second in managerial importance was "getting to the heart of problems rather than dealing with less imporant issues," a finding that seems to show up in all such studies. Most of the remaining eight management practices were related directly or indirectly to decision making.

(*Source*: Condensed from *Stars and Stripes*, May 10, 1987.)

---

spend more time on planning activities instead of "putting out fires." AI technologies can enable many managers to become real managers rather than "paper shufflers."

Another aspect of the management challenge lies in the ability of AI to *support* the decision process in general and strategic planning and control decisions in particular. AI could change the decision-making process and even decision-making styles. For example, information gathering for decision making will be much quicker. AI technologies are being used now to improve environmental scanning of information (e.g., see Elofson and Konsynski [12]). As a result, managers may change their approach to problem solving. Research indicates (e.g., see Mintzberg [26]) that most managers currently work on a large number of problems simultaneously, moving from one to another as they wait for more information on their current problem or until some external event "interrupts" them. AI tends to reduce the time necessary to complete any step in the decision-making process. Therefore, managers will work on fewer tasks during the day but complete more of them. The reduction of startup time associated with moving from task to task could be the most important source of increased managerial productivity.

There is no doubt that AI applications could save managers a considerable amount of time by freeing them from routine tasks. An ES, for example, could save time currently being spent on checking manuals and directories. Analysis of reports could be expedited by an ES, and training inexperienced managers could be delegated to a computer-aided instruction system.

Another possible impact on the manager's job could be a change in leadership requirements. What are generally considered to be good qualities of leadership may be significantly altered with the use of AI. For example, when face-to-face communication is replaced by electronic mail and computerized conferencing, leadership qualities attributed to physical appearance could be less important.

Even if managers' jobs do not change dramatically, the methods that managers use to do their jobs will. For example, an increasing number of CEOs no longer use intermediaries; instead, they work directly with computers. Once voice understanding is economically feasible, we may see a real revolution in the manner that computers are used by managers.

17.8 Organizational Intelligence and Institutional Knowledge Bases

The availability of AI technology implies the possible development of very large and complex knowledge bases that require trained expertise to use and maintain. (For a detailed discussion see Holsapple and Whinston [15].) In other words, **organizational intelligence** will become a critical issue.

Institutional information bases are maintained by written documentation and experts in methods of accessing and interpreting information. The information that makes up these knowledge bases is accumulating at an ever-increasing rate. The ability of human experts to work with this knowledge base is becoming strained. In many cases, work is limited to a few individuals who have a tremendous amount of training and experience. The use of AI could greatly facilitate both the maintenance and use of institutional knowledge bases.

As system integration continues to expand in organizations, the volume of accessible data and knowledge will grow considerably. Powerful filtering and reporting systems that can be used by nonprogrammers will be a necessity. Problem determination and analysis will be much faster than what is now available with the traditional MIS approach. Some questions that need to be addressed include the following:

☐ How will the availability of knowledge affect strategic plans?
☐ How will the communication stream be affected? Will results of decisions be as readily communicated to peers, subordinates, and superiors by

managers, who may assume that these people *have* and *take advantage* of the access to knowledge bases?

□ How will managers be trained to make *effective* use of these new tools? The tools themselves are only aids; they are not surrogates for native intelligence or sound managerial practices.

□ What needs to be done to assess the current competency of managers and to match the tools to these competencies?

17.9   Legal Implications and Privacy

The introduction of AI, and especially ES, may compound a host of legal issues already relevant to computer systems. Some of the issues surrounding computers and artificial intelligence will be settled in the courtrooms, not in the research centers or user communities. The expensive, prolonged litigation of IBM's antitrust case and the restructuring of AT&T are two prominent examples. Questions concerning liability for the actions of intelligent machines in the world of industry, business, and commerce are just beginning to be considered. The issue of a computer as a form of unfair competition in business has already been raised in a recent dispute over the practices of airline reservation systems.

In addition to resolving disputes over the unexpected and possibly damaging results of some AI systems, other complex issues may surface. For example, who is liable if an enterprise finds itself bankrupt as a result of using the advice of ES? Will the enterprise itself be held responsible for not testing such systems adequately before entrusting them with sensitive issues? Will auditing and accounting firms, which are just beginning to use AI, share the liability for failing to apply adequate auditing tests? Will the manufacturers of such systems be jointly liable? Consider these specific issues that may be encountered:

□ What is the value of an expert opinion in court when the expert is a computer?

□ Who is liable for wrong advice (or information) provided by an ES? For example, what happens if a physician accepts an incorrect diagnosis made by a computer and performs an act that results in the death of a patient?

□ What happens if a manager enters an incorrect judgment value into an AI system and the result is damage or a disaster?

□ Who owns the knowledge in a knowledge base?

□ Should royalties be paid to experts, and if so how much?

□ Can management force experts to contribute their expertise?

For a discussion of these and other issues consult Mykytyn et al. [28] and Tuthill [46].

The issue of privacy, which is important to other computer-based information systems as well, will surface in AI systems and become even more difficult to control because there will be knowledge bases in addition to corporate databases.

Modern computer systems can economically collect, store, integrate, interchange, and retrieve information and knowledge. This ability can affect every individual's right to privacy. Confidential information on individuals contained in knowledge bases (e.g., how they are likely to react to certain actions) could be misused and result in invasion of privacy and other injustices. Unauthorized use of such information would seriously invade the privacy of individuals, while errors in data or knowledge files could seriously hurt their reputation.

The use of ES in the administration and enforcement of laws and regulations may increase public concern regarding privacy of information. These fears, generated by the perceived abilities of ES, whether real or not, will have to be addressed at the outset of almost any ES development efforts.

17.10   Economic Impacts

AI technology may have profound economic impacts on the national level as well as worldwide. Three areas that could be affected significantly are discussed next.

First, the *structure of the economy* can be changed drastically. For example, recent AI innovations (such as automatic help desks and automatic telephone switching) could reduce the size of the service sector. On the other hand, the proportion of the work force engaged in the leisure industry may be increased due to the many innovations that increase opportunities to participate in leisure activities at affordable costs.

Second, the *general form of organizations* may change. AI innovations already have changed the structure of organizations (as discussed earlier). Another result, for example, could be elimination of certain types of industries or organizations—perhaps a small company will be unable to survive. The proportion of white-collar and blue-collar workers could also be affected.

Third, the *position of the national economy on a global scale* could change. There is intense competition among all major industrial countries on who will be the leader of AI technologies (see discussion in Chapter 19). One example is Japan's Fifth-generation Project.

17.11   Fifth-generation Project

The Fifth-generation Project was announced in 1982 by the Japanese government. The Japanese have marshaled an impressive array of resources in an attempt to change their image from implementers of technology to developers and innovators (see Box 17.7). For the first several years, the project did not require private funding; $450 million of financing was provided by Japan's powerful Ministry of International Trade and Industry. By the time it is complete, the Fifth-generation Project may require more than $1 billion in a typical Japanese combination of public and private funding. The Institute for New Generation

Box 17.7: The Japanese—Only Implementors of Others' Innovations?

The United States traditionally has been the greatest source of technological innovation in the world. More recently, the Japanese have founded their own "tradition" in what has been called their "economic miracle"; during the years since World War II, they have become the acknowledged leaders at the implementation of technology. The following examples will probably be familiar:

- The automobile was first mass-produced in the United States; but by applying American technology and management techniques in innovative ways, Japanese automobile manufacturers have made an impact on the American automobile industry that is dramatic and irrevocable.
- It is becoming increasingly difficult to purchase a high-quality stereo, television, or other electronic device that is not manufactured in Japan.
- Although handheld calculators and digital watches were invented in the United States, creative Japanese competition has driven nearly every American manufacturer out of those markets.
- The process of electronic miniaturization was created in the United States, first with transistors and then with integrated circuits. Japanese companies are now among the largest producers of chips in the world and may be on the verge of dominating that market.
- The manufacture of cameras and other optical instruments, previously dominated by Germany, is now dominated by Japan.

If these kinds of trends were to continue, you might expect the Japanese to wait until American manufacturers had commercialized AI successfully and developed a wide range of AI products. Then, according to past scenarios, Japanese companies would develop clever, creative, and inexpensive products based on the mature American technology. This time, however, the Japanese have served notice that they are no longer content to create innovative uses for American technology. This time they intend to develop the technology themselves; this time, they plan to make their own discoveries. (Note: The Japanese are already using fuzzy-logic-based expert systems in many consumer products.)

Computer Technology (ICOT) was established in Tokyo to bring the project to fruition. Forty of the brightest young computer researchers in Japan have been brought together at ICOT. Over 150 other researchers in various locations contribute to the project under contract to ICOT.

Fifth-generation Technology

The ultimate aim of the project is the development of fifth-generation computers. To achieve this goal, the Japanese have divided the project into the following four parts.

Data Access. AI programs typically require large amounts of data. The ability to retrieve information as needed is just as important as the ability to store the information in the first place. The Fifth-generation Project has developed a prototype computer, called the Relational Database Machine, that is designed specifically to facilitate the storage and retrieval of information.

Inference. An inference engine is an essential component of a knowledge-based system. The Fifth-generation Project is developing a prototype computer, known as the Personal Sequential Inference Machine, to provide inference capabilities in PROLOG. When ready, the inference machine will be used by researchers as a tool to write programs for other parts of the project.

Ease of Use. The Fifth-generation Project includes research in several areas of AI that investigate ways of making computers easier to use: computer vision, speech recognition, and natural language processing.

Intelligent Programming. Intelligent computer programming tools are being developed to expedite the programming efforts in all phases of the project.

Knowledge Is Power

Why are the Japanese so intent on supplanting the United States by becoming the world leader in computer technology? What is it about intelligent machines that is leading them to devote so many resources to their development? Why is it so important to be first?

Quite simply, the Japanese believe that knowledge, supplied by a new generation of intelligent machines, is poised to become the basis of a new economic order. They believe that the world is evolving toward a postindustrial society in which the wealth of nations will be measured not in terms of gold or oil but information. The Japanese believe the nation that is first to commercialize AI technology successfully will gain an enormous economic advantage over other nations. First place will not only give that nation an obvious advantage in the computer industry, it will have repercussions throughout a wide range of human affairs.

The United States currently dominates the worldwide processing of information by computers. Because information processing in the United States is a $200 billion industry (annually), it is a dominance that the country can scarcely afford to lose. Gaining the preeminent position in the computer industry might be just the tip of the iceberg for Japan, merely the most obvious of the widespread economic advantages that the Japanese hope the Fifth-generation Project (as well as the Sixth- and the Seventh-generation Projects—see Chapter 19) will provide them. The successful development, implementation, and proliferation of AI technology (according to Feigenbaum and McCorduck [13]) could render all Japanese products so much better than their competitors', thanks to the degree of knowledge that will be brought to bear on their design and manufacture, that the Japanese will dominate markets in conventional products, too.

Although many AI researchers in the United States do not believe that the Fifth-generation Project (and its extensions) will be a complete success, no one is prepared to discount its prospects with complete confidence. Even if the goals for the project are realized only in part, the Japanese will have developed technologies that will make their competition as formidable in the information age as it currently is in the industrial age.

17.12 Automation and Employment

The Industrial Revolution of the eighteenth century saw machines replace muscle power.[1] This was the beginning of automation: the automatic transfer and positioning of work by machines, or the automatic operation and control of a production process by machines. The assembly line operation of automobile manufacturing is a typical example of automation.

The impact of computers on employment and productivity is directly related to the use of computers for achieving automation. There can be no doubt that computers have created new jobs and increased productivity; they have also, however, caused a significant reduction in some types of job opportunities. Computers used for office information processing or for numeric control of machine tools are accomplishing tasks formerly performed by clerks and machinists. Jobs created by computers require different types of skills and education than those jobs eliminated by computers. Therefore, specific individuals within an organization will become unemployed unless they are retrained for new positions or new responsibilities.

The productivity of many individual workers has been increased significantly by computerization. One worker can now do the work of several, and the time required to perform certain tasks has been drastically reduced. Increased productivity has led to lower labor costs and prices, which in turn have increased demand for products and services and, thus, have increased employment. The higher profits caused by increases in productivity also have stimulated more investment in the expansion of production facilities, resulting in further increased employment.

Another point to remember is that the higher standard of living caused by increased productivity generates *more* rather than *less* demand for more types and amounts of goods and services (at least up to a certain limit). "Yesterday's luxuries become today's necessities" is a statement that emphasizes the almost

---

[1] This section is based on O'Brien's work (31).

unlimited demand for goods and services our society seems to exhibit. This phenomenon is related to the impact of computers on employment, because a desire to increase the standard of living leads to an expanded demand for goods and services, and results in an increase in employment opportunities.

The computer industry has created a host of new job opportunities for the manufacture, sale, and maintenance of computer hardware, software, and other computer services. Many new jobs (system analysts, knowledge engineers, computer operators) have been created. Additional jobs have been created because the computer makes possible the production of complex industrial and technical goods and services that would otherwise be impossible or uneconomical to produce.

The controversy over the effect of computers on employment will continue as long as activities formerly performed by people are computerized. Unemployment figures are more than statistics; office and factory workers whose jobs have been eliminated by computerization are real people with real employment needs. Such people will take little comfort in the fact that computers have many beneficial effects on employment in general. Business firms and other computer-using organizations, labor unions, and government agencies must continue to provide job opportunities for people displaced by computers. This includes transfers to other positions, relocation to other facilities, or training for new responsibilities. Only if society continues to take positive steps to provide jobs for people displaced by computers can we take pride in the increase in employment caused by computer usage. Finally, education, starting at elementary schools and ending at universities, must keep up with technology to prevent massive unemployment.

17.13 AI and Employment

The previous section presented an overview of the issue of computer systems, productivity, and employment. There is very little information on the relationship of AI to these topics. However, both AI and ES have the potential of significantly affecting the productivity and employment of many types of employees. The material in this section summarizes the position of some of the country's top experts with regard to the potential impact of AI on productivity and unemployment.[2]

Although the impact of AI may take decades to materialize, there is agreement among researchers that AI in general, and ES in particular, will increase the productivity of **knowledge employees.** (For a comprehensive discussion of knowledge employees and their role in organizations see Holsapple and Whinston [15].) Technology will be relatively inexpensive and thus create substantial shifts in jobs and job contents. Researchers disagree about the potential impact of AI technologies on the aggregate employment (or unemploy-

---

[2] This discussion is based on Nilsson (30). For extended discussion see Partridge (34).

ment) level. The two extreme positions are (1) massive unemployment and (2) increased employment (or at worst, no change in the employment level). These positions have been supported by two Nobel prize winners: Wassily Leontief [23], who supports the massive unemployment argument, and Herbert Simon, who takes the other position. Now, let us examine the major arguments of the opposing parties.

Massive Unemployment

Massive unemployment as a result of AI is predicted for the following seven reasons:

1. The need for human labor will be reduced significantly.
2. The skill levels of people performing jobs with the help of AI will be low.

Box 17.8: Survey: Computers Cause Joblessness

Unemployment is the greatest concern among a polled population in France, Germany, Great Britain, Norway, Spain, and the United States. And in every one of those countries—except the United States—respondents believed that increased use of computers would worsen the unemployment problem.

The poll further showed Japan as the exception: respondents did *not* believe unemployment was "the greatest concern for yourself and your country today."

The poll, titled "The Impact of Technological Change in the Industrial Democracies," was conducted by Louis Harris International for the Atlantic Institute. The study also indicated a large measure of agreement in all the countries polled that the use of computer data banks would facilitate infringement on personal privacy.

The conclusions that the Atlantic Institute made from the data are "unexpected." According to the Atlantic Institute, France, Britain, Spain, and, to a lesser extent, Italy reflect a high degree of optimism about computer and word processing systems, whereas Japan and Germany seem to generate considerable and widespread negativism about their use. The United States, it feels, is a case apart, with Americans already much more attuned to the perceived advantages of the technologies. The Atlantic Institute for International Affairs, headquartered in Paris, is a private, independent and nongovernment center for research and discussion.

(*Source:* Condensed from *MIS Week*, August 28, 1985.)

---

3. AI will affect both blue- and white-collar employees (professionals and managers, too) in all sectors, including service industries and high-technology companies. In the past, service industries and the high-technology sector absorbed employees replaced by automation in other sectors.
4. The signs are already written on the wall. In the past few years several industries such as banking and insurance have laid off many employees or announced their intentions of doing so.
5. Industry, government, and services already have a substantial amount of **hidden unemployment;** that is, companies retain many employees who are not needed or fully utilized for humanitarian reasons, union pressures, or governmental policies.
6. Unemployment levels have grown steadily in the past decade in spite of increased computerization (see Box 17.8).
7. The per capita amount of goods and services that people can consume is limited and sooner or later may stop growing.

Increased Employment Levels

Increased employment levels are predicted for several reasons:

1. Historically, automation has always resulted in increased employment, in the macro sense (see Box 17.9).
2. Unemployment is worse in unindustrialized countries.
3. Work, especially the professional and managerial kind, can always be expanded, so there will be work for everyone.
4. The task of converting to automated factories and offices is complex and may take several generations.
5. Many tasks cannot be fully automated (e.g., top management, nursing, marriage counseling, surgery, the performing arts, and the creative arts).
6. Machines and people can be fully employed, each where its comparative advantage is strongest.
7. Real wages may be reduced, however, because people will have income from other sources (assuming that the government will control the distribution of wealth); people will have enough money to spend and thus will help create more jobs.
8. The cost of goods and services will be so low that the demand for them will increase significantly. Automation will never catch up with the increased demand.

This debate about how AI will affect employment raises a few other questions: Is some unemployment really socially desirable? (People could have more leisure time.) Should the government intervene more in the distribution of income and in the determination of the employment level? Can the "invisible hand" in the economy, which has worked so well in the past, continue to be

Box 17.9: New or Expanded AI-related Jobs

- □ AI computer lawyer
- □ AI headhunter
- □ AI project manager
- □ AI hardware architecture specialist
- □ AI venture capitalist
- □ AI user training specialist
- □ Expert system shell developer and vendor
- □ Industrial robotics supervisor/manager
- □ Knowledge acquisition and maintenance specialist
- □ Robotic maintenance engineer

(*Source:* J. Liebowitz, "Possible Societal Impacts of Artificial Intelligence," *Information Age* [July 1989].)

successful in the future? Will AI make most of us idle but wealthy? (Robots will do the work; people will enjoy life.) Should the issue of income be completely separated from that of employment?

17.14   Training, Retraining, and Education

The increasingly reduced costs of AI systems will be accompanied by a boost in productivity. As a result, AI could change the ways that people do their jobs—not only blue-collar employees, but supervisors, managers, and technical experts as well. The greater the change, the greater the amount of training and education (retraining) that will be required.

People react differently to the need for training according to factors such as their education, time elapsed since previous educational experience, time since previous training, job security, proximity to retirement, ability to ignore competing commitments, age, family status, and income needs. Because of these influences, questions such as the following arise: What kind of employment policies are most conducive to successful training for new technology? If it is in the national interest to foster rapid, well-integrated technical change, should the government finance and assist massive training efforts? What roles should private and public educational institutions play in these efforts? These and other questions are being considered by management, unions, and the government.

Management's Position

The position of management varies from company to company. Some companies (e.g., the auto industry) have instituted extensive retraining programs. In other cases, nothing is being done. Management's position is strongly influenced by the position taken by unions.

Trade Unions' Position

Most unions respond to technological change with opposition or at best with unwilling acceptance. Very few unions welcome technological change (see Rosow [36]). However, studies indicate that union opposition is usually followed by adjustment and accommodation. A union is likely to adapt when satisfactory trade-offs can be made. Union accommodation usually occurs under the following circumstances:

- Union leadership sees that the technological change is inevitable.
- The membership base is notably larger than the group affected by technological changes.
- Management has given detailed consideration to the union's political circumstances and has developed trade-off routes into which union response can be channeled.

Several techniques are commonly used to lessen the impact of unemployment:

- Early warning systems regarding layoffs linked to business planning (at least six months to one year ahead)
- Work force reduction accomplished only by voluntary resignation or early retirement
- Contractually provided special rights to training and retraining, transfer to other jobs or other functions (including relocation), wage retention after bumping or transfer ("red circling"). For example, the federal government grants two-year pay protection.
- Severance pay, supplemental unemployment benefits, and integration with unemployment insurance programs

Government's Position

The federal government has not been active in the area of training and retraining. It considers the problem that of the states, counties, and cities. One of the few government programs that is related to unemployment is the **Job Training Partnership Act** (JTPA). The JTPA supplements the federal Comprehensive Employment and Training Act (CETA). Although primarily targeted at the economically and culturally disadvantaged, the JTPA includes provisions (Title III) for retraining displaced workers. In essence, the act provides grants to the states, which, in cooperation with the private sector, set up and run local training programs. A main goal of the JTPA is to move retraining and job creation into the private sector, in contrast to CETA, which focused on public-sector support and positions. The JTPA represents the first time that the federal government, through national legislation, has identified dislocated workers as a pervasive problem.

17.15   Other Societal Impacts

Several other positive and negative social implications of AI systems could be far-reaching. (For an overview see Partridge [34].) AI systems already have had many direct beneficial effects on society when they have been used for complicated human and social problems such as medical diagnosis, computer-assisted instruction, government program planning, environmental quality control, and law enforcement. Problems in these areas could not have been solved economically (or solved at all) by other types of computer systems. Specific areas of *potential* impact are discussed next.

Work in Hazardous Environment. Expert systems, especially when combined with sensors and robots, can reduce or even eliminate the need for a human presence in dangerous or uncomfortable environments (e.g., see Oxman's work on cleaning chemical spills [33]).

Opportunities for the Disabled. The integration of some AI technologies (speech recognition, vision recognition) into a CBIS could create new employment opportunities for disabled people. For example, those who cannot type would be able to use a voice-operated typewriter, and those who cannot travel could work at home. Boeing Co. is developing several ES that help disabled employees perform tasks.

Changing Role of Women. AI technologies could change the traditional role of women at the workplace. For example, the opportunity to work at home and the need for less travel (e.g., due to teleconferencing) could help women assume more responsible (and demanding) managerial positions in organizations.

Working at Home (Telecommuting). Another trend gaining momentum is working at home. This phenomenon, called **cottage industry** in the past, is now referred to as *telecommuting*. Employees work at home on a computer or a terminal linked to their place of employment. The first telecommuters to work at home were typists and bookkeepers, but now a growing number of professionals do a significant part of their work at home (see Newman [29], Cross and Raizman [9], and Kelly [20]). The advantages of telecommuting are more flexible hours, less time spent traveling, less need for office and parking space, and the ability of the housebound to hold a job. As usual, there are some disadvantages: difficulties in supervising work, lack of human interaction, and increased isolation. (For a discussion of these and other negative factors see [47].)

Aids for the Consumer. Several AI products are in place, and many more will be developed, to help the layperson perform skilled or not so desirable tasks. For example, Dan is an ES that can help in tax preparation; Willmaster is an ES that helps a layperson draft a simple will; and Wines on Disk advises the consumer on how to select wines. Intelligent robots will clean the house and mow the lawn. These and many other improvements will contribute to the quality of life.

Improvements in Health. Several early expert systems were designed to improve the delivery of health care (e.g., MYCIN). Since that time we have seen a growing role for AI technologies in supporting various tasks carried out by physicians and other health-care workers. Of special interest are expert systems that support diagnosis of diseases and the use of machine vision in radiology (see Chapter 9).

Quality of Life. On a broader scale, AI technologies have implications for the **quality of life** in general (see Krout et al. [22]). Improved organizational efficiency may result in more leisure time, at least for the white-collar work force. The workplace can be expanded from the traditional nine to five at a central location to twenty-four hours a day at *any* location. This expansion provides flexibility that can significantly improve the quality of leisure time, even if the total amount of leisure time is not increased. For example, not having to commute every day or the ability to commute during nonrush hours would immediately improve the quality of life for many people!

Negative Effects

Improvements in quality of life may be accompanied by some negative effects. In addition to unemployment and the creation of large economic gaps among people, AI technologies may result in other negative situations, some of which are common to other computer systems.

Computer Crime. Fraud and embezzlement by "electronic criminals" is increasing. The American Bar Association estimates that losses from theft of tangible and intangible assets (including software), destruction of data, embezzlement of funds, and fraud at as much as $45 billion annually [1]. With ES, there is a possibility of deliberately providing bad advice (e.g., to advise employees to opt for early retirement in cases in which they really should stay on). On the other hand, ES can be used to prevent computer crimes. For a discussion, see Tener [43].

Too Much Power. Integrated information systems that allow greater centralization in decision making and control of an organization may give some individuals or governmental agencies too much power over other people. Power may be used in an unethical manner; see Dejoie et al. [10].

Blaming the Computer Phenomenon. Many people tend to blame the computer in order to cover up human errors or wrongdoing. You may hear "but the expert system told us to do it" to justify some action that otherwise would be unjustifiable.

17.16 Managerial Implications and Social Responsibilities

The potential societal as well as organizational impacts of AI discussed in this chapter raise the issue of what management can do about all the changes. How do we anticipate the broad societal effects of AI and the things it makes possible? What can we do to ensure that people's attitudes toward AI techniques are well founded and that their expectations about what these systems can and cannot do are accurate? How do we determine the potential positive and negative effects of AI systems before they become realities?

The examples presented in this chapter show that widespread application of AI could have subtle yet profound and varying influences on society. Moreover, AI could foster a general view of humanity as either mechanistic or nonmechanistic, depending on how AI is interpreted by the public. The most common interpretation is that AI makes us "mere machines," with no free choice or moral responsibility. Because this image could have socially pernicious effects, people should be encouraged to understand that it is fundamentally wrong. Perhaps education in computer and AI literacy could reshape perceptions. More generally, we should start thinking now about what the optimal social arrangements might be for a post-industrial information society. In addition to general issues such as the universality of human knowledge and human needs (see Gill [14]), the following specific areas must be considered.

Social Responsibility. Organizations need to be motivated to utilize AI to improve the quality of life in general. They should design their AI systems to minimize negative working conditions. This challenge relates not only to companies that produce AI hardware and software, but also to companies that use these technologies. Properly designed systems can be implemented and used in ways that are either positive or negative.

Public Pressure. Increased exposure to the concepts and actual use of AI will bring some pressure on public agencies and corporations to employ the latest capabilities for solving social problems. At the same time, conflicting public pressures may rise to suppress the use of AI because of concerns about privacy and "big brother" government.

Computer and Staff Resources. Obvious implications of the introduction of AI involve the increased need for computer resources and people with computer and AI skills. AI may not be the dominant factor in the expected future growth of computer resources, but it will be a significant one. Depending on the level of involvement in AI, significant impacts could be expected on the recruitment of personnel and training. Some researchers forecast that it will be very difficult to find skilled AI practitioners, and especially knowledge engineers, in the next five to ten years.

Planning. Management must be ready for all the potential impacts of AI— they may come faster than most of us think. Managers should plan the introduction of AI after analyzing its potential impacts (see Weitz [48]). Smart machines can change our world (see Zuboff [51]); let's be ready to make the best of them.

Chapter Highlights

- □ AI technologies can affect organizations in many ways, either as stand-alone systems and/or integrated with other computer-based information systems.
- □ Flatter organizational hierarchies are expected, but the ratio of staff to line workers may decrease.
- □ The impact of AI technology on the degree of centralization of power and authority is inconclusive. Distributed AI systems may increase decentralization.
- □ AI could cause a power redistribution. Advisory professionals may be the losers as power shifts to administrators and managers.
- □ Special AI units and departments are likely to appear in many organizations.
- □ Many jobs will require fewer skills when supported by AI.
- □ The job of the surviving expert will become more important as it becomes one of custodian of the expert system and the knowledge base.
- □ Expertise will be much easier to acquire (shorter time).
- □ AI technologies could reduce the need for management supervision by providing more guidelines to employees through electronic means.
- □ The impact of AI on individuals is unclear; it can be either positive or negative.
- □ Organizational knowledge bases and intelligence will be critical issues as AI technology becomes more available.
- □ Serious legal issues may develop with the introduction of AI; liability and privacy are the dominant problem areas.
- □ In one view, AI will cause massive unemployment because of increased productivity, reduced required skill levels, and impacts on all sectors of the economy.
- □ In another view, AI will increase employment levels because automation makes products and services more affordable and so demand increases, and the process of disseminating automation is slow enough to allow the economy to adjust to AI technologies.

□ Training and retraining for new technologies are important concerns and should be supported by organizations and governments.

□ Many positive social implications can be expected from AI systems. They range from providing opportunities to the handicapped to reducing the exposure of people to hazardous situations.

□ Quality of life, both of work and at home, is likely to improve as a result of AI technologies

□ Managers need to plan for the AI systems of the future so they are ready to make the best of them.

Key Terms

cottage industry	knowledge employee	role ambiguity
hidden unemployment	organizational	span of control
job content	intelligence	telecommuting
Job Training	quality of life	
Partnership Act		

Questions for Review

1. Explain why organizations might have fewer managerial layers (or levels) because of AI. Give at least two reasons.
2. Why might the ratio of staff to line workers decrease in the future?
3. How can AI increase the trend toward decentralization?
4. Explain the impact of microcomputers on the degree of organizational decentralization.
5. List some of the major forces that created user-oriented computing.
6. Describe the potential power shift in organizations when expert systems are used.
7. Describe some potential changes in jobs and job descriptions in organizations that plan to use AI extensively.
8. What are some of the issues related to human-computer interactions?
9. List some of the reasons why an expert may not be able or willing to contribute his or her expertise to an ES.
10. Why will managers in the future work on fewer problems simultaneously?
11. What is organizational intelligence?
12. Describe some of the legal implications of ES.
13. List three reasons why AI could result in massive unemployment.
14. Give three arguments to counter the arguments in the previous question.
15. What actions can management take to reduce the impact of employee replacement by a computer?
16. What is the Job Training Partnership Act?
17. List some potential social benefits of AI.
18. Why could work done at home be increased through AI?
19. How can telecommuting improve the quality of life?
20. List some possible negative effects of AI technologies.

21. Could AI provide more managerial opportunities for the handicapped and minorities? Why or why not?

Questions for Discussion

1. Some say AI in general and ES in particular dehumanize managerial activities and others say they don't. Discuss arguments for both points of view.
2. Explain why you agree or disagree with the following statement: AI technologies will increase organizational productivity.
3. Describe the manager of the future in a workplace that uses AI extensively.
4. Should top managers who use ES instead of a human assistant be paid more or less for their job? Why?
5. How can an ES increase the span of control of a manager?
6. The following story was published in the November 1974 issue of *Infosystems:*

   I've seen the ablest executives insist on increased productivity by a plant manager, lean on accounting for improved performance, and lay it on purchasing in no uncertain terms to cut its staff. But when these same executives turn to EDP they stumble to an uncertain halt, baffled by the blizzard of computer jargon. They accept the presumed sophistication and differences that are said to make EDP activities somehow immune from normal management demands. They are stopped by all this nonsense, uncertainty about what's reasonable to expect, and what they can insist upon. They become confused and then retreat, uttering about how to get a handle on this blasted situation.

   Discuss how AI technologies can change such a situation.
7. The Department of Transportation in a large metropolitan area has an expert system that advises an investigator about whether to open an investigation on a reported car accident. (This system, which includes 300 rules, was developed by Dr. Nagy at George Washington University.) Discuss the following questions:
   a. Should the people involved in an accident be informed that an ES decides about the investigation?
   b. What are some of the potential legal implications?
   c. In general, what do you think of such a system?
8. Diagnosing infections and prescribing pharmaceuticals are weak points of many practicing physicians (according to Dr. Shortliffe, one of the developers of MYCIN). It seems, therefore, that society would be well served if MYCIN (and other expert systems) were used extensively. But few physicians use MYCIN. Discuss these questions:
   a. Why do you think MYCIN is little used by physicians?
   b. Assume that you are a hospital administrator whose physicians are salaried and report to you. What would you do to influence and persuade these physicians to use MYCIN?
   c. If the potential benefits to society are so great, can society do something that will increase the use of MYCIN by doctors?

Exercises

1. Write a short essay that describes the major similarities and differences between the Industrial Revolution and the Information Revolution.
2. Read the article "The Molting of America" by J. Cook in *Forbes*, November 22, 1982. Relate the development of AI to the future of America as projected in this article. Specifically, consider the national benefits of AI.
3. Debate the following issues:
    a. Are we relying too much on computers?
    b. Are we becoming too dependent on intelligent computers that are doing all the thinking?
    c. Many jobs will require fewer skills when supported by AI. Debate the positive and negative implications of such an impact.
    d. Telecommuting is liked by many, but others think that it is undesirable and unprofitable. Present the positions of both sides.
    e. The skill requirements for many jobs performed with AI support will be reduced. For example, a technician will be able to do the job of an engineer. Should we pay the technician more than he or she is making today, the same, or less? (Refer to Senker [39].)

References and Bibliography

1. American Bar Association Computer Crime Task Force, White Collar Crime Committee, Criminal Justice Section. *Report on Computer Crime.* Washington, D.C.: American Bar Association, 1984.
2. Argyris, C. "Management Information Systems: The Challenge to Rationality and Emotionality." *Management Science* (February 1971).
3. Barb, J.F. "An Assessment of Industrial Robots: Capabilities, Economics and Impacts." *Journal of Operations Management* (February 1987).
4. Beerel, A.C. *Expert Systems: Strategic Implications and Applications.* New York: Ellis Horwood/John Wiley & Sons, 1987.
5. Benjamin, R.I., and M.S. Scott-Morton. "Information Technology Integration and Organizational Change." *Interfaces* (May-June 1988).
6. Berry, D., and A. Hart. *Expert Systems: Human Issues.* Cambridge, Mass.: MIT Press, 1990.
7. Buckland, M.K. "Information Handling, Organizational Structure, and Power." *Journal of American Society of Information Science* (September 1989).
8. Child, J. "Information Technology, Organization, and the Response to Strategic Challenges." *California Management Review* (Fall 1987).
9. Cross, T.B., and M. Raizman. *Telecommuting: The Future Technology at Work.* Homewood, Ill.: Dow-Jones/Irwin, 1986.
10. Dejoie, R.M., et al. *Ethical Issues in Information Systems.* Cincinnati: Boyd & Fraser Publishing, 1991.
11. DeSalvo, D.A., and J. Liebowitz, eds. *Managing AI and Expert Systems.* Englewood Cliffs, N.J.: Yourdon Press, 1990.

12. Elofson, G.S., and B.R. Konsynski. "Supporting Knowledge Sharing in Environment Scanning." In *Proceedings, 23rd HICSS*. Hawaii, 1990.

13. Feigenbaum, E.A., and E.P. McCorduck. *The Fifth Generation Computer*. Reading, Mass.: Addison-Wesley, 1983.

14. Gill, K.S. *Artificial Intelligence and Society*. New York: John Wiley & Sons, 1986.

15. Holsapple, C.W., and A.B. Whinston. *Business Expert Systems*. Homewood, Ill.: Richard D. Irwin, 1987.

16. Huber, G.P. "The Nature and Design of Post Industrial Organizations." *Management Science* 30 (no. 8, 1984).

17. Huber, G.P. "A Theory of the Effects of Advanced Information Technologies on Organizational Design, Intelligence, and Decision Making." *Academy of Management Review* 15 (no. 1, 1990).

18. Jacobson, A., and P. Klahr. "Decision Automation: Case Studies in the Successful Development of Mission-Critical Expert Systems." In *Proceedings, Forum on AI in Management*. Monterey, Calif.: Defense Management College, 1990.

19. Katz, D., and R.L. Kahn. *The Social Psychology of Organizations*, 4th ed. New York: John Wiley & Sons, 1986.

20. Kelly, M.M. "The Work at Home Revolution." *The Futurist* (November-December 1988).

21. Keyes, J. "Expert Help Desks: Expert Help for the 90's." *AI Expert* (September 1990).

22. Krout, R., et al. "Computerization, Productivity and Quality of Work Life." *Communications of ACM* (February 1989).

23. Leontief, W. *The Future Compact of Automation on Workers*. Oxford: Oxford Univ. Press, 1986.

24. Liebowitz, J. "Possible Societal Impacts of Artificial Intelligence." *Information Age* (July 1989).

25. Lucas, H.C., Jr. "Organizational Power and the Information Services Department." *Communications of ACM* (January 1984).

26. Mintzberg, H. *The Nature of Managerial Work*. New York: Harper & Row, 1973.

27. Monger, R.F. "AI Applications: What's Their Competitive Potential?" *Journal of Information Systems Management* (Summer 1988).

28. Mykytyn, K., et al. "Expert Systems: A Question of Liability?" *MIS Quarterly* (March 1990).

29. Newman, S. "Telecommuters Bring the Office Home." *Management Review* (December 1989).

30. Nilsson, N.I. "Artificial Intelligence: Employment and Income." *AI Magazine* (Summer 1984).

31. O'Brien, J.A. *Computers in Business Management*, 6th ed. Homewood, Ill.: Richard D. Irwin, 1991.

32. O'Leary, D., and E. Turban. "The Organizational Impact of Expert Systems." *Human System Management* 7 (Spring 1987).

33. Oxman, S.W. "Reporting Chemical Spills: An Expert Solution." *AI Expert* (May 1991).
34. Partridge, D. "Social Implication of AI." In *AI Principles and Applications*, M. Yazdani, ed. New York: Chapman and Hall, 1988.
35. "The Recovery Skips Middle Managers." *Fortune* (February 6, 1984).
36. Rosow, J.M. "People vs. High Tech Adapting New Technologies to the Workplace." *Management Review* (September 1984).
37. Ryan, J. "Expert Systems in the Future: The Redistribution of Power." *Journal of Systems Management* (April 1988).
38. Scott-Morton, M. "DSS Revisited for the 1990s." Paper presented at DSS 1986. Washington, D.C., April 1986.
39. Senker, P. "Implications of Expert Systems for Skill Requirements and Working Life." *AI and Society* 3 (1989).
40. Sharma, R.S. "A Socio-Technical Model for Deploying Expert Systems— Part I: The General Theory." *IEEE Transactions on Engineering Management* (February 1991).
41. Sviokla, J.J. "An Examination of the Impact of Expert Systems on the Firm: The Case XCON." *MIS Quarterly* (June 1990).
42. Szewczak, E.J., et al. *Management Impacts of Information Technology*. Hershey, Pa.: Idea Group Publishers, 1991.
43. Tener, W.T. "Expert Systems for Computer Security." *Expert Systems Review* (March 1988).
44. Trappl, R., ed. *Impacts of AI: Scientific, Technological, Military, Economic, Social, Cultural, Political*. New York: Elsevier, 1986.
45. Turban, E., and J. Liebowitz. *Managing Expert Systems*. Hershey, Pa.: Idea Group Publishers, 1991.
46. Tuthill, S.G. "Legal Liabilities and Expert Systems." *AI Expert* (March 1991).
47. *Wall Street Journal*, March 30, 1986, p. 25.
48. Weitz, R.R. "Technology, Work and the Organization: The Impact of Expert Systems." *AI Magazine* (Summer 1990).
49. Wijnhoven, A.B.J.M., and D.A. Wassenarr. "Impact of Information Technology on Organizations: The State of the Art." *International Journal of Information Management* 10 (1990).
50. Wysocki, R.K., and J. Young. *Information Systems: Management Principles in Action*. New York: John Wiley & Sons, 1990.
51. Zuboff, S. *In the Age of the Smart Machine*. New York: Basic Books, 1988.

Part 6

Advanced Topics and the Future

Extensive research and development work are part of applied AI. New methods, approaches, and theories are constantly under investigation. Successes are reported frequently and transfers from the labs to the real world occur often.

Neural computing, which is described in Chapter 18, is not considered to be an AI technology by some, but others believe that it is. Regardless of its classification, neural computing can be used as a substitute for expert systems and/or as a faithful companion. Neural computing can also enhance the effectiveness of all AI technologies whenever pattern recognition is used (natural language processing, expert systems, speech understanding, machine vision). Therefore, an understanding of the technology and its interface with AI is essential.

In assessing the future of AI we must look at technological developments such as very-large-scale integration (VLSI), parallel processing, and optical computing; detailed consideration of these topics, however, is outside the scope of this book. Some of the many important topics of machine learning are briefly described in Chapter 19. National research efforts and special topics that could affect the direction of AI in the future are also assessed in the chapter.

Chapter 18

Neural Computing
and AI

Neural computing is an approach that attempts to mimic the manner in which our brain works. It is not considered a subarea of AI (because it does not possess the major characteristics of AI as presented in Chapter 1), but it is closely associated with AI activities such as knowledge acquisition, inferencing, and machine learning. Even though many applications of neural computing are not related to AI, others either complement AI technologies or can be used as a substitute for them. Therefore, it is important to understand neural computing and how it interfaces with AI. We will discuss the subject in the following specific sections:

Most of the material in this chapter was written by Professor Larry Medsker from the American University, Washington, D.C.

621

18.1   Introduction

Over the past four decades, the field of artificial intelligence has made great progress toward computerizing human reasoning. Nevertheless, the tools of AI have been mostly restricted to sequential processing and only certain representations of knowledge and logic. A different approach to intelligent systems involves constructing computers with architectures and processing capabilities that mimic some processing capabilities of the brain. The results may be knowledge representations based on massive parallel processing, fast retrieval of large amounts of information, and the ability to recognize patterns based on experience. The technology that attempts to achieve these results is called **neural computing,** or **artificial neural networks** (ANNs).

Artificial neural networks are an information processing technology inspired by studies of the brain and nervous system (according to C. C. Klimasauskas of NeuralWare, Inc.). After falling into disfavor in the 1970s, the field of neural networks experienced a dramatic resurgence in the late 1980s. The renewed interest developed because of the need for brainlike information processing, advances in computer technology, and progress in neuroscience toward better understanding of the mechanisms of the brain. Declared the Decade of the Brain by the U.S. government, the 1990s look extremely promising for understanding the brain and the mind. Neural computing should have an important role in this research area, which initially was oriented toward medical research.

In some cases, ANNs are taking the place of expert systems and other AI solutions to problems. In other applications, ANNs provide features not possible with conventional AI systems. Perhaps they will provide aspects of intelligent behavior that have thus far eluded the AI symbolic/logical approach.

The content of this chapter falls into two distinct parts. In the first part (sections 18.2–18.16), we describe what ANNs are, how they work, how to build them, and in what applications they excel. In the second part (sections 18.17–18.23), we discuss the relationships between ANNs and AI technologies, especially expert systems.

18.2   The Biological Analogy

Biological Neural Networks

The human (and animal) brain is composed of special cells called **neurons.** These cells are special because they do not die (all other cells reproduce to replace themselves, then die). This phenomenon may explain why we retain information. Estimates of the number of neurons in a human brain cover a wide range—up to 100 billion—and there are more than a hundred different kinds. Neurons are separated into groups called networks. Each group contains several thousand neurons that are highly interconnected. Thus, the brain can be viewed as a collection of neural networks.

Thinking and intelligent behavior are controlled by the brain and the central nervous system. The ability to learn and react to changes in our environment requires intelligence. Those who suffer brain damage, for example, have difficulties learning and reacting to changing environments.

A portion of a network composed of two cells is shown in Figure 18.1. The cell itself includes a **nucleus** (at the center). On the left of cell 1, note the **dendrites,** which provide inputs to the cell. On the right is the **axon,** which sends signals (outputs) via the axon terminals to cell 2. These axon terminals

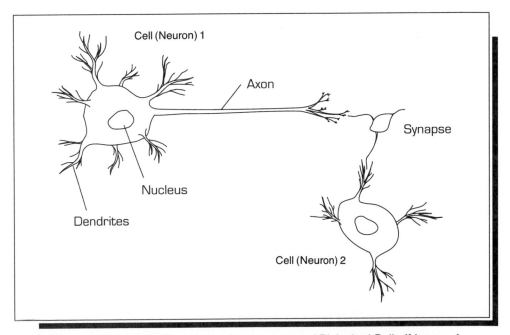

FIGURE 18.1   Portion of a Network: Two Interconnected Biological Cells (Neurons)

are shown merging with the dendrites of cell 2. Signals can be transmitted unchanged, or they can be transmitted over synapses. A **synapse** is able to increase or decrease its strength of connection and causes excitation or inhibition of a subsequent neuron.

Artificial Neural Networks

An *artificial* neural network is a *model* that emulates a biological neural network. As you will see, today's neural computing uses a very limited set of concepts from biological neural systems. The concepts are used to implement software simulations of massively parallel processes involving processing elements (also called artificial neurons or neurodes) interconnected in a network architecture. The artificial neuron is analogous to the biological neuron: The artificial neuron receives inputs that are analogous to the electrochemical impulses that the dendrites of biological neurons receive from other neurons. The output of the artificial neuron corresponds to signals sent out from a biological neuron over its axon. These artificial signals can be changed similarly to the change occurring at the synapses.

The state of the art in neural computing rests on our current understanding of biological neural networks. Despite extensive research in neurobiology and psychology, important questions remain about how the brain and the mind work. This is just one reason why neural computing models are not very close to actual biological systems. Nevertheless, research and development in the area of ANNs is producing interesting and useful systems that borrow some features from biological systems. We are, however, far from having an artificial, brainlike machine.

18.3   Neural Network Fundamentals

Components and Structure

A network is composed of processing elements, organized in different ways to form the network's structure.

Processing Elements. An ANN is composed of artificial neurons (to be referred to as neurons); these are the **processing elements** (PEs). Each of the neurons receives input(s), processes the input(s), and delivers a single output. This process is shown in Figure 18.2. The input can be raw data or output of other processing elements. The output can be the final product or it can be an input to another neuron.

A Network. Each ANN is composed of a collection of neurons that are grouped in layers. The basic structures are shown in Figure 18.3. Note the three layers: input, intermediate (called the **hidden layer**), and output.

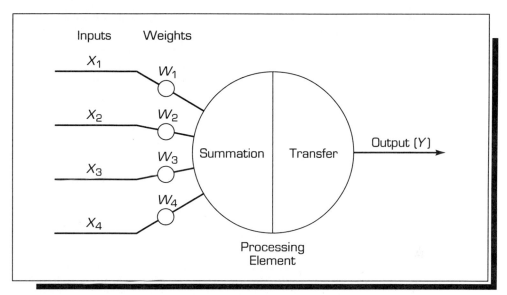

FIGURE 18.2 Processing Information in an Artificial Neuron

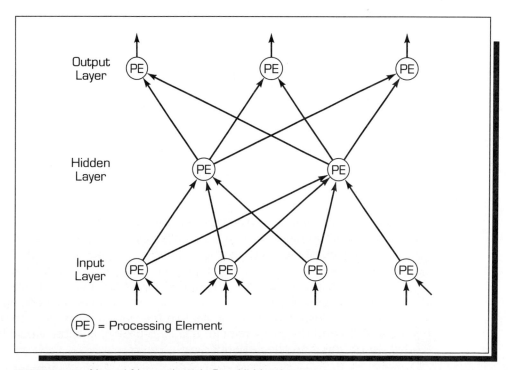

FIGURE 18.3 Neural Network with One Hidden Layer

Structure of the Network. Similar to biological networks, an ANN can be organized in several different ways (topologies); that is, the neurons can be interconnected in different ways. Therefore, ANNs appear in many shapes (see section 18.9). In processing information, many of the processing elements perform their computations at the same time. This **parallel processing** resembles the way the brain works, and it differs from the serial processing of conventional computing.

Processing Information in the Network

Once the structure of a network is established, information can be processed. Several major elements participate in the process (see Figure 18.2).

Inputs. Each input corresponds to a single attribute. For example, if the problem is to decide on the approval or disapproval of a loan, an attribute can be an income level, age, or ownership of a house. The *value* of an attribute is the input to the network. Several types of data can be used as inputs (see Box 18.1).

Outputs. The output of the network is the solution to a problem. For example, in the case of a loan application it may be "yes" or "no." The ANN assigns numeric values, for example, +1 for yes and 0 for no. The purpose of the network is to compute the values of the output.

Weights. A key element in an ANN is the **weight.** Weights express the *relative strength* (or mathematical value) of the initial entering data or the various connections that transfer data from layer to layer. In other words, the weights express the *relative importance* of each input to a processing element. Weights are crucial; it is through repeated adjustments of weights that the network "learns."

Box 18.1: Input to Neural Networks

Neural computing can only process numbers. If a problem involves qualitative attributes or pictures, they must be preprocessed to numeric equivalences before they can be treated by the artificial neural network.

Examples of inputs to neural networks are pixel values of characters and other graphics, digitized images and voice patterns, digitized signals from monitoring equipment, and coded data from loan applications. In all cases, an important initial step is the design of a suitable coding system so that the data can be presented to the neural network, commonly as sets of 1s and 0s. For example, a 6-by-8-pixel character would be a 48-bit vector input to the network.

Summation Function. The **summation function** finds the weighted average of all the input elements to each processing element. A summation function multiplies each input value (X_i) by its weight (W_i) and totals them together for a weighted sum, Y. The formula for n inputs in one processing element (Figure 18.4a) is:

$$Y = \sum_i^n X_i W_i$$

For several (j) processing neurons (Figure 18.4b), the formula is:

$$Y_j = \sum_j^n X_i W_{ij}$$

Transformation (Transfer) Function. The summation function computes the internal stimulation, or activation level, of the neuron. (Sometimes it is referred to as the activation function.) Based on this level, the neuron may or may not produce an output. The relationship between the internal activation level and the output may be linear or nonlinear. Such relationships are expressed by a **transformation (transfer) function**, and there are several different types. The selection of the specific function determines the network's operation. One

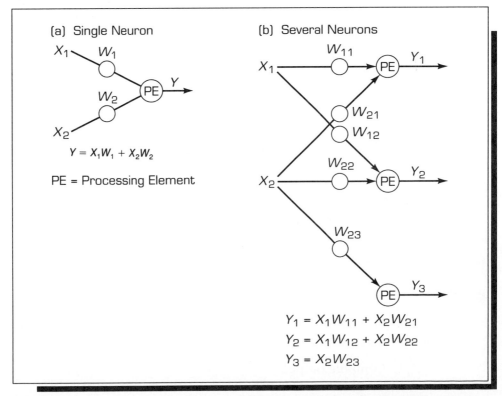

FIGURE 18.4 Summation Function for Single Neuron (a) and Several Neurons (b)

Box 18.2: Example of ANN Functions

$X_1 = 3$ $\dfrac{W_1 = 0.2}{\longrightarrow}$

$X_2 = 1$ $\dfrac{W_2 = 0.4}{\longrightarrow}$ (Processing Element) $\dfrac{Y = 1.2}{\longrightarrow}$

$X_3 = 2$ $\dfrac{W_3 = 0.1}{\longrightarrow}$

Summation function:

$$Y = 3(0.2) + 1(0.4) + 2(0.1) = 1.2$$

Transformation (transfer) function:

$$Y_T = \frac{1}{1 + e^{-1.2}} = 0.77$$

popular nonlinear transfer function is called a **sigmoid function** (or logical activation function):

$$Y_T = \frac{1}{1 + e^{-Y}}$$

where Y_T is the transformed (or normalized) value of Y (see Box 18.2).

The purpose of this transformation is to modify the output levels to a reasonable value (e.g., between zero and one). This transformation is done *before* the output reaches the next level. Without such transformation, the value of the output may be very large, especially when several layers are involved. Sometimes instead of a transformation function, a *threshold value* is used. For example, any value of 0.5 (or other fixed number) or less is changed to zero; any value above 0.5 is changed to one.

A transformation can occur at the output of each processing element, or it can be performed at the final output of the network.

Learning

An ANN learns from its mistakes. The usual process of learning (or training) involves three tasks (Figure 18.5):

1. Compute outputs.
2. Compare outputs with desired targets.
3. Adjust the weights and repeat the process.

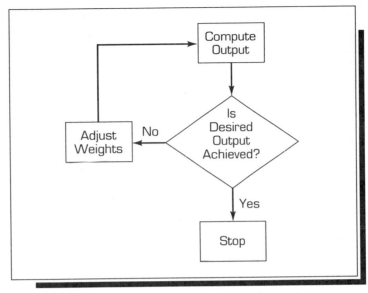

FIGURE 18.5   Learning Process of an Artificial Neural Network

The learning process starts by setting the weights randomly. The difference between the actual output (Y or Y_T) and the desired output (Z) is called delta. The objective is to minimize delta (or better, to reduce it to zero). The reduction of delta is done by changing the weights. The trick is to change the weights in the *right* direction, that is, to make changes that further reduce delta.

Information processing with an ANN consists of analyzing patterns of activities (**pattern recognition**) with learned information stored as the neuron's connection weights. A common characteristic of systems is the ability to classify streams of input data without the explicit knowledge of rules and to use arbitrary patterns of weights (see Box 18.3). During the learning stages, the interconnecting weights change in response to training data presented to the system.

Different ANNs compute the error in different ways depending on the learning algorithm that is being used. More than a hundred learning algorithms are available for various situations and configurations; these are discussed in section 18.9.

18.4   Developing Neural Network Applications

Neural network applications are in use enough to allow identification of practical guidelines for their development. Although the development process is similar to the structured design methodologies of traditional computer-based information systems, some steps are unique to neural network applications or have additional considerations. In the process described here, we assume that preliminary steps of system development, such as determining information requirements and

Box 18.3: How Patterns Are Presented and Recognized

This box shows seven ideal desired outputs. Actual cases can be exactly the same, or they can differ. The problem is to clarify each pattern to a class (the interpretation).

The historical cases show how interpretation decisions were made. These cases are divided into two categories: test cases and training cases.

Desired Outputs

Pattern	Interpretation
0 0 0 0 0 0 0 0 0 0	down
1 1 1 1 0 0 0 0 0 0	left
1 1 1 0 0 0 0 1 1 1	valley
0 1 0 1 0 1 0 1 0 1	alternating
0 0 0 0 0 0 1 1 1 1	right
0 0 0 1 1 1 1 0 0 0	hill
1 1 1 1 1 1 1 1 1 1	up

Historical Cases

	Pattern	Interpretation
Test cases		
#1	1 1 0 0 1 1 0 0 1 1	alternating
#2	0 0 0 0 0 1 0 0 0 1	right
#3	1 1 0 1 1 1 0 0 0 0	left
#4	0 0 1 1 0 1 0 1 0 1	alternating
#5	0 0 0 1 1 0 1 1 0 0	alternating
Training cases		
#6	1 1 1 0 1 1 1 0 1 1	alternating
#7	0 0 1 0 0 0 1 1 1 1	right
#8	0 1 0 1 1 0 1 1 0 0	alternating
#9	1 1 1 0 0 0 0 0 0 0	left
#10	1 1 1 1 0 0 1 1 1 1	valley

Notice that the historical cases may deviate from the desired output. The ANN will try to minimize the difference and give an interpretation as close as possible to the desired pattern.

(*Source:* C.W. Engel and M. Cran, "Pattern Classifications: A Neural Network Competes with Humans," *PC AI* [May/June 1991].)

conducting the feasibility analysis for the project, have been completed successfully. Such steps are generic to *any* information system.

As shown in Figure 18.6, the development process for an ANN application has nine steps. In *steps 1 and 2* the data to be used for training and testing are collected. Important considerations are that the particular problem is amenable to neural network solution and that adequate data exist and can be obtained. Training data must be identified, and a plan must be made for testing the performance of the network.

In *steps 3 and 4* a network architecture and a learning method are selected. The availability of a particular development tool or the capabilities of the development personnel may determine the type of neural network. Important considerations are the particular number of neurons and the number of layers to be used.

Current neural network models have various parameters available for tuning the network to the desired performance level. Part of the process in *step 5* is initialization of the network weights and parameters, followed by modification of the parameters as performance feedback is received. In many cases, the initial values are important for determining the efficiency and length of the training.

The next step, *number 6*, is to transform the application data into the type and format required by the neural network. This may mean writing software for preprocessing the data. Data storage and manipulation techniques and processes need to be designed for conveniently and efficiently retraining the neural network when needed. Also, the way the application data is represented and ordered often determines the efficiency and possibly the accuracy of results from the network.

In *Steps 7 and 8*, training is conducted as an iterative process of presenting input and desired output data to the network. The network computes the actual outputs and adjusts the weights until the actual outputs match what is desired. The desired outputs and their relationships to input data are derived from historical data (a portion of data collected in step 1).

At *step 9* in the process, a stable set of weights has been obtained. Now the network can reproduce the desired outputs given inputs like those in the training set. The network is ready for use as a stand-alone system or as part of another software system.

Now let's look at these nine steps in detail.

18.5   Data Collection and Preparation

The first two steps in the ANN development process involve collecting data and separating them into a training set and a test set. These tasks must be based on a thorough analysis of the application so that the problem is well bounded and the functionality of the system and the context of the neural network are well understood.

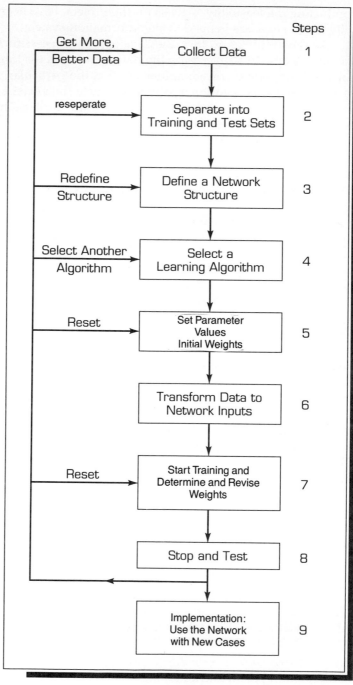

FIGURE 18.6 Flow Diagram of the Development Process of an Artificial Neural Network

In conjunction with a domain expert, the developer must identify and clarify data relevant to the problem. This means formulating and conceptualizing the task in a data-oriented way that will be amenable to a neural network solution. For example, textual descriptions need to be reformulated to allow the knowledge to be described numerically. The developer needs to avoid biases due to the particular way the data are represented. Other considerations are the stability of the input and the extent to which environmental conditions might require changes in the number of input nodes to the neural network. At this point, a difficulty in expressing data in the form needed for a neural network might lead to cancellation of the project.

The anticipated structure of the neural network and the learning algorithm determine the data type, such as binary or continuous. High-quality data collection requires care to minimize ambiguity, errors, and randomness in data. The data should be collected to cover the widest range of the problem domain; data should cover not only routine operations, but also exceptions and conditions at the boundaries of the problem domain. Another task is to confirm reliability by using multiple sources of data; even so, ambiguities will have to be resolved. In general, the more data used, the better—as long as quality is not sacrificed. Larger data sets increase processing times during training, and also improves the accuracy of the training and could lead to faster convergence to a good set of weights.

The data sets are randomly separated into two categories: training cases and testing cases. The training cases are used to adjust the weight. The test cases are used for validation of the network.

18.6 Network Structures

Many different neural network models and implementations (step 2) are being developed and studied today [2, 4, 8, 20]. Three representative architectures (with appropriate learning algorithms) are shown in Figure 18.7 and are discussed next.

Associative Memory Systems

Associative memory refers to the ability of recalling complete situations from partial information. These systems correlate input data with information stored in memory. Information can be recalled from incomplete or "noisy" input, and performance degrades only slowly as neurons fail. Associative memory systems can detect similarities between new input and stored patterns. Most neural network architectures can be used as associative memories, and a prime example of a single-layer system is the Hopfield network [22], which uses the collective properties of the network and minimization of an energy function to classify input patterns.

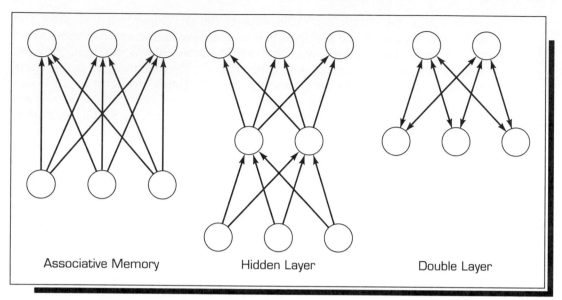

FIGURE 18.7   Neural Network Structures

Hidden Layer

Associative memory systems can have one or more intermediate (hidden) layers. An example of a simple network was shown in Figure 18.2. Many of today's multilayer networks use the backpropagation learning algorithm. Another type of unsupervised learning, competitive filter associative memory, has capabilities for learning by changing its weights in recognition of categories of input data without being provided examples by an external trainer. A leading example of such a single-layer, self-organizing system for a fixed number of classes in the inputs is the Kohonen network [28].

Double-Layer Structure

A double-layer structure, exemplified by the adaptive resonance theory (ART) approach (e.g. Carpenter and Grossberg [7]), does not require the knowledge of a precise number of classes in the training data. Instead, it uses feed forward and feed backward to adjust parameters as data are analyzed to establish arbitrary numbers of categories that represent the data presented to the system. Parameters can be adjusted to tune the sensitivity of the system and produce meaningful categories.

For more complex neural computing applications, neurons are combined together in various architectures useful for information processing. Practical applications require one or more (hidden) layers between the input and output neurons and a correspondingly large number of weights. Most commercial ΛNNs include three, and rarely four or five layers, with each containing from

10 to 1,000 processing elements. Some experimental ANNs include millions of processing elements. The use of more than three layers is not necessary in most commercial systems. The amount of computation added with each layer increases exponentially very rapidly.

18.7 Preparation

In preparation for the training, it is necessary first to decide on what learning algorithm to use (step 4, see section 18.9). This decision is related to the software tools that are going to be used (see section 18.12). A decision must be made at this stage because the structure and data preparation may have to be adjusted to fit the learning algorithm (especially if a software tool is used).

Selecting a learning algorithm is necessary but not sufficient. Before the training starts, several parameters must be determined (step 5). One parameter determines the rate of learning (as will be shown in section 18.9). It can be set to be high or it can be low. Another parameter is the threshold value that determines the form of the output (an example is given in section 18.9). Finally, the initial values of the weights need to be set. Several other parameters that deal with validation and testing can also be determined during preparation.

The last task of preparation is transforming the training and test data to the format required by the network and its algorithm (step 6). This step is especially important when a software tool is used.

18.8 Training the Network

This phase (step 7) consists of presenting the training data set to the network so that the weights can be adjusted to produce the desired output for each of the inputs. Weights are adjusted after each input vector is presented, so several iterations of the complete training set will be required until a consistent set of weights that works for *all* the training data is derived.

The choice of the network's structure (e.g., the number of nodes and layers), as well as the selection of the initial conditions of the network, determines the length of time for the training. Therefore, these choices are important and require careful consideration at the outset of the process.

In the ideal case, the network can learn the features of the input data without learning irrelevant details. Thus, with the presentation of novel inputs that are not identical to those in the training set, the network would be able to make correct classifications.

18.9 Learning Algorithms

An important consideration in ANN is the appropriate use of algorithms for learning (or training). Such algorithms are called **learning algorithms** and there are more than a hundred of them. A taxonomy of these algorithms has been proposed by Lippman [31], who distinguishes between two major categories based on the input format: binary-valued input (0s and 1s) or continuous-valued input. Each of these can be further divided (Figure 18.8) into two basic categories: supervised learning and unsupervised learning.

Supervised learning uses a set of inputs for which the appropriate (desired) outputs are known. In one type, the difference between the desired and actual output is used to calculate corrections to the weights of the neural network. A variation of that approach simply acknowledges for each input trial whether or not the output is correct as the network adjusts weights in an attempt to achieve correct results. Examples of this type of learning are backpropagation and the Hopfield network.

In **unsupervised learning,** only input stimuli are shown to the network. The network is self-organizing; that is, it organizes itself internally so that each hidden processing element responds strategically to a different set of input stimuli (or groups of stimuli). No knowledge is supplied about what classifications (outputs) are correct, and those that the network derives may or may not be meaningful to the person training the network. However, the number of categories into which the network classifies the inputs can be controlled by varying certain parameters in the model. In any case, a human must examine the final categories to assign meaning and to determine the usefulness of the results. Examples of this type of learning are the Adaptive Resonance Theory (ART) and Kohonen self-organizing feature maps.

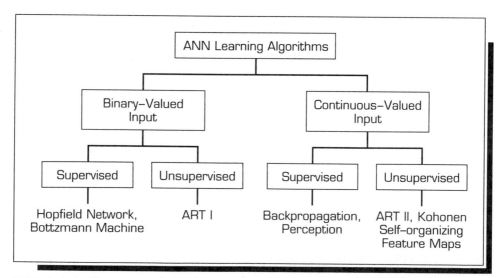

FIGURE 18.8 Taxonomy of Artificial Neural Network Learning Algorithms (*Source:* Modified from R. P. Lippman, "Review of Neural Networks for Speech Recognition," *Neural Computing* 1 [no. 1, 1989].)

How a Network Learns

Consider a single neuron that learns the inclusive OR operation—a classical problem in symbolic logic. There are two input elements, X_1 and X_2. If either of them or both have a positive value (or a certain value), then the result is also positive. This can be shown as follows:

	Inputs		
Case	X_1	X_2	**Desired Results**
1	0	0	0
2	0	1	1 (positive)
3	1	0	1 (positive)
4	1	1	1 (positive)

The neuron must be trained to recognize the input patterns and classify them to give the corresponding outputs. The procedure is to present to the neuron the sequence of the four input patterns so that the weights are adjusted by the computer after each iteration. This step is repeated until the weights converge to a uniform set of values that allow the neuron to classify correctly each of the four inputs. The results shown in Table 18.1 were produced by using the Excel spreadsheet software to execute the calculations. In this simple example, a step function is used to evaluate the summation of input values. After calculating outputs, a measure of the error (delta) between the output and the desired values is used to update the weights, subsequently reinforcing correct results. At any step in the process for a neuron, j, we get

$$delta = Z_j - Y_j$$

where Z and Y are the desired and actual outputs, respectively. Then, the updated weights are

$$W_i \text{(final)} = W_i \text{(initial)} + alpha*delta*X_1$$

where alpha is a parameter that controls how fast the learning takes place.

As shown in Table 18.1, each calculation uses one of the X_1 and X_2 pairs and the corresponding value for the OR operation along with initial values, W_1 and W_2, of the neuron's weights. In this example, the weights are assigned random values at the beginning, and a *learning rate* (a parameter), alpha, is set to be relatively low. Delta is used to derive the final weights, which then become the initial weights in the next row.

The initial values of weights for each input are transformed using the equation above to values that are used with the next input (row). The threshold value (another parameter) causes the Y value to be 1 in the next row if the weighted sum of inputs is greater than 0.5; otherwise, the output is set to 0. In this example, in the first step two of the four outputs are incorrect (delta = 1) and no consistent set of weights has been found. In the subsequent steps, the

TABLE 18.1   Example of Supervised Learning

Step	X_1	X_2	Z	Initial W_1	W_2	Y	Delta	Final W_1	W_2
1	0	0	0	0.1	0.3	0	0.0	0.1	0.3
	0	1	1	0.1	0.3	0	1.0	0.1	0.5
	1	0	1	0.1	0.5	0	1.0	0.3	0.5
	1	1	1	0.3	0.5	1	0.0	0.3	0.5
2	0	0	0	0.3	0.5	0	0.0	0.3	0.5
	0	1	1	0.3	0.5	0	1.0	0.3	0.7
	1	0	1	0.3	0.7	0	1.0	0.5	0.7
	1	1	1	0.5	0.7	1	0.0	0.5	0.7
3	0	0	0	0.5	0.7	0	0.0	0.5	0.7
	0	1	1	0.5	0.7	1	0.0	0.5	0.7
	1	0	1	0.5	0.7	0	1.0	0.7	0.7
	1	1	1	0.7	0.7	1	0.0	0.7	0.7
4	0	0	0	0.7	0.7	0	0.0	0.7	0.7
	0	1	1	0.7	0.7	1	0.0	0.7	0.7
	1	0	1	0.7	0.7	1	0.0	0.7	0.7
	1	1	1	0.7	0.7	1	0.0	0.7	0.7

Parameters: alpha = 0.2; threshold = 0.5.

learning algorithm improves the results until it finally produces a set of weights that give the correct results (in step 4). Once determined, a neuron with those weight values can quickly perform the OR operation.

In developing ANN, an attempt is made to fit the problem characteristic to one of the known learning algorithms. Software programs exist for all the different algorithms, but it is best to use a well-known and well-characterized one, such as backpropagation, which will be described next.

18.10   Backpropagation

Backpropagation (or back-error propagation) is the most widely used learning algorithm (see Hecht-Nielsen [20]). It is a very popular technique that is relatively easy to implement. It does require training data for conditioning the network before using it for processing other data. A backpropagation network includes one or more hidden layers. The network is considered a *feed forward*, since there are no interconnections between the output of a processing element and the input of a node on the same layer or on a preceding layer. Externally provided correct patterns are compared with the neural network output during training (i.e., it is a supervised training), and feedback is used to adjust the weights until all training patterns are correctly categorized by the network.

Starting with the output layer, errors between the actual and desired outputs are used to correct the weights for the connections to the previous layer. It has been shown that for any output neuron, j, the error (delta) = $(Z_j - Y_j)*(df/dx)$, where Z and Y are the desired and actual outputs. It is useful to choose the sigmoid function, $f = [1 + \exp(-x)]^{-1}$, to represent the output of a neuron, where x is proportional to the sum of the weighted inputs to that neuron. In this way, $df/dx = f(1 - f)$ and the error is a simple function of the desired and actual outputs. The factor $f(1 - f)$ is the logistic function, which serves to keep the error correction well bounded. The weights of each input to the jth neuron are then changed in proportion to this calculated error. A more complicated expression can be derived to work backwards in a similar way from the output neurons through the inner layers to calculate the corrections to the associated weights of the inner neurons.

The procedure for executing the learning algorithm is as follows: initialize weights and other parameters by giving them random values. Then read in the input vector and the desired output. Compute actual output via the calculations forward through the layers; change the weights by calculating *backward* from the output layer through the hidden layers. This procedure is repeated for all the input vectors until the desired and actual outputs agree within some predetermined tolerance. Given the amount of calculation for one iteration, a large network can take a very long time to train. Current research is aimed at developing algorithms to improve this process.

18.11 Testing

In the second step of the development process, the available data were divided into training and testing data. Now that the training has been performed, it is necessary to test the network. The testing phase (step 8) examines the performance of the network using the derived weights by measuring the ability of the network to classify the test data correctly. Black-box testing (comparing test results to actual historical results) is the primary approach to verify that inputs produce the appropriate outputs.

In many cases, the network is not expected to perform perfectly, and only a certain level of quality is required. Usually, the neural network application is an alternative to another method that can be used as a standard. For example, a statistical technique or other quantitative methods may be known to classify inputs correctly 70 percent of the time. The neural network implementation often improves on that percentage. If the neural network is replacing manual operations, performance levels of human processing may be the standard for deciding if the testing phase is successful.

The test plan should include routine cases as well as potentially problematic situations, for example, at the boundaries of the problem domain. If the testing reveals large deviations, the training set needs to be reexamined and the training process may have to be reactivated.

In some cases, other methods can supplement black-box testing. For example, the weights can be analyzed statistically to look for unusually large values that indicate overtraining or unusually small weights that indicate unnecessary nodes. Also, certain weights that represent major factors in the input vector can be selectively activated to make sure that corresponding outputs respond properly.

Even at a performance level equal to that of a traditional method, the ANN may have other advantages. For example, the network is easily modified by retraining with new data. Other computerized techniques may require extensive reprogramming when changes are needed.

18.12 Implementation

The implementation of the ANN (step 9) frequently requires proper interfaces with other computer-based information systems and training of the users. Ongoing monitoring and feedback to the developers are recommended for system improvements and long-term success. An important consideration is to gain confidence of the users and management early in the deployment to ensure that the system is accepted and used properly.

If it is a part of a larger system, the ANN will need convenient interfaces to other information systems, input/output (I/O) devices, and manual operations for the users. The system may need I/O manipulation subsystems such as signal digitizers and file conversion modules. Good documentation and user training are necessary to ensure successful integration into the mainstream operations. A convenient procedure must be planned for updating the training sets and initiating periodic retraining of the network. This includes the ability to recognize and include new cases that are discovered when the system is used routinely.

Ongoing monitoring and feedback to the developers is necessary for maintaining the neural network system. Periodic evaluation of system performance may reveal environmental changes or previously missed bugs that require changes in the network. Enhancements may be suggested as users become more familiar with the system, and feedback may be useful in the design of future versions or in new products.

Neural Computing Paradigms. In building an artificial neural network, the builder must make many decisions:

- Size of training and test data
- Learning algorithms
- Topology: number of processing elements and their configurations (inputs, layers, outputs)
- Transformation (transfer) function to be used
- Learning rate for each layer
- Diagnostic and validation tools

A specific configuration determined by these decisions is referred to as the network's paradigm.

18.13   Programming Neural Networks

Artificial neural networks are basically software applications that need to be programmed. Like any other application, an ANN can be programmed with a programming language, a tool, or both.

A major portion of the programming deals with the training algorithms and the transfer and summation functions. It makes sense, therefore, to use development tools in which these standard computations are preprogrammed. Indeed, several dozen development tools are on the market (Table 18.2). Some of these tools are similar to expert system shells. Even with the help of tools, however, the job of developing a neural network may not be so simple. Specifically, it may be necessary to program the layout of the database, to partition the data (test data, training data), and to transfer the data to files suitable for input to an ANN tool (see Box 18.4).

Box 18.4: How Simple Is It?

In principle, a neural network should be very simple to build. These steps are followed:

□ A processing element (PE) takes all its incoming signals (usually given in a binary code).
□ The PE multiplies them by the weights of the connections over which they entered.
□ The PE adds up the intermediate answers and multiplies the total by a nonlinear transfer function. This provides a single output.

Sounds simple? Not necessarily. Here are some unrelated portions of a neural network program written in C:

```
NPCat = Stats[0][0] − Stats[1][1];
for(wx = 1; wx < 3; wx+ +){
wi = Stats[wx][0] − Stats[wx][1];/* # of items left */
if (wi < NPCat)
NPCat = wi;/* pick smallest */

if (CatLeft[wx] > 0 && rand() < CatThresh[wx]){
/*—add this record to training data-base—*/
fputs ((char*)dbP, TrFP);/* output record*/
CatLeft[wx]—;/* decrement remaining */
BITSET(RecUsed,RecNumber);/* claim the record*/
ClassifyRec(dbP,2);/* classify it*/
```

(*Source of the program:* C. C. Klimasauskas, "Applying Neural Networks Part II," *PC AI* [March/April 1991].)

TABLE 18.2 Representative Neural Computing Development Tools

Tool	Vendor
BrainMaker	California Scientific Software, Grass Valley, Calif.
ExploreNet	Hecht-Nielsen Neurocomputer Corp., San Diego, Calif.
Explorer NeuralWorks Professional I, II, Plus	NeuralWare, Pittsburgh, Pa.
Plexi	Lucid Inc., Menlo Park, Calif.
NeuroShell	Ward Systems Group, Frederick, Md.
MacBrain	Neurix, Boston, Mass.
N-NETEX, N-NET 600	Al Ware, Cleveland, Ohio
Nestor Development System	NESTOR Corp., Providence, R.I.

For a complete list, see "Neural-Net Resource Guide," *AI Expert* (July 1991): 60–68.

Most development tools can support several network paradigms (up to several dozens). In addition to the standard products, there are many special products. For example, several products are based on spreadsheets (e.g., NNetSheet). Other products are designed to work with expert systems as hybrid development products (e.g., KnowledgeNet) and NeuroSMARTS. For a list of ANN tools, see [23].

The user of ANN tools is constrained by the configuration of the tool. Therefore, builders may prefer to use programming languages such as C or to use spreadsheets to program the model and execute the calculations.

18.14   Neural Network Hardware

Most current neural network applications involve software simulations that run on conventional sequential processors. Simulating a neural network means mathematically defining the nodes and weights assigned to it. So instead of using one CPU for each neuron, one CPU is used for all of the neurons. This simulation may take long processing times. Advances in hardware technology will greatly enhance the performance of future neural network systems by exploiting the inherent advantage of **massively parallel processing.** Hardware improvements will meet the higher requirements for memory and processing speed and thus allow shorter training times of larger networks.

Each processing element computes node outputs from the weights and input signals from other processors. Together, the network of neurons can store information that may be recalled to interpret and classify future inputs to the network.

To reduce the computational work of an ANN, which can consist of hundreds of thousands of manipulations, when the work is done on regular computers, one of three approaches is applicable:

1. *Faster machines:* For example, a machine with the Intel 80486 processor supplemented by a math coprocessor can expedite work, but not too much (e.g., between two to ten times faster).

2. *Neural chips:* Most of today's special chips can execute computations very fast, but they cannot be used to train the network. So it is necessary to "train off the chip." This problem is expected to be corrected soon. (In the interim, acceleration boards are practical.) The idea of a chip is to provide implementation of neural network data structures on a chip—an analog chip (e.g., Intel 80170 Electronically Trainable ANN) or a digital chip, or even an optical one. (See Caudill [10] for details.) Most neural chips are still in the developmental stage.

3. *Acceleration boards:* These are dedicated processors that can be added to regular computers, similar to a math coprocessor. Because they are especially designed for an ANN, they work very fast. (For example, such a processor can be ten to a hundred times faster than the 20 MHZ 80386/387 processor.) Acceleration boards are currently the best approach to speeding up computations. Some examples are BrainMaker Accelerator Board, Balboa/860 boards, and NeuroBoard, which is at least a hundred times faster than the 80386/387 processor. Acceleration boards are extremely useful because they reduce training time, which is usually long. For example, an independent testing with NeuroBoard showed a reduced training time from seven minutes to one second.

18.15 Benefits of Neural Networks

The value of neural network technology includes its usefulness for pattern recognition, learning, classification, generalization and abstraction, and the interpretation of incomplete and noisy inputs. A natural overlap with traditional AI applications thus occurs in the area of pattern recognition for character, speech, and visual recognition. Systems that learn are more natural interfaces to the real world than systems that must be programmed, and speed considerations point to the need to take advantage of parallel processing implementations.

Neural networks have the potential to provide some of the human characteristics of problem solving that are difficult to simulate using the logical, analytical techniques of expert system and standard software technologies. For example, neural networks can analyze large quantities of data to establish patterns and characteristics in situations where rules are not known. Neural networks may be useful for financial applications such as measuring stock fluctuations for determining an appropriate portfolio mix. Likewise, neural networks can provide the human characteristic of making sense of incomplete or noisy data. These features have thus far proven too difficult for the symbolic/logical approach of traditional AI.

Neural networks have several other benefits:

□ *Fault tolerance:* Since there are many processing nodes, each with primarily local connections, damage to a few nodes or links does not bring the system to a halt.

□ *Generalization:* When a neural network is presented with noisy, incomplete, or previously unseen input, it generates a reasonable response.
□ *Adaptability:* The network learns in new environments.

Thus, neural computing differs from traditional computing methods in many ways, and the differences can be exploited by the application developer. Neural networks can be applied in areas where data are multivariate with a high degree of interdependence between attributes, data are noisy or incomplete, or many hypotheses are to be pursued in parallel and high computational rates required.

Beyond its role as an alternative, neural computing can be combined with conventional software to produce powerful hybrid systems. Such integrated systems could include database, expert system, neural network, and other technologies to produce computerized solutions to complex problems. Thus, computerized systems could eventually mimic human decision making, even under conditions of uncertainty and in which information is incomplete or contains mistakes. A popular goal is to produce systems with components such as neural computing that exhibit mindlike behavior in order to handle information as flexibly and powerfully as humans do.

18.16   Limitations of Neural Networks

The current applicability of artificial neural networks is limited by the present state of research and development and possibly by some inherent characteristics. In general, ANNs do not do well at tasks that are not done well by people. For example, arithmetic and data processing tasks are not suitable for ANNs and are best accomplished by conventional computers. Current applications of ANNs excel in the areas of classification and pattern recognition.

Most neural network systems lack explanation facilities. Justifications for results are difficult to obtain because the connection weights do not usually have obvious interpretations. This is particularly true in pattern recognition where it is very difficult or even impossible to explain the logic behind specific decisions. The limitations and expense of current parallel hardware technology restrict most applications to software simulations. Research and development continues to find better learning algorithms, system architectures, and development methodologies. With current technologies, training times can be excessive and tedious; thus, the need for frequent retraining may make a particular application impractical. The best way to represent input data and the choice of architecture are still mostly subject to trial and error. Methods for handling temporal aspects of data are still in the research stage. Finally, neural computing usually requires large amounts of data and lengthy training time.

Most of these problems are the subject of current research and development efforts. Current applications focus on the areas that are done well and easily with neural networks. Further uses await the many technological advances on the horizon.

18.17   Neural Networks and Expert Systems

When ANNs were revived in recent years, they were labeled by some as sixth-generation computing. This labeling gave the erroneous impression that the fifth-generation computing, of which expert systems are a major part, is going to be replaced. As a matter of fact, while in some cases ANNs can perform tasks better (or faster) than ES, in most instances the two technologies are not in competition. Furthermore, the characteristics of the technologies are so different that they can *complement* each other rather nicely in some cases. The purpose of this section is to provide an overview of the relationship between the two technologies. In section 18.19 we will discuss the potential integration of the two technologies.

In principle, expert systems represent a logical, symbolic approach, whereas neural networks use numeric and associative processing to mimic models of biological systems. The main features of each approach are summarized in Table 18.3.

Expert Systems

Expert systems perform reasoning using preestablished rules for a well-defined and narrow domain. They combine knowledge bases of rules and domain-specific facts with information from clients or users about specific instances of problems in the knowledge domains of the expert systems. Ideally, reasoning can be explained and the knowledge bases can be easily modified, independently of the inference engine, as new rules become known.

Expert systems are especially good for closed-system applications for which inputs are literal and precise and lead to logical outputs. They are especially useful for interacting with the client/user to define a specific problem and bring in facts peculiar to the problem being solved. Expert systems reason by using established facts and preestablished rules.

TABLE 18.3   Major Characteristics of Expert Systems and Artificial Neural Networks

Characteristic	Expert Systems	Neural Networks
Approach	Symbolic (mainly)	Numeric
Reasoning	Logical	Associative
Operations	Mechanical	Biologicallike
Explanation	Available	Not available
Processing	Sequential	Parallel
System	Closed	Self-organizing
Validation and verification	Slow, difficult	Fast
Driven by	Knowledge	Data
Maintenance	Difficult	Easy

Box 18.5: A Neural Network View

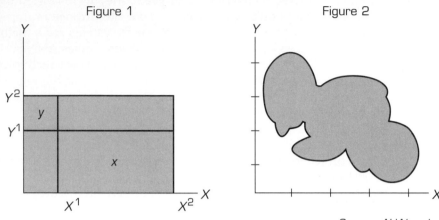

Figure 1

Figure 2

Source: AI Ware Inc.

Generally, conventional computing systems solve problems in a sequential manner—solve problem A by performing steps 1 through 10, in order. An expert system tackles the same 10 steps, but might do step 9 first, then step 6, then step 1, in whatever order its chain of reasoning determines to be most efficient. A neural network looks at all 10 steps simultaneously, and maps a pattern representing an acceptable solution. This simplified decision model shows the differences between the way an expert system and a neural network view a quality control problem. In this sample, only two test criteria, X and Y, are involved. The shaded area represents an acceptable relationship between X and Y (the tested parts are good); an unshaded area represents unacceptable parts. This simple yes/no quality problem could be easily handled by a rule-based expert system (Figure 1). In an actual industrial situation, however, with real-world data, the actual relationship between X and Y might look more like Figure 2, where it is not clearly obvious which parts fall into the acceptable range and which do not. And, of course, it is more likely that many criteria would be involved rather than just two. By learning to recognize shapes or patterns—in this case, depicting part acceptability—neural networks can efficiently handle problems of complex relationships involving many variables.

(*Source:* B. Francett, "Neural Nets Arrive," *Computer Decisions* [January 1989]: 2.)

A major limitation of the expert system approach arises from the fact that experts do not always think in terms of rules. Also, experts may not be able to explain their line of reasoning, or they may explain it incorrectly. Thus, in many cases, it is difficult or even impossible to build the necessary knowledge base.

To overcome this and other limitations, neural computing may be attempted (see Box 18.5).

Neural Computing

Neural networks rely on training data to "program" the system. Particular applications are developed by establishing an appropriate training set that allows the system to learn and generalize for operation on future input data. Inputs that match the training data exactly are recognized and identified, while new data (or incomplete and noisy versions of the training data) can be matched closely to patterns recognized by the system.

Comparison of Characteristics

For stable applications with well-defined rules, expert systems can be developed to provide good performance. Furthermore, most ES development software packages allow the creation of explanations to help the user understand questions being asked or conclusions and reasoning processes. In contrast, in ANNs, knowledge is represented as numeric weights; therefore, the rules and the reasoning process are not readily explainable.

Neural networks can be preferable to expert systems when rules are not known either because the topic is too complex or no human expert is available. If training data can be generated, the system may be able to learn enough information to function as well as, or better than, an expert system. This approach also has the benefit of easy maintenance. Modifications are exercised by retraining with an updated data set, thereby eliminating programming changes and rule reconstruction. The data-driven property of neural networks allows adjustment of changing environments and events. (Expert systems are knowledge driven, so changes can be made only if the knowledge is changed.) Another advantage of the neural network implementation is the speed of operation after the network has been trained. The natural use of parallel systems and neural boards and chips enhances this aspect dramatically.

Comparison of Development Processes

The processes for developing expert systems and neural networks have important parallels, as shown in Figure 18.9. Knowledge engineers and neurocomputing engineers each have to represent a body of knowledge in either facts and rules or as data sets. In either case, domain experts need to be involved to ensure the accuracy of the rules or data sets. However, the required involvement in ANNs is significantly less.

The builders spend considerable time and effort either in formulating and testing rules or in creating accurate data sets with the proper format to present to the neural network for training. In each case, validation and verification of

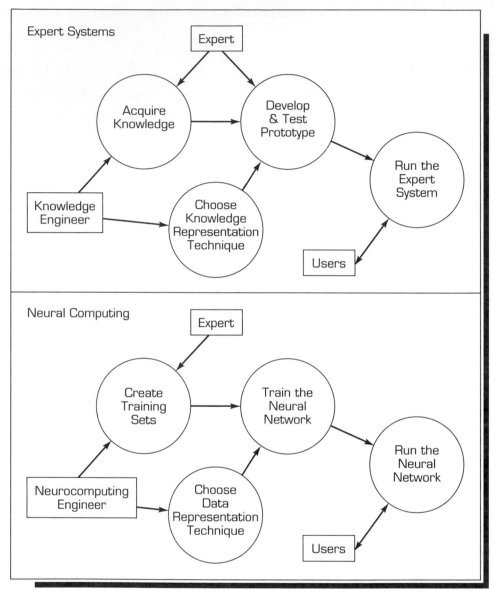

FIGURE 18.9 Development Processes for Expert Systems and Artificial Neural Networks

the system is an important and difficult task. (It is more difficult in expert systems.)

The parallels between expert system and neural network development and their complementary nature make hybrid systems a promising area for research and development. The *integration* of these and possibly other intelligent components with conventional systems promises to be an important area for both research and development and for implementation in the 1990s.

18.18   Neural Networks in Knowledge Acquisition

As pointed out earlier, a major limitation of expert systems is knowledge acquisition. Therefore, it makes sense to use ANNs to acquire knowledge that later can be used in an ES. An artificial neural network can execute an automatic knowledge acquisition task for situations in which historical data are available. In principle, the approach is similar to rule-induction or case-based reasoning. However, rule induction requires an initial set of *attributes,* and these may not be available if experts are not available to produce them or if the experts can not identify all the relevant attributes. Also, the input data must be unambiguous and missing data may prevent rule induction. Case-based reasoning is a new technology with limited real-life applications reported to date.

In situations where rules cannot be determined directly, or where it may take too long to solicit them, an ANN can be useful for fast identification of implicit knowledge by automatically analyzing cases of historical data. The ANN analyzes the data sets to identify *patterns* and relationships that may subsequently lead to rules for expert systems. The ANN may be the sole technique for knowledge acquisition or it may supplement explicit rules derived by other techniques (such as interviews or rule induction).

Another possible contribution of ANNs to knowledge acquisition occurs when the interface with an expert may best be accomplished with an expert system module that asks questions and directs the data gathering from the expert efficiently and comprehensively. A trained neural network can then rapidly process information to produce associated facts and consequences. Next, an expert system module can perform further analysis and report results. Thus, fewer explicit rules may be necessary since the neural network contains general knowledge embedded in its connection weights and produces specific knowledge relevant to the user's specific problem.

Work by Taber and Siegel [44] uses fuzzy cognitive maps as associative memory to assist in knowledge acquisition. The technique allows the knowledge engineer to create analysis diagrams that help identify causal connections in knowledge and dynamic systems. This diagrammatic technique assists the knowledge engineer in translating knowledge into rules or neural networks.

18.19   Integrating Neural Networks and Expert Systems

The complementary nature of artificial neural networks and expert systems allows novel applications and solutions to more complex problems when the two technologies are combined. There are two basic ways of using expert systems and neural networks: embedded systems and distributed systems.

Embedded Systems

In the embedded system configuration, the expert system and neural network are *integrated* or *tightly coupled* components of the same system. For example, the neural network component could represent the knowledge base implicitly as connection weights. The system could be designed so that the weights represent branches in the logic of the rule base so that the lines of reasoning can be explained. Alternatively, the neural network associative memory may just store relationships between patterns of inputs and corresponding conclusions. For example, Gallant [16] has designed connectionist networks for use as expert systems, and Dietz et al. [12] have created an expert system using a neural network for jet and rocket engine diagnostics.

Distributed Intelligent Systems

A relatively straightforward approach is the *loose coupling* of expert systems with neural networks and possibly databases in which individual subsystems are capable of *functioning independently*. They can interface with each other via communication lines (e.g., by transfer of data). Neural network components can also be coupled more *tightly* with other software to provide specialized functions or subroutines to the overall system. Thus, distributed systems may communicate information by file transfer or by means of the internal memory and data structures of the overall system.

One type of distributed system involves pre- and post-processing with standard or expert system software to interface with neural network components. This configuration uses an expert system component, for example, for collecting data from a user and also for the reasoning required to present final conclusions. The neural network component analyzes data to supply information needed by the expert system for a complete analysis. One advantage of this model is the ability to use files of training data to change system behavior without knowing or changing rules in the knowledge base. An interesting variation is the inclusion of a case base that serves as training input for the neural network but can be updated easily as new knowledge is discovered and used periodically to retrain the network.

Examples of Integrated Systems

A prototype system using the expert system shell AUBREY and the neural network tool NeuroShell has been designed to advise users on resource requirements for developing database systems (Caudill [11]). The neural network analyzes experiential data on the amount of time and effort required to finish previous database projects. The system provides the flexibility of presenting new data files to supply information without having to enter new rules or information extracted from separate data analysis.

A system developed by Hanson and Brekke [18] projects personnel resource requirements for maintaining networks or workstations at NASA. A rule-based system determines the final resource projections, but an ANN provides project completion times for services requested. The projections are based on historical cases and the current service request activity list. The neural network is easily *retrained* via new data sets on completion times for recent services (Figure 18.10).

Bhogal et al. [5] have developed an integrated system called CAPS, which translates production systems written in OPS5 into neural network implementations. Fully trained neural networks can then perform as rule-based, symbolic reasoning systems. This translation facility increases the feasibility of hardware implementations.

Pham and Degoult [37] describe an approach called Macro-connectionist Organization System for Artificial Intelligence Computation (MOSAIC), which they have devised to integrate different kinds of cognitive functions. MOSAIC allows the management of complex, structured knowledge by means of numeric connectionist networks. Several inference strategies can be used to acquire knowledge explicitly or by fast, unsupervised learning.

In an expert system that is a front-end to an ANN, the data needed for the ANN is *preprocessed* by the ES. Organizing data available in cases into the manner required by the specific ANN model can be a tedious and repetitive

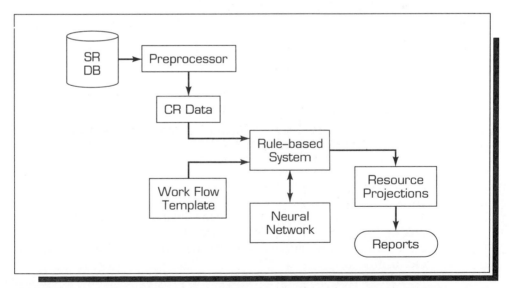

FIGURE 18.10 Hybrid System for Resource Requirements (*Source:* Drawn by L. Medsker, based on M. A. Hanson and R. L. Brekke, "Workload Management Expert System—Combining Neural Networks and Rule Based Programming in an Operational Application," special report published by the Instrument Society of America, 1988, pp. 1721–1726.)

job. Sherald [42] describes a window design system developed by Du Pont which is based on such a configuration. In addition to an ES and ANN, the system includes a customized file reader for displaying text, programmed in C (in this system there are two ANNs). The expert system can provide explanations if needed. The system builder used the Level5 ES shell and the NeuroShell product for building the ANN.

18.20   Neural Networks in Natural Language Processing

Neural networks are well suited to support speech recognition by storing trained information on speech parts and rapidly matching them with input patterns. A front-end ANN recognizes short phonemelike fragments of speech, and another ANN constructs words from combinations of the fragments. Finally, another component clarifies ambiguities between words with similar sounds. For example, a system developed by Kohonen [28] has the highest accuracy and the largest vocabulary currently available.

A system called NETtalk, is a three-layer network that synthesizes speech from text. The system has no programmed rules and can pronounce an unrestricted range of English text. The steps of the training phase mimic the developmental phases of children learning to speak.

An important requirement for language processing systems is to discriminate meanings of words dependent on the textual setting. Neural networks can be used to establish associations between words commonly used together. During operation, the ANN checks these linkages for words in the particular sentence being analyzed and chooses the best interpretation.

18.21   Signal Processing, Machine Vision, and Robotics

Autonomous machines have long been a goal of artificial intelligence research and development. Aspects of this area include processing and understanding of sensory data, coordination between visual perception and mechanical actions, sensing the context of the local environment, and the ability to learn and adapt to a changing environment. Clearly, neural computing can play an important role in this area.

Although the use of ANNs for improving machine vision makes sense, implementation may not be simple, as evidenced in the anecdote about the tank and the rock in Box 18.6.

Much of the work in robotic learning (e.g., error recovery, see Chapter 11) is in the experimental/prototype stage; however, research results are

Box 18.6: The Tank and the Rock: Believe It or Not

For many years the military has been experimenting with technologies that will enable machines to identify objects on the battlefield at night or from a long distance. The basic issue is automatic interpretation of pictures or other signals provided by various sensing devices.

Neural computing seemed to be an excellent solution for such a task. However, as reported by Loofbourrow [32], even ANNs may fail. The story goes like this: A scanner attached to an ANN was shown thousands of photographs of tanks, rocks, and other objects in the battlefield. The system was told what was in each photograph. The purpose was to train the ANN. Indeed, after extensive training, the ANN was able to correctly distinguish a *photo* of a tank from that of a rock nearly 100 percent of the time.

Later someone discovered that all the photos of tanks had been taken with one camera and that these photos were all slightly darker than the photos of other objects. The Army had built a near-perfect ANN for identifying the camera used to take a picture. The system had learned nothing about tanks. Had the same camera been used for *all* photos, the ANN could have been a tank identifier instead of a camera identifier.

encouraging. Recent work concerns systems that can interpolate learned data to create smoother motions and can vary speeds as needed in specific situations. In the area of robot control, two aspects under intense study are path and trajectory planning and nonlinear control of motors and gears. Systems are also being developed for obstacle detection and adaptive response and for coordination of robot arms with input from cameras.

One example of the integration of ANNs into robotic systems is the work on autonomous learning machines by Handelman et al. [17]. Their work takes advantage of the complementary features of expert systems and ANNs to build subsystems appropriate to the task at hand. The systems combine the reflexive type of knowledge typical of motor skills and ANNs with a declarative mode that modifies the system when the robotic arm starts to deviate from the desired motion. A rule-based module monitors other tasks and invokes rule-based or neural computing components, depending on whether steady-state operations are appropriate or adjustments need to be made. Initially, the rule-based module supervises the training of the ANN, which generalizes the data about arm movement. Subsequently, in operational mode, the ANN can associate given inputs with relevant outputs and therefore be more sensitive to small changes in motion.

In the vision component of robotic or other systems, neural networks can use the associative memory feature to learn to interpret digitized visual data such as partially obscured faces or objects and choose a close match with an image in memory. The systems take incoming visual data and extract features as subtasks of larger systems that use the feature extraction information. The availability of chips for parallel processing of ANNs will allow easy integration with robotic hardware.

18.22   Handwriting Recognition

The recognition of handwritten characters has several important applications. For example, automatic verification of signatures on checks and other documents could save processing costs and reduce losses due to unauthorized transactions. Another example is machine reading of forms filled out in handwriting, which could be advantageous because people do not always have access to typewriters and because they tend to make fewer mistakes if they fill in forms by hand. Finally, postal systems could save billions of dollars if machines were able to read handwritten addresses.

Most ANN vendors are working on systems to recognize handwritten characters. The range of characters that can be analyzed includes graphic symbols and even Chinese characters. Some systems read words directly from paper documents so that a person does not have to reenter data. Other systems have a person use a light pen or write on a sensitive panel with a stylus for data entry.

One system, developed by Fukushima and Miyaki [15], uses an ANN model called "The Neocognitron." This system achieved 95 percent accuracy in recognizing hand-printed characters. Because ANNs are tolerant of variations in input, the system is successful even with a certain amount of shift in the characters' positions, size, and clarity.

Another example is the Intelligent Character Recognition System developed by NYNEX Corp. to process business checks. The system can determine if the amounts written on checks are within predetermined limits.

Other applications under development include systems to read zip codes from letters and packages, process insurance forms, and read numbers from credit-card slips.

18.23   Decision Support Systems

The objective of a decision support system is to provide computerized support to decision makers, especially at the middle and top levels of management, as well as to support staff analysts. The domain of applicability includes semistructured and unstructured situations involving dynamic and open systems, which could involve considerable uncertainty and risk. Problems addressed by such systems tend not to be well structured, and exact solutions and data requirements are difficult to anticipate (see Turban [46]).

Increasingly, ES applications have played a role along with traditional decision support systems in providing personal tools that are adaptable to the needs of individual managerial decision makers. Because of their complementary nature, ANNs can provide capabilities not available in either type of system. Some of the capabilities ANNs provide are similar to human qualities and allow decision makers to perform much better than computer systems. Specifically, ANNs can provide the ability to adapt to the new situations that are typical of open systems and the ability to generalize from experience and interpolate from facts to recognize similar situations. Thus, ANN components can reduce the need for systems to provide a complete set of solutions that anticipate all possible configurations that a manager may encounter.

A basic model of the behavior of decision makers (according to H. Simon, see Turban [46]) starts with an *intelligence* phase in which information is gathered and structured in order to identify problems and opportunities that require decisions. Subsequently, the decision maker *designs* alternate potential solutions and sets criteria for testing and evaluating these alternatives. Finally, the decision maker *chooses* the best (or good enough) alternative. The execution of all three phases can be complicated because of the unstructuredness of problems solved by decision support systems. A natural application of neural networks could be in the processing of large and/or fuzzy data sets to identify patterns and features that require further analysis by a DSS. Thus, the intelligence phase can be greatly enhanced. Also, in the design phase, proposed solutions may be evaluated by matching results with solution criteria. Finally, ANNs can help in the choice phase by analyzing historical cases for their solutions.

Examples of Applications

In financial analysis ANNs can preprocess information from large databases to look for patterns and trends. Results can be used in investment decisions (e.g., see Trippi and Turban [45]).

Artificial neural networks can be useful in the structured models of statistics and operations research/management science. They can help solve very difficult optimization and allocation problems that are not solvable with standard models. Here are three examples:

1. Optimization—use of neural network models to find optimal solutions to problems involving many parameters (For example, an ANN was used to solve the classic Traveling Salesman Problem—see Port [38].)
2. Resource allocation based on historical, experiential data
3. Standard statistical analyses—hybrid systems perform such analyses on data sets selected by the neural network

Research by Kaduba et al. [25] provides an interesting example of the use of hybrid systems in areas of traditional operations research and decision analysis. The researchers developed a system called XROUTE, an exploratory framework that combines an ANN with capabilities for mathematical modeling, knowledge-based systems, and genetic algorithms (Chapter 19). They have applied their model to a combinatorial problem known as the NP-complete vehicle routing problem.

In connection with the database aspect of decision support, future systems will increasingly need flexible and convenient access to heterogeneous distributed databases. The intelligent features of these systems will be provided by a variety of technologies including expert systems, object orientation, and neural networks. Neural networks could be a component of database management systems that run in the background to look for special data or interesting correlations in a database that may be of interest to a decision maker. A goal for intelligent database systems (see Parsaye et al. [36]) is to handle information and decision making similarly to the way humans do. Neural network components may be crucial for finding patterns in data, identifying approximate matches, making best-guess estimates, and facilitating inexact queries.

Chapter Highlights

- □ Neural computing attempts to mimic the manner in which the brain works. It uses procedures similar to those that function in biological systems.
- □ The human brain is composed of billions of cells called neurons, which are grouped in interconnected clusters.
- □ Neural systems are composed of processing elements called artificial neurons. They are interconnected and receive, process, and deliver information (usually in binary code). A group of connected neurons forms an artificial neural network.
- □ An artificial neural network can be organized in many different ways, but the major elements are the processing elements, the contacts among the processing elements, the inputs, the outputs, and the weights.
- □ Weights express the relative strength (or importance) given to input data before it is processed.
- □ Each neuron has an activation value that is expressed by summarizing the input values multiplied by their weights.
- □ An activation value is translated to an output by going through a transformation (transfer) function. The output can be related in a linear or nonlinear manner or via a threshold value.
- □ Artificial neural networks learn from historical cases. The learning (training) produces the required values of the weights, which make the computed outputs equal (or close) to desired outputs.
- □ The learning process is carried out with algorithms. There are more than a hundred, and they are easy to computerize.
- □ Supervised learning refers to a situation in which computed outputs are compared to standards that have been input. In unsupervised learning, the network is self-organized to produce categories (patterns) into which a series of inputs falls.

□ Testing is done by using historical data and running it on adjusted weights to see if the outputs match the standards.

□ Neural computing is frequently integrated with traditional computer-based information systems and with expert systems.

□ Most ANNs are being built with tools that include the learning algorithm(s) and other computational procedures.

□ Artificial neural networks lend themselves to parallel processing. However, the current state of the art of parallel processing involves nonconnected processors. Therefore, current ANNs are solved on regular computers where multiprocessing is simulated on a single processor.

□ Special boards have been developed for expediting the computational work of computers; these boards can be easily added to standard computers.

□ Neural computing excels in pattern recognition, learning, classification, generalization and abstraction, and interpretation of incomplete input data.

□ Artificial neural networks do well at tasks done well by people and *not* so well at tasks that are done well by traditional computer systems (e.g., transaction processing, nonrepetitive scientific computing).

□ ANNs are especially supportive of natural language processing and speech understanding because of their pattern recognition capabilities.

□ ANNs are suitable for interpreting machine vision and signals from different sensors, and they can enhance robotic learning.

□ ANNs being used in simple handwriting recognition could eventually save the postal system billions of dollars.

□ ANNs integrated with decision support systems provide decision makers with powerful new tools.

Key Terms

artificial neural
   network
associative memory
axon
backpropagation
dendrites
hidden layer
learning algorithm
massively parallel
   processing

neural computing
neuron
nucleus
parallel processing
pattern recognition
processing element
self-organizing
sigmoid (logical
   activation) function

summation function
supervised learning
synapse
transformation
   (transfer) function
unsupervised learning
weight

Questions for Review

1. What is an artificial neural network?
2. Explain the following terms: *neuron, axon, dendrite,* and *synapse.*
3. Describe biological and artificial neural networks.

4. What is a hidden layer?
5. How do weights function in an artificial neural network?
6. Describe the role of the summation function.
7. Describe the role of the transformation function.
8. What is a threshold value?
9. Why are learning algorithms important to an ANN?
10. Define associative memory.
11. Briefly describe backpropagation.
12. Explain how acceleration boards aid computers.
13. List the major benefits of neural computing.
14. List the major limitations of neural computing.

Questions for Discussion

1. Compare artificial and biological neural networks. What aspects of biological networks are not mimicked by the artificial ones? What aspects are similar?
2. Draw a picture of a neuron and explain the flow of information.
3. Compare and contrast neural computing and conventional computing.
4. Why is parallelism related to ANNs? How can an ANN be developed and run on one processor?
5. Discuss the role of weights in ANNs.
6. Explain the combined effects of the summation and transformation functions.
7. Discuss the relationship between a transformation function and a threshold value.
8. Explain how ANNs learn in a supervised and in an unsupervised mode.
9. Why is an ANN related so closely to pattern recognition?
10. Explain how learning (training) is executed and why there are so many different learning algorithms.
11. Review the development process of ANNs. Compare it to the development process of expert systems.
12. What is meant by "initialization of the parameters of the network"?
13. Discuss the major advantages of ANNs.
14. Explain the difference between a training set and a testing set. Can the same set be used for both purposes? Why or why not?
15. Why is it said that it is much easier to maintain an ANN than an expert system?
16. Compare and contrast a neural chip and an acceleration board.
17. What deficiencies of expert systems can be overcome by artificial neural networks?
18. Explain why a major contribution of ANNs is in knowledge acquisition.
19. Expert systems and ANNs can complement each other very nicely. Explain why and be specific!
20. Explain how an ANN can improve natural language processing and speech understanding.

21. Explain how an ANN can improve machine vision.
22. What contributions can ANNs make to robotics?
23. One of the greatest areas for applied ANNs is handwriting recognition. Why?
24. Explain the support an ANN can give to a decision support system.

Exercises

1. Using the algorithm discussed in the chapter, calculate the weight changes as a single neuron learns the following:
   a. the AND operator
   b. a diagonal line in a 4-pixel display
2. For the following applications, which would be better—neural networks or expert systems? Explain your answers, including possible exceptions or special conditions.
   a. Diagnosis of a well-established, but complex disease
   b. Price-lookup subsystem for a high-volume merchandise sales
   c. Automated voice-inquiry processing system
3. List three known applications of expert systems. (You may consult Chapter 20.) For each of them, answer these questions:
   a. How might each application be implemented with neural networks?
   b. Are there advantages and disadvantages of the neural network alternatives?
4. Give possible applications of neural networks for the following:
   a. Character recognition
   b. Transaction processing
   c. Decision support
5. Several companies are flooded by hundreds and even thousands of job applications. Prepare a conceptual design of an integrated ANN and ES that will help in the screening process of a company for which security considerations are important.
6. Review this neural network and compute as directed on page 660.

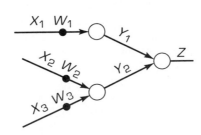

where:

$$X_1 = 15, X_2 = 8, X_3 = 14$$
$$W_1 = 0.6, W_2 = 0.3, W_3 = 0.1$$
$$\text{weight for } Y_1 = 0.6, \text{ for } Y_2 = 0.45$$

   a. Compute the value of Z without any transfer function.
   b. Compute the value of Z with a threshold function. If the value is 5 or less, call it 0; otherwise call it 1.
   c. Figure the value of Z with the sigmoid transfer function employed at all neurons.
7. Develop an example of backpropagation.

References and Bibliography

1. Allman, W. *Apprentices of Wonder*. New York: Bantam Books, 1989.
2. Bailey, D.L., and D.M. Thompson. "Developing Neural-Network Applications." *AI Expert* (September 1990): 34–41.
3. Beale, R., and T. Jackson. *Neural Computing*. Bristol, England: Adam Hilger, 1990.
4. Benachenhou, D., et al. "Neural Networks for Computing Invariant Clustering of a Large Open Set of DNA-PCR Primers Generated by a Feature-Knowledge Based System." In *Proceedings, International Joint Conference on Neural Networks*. San Diego, June 1990.
5. Bhogal, A.S., et al. "Towards Connectionist Production Systems." *Expert Systems with Applications* (special issue). 2 (no. 1, 1991).
6. Bigus, J.P., and K. Goolesby. "Integrating Neural Networks and Knowledge Based Systems in a Commercial Environment." In *Proceedings, IJCNN*. Washington, D.C., 1990. Hillside, N.J.: Lawrence Erlbaum Associates, 1990.
7. Carpenter, G., and S. Grossberg. "A Massively Parallel Architecture for a Self-Organizing Neural Pattern Recognition Machine." *Computer Vision, Graphics and Image Processing* 37 (1987): 54–115.
8. Caudill, M., and C. Butler. *Naturally Intelligent Systems*. Cambridge, Mass.: MIT Press, 1990.
9. Caudill, M. "Using Neural Nets." (six parts) *AI Expert* (December 1989, April 1990, June 1990, July 1990, September 1990, December 1990).
10. Caudill, M. "Embedded Neural Networks." *AI Expert* (April 1991).
11. Caudill, M. "Using Neural Nets: Hybrid Expert Networks." *AI Expert* (November 1990): 49–54.
12. Dietz, W.E., et al. "Jet and Rocket Engine Fault Diagnosis in Real Time." *Journal of Neural Network Computing* 1 (no. 1): 5–18.
13. Eberhart, R., and R. Dobbins. *Neural Network PC Tools*. San Diego: Academic Press, 1990.

14. Engel, C.W., and M. Cran. "Pattern Classifications: A Neural Network Competes with Humans." *PC AI* (May/June 1991).

15. Fukushima, K., and S. Miyaki. "Neocognition: A New Algorithm for Pattern Recognition Tolerant of Deformation and Shifts in Position." *Pattern Recognition* 15 (June 1982): 455–469.

16. Gallant, S. "Connectionist Expert Systems." *Communications of ACM* (February 1988).

17. Handelman, D. A., et al. "Integration of Knowledge Based System and Neural Network Techniques for Autonomous Learning Machines." In *Proceedings, International Joint Conference on Neural Networks.* San Diego, 1990.

18. Hanson, M.A., and R.L. Brekke. "Workload Management Expert System—Combining Neural Networks and Rule Based Programming in an Operational Application." Special report published by the Instrument Society of America, 1988, pp. 1721—1726.

19. Hawley, D.D., et al. "Artificial Neural Systems: A New Tool for Decision Making." *Financial Analyst.* 46 (November 1990): 63–72.

20. Hecht-Nielsen, R. *Neurocomputing.* Reading, Mass.: Addison-Wesley, 1990.

21. Hillman, D.V. "Integrating Neural Networks and Expert Systems." *AI Expert* (June 1990): 54–59.

22. Hopfield, J. "Neural Networks and Physical Systems with Emergent Collective Computational Abilities." *Proc. Natl. Acad. Sci. USA* 79 (1985): 141–152.

23. *Intelligent Software Strategies* 7 (June 1991): 8–12.

24. Josin, G. "Integrating Neural Networks with Robotics." *AI Expert* (August 1988).

25. Kaduba, N., et al. "Integration of Adaptive Machine Learning and Knowledge-based Systems for Routing and Scheduling Applications." *Expert Systems with Applications* (special issue) (no. 1, 1991).

26. Khanna, T. *Foundations of Neural Networks.* Reading, Mass: Addison-Wesley, 1990.

27. Klimasauskas, C.C. "Applying Neural Networks—Part 2." *PC AI* (March/April 1991).

28. Kohonen, T. *Self-Organization and Associative Memory.* Berlin: Springer-Verlag, 1984.

29. Kohonen, T. "An Introduction to Neural Computing." *Neural Networks* 1 (no. 1, 1988): 3–16.

30. Kosko, B. *Neural Nets and Fuzzy Systems.* Englewood Cliffs, N.J.: Prentice-Hall, 1991.

31. Lippman, R.P. "Review of Neural Networks for Speech Recognition." *Neural Computation* 1 (no. 1, 1989): 1–38.

32. Loofbourrow, T.H. "Expert Systems and Neural Networks: The Hatfields and the McCoys?" *Expert Systems* (Fall 1990).

33. Medsker, L.R., ed. Special issue of *Expert Systems with Applications* 2 (no. 1, 1991).

34. Medsker, L. "The Synergism of Expert Systems and Neural Network Technologies." *Expert Systems with Applications* (special issue) (no. 1, 1991).

35. Minsky, M., and S.A. Papert. *Perceptions*. Cambridge, Mass.: MIT Press, 1969.
36. Parsaye, K., et al. *Intelligent Databases*. New York: John Wiley & Sons, 1989.
37. Pham, K.M., and P. Degoult. "MOSAIC: A Macro-Connectionist Expert Systems Generator." *Expert Systems with Applications* (special issue) (no. 1, 1991).
38. Port, O. "Computers that Come Awfully Close to Thinking." *Business Week* (June 2, 1986).
39. Schwartz, T.J. "A Neural Chips Survey." *AI Expert* (December 1990).
40. Sejnowski, T., and C. Rosenberg. "Parallel Networks that Learn to Pronounce English Text." *Complex Systems* 1 (1987): 145–168.
41. Sherald, M. "Neural Networks Vs. Expert Systems: Is There Room for Both?" *PC AI* (July/August 1989).
42. Sherald, M. "Mission Possible—If You Combine Neural Networks and Expert Systems." *PC AI* (May/June 1991).
43. Simpson, P.K. *Neural Networks: Research and Applications Series*. New York: Pergamon Press, 1990.
44. Taber, R., and M. Siegel. "Estimation of Expert Credibility Weights Using Fuzzy Cognitive Maps." In *Proceedings, IEEE First International Conference on Neural Nets*. San Diego, 1987.
45. Trippi, R., and E. Turban. *Neural Network Applications in Investment and Financial Services*. Chicago: Probus Publishers, 1992.
46. Turban, E. *Decision Support and Expert Systems*, 2nd ed. New York: Macmillan Publishing, 1990.
47. Wasserman, P. "Neural Computing: Theory and Practice." New York: Van Nostrand Reinhold, 1989.
48. Werbos, P. "Back-Propagation and Neurocontrol: A Review and Prospectus." In *Proceedings, International Joint Conference on Neural Networks*. Washington, D.C., June 1989.
49. Zeidenberg, M. *Neural Networks in Artificial Intelligence*. Englewood Cliffs, N.J.: Prentice-Hall, 1990.

Appendix A: Application Areas for Neural Computing

1. Pattern recognition, speech generation—systems that learn phonemes in order to pronounce English text

   Data transmission—fast matching of patterns of data used in compression techniques for transmission of voice, image, and text

   Motion detection for military applications—aircraft identification, terrain analysis, recognition of underwater targets from sonar signals

Robot learning—hand-eye coordination through training for grasping objects; possible use with space-station assembly systems

Automation of operations in hazardous environments—earth observatory, power plants, undersea vehicles

Character recognition—typewritten and handwritten, even if distorted; verification of signatures on checks and recognition of zip codes

Voice recognition systems—voice-activated control of devices, voice typewriter

Diagnosis of defective equipment—analysis, based on training cases, of monitored data to identify malfunctions in electrical circuits and so forth

2. *Interpretation of data where analytical tools are needed to make generalizations or draw conclusions from large amounts of data from different sources or from sensors:*

Financial services—identification of patterns in stock market data and assistance in bond trading strategies

Loan application evaluation—judging worthiness of loan application based on patterns in previous application information

Jet and rocket engine diagnostics—training neural networks with sensor data

Medical diagnosis—training neural networks with cases of previous patients

Credit-card information—fast detection of fraud from purchasing patterns

DNA sequencing—analysis of patterns in DNA structures and rapid comparison of patterns in new sequences

Airline forecasting—prediction of seat demand after training with historical data; rapid modification by retraining with new data as it becomes available

Evaluation of personnel and job candidates—matching personnel data to job requirements and performance criteria; allows flexibility and tolerance of incomplete information

3. Optimization—Techniques such as the Boltzmann machine and simulated annealing that find acceptable solutions to problems involving many parameters

Chapter 19

The Future of AI and Expert Systems

Applied AI technologies are very exciting. Many organizations are using expert systems, natural language processing, and intelligent robotics to improve their operations and increase their competitiveness. But applied AI is still very far from real intelligence. In this chapter, we consider some topics that are being studied and projects that are being conducted at various research laboratories. We also review relevant technological developments to get some idea of the direction of the field. The following specific topics are discussed:

19.1   Introduction

The AI field is about thirty-five years old. Commercial applications started only about ten years ago. Yet the progress is overwhelming. Although no one knows exactly how many expert systems have been implemented, we do know that we are not talking about a few hundred any longer (the estimated number in the mid-1980s). Some experts believe that several hundred thousand systems are up and running. Slower progress has been reported in natural language processing, voice technologies, intelligent robotics, and other AI applications. Where are we heading? What will be the role of AI and ES in the future? What impact will AI have on society? How smart can a machine be?

In this chapter, we will attempt to answer some of these questions by looking at relevant technological trends as well as work in progress at AI laboratories. We also will present contradictory opinions: some believe that machines are going to approach human intelligence very soon and others believe that this will never happen.

Our discussion starts with the concept of machine learning and one of its most promising techniques—genetic algorithms. Then, we present some advanced reasoning systems. After reviewing the latest technological trends, we look at the future of ES, voice technologies, and other AI technologies. Finally, we discuss the limits of artificial intelligence.

19.2   Machine Learning

Overview

Even though expert systems aim to mimic human experts, they lack an extremely important capability of human intelligence: the ability to learn from experience. With the exception of simple induction systems (which can handle only classification-type problems) and some simple tasks executed by case-based reasoning and neural computing, there is very little today that resembles human learning capabilities. **Machine learning** capabilities are essential in situations where environments change (e.g., the breakdown of a robotics system), in situations where standards of expertise are changing, and in situations where there is no historical data and learning occurs as a task is performed.

Machine learning is also important in knowledge acquisition. The objective is to reduce costs and save time by minimizing the use of experts. The machine is expected to learn from historical cases. Machine learning can also reduce reliance on knowledge engineers, and in some cases it can increase the quality of collected knowledge.

Automated problem solving has been a target for generations, long before computers were invented. Consider these examples: statistical models such as regression or forecasting, management science models such as inventory level determination and allocation of resources, and financial models such as make versus buy decisions and equipment replacement schedules. Unfortunately, such methods deal with what is called shallow knowledge, or **knowledge-poor procedures.** When problems are complex, they cannot be solved by these standard models. Instead, additional knowledge is needed. Such knowledge can be provided by expert systems. Indeed, expert systems are already being combined with traditional models (as discussed in Chapter 15); however, integration is being done manually and the level of knowledge is not too deep.

Thus, there are many incentives to develop automatic machine learning capabilities. The task, however, is not simple. One problem is that there are many models of learning. For example, neural computing involves learning and so do genetic algorithms (which will be discussed in the next section). Sometimes it is difficult to match the learning model with the type of problem (e.g., job scheduling) that needs to be solved.

Learning

Until recently, machine learning has not been a major concern for applied AI. Most AI researchers initially felt that it was necessary to concentrate on how to make a computer program do something before figuring out how the program could learn to improve its performance. Now machine learning is taking on an ever-increasing significance in AI.

Early examples of machine learning are the well-publicized checkers- and chess-playing programs. These programs improve their performance with experience. Learning is done by using analogy, by discovery, through special procedures, by observing, or by analyzing examples. Learning can improve the performance of AI products like expert systems and robotics.

Learning is a "support" area of AI because it is an investigation into the basic principles underlying intelligence rather than an application itself. The following four observations are relevant to learning as it relates to AI:

1. Learning systems demonstrate interesting learning behaviors, some of which (e.g., the checkers-playing program) obviously challenge the performance of humans.
2. Although human-level learning capabilities are sometimes matched, no claims have been made about being able to learn as well as humans or in the same way that humans do (e.g., the checkers-playing program learns quite differently from humans).
3. Learning systems are not anchored in any formal bedrock; thus their implications are not well understood. Many systems have been exhaustively tested, but exactly why they succeed or fail is not precisely clear.

4. A common thread running through most AI approaches to learning (and distinguishing them from non-AI learning approaches) is that learning in AI involves the manipulation of structures rather than numeric parameters.

Methods

Large numbers of AI learning methods and algorithms have been developed. Most of them are still in research labs. Here are some examples:

- **Inductive learning:** This approach is used in knowledge acquisition (described in Chapter 4).
- **Case-based reasoning and analogical reasoning.** This approach is used in knowledge acquisition and in inferencing (described in Chapter 6).
- **Neural nets:** This approach can be used for knowledge acquisition and for inferencing (the subject of Chapter 18). It is just beginning to be commercialized.
- **Explanation-based learning:** This approach, as outlined by Mitchell et al. [28], assumes that there is enough existing theory to provide rationalization of why one instance is or is not a prototypical member of a class. This promising approach has not yet been applied in the real world.
- **Genetic algorithms:** Biological systems are excellent learners. Genetic algorithms attempt to follow some of their procedures (the topic of the next section of this chapter).
- **Statistical methods:** Although more suitable to knowledge-poor situations, statistical methods have been applied to knowledge acquisition and problem solving. For details, see Liang et al. [24].

The Cyc project at the Microelectronics Computer Technology Corp. (see section 19.7) is a large-scale research effort intended to make expert systems "smarter." The project includes a machine learning module that uses symbolic learning in addition to other learning modes. For details see Guha and Lenat [16].

19.3 Genetic Algorithms

A basic goal of genetic algorithms is to develop systems that demonstrate self-organization and adaptation on the sole basis of exposure to the environment, similar to biological organisms. Attaining such a goal would provide special capabilities in pattern recognition, categorization, and association; that is, the system would be able to learn to adapt to changes.

An algorithm is a set of instructions that is repeated to solve a problem. The word *genetic* refers to a behavior of algorithms that would be similar to biological processes of evolution.

A Game Called Vector

To illustrate how genetic algorithms work, let us review a special game, called Vector, devised by Walbridge [38].

Description. You play the game against an opponent who secretly writes down a string of six digits. Each of the digits can be either 0 or 1. For this example, the secret number is 001010. You must try to guess this number as quickly as possible. All you can do is present a number to your opponent and he or she will tell you how many of the digits (but not which ones) that you guessed are correct. For example, a guess 110101 has no correct digits (score = 0). A guess 111101 has only one correct digit (the third one). Thus, the score = 1.

Random Trial and Error. There are sixty-four possible six-digit strings of numbers. If you just pick numbers at random, on the average, it will take up to thirty-two guesses to find the right string. Can you do it faster? Sure, if you can make sense of the feedback provided to you by your opponent. This is exactly what the genetic algorithm does.

Genetic Algorithm Solution. *Step 1:* Present to your opponent four strings selected by random trial. Four were selected arbitrarily for this presentation; through experimentation, you may find that five or six would be better. You selected these four:

> ☐ (A) 110100, of which you scored 1 digit correctly
> ☐ (B) 111101, of which you scored 1 digit correctly
> ☐ (C) 011011, of which you scored 4 digits correctly
> ☐ (D) 101100, of which you scored 3 digits correctly

Since none of the strings is entirely correct (a score of 6 would be perfect), continue.

Step 2: Delete (A) and (B) for having low scores. Call (C) and (D) parents.

Step 3: Mate the parent's "genes" through *crossover*. This is done by splitting each number as shown:

> ☐ (C) 01:1011
> ☐ (D) 10:1100

Now, crossover the first two digits of (C) with the last four of (D). The result is (E), the first offspring:

> ☐ (E) 011100; score = 3

Similarly, crossover the first two digits of (D) with the last four of (C). The result is (F), the second offspring:

    □ (F) 101011; score = 4

It looks as though the offspring are not doing much better than the parents.

Step 4: Now copy the original (C) and (D).

Step 5: Mate and crossover the new parents, but use a different split. You get two new offspring (G) and (H):

    □ (C) 0110:11
    □ (D) 1011:00
    □ (G) 0110:00; score = 4
    □ (H) 1011:11, score = 3

Next, repeat step 2; select the best "couple" to reproduce. Obviously, one is G; (the best), the other is (C). However, a crossover here will not be successful. (C) and (G) will reproduce themselves. Therefore, we select (G) and (F). Now duplicate and crossover. Here are the results:

    □ (F) 1:01011
    □ (G) 0:11000
    □ (I) 111000; score = 3
    □ (J) 001011; score = 5

Also, you may generate more offsprings:

    □ (F) 101:011
    □ (G) 011:000
    □ (K) 101000; score = 4
    □ (L) 011011; score = 4

Now repeat the processes with (J) and (K) as parents; duplicate and crossover:

    □ (J) 00101:1
    □ (K) 10100:0
    □ (M) 001010; score = 6

This is it; you reached the solution after thirteen guesses. Not bad when compared to thirty-two for a random guess.

The process exercised in this game is shown in Figure 19.1. Essentially, this is what is done in genetic algorithms. Of course there are additional operations, and the problems can be much more complex.

Definition and Applications

Grefenstette [15] defines a genetic algorithm as "an iterative procedure maintaining a population of structures that are candidate solutions to specific domain

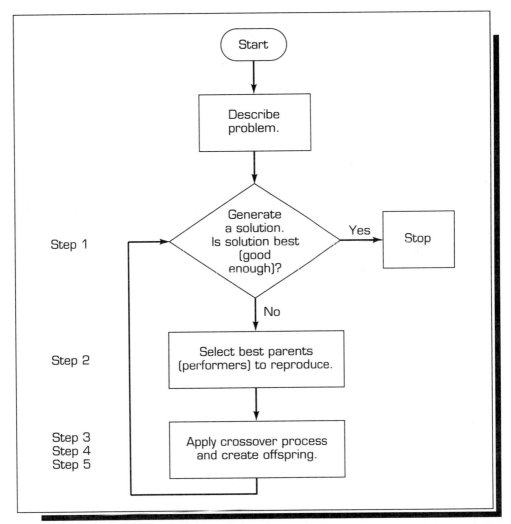

FIGURE 19.1 Flow Diagram of the Genetic Algorithm Process

challenges. During each temporal increment (called a *generation*), the structures in the current population are rated for their effectiveness as domain solutions, and on the basis of these evaluations, a new population of candidate solutions is formed using specific 'genetic operators' such as reproduction, crossover and mutation."

Most genetic algorithms use three primary operators:

1. **Reproduction:** Genetic algorithms produce new generations of improved solutions by selecting parents with higher fitness rating (or by giving such parents greater probability to be contributors).

2. **Crossover:** Many genetic algorithms use strings of binary symbols, as in our game, to represent solutions. Crossover means choosing a random position on the string (e.g., after two digits) and exchanging the segments either to the right or to the left of this point with another string partitioned similarly.

3. **Mutation:** This genetic operator was not shown in the game. Mutation is an arbitrary change in a situation. Sometimes it is needed to keep the algorithm from getting "stuck.") The procedure changes a 1 to 0 or a 0 to 1 instead of duplicating them. However, such a change occurs at a very low probability (say, one in a thousand).

Genetic algorithms can be viewed as a type of machine learning for automatically solving complex problems. They provide a set of efficient, domain-independent search heuristics for a broad spectrum of applications. Austin [3] has indicated some general areas of applications:

- Dynamic process control
- Induction of optimization of rules
- Discovering new connectivity topologies (e.g., neural computing connections)
- Simulating biological models of behavior and evolution
- Complex design of engineering structures
- Pattern recognition

A genetic algorithm is an exciting tool. It can even do what an expert system cannot: it can learn from experience. It receives information that enables it to reject inferior solutions and to accumulate good ones. Also, a genetic algorithm can be one of the most advanced tools of AI because of its suitability for parallel processing; thus it is closely related to neural computing (see Austin [3]). Finally, genetic algorithms are also related to **fuzzy logic** (see Karr [19]).

19.4 Advanced Reasoning Systems: Truth Maintenance, Constraint Satisfaction, and Hypothetical Reasoning

The reasoning methods described in Chapter 6 were fairly straightforward, and most commercial systems employ those methods. In research laboratories, efforts are being made to deal with more complex situations that require advanced reasoning methods. Even though these methods have only limited practical value today, they could play an important role in tomorrow's AI. Three such methods are described in this section: truth maintenance, constraint satisfaction, and hypothetical reasoning.

Truth Maintenance Systems

Most expert systems deal with monotonic (static) situations. However, certain problems in scheduling, production planning and control, and similar areas involve **nonmonotonic reasoning.** In such situations problem solvers often augment *absolute truth* with beliefs that are subject to change given additional information. Such beliefs are held, in some cases, in light of lack of evidence to the contrary. A **truth maintenance system** (TMS) is an implementation of nonmonotonic reasoning. Its major function is to maintain the consistency (or truth) of contexts with respect to subsequent contexts ("children"). For this reason, the TMS is also called a **consistency management system.** The TMS operates as a knowledge-based management system that is activated every time the reasoning system generates a new truth value. The TMS modifies beliefs to maintain consistency in the knowledge base. Thus, the TMS plays a passive role.

The revision of conclusions drawn during reasoning is an important aspect of intelligent behavior. The TMS is a collection of techniques for doing such belief revision. The major task of a TMS is to maintain a set of beliefs in such a way that (1) they are not known to be contradictory and (2) no belief is kept without a reason.

The TMS process can be handled in a variety of ways; therefore, there are many techniques to execute the job. Three of the major types are the justification TMS, the logic-based TMS, and the assumption-based TMS. A description of these methods and the manner in which they are selected and implemented are beyond the scope of this book. For more information consult De Kleer [9], Doyle [10], and Martins [25].

According to Martins [25], the major applications for truth maintenance systems are in reasoning, diagnosis, planning, search, user modeling, and constraint satisfaction. Of special interest is the last topic, which will be discussed next.

Constraint Satisfaction Problems

Constraint satisfaction problems (also known as consistent-labeling problems) have a wide range of applications in complex AI problem-solving areas such as scheduling, designing, and planning (see Box 19.1). These problems require that values be assigned to variables subject to a set of constraints.

Several representation forms exist for each constraint satisfaction problem. Choosing the best representation for a specific class of problems is extremely important because the representation determines the efficiency of the search. Several search procedures have been developed to solve this class of problems (e.g., see Nadel [31] and Nachtsheim [30]). One of the successful approaches is the truth maintenance system we just discussed.

Box 19.1: The Four Queens Problem

The objective of this classic problem of demonstrating constraint satisfaction is to place four queens on a square board (four positions per side) such that no two queens occupy the same row, column, diagonal, or crossdiagonal. The solution to the problem, which is illustrated in the accompanying figure, can be found quickly by trial and error. However, when there are more than four queens (*n* queens, where *n* > 4), the solution may not be simple at all. Try to do it with six or seven queens—good luck!

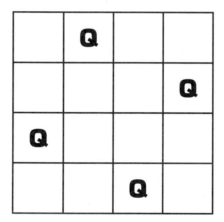

Hypothetical Reasoning

Hypothetical reasoning is a sophisticated inferencing tool that deals with countervailing factors to reach a conclusion. Such situations were described in Chapter 7 on uncertainty. Here, uncertainty is expressed in *conflicting* evidence. One way to resolve conflicts is to do it during the knowledge acquisition process (see discussion in Chapter 4 about multiple experts). If you resolve a conflict during knowledge acquisition, then you will not have a problem during inferencing. However, such a resolution may not be desirable or even possible. For example, in real-time expert systems, you may not have time to resolve knowledge conflicts. Also, in real-time systems the symptoms collected may be in a conflict. For such situations, hypothetical reasoning can be very beneficial.

Complex problems such as scheduling, planning, and distribution, even if they are not operating on a real-time basis, need to be solved by hypothetical reasoning. In rule-based systems, inferencing is done in three steps:

1. Compute which rule(s) could fire. If more than one is eligible, you have a conflict set.
2. Determine which specific rule to fire (conflict resolution). (In forward or backward chaining, conflict resolution is usually done completely arbitrarily.)
3. Fire the selected rule.

Hypothetical reasoning is built around existing backward or forward mechanisms. The hypothetical reasoning program maintains multiple states within which the normal chaining takes place. The conflict set is composed of states that could be logically pursued to find a solution. The program determines which state to investigate next. Once this is done, the normal chaining process is activated. As soon as the inference engine goes back to the first step, the process repeats itself.

Executing the hypothetical reasoning method is fairly complex. It depends on the problem to be solved and on the algorithm or heuristic that is used (for an example see Harris [18]). Complex scheduling and work-flow applications are suitable to the technique, which can easily be supported by object-oriented graphics. Routing, stock portfolio, distribution, dynamic investment, and other problems that may have a very large number (astronomical in some instances) of possible solutions are most suitable. Typically such problems are formulated as linear (or integer) programming where hypothetical reasoning may be used to react to sudden changes such as machine breakdowns. Often, though, linear programming cannot be run quickly enough to react to sudden changes. (The hypothetical reassessing mechanism is often combined with heuristics so only a good enough solution is achieved instead of an optimal one.)

19.5 Trends in Computer Technology

Developments in AI, and especially in the area of ES, are occurring rapidly. At no other time in history have we witnessed such accelerated technological progress. Some commercial AI products become obsolete as soon as (or even before) they are fully developed. In addition, developments in computer technology have a profound effect on progress in AI and on the implementation of its applied technologies. Our objective in this section is to briefly describe trends in computer technology that are likely to affect the development of AI. In addition, we will attempt to predict future directions of the technologies from a broad, general view.

Advances in AI depend on advances in computer technology.[1] Large, complex AI applications generally require more computer resources than management information system projects. Computer technology, for example, has been an especially limiting factor for ES implementation. Therefore, an

---

[1]Condensed from Mishkoff [27].

awareness of trends and advances in computer technology is essential for understanding the future of AI. Specifically, three topics are most relevant: parallel processing, neural computing, and **very-large-scale integration** (VLSI). The first two topics were discussed in Chapters 15 and 18. VSLI is discussed next.

Very-Large-Scale Integration (VLSI)

The process of combining electronic components into a single compact device is known as **integration,** and the devices containing multiple electronic components are **integrated circuits,** or **chips.** Since the invention of the chip in the late 1950s, computer scientists have been trying to include more and more components on a single silicon chip that is about a quarter of an inch square. Because integration can *increase* processing speeds and *decrease* costs at the same time, advances in integration often are accompanied by the development of more powerful computers.

In the 1970s, the techniques of large-scale integration (LSI) allowed chip manufacturers to combine the functions of several thousand components on a single chip. The modern techniques of VLSI allow several hundred thousand, or even several millions, of electronic components to be combined on a single chip. Advanced VLSI techniques may allow computers to feature the large memory and high processing speeds essential for many AI applications. For example, Japan's **Fifth-generation Project** hopes to develop computers with memories as large as 1,000 gigabytes (1,000,000,000,000 characters) and with processing speeds of up to 1 billion logical inferences per second. **Logical inferences per second** (LIPS) is a measure of the speed of computers used for AI applications. A logical inference usually consists of from 100 to 1,000 computer instructions; therefore, a computer operating at 1 billion LIPS could execute from 100 billion to 1,000 billion computer instructions per second. In the mid-1980s, by way of contrast, an exceptionally high-speed computer might have operated at a mere 20 million instructions per second.

In 1987, Texas Instruments developed a custom LISP processor using its proprietary VLSI semiconductor design and processing capabilities. The chip provides two to ten times the processing power of commercial symbolic processors available in 1987. Other companies also developed expert systems on a chip (see Box 19.2).

Megachip Technology

Megachip technology is a concept developed by Texas Instruments. It relates to a single chip, process, or service, but it is a culmination of new requirements for creating, manufacturing, and supporting highly sophisticated integrated circuits. A megachip circuit can include over 1 million components (for example, the Intel 486 chip contains 1.2 million components). These chips are being manufactured with the aid of AI technologies and extensive automation.

Box 19.2: AT&T Develops Expert System on a Chip

Combining custom hardware design and fuzzy logic, scientists at AT&T Bell Laboratories built in 1985 the first expert system on a chip for *real-time* response applications such as missile command and control, robotics, and manufacturing operations. Since then, many improvements have been made and the chip is significantly faster than conventional expert systems. Many expert system applications require a fast and reasonable response, but the data isn't precise. The expert system on a chip can handle many of these situations.

The AT&T chip's initial use was for control of a robot arm. The chip can, for example, guide a robot hand to a part rolling around on a conveyor belt. It can also decide when and by how much to reduce the temperature during a chemical process.

In developing the chip, the researchers built the operating instructions of the expert system into the chip's circuitry rather than writing them in software. This avoids time-consuming retrieval of instructions from external memory. Fuzzy logic reduces the number of rules required to act on problems. Combining these techniques, the researchers achieved a chip speed of 80,000 fuzzy logic inferences per second, which is about 10,000 times faster than conventional expert systems.

Using fuzzy logic, the expert system on a chip accepts vague data, compares it to all the rules in its memory simultaneously, and assigns each rule a weight. The highest weights are given to the rules that best match the data. A decision is based on the combined recommendations of these rules.

(*Source:* Based on material reported in *Applied AI Reporter* [January 1986].)

Other Developments

Several other developments in computer technology can enhance the progress of AI. One important area is computer storage. An emerging technology is the computer disk. For example, a single CD-ROM (computer disk, read-only memory) can hold as many as 550 megabytes of data. (To hold the same amount of information on floppy disks, you would need about 1,500 regular $5\frac{1}{4}$-inch disks.) Data is read by a laser beam. The technology is already being used to store large public databases that are important for multimedia integration with expert systems (refer to Chapter 14).

Optical Computers. Recent developments of **optical computers** could lead the next generation of computer technology. These computers process information encoded in light beams; thus, the computers have the potential of computing at the speed of light. In addition, optical lenses can perform mathematical calculations that are very difficult to do digitally. Finally, these computers will have a high storage capacity and will be much easier to maintain. Optical computers could provide a major boost to ES development. Commercialization is expected in the early to mid-1990s. For further information see Miller [26] and Feitelson [13].

Molecular Computing. The technology of **molecular computing** aims to use genetic engineering techniques (among others) to create substances capable of computation at molecular scales. This technology, which is still in its infancy, could increase the number of transistors (and other units) that can be placed on one chip by a large factor (see Langton [22] for details).

19.6   Large-scale Research Efforts

The combination of parallel processing with VLSI and other developments could significantly advance AI technology. Several large-scale national and international research efforts are capitalizing on these developments. This section explores these research efforts, which may have profound implications for the future of AI.[2]

DARPA Strategic Computing Program

In 1983, the Defense Advanced Research Projects Agency (DARPA) announced one of the most ambitious scientific research projects ever attempted: the Strategic Computing Program (SCP). The program, which began in 1984, was scheduled to last five years. Now it has been extended into the 1990s with a major emphasis on neural computing.

Figure 19.2 presents the structure and goals of the program. The program actually contains a number of projects in a wide range of AI and other computing areas. Its ultimate goal is to provide the United States with a broad line of machine intelligence technology and to develop applications of the technology for critical problems in defense. At a later time, the technology may transfer from defense to nondefense sectors.

Fifth-generation Project

The Fifth-generation Project is a large-scale national research and development project in Japan directed at developing computer systems for the 1990s. The computers are intended to learn, associate, and make decisions similar to the way humans perform these tasks. The Japanese intend to develop both hardware

---

[2]Some of the material in this section was condensed from Mishkoff [27].

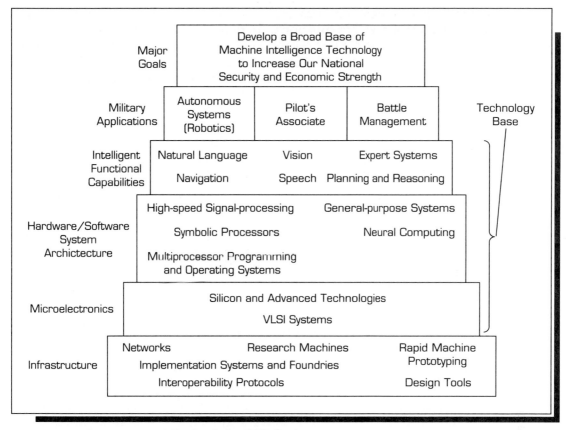

FIGURE 19.2 Structure and Goals of the SCP Project

and software that will be conceptually and functionally different from what currently exists. Intelligent interface machines are planned to replace the input-output devices of the fourth-generation computer. (The project has been described in Chapters 15 and 17 of this book.)

Sixth- and Seventh-generation Projects

The Sixth-generation Project in Japan deals with neural computing, and the Seventh-generation Project deals with molecular computing. Both projects are sponsored by the Japanese government and both are in the early stages of development.

Microelectronics and Computer Technology Corp. (MCC)

Established in 1983, MCC can be considered a response to the Japanese challenge. It is a consortium of twenty-one major U.S. corporations in the computer and computer-related industries.[3] Currently, MCC is engaged in four long-term projects with a common goal: to provide the technology necessary to make computers faster, more reliable, and capable of performing more complex tasks at a higher level of quality and much lower cost. By concentrating on long-term goals rather than seeking an immediate profit, MCC is free to follow a long-range strategy that might have been difficult for its members to pursue individually. Corporations often are under intense stockholder pressure to generate short-term profits, frequently at the expense of long-term goals.

MCC sponsors several advanced projects in the areas of neural and molecular computing. It also sponsors the expert system Cyc project discussed earlier. The programs undertaken by MCC fall into four major areas:

1. *Packaging:* The packaging project aims to advance the state of the art of semiconductor packaging and interconnect technology.
2. *Software technology:* The software effort aims to develop new techniques, procedures, and tools that can be used to improve the productivity of the software development process by one or two orders of magnitude.
3. *VLSI/computer-aided design:* MCC's program in this area aims to improve computer-aided design technology and to develop an integrated set of tools that will have particular application to complex systems and the very complex VLSI chips from which they will be built.
4. *Advanced computer architecture:* The most complex and ambitious of the MCC programs is a ten-year effort focusing on the following projects and goals:

   □ AI/knowledge-based systems to realize the computer's problem-solving potential by developing new ways to represent human knowledge and thought concepts as well as new engineering and managerial models and tools to apply human expertise to a wide range of problems
   □ Database system management to improve database design and storage methods and capacities to permit more flexible storage and faster retrieval of a broader range of more complex information
   □ Human factors technology to improve the relationship between people and computers by simplifying computer use through techniques like improved voice technology, character recognition, and natural languages.
   □ Parallel processing to develop the languages and architectures that will allow computers to perform tasks simultaneously instead of sequentially, with corresponding increases in processing speed.

---

[3]The original corporations were Advanced Micro Devices; Allied Corp.; Bell Communications Research (Bellcore); BMC Industries, Inc.; Boeing Co.; Control Data Corp.; Digital Equipment Corp.; Eastman Kodak Co.; Gould, Inc.; Harris Corp.; Honeywell, Inc.; Lockheed Corp.; Martin Marietta Corp.; Mostek Corp.; Motorola, Inc.; National Semiconductor Corp.; NCR Corp.; RCA Corp.; Rockwell International Corp.; Sperry Corp.; and 3M.

Alvey Program

The British government is backing a research effort called the Alvey Program. The main areas of research are (1) expert systems, (2) VLSI, (3) software engineering, and (4) the interface of humans and machines. The primary aim of the program is to provide the British information technology industry with technical lead over rivals in other countries. For a discussion of the Alvey Program and the development of ES in the United Kingdom see [33].

European ESPRIT Program

A joint research effort by several West European countries commenced in 1984 for an initial period of five years and was extended in 1989. The European Strategic Programme for Research and Development in Information Technologies (ESPRIT) is conducting research in the areas mentioned under the Alvey Program. It deals also with topics directly related to office automation and computer-integrated manufacturing (CIM, CAD, CAM, robotics, etc.)

19.7 Voice Technologies and Natural Language Processing

One of the major obstacles to the wide use of computers by managers and professionals is the required manual data entry via keyboards. For some it remains a clerical function; to others it is "just a waste of time." Menus, icons, touch screens, and the like have simplified the problem but they have not eliminated it.

Whenever human-machine communication becomes possible in a natural language and by voice, the use of computers will explode. Recent efforts of vendors clearly point to this direction. Several companies are developing voice and natural language processing front-end packages to AI and conventional computing development tools. Natural language processors to databases are being marketed by about a dozen vendors. Once voice is added, these systems could be embraced by ten times as many users.

The technical developments discussed earlier could provide the mechanisms that will make natural language processing and speech understanding an integral part of many computer systems. It is only a question of time; progress, however, has been fairly slow. Large-scale commercialization of such technologies will probably not happen in this century.

19.8 Distributed Systems

Distributed data processing systems offer a means of solving complex problems that affect a large physical area such as a plant or city. By use of local area networks, different components and participants of an AI application are able to communicate and cooperate with one another. It is reasonable to assume that in the future there will be a larger use of distributed data processing for the following reasons:

- ☐ Hardware technology has improved, so the building of very large distributive networks is becoming technologically and economically feasible.
- ☐ A large number of AI and AI-supported applications need distributive technology to succeed or to be more efficient. Many real-world information systems are already distributed.

Through the intelligent use of AI techniques, it is now possible to develop an infinitely expandable system than can address the time-critical needs of the real-world environment. For example, an expert system will be able to provide the knowledge for an intelligent distribution of other expert systems over the network.

Developments in communication networks, both local and global, could enhance the spread of AI. Someday it will be economically and technically feasible to access a computer by voice from almost any place in the world. People will be able to seek the advice of intelligent computers simply by picking up the telephone and asking for it. Advice will be provided on hundreds of topics, both organizational and personal.

Related to these developments is the merging of voice and data. Such a merger could greatly reduce the cost of communication, thereby enhancing the use of AI technologies in remote locations.

19.9 Future of Expert Systems

The present enthusiasm for expert systems must be placed in perspective before we consider the future.[4] The recent interest in this topic can be viewed as an interplay of both technical and social factors. Artificial intelligence research is a young field—in its infancy compared with other scientific endeavors. It is unrealistic to expect immediate practical results. Yet, as many AI researchers started to deal with real-world problems, they noticed that they were achieving some degree of success in modeling expert behavior. Although many projects began as basic research for knowledge representation, they evolved into realistic schemes for solving highly bounded problems. We already see definite technical achievement, and the potential for developing even more powerful and imaginative expert systems is not hard to foresee.

Does this mean that developing ES is now routine? Hardly! Designing and building an ES usually involve difficult and intensive efforts. Recall the distinction between expert and knowledge systems. Building a system that uses

---

[4]The material in this section was condensed from Weiss and Kulikowski [40], pp. 157–165.

only documented knowledge does not qualify the resulting system as an ES. However, we can expect more and more ES to be developed, together with a very large number of knowledge systems.

Most early developmental work in AI has taken place on relatively large, time-shared computers. These machines, which are beyond the means of many users, tend to become heavily loaded with competing applications and therefore limit the applicability of most ES that may be developed. Now we are seeing small machines at a relatively modest cost with large memories (some with virtual memories), more guaranteed (that is, noncompetitive) CPU time, large amounts of disk space, and high-speed graphic capabilities. Machines with some or all of these characteristics should not only enhance our ability to develop ES, but also increase the possibilities for wider dissemination.

The state-of-the-art technology in building ES is still what is called the **classification model.** A number of generalized tools have been developed to help design and implement this model. The typical classification model uses production rules and covers a highly bounded problem.

Not all problems can be represented by the classification model, and alternative approaches are necessary. The recent trend to develop hybrid tools that can handle multiple reasoning techniques, multiple sources of knowledge, and less bounded problems will enable us to address many new areas. Currently, there are many research topics under investigation at various laboratories and institutions. The following topics could have the greatest impact in advancing expert systems.

Adding New Types of Knowledge to the System

Not all knowledge can be captured by production rules. Experts use other forms of knowledge in their reasoning. For example, they may use causal information or mathematical relationships, neither of which is easily captured by production rules. The classification model falls into what is called a **shallow** (or **surface**) **model** category, whereas models that capture other types of knowledge are described as **deep models**.

Surface models are relatively easy to represent and design. In contrast, deep models are much harder to describe and use. As we try to increase the power and scope of the surface model, we see its limitations and have difficulty in extending its performance. The problem is that there are trade-offs between the two types of models. The surface model is much easier to specify and use. Also, some problems may be simple enough for the surface model to be adequate. Furthermore, even if we knew how to build the deep model, in the final analysis it might not be worth the effort.

To date, no one has demonstrated generalized approaches or tools for the deep models that are analogous to those that exist for the classification models. However, the use of object-oriented programming has greatly contributed to this area. Other possible contributions could come from neural computing, machine learning methods, and advanced reasoning methodologies.

Easing the Knowledge Acquisition Task

The ultimate design goal for knowledge acquisition is to allow experts to encode their own knowledge directly into the computer, thereby removing the role of the knowledge engineer from the knowledge acquisition phase. Moreover, experts should spend as little time as possible in encoding their knowledge. It is not likely, however, that we will see any revolutionary change in the current balance between knowledge engineering and experts in the near future. Rather, we can expect a gradual evolution in the development of tools to facilitate the building of a knowledge base that will speed up the process of developing an ES.

Improved hardware at lower costs will make ES more practical and more widespread. Improved software, particularly specialized knowledge engineering packages, can ease the task of knowledge representation. But for now, the role of the knowledge engineer, which is of prime importance, cannot be automated. The knowledge engineer is an artist who cannot be reproduced by supplying another individual with high-quality paints and brushes.

Learning from Practical Experience

Most of the practical lessons in the near future are likely to come from applying current ES technology to real-world problems. Such applications are also likely to lead to a better understanding of the types of problems we understand well versus those that require further research. This in turn will lead to gradual extensions of the basic classification model and an improved set of developmental tools. One area of great potential, but as yet unfulfilled promise, involves systems that learn from experience (see section 19.2). Nevertheless, today we are far from ready to supplant the knowledge engineer and the expert with a system that automatically learns rules from experience and automatically improves and expands the ES itself. For a survey and analysis, see Rauch-Hindin [34].

Incorporating Time and Location Relationships

One important issue is the influence of time relationships on decision making. The classification model has no direct statement of time, although the observations used in the model could be made over time. Most classification models assume that all past information is summarized in a current snapshot. This situation can be quite complicated, and there is much room for improvement in how time is to be incorporated in these models. Although the snapshot assumption summarizes the past, this is not the usual way of gathering information. Expert systems of the future will have to handle dynamic situations. Real-time systems deal with dynamic situations, and they are more difficult to construct than static systems.

An issue related to time is space. Most of the real-world classification models are one dimensional. In some cases, though, a system must reason with multiple instances of the same item. For example, a car repair ES is a typical classification model. But a car may have many instances of the same object, such as four tires and six cylinders. If these multiple instances can be treated independently, solutions are straightforward. However, generalized solutions tend to grow more complex with increasing numbers of interactions among the multiple instances (or locations) of objects.

Other Topics

Several other topics are of concern for the next generation of ES:

- Use of multiple sources of expertise
- Integration with other computer systems
- Development of more capable hybrid environments
- Multiple expert systems that cooperate with each other
- Increased machine learning capabilities
- Improved reasoning capabilities (deeper knowledge)
- More miniaturization of ES on chips at a reasonable cost
- Proliferation of ready-made ES

19.10 Features for Enhancing Computer-based Information Systems[5]

Several features will be important in the future as ways to enhance computer-based information systems.

Toolbox for Building Customized Systems. In order to quickly develop an AI or conventional system, the builder needs a toolbox of graphic and analytical objects that can be easily linked together to produce the system. In the future, AI systems are likely to provide toolboxes like intelligent hypertext and intelligent CASE packages for building visual and graphic front-ends.

Multimedia Support. The development of many AI applications requires support of multiple modes of input and output. The current generation basically provides text and graphic output with touch-screen, mouse, or keyboard input. The rapid proliferation of databases supporting image data and the slow but sure appearance of video, as well as voice I/O, will probably mean that future ES applications will be multimedia in nature. For example, in the next generation of ES, a user may sit in front of a high-resolution map of the company's sales regions. By touching one of these regions, the user might be presented with an animated display of the regions, revenue and expense figures over the past few

---

[5]This section was condensed from an unpublished work of D. King of Execucom Systems Corp.

Box 19.3: The Knowledge Navigator—A Vision

Artificial intelligence is the cornerstone of the information age. It is also the key to what I believe will be a revolutionary development early in the next century—a Knowledge Navigator that will be a tool for unprecedented creativity and innovation.

A Vision. The Knowledge Navigator is a vision for what personal computers could be several decades from now. It assumes technological breakthroughs that are yet to come.

The Navigator will be an intelligent librarian with the world at its fingertips. To access source material from anywhere, with the internal artificial intelligence to draw links between ideas from totally different fields, a machine like the Navigator will require a network of informational highways.

This will become possible as tomorrow's users find themselves able to hook into a telephone "highway" (an intelligent network) to get streams of information—voice, text, and images—over the same wire simultaneously. Today, we're limited by slow modems, long log-on times, and hard-to-memorize commands to get costly information from only a few sources. By the early part of the next century, few limitations will prevail and the process will become transparent. Users won't even have to give a moment's thought to where the information resides—the tool will navigate its own way through these highways to capture it.

The Navigator will not only travel such highways, it will also perform content analysis of the information, meaning that it will tailor information to your precise needs. That's an important feature, because the quantity of information in the world is doubling every three to four years.

The Ultimate Observer. Artificial intelligence will play an important role in the Knowledge Navigator. Inside the soul of the computer will be intelligent software "agents."

The agent will be your opinion surrogate, the ultimate objective observer. It will wander around throughout dozens of databases, pulling together whatever it thinks you, the user, are interested in. You won't have to search through the stacks of libraries—the world's largest library will exist on your desktop or lap.

Over time, the agents will become smart enough to learn that you like certain types of information presented in certain ways. The agents will learn along with you and work invisibly, turning information into useful knowledge for you.

(*Source:* Condensed from a speech delivered by John Sculley, president, Apple Computer, Inc., published in *PC AI* [January/February 1989].)

years, and a voice summary of the results from the regional sales directors. Not only does this mean that the workstation will have to support the storage and display of multimedia objects, but it also means that the network will have to support the transfer of these objects.

Automated Support and Intelligent Assistance. Expert systems and other AI technologies (e.g., natural language processing) are currently being embedded or integrated with existing computer systems. Clearly, this adds more automated support and assistance to the analytical engines underlying decision support systems. We are also likely to see other forms of intelligent or automated assistance. One such form is the **intelligent agent.** Think of an agent as a small, individualized, knowledge-based system designed to carry out a few rudimentary tasks. For example, a mail agent might monitor incoming electronic mail and, based on various built-in rules, place the mail in appropriate slots. Thus, instead of thinking of an intelligent computer-based information system as a single program or system, we might think of the system as a society of agents whose actions need to be coordinated. Although the concept of an agent may appear a bit foreign, it is currently being touted as the foundation for Apple's Knowledge Navigator—the ultimate intelligent computer system of the future (see Box 19.3).

19.11 Human-Machine Interaction and Knowledge Codification

What may be the most important factor in increasing the acceptance of AI is society's changing view of computers as a result of the microcomputer revolution and the advent of personal computers. Professionals in particular view computers mostly as aids to increasing their own productivity and creativity. The tasks performed by the computers may be simple, time-saving efforts such as personal financial planning, or they may be economically productive efforts such as configuring insurance policies. Just a short time ago computers were viewed by the majority of people as a machine to be distrusted and possibly even feared. Now computers have become so familiar that *Time* magazine changed the Man of the Year selection for 1982 to a Machine of the Year. Computer programming has become mandatory for many students in secondary education, and the number of jobs in computer-related industries is growing rapidly.

Still, not all people welcome computers with open arms. Many professionals and managers may feel that their jobs are threatened. This feeling is often cited as a negative factor in assessing the impact of computers on society. It is true that many people, particularly those in clerical jobs, have been forced to retrain or become unemployed as new technologies displace old ones. With AI applications, still other groups of individuals may feel threatened. Our society has become increasingly more specialized; new skills and professions dominate many fields. Individuals may be protective of their experience and knowledge, unwilling to share it with others. Their knowledge, particularly if it involves tricks of the trade that have never been explicitly formulated, may be of great economic value to them. Perhaps the greatest benefit of AI is the potential for formalizing (or codifying) knowledge in areas where knowledge is mostly experimental and not widely disseminated because of economic reasons and because people may have no formal structure with which to contribute their knowledge.

Thus one of the most important by-products of ES development will be the codification of knowledge. As developers construct large, sophisticated knowledge bases, a market will develop for the knowledge itself, independent of any associated computer system. Tutoring facilities will be developed to help disseminate this information to students trying to learn about the application domain, and "knowledge decompilers" will be designed to translate the knowledge bases into coherent books or written reports. Because metaknowledge—knowledge about effective strategies and procedures for using the domain knowledge—will be used more extensively in future ES, it too will become an important commodity. From the social point of view, ES are likely, in the next two decades, to help systematize the better-established reasoning procedures used by experts. They will not replace the experts, but rather help people to move into more intellectually challenging activities where the knowledge encoded in an ES is another routine source of information. On the positive side, this ought to spur experts into more creative jobs; but given human nature, this change is bound to meet resistance and resentment, just as previous technological innovation has. How far can all this go? Can computers take over? Some provocative discussion is provided in the forthcoming section.

19.12   Is There a Limit?

How intelligent can a computer be? Is there a limit? To what extent can ES replace experts? It is difficult to answer these questions (for a discussion, see Davis [6]). Several scientists believe that there are major limitations to ES and intelligent computer-based information systems, even in the distant future.

In a challenging book titled *Mind over Machine*, Huber Dreyfus and Stuart Dreyfus [11] make the following nineteen statements:

1. Real-life situations rely on less than 100 percent predictability.
2. Machine intelligence cannot replace human reasoning ability.
3. Humans possess know-how based on practice and past experience. These are not quantifiable into rules.
4. Certain daily skills (e.g., conversing at a party, walking) are too complex to explain with rules.
5. Many daily skills are not innate and must be learned by trial and error or from someone we consider proficient (experience-based knowledge versus knowing how).

6. Computers cannot progress to the expert level of human skill because experts do not rely mainly on rules but rely more on practical understanding and intuition.
7. Experts are able to react to changing and new situations. Computers cannot.
8. Computers can't relate to "world" knowledge. They are restricted to microworlds, isolated domains that cannot be combined and extended to reflect daily life.
9. Computers cannot incorporate human belief systems into decisions.
10. Computers cannot be programmed for context.
11. Computers cannot use common sense rules (i.e., under normal conditions . . .).
12. Computers cannot selectively choose only rules that apply in a particular situation.
13. It is impossible to include all possible exceptions to rules.
14. In real life, no set of rules is complete.
15. People use images, not descriptions, to understand and respond to situations.
16. Computers make inferences only from a list of facts.
17. Computers cannot recognize emotions portrayed visually.
18. Computers cannot anticipate social consequences of situations with simulations.
19. Computers cannot deal with uncertain data.

Another point has been raised by Zadeh [41], who advocates the use of fuzzy logic for ES. Zadeh is less impressed about the potential of AI to surpass the ability of human decision makers in the foreseeable future. One of the challenging problems is that of writing programs that allow a machine to understand problems. The ability to understand can be demonstrated by "summarization," as Zadeh says—understanding the meaning of some material (text, data, graphics) and summarizing it. Having a very-high-speed computer capable of performing millions of LIPS will not help in itself, because no one yet knows how to write a program that will enable a machine to truly summarize information.

Furthermore, Zadeh is not at all sure that the AI research community is approaching the problem in a way that is likely to produce the desired ability to understand. Most of the research is based on the use of two-valued yes-no logic; something is either right or wrong, true or false. Zadeh advocates the use of fuzzy logic, which humans use most of the time. Two-valued logic cannot deal with fuzzy quantifiers such as *few, many, several, most,* and *tall.* Most of what is common-sense reasoning uses fuzzy logic, he says. Two-valued logic is much too precise and much too confining to serve as a good model for common-sense reasoning. "The reason why humans can do many things that present-day computers cannot do well, or perhaps even at all, is because existing computers employ two-valued logic," Zadeh says. And the design of the new,

Box 19.4: Computers Will Understand Body Language

Researchers at Nippon Telegraph & Telephone (Japan) are developing computers that may understand body language. For example, by looking at your face, the computer will know if you look puzzled, unhappy, or even sick.

A digitized image of the user's face is taken by a video camera and is analyzed by an expert system. When fully developed, the system will be able to "read" not only people's faces, but also other body movements.

When such systems are commercialized, they could significantly increase the effectiveness of the human-machine interface. They will also be helpful in medical diagnosis, personal interviews, and criminal investigations.

(*Source:* Based on a story by R.C. Wood published in *High Technology Business* [December 1988].)

very-high-speed computers apparently will continue to use the two-valued logic.

The arguments raised by the Dreyfus brothers and Zadeh may not hold for a long time given the developments in computer technology discussed earlier—especially neural computing and machine learning. Should such developments be successful, computers may act like humans in a manner that surpasses our present-day imagination (see Box 19.4).

Counterarguments to the Dreyfuses' Claims

The position of the Dreyfus brothers is based on a comparison of "imperfect" computers with "perfect" humans. Neither of these assumptions is totally accurate. Table 19.1 attempts to refute their nineteen points, based on the assumption of success in technological developments. Several researchers believe that neural, optical, and molecular computing will make it possible, within one generation, to build neural computers with as many neurons as there are in the human brain; and in two generations, they believe these computers will be applied in an extremely intelligent manner (see Waltz [39]). So, many of the Dreyfus brothers' arguments will not be valid any more.

19.13   Conclusion

Latest developments in computer technology lead us to believe that the Dreyfus brothers' predictions are not valid any longer. Although we are not sure about predictions such as "intelligent machines will replace almost all workers" (see Toth [37]), we do believe that intelligent machines will perform many tasks that are now being performed by people. We do believe that AI and ES will play a major role in improving the quality of life. Will intelligent machines take over our planet as we read in some science fiction literature? Probably not. However, their impacts on our life in the twenty-first century, as presented by De Garris [8], could be drastic. The Desert Storm war gave us some idea of what intelligent weapons can do. For one thing, the manner in which wars are conducted has been changed completely. A similar impact may be observed in industry and services.

TABLE 19.1 Refuting the Dreyfus Brothers' Statements

Statement No.	Counterarguments: Why These Statements May Not Hold
1	Certainty factors and fuzzy logic could decrease uncertainty.
2	Future developments in AI, metaknowledge, and learning will improve reasoning.
3	Future expert systems may approach humans' know-how.
4	True, at least in the short run.
5	Expert systems have had limited success—more to come.
6	True in complex situations; ES are successful in narrow domains. Deep knowledge technology could change this situation.
7	Expert systems have had limited success in some areas. Neural computing could solve the problem.
8	True; however neural computing could solve the problem. Also, distributed AI might help.
9	True; however, intelligent systems can solve the problem.
10	Not yet; more storage, higher speed, and better representation techniques will do.
11	True; however, heuristics could be used to discover common-sense rules.
12	Neural networks can help.
13	Humans don't do this either (especially one person).
14	This is true for humans (especially one person) too.
15	Hopfield's laser and holographs can solve the problem (but it will be a long time before commercialization).
16	Neural computing and AI pattern recognition could change this situation.
17	Computer vision will do it, in the far future.
18	Humans cannot do it accurately either.
19	No one really can; however, fuzzy logic can help.

Chapter Highlights

- Applied AI systems today do not have much intelligence.
- Machine learning describes the many techniques that enable computers to learn from experience.
- Machine learning is used in knowledge acquisition as well as in inferencing and problem solving.
- Machines learn differently from the way people do and not as well.
- Common commercial machine learning methods are inductive learning and case-based reasoning. The neural net method is just starting to be commercialized.
- Genetic algorithms use a three-step iterative process: test a solution to see how good it is, select the best "parents," and generate offspring. The procedure learns to improve based on accumulated knowledge.
- Truth maintenance systems are designed to revise beliefs so that consistency in reasoning is maintained.
- Constraint satisfaction problems attempt to solve complex problems that may have an extremely large number of possible solutions.
- Hypothetical reasoning is designed to resolve conflicts in rule-based systems by using logical (or heuristic) procedures.
- Integrated circuits (chips) include several hundred thousands of electronic components on a small (quarter inch, squared) silicon chip. The method of placing such a large number of components is called very-large-scale integration (VLSI).
- A complete expert system program that uses fuzzy logic is available on a single chip.
- The two newest computing technologies are optical computing and molecular computing.
- Large-scale AI research efforts are being performed in the United States, Japan, United Kingdom, and Western Europe.
- Japan is a leader in AI research with several major projects underway.
- Advances in voice technologies and natural language processing could improve the human-machine interface. Progress is fairly slow, however.
- Distributed systems and networks will help to disseminate AI technologies at a reasonable cost worldwide.
- Expert systems of the future will be easier to build (automating knowledge acquisition) and will deal with "deeper" types of knowledge (using machine learning). They will incorporate time and location relationships and will be integrated with other computer systems.
- Computer-based information systems of the future will have intelligent agents, or knowledge bases, embedded in them.
- The debate about how intelligent a computer can be continues. On one side are those who believe in human superiority that will remain for many generations. On the other side are those who predict that in one generation

computers will behave in a manner that will closely approximate human intelligence.
   □ Recent technological developments could make computers very smart— perhaps earlier than most of us think.

Key Terms

analogical reasoning
case-based reasoning
chip
classification model
consistency
   management system
constraint satisfaction
   problem
crossover
deep model
explanation-based
   learning
Fifth-generation Project
fuzzy logic
genetic algorithm
human factors
   technology

hypothetical reasoning
inductive learning
integrated circuit
integration
intelligent agent
knowledge-poor
   procedure
logical inferences per
   second (LIPS)
machine learning
megachip technology
Microelectronics and
   Computer
   Technology Corp.
molecular computing
mutation
neural net

nonmonotonic
   reasoning
optical computer
parallel processing
reproduction
Seventh-generation
   Project
shallow (surface)
   model
Sixth-generation
   Project
truth maintenance
   system
very-large-scale
   integration

Questions for Review

1. What is machine learning? List its major technologies.
2. What are the major objectives of machine learning? Why is there such an interest in the topic?
3. Describe the learning process in genetic algorithms. Why is it similar to a biological process?
4. Describe the major genetic algorithm operators.
5. Define truth maintenance system and explain its major purpose.
6. Describe the constraint satisfaction problem. Why is it difficult to solve?
7. Define hypothetical reasoning and explain how it works.
8. Why is parallel processing so important for ES development?
9. How can the developments in VLSI and parallel processing assist the developments of AI technologies?
10. Why is it easier for MCC to pursue a long-term strategy than for the individual companies that compose MCC?
11. What is the Knowledge Navigator? Why is it important? How can it be helped by AI technologies?

Questions for Discussion

1. Read some recent information about the Fifth-generation Project. Assess the progress of the project.
2. Knowledge acquisition is considered a major (perhaps *the* major) obstacle for wide use of expert systems. Find a recent article on advances in this area and discuss it.
3. The expert systems being installed on a chip can be implanted in a robot. In your opinion, what could be the impact of such an installation?
4. Review the statements of the Dreyfus brothers. How do you feel about each statement? Prepare a table similar to Table 19.1 for your responses. (Consider the newest technologies.)
5. You are playing a game in which your opponent thinks about an object and you ask questions that will guide you to an answer. To what AI technology is this game similar and why?

Exercises

1. You are trying to identify a specific number in the set of 1 to 16. You can ask questions such as, "Is this number in the set 1–8?" The answer can either be yes or no. In either case, you continue to ask more questions until you can identify the number.[6]
   a. How many questions are needed, in the worst and the best possible cases, to identify such a number?
   b. Is the problem suitable for parallel processing? Why or why not?
   c. Can you relate this problem to a genetic algorithm?
2. A set of five letters from the alphabet is given to you (say, B, E, M, S, and T). Your task is to compose as many words as possible from these letters. One way to do it is to write a computer program that will try to match each combination of these letters to words in a dictionary.
   a. Describe the process that a regular computer will go through.
   b. Is the problem suitable for parallel processing? Why or why not?
3. Identify the constraint(s) in the four queens problem (Box 19.1).

References and Bibliography

1. Almasi, G.S., and A. Gottieb. *Highly Parallel Computing*. Redwood City, Calif.: Benjamin-Cummings, 1989.
2. Austin, S. "An Introduction to Genetic Algorithms." *AI Expert* (March 1990).
3. Austin, S. "Genetic Solution to XOR Problems." *AI Expert* (December 1990).

---

[6] This problem and the next appeared in the April 15, 1988 issue of *AI Week* (contributed by D. B. Hertz).

4. Cohen, P., and E.A. Feigenbaum. *The Handbook of Artificial Intelligence,* vol. III. Reading, Mass.: Addison-Wesley, 1982.

5. Davis, E. *Representations of Commonsense Knowledge.* San Mateo, Calif.: Morgan Kaufman, 1990.

6. Davis, R. "Expert Systems: How Far Can They Go?" *AI Magazine.* Part I (Spring 1989); Part II (Summer 1989).

7. Davis, L. *Handbook of Genetic Algorithms.* New York: Van Nostrand Reinhold, 1989.

8. De Garris, H. "What If AI Succeeds? The Rise of the 21st Century Artilect." *AI Magazine* (Summer 1989).

9. De Kleer, J. "An Assumption-based Truth Maintenance System." *Artificial Intelligence* 28 (1986).

10. Doyle, J. "A Truth Maintenance System." *Artificial Intelligence* 12 (no. 3, 1979).

11. Dreyfus, H., and S. Dreyfus. *Mind Over Machine.* New York: Free Press, 1986.

12. Dreyfus, H., and S. Dreyfus. "Why Computers May Never Think Like People." *Technology Review* (January 1986).

13. Feitelson, D. *Optical Computing: A Survey for Computer Scientists.* Cambridge, Mass.: MIT Press 1988.

14. Goldberg, D.E. *Genetic Algorithms In Search, Optimization and Machine Learning.* Reading, Mass.: Addison-Wesley, 1989.

15. Grefenstette, J. "Optimization of Control Parameters for Genetic Algorithms." *IEEE Transactions on Systems Management and Cybernetics* 16 (no. 1, 1982).

16. Guha, R.V., and D.B. Lenat. "CYC: A Mid-Term Report." *AI Magazine* (Fall 1990).

17. Gusgen, J. *CONSAT—A System for Constraint Satisfaction.* San Mateo, Calif.: Morgan Kaufman, 1989.

18. Harris, L.R. "Hypothetical Reasoning." *AI Expert* (June 1989).

19. Karr, C. "Applying Genetics to Fuzzy Logic." *AI Expert* (March 1991).

20. Karr, C. "Genetic Algorithms for Fuzzy Controllers." *AI Expert* (February 1991 and March 1991).

21. Kodratoff, Y. *Introduction to Machine Learning.* San Mateo, Calif.: Morgan Kaufman, 1989.

22. Langton, C.G., ed. *Artificial Life: The Synthesis and Simulation of Living Systems.* Reading, Mass.: Addison-Wesley, 1989.

23. Lenat, D., and Guha, R.V. *Building Large Knowledge-based Systems, Representation and Inference in the CYC Project.* Reading, Mass.: Addison-Wesley, 1990.

24. Liang, T.P., et al. *Automatic Methods of Knowledge Acquisition.* San Mateo, Calif.: Morgan Kaufman, 1992.

25. Martins, J.P. "The Truth, the Whole Truth, and Nothing But the Truth." *AI Magazine* (January 1991).

26. Miller, R.K. *Optical Computing: The Next Frontier in Computing.* Madison, Ga.: SEAI Technical Pub., 1986.

27. Mishkoff, H.C. *Understanding Artificial Intelligence.* Dallas: Texas Instruments, 1985.
28. Mitchell, T.M., et al. "Explanation-based Generalization: A Unifying View." *Machine Learning* (no. 1, 1986).
29. Moravec, H. *Mind Children—The Future of Robot and Human Intelligence.* Cambridge, Mass.: Harvard Univ. Press, 1988.
30. Nachtsheim, P.R. "Solving Constraint Satisfaction Problems." *AI Expert* (June 1989).
31. Nadel, B.A. "Representation Selection for Constraint Satisfaction: A Case Study Using *n*-Queens." *IEEE Expert* (June 1990).
32. Nadel, B.A. "Constraint Satisfaction Algorithms." *Computational Intelligence* (November 1988).
33. *R&D Management.* Special Issue (April 1985).
34. Rauch-Hindin, W.B. *A Guide to Commercial AI.* Englewood Cliffs, N.J.: Prentice-Hall, 1988.
35. Rawlins, G., ed. *Foundation of Genetic Algorithms.* San Mateo, Calif.: Morgan Kaufman, 1991.
36. Rice, J. "The Advanced Architectures Project." *AI Magazine* (Winter 1989).
37. Toth, K.A. "The Workless Society." *The Futurist* (May-June 1990).
38. Walbridge, C.T. "Genetic Algorithms: What Computers Can Learn From Darwin." *Technology Review* (June 1989).
39. Waltz, D. "The Prospects for Building Truly Intelligent Machines." In *True Artificial Intelligence Debate*, D. Waltz, ed. Cambridge, Mass.: MIT Press, 1988.
40. Weiss, S.M., and C.A. Kulikowski. *A Practical Guide to Designing Expert Systems.* Totowa, N.J.: Rowman and Allanheld, 1984.
41. Zadeh, L.A. "The Management of Uncertainty in Expert Systems." In *Proceedings, 1st Symposium on Application of Expert Systems in Emergency Management Operations, FEMA/NBS.* Washington, D.C., April, 1985.

Part 7

Applications and Cases

Now that you are familiar with AI theory, concepts, basic foundations, and ideas, it is time to see everything in action. Part 7 presents actual applications of expert systems (recall that some applications of other technologies were discussed in Part 3).

In Chapter 20, expert systems in a variety of fields are described along with an analysis of each application. An example of a student project is provided in Chapter 21; this simple project has been implemented. In contrast, the second case discussed in Chapter 21 was not implemented. It is introduced to show *why* some systems are not implemented, and to illustrate the design of an extremely complex system involving several AI techniques and other computer-based information systems.

Finally, we look at those who practice what we preach—the practitioners of AI technology. Two AI specialists from Inference Corp. contributed the closing chapter of this book. In it, they describe the successful application of three mission-critical systems.

Chapter 20

Expert Systems: Illustrative Applications

In the previous chapters, the fundamentals of expert systems were described and the construction process was introduced. In this chapter, we present brief, illustrative ES applications in the following sections:

20.1 Introduction

Expert systems are being developed and implemented today at an accelerated
rate. Many thousands of such systems exist in various stages of development
in the United States, Japan, and Europe. The application cases presented in this
chapter (see Table 20.1 for a summary and brief description) have several goals:

☐ Reinforce concepts and ideas presented in the previous chapters through
   the cases themselves and through the questions at the end of the chapter.
☐ Show the potential use of ES in various industries and functional areas.
☐ Raise some issues concerning the development and use of such systems.
☐ Analyze some commonalities and differences among the systems.

A major problem confronts us in collecting information about successful,
commercial ES. Because such systems sometimes give their user a significant
competitive advantage, companies do not like to share information about them.
Furthermore, many ES are still being developed and the monetary results are
not clear. Developers of such systems are reluctant to release any information
that would increase expectations in their own organizations. Finally, several
systems presented in the literature as ES are not true expert systems.

At the end of the chapter the Balsams Grand Resort Hotel case is presented
as a summary case with specific questions for analysis and discussion.

20.2 Case 1: An Intelligent Help Desk

Problem

Help desks have traditionally been employed by private and public organizations
to provide assistance or information in person or via the telephone to customers,
employees, or other interested parties. Managing help desks is becoming difficult
because of the following trends:

☐ The volume of calls to help desks is increasing.
☐ The complexity of the required information is increasing.

TABLE 20.1 List of Cases

Case	Area	Developing or User Organization	Brief Description
1. Help Desk	Maintenance	Harris Corp.	Troubleshooting at help desk
2. DustPro	Environmental safety	U.S. Bureau of Mines	Environmental control analysis
3. GADS	Transportation scheduling	United Airlines	Scheduling aircraft at airport gates
4. ISIS-II	Operations management	Westinghouse Corp.	Scheduling jobs, factory automation
5. PROSPECT	Marketing	USC (student project)	Selecting method for contacting customers
6. COMPASS	Maintenance and repair	GTE	Analyzing maintenance reports
7. AIG/DIC	Insurance	American International Group	Underwriting complex insurance policies
8. Hostages	Police management	University of Arizona	Advising on how to handle hostage-taking incidents
9. Loan analysis	Banking, loans	ABC Bank	Estimating chances of approving large loans
10. CARGEX	Transportation	Lufthansa (Germany)	Configuring cargo, scheduling
11. Energy management	Maintenance of an electrical distribution network	Spanish electrical utility (Spain)	Troubleshooting and recommending repairs in real time
12. EXSOFS	Construction operations	NanYang Technological University (Singapore)	Selecting best construction method based on costs and constraints
13. SUTA	International trade with Soviet Union	Deloitte and Touche	Advising business people on trade opportunities in the Soviet Union
14. Management Edge	Personnel management	Human Edge, Inc.	Personnel managing situations

□ The quality of the personnel who provide the help is not improving (it's even decreasing).
□ The cost of operating the help desks is increasing.

Help desks are especially important in providing technical information about procedures and regulations (e.g., answering questions regarding taxes).

Many attempts are being made to increase the efficiency and effectiveness of help desks; automation is the most serious one. Traditional computerized solutions include searching databases. However, because of the increased complexity and quantity of the stored information, this approach is becoming less effective.

Solution

The basic idea is to create an expert system that will "assist the assistors." An example is the help desk at Harris Corp.'s headquarters (Melbourne, Fla.).[1] This help desk provides a hot line for employees to troubleshoot problems in computer hardware and networks. (The system is composed of 6,000 pieces of hardware.) This is how the help desk works: Requests are made by phone (from a plant seven miles away). Help desk operators call an ES for help. The information provided by the employee (e.g., the type of equipment) is keyed in using a simple menu system. The ES then asks a few questions and provides brief procedures to help diagnose the problem. The ES provides a diagnosis and instructions on what to do next. The consultation takes about ten minutes.

Development. The system (rule based and personal computer based) was developed in 1988 using the Insight2+ shell (now called Level5). The system interacts directly with the Virtual Telecommunication Access Method network to get information about the specific device experiencing the problem and the current status of the device. The interface was written in Turbo Pascal. The system includes 200 rules.

Benefits. The system expedites the work of the help desk operators, but more than that, it allows the operators to diagnose problems that previously were directed to a higher level of experts (system programmers). This is a significant saving since a problem that took four hours of a system programmer's time is now being solved in ten minutes by an operator. (The number of difficult cases transferred to system programmers has been reduced by 80 percent.)

The system is also used for *training* help desk workers. Harris Corp. is considering developing similar systems for its customers. Intelligent help desk systems are being used by many corporations (e.g., see Bonafield [3] and Eskow [5]).

Future Developments

Voice technologies could make the job of the help desk operator obsolete. Even today, if clients have accessibility to a personal computer, there is no need for a help desk operator (or, his or her services are minimized). Abraham et al. [1] provide a complete discussion of the topic and suggest the following basic features for any system:

☐ Provide assistance to a user reporting a problem
☐ Collect information from the network user

---

[1]Condensed from P. Karon, "Help Desk Gets Help from Trouble-Shooting System," *PC Week* (January 26, 1988).

□ Store the user information in a database
□ Use stored data from past consultations to personalize the current session
□ Use data from past consultations to induce new rules and thus facilitate system learning over time
□ Use the historical data to create advisory reports for management (Reports would be designed to highlight trends, clustered problems, and unusual events that merit notice by management.)

Finally, Barr [2], a consultant specializing in the automation of help desks, believes that intelligent help desk systems provide one of the most cost-efficient means of knowledge distribution.

20.3   Case 2: DustPro: Environmental Control in Mines

Problem

The majority of the 2,000 active mines in the United States are medium or small, so they cannot afford a full-time dust control engineer whose major job is to reevaluate and reassign facilities each time operating conditions change.[2] If a dust control engineer is not readily available, the mine must be shut off until an expert arrives. This can be very costly since experts are expensive and so is downtime. Operating without appropriate testing and interpretation of results is a violation of federal regulations.

Solution

DustPro is a small rule-based system developed by the U.S. Bureau of Mines. It includes about 200 rules and was developed with a Level5 shell on a microcomputer. It took 500 hours to develop the system. The system is now in operation in more than 200 mines. It is so successful that more than ten countries have requested permission to use the system in their mines.

System Characteristics. DustPro advises in three areas: control of methane gas emission, ventilation in continuous operations, and dust control for the mine's machines. The system is completely independent. Data on air quality is entered manually. The user interface is very friendly. The system is composed of thirteen subareas of expertise, and the average consultation time is ten to fifteen minutes.

---

[2]Courtesy of Information Builders, Inc., corporate publication, 1988.

System Use. DustPro, through a series of questions, determines what types of ventilations are used, what the dust standard is, and which group of mines is most affected by the dust. Thus, the system can advise the operators about what to do. The system and its variants are used at the U.S. Bureau of Mines (Pittsburgh Research Center) to diagnose problems telephoned in by operators of mines. This saves bureau staff time and travel expense. Also, the staff can respond more quickly and can devote more time to research and development.

20.4   Case 3: Gate Assignment Display System (GADS)

Problem

Gate assignment, the responsibility of gate controllers and their assistants, is a most complex and demanding task.[3] At O'Hare airport in Chicago, for example, two gate controllers typically plan berthing for about 400 flights a day at some fifty gates. Flights arrive in clusters for the convenience of customers who must transfer to connecting flights, so the controllers must accommodate a cluster of thirty or forty planes in twenty or thirty minutes. To complicate the matter, each flight is scheduled to remain at its gate a different length of time, depending on the schedules of connecting flights and the amount of servicing needed. Mix those problems with the need to juggle gates constantly because of flight delays caused by weather and other factors, and you get some idea of the challenges.

Solution

In November 1986, a United Airlines/TI team went to work on the problem. By the end of June 1987, they had the first fully operational ES in daily use at Denver's airport. The second system was implemented at O'Hare in August 1987. The system is integrated with the United Mainframe Operation Information System.

System Capabilities. The new system does everything the old magnetic display did—except fall apart when somebody brushes against it. It is faster to set up and reschedule, and it carries far more information. Its superb graphic display shows clock/times and gate numbers. The aircraft are symbolized as colored bars; each bar's position indicates the gate assigned, and its length indicates the length of time the plane is expected to occupy the gate. Bars with pointed ends identify arrival-departure flights; square ends are used for originator-terminator flights.

---

[3]Condensed from *Artificial Intelligence Letter*, Texas Instruments, Data Systems Group, Austin, Tex., January 1988.

That much symbology already carries more information than the old system did, because the length of the bar is now variable. But that's just the beginning. GADS also shows, in words and numbers near each bar, the flight number, arrival and departure times, plane number (with a letter code to indicate the precise configuration), present fuel load, flight status, ground status, and more.

Ground status alone presents a wealth of split-second information not available on the old display. Each United aircraft carries a small radio transmitter that automatically reports to the mainframe system when the nose wheel touches down at the field. GADS immediately changes that plane's bar from "off," meaning "off the field," to "on," meaning "on the field." When the plane is stopped at its gate, the code changes to "in." So gate controllers have up-to-the-second ground status on every flight in their display.

GADS also has a number of built-in reminder systems. It won't permit an aircraft to be assigned to the wrong kind of gate, for instance, and explains why it can't. The controller can manually override such a decision to meet an unusual situation. The system also keeps its eye on the clock—when an incoming flight is on the field and its gate hasn't been assigned yet, flashing red lines bracket the time to alert the controller.

GADS affords both historical and future views. Historical logs are kept automatically for analysis that can improve future scheduling.

Benefits of the Program. Three major benefits have been identified. First, the assistant gate controller can start scheduling the next day's operations four or five hours earlier than was possible before GADS. Second, the ES is also used by zone controllers. At O'Hare, each of the ten zone controllers is responsible for all activities at a number of gates—fueling, baggage handling, catering service, crew assignment, and the rest. Decisions in these areas are supported by GADS. Third, super reliability is built into GADS. There are two Explorer computers (AI workstations from TI) for the gate controllers and five for the zone controllers. Any one of the seven Explorers can take over the job when any of the others has a problem. Furthermore, if the mainframe system, with which the explorers are linked, should ever go down, all the Explorers shift automatically into a stand-alone mode, which allows operations to continue.

20.5   Case 4: Intelligent Scheduling and Information System (ISIS-II)

Scheduling complex work orders on a factory floor will become more efficient and cost-effective if ISIS-II, an expert system developed at Westinghouse's Productivity and Quality Center in Pittsburgh, lives up to its early promise.[4] ISIS-II schedules work orders of an individual factory work center. Westinghouse

---

[4]Based on Fox and Smith [6].

envisions that each work center, or job shop, within its factories will eventually have its own ISIS-II to schedule its orders. Westinghouse founded the ISIS project in conjunction with the Robotics Institute of Carnegie-Mellon University in the spring of 1983 to learn more about how AI could benefit the company.

ISIS-II uses KEE software on a dedicated AI computer to generate, compare, and rate alternative schedules for a job shop. Results are superior to schedules generated with conventional scheduling methods, even those supported by management science models and computers, because ISIS-II can consider *all* the complex factors and constraints encountered in a job shop situation. ISIS-II generates a prioritized list of work orders. Each order includes the machine that will process the order, the operation to be performed, and the time and date of operation.

The system considers five types of constraints (Table 20.2). The constraints are represented in the KEE system as rules and are ranked by the order of their importance, which may vary over time.

Machines, production processes, orders, and other aspects of the job shop are represented as frames. ISIS-II's user interface utilizes the KEE system's ActiveImages.

TABLE 20.2   Scheduling Constraints

Type of Constraint	Examples of Constraints
Organizational goals and policies	Due date Work in process Shop stability Shifts Cost Productivity goals Quality Relative priorities of jobs
Physical constraints	Machine physical constraints (e.g., capabilities and tooling) Setup times Processing time Quality
Causal restrictions	Operation alternatives Machine alternatives Tool requirements Material requirements Personnel requirements Interoperation transfer times
Availability constraints	Resources reservations Machine downtime Shifts Inventories
Preference constraints	Operation preferences Machine preferences Sequencing preferences

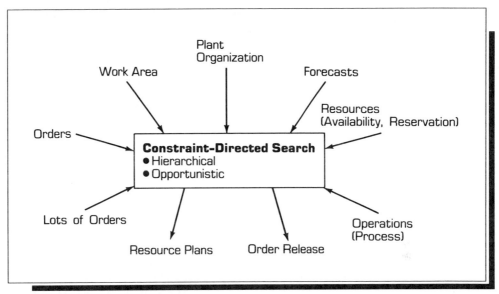

FIGURE 20.1 Inputs, Constraints, and Outputs to ISIS-II

The availability of both rule-based and frame-based components in the KEE package was found to be a major advantage in the development work. The use of ActiveImages for creating a user interface saved a great deal of time and freed the ES builder to work on the more interesting and difficult parts of the application.

ISIS-II has been highly rated by expert schedulers in a factory environment. The system is also of particular importance to facility design where it is being used in simulation (or in analytic performance) models for postanalysis of facility design output. The system can model a manufacturing plant with a high level of detail, from physical machine descriptions to process descriptions to organizational structures and relations (Figure 20.1).

20.6   Case 5: Selecting the Form of Marketing Contacts

A prototype marketing expert system called PROSPECT was developed to help the sales representatives of a corrugated container company decide which is the most appropriate form of contact: telephone, mail, or personal sales calls.[5] This system was constructed by using a rule induction approach with a shell called Expert Ease (now called Expert One).

---

[5]This case was developed as a term paper by Steve Durale, an MBA student at the University of Southern California, Los Angeles (1985).

There are three major steps involved in the construction and use of the system.

Step 1: Listing the Attributes. This step involves listing all the attributes that are necessary in the development and operation of the ES. Figure 20.2 shows a simplified example of data input during the development of the program. In this case there are three attributes: reason, potential, and buy criteria. Each attribute can assume different values. The attributes with their values are given next along with the possible methods:

```
EXPERT-EASE Attribute Listing, Problem: PROSPECT
REASON        :
      R1            :   Respond to a request for quote that
                        does not require inspection.
      R2            :   Request for quote on item that requires
                        inspection.
      Qualify       :

      Present       :
      QandP         :   Qualify and present is your objective.
      Initiate      :
POTENTIAL   :
      SMALL         :   Small-Less than 250 MSF/Month
      MEDIUM        :   Medium-Between 250-500 MSF/Month
      LARGE         :   Large-Greater than 500 MSF/Month

BuyCriteria:
      Design        :   Design is an important criteria for a
                        buy decision.
      Price         :   Price is the most important buying
                        decision and design is not involved.
      QSC           :   Quality, service and company reputation
                        is most important and design is not
                        involved.
      DK            :   Don't know yet what is important to the
                        buyer.
METHOD      :
      TELEPHONE   :
      MAIL        :
      PERSONAL    :
      TandM       :   Telephone and Mail combination
```

FIGURE 20.2   List of Attributes from Prototype Marketing Expert System

□ *Reason*: This is the list of six possible reasons why a contact is made. For example, R1 is an abbreviation for "respond to a request for quote that does not require inspection." Some of the reasons are not defined, just listed, because they are terms known to the user.

□ *Potential*: There are three possible volumes of sales to a client: small, medium, and large.

□ *Buy criteria*: Four criteria important for buyers are listed here as examples: design, price, quality, and not sure.

□ *Method*: Once the decision attributes are listed, it is necessary to list the alternative decisions. In this case, four alternative methods of contact are defined: telephone, mail, personal, and telephone combined with mail.

Step 2: Analyzing Cases (Example Listing). In this step the computer is presented with different cases. Figure 20.3 shows seventeen. In each case a combination of three values of each of the three attributes is shown. For example, case 1 involves "qualify" (a reason attribute), "large" number of contacts (for the potential attribute), and "price" (as the most important buying criteria attribute).

```
     EXPERT-EASE Example Listing, Problem: PROSPECT

     REASON        POTENTIAL      BuyCriteri     METHOD
     logical       logical        logical        logical
     --------      ---------      ----------     ---------
  1  Qualify       LARGE          Price          PERSONAL
  2  R1            SMALL          Design         PERSONAL
  3  R1            SMALL          Price          TELEPHONE
  4  Qualify       MEDIUM         DK             TELEPHONE
  5  Present       MEDIUM         Price          PERSONAL
  6  Present       SMALL          Price          TELEPHONE
  7  Qualify       SMALL          DK             TELEPHONE
  8  Present       SMALL          Design         PERSONAL
  9  R2            SMALL          Price          PERSONAL
 10  Present       LARGE          DK             PERSONAL
 11  Present       SMALL          QSC            MAIL
 12  Initiate      LARGE          DK             PERSONAL
 13  Initiate      MEDIUM         DK             TELEPHONE
 14  Initiate      SMALL          DK             MAIL
 15  R1            MEDIUM         QSC            TandM
 16  R1            SMALL          QSC            TandM
 17  R1            MEDIUM         Price          PERSONAL
```

FIGURE 20.3 List of Cases from Prototype Marketing Expert System

```
EXPERT-EASE Rule Listing, Problem: PROSPECT
BuyCriteria
     Design : PERSONAL
      Price : POTENTIAL
             SMALL : REASON
                            R1 : TELEPHONE
                            R2 : PERSONAL
                  Qualify : null
                  Present : TELEPHONE
                     QandP : null
                  Initiate : null
            MEDIUM : PERSONAL
             LARGE : PERSONAL
        QSC : REASON
             R1 : TandM
             R2 : null
         Qualify : null
         Present : MAIL
            QandP : null
       Initiate : null
        DK : POTENTIAL
           SMALL : REASON
                          R1 : null
                          R2 : null
                Qualify : TELEPHONE
                Present : null
                   QandP : null
                Initiate : MAIL
             :MEDIUM : TELEPHONE
              LARGE : PERSONAL
```

FIGURE 20.4   Rules as Generated by the Computer Program from Prototype Marketing Expert System

When the system was being developed, a human expert was asked to suggest a contact method for such a combination of values. The expert recommended, in case 1, a "personal" contact. However, instead of interrogating a human expert, cases can be derived from historical files.

Step 3: Rule Listing. In this step the computer creates the rules. Figure 20.4 is an example of rules generated by the computer. The prototype is sufficient to generate advice. As more cases are added, rules are added or previous rules are modified. The program will identify inconsistencies in the rules as new rules are generated.

The next four figures demonstrate a consultation session between a potential user and the computer. Figure 20.5 shows the first question posed to the user:

```
┌─────────────────────────────────────────────────────────────────────┐
│  ┌───────────────────────────────────────────────────────────────┐  │
│  │  EXPERT-EASE   file: PROSPECT    43958 bytes left      1 : REASON │  │
│  ├───────────────────────────────────────────────────────────────┤  │
│  │  What is the value of BuyCriteria?                            │  │
│  │                                                               │  │
│  │    1. Design is an important criterion for a buy decision.    │  │
│  │                                                               │  │
│  │    2. Price is the most important buying decision and design is not │  │
│  │       involved.                                               │  │
│  │                                                               │  │
│  │    3. Quality, service, and company reputation is most important and │  │
│  │       design is not involved.                                 │  │
│  │                                                               │  │
│  │    4. Don't know yet what is important to the buyer           │  │
│  │                                                               │  │
│  ├───────────────────────────────────────────────────────────────┤  │
│  │  running PROSPECT                                             │  │
│  │  Enter value 1..4                                             │  │
│  │  >                                                            │  │
│  └───────────────────────────────────────────────────────────────┘  │
└─────────────────────────────────────────────────────────────────────┘
```

FIGURE 20.5 First Question Posed to User—Buy Criteria—by Marketing Expert System

"What is the value of BuyCriteria?" The user selects item 4 from the menu. In Figure 20.6, the user selects item 3 for the "potential" question (i.e., there is a potential for large sales). Figure 20.7 asks the reason for the contact. The user selects item 6 (an initial contact). Now the computer arrives at a conclusion—the use of the telephone (Figure 20.8).

Expert Ease can display for the user the rules used to arrive at any appropriate recommendation. At present, the software can take only a small number of attributes and values. All the information is assumed to be under certainty; that is, no certainty factors or probabilistic values are permitted.

20.7 Case 6: COMPASS: A Telephone Switch Maintenance System

COMPASS (Central Office Maintenance Printout Analysis and Suggestion System) analyzes maintenance printouts of telephone company control switching equipment and suggests maintenance actions to be performed.[6] A central office telephone switch system connects thousands or tens of thousands of telephone lines to one another or external trunks (interconnections among central offices).

---

[6]Based on Goyal et al. [7].

```
EXPERT-EASE   file: PROSPECT    43958 bytes left              1 : REASON

What is the value of POTENTIAL ?

    1. Small - Less than 250 MSF/Month

    2. Medium - Between 250 - 500 MSF/Month

    3. Large - Greater than 500 MSF/Month




running PROSPECT
Enter value 1..3
>
```

FIGURE 20.6   Question of Potential Posed by Marketing Expert System

```
EXPERT-EASE   file: PROSPECT    43958 bytes left              1 : REASON

What is the value of REASON ?

    1. Respond to a request for quote that does not require inspection.

    2. Request for quote on item that requires inspection.

    3. Qualify

    4. Present

    5. Qualify and present is your objective.

    6. Initiate



running PROSPECT
Enter value 1..6
>
```

FIGURE 20.7   Question of Reason Posed by Marketing Expert System

```
┌─────────────────────────────────────────────────────────────────────┐
│  ┌───────────────────────────────────────────────────────────────┐  │
│  │ EXPERT- EASE   file: PROSPECT      43958 bytes left        1 : REASON │
│  │                                                               │  │
│  │ The value of METHOD is TELEPHONE                              │  │
│  │                                                               │  │
│  │ do you want to run  PROSPECT again (y or n) ?                 │  │
│  │ >                                                             │  │
│  │                                                               │  │
│  └───────────────────────────────────────────────────────────────┘  │
└─────────────────────────────────────────────────────────────────────┘
```

FIGURE 20.8 Conclusion Reached by the Computer in the Marketing Expert System

Such a switch system can produce hundreds of maintenance messages daily. The messages are analyzed to determine what actions are necessary to maintain the switch.

GTE developed COMPASS, an ES, to perform an analysis of maintenance messages for its No. 2 Electronic Automatic Exchange (EAX). The No. 2 EAX was selected because its technology is stable, widely used, and scheduled to be in use for several years. In addition, the available expertise in No. 2 EAX maintenance and administration is likely to diminish as technicians work on newer situations.

A GTE software system called Remote Monitor and Control System (RMCS) monitors the output messages of several telephone switches. The maintenance printouts from RMCS are analyzed to determine what maintenance actions should be taken. A maintenance message describes an error situation that occurred during the telephone call-processing operation of the switch, but it gives no indication as to where the problem could be. Problem patterns appear only by collecting a series of messages over an extended time. Expertise is required to analyze and act on the printouts of the RMCS, and there are several levels of expertise. People with less expertise perform the job less well and more slowly than those with greater expertise. Internal consultants with great expertise are consulted when those with less expertise cannot solve a problem. The expertise involves judgment and rules of thumb accumulated over many years. In maintaining older switches, corporate expertise is lost as experts move on to work on newer switches. Thus, the need for an expert system exists and will grow in the future.

A great amount of expertise is required to analyze a No. 2 EAX maintenance printout (Figure 20.9) and determine and prioritize maintenance actions such as these:

☐ Identifying groups of maintenance messages that are likely to be caused by the same switch fault
☐ Analyzing the messages in each group, along with any related information, to determine the possible specific faults in the switch that could be causing those maintenance messages

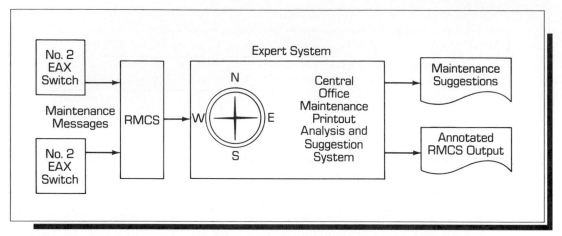

FIGURE 20.9 Procedure of Analysis for GTE Maintenance Printout (*Source:* S. I. Goyal, et al., "COMPASS: An Expert System for Telephone Switch Maintenance," *Expert Systems* [July 1985].)

- □ Estimating the likelihood of recurrence of the possible faults
- □ Determining the possible maintenance actions that could be suggested to the switch maintenance person to enable these faults to be verified and remedied
- □ Prioritizing the list of suggested actions by taking into account such considerations as the likelihood of the fault and the ease of performing the corrective action
- □ Making the system's suggestions known to the user in the most user-friendly way.

COMPASS includes all these areas of expertise.

System Development

The system was developed on a Xerox 1108 AI workstation using the KEE development tool. The prototyping, which involved several person-years of effort, lasted about a year of elapsed time. The entire development process is documented by Goyal et al. [7]. Some of the lessons learned from the construction of the system were presented in Chapter 12.

Testing and Validation

Initial field use of this system has been successful. In one field trial, COMPASS analyzed the maintenance messages and suggested maintenance actions for four No. 2 EAX switches (two in Texas and two in Florida). These switches service over 100,000 lines of customer phones and trunks. For each switch,

COMPASS was run once a day for three to five days. COMPASS found a total of fifty-one switch problems. During the time allotted for the trial, switch maintenance personnel were able to execute the recommended set of actions for thirty-three of the fifty-one problems. In all thirty-three cases the recommended actions fixed the switch problem. In most cases the problem was fixed by COMPASS's first recommendation (if the first recommendation does not help, a second one is issued, etc.).

In addition to the field trials, COMPASS's analyses, rules, and procedures were examined in detail by a group of four No. 2 EAX switch experts (peers of the project's domain expert). The group strongly endorsed COMPASS. Generally, they came to the same conclusions as COMPASS, though sometimes by a slightly different procedure. In one test case, the experts agreed that COMPASS had correctly identified a switch problem that none of them had identified in their analyses.

Results of the field trials and expert analyses convinced telephone switch operating personnel to request that the present version of COMPASS be quickly installed in a field location. It is used to analyze maintenance problems for GTE's No. 2 EAX switches throughout the country. (There are more than 150 such switches nationwide.) More importantly, COMPASS will provide the basis for studying the impact of ES on human resources and for quantifying the costs and benefits of such systems.

Potential Advantages, Payoffs, and Expansions

COMPASS affords several potential advantages to users:

- □ It supports better telephone switch performance, yielding higher-quality service to telephone customers.
- □ It increases the productivity of experienced switch maintenance persons.
- □ It upgrades the performance of less experienced personnel.
- □ It provides guaranteed maintenance of existing switches by capturing expertise that may not be available in the future.

COMPASS can perform certain tasks better than the best human experts. For example, COMPASS can analyze a complete situation (which is difficult for even the best human expert), automate present maintenance procedures that involve laborious and error-prone table lookups and calculations, analyze each situation without bias, and perform equally well any day or any hour.

One of the positive aspects of COMPASS is long-term growth potential. COMPASS can be expanded to include the following tasks:

- □ Covering maintenance messages from other types of switches
- □ Combining RMCS information with information from other local indicators, such as switch alarm systems

□ Adding network traffic information to allow analysis on a more global basis

□ Learning from experience to upgrade performance, such as learning better values for the frequency of switch faults

Early in its use, the elapsed time for a typical COMPASS run was about one-half hour; this time is decreasing rapidly (to a few minutes) with improved technology. Depending on their level of expertise, No. 2 EAX maintenance personnel would take five minutes to two hours to perform a similar analysis (which in many cases was not as accurate or complete as that of COMPASS).

20.8   Case 7: AIG's Underwriting System

American International Group, Inc. (AIG, New York) is the nation's seventh largest insurance company (more than \$11 billion in assets).[7] The company operates in 130 countries, primarily writing custom-made policies for major corporations. Many clients (such as aerospace companies) encounter unusual risk problems. Underwriting the policies, therefore, requires experienced individuals with flexible thinking capabilities.

Development

The ES was developed at the American Home Inland Marine division, which insures literally "anything that moves," from telecommunication signals to registered mail. The system was developed by Syntelligence, Inc. to mimic a top AIG risk manager. The division operates fourteen offices nationwide; the prototype was developed in one office only. Once the system is fully implemented, it will be equivalent to having another top underwriter in each of the fourteen offices.

The prototype was initially done on one product (out of nine major products). This product, called DIC, deals with an insurance policy that covers all types of perils, including earthquakes and floods. The ES was structured with a construction tool called Syntel (developed by Syntelligence, Inc., for building financial expert systems). The software runs on a Xerox 1108 AI workstation.

Development took about a year with numerous iterations, each of which improved the system's performance. The system initially covered 95 percent of the expert's knowledge, and it was continually being improved. Many knowledge acquisition sessions were required (see Box 20.1) to extract the knowledge from the top risk managers.

---

[7]This section is based on Shamoon [12].

Box 20.1: A Sample of Knowledge Acquisition Dialogue

Q = Questions by the knowledge engineer
A = Answers by the expert

Q: How do you determine a premium?
A: I . . .

Q: It doesn't just come out of the air magically. You think about a lot of things, don't you?
A: Yes, I do. I think about flood exposure, earthquake exposure, collapse, burglary.

Q: What do you think about when you think about burglary?
A: I think about the commodity—whether it's liquor and cigarettes or widgets.
Q: If it's liquor or cigarettes, is that good or bad compared with widgets? Which would you rather have and why?

Capabilities

The system is designed to help the company's staff explore how a risk manager should think about insurance, or size up risks and price them—which is basically what underwriters do. In contrast to ready-made, off-the-shelf expert systems, the AIG system can think as top experts at AIG think. The system advises, for example, whether to accept a client and what the premium should be. The system is also being used as a training device for new underwriters, who work with the machine on actual cases under the supervision of a top expert.

The ES uses the certainty factor approach for assigning weights to the recommendations. In addition, the system takes into account geographical differences. It knows, for example, how AIG experts think about earthquake chances in Los Angeles as compared with those in San Francisco.

More than a hundred AIG employees with personal computers can tap into the company's mainframe and use the ES.

Facts and Issues

☐ The prototype ES has influenced AIG in many ways and will continue to do so. The system cost about $2 million. The company estimates a payback period of two and a half years. This estimate is based on saving the salary of fourteen senior risk managers (one in each office). At $60,000 a person, the annual savings is $840,000.

- Risk managers will not be fired; however, over the next two to three years, the computer will be able to handle a substantially increased volume of business with existing personnel.
- Senior managers who were skeptical at the beginning now think the system is great, and has a lot of potential.
- Eight experts were interviewed to ensure that expertise in diversified topics is covered.
- Once the first product line is operational, the company will prototype the other eight product lines.
- Some employees fear that expert systems will replace human experts. Management is currently seeking a way to deal with their fears.
- Expert systems improve corporate decision making by speeding it up and making it more consistent than is normally possible for humans.
- Intelligent systems can be used as tools to train new or junior people in an organization.

20.9 Case 8: Expert System in Law Enforcement

Problem

One of the most difficult decision-making situations occurs when law enforcement officials are involved in stressful circumstances such as responding to hostage-taking incidents.[8] Police officers must make critical, emotionally charged decisions under conditions of high stress and great uncertainty. Most officers who are involved in such incidents have little experience. The few trained and experienced officers cannot be brought fast enough to all places that require them. Therefore, the availability of an expert on a disk in each police station holds great promise.

Methodology

The first step in developing this system at the University of Arizona was a feasibility study to make sure that an ES was justifiable. Once the criteria were satisfied, a model of the situation was developed; this model is shown in Figure 20.10. As you can see, the purpose of the ES is to advise the officer about what to do. The recommendation is filtered through the human value system and the officer makes the final decision.

The system was developed initially to handle forty-one different scenarios, each of which may develop during a hostage-taking incident. Knowledge was solicited from human experts.

---

[8]Based on Vedder and Mason [15].

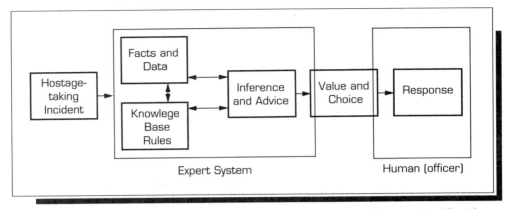

FIGURE 20.10 Model for Expert System for Law Enforcement (*Source:* Modified from R. G. Vedder and R. O. Mason, "An Expert System Application for Decision Support in Law Enforcement," *Decisions Sciences* [Summer 1987].)

Development

The system is rule based and it can assist several different decision makers simultaneously. It was developed with a simple rule-based shell and was run on a VAL 11/785 (superminicomputer).

The first prototype was developed fast, and its recommendations and rules were evaluated by an expert officer. The officer found the first prototype to be "too academic." For example, the information required by the system took too long to collect. There also was a problem with four different decision makers who needed to coordinate their activities.

The second prototype incorporated many of the suggestions of the evaluator. Yet, the results were far from satisfactory. Next, the prototype was tested on a simulated hostage-taking incident. A student used the expert system to make decisions that were evaluated, on the scene, by an expert. The system performed fairly well and currently it is being used as a training tool.

Several additional iterations are necessary, however, before the system could be used in real incidents. Also, the system should run on a microcomputer so that it can be used in many locations.

20.10   Case 9: High-value Loan Analysis

Problem

ABC Bank (so-called to maintain anonymity) specializes in loans of over $30 million each. Such loans are typically made for major construction projects. The funding money in many cases comes from the federal government and there are extensive regulations on the loans. Before a loan can be approved, a lengthy and expensive study must be conducted. Typically, the study is about 3,200 pages long, takes six months to complete, and costs about $250,000. The bank recovers the cost of doing the study as part of the cost of issuing the loan; however, the cost is recovered *only* if the bank issues the loan. If after doing the study, the bank decides not to issue the loan, it loses the money it spent. Consequently, there is a great deal of pressure to issue the loan, even if the situation is not as secure as desired.

Solution

To solve this problem, the bank had an expert system developed by Micro Support Inc., using the EXSYS shell. The ES uses data that can be obtained at low cost. A bank employee can run the expert system on a laptop computer on site. The results from the expert system are sent to the bank via modem for examination by the chief underwriter.

The expert system uses the data to predict if the full study will result in a loan that can or should be issued. The system divides loans into three categories: likely to be issued, unlikely to issued, and "gray area." Loans that are unlikely to be issued can be dropped before expending the time, resources, and dollars on the full study. This has resulted in tremendous savings. Since the system can explain why the loan was rejected, the borrower knows specifically what would have to be corrected to successfully reapply for the loan. The loans likely to be issued can be pursued with confidence that the costs will be recovered. The gray area loans are examined by human experts. They analyze the conclusions of the expert system to determine if they should proceed with the full study.

In addition, the expert system determines the most appropriate money source for the potential loan—the Ginnie Mae, Fannie Mae, Freddie Mac, or private funds—by evaluating the many requirements associated with each loan. The system contains 380 rules and was developed over three months. It uses a wide range of analysis techniques including Delphi studies conducted during the knowledge acquisition phase and decision modeling to establish the probability factors used during rule generation.

20.11   Case 10: CARGEX: Cargo Expert System

Problem

The German airline Lufthansa concentrates on airfreight consolidation processes.[9] Worldwide, all airfreight applications are routed into the cargo center in Frankfurt. A "traditional" electronic data processing system makes automatic

---

[9]Condensed from W. Koenig, et al., "Building on an Expert System to Create an Active DSS," In *Proceedings HICSS*, 1988.

loading decisions, as long as (1) freight is standard and (2) some threshold values on loading an aircraft are not exceeded.

Applications that cannot be handled by this system are routed on the screen to experts who decide (1) whether an application is acceptable, and if it is, at what price, and (2) on which specific flights the airfreight should be loaded. The last decision is not a trivial one because of the following four facts:

1. Aircraft are loaded by both weight and volume. Various aircraft types differ in the optimal ratio of weight to volume. The employment of mixed-mode aircraft (e.g., 74M) allows short-term decisions on the distribution of passengers and freight on the passenger deck. It is the task of the consolidator to properly accept new freight into an aircraft so that (1) the amount of chargeable kilograms of freight is maximized and (2) the total ratio of weight to volume of the aircraft is near the optimum.
2. Various freight types interact heavily, for example, living animals (which require special handling and cannot be loaded side by side in a lot of cases), valuable goods (which require particular loading/unloading procedures), and dangerous chemicals.
3. Although the airline has a one-hub network, there is considerable complexity in each branch out of (and into) Frankfurt. Moreover, in cases of capacity bottlenecks, the airline employs trucking between two airports. Freight may also be stored and shipped later to achieve better loading configurations; however, some freight types require immediate transport (e.g., live fish, flowers).
4. Many qualitative conditions are relevant in an actual decision, for example, customer priority (which may overrule other decision parameters in certain cases), assessment of the accuracy of freight delivery to the airport, and assessment of the level of the actual airfreight market.

Solution

CARGEX is an ES constructed to assist in making loading decisions. The user interface of CARGEX is shown in Figure 20.11. The screen is subdivided into three zones called north, central, and south. The northern part contains a calendar, the required destination of each flight, the specification of the season (which influences the market level), and the sender. Moreover, the freight is specified by an airway bill number (identification), type of freight, origin, allotment, weight, volume, type of container, number of pieces, whether a split is allowed between various flights, whether it is a must-go freight, and information about charges.

The central part shows both graphically and numerically the actual loading situation of the respective flight, subdivided into weight and volume for the scheduled aircraft. In mixed-mode aircraft, the distribution of the passenger deck is also included in these calculations. Moreover, the usage of various container types for the respective aircraft is shown.

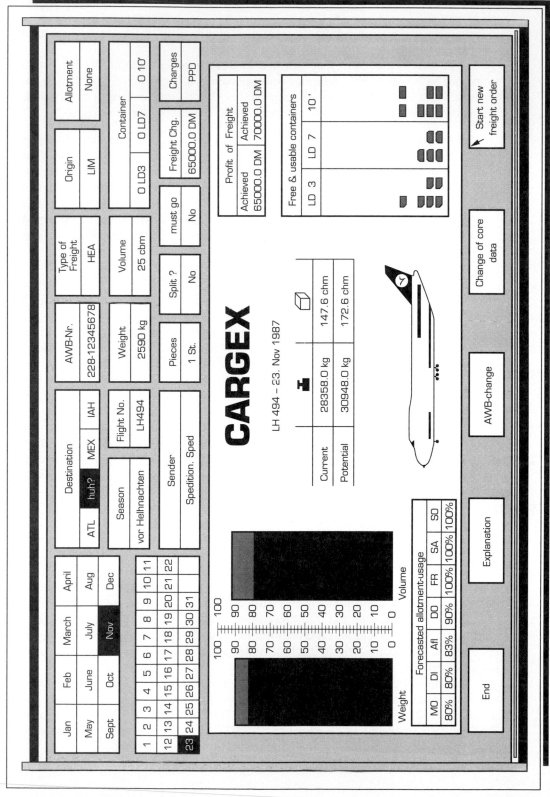

FIGURE 20.11 User Interface of CARGEX: Typical Screen (*Source:* W. Koenig, et al., "Building an Expert System to Create an Active DSS," In *Proceedings, HICCS*, 1988.)

The southern part contains the command line where the user can conduct these activities:

- Quit the expert system
- Ask for an explanation of a proposal, which shows the rules and their hierarchy
- Require investigations (look up of particular airway bills which have to be rescheduled)
- Change environmental data

CARGEX actually supports the segments of the interface from Frankfurt, Atlanta, Dallas/Fort Worth, Houston, and Mexico. The system contains approximately 300 rules that are described in about 6,000 lines of code. The basic goal of the application of CARGEX is increased productivity of the consolidation system; it is expressed in two objectives:

1. Maximize the amount of kilogram chargeable per aircraft. This measure is computed as the sum of the actual weights of the goods and the virtual weights of voluminous goods.
2. Handle an increasing amount of airfreight business with a substantially smaller increase of consolidation personnel.

CARGEX successfully underwent two field tests at the airline's cargo center. The tests revealed that in standardized decision situations, which account for 90 percent of all cases, CARGEX was able to create a decision of a quality similar to or in some cases even better than a human expert. Moreover, the consolidation people are convinced that these techniques will help them to handle more applications per period, thus reducing the actual time required for working on really hard problems.

20.12 Case 11: Energy Management in a Hydroelectric Plant

Problem

A large hydroelectric plant in Spain (Iberduero-Labein) serves more than 7 million customers.[10] Electricity is provided via a large, centrally controlled network. Decisions are based on information collected from 2,500 data points. Whenever a major problem occurs in the system (e.g., due to a storm), more than 100 alarms are activated in less than a minute. The problem is to properly analyze and quickly interpret the information collected by the alarms. The high

---

[10]Condensed from *Artificial Intelligence Letter* V (no. 10, October 1989), published by Texas Instruments, Data Systems Group, Austin, Tex.

volume of messages and the potential uncertainty caused by the thousand possible combinations of signals make the situation ideal for an ES application.

Solution

The utility needed a real-time ES integrated with a signaling system as well as with existing databases. Links were done via communication lines. The system, which was developed on a Texas Instruments workstation (Explorer), began as an initial prototype with 400 rules, 1,500 objects, and 200 LISP functions. It was developed with LISP-related language and fully implemented after two years (in 1989). The system uses a model base (see Chapter 6) in addition to the rule base.

System capabilities include (1) detecting a disturbance when it happens, (2) locating the element of the fault, (3) tracking the location of the disturbance, and (4) recommending repairs (and justifying them). Working in its online mode, the expert system assesses alarms, generates several hypotheses about fault location, selects the most likely, and sends its conclusions to the human operator. In its off-line mode, it becomes more thoughtful; after the disturbance has been resolved and all possible information about it has been amassed, the expert system reasons about it. The system explains the chain of reasoning it followed in selecting its hypotheses, monitors the operation of the protective relays to assist the maintenance engineers, and presents a statistical evaluation of the disturbance. The statistics include such things as the length of times consumers experienced outages, the number of tests performed by the breakers to restore service, and a list of breakers that remained open when the disturbance reached a steady state.

20.13   Case 12: EXSOFS: Expert System in Building Construction

Problem

Construction costs in Singapore are escalating.[11] Builders are attempting various cost-reduction approaches. Because many of the buildings are underpinned by concrete structures, the selection of an appropriate formwork is especially important. A selection can be made from six possible methods. The problem is to find the most appropriate method for the construction of concrete slabs of each individual building. Both building conditions and site conditions influence the selection of the appropriate method. Their relationships are complex, including both qualitative and quantitative factors. Thus, considerable expertise is needed.

---

[11]Condensed from Tiong and Koo [14].

Solution

A system, called EXSOFS, was constructed with an expert system shell named Xi Plus (from Inference Corp.). The shell includes both frame and rule representation. Knowledge was acquired from experts in industry and academia.

A schematic view of the system is shown in Figure 20.12. The knowledge is contained in eleven different knowledge bases. The system interfaces with a database that is managed by dBASE IV and is supported by a spreadsheet. There, calculations are performed and reports are generated. The knowledge is represented either as rules or as "when-then" demons. To expedite calculations, the program has an interface with BASIC. This external program is designed to calculate costs quickly. The DBMS allows cost-management programs (e.g., updating, comparing). Extensive graphics can be accessed by Xi Plus to provide vivid consultation; special procedures were developed to allow presentation of graphs and even pictures.

Structure of the System.   The system is composed of the following modules:

- The formwork selection module—selects one of the six methods
- The cost-calculation module (using the BASIC program)—calculates the ownership cost
- Cost calculation for a rented formwork system
- Cost of using a conventional formwork system
- Graphic presentation
- Database management module

Several of the modules include more than one knowledge base. The system, which is really a combination of a decision support system and an expert system, allows DSS analysis (e.g., what-if). It has been successfully validated against recommendations provided by human experts.

Application.   The system, which runs on a personal computer, can be used by relatively inexperienced construction engineers. Experienced engineers can run quick consultations to validate their judgments. Also, the experienced engineers saved time in executing support calculations.

20.14   Case 13: Soviet Union Trade Advisor (SUTA)

Problem

The economic and political changes in the Soviet Union may provide an opportunity for many companies to trade with the country.[12] However, there

---

[12]Condensed from Szuprowicz [13].

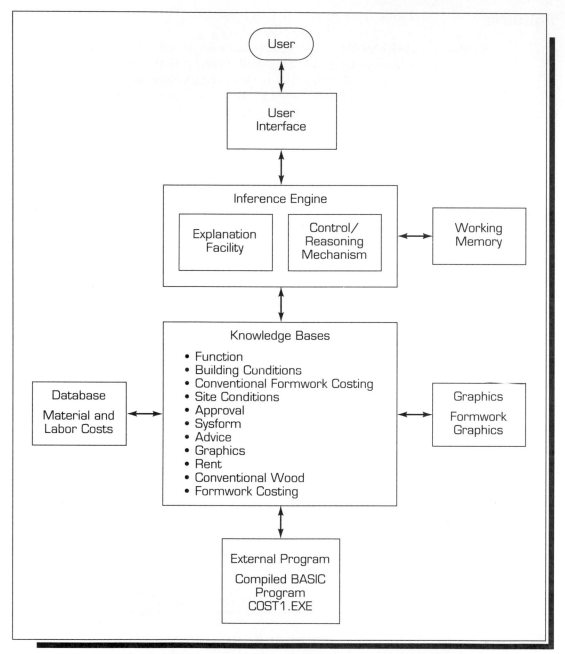

FIGURE 20.12 System Structure of the Expert System Called EXSOFS (*Source:* R. Tiong and T. K. Koo, "Selecting Construction Formwork: An Expert System Adds Economy," Reprinted from *Expert Systems* [New York: Auerbach Publishers]. © 1991 Warren, Gorham, & Lamont Inc. Used with permission.)

is little expertise in Western countries on what is really going on in the Soviet Union. So while there are opportunities, there are also risks. The situation is clouded by a stream of incomplete and frequently contradictory and even incorrect data. Businesspeople want quick and reliable advice, but it is rarely available. (The U.S. Department of Commerce is flooded with such requests.)

Solution

An expert system called Soviet Union Trade Advisor (SUTA) was developed by Deloitte and Touche, a large management consulting (and CPA) company. The major objective of the system is to provide advice on trade opportunities and licensing requirements for medium- to high-technology products. The system started as an advisory service to the company's employees (consultants, auditors). Now it is being further developed so it can be marketed (for a fee) to potential traders.

System Development. SUTA contains many knowledge bases and since the domain is very complex, subdivision is essential. The builder prepared a list of preliminary questions most frequently asked (e.g., what products are needed, what is the competition, and what are the export and import controls). In addition, traders like to find the prospective buyers. The first module of SUTA was developed to provide this kind of information.

Knowledge was difficult to accumulate. Therefore, a small prototype was constructed first with the Crystal shell (from Intelligent Environments, Inc.). Soviet experts were identified and the knowledge was validated. Also, the ES had to interface with several databases (some of which are online). The system was expanded to deal with export licensing requirements and provides a facsimile of an application for export license (displayed on the screen with instructions on how to complete it). The system is supported by hypertext that navigates through the complex forms.

Use. The system is very user-friendly; it is based on simple sets of menus. The market is divided into twelve sectors with which potential products are matched. The system assesses the opportunities for general classes of products and then for specific ones. Then, potential buyers are identified together with procedures for making contacts. Explanations are provided on request. Several other types of valuable information are provided by the system. The system is being improved in cooperation with Soviet sources.

20.15 Overview of Ready-made Expert Systems

An increasing number of software packages address generic problems that trouble people. Such problems range from selecting an appropriate wine for

TABLE 20.3 Representative Ready-made Expert Systems

Name	Area	Vendor
Alacrity-Strategy	Strategic management decisions	Alacritous, Inc.
BuySmart	Advice on buying technological products	Expert Buying Systems, Inc.
CAD/CAE/CAM	Automated engineering design	Carnegie Group, Inc.
Communications Edge	Management	Human Edge, Inc.
Concept	Marketing simulation, consumer behavior, integration of DSS/ES	Timeshare Systems, Inc.
Experimental Design	Consulting statistician: select most appropriate experimental design	Statistical Programs
Hyper's Estimator	Estimation for builders and architects; estimates of construction costs	Turtle Creek Software
Leading-Effectively	Effectiveness, productivity	Thoughtware, Inc.
Logician	Electronic design	Daisy Systems, Inc.
MORE	Selecting potential customers from large lists	American Express
Mortgage Lender/Broker	Management of lending for mortgages; management of broker's job	Synthetic Intelligence Corp.
MUS	Mortgage underwriting	Cognesys
Negotiation Edge	Personnel and labor relations	Human Edge
PC-Stockcast	Stockmarket forecasting	Micro Applications
Performance	Performance analysis	Performance Mentor
PLUS	Personal insurance underwriting	Cognesys
Production	Integrated factory management	Carnegie Group, Inc.
Project-Management	Software project management	Carnegie Group, Inc.
Questware	Selecting PC hardware and software	Dynaquest
Resource 1	Productivity, time management	Resource 1
ROI Expert	Investment analysis	Microtext Services
Sales Edge	Advertising	Human Edge
SMP/MACSYMA	Mathematical problem solving	Inference, Inc. & Symbolic, Inc.
StreetSmart	Finding the best route to take between two points in cities and counties	Street Map Software
Teckchek	Help in hiring and training	Bookman Consulting
TRILOGY	Automatic construction of courseware	Metavision, Inc.

dinner to maintaining software and hardware. Like any other off-the-shelf application packages, these systems have standard features. They do not perfectly match specific problems, but they are much cheaper than custom-made systems and they can be used instantaneously. Such packages are being developed by vendors of shells or by third-party firms who buy development tools (or shells), develop a knowledge base for a specific application, and then sell it to the end-user. Instead of buying a shell and then developing an ES using their own experts, end-users buy computerized expertise. The use of such systems is expanding rapidly in areas ranging from investment (e.g., capital budgeting) and financial planning to admission decisions in universities. Table 20.3 lists examples.

There is a major limitation to the use of ready-made systems. Since the experts who are employed to build such systems have no idea about the specific circumstances of the end-users, they tend to give general (and somewhat vague) recommendations. Therefore, several of the reviews of these products (especially those that are based on microcomputers) are critical of their value. On the other hand, these programs, like any other ES, are improving with time and their quality is expected to rise in the future. Some of the more expensive packages can be modified to fit users' needs more closely as well. The following sections contain brief descriptions of several ready-made packages.

20.16 Case 14: Management Edge

The Management Edge (from Human Edge, Inc.) offers a method of understanding and communicating with coworkers, subordinates, and superiors by presenting expert management advice in specific situations. The program is composed of several steps. First, the user is asked to conduct a self-assessment through a list of eighty statements with which the user can either agree or disagree (Figure 20.13). This approach is similar to a standard psychological test like MMPI (Minnesota Multiphasic Personality Inventory). Administration of the self-assessment enables the computer to "learn" about users and their attitudes and beliefs. Users can then receive advice about (1) a relationship with a subordinate, (2) a relationship with a superior, (3) assessment of their managerial skills, and (4) assessment of their organization. For each of these four categories, users answer several dozen additional questions.

The assessment given by the system is based on pattern recognition. If the answers of a user show a certain pattern (or profile), a matching assessment (or recommendation) is given. There is a limited number of possible computer outputs. Sample questions for an assessment of the user's organization are shown in Figure 20.14. A typical assessment produced by the computer is shown in Figure 20.15.

```
 File  Edit  Self


                          ASSESSING YOURSELF        AGREE DISAGREE
  I usually arrive early for work.                   ☒     ☐
  Being popular at work is important to me.          ☒     ☐
  I am overly sensitive to criticism on the job.     ☐     ☒
  I often am critical of fellow employees.           ☐     ☒
  Others on the job count on me to stir up some action ☒   ☐
  Often I feel tense at work for no good reason.     ☐     ☒
  I like being feared by other employees.            ☐     ☒
  I am friendly when meeting other employees.        ☒     ☐
  I am more nervous than most other employees.       ☐     ☐

  ┌────┐ ┌──────────┐
  │Next│ │Previous  │
  └────┘ └──────────┘
  Please check AGREE or DISAGREE for each item.
```

FIGURE 20.13   Sample Questions from the Self-assessment Program of Management Edge

```
                                                     Agree Disagree
  1. Employees seem to get along very well             ☒     ☐
  2. The majority of employees strive to power         ☒     ☐
  3. The organization has a goal of high growth        ☐     ☒
  4. Employees do not socialize among themselves       ☒     ☐
  5. The company can be described as risk-taking       ☐     ☒
```

FIGURE 20.14   Sample Questions Concerning an Organization, from Management Edge

20.17   Miscellaneous Ready-made Systems

Wheat Counsellor

Wheat Counsellor, a system developed by ICI (England), advises on the control of disease in winter wheat. It includes recommendations about which chemicals to use when treating diseases. Because ICI markets many agrichemicals, it is interested in ensuring that farmers use them correctly.

```
            * * * * * * * * * * * * * * * * * * *
            *   THE  MANAGEMENT  EDGE    *
            * * * * * * * * * * * * * * * * * *


                    - - - - - - - - - - - - - - - -
                    YOUR ORGANIZATION
                    - - - - - - - - - - - - - - - -


You have described your overall organization as stable and
formally organized. Rules and authority tend to be formalized,
and employee responsibilities are well defined. Compliance and
commitment are valued assets. It is likely that you work within
bureaucratic structure. Because of your flexible nature, you will
work well in this organization. Although you might find some
things about a bureaucracy frustrating, in general, you are a
good match for this company.


The organization you work in also values achievement. High
productivity and independent action are emphasized. Individuals
are motivated to succeed through their own hard effort. In this
organization, you will perform to the extent of your capacity. It
is likely that the emphasis placed on achievement will raise your
motivation and productivity. Your reliable and consistent work
habits will help you to succeed in this setting.
```

FIGURE 20.15 Typical Output from Management Edge

Wheat Counsellor first evaluates the risks of fungal diseases in a crop by asking for information about the variety of wheat being grown, its location, the soil type, local weather, and so on. It then draws on crop-growth data from several organizations and states the expected loss if no treatment is given. Next, Wheat Counsellor examines the range of fungicides sold by ICI and other manufacturers and recommends treatment from this range. Finally, it provides costs for these and states the likely return on investment.

Wheat Counsellor is interesting because it is attached to videotex. The expert system itself runs on a PDP-11. ICI uses a private videotex system called Grapevine, which is similar to the public British system Prestel. An ordinary telephone is sufficient to connect an adapted television set or other terminal to Grapevine; Wheat Counsellor can then interact with that terminal. Wheat Counsellor provides the usual explanation facilities. Because it is used by computer-naive users, ICI has taken care to make its output comprehensible.

Questware

A system that advises on the purchase of computer software and hardware is available from Dynaquest Corp. The system, called Questware, is being expanded for diagnostic sessions regarding computer systems. Advice is given only online via telephone lines.

MIKE

MIKE, developed by the Mandell Institute, is the automated admissions representative of Brandeis University. Built to expand the pool of high-quality applicants for the school, the system is designed to be used by high school seniors who are narrowing their choice of colleges.

MIKE explains all the academic and extracurricular programs in which the prospective applicant has an interest. It also uses its video base to take the student on a tour of the campus. Once the system has the student's interest, it even gives feedback concerning the likelihood of admission and the type and amount of financial aid. At this point, the student's name and address are taken for transmission to the campus-based computer for follow-up.

A new, enhanced MIKE will be able to do detailed financial aid planning with prospective applicants and their parents and will even provide a customized catalog for students. The catalog will focus on the areas in which the student showed the greatest interest, in the judgment of MIKE.

Fair-Cost

This Fair-Cost system (from DM Data, Inc.) provides an interactive planning aid for strategic planning, system costing, engineering, and purchasing involved in obtaining custom VLSI circuits for electronic systems.

FS

The FS system (from Athena Group) advises on foreign exchange trading activity. It supports a number of different analysis techniques and provides probabilistic decision support. Thus it can be considered a DSS/ES combination. The system contains several trading, hedging, and risk-control strategies.

PM and SO

The expert system packages called PM and SO (from Athena Group) help stock portfolio management (PM) and stock option (SO) strategies.

PEANUTS

PEANUTS is an irrigation management ES written with EXSYS that is being tested in the southeastern United States. The user supplies soil type, growth stage of the peanut plant, and general information about the soil temperature, the amount of water applied, and the predicted weather. The system responds with a recommendation to irrigate or not and gives extensive information about why the decision was reached. It also uses the same input to issue warnings if conditions indicate possible problems with pests. The system is being developed by the United States Department of Agriculture, Peanut Research Laboratory (Dawson, Ga.) and the U.S. Department of Agriculture, Agricultural Research Services (Temple, Tex.).

Wines on Disk

Wines on Disk is a ready-made ES that provides advice on how to select American wines to suit any occasion. The wine inventory includes 600 choices and the expert is an internationally acknowledged wine expert. The ES provides information about the wine's varietal, vineyard, year, price range, rating, and tasting comments. It is available in many liquor stores and vineyards.

Paint Advisor

The system called Paint Advisor advises customers in Europe about do-it-yourself paint jobs and appropriate products. It tells the user how to prepare for painting, cleaning up, and doing the job under different conditions.

The program, which includes about 300 rules, is programmed in KES. It is available in a chain of department stores in Europe for free use by potential buyers of paint products.

20.18 Summary

The case applications discussed in this chapter present a diversified sample of expert systems developed fairly recently in various types of organizations. Most of these systems are pure rule-based systems. Some include an explanation facility. Most were constructed with shells or construction packages. Here is where the similarity among the systems ends. Each system was constructed for a different purpose and therefore exhibits unique characteristics. The questions for discussion that follow are designed to explore some of the similarities and differences among the systems.

Questions for Discussion

1. Why are tasks performed by help desks ideal for AI automation?
2. Can DustPro be considered a ready-made system? Why?
3. Review the tasks that were automated in GADS. What are the major before-after differences?
4. Both YES/MVS and ISIS-II deal with scheduling problems in a manufacturing environment. What are the similarities and differences between the systems?

5. Describe some of the advantages and disadvantages of rule induction in a shell such as Expert Ease. Are there situations in which rules cannot be authored by a computer?

6. Review the development process of COMPASS. Compare it with the process suggested in Chapter 12. What phases in the process can you identify in this case?

7. What is a real-time expert system? Why is AIG/DIC *not* such a system?

8. Why may an ES help in hostage-taking incidents?

9. Why is the ES described in case 8 currently good only for training and not for actual use?

10. Justify the need for an ES in case 9.

11. Why is EXSYS (a small rule-based system) sufficient for case 9?

12. Is CARGEX an ES or ES/DSS? Explain.

13. Some people do not consider Management Edge an expert system. Others say that it is a typical rule-based system and an explanation capability can be easily added. What do you think?

14. Refer to the ten generic areas of expert systems (Chapter 3) and relate each of the systems in this chapter to one (or more) of the areas.

15. It is said that most knowledge can be presented as rules. Review all the cases in this chapter and identify all the rule-based systems. Also identify the systems that use presentations other than rules (or in addition to rules). Do you think that most knowledge can be represented as rules? Why or why not?

16. Review all the cases and identify those systems constructed with shells. List the shells and review the reasons (whenever possible) why these shells were selected. Which of the systems were constructed from scratch? Why?

17. Identify the iterative approach in the systems in this chapter. Prepare a table that lists the cases where the iterative process is described, and explain how the initial prototyping was expanded.

18. Rapid prototyping is an essential approach in developing ES. Why is this so? In what cases is there evidence of rapid prototyping?

19. Most systems described in this chapter were executed in very large corporations or in research institutions. This situation is changing now, and ES can be developed economically in a small business. What caused the change?

20. Several of the systems described in this chapter were developed as a joint venture of two partners. List all the systems that were constructed in this way, identify the nature of the partners, and assess the potential benefits to each of them.

21. Identify the real-time systems in this chapter. List commonalities.

22. Identify the trends in ES development by comparing the features of systems built in the mid-1980s with those built around 1990.

23. Relate the major benefits of ES to the systems described in this chapter. Develop your own table using Table 20.4 as a guide. Use check marks to designate a capability-system relationship. (Add more benefits and more systems to your table.)

TABLE 20.4

	Capabilities		
System	**Increase Productivity**	**Increase Quality**	**Preserve Expertise**
Help Desk			
DustPro			
PROSPECT			

Exercise

1. Some sociologists have warned us that computers are reducing people to numbers. On the other hand, technologists assure us that computers will give us more individualized products and services than kings have enjoyed in the past. Based on the examples provided in this chapter, as well as your experiences with expert systems, debate the pros and cons of each position.

Case Study: Eloquent System Helps Balsams Grand Resort Hotel

Problem

Providing personalized service is essential in the hospitality industry, especially in expensive hotels and restaurants.[13] However, labor costs are increasing constantly and so is competition among hotels and restaurants. Thus, personalized service is essential, yet expensive, if provided manually.

Solution

Computers that use artificial intelligence to provide personalized service are entering the hospitality industry. The first hotel in the United States to use the Eloquent System (developed by Eloquent Systems Corp.) is the Balsams Grand Resort Hotel (Dixville Notch, N.H.).

The Balsams has been a posh resort for 113 years. Located on 15,000 acres just fifteen miles from Canada, it's a sprawling 232-room hotel that offers golf, tennis, swimming, ice skating, skiing, dancing, and more. It's the only resort hotel in New England rated Four Stars by Mobil, and Four Diamonds by the AAA. Its managing director, Stephen Barba, is considered a hotelier's hotelier.

Guests at the Balsams are all treated as VIPs, and occupancy consistently runs close to 100 percent during the summer season. But true champions are

[13]Source: Condensed from *Artificial Intelligence Letter* (September 1987), published by Texas Instruments, Data Systems Group, Austin, Tex.

never satisfied. Management felt they could sell even more effectively if their reservationists could quickly match a specific room (each room is unique) to each guest's preferences (during one brief phone call), and also reserve tee times on the golf course, make other special arrangements, and send the guest a written confirmation the same day. They also knew that such a system could help them avoid the one- and two-day gaps in a room's occupancy that often occur with manual systems. Resort hotels rarely have short-stay guests, so these gaps are frequently left unsold.

In January 1986, the Balsams installed an ES. This highly flexible and versatile system helps to service inquiries, make reservations, assign rooms, generate confirmations and other correspondence, handle deposits, do market analysis, and create management reports. The physical system includes eight Macintosh Plus personal computers and several printers connected to an Explorer workstation.

The Explorer AI computer has optical disk storage that can hold up to a million guest histories. Presently, it holds information on Balsams guests and stays since 1971—so a reservationist might tell a caller, "I can give you the same room you had in 1981, if you liked it." Only the best concierges in Europe have memories like that.

The system rests on three foundations: the continually updated history of guest stays, complete characteristics of each room, and management's strategies and policies for running the hotel.

In practice, when a guest calls, the reservationist quickly types the guest's name and the display shows all previous stays and the guest's preferences. As soon as a bit of conversation has made the guest "feel at home," the reservationist can switch to a display form and enter the guests needs and wants—in plain English, an important feature of this easy-to-use system.

Information entered includes dates of stay, rate class, bed type, number of adults and children, section of the hotel preferred, view preferred, and the like. When this is complete, the reservationist enters the one-touch command "Suggest Rooms." The computer reviews its inventory of rooms available on those dates, selects the ones that best fit the guest's wishes *and* the hotel's need to avoid gaps, and lists them in descending rank—with the recommendations that will make everybody happy at the top.

Each room on the recommended list is described, so the reservationist can say, "We can give you room 262, which is our superior class, has a king-size bed, has handicap access as you requested, has a door to room 263, and has a lovely view of our flower gardens, the pool, and the tennis courts." The reservationist is also informed by the display that this stay will fit perfectly between two others, without a gap. Other recommendations may show gaps, and they're better left to guests whose stays will leave no gaps.

Once the guest makes the final decision, the reservationist prints out a confirmation form that's ready to go out in the next mail. It confirms the basic reservation, as all hotels do, but also confirms all the other special arrangements being made for the guest's convenience and enjoyment—and it's signed personally by the reservationist.

Jerry Owen, reservation manager, says, "We're offering the guests better service by meeting their requests and handling the paperwork. And we have much better business forecasts than ever before. I sleep better at night." Owens reports that the system has eliminated the hotel keeper's nightmare, accidental double booking, that is, promising the same room for the same night to two different guests. But the big profit maker is the feature of gap reduction: In the first season, the system cut single-night vacancies more than 50 percent, which translates into roughly six extra guest-nights a day, which means almost $1,000 added profit per day. Management estimates that the system produced $50,000 in its first season. The second season, with the system in full use, looked even better (saving almost $3,000 added profit per day).

The system is popular with the reservationists, too. With the old manual system and a welter of practices, procedures, special rate discounts, and frequent changes, it typically took two months to train a new reservationist. The first reservationist to start work after the Eloquent System was installed became proficient in a week. Probably more important, reservationists are now free to concentrate on extending gracious and creative hospitality rather than being preoccupied with the hectic business of making the manual scheduling system work.

The artificial intelligence approach that makes the system so easy to learn also makes it easy to change as the market changes (without the need for a programmer). Management can easily modify rates, introduce new packages, modify minimum stays, adjust deposit policies, and try new room assignment guidelines. Owen says, "We can quickly make changes. It doesn't take long, and it doesn't screw up existing operations."

Balsams management is known for creative marketing skill, and the system serves marketing well. To cite just one of many examples, management is seeking to increase group business. The system is an excellent tool for this, because it provides an excellent database for cross-marketing—identifying which social guests may be contacts for obtaining group business, and which group guests to invite back as social guests.

There's a nice symmetry to this application of artificial intelligence: The most human-oriented computer concept is now serving one of the most human-oriented businesses, and delighting all the humans it touches.

Some additional facts about Eloquent System follows:

1. The system is rule based, written in TI's shell. This allows hotel management to maintain the system; there is no need for a programmer.
2. The total development cost of the system is estimated to be about $100,000.
3. The initial needs assessment for the system pointed out a possibility of automating food-service management. A good food-service manager is "worth" between $200,000 and $400,000 in profit in hotels. AI technology is not appropriate, however, since there are many restaurant computer systems on the market that are fairly useful.

Questions

1. Identify the various AI technologies used in this system.
2. Identify the multimedia portions of the system.
3. Why is there a need for both the Macintosh Plus and the Explorer machines?
4. List the benefits to the customers.
5. List the benefits to the company.
6. What type of system is this?
7. The system increases the productivity of the reservationists. Why are they happy with the system?
8. Discuss the decision support opportunities in this system.
9. Why is AI considered the "most human-oriented computer concept"?
10. Discuss the relationship between the software vendor and the Balsams.
11. It is said that the system provides tight control yet more flexibility to management. Explain.
12. Why is AI inappropriate for food service management?

References and Bibliography

1. Abraham, D.M., et al. "Expertech: Issues and Development of an Intelligent Help Desk System." *Expert Systems with Applications* 2 (no. 4, 1991).
2. Barr, A. *The Evolution of Expert Systems.* Palo Alto, Calif.: Aldo Ventures, 1990.
3. Bonafield, C. "Net Management Links Grow." *Communications Week* 280 (no. 6, 1989).
4. Brazile, R.P., and K.M. Swigger. "Gates—An Airliner Gate Assignment and Tracking Expert System." *IEEE Expert* (Summer 1988).
5. Eskow, D. "Firms Unite to Give Help Desk the Help They Need." *PC Week* 7 (no. 7, 1990).
6. Fox, M.S., and S.F. Smith. "ISIS—A Knowledge-Based System for Factory Scheduling." *Expert Systems* 1 (no. 1, 1984).
7. Goyal, S.I., et al. "COMPASS: An Expert System for Telephone Switch Maintenance." *Expert Systems* (July 1985).
8. IBM Research Division Laboratory. "Artificial Intelligence Topics of IBM." *IBM Research Highlights* 2 (1984).
9. Keyes, J. "Expert Help Desks: Expert Help for the 90's." *AI Expert* (September 1990).
10. O'Connor, D.E. "Using Expert Systems to Manage Change and Complexity in Manufacturing." In *Artificial Intelligence Application for Business*, W. Reitman, ed. Norwood, N.J.: Ablex Publishing Corp. 1984.
11. Rubinger, B. *Applied AI in Japan.* New York: Hemisphere Publishing, 1989.
12. Shamoon, S. "The 'Expert' That Thinks Like an Underwriter." *Management Technology* (February 1985).
13. Szuprowicz, B.O. "The Soviet Union Trade Advisor." *Expert Systems* (Spring 1991).

14. Tiong, R., and T.K. Koo. "Selecting Construction Formwork: An Expert System Adds Economy." *Expert Systems* (Spring 1991).
15. Vedder, R.G., and R.O. Mason. "An Expert System Application for Decision Support in Law Enforcement." *Decision Sciences* (Summer 1987).
16. Waterman, D. *A Guide to Expert Systems.* Reading, Mass.: Addison-Wesley, 1986.

Appendix A: Representative List of Commercial ES Applications[14]

Financial services

- Claim estimation
- Credit analysis
- Tax advisor
- Financial statement analysis
- Financial planning advisor
- Retail bank services advisor

Data processing and MIS

- Front-end to statistical analysis package
- Front-end to a large software package (several applications)
- Database management system selection
- Software services consultant

Finance and administration

- Legal analysis of contract claims
- Loan application assistant for school administrators
- Performance evaluation of dealerships
- Conflict-of-interest consultant
- Inventory management advisor

Manufacturing

- Maintenance advisor for multimillion-dollar hydraulic system
- Continuous-process manufacturing advisor
- Tooling selection for machining (several applications)
- Drilling advisor for machining

---

[14]Source: *TRANSFER*, IJCAI show edition, Teknowledge, Inc., August 1985.
Note: For additional list of systems see T.C. Walker and R.K. Miller, *Expert Systems 1990, An Assessment of Technology and Applications* (SEAI Technical Publications, 1990 and 1991) and *The CRI Directory of Expert Systems* (Medford, N.J.: Learned Information, 1986).

☐ Material selection (chemical)
☐ Procedure advisor for oil-well drilling operations (several applications)
☐ Electrical system fault diagnosis
☐ Gas turbine engine fault diagnosis
☐ Electronic equipment fault diagnosis (several applications)
☐ Power supply fault diagnosis
☐ Mechanical equipment fault diagnosis (several applications)
☐ Refinery process control
☐ Sensor verification for power generation equipment

Field service

☐ Software system troubleshooter
☐ Fault diagnosis of electronic systems from event tracers (several applications)
☐ Fault diagnosis of automotive subsystems (several applications)
☐ Computer network fault diagnosis

Education

☐ Problem diagnosis training aid
☐ Speech pathology advisor
☐ Test results interpreter
☐ Worksheet generation based on student's prior performance
☐ Student behavior consultant
☐ Learning disability classification advisor
☐ Textbook selection advisor

Sales and marketing

☐ Selection of components from an engineering catalog
☐ Qualification of sales leads

Engineering

☐ Design of motor components (outputs engineering drawings)
☐ Fastener selection (several applications)
☐ Material selection for manufacturing process (several applications)
☐ Front-end for complex computer simulation program
☐ Front-end for engineering design package
☐ Engineering change order manager
☐ Weight estimator for evolving designs
☐ Statistical analysis tool selector
☐ Front-end to structural analysis software system
☐ Construction project planning and evaluation
☐ Structural analysis of buildings
☐ Sensor interpretation for drilling
☐ Robot sensor interpretation

Chapter 21

A Student Project and a Major Case Study

The two cases in this chapter are intended to help you reinforce your knowledge of the applicability of artificial intelligence and expert systems. First, a small expert system, which was developed as a student project, demonstrates *how* to develop a successful project. Second, a very-large-scale integrated project is presented. The project, which includes a decision support system, an expert system, and natural language processing, was developed for the U.S. Securities and Exchange Commission.

STUDENT PROJECT: EXPERT TELEPHONE CONFIGURATION SYSTEM[1]

21.1   Introduction

Tripler Army Medical Center Expert Telephone Configuration System (EXTELC-SYS) was designed to aid Tripler Information Management Division personnel, U.S. Army Information Systems Command Signal Battalion Liaison personnel, and telephone users. It helps them select appropriate telephone equipment and configure a hospital department, division, or separate service telephone system to meet users' needs within constraints imposed by Army regulations, budget, equipment available, and the ongoing hospital renovation project.

The system was developed using EXSYS during the summer of 1988. Knowledge required to develop the system rules was acquired from current personnel and from the system developer. The system was installed on an existing Zenith 248 personal computer. The liaison office staff uses the system to develop, modify, or confirm telephone equipment configurations associated with telephone move and change requests received from Tripler customers.

EXTELCSYS is expected to simplify training required for new personnel as well as expedite processing of telephone moves and changes associated with the hospital renovation project. Future enhancements planned for the system include adding the capability to produce a consolidated listing of all the equipment required, by room number, for an entire department or division telephone system.

21.2   Problem Domain

The Tripler Army Medical Center Information Management Division in Hawaii is responsible for overseeing all aspects of the five components of the Army's Information Mission Area within the medical center. These include automation, communications, visual information, records management, and printing/pub-

---

[1]The project was developed by Major Gary Gilbert, formerly a graduate student at the University of Southern California. He also wrote this case.

lishing. Communications support is provided to the medical center by the Army Information Systems Command Signal Battalion–Hawaii. Voice, data, and radio communications support are included. The battalion provides support on a day-to-day basis through a signal liaison office at the hospital composed of an officer, a noncommissioned officer, and two or three enlisted soldiers. They receive and process all requests from the medical center for communications support; they are required to evaluate each request and determine the best method of providing the support. Their recommendations are then reviewed and approved by the medical center's information management officer before being forwarded for execution.

By far, the biggest job of the signal liaison office staff is to review requests for telephone moves and changes associated with the massive hospital renovation project, which began in 1984 and is scheduled for completion in 1992. Because each hospital activity must move one or more times on an interim or permanent basis, hundreds of telephone move or change requests are generated.

Two different telephone companies provide service to the hospital. The old sections of the hospital and the outlying buildings are serviced by Hawaiian Telephone Company. The newly renovated sections of the hospital are serviced by Tel-a-Com Hawaii. Telephone configurations are complicated by the two-contractor situation. All of the telephone lines provided by Hawaiian Telephone in the old and outlying areas must be serviced by the new Tel-a-Com Hawaii switch, and all off-post (nonmilitary) and commercial access requires access to trunks provided by Hawaiian Telephone Company. Telephone equipment provided by Tel-a-Com Hawaii is made by Rolm, Inc.; telephone equipment provided by Hawaiian Telephone is made by GTE. In addition, the Hawaiian Telephone equipment is all analog equipment, while the new switch and the majority of the Tel-a-Com Hawaii telephone equipment is digital. Digital instruments will not work on analog lines and vice versa. Many telephone instrument features are available through the new switch; some can be provided with the old equipment but some cannot.

A significant amount of training and experience is required to familiarize the signal liaison personnel with the complicated hospital telephone system so they can do an adequate job of configuring telephones. The medical center's information management officer must have similar knowledge to adequately review proposed telephone configurations and ensure that they are within regulatory and budget constraints while meeting the hospital's needs. Since the information management officer belongs to the Medical Service Corps, he or she most likely has little technical communications training.

Because the signal liaison personnel and the information management officer are military, their tenure is limited to the length of their assignments in Hawaii—usually four years or less. In addition, military career management practices favor reassigning officers and noncommissioned officers after eighteen months to two years in a job in order to broaden their experience. The result is a significant problem in maintaining sufficient expertise within the signal liaison and the information management staffs to be able to competently configure telephones. Therefore, the purpose of this expert system is to "capture" and maintain telephone configuration expertise. To save money and to develop the system rapidly, an ES shell called EXSYS was used.

21.3   Feasibility Study

Necessary Requirements for Expert System Development

Six specific requirements must be validated to develop the expert system (using EXSYS):

1. This task requires more than simple numeric analysis or application of common sense for solution. The task requires real knowledge about the various Tripler telephone systems, the renovation project, budget and regulatory constraints, and interdepartmental politics along with the ability to make heuristic judgments and/or decisions based on that knowledge.
2. The task requires only cognitive skills, rather than physical or mechanical skills, to be able to reason or infer a solution. For this task, all technical/ mechanical skills are cognitive.
3. A genuine expert is available. The current signal liaison officer, noncommissioned officer, and information management officer (system designer and author of this case) are sufficiently knowledgeable and experienced to be considered "experts" in this narrow area of telephone communication engineering. All three are scheduled for imminent reassignments.
4. The experts can articulate their methods of problem solving, and in the case of EXSYS they can express them in the form of heuristic rules. The telephone configuration process is just application of a variety of "rules" to the specific requirements and constraints of a particular situation.
5. The problem at hand is not so difficult or complex as to warrant it unsolvable by a well-trained human expert. The task is well understood and is clearly defined. The current experienced experts previously mentioned solve the telephone configuration problems every day. The problem (as defined earlier in the section on problem domain) is sufficiently narrow in scope.
6. Computer equipment and staff resources or funding are available to complete the project. An IBM/MS-DOS-compatible personal computer and EXSYS software are available for development and for installation and operation. The available system developer is sufficiently trained to use the EXSYS development tool, and computer-assisted tutorials are available for both development and operational training.

Appropriateness of the System

1. Nature of the problem: Heuristic rules are used to configure telephones. The rules often change because of changes in regulations, changes in availability of funds, changes in command policies, and progress in the renovation project. Therefore, a rule-based system that can easily be modified is appropriate.
2. Complexity of the task: The task is not overly complex or difficult for a "trained expert." However, the constant turnover of personnel makes it very difficult to maintain staff expertise. Because there are so many variables, and the "rules" are subject to interpretation by the individual doing the configuration analysis, results are not consistent.
3. Scope of the problem: Because this problem is rather narrow and has a small number of rules, it is appropriate for development and installation on a microcomputer through the use of a simple, rule-based, expert system development tool.

Justification for Development

1. Improved performance: Since the system will apply the rules in a more consistent manner than do most of the employees, especially new ones, the results obtained should be less likely to omit requirements and should provide for more consistent and efficient telephone configurations.
2. Faster configurations: The system will produce a recommended configuration much faster than staff members can. Since the information management officer will have more confidence in the configuration recommendations, he or she can spend less time reviewing them before approving them. This will free the signal liaison staff and information management officer to perform other tasks.
3. Reduced requirements for training: Since the system can be operated by nonexperts, who can use the explanation capability to learn on the job, training requirements are significantly reduced.
4. Easy maintenance: It is easy to modify the rules, the goals (choices), and the qualifiers in an EXSYS-based system. Therefore, maintenance and updates to the system can be performed easily.

21.4 EXTELCSYS

Conceptual Design and Feasibility

Selection of an Expert. The currently assigned signal liaison officer, noncommissioned officer, and information management officer are sufficiently knowledgeable to be considered experts in this narrowly focused problem area. Together, they have more than seven years of experience with the Tripler telephone system, and more than thirty years of telephone communications work experience.

System Developer. The system developer has a master's degree in management of computer systems applications, ten years of automation management and computer system design experience, and three years of experience at preparing, reviewing, and/or approving telephone configurations at Tripler.

Development Strategy. Rapid prototyping was used to develop the system. At the first cut, a fifteen-rule system was developed. The system was then revised and expanded to include more features and situations until enough rules were included to provide satisfactory results in at least 90 percent of the specific consultations tested.

Selection of Hardware and Software. The system was developed on a laptop Zenith 184 microcomputer using EXSYS. Once completed, the system was transported and operated on a Zenith 248 microcomputer.

Project Development Costs

Hardware (currently in place and operational)
Zenith 248 PC with dot matrix printer	$1,900

Software
EXSYS program	$395
DOS (bundled with hardware)	0
Total	$2,295

Personnel person-hours (military personnel provided)
Information management officer	25
Signal liaison staff experts	12
Total person-hours	37

Cost/Benefit Analysis. This system will be very inexpensive to fully develop and use in the field, especially since the computer hardware is already in place, and military personnel will be used for both the developer and knowledge acquisition. Even if those costs are included, the benefits of this system far outweigh the costs. Most significant are the reduction in training requirements and the reduction in time required by the signal liaison staff to prepare telephone configurations and by the information management officer to review and approve them. If the increase in quality and consistency of the final product is also considered, this system will pay for itself in less than a month.

21.5   Knowledge Acquisition Methodology

In the development of EXTELCSYS, the system developer is also an expert. This is an excellent example of a user-developed system in which the expert's task is to capture his or her own expertise. Often, this type of expert system development results in a better product than one in which the system developer or knowledge engineer must extract the knowledge from some expert, especially if the expert is uncooperative.

Since pooling knowledge from several experts could result in synergy, the EXTELCSYS system developer also interviewed the other experts from the signal liaison staff to add any additional information to the knowledge base. The developer also tested the system with the staff during and after completion of development to ensure that rules were clearly stated, accurate, and unambiguous.

21.6   Rapid Prototyping Procedures

EXTELCSYS was built using the rapid prototyping methodology. A simple prototype was built using fifteen rules and ten choices. This prototype was able to determine many features: what type of instrument should be installed (digital or analog); what make (Rolm or GTE); what model (multi- or single-line, push-button or rotary dial, etc.); if the line(s) should be capable of receiving incoming calls from off post (direct inward dial); how it should be installed (wall mounted or on a desk) depending on the required location within the medical center; and a selection of user requirements. Seven qualifiers were used in the first prototype. The basic rules, choices, and qualifiers still exist in the final version of the system, although they have been significantly modified.

After the first prototype was tested, new rules, qualifiers, variables, values, choices, and so forth, were continually added until all the basic features and/or requirements known to the experts were included. Some features that are automatically included with installation of a new telephone were not included.

The final (1988) system includes fifty rules, fifteen qualifiers, four mathematical variables, and thirty-five choices.[2] The user (or the inference engine) can select from seventeen different features, including headset, speaker phones, commercial long distance, military long distance (called AUTOVON), internal department and/or hospitalwide intercom, group teleconferencing, computer modem, telefax, autoanswering machine, hunt groups (rings the next line in an office when one is busy), pick groups (enables any line in an office to be answered from any telephone), digital radio paging, and a 25-foot extension cord.

---

[2]After the completion of the case, the system was further developed before it was fielded. It includes more than a hundred rules in its fielded version.

21.7   Training and Implementation Plan

Implementation of EXTELCSYS involves three steps: (1) transporting the system to the Zenith 248 personnel computer in the signal liaison office; (2) training the signal liaison staff on the system; and (3) changing the standing operating procedures for processing telephone moves and changes or preparing and reviewing telephone configuration plans.

1. Transporting EXTELCSYS simply requires that a copy of EXSYS "run-time" and EXTELCSYS rules and text files be loaded on the Zenith 248. Since the system was developed on a Zenith 184 laptop computer, there should be no compatibility problems between the two systems. In fact, the EXTELCSYS was tested on the Zenith 248 as part of the rapid prototyping process and expert review/testing.

2. The signal liaison staff are the primary users. Initial training was conducted by the information management officer. Training of new personnel will be conducted by the signal liaison staff. The EXSYS help features and the tutorial demos will also be used for refresher or remedial training. The information management officer will train his replacement and cross-train another information management division staff member on both operation and maintenance of the system. EXSYS demo tutorials will also be used to conduct system maintenance training.

3. The information management officer issued instructions to the staff for updating standard operation procedures. A complete EXSYS/EXTELC-SYS consultation printout for each recommended telephone instrument configuration is required to be included with all telephone move or change requests, which are forwarded to the information management officer by the signal liaison staff for approval.

21.8   Documentation, Maintenance, and Continued Program Plans

Documentation

EXTELCSYS user documentation consists of the EXSYS user documentation itself, the starting and ending texts (see Appendix A to this case), two sample consultation printouts (Appendix B to this case), and printouts of the choices (possible recommendations) and rules (Appendices C and D to this case). The EXSYS "runtime" module also has built-in help modules that can be printed or called up by the user during a consultation. System maintenance documentation consists of the EDITXS user documentation, the EDITDEMO tutorials and software, the user documentation listed previously and contained in the appendices, plus the EXTELCSYS rules and text files.

System Maintenance

System maintenance consists of updating the rules, choices, qualifiers, or variables to meet new user needs or changes in procedures, regulations, or equipment available. Maintenance will be performed by the information management officer rather than by the signal liaison user personnel. This will enable the officer to maintain control of and familiarity with the rules, choices, and qualifiers, which are the basis for system recommendations. For this plan to be successful, the information management officer must consult regularly with the signal liaison user personnel to ensure that rules are revised or new rules are developed for any situation for which the system does not produce a satisfactory recommendation.

Continued Program Plans

The information management officer will continue to revise and expand EXTELCSYS to incorporate rules and choices for configuring those standard features not included in the current version. Although those features (transfer, call forward, hold, camp-on-busy, park, conference, system speed dial, etc.) are automatically included with each telephone configuration, the user does have an option of including a button for each feature on his or her instrument or using a series of pound sign (#) or star (*) commands to execute them. For the sake of system development expedience, these options were not included in the current version. In addition, the information management officer plans to expand the system to enable signal liaison personnel to run EXTELCSYS for an entire department at one time and produce a consolidated listing of all telephone instrument configurations required for a department. The current version must be run individually for each instrument required. This extension will require increased use of the EXSYS math functions and interface to a database. Finally, the information management officer plans to produce a database of all telephone equipment currently installed or in storage. EXTELCSYS would then be modified to automatically update the database any time a telephone move or change is approved and executed.

21.9   Security and Integrity

EXTELCSYS does not contain any sensitive information; therefore, security of the system is not of great concern. The software is of some value because several person-hours have gone into producing it. However, it can easily be developed again if lost or destroyed. The knowledge base, however, cannot be recreated if the experts are no longer available because they have been reassigned (which will occur shortly). Therefore, security of the system entails carefully backing up the knowledge base rules and text files and storing backups in a secure location away from the work site. Complete copies of the EXTELCSYS files and documentation will be stored in the Tripler Data Processing Center computer magnetic media library and at Tripler's alternate storage site at the Fort Shafter Data Processing Center.

System integrity will be maintained by providing only the EXSYS runtime module and the EXTELCSYS rules and text files to the signal liaison staff personnel. They will not be provided the EDITXS or EDITDEMO editing software. They will thereby be unable to modify the rules or choices without contacting the information management officer. The information management officer will occasionally require the signal liaison staff to provide an expanded consultation printout that includes the rules used by EXSYS to make the recommendations. The officer will then be able to spot-check the rules to make sure no unauthorized changes have been made to the system.

21.10   Problems and Lessons Learned

Conversion of heuristic rules of thumb into IF-THEN-ELSE rules is not easy, even when a system such as EXTELCSYS is well suited for a rule-based expert system. It is difficult even if the developer, knowledge engineer, and expert are all the same person; it is even more difficult when they are different persons.

Since the EDITDEMO (student) version of EXSYS was available to the developer during development of the initial prototype, the knowledge base includes only fifty rules. The full-blown EDITXS is needed to expand and include the additional requirements and telephone feature options mentioned.

Because the EXSYS inference engine uses backward chaining exclusively, there are some situations that occur within EXTELCSYS in which user input to EXSYS questions does not result in all the appropriate choices being selected. This usually occurs after the system has determined its own answers to some qualifier without asking the user, and then asks the user a question that would allow him or her to add a requirement for a feature that may have been inadvertently omitted earlier. Examples are rules 34–44 which, before modification, asked the user about modem, telefax, or answering machine features. A rule could have been invoked because the user selected an answering machine but not a modem or telefax machine. However, when the user saw the qualifier's fifteen questions, which included answers pertaining only to modems or telefax machines, he or she may have remembered that a modem was needed and selected some answers that pertain to modems. This situation required the rules to be modified.

As with any automated development or editing tool, the developer should save work at regular intervals to avoid loss of significant work effort because the computer or software system "hung." Failure to follow that simple procedure resulted in the developer being required to do extra work more than once.

Maintenance of backup copies of the rules and text files during development can save redoing development work because the master rule or text files become corrupted. This occasionally happens while files are being saved to disk. Again, failure to follow this simple rule resulted in extra work during the EXTELCSYS development effort.

21.11 Conclusion

EXTELCSYS provides the Tripler Army Medical Center Information Management Division staff with a workable expert system that reduces the time involved in preparing and reviewing telephone configurations. Expertise previously available only from existing staff members has been preserved.

Note: This project was extremely helpful to its developer and his organization. However, for a better student project, interfaces for databases and/or spreadsheets are desirable.

Questions for Discussion

1. What are the factors that created the need for this system?
2. Describe the process of requesting equipment and approving it. Explain how the ES is used in this process.
3. List some of the necessary requirements (feasibility) for this project.
4. What are the project's major justification points?
5. Describe how rapid prototyping was executed.
6. Discuss the implementation and training plan. Can it be improved?
7. Briefly summarize the lessons learned from this project.
8. The grade for this project was an A. What would you do to elevate it to an A+?
9. The use of multiple experts in this case was beneficial. How does it differ from a typical multiple expert case?

Appendix A: Starting and Ending Texts

Starting Text

Tripler Army Medical Center Expert Telephone Configuration System (EXTELC-SYS) is designed to aid information management division personnel, signal battalion liaison personnel, and telephone users in configuring an office telephone system to meet their department, division, or separate service needs. The system is designed to select an appropriate telephone instrument with features required to perform the functions desired by the user depending on the user's office, clinic, or ward location within the medical center installation. It is to be used to plan telephone moves and changes associated with the renovation program. In many cases user activities will be converted from the existing rotary dial analog telephone system provided under lease contract from Hawaiian Telephone Company to the digital telephone system being installed by Tel-a-Com Hawaii Corp. For those activity moves that are only temporary, the existing rotary equipment will be moved or an electronic key push-button system may be temporarily leased from Hawaiian Telephone if funds are available.

EXTELCSYS should be run for each new telephone you need and/or for each old telephone you are moving. The system will recommend the type of telephone and associated features which will best fit the needs of the user in the new location.

Instructions: Select *one* or *more* answers to each question EXTELCSYS asks you, and enter the numbers of the selections separated by commas.

Ending Text

EXTELCSYS will now recommend the type of telephone instrument and associated features best suited to the user's needs as provided by the answers you gave to the questions the system asked of you. *Remember*, this is only a recommendation. If the user is not satisfied, he or she may submit a request for exception with justification to the chief, information management division.

To see why EXTELCSYS made a recommendation, enter the number of the recommendation.

Appendix B: Sample Consultation

This appendix contains a sample of EXTELCSYS consultations for which the computer screens have been printed out as they would appear to the user.

The consultation is an example of a telephone installation required for a user located in the old section of the hospital, which is serviced by Hawaiian Telephone using GTE rotary dial equipment. The user is a department chief; therefore, certain features and options are automatically approved or provided even if the user does not select them. An example of the logic employed by the system is contained in the choice, external keypad. The user did not select push-button dial, and a rotary instrument is provided in the old section of the hospital; but the user did select digital paging, which requires a push-button dial. Therefore, EXTELCSYS included an external keypad.

Example: The user is asked four questions:

    1. Instrument location is
            1. in new/renovated section of main hospital
            2. in old section of main hospital
            3. in outlying buildings of Medical Center installation
            4. in an office
            5. in a reception area

      6. in a treatment room
      7. in a patient room
      8. on a desk
      9. mounted on the wall
    10. unknown at this time
    11. in a conference room

    2, 4, 8 = answer

2. Feature(s) desired is/are
      1. push-button dial
      2. headset
      3. pick group
      4. external speaker
      5. microphone
      6. commercial long distance
      7. Autovon
      8. off-post dialing
      9. ability to receive calls from off post
    10. internal (activity) intercom
    11. group teleconferencing with speaker phone
    12. computer modem
    13. telefax machine
    14. answering machine
    15. 25-foot extension cord
    16. digital paging
    17. hunt group
    18. none of the above

    7, 8, 9, 12, 16, 17 = answer

3. User is
      1. a department or division chief
      2. not a department or division chief
      3. status unknown

    1 = answer

4. Computer modem or telefax machine is
      1. on primary line
      2. on extension line
      3. required to dial off post
      4. required to make Autovon calls
      5. required to make long distance calls
      6. required to receive calls from off post
      7. on post only
      8. operates at speeds greater than 2,400 baud
      9. not required
    10. none of the above

    1, 3, 6 = answer

TABLE 21B.1 Recommendation Made by EXTELCSYS

Values Based on −100 to +100 System	Original Value	New
1. Hawaiian Telephone rotary instrument	100	−90
2. RJ 11 jack required	80	80
3. Primary line is Priority AUTOVAN (AVP)	70	70
4. Additional line is Direct Inward Dial (DID)	70	70
5. External keypad	60	60
6. Primary line is Direct Inward Dial (DID)	60	None
7. Additional C line	55	55
8. Hunt group	50	50
9. Primary line is extension	50	−20
10. PAX Intercom required	50	50
11. Additional line is an extension line	20	20
12. Department/Division/Activity Intercom	10	10
13. Analog extension required	None	80
14. Rolm single-line digital instrument	None	100

Results and Sensitivity Analysis

Results. The system's recommendations are shown in Table 21B.1. Twelve items are recommended, starting with CF (certainty factor) = 100 (Hawaiian Telephone rotary instrument) to CF = 10 for item 12 (in the column titled Original Value). It is now up to the liaison office staff to determine what to approve.

Sensitivity Analysis. By pressing "C" it is possible to change any of the input data. As an illustration, we changed the location from the old location to the renovated one. The system asked us more questions and then displayed new recommendations side by side with the original one (column titled New was added in Table 21B.1). Notice that new items appear on the list and negative values appear on some of the original items. These items should *not* be included in the package.

Appendix C: Sample Choices (out of 35)

Choices

1. Hawaiian Telephone rotary instrument
   Used in rules(s): (0005)(0006)(0007)(0009)(0010)(0011)(0049)
2. Hawaiian Telephone electronic push-button instrument
   Used in rule(s): (0009)(0010)
3. Rolm single-line digital instrument
   Used in rule(s): (0006)(0024)

Appendix D: Sample Rules (out of 50)

RULE 1

IF   Instrument location is in old section of main hospital or in outlying
        buildings of medical center installation
THEN   the instrument type is analog
        AND
        Equipment make is GTE (Hawaiian Telephone)
        AND
        Primary line is extension—probability = 50/100
        AND
        Primary line is private—probability = −20/100
ELSE   Equipment make is Rolm
        AND
        Primary line is private—probability = 20/100
        AND
        Primary line is extension—probability = −20/100

Note: Digital Rolm phones cannot be installed in outlying buildings because
existing cables will not support the digital system. Digital Rolm phones will not
be installed in the old part of the hospital.

Reference: TAMC Telephone Switch Installation Contract

RULE 2

IF   Instrument location is in old section of main hospital
        AND
        Instrument location is in patient room
THEN   Telephones will not be installed in patient rooms located in the old
        hospital or outlying building

RULE 3

IF   Instrument location is NOT in new renovated section of main hospital
        or unknown at this time
        AND
        Instrument location is NOT in old section of main hospital
        AND
        Instrument location is NOT in outlying buildings of medical center
        installation
THEN   Proposed location of instrument must be determined before configura-
        tion can be completed

CASE STUDY: INTELLIGENT FINANCIAL STATEMENT GATHERING, ANALYZING, AND RETRIEVING AT THE SEC[3]

21.12 Introduction

The SEC

The U.S. Securities and Exchange Commission (SEC) has experimented with a very sophisticated computerized system to monitor, analyze, and retrieve information from financial statements submitted periodically by publicly held companies. These financial statements contain over 12 million pages. This means that the SEC must (carefully!) read and analyze about 50,000 pages a day. To expedite this process, the SEC experimented with a system intended to automate several aspects of the process.

The purpose of this case is to illustrate the conceptual design of and the experimentation with a highly integrated AI system, which was never implemented. The case illustrates the opportunities as well as the difficulties in building a complex AI-supported system.

Background

The SEC is a federal agency whose function is to collect performance and status information from all publicly held corporations. Most famous is the 10-K report which is submitted once a year by such corporations. The 10-Q reports are submitted quarterly; 8-K, 13-D, S-1, S-4, and many file-as-needed reports are submitted occasionally. The SEC monitors the submission of such reports (for example, even a violation of the submission date is made public to alert investors). These reports submitted to the SEC are placed in the public domain. Investors, loaners, and stocks and bonds rating agencies analyze the reports continually. Also, the SEC's staff conducts many studies to assure compliance with government regulations.

Information overload, which is becoming a serious problem for many organizations, is clearly a problem for the SEC. Computerization is a potential solution in an environment where the trend is for labor cost to increase and for computer costs to decrease. For this reason, the SEC decided to experiment, since the early 1980s, with several computerized systems. Three of these systems will be described in this case:

---

[3]This case was developed from information provided in the following sources: ELOISE [1], Keyes [2], McGee and Porter [3], Mui and McCarthy [4], and Texas Instruments [5].

1. EDGAR (Electronic Data Gathering, Analysis, and Retrieval): This is a basic information system for collecting and processing information.
2. FSA (Financial Statements Analyzer): This is an ES whose major purpose is to perform financial analyses (such as ratio analysis).
3. ELOISE (English Language-Oriented Indexing System for EDGAR): This is a natural language processing component that can improve the performance of EDGAR. A separate NLP was written specifically for FSA.

EDGAR

EDGAR is an experimental system that electronically receives SEC filings directly from about 1,500 companies. The purpose of the system is to enable corporations to file their periodic reports electronically (as opposed to paper submissions). Eventually, most corporations will submit the reports via electronic mail or will ship a disk or a tape. This paperless submission would have several advantages:

1. Save physical storage space for the reports
2. Eliminate the need to manually input data from the report to a computer for analysis purposes
3. Make information available to the public for easy access (potentially by electronic dialing) at a reasonable cost
4. Permit a quick and inexpensive monitoring of filings for compliance with the SEC

EDGAR "speaks" fluent word processing (about eighty-five dialects), so it can accept almost 100 percent of the submissions electronically. EDGAR also has a powerful DBMS and storage and retrieval capabilities.

EDGAR's main tasks, as its name indicates, are data *gathering, analysis,* and *retrieval.* To enhance the analysis and retrieval, two AI components were added: an expert system (FSA), and a natural language processor (ELOISE). The experimentation of the AI technologies was performed by Andersen Consulting (previously Arthur Andersen & Co.).

21.13   An Intelligent Financial Statements Analyzer

FSA

FSA is an experimental ES whose major objective is to perform a *ratio analysis* using the corporation's annual 10-K report as the major source of information. (This information is available at EDGAR's database.) The knowledge in FSA consists of *accounting knowledge,* needed to understand financial statements, and *financial knowledge,* needed to perform ratio analysis. A schematic view of how FSA is integrated is given in Figure 21.1.

The data collected by EDGAR is stored in its database. FSA uses the data as input. A special natural language processor can help in preparing some of

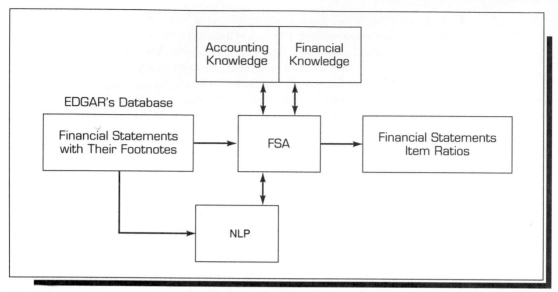

FIGURE 21.1   Schematic View of the Experimental Expert System Called FSA

some of the data in EDGAR in a manner understandable to FSA. (The natural language parser allows FSA to understand highly detailed footnotes and parenthetical notes.) Utilizing its knowledge base, the ES can perform calculations of standard ratios.

Financial Statements and Ratios

A financial statement is a summary of the company's financial status. The two most common financial statements are the balance sheet, which summarizes the assets and the liabilities of the corporation, and the income statement, which summarizes income and profit (or loss). Each statement is divided into sections. For example, the assets are divided into current assets, accounts and notes receivable, prepaid expenses, and so on. Each section is divided into line item captions, such as cash (part of current assets).

Financial ratios are computed by dividing one line item (or a combination of line items) by another one. For example, the *current debt to equity* ratio is the division of the current debt by a shareholder's equity. (This ratio measures the extent to which a firm is financed by a short-term debt.) Frequently computed is the *quick* ratio (add company's cash to its receivables and divide the sum by the current liabilities), which measures the firm's ability to pay short-term obligations without relying on sale of inventory.

Reports submitted to the SEC do not include any ratios. The difficulty in computing the ratios is the lack of an appropriate definition of the line items (which may appear under different names) and the need to consider the *footnotes* that appear in most financial statements.

The SEC is reluctant to force all reports into strictly standard formats, including that of the footnotes. Therefore, the task of making sense of the nearly 250,000 reports that are submitted by almost 20,000 companies every year can be really formidable.

How FSA Works

The major task of FSA is to match existing text with the standard terminology required for each ratio. For example, to compute the quick ratio, it is necessary to compute all the receivables. In many statements receivables are subdivided. For example, a line "other" means "other receivables" if it is listed in subdivision receivables. In many cases, interpretation depends on what is written in the relevant footnote. This is where NLP may help by interpreting natural language statements into standard financial statement terminology.

Although the initial task of FSA is to determine the appropriate input information for the financial ratios (what data to look for and where to find them), it has two other functions (Figure 21.2). Once the item lines for the ratios are known, finding the ratios requires simple calculations. More difficult, however, is the interpretation of the ratios (e.g., by comparing them to standards or to historical ratios). The ES may, for example, look for situations in which an unusual balance is carried in a specific line item (either high or low).

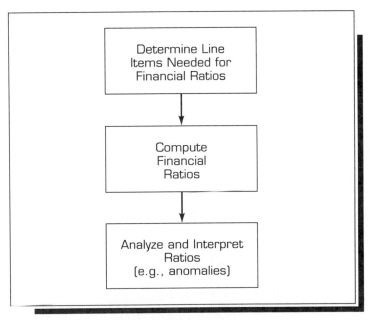

FIGURE 21.2 Three Functions of the FSA System

System Development and Testing

The initial prototype was built in 1985 with the state-of-the-art equipment at that time. The builders used a symbolic 3600 workstation and the KEE environment, which enabled them to use frames for knowledge representation also, LISP was used for the NLP. The system operates interactively, where the developer or the user could add a new ratio, for example.

The FSA correctly computed 94 percent of the tested cases. The remaining 6 percent included very complicated footnotes, wording, or cases that required judgment calls which the SEC analysts themselves were unable to agree upon.

21.14 ELOISE

Description

ELOISE is a natural language processor for indexing 10-K reports. It was designed to work together with EDGAR initially in the area of proxy statements (Figure 21.3). The purpose of ELOISE is to analyze electronically stored text to detect the presence of predefined *concepts* of interest to the SEC. Its features include:

- Indexing SEC documents according to concepts
- Identifying which companies are proposing anti-takeover measures
- Determining if other companies are proposing similar measures
- Finding out if any company is proposing unusual bylaw changes

How ELOISE Works

ELOISE's knowledge base includes knowledge about (1) the concept sought and the vocabulary used and (2) the English language—word meaning, sentence structure, grammar, and so forth.

To illustrate how the system works, let's look at an example. Let's assume that a concept can be expressed as: "Changes to a company's bylaws to accommodate the authorization or disposal of securities." Now, let us assume that two companies submit a document called *proxy statement* in which they deal with the same concept:

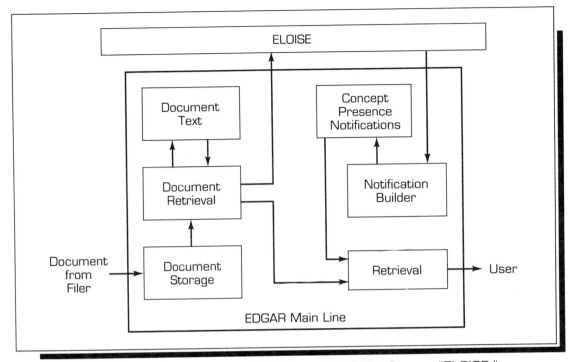

FIGURE 21.3 Integrated Functioning of ELOISE and EDGAR (*Source:* "ELOISE," *AI Application Notes*, Andersen Consulting, 1987. All rights reserved. Reprinted with permission.

□ *Company A:* Proposed charter Amendment 2 would increase the authorized shares from 6 million to 20 million

□ *Company B:* A proposal to amend the company's restated Articles of Incorporation to increase the number of authorized shares of series preferred stock from 150,000 to 1,500,000 and to make certain changes in the terms of the series preferred stock.

ELOISE will look at a proxy statement and identify that the material is related to a specific concept by highlighting it. The detection of the appropriate sentences that match a specific concept is done by using a natural language processing technique; the technique is not merely a word recognizer, but it handles complete sentences.

ELOISE enables people to quickly get answers to questions such as: "Which of this year's proxy statements contain changes to bylaws to create a new class of stock?"

The ELOISE process is composed of five steps, as shown in Figure 21.4. Tests conducted with ELOISE showed a success rate of over 85 percent.

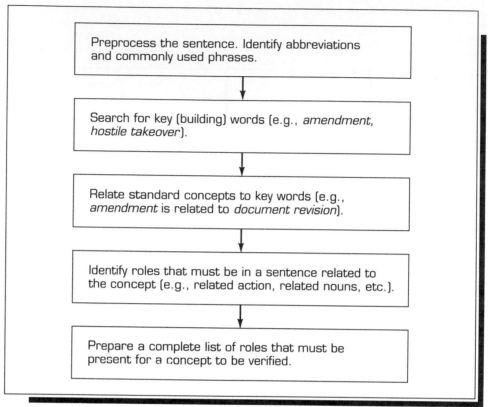

FIGURE 21.4 Five Steps in the ELOISE Process

21.15 From Prototypes to System Development

Although the data gathering and retrieval activities of EDGAR were approved for further development, FSA and ELOISE were not. Here are some of the issues and concerns related to the no-go decision:

- The required total cost, including maintenance, seemed prohibitive to the SEC (no formal cost-benefit analysis was conducted).
- The time scale of the developer was prohibitive.
- Fiscal belt-tightening policies in the federal government prevented continuation of the project.
- It was not clear if the system would run on AI workstations or on conventional hardware.
- There was no conclusion regarding the interfaces among EDGAR, ELOISE, and FSA.

☐ The automatic transfer of data from EDGAR to FSA seemed to be difficult. Such a transfer would need the capability to distinguish the beginnings and ends of sections, captions, embedded footnotes, and so on in a very large variety of layouts of financial statements submitted by corporations.

☐ Since there are about 18,000 different companies in several industries, it would be necessary to have several databases that could be organized and accessed in different ways.

☐ There was a question about who was going to maintain and enhance the knowledge bases.

☐ Issues of control of information, privacy, security, and accessibility need to be answered.

Questions for Discussion

1. Who are the potential clients of EDGAR?
2. How can the public be served by a combined EDGAR-ELOISE-FSA (EEF) system?
3. Review the development process of Chapter 12. Do you think anything was not done properly in the EEF project?
4. In what ways does ELOISE support EDGAR? In what ways does it support FSA?
5. How are financial ratios used? Why does an expert system need to compute them?
6. FSA was built with KEE and run on symbolic machines. If you were to develop FSA today, what would you do differently?
7. Discuss the questions that follow this statement by Keyes [2]:

> Had FSA been deployed in the business community, it might have detected the financial statement doctoring of MiniScribe Corp., a computer disk-drive maker based in Colorado. MiniScribe was caught with its fingers in the balance sheet cookie jar. "The balance sheet was scary," says MiniScribe director William Hambrecht of the sudden jump in receivables from $109 million to $173 million. Inventories were similarly doctored from $93 million to $173 million.
>
> Until early 1989, neither the board of directors nor the company's accounting firm nor any of the various regulators noticed anything amiss. By the time *The Wall Street Journal* reported the case, the company was questioning its ability to produce accurate financial statements for the previous three years.

   a. Why does the author believe that FSA could have detected the problem that humans did not detect?
   b. How could FSA have made such a discovery?

References

1. "ELOISE." *AI Application Notes.* Arthur Andersen & Co., 1987.
2. Keyes, J. "An Intelligent Financial Statement Analyzer." *Expert Systems* (Summer 1990).
3. McGee, J.V., and L.K. Porter. "The SEC: Application of Expert Systems Technologies." Harvard Business School, Case #9-186-279, 1986.
4. Mui, C., and W.E. McCarthy. "FSA: Applying AI Techniques to the Familiarization Phase of Financial Decision Making." *IEEE Expert* (Fall 1987).
5. Texas Instruments. "Can Arthur's ELOISE Help EDGAR Protect the SEC from Overwork?" *AI Letter* IV (no. 7, July 1987). Published by Texas Instruments, Data Systems Group, Austin, Tex.

Chapter 22

Decision Automation: Mission-Critical Expert Systems

Some expert systems can significantly change the manner in which business is being conducted. The introduction of such systems is not easy and the development process is not simple. However, the payoffs to the organization can be extraordinary. Such systems are called mission-critical systems because they do provide a competitive advantage in the company's core operations. Such systems are usually integrated with decision support systems and/or databases. Three illustrative examples are provided in this chapter:

- □ American Express—credit-card authorization
- □ American Airlines—airplane maintenance scheduling
- □ American President Companies—freight scheduling

This chapter was written by Alexander Jacobson and Philip Klahr of Inference Corp. (550 N. Continental Blvd., El Segundo, CA 90245, 213-322-0200). It is based on keynote addresses made by the first author at the Forum on Artificial Intelligence in Management in Monterey, Calif. in May 1990, and by the second author at the Third International Symposium on Expert Systems in Business, Finance and Accounting in Laguna Niguel, Calif. in September 1990.

The chapter also describes the organizational climate necessary for developing such systems, and it traces the improvements in building them over time.

22.1   Introduction

During its first decade of life the expert system industry went from the early days of hype and overpromise (the mid-1980s), to a period of disillusionment that expert systems could not integrate into mainstream corporate business (1987–1988), to a resurgence and reemergence in 1990–1991 following a number of successes in critical business applications (Schorr and Rappaport [3], Rappaport and Smith [2], Smith and Scott [4]).

As a result of this history, many judgments have been offered about the status of the industry today and what its prospects are for success. Inference Corp. is one of the pioneering organizations that helped to create this new expert systems industry. We have experienced the ups and downs of the industry, and we have seen companies grow and we have seen companies fail. Through all of this history we have developed an insider's perspective on the fortunes and the potential of this new industry. This chapter presents our assessment of the current state of health of the industry and our prognosis for its future.

The centerpiece of the chapter is three case studies describing mission-critical systems that Inference Corp. has built in conjunction with major clients. We have focused on mission-critical applications—rather than on smaller, more adjunct expert systems of which there are thousands currently providing business benefit (albeit on a small scale)—because we wish to highlight that this new technology offers something special. It offers the ability to gain competitive advantage by automating knowledge workers. We characterize as *mission critical* those expert systems that are applied to a company's core business operation; that are business knowledge intensive, providing a qualitatively greater level of decision automation; that are deeply integrated with business operations and with the company's computer systems' infrastructure; and that are valuable to the extent that, once installed, their removal would be a major setback to the business.

These case studies show two things: (1) Expert systems are capable of serving major corporations in highly visible and important business ways. (2) Applications of this technology by these businesses have evolved considerably over the history of the industry. In particular, we demonstrate the industry's evolution along several dimensions:

- The early use of highly specialized languages and machines that were difficult to integrate and required a high level of sophistication to use has turned to *mainstream* languages, operating systems, and machines for both development and deployment.
- As the technology has become more integrated and embeddable, companies no longer are using their research organizations to experiment and introduce the technology internally. Expert systems have begun to find a permanent home in both business operations and MIS organizations. Expert systems are now being designed and built for production deployment and business exploitation, not for test and experimentation.
- The time frame for designing and building successful expert systems is being dramatically reduced as a result of more informed development procedures and an up-front willingness to commit the technology to an operational role without recourse to extraordinary test and validation. Direct integration of expert system software has also contributed to reduced development time.
- Because the technology is still relatively new, the risks need to be managed carefully. In-house champions are still needed to overcome organizational and cultural hurdles that inevitably arise to thwart new technology industries. However, as the number and impact of business successes increase, we anticipate that the technology will become increasingly integrated within corporate MIS organizations.

This evolutionary profile is typical of the process whereby new technology is adopted commercially by business. Hence, these case studies support our thesis that the expert system industry, although young, is prospering, is developing well, and is delivering substantial benefit to the businesses that are exploiting its products and services.

22.2 Barriers to Success: The Need for Innovation

If the expert system industry is indeed healthy, why aren't there more expert systems of consequence in existence and why isn't the industry growing faster? We believe the answers to these questions are connected with the notion of innovation. Significant expert systems require, in our opinion, two sorts of innovation to become effective for business use. The first is *innovation in programming*, and the second is *innovation in end-user operations*.

At the programming level, rule-based programming is a nonprocedural method. Therefore, it is fundamentally different from the conventional method of programming done in virtually all MIS organizations. To use rule-based programming requires that MIS people, who are the application programmers of their companies, write their applications in a new way. Given that we are dealing with language, we are asking these programmers to change their professional language in order to realize the extraordinary benefits of expert systems. This is a challenging request for them to meet. It is not at all surprising that there is resistance to the adoption of this new technology, even though it offers great promise.

The second innovation hurdle that must be overcome occurs when the application is deployed to the end-user organization. Mission-critical expert systems tend to incorporate much more business knowledge and functionality than do even the most robust conventional applications. Consequently, the level of automation expert systems bring to the end-user organization is significantly higher. This implies that the change in operations such automation creates can be extensive, making the integration of significant expert systems into business operations unusually challenging. On the other hand, it is exactly these changes that are sought by the businesses that have built mission-critical expert systems. Hence it is not surprising, once again, that this new technology, as effective and beneficial as many users have found it, meets with ambivalence in the market. This ambivalence reflects the reaction of businesses to the challenge of having to manage the risk of change. In the case of mission-critical expert systems, this risk is to core business units of the company.

Yet another challenge must be met by corporations in order to adopt expert systems for routine business use. Expert systems, which contain more business knowledge and functionality than conventional applications, require much more intensive cooperation between business operations personnel (i.e., "experts") and MIS professionals (i.e., developers) throughout the application life cycle than has been required with conventional application software. This cooperation must occur during project conception, through development and deployment, and into the maintenance period. It is no longer a matter of business operations listing the specifications and MIS designing and developing the software. The entire process must be done conjointly. What is important here is that the introduction of significant expert systems into production use requires MIS and business operations to operate in a new relationship to each other. This, once again, requires change, which implies further risk.

To manage these risks, companies move more slowly with a new technology like expert systems than they do with already adopted technologies. Cautious commitment to expert systems does not reflect skepticism about its value. Expert systems, like every other new technology, require that businesses manage change as they proceed with adoption. Inevitably, this results in slow acceptance in the early phases of adoption. Even though the benefits of using the technology are likely to be extraordinary, businesspeople find it difficult to accept and manage the change that use of the new technology requires. As a consequence, businesses tend to achieve results with new technology slowly, not because the technology is not valuable, not because they do not know how to use it, not because they do not want it, but simply because they are being careful with something that is novel and that requires them to operate in new ways.

22.3   American Express's Authorizer's Assistant

The Authorizer's Assistant (AA) is an expert system that supports the process of authorizing credit on American Express charge-card transactions (Dzierzanow-ski et al. [1]). It has been in daily use on a routine basis since November 1988.

Problem

The process of deciding on a charge-card transaction for American Express is more difficult than that of many of its competitors, primarily because the American Express card has no preset credit limit. In other words, for any given transaction American Express extends credit based on the company's judgment of the creditworthiness of the customer at the time the transaction is made. Thus, for each transaction, there is an online evaluation of the cardholder's creditworthiness to determine whether to approve the charge. In addition to credit issues, fraud issues must also be considered.

Financial losses due to credit and fraud problems are significant at American Express, as they are throughout the credit-card industry. Even small improvements in decision quality and consistency can contribute significantly to the bottom-line profits of the company.

Prior to the AA project, the authorization process relied on a statistical software system, running on an IBM 3093, called the Credit Authorization System (CAS), which handled a large percentage of the cases—all of those that were straightforward. However, the complicated transactions were referred, by CAS, to online human authorizers, of whom there were several hundred operating at four domestic centers.

American Express decided to build an expert system because the credit authorizers faced a very difficult operating problem. The authorization environment is complex and laden with pressures. For each transaction decision (of which there are millions each day), the decision support data (i.e., the data needed to make the online credit decision) resides on all or some of a dozen outlying databases connected to CAS via SNA. An authorizer sits at a 3270 terminal connected to these dozen outlying databases and has a telephone hookup to talk to the merchant and card member. The authorizer gets a case, goes out to the databases, retrieves screens of data from each database, finds and digests the relevant data (some of which conflict because the databases are managed independently), and makes a decision to grant or reject the charge, or else goes to the merchant or card member to ask questions in order to reach the decision.

In addition, each decision for creditworthiness has to be made in real time, quickly (within ninety seconds), while merchants and cardholders stand waiting. The large data load and the very short time for decisions place a heavy demand on these authorizers. Furthermore, correct credit judgment is a skill-intensive process—some people are better at it than others—which leads to uneven performance among the authorizers. In this environment, it is not uncommon for mistakes to be made.

Solution

American Express wanted to build an expert system that provided the authorizers with decision automation, as opposed to the decision support they already had. Decision automation is the capability to make automatically the same level of business decision as a human does, and do it with the same or better accuracy than the most expert humans at the task. This, in fact, is what the Authorizer's Assistant expert system does (Figure 22.1).

When a transaction comes in to CAS, the complicated cases are now referred to the AA instead of to a human authorizer. The AA goes to the outlying databases, retrieves and collects all the required data, and automatically builds an internal model of a given card transaction—a data model of the cardholder and the specific transaction under consideration. The AA resolves any conflicts or inconsistencies that may exist in the information in the databases based on the same rules, practices, and policies that the human authorizers use. The AA then creates a *single screen* for the authorizer containing only the relevant information needed to resolve the transaction and applies its built-in credit authorization logic and judgment to make the credit decision or to decide to get more information. In the latter case, the AA supports the human authorizer in interacting with the appropriate person (e.g., the customer at the merchant's store) to obtain the needed information. The human authorizer is free either to accept the system's judgment (which is *explained* by means of a backup screen) or to override it. Thus, the AA is a true decision automation system. It does automatically what a human does (except for the vocal communication of any needed questions), and yet gives the human authorizers override capabilities that allow them to interrogate the model, question the credit logic, and override the judgment, if they choose.

The credit logic built into the AA is based on the credit expertise and judgment of American Express's most expert credit authorizers. Essentially, the credit expertise of American Express's best authorizers is explicitly represented in over 900 rules within the AA, and, by means of the AA, is distributed throughout the entire authorization organization. Furthermore, the AA exceeded its performance goals: it requires only several seconds on the average to do its analysis and formulate its decision, and, more importantly, it makes decisions that are correct for more than three-fourths of the accuracy difference between the average authorizer and the best expert authorizers.

Benefits

Before deciding to put the AA into production use, American Express did a return-on-investment (ROI) analysis to determine the potential payback. To do this, they took 2,500 actual card transactions that had already been decided by the human authorizers and put them through the AA. Four months later they

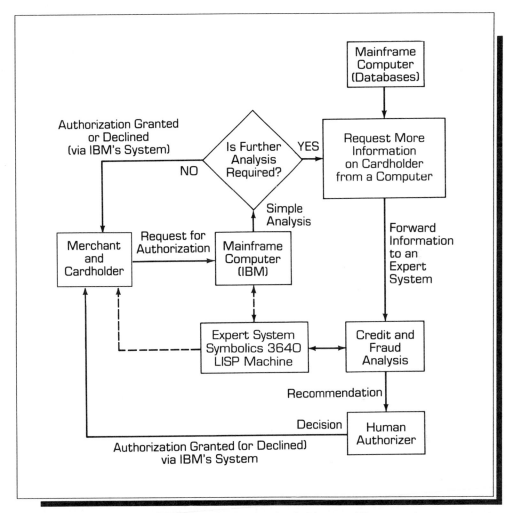

FIGURE 22.1 American Express's Authorizer's Assistant. The merchant requests authorization from the mainframe computer. The computer checks credit availability and performs a simple analysis (e.g., checking the cardholder's normal charging pattern). If no further analysis is needed, the authorization is either granted or declined. If further analysis is necessary, the computer collects more information about the cardholder from another mainframe computer. The initial information and new information are forwarded to a rule-based expert system. The expert system may request more information from the cardholder if necessary; then it provides a recommendation to the human authorizer. (*Source:* Based on information provided by Inference Corp. and American Express.)

evaluated the status of those accounts to see whether the accounts were current (earlier charges were paid) or delinquent, or possibly in collections (earlier charges were not paid). This study proved clearly that the AA was capable of creating enormous savings. American Express found, first of all, that the AA recommended one-third fewer declines than did human authorizers. This meant more revenue to American Express, which makes its money by approving charges, not by refusing them. Every time a transaction is declined, it represents a loss of revenue as well as a loss of customer goodwill, which can result in the loss of the customer. Despite accepting more transactions, American Express found that the AA was twice as accurate both on those declines it did make as well as on its acceptances than were the human authorizers. The result represents a *quantum leap* in functionality and a savings of many millions of dollars per year. Based on these results, the decision was made to deploy the AA.

As a result of the AA, American Express has improved its authorization process in many ways. Authorization decisions are better and more consistent and they yield significant business returns and improved customer relations. The service time to resolve transactions has decreased, providing better customer service to merchants and cardholders. The learning curve for new authorizers has been dramatically reduced now that the AA does the bulk of the routine and cumbersome work for them. And, finally, the AA has provided American Express with improved management of the credit authorization function because, for the first time, the company's credit decision expertise and judgment is displayed and is available explicitly, online. Managers can examine it, agree or disagree with it, and modify it as appropriate. The authorization logic no longer resides only in people's heads; it is now documented and embodied in software, where it is maintained as a corporate asset.

It is worth noting that the cost savings to American Express gained from the AA's speed in making decisions is minuscule compared to the earnings realized from the improvement in accuracy of the AA's decisions over that of the average human authorizer. Speed improvements create productivity gains, whereas accuracy creates improvement in quality, which translates directly to greater competitive edge.

Development Process

The AA project began in 1985, early in the history of the expert system industry. It was a three-phase project consisting of a research and development (R&D) pilot phase (i.e., the project was financed by R&D funds), an ROI evaluation phase, and an integration/installation phase. The development of the pilot began in November 1985 and was completed in January 1987. The pilot contained all of the required functionality and expertise and was operational in a live, real-time setting, but it was not at production-level quality, particularly in its integration and performance. The pilot was sufficient, however, to allow American Express to conduct the ROI analysis and evaluation, which lasted eight months. Having concluded that the payback warranted deployment, American Express embarked on the system integration and deployment phase. That phase required approximately thirteen months for completion and resulted in a production-quality system released for nationwide use in November 1988.

Certain issues relative to the development process are important to note. First of all, the project was managed by a strong champion without whom the project would most likely not have been completed successfully. His project management prowess, his understanding of corporate culture and politics, and his drive and commitment to success all were vital to the completion of the project.

Secondly, the project started in R&D which immediately led to a special requirement—a technology transfer process within American Express. The people who sponsored the pilot were not the people who sponsored the deployed application, which created a formidable internal hurdle to overcome before the system could be deployed.

Thirdly, because expert systems were regarded to be an experimental technology, the person who made the final decision to deploy the expert system into production use was the businessperson who ran the entire American Express card business—a multibillion dollar a year business. It is unusual for a software application deployment decision the size of the AA to be made at that level.

Finally, because it was early in the history of the expert system industry, the AA was built and still runs (1992) on dedicated LISP machines operating as coprocessors and connected to the IBM 3093 that runs CAS. Thus, there are dozens of LISP machines operating on a dedicated network within one of the country's largest mainframe shops containing dozens of IBM mainframes. Acceptance of the LISP machines by the data center professionals was unusual and was a testimony both to the promised payback and to the flexibility of American Express's data center management.

The AA was, and continues to be, a major success for American Express and for the expert system industry. But it resulted from a difficult and time-consuming development process because it occurred so early in the history of the industry. American Express is to be commended for its willingness to pioneer new business solutions.

22.4 American Airlines' MOCA

MOCA is an expert system that schedules American Airlines' airplanes for maintenance (Smits and Pracht [5]). It has been in daily use on a routine basis since April 1990.

Problem

American Airlines schedules its aircraft for maintenance according to a rigorous formula regulated by the federal government, yet it must do so in a way to minimize the time that an airplane is out of service. As a result, airplanes are not removed from passenger routes to receive routine maintenance. For example, if an airplane is completing its current day's routing at Dallas airport and needs a particular maintenance procedure that can be done in Dallas, the work is performed overnight in time for the airplane's scheduled departure the next morning. Performing maintenance as part of an aircraft's routing, rather than having it done at a remote site, translates into substantially reduced costs. As a consequence, however, maintenance scheduling becomes inextricably intertwined with the scheduling of the aircraft for passenger routing.

The scheduling of airplanes on their routes is an enormously complex process that is made even more difficult by the dynamic, constantly changing environment of air travel. In fact, an aircraft usually remains on a given planned route for three days or less before some unplanned change to the routing occurs because of bad weather, airport closures, crew constraints, canceled flights, unanticipated maintenance problems, air traffic control restrictions, or other events. Moreover, in assigning airplanes for maintenance, each plane must be passed through the proper maintenance center, at the right flight mileage, at the right airport. The result is a complex, dynamic, resource allocation process that must be managed in a rapidly changing, highly constrained environment. Airlines such as American do this routinely every day.

Prior to MOCA, the maintenance scheduling process was based on a decision support system. All the data required to do the scheduling was made available online, but the system was unable to adapt in real time to changes in the flight environment; it did not provide scheduling updates. The maintenance operations controllers had to reschedule affected aircraft manually. In 1988, the schedulers operating the four fleets in American's inventory (MD-80, 727, DC-10, and the other wide bodies) were already at their maximum level of performance. Despite this, the management of American Airlines felt they had to set as a strategic objective the task of increasing the size of their fleet in order to take advantage of the enormous growth in air travel anticipated in the 1990s. Further, management believed that the scheduling overload problem could not be solved simply by adding more schedulers. Experience showed them that assigning more than one scheduler per fleet increased the airline's exposure to uncontrolled disruption and to maintenance violations. Thus, the system for scheduling and routing aircraft had become a bottleneck to the growth of the airline, and management came to the conclusion that only by directly automating the existing schedulers could the bottleneck be broken.

Solution

American Airlines first attempted several conventional approaches to automate the scheduling process using traditional operations research and conventional programming techniques. Both of these attempts were unsuccessful due to the complexity of the problem. Coincidentally, American Airlines had been studying the general utility of expert systems technology to its business requirements. These studies, which had been going on for almost two years, led them to try expert systems technology to provide the schedulers with decision automation. The result was MOCA, which automatically processes all real-time data (just like the American Express application), formulates the daily plan for assigning aircraft to flight segments, and dynamically updates aircraft flight assignments in real time as disrupting events occur, regardless of their complexity. In this task, MOCA automatically ensures that all maintenance constraints and required procedures are satisfied, and it works to minimize costs. In short, MOCA automates the schedulers' decision process online to create the capability for them to accept additional airplanes in their respective fleets.

Benefits

Clearly, there are direct cost savings in using MOCA; these include personnel productivity, reduction in the number of flight breaks, and improved aircraft utilization. But, like the American Express application, the real benefit is not simply cost savings—it is the competitive edge. MOCA breaks the information systems bottleneck to airline growth. This is a mission-critical expert system. It enables American Airlines to grow and thus is central to the success of American Airlines' core business.

The strategic importance of MOCA was clearly evident in the project justification studies conducted before the onset of work. A cost-benefit analysis showed that direct cost savings alone would justify development of the system. However, the project was funded not on the basis of the ROI analysis, but because it was deemed to be an operational necessity required to achieve the strategic growth plan of the airline.

Development Process

The expert system development process was quite different for American Airlines than it was for American Express. This was due, in part, to the fact that the corporate cultures are different. Also, the American Airlines project was undertaken considerably later in the history of the expert systems industry. At American Express, the project was brought in through R&D, as an experiment, and then driven into the heart of the company through a formal technology transfer process. At American Airlines, the project was done on the basis of a careful study conducted entirely within the MIS organization without recourse to an R&D phase. Conventional approaches had been attempted first and had failed. A prototype expert system was developed in late 1987 and early 1988 by another vendor; the technology of expert systems was accepted, but the vendor was not. Inference Corp. was approached on the basis of its then recent introduction of its products on IBM equipment. To qualify for the task, Inference was asked by American Airlines to build a small-scale, but different, application that was designed for deployment on personal computers. After six weeks of development, the small system was successfully put into production and Inference's qualifications to do MOCA were deemed sufficient.

The MOCA project began just one month after the successful deployment of the personal computer application. The initial phase, which lasted three months, resulted in a detailed design. It was followed by eleven months of developing the knowledge base; the relevant knowledge of the human schedulers was captured and coded. The systems integration phase, which was contiguous with the knowledge base development phase (unlike at American Express), required an additional seven months. The project duration was reduced by more than 40 percent from that of the American Express system, even though it led to a system of about the same size.

Again, the project was managed by a strong champion, without whom it could easily have failed. It was done this time, however, entirely within MIS, which is one reason why it went faster. There was no technology transfer required from one organization to another within the company. Like the AA at American Express, it was given intense, high-level scrutiny throughout, even at the CEO level.

MOCA was deployed in April 1990, has been operational ever since, and has exceeded all expectations in terms of its performance and payback. In fact, the airline reported publicly (Rappaport and Smith [2]) that MOCA had directly contributed to significant improvements in aircraft utilization—an operations performance parameter that has a major impact on airline profitability. This was presented as a collateral benefit to the system's intended purpose, that is, to enable American Airlines to grow.

22.5   American President Companies' SMART

SMART is an expert system that allows American President Companies (APC) to decide where to place a client's freight, both in the shipping yard and on the ship, to ensure that the freight will meet its delivery schedule to the customer. SMART has been fully operational since May 1990.

Problem

APC customer service agents work with clients of APC to arrange for the shipment of freight. For each booking, the client specifies what the freight is, where it is to go, when it has to be delivered, and so forth. The customer service agent then calls a ship planner, of which there are only two, one in Oakland, Calif. at APC's headquarters and one on the east coast of Asia. These planners determine where freight is to be placed in the yard and on the ship to arrive at its destination exactly when the client wants it. Planning is often complicated by freight having to be transferred from ship to ship or from ship to train, or even from ship to train to truck, as it moves from Asia to its destination in the United States (e.g., a shipment originating in Madras, India, can be transferred to another ship in Singapore and then to another ship in Kaohsiung, Taiwan, to arrive in San Pedro, Calif., where it is transferred to a train that takes it to Baltimore where it is transferred to a truck for delivery to the customer).

Containers that miss their train connections, for example, are often a week late in being delivered to the customer. This is highly undesirable for APC. Just-in-time manufacturing means that arrival too late could be a disaster, whereas arrival too early increases storage and handling costs. Customer satisfaction has become the dominant competitive issue in the shipping industry. All transport connections must be made successfully for a given shipment in the presence of thousands of other shipments all of which are going to different final destinations. This is another highly dynamic, overconstrained, decision-critical process.

Accurate delivery schedules require that APC personnel stow a customer's freight properly in the yard and on the ship to ensure proper loading and unloading and to meet connecting transportation. Individual load planning decisions are modified as new freight is added to a given shipload. All of these elements can change if already consigned customers modify their shipping plans, which they often do. Load planning decisions must be modified repeatedly as new information accumulates about a shipment. This can occur even while the shipment is en route; phoned-in changes can occur at any time.

Several problems make this complex planning process even more difficult. First of all, often only partial information about a shipment is available at the time loading decisions are made. Planners have developed expertise about filling in missing details. They know the customers and often they can anticipate what is going to happen. They have rules of practice about how to do their business; they have learned how to guess missing details correctly. Such aggressive guessing is critical to the success of the company.

Secondly, as they gain experience, as world events change, and as random business changes occur (e.g., ship routing changes caused by bad weather or labor strikes), planners are forced to revise not only their specific decisions, but also the planning policies themselves. As a result, they find that they are constantly updating their expertise.

Thirdly, before SMART was deployed, load planning was done manually. Planners would make their decisions and then send them on paper, or via telephonic messages, to the shipping agents in the various yards around the world to get the work done. Because of the planning complexity and the dynamic changes that occur, planners were operating in a complex, ever-changing, crisis-ridden working environment. Even when the shipping process works smoothly, the planners are overloaded just by the sheer number of loading decisions and the speed with which the business must be done.

Solution

The SMART expert system was built to provide the two planners with decision automation. SMART contains the knowledge and expertise of the APC planners and applies this knowledge automatically to determine and update the appropriate priority and load region for each piece of freight in the yard and on the ship. SMART operates online and is embedded in a high-volume, real-time IBM mainframe transaction processing environment. It now provides real-time support for hundreds of customer service agents on computer terminals around the Pacific Rim.

The planners monitor the routinely used system to ensure that it is operating properly. But, more importantly, they work to keep SMART current by implementing one of the very important capabilities of expert systems technology—online maintenance and enhancement of the knowledge base. Stowage planning rules change frequently. As a result, SMART was designed from the outset to support a customized end-user maintenance facility that allows the planners to modify, create, and maintain new freight assignment rules, policies, and expertise online. This end-user tool was built with an interface that allows the planners to modify and enhance SMART's knowledge base in a way that was natural to them, that is, in the same table-oriented format with which they had been working for years. The planners were not required to learn a specialized "programming" language, and thus they were able to use the SMART maintenance facility immediately, with no training.

Benefits

SMART has lead to improved employee productivity through the automation of the freight-region assignment decision process. Consequently, the cost of yard operations has been reduced, load planning has been streamlined, operational flows and reliability have been improved, dependency on paper and electronic messages has been eliminated, and stowage efficiency has increased. But once again, the real benefit to APC is not merely productivity gains. Rather, it is the intangible benefit of substantively improved customer service, which is directly realized through more accurate and timely deliveries. In the shipping industry this translates into competitive advantage. SMART is a mission-critical application at APC.

Development Process

The project started in June 1989, relatively recently in the history of the expert system industry. The American Express system was written in a LISP-based expert system tool on LISP machines and was deployed on LISP machines. The American Airlines system was built in a LISP-based expert system tool as well, but was deployed on Texas Instruments' Micro-Explorer (an Apple MAC II computer containing a LISP machine board). This represents a change in the market's demand for the delivery of the technology, but still it was a LISP-based product. The SMART system at APC, however, was built on personal computers in a C-based expert system tool (ART-IM) and deployed in an online transactional environment on an IBM mainframe. This represents a major leap in the commercialization of the technology over five years. SMART was implemented by much the same process as are conventional business applications.

The project originated in a CEO-to-CEO contact between Inference Corp. and APC. Initially, the idea was for APC to try out expert system technology by building a significant business application with the technology. The project was handed to a project manager within APC's MIS organization. It was decided from the outset to manage the project as a conventional MIS initiative. A top-down, two-month business analysis process was formed to select an expert system application that would be high impact, economically rewarding, and technically manageable, and that could meet the budget constraints set by APC for this project. The business analysis process, done jointly by APC and Inference Corp., took into consideration over thirty potential alternative projects and led to the selection of SMART as the preferred application. Development of SMART was implemented in three phases: a one-month design phase, a three-month knowledge base development phase, and a six-month system integration and testing phase. The total project was completed and deployed in the transactional mainframe environment in less than one year.

System integration turned out to be the most important issue; it encompassed more than half of the project's time frame. A great deal of forethought was given to the integration design. The lesson that we have learned repeatedly in building production-worthy expert systems is clear: to be successful, the integration issue must be faced early and thoroughly.

This project was managed by an MIS project manager, not by an expert system champion. However, a champion, who played an important role in completing the project, did emerge during the development process. He was the corporate database administrator who proved to be a vital supporter during the system integration phase. However, there was no overall project champion. The project was managed more as a routine, albeit complex, MIS project. In addition, SMART underwent the same rigorous testing and computer resource analysis that is typical of any application installed in a mainstream transactional computer environment. In the case of SMART, Inference Corp. had built an expert system by means of a process that looks just like that used to develop conventional application software.

22.6 Keys to Success

From these examples, and the many others in which Inference Corp. has participated or watched its customers implement, we feel that developing mission-critical expert systems can be done systematically provided certain key steps are carefully observed:

- □ *Select a project that is driven by the needs of the business.* It is critical to define and select the correct application. The first consideration is business relevance; this then needs to be matched to the technology.
- □ *Create strong project management by an effective champion, if at all possible.* Expert system technology is still regarded to be an experimental technology by many MIS professionals. Hence strong champions are still critical if projects are to avoid cultural, political, or organizational pitfalls.
- □ *Form and manage a cooperative working relationship between business operations and MIS throughout the project.* Create an integrated project team that includes both strong knowledge engineering and system engineering capabilities.

□ *Provide for sufficient end-user involvement throughout the project.* Inadequate access to relevant experts and users is a sure way to defeat an expert system project.

□ *Build the system with the aid of a structured expert system development methodology.* Choose a methodology that integrates the traditional software methodologies in use by many companies today with the needs of iterative knowledge acquisition and refinement, which are required specifically for the development of the knowledge base. The integrated methodology should include processes to develop knowledge base specifications, effective expert system solution architectures and designs, and mechanisms for knowledge base maintenance. Rapid prototyping methodology may be fine for understanding requirements and exploring design alternatives, but it doesn't necessarily scale up to supporting the knowledge base of a large or sophisticated mission-critical expert system.

□ *Build the expert system on a powerful and embeddable expert system technology base.* Use an expert system tool that has a powerful knowledge representation capability, production quality performance at runtime (regardless of the size of the knowledge base), and easy integration, and that offers a productive development environment. Do not try to develop significant expert systems for production use without a strong, fully proven (i.e., production qualified) expert system tool. Just as with any other technology, using the wrong tools usually leads to suboptimal results, if not to outright failure.

22.7   Summary

Expert systems bring a new dimension of productivity and capability to the writing of business software. This new capability provides far more than an incremental advantage. Properly implemented, it provides a quantum leap in business functionality and payback. Companies are achieving these results today in applications that give them significant competitive advantage.

A technology transfer process burdens adoption of the technology. Expert system technology is developed and used differently from conventional computer technology, and companies must be sensitive to and manage these differences effectively. Furthermore, companies need to understand the organizational and operational impact of the technology and how to adjust to it. Despite these challenges to its customers, we believe that the expert system industry is healthy and that adoption of the technology is progressing well—witness the many major companies that are benefiting from it today. The mainstream MIS market has begun to show real interest in this new technology and represents the potential for significant growth over the next several years. Even so, the real impact of expert systems is yet to come.

Questions for Discussion

1. What are the major characteristics of mission-critical expert systems?
2. Why do we need more cooperation between end-users (including experts) and MIS professionals when we build and use expert systems?
3. Why is the introduction of mission-critical systems into the business environment more difficult than the introduction of conventional applications?
4. What are the major barriers to the introduction of expert systems into organizations?
5. Why do MIS people find it difficult to adjust to AI technology?
6. Review the development process of Chapter 12. Which phases were emphasized in each of the three systems in this chapter and why?
7. Describe the integration that took part in all three systems. What lessons can be learned from such integration?
8. Top management support was critical in all three systems. Describe the support and discuss it.
9. For each system, prepare a table with the benefits that justified that system.
10. Review the capabilities of ART as described in the appendix to this chapter. Prepare a list of characteristics of each of the three systems and suggest which of ART's capabilities are most appropriate to handle the special complexities of each.

References

1. Dzierzanowski, J.M., K.R. Chrisman, G.J. MacKinnon, and P. Klahr. "The Authorizer's Assistant: A Knowledge-Based Credit Authorization System for American Express." In *Innovative Applications of Artificial Intelligence*, H. Schorr and A. Rappaport, eds. Menlo Park, Calif.: AAAI Press, 1989.
2. Rappaport, A., and R. Smith. *Innovative Applications of Artificial Intelligence II.* Menlo Park, Calif.: AAAI Press, 1990.
3. Schorr, H., and A. Rappaport. *Innovative Applications of Artificial Intelligence.* Menlo Park, Calif.: AAAI Press, 1989.
4. Smith, R., and C. Scott. *Innovative Applications of Artificial Intelligence III.* Menlo Park, Calif.: AAAI Press, 1991.
5. Smits, S., and D. Pracht. "MOCA: The Maintenance Operations Control Advisor." In *Innovative Applications of Artificial Intelligence III.* Menlo Park, Calif.: AAAI Press, 1991.

Appendix A: Automated Reasoning Tool for Information Management (ART-IM)

The language of ART-IM is used to define applications in terms of the basic elements of the technology: objects, rules, procedures, and cases. Objects are used to represent and maintain all information used by the ART-IM application during an analysis. Analysis can be performed by rules and/or procedures.

An ART-IM application functions by using one or more integrated processing capabilities: data-driven inferencing, object-oriented programming, case-based reasoning, or hypothetical reasoning with consistency management. Data-driven inferencing automatically selects and sequences rules that define the correct conclusions and responses to inputs received by the application within its objects. Object-oriented programming supports the attachment of procedures to objects in order to give the objects behaviors. Case-based reasoning solves new problems by selecting and adapting known correct solutions to similar

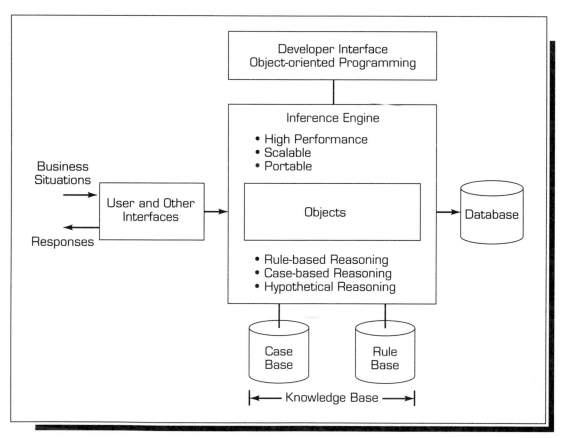

FIGURE 22A.1 Graphic Presentation of ART-IM (*Source:* Courtesy of Inference Corp.)

problems that have already been solved. Hypothetical reasoning with consistency management allows a knowledge base system to explore possible, but uncertain, assumptions and to automatically update its conclusions to keep them consistent as assumptions are varied.

ART-IM is implemented within an open, highly portable architecture. This allows ART-IM applications to be easily integrated with other application components, including databases, user interface packages, and modules written in conventional programming languages and deployed on any type of hardware platform. Figure 22A.1 shows a graphic representation of ART-IM including the functionality mentioned, its connection to external systems and/or users, and the development environment described next.

ART-IM's development environment supports high-productivity application development. Development and testing of the application are performed simultaneously. Application changes and additions are compiled incrementally into the current test environment and are immediately available for iterative testing and analysis by the developer. This mechanism supports rapid prototyping and cooperative development between software engineers and business experts or users. In addition, productivity tools are provided to simplify and/or automate user interface development and systems integration, particularly the integration of knowledge-based applications with databases. This allows the application developer to focus on defining the policy and business knowledge of the application within rules and cases. ART-IM is written in the C programming language.

In addition to the features mentioned, ART-IM includes multiple inheritance, truth maintenance, extensible pattern matching, automatic conversion to/from external data sources, hypertext, graphic interface (including to end-user), blackboard modeling, and object-oriented programming. These features are essential to the successful development and deployment of mission-critical applications such as those presented in this chapter.

Glossary

Access-oriented Programming   Variation of object-oriented programming in which gathering or sorting data can cause procedures to be invoked.

Action Language   User's action (e.g., input data, query, etc.).

Actuator   Power source of a robot.

ADC   Analog-to-digital converter.

AI Workstation   Workstation designed specifically to execute AI work (e.g., LISP machine or DEC station with added-on capabilities).

Algorithm   Step-by-step search in which improvement is made in every step until the best solution is found.

Analogical Reasoning   Determining the outcome of a problem by the use of analogies. A procedure for drawing conclusions about a problem by using past experience.

AND/OR Branch   Graphic presentation of knowledge in which two or more, or at least one, IF statements determine the THEN part of a rule.

Android   Synthetic humanlike machine with mechanical limbs and electronic brain.

Application Software   Programs that can perform specific, user-oriented tasks.

785

Artificial Intelligence (AI)   Subfield of computer science that is concerned with symbolic reasoning and problem solving.

Artificial Neural Network (ANN)   (*See* Associative Memory Technology.)

Assertion   Database or fact part of the knowledge base. It includes rules that are known to be true or false and any other information.

Associative Memory Technology   Experimental computer technology that attempts to build computers that will operate like a human brain. The machines possess simultaneous memory storage and work with ambiguous information.

Automated Guided Vehicle (AGV)   Mobil robot with legs, or one mounted on a vehicle.

Autonomous Robot   (*See* Intelligent Robot.)

Axon   Outgoing terminal from a biological neuron.

Backpropagation   The most known learning algorithm in neural computing. Learning is done by comparing inputs to desired outputs of historical cases (*See* Supervised Learning.)

Backtracking   Technique used in tree searches. The process of working backward from a failed objective or an incorrect result to examine unexplored alternatives.

Backward Chaining   Search technique used in production (IF-THEN rule) systems that begins with a possible goal or hypothesis (the action clause of a rule) and works "backward" through a chain of rules in an attempt to find a verifiable set of condition clauses. It is a goal-driven procedure.

Bayesian Formula   Statistical formula that allows revision of prior probabilities based on additional evidence.

Belief Function   Representation of uncertainty without the need to specify exact probabilities.

Best-first Approach   A heuristic search algorithm that looks for the best possible value in the immediate vicinity of the search point.

Binary Code   System of numbering in base 2, which uses only 1s and 0s as digits. Because of the simple correspondence to the on–off states of electronic switches, the binary number system is used to "code" information and instructions inside a computer.

Blackboard Architecture   Architecture that enables independent knowledge sources (and representations) to communicate through a central database called a blackboard.

Blind Search   Search approach that makes use of no knowledge or heuristics to help speed up the search process. A time-consuming and arbitrary search process that attempts to exhaust all possibilities.

Breadth-first Search   Search technique that evaluates every item at a given level of the search space before proceeding to the next level.

Case-based Reasoning   Methodology in which knowledge and/or inferences are derived from historical cases.

Certainty Factor   A percentage supplied by an expert system that indicates the probability that the conclusion reached by the system is correct. Also, the degree of belief of the expert that a certain conclusion will occur if a certain premise is true.

Certainty Theory   (*See* Certainty Factor.)

Champion   A person with authority and power who "pushes" AI projects.

Charged Coupled Device (CCD)   Device that converts light to electronic signals.

Chip   Single device consisting of transistors, diodes, and other components forming a complex circuit on a $\frac{1}{4}$-by-$\frac{1}{4}$-inch section of a wafer sliced from a crystal of silicon.

Chunk of Information   A collection of facts stored and retrieved as a single unit. The limitations of working memory are usually defined in terms of the number of chunks that can be handled simultaneously.

Class   Term used in object-oriented programming to designate a group of items with the same characteristics. (For example, the car Mustang is in a class of transportation.)

Classification Model   Model used in building expert systems that uses production rules and covers a highly bounded problem. (For example, diagnosing a problem when the list of possible problems is given, or selecting a candidate from a given list.)

Cognitive Style (Cognition)   Subjective process through which individuals organize and change information during the decision-making process.

Cognitive Subsystem   Portion of an information processing model.

Combinatorial Explosion   Problem in which adding one variable, or even one value to a variable, increases the size of the problem exponentially, resulting in an astronomical number of potential solutions to the problem.

Complete Enumeration   Process of checking *every* feasible solution to a problem.

Computer-aided Instruction   In general, the use of the computer as a teaching tool. Synonymous with computer-based instruction, computer-assisted learning, and computer-based training.

Conceptual Dependency   Translation of sentences in natural language processing into basic concepts.

Conflict Resolution (of Rules)   Selecting a procedure from a conflicting set of applicable competing procedures or rules.

Consistency Management System   (*See* Truth Maintenance.)

Constraint Satisfaction Problem   A problem with many, many possible solutions, subject to some constraints.

Consultation Environment   Part of the expert system that is used by the nonexpert to obtain expert knowledge and advice. It includes the workplace, inference engine, explanation facility, the recommended action, and the user interface.

Continuous Speech   Ability to recognize several words connected together without the need for a long pause after each word.

Control Strategy   Method for selecting the inference steps (procedures). (For example, a backward chaining is a control strategy.)

Crossover   Combination of parts from two superior solutions in a genetic algorithm in an attempt to produce even better solutions.

Cyborg   Human being supplemented by some type of electromechanical device.

Database   The organization of files into related units that are then viewed as a single storage concept. The data is then made available to a wide range of users.

Database Management System (DBMS)   Software that establishes, updates, or queries a database.

Data-directed (or driven) Search   Search procedure that starts with the evidence (e.g., symptoms, facts) and attempts to find the cause (solution); that is, inference is done from the input data.

Decision Style   Manner in which decision makers think and react to problems. It includes their perceptions, cognitive responses, values, and beliefs.

Decision Support System (DSS)   Computer-based information system that combines models and data in an attempt to solve nonstructured problems with extensive user involvement.

Decision Table   Table that is used to represent knowledge and prepare it for analysis.

Decision Tree   Graphic presentation of a sequence of interrelated decisions to be made under assumed risk.

Declarative Knowledge Representation   Representation of facts and assertions.

Deductive Reasoning   In logic, reasoning from the general to the specific. Conclusions follow premises. Consequent reasoning.

Deep Representation   Model that captures all the forms of knowledge used by experts in their reasoning.

Default Value   Value given to a symbol or variable automatically if no other value is defined by the programmer or user.

Demon   Procedure that is automatically activated if a specific, predefined state is recognized.

Dendrite   Incoming connection to a biological neuron.

Depth-first Search   Search procedure that explores each branch of a search tree to its full vertical length. Each branch is searched for a solution and if none is found, a new vertical branch is searched to its depth, and so on.

Development Environment   That part of the expert system that is used by the builder. It includes the knowledge base, the inference engine, knowledge acquisition, and improving reasoning capability. The knowledge engineer and the expert are considered a part of this environment.

Disbelief   Degree of belief that something is *not* going to happen.

Dissemination Strategy   Strategy of how to use systems throughout an organization.

Distributed AI Splitting of a problem to multiple cooperating systems for deriving a solution.

Domain Area of knowledge or expertise.

Domain Expert Person with expertise in the domain in which the expert system is being developed. The domain expert works closely with the knowledge engineer to capture the expert's knowledge in a knowledge base.

Domain-specific Tool Expert system development tool for special situations (e.g., for diagnosis or for real-time processing).

Dynamic Explanation Explanation that fits the execution pattern of the rules.

Dynamic Programming Path-finding algorithm in speech recognition.

Elicitation of Knowledge Acquisition of knowledge by people and from people. The term is frequently used interchangeably with knowledge acquisition in general.

Embedded Systems Inclusion of one system inside another one. No distinction among the composing parts is visible.

EMYCIN Nonspecific part (called shell) of MYCIN consisting of what is left when the knowledge is removed. EMYCIN becomes a new problem solver by adding the knowledge (using rules) for a different problem domain.

Encapsulation Coupling of data and procedures in object-oriented programming.

End-effector Device attached to the end of robot's arm (e.g., a gripper).

End-user Computing Development of one's own information system by a computer user.

English-like Language A computer language that is very similar to the everyday, ordinary English.

Enumeration (Complete) Listing of *all* possible solutions and the comparison of their results to find the best solution.

Epistemic Information Information that was constructed from vague perceptions.

Error Recovery A robot's ability to self-correct errors, to properly operate even if the environment is changing.

Exhaustive Search (*See* Complete Enumeration.)

Explanation-based Learning Experimental approach which assumes that if there is enough exiting theory, then learning can occur automatically.

Explanation Facility Component of an expert system that can explain the system's reasoning and justify its conclusions.

Expertise Set of capabilities that underlines the performance of human experts, including extensive domain knowledge, heuristic rules that simplify and improve approaches to problem solving, metaknowledge and metacognition, and compiled forms of behavior that afford great economy in skilled performance.

Expert System (ES)   Computer system that applies reasoning methodologies on knowledge in a specific domain in order to render advice or recommendations, much like a human expert. A computer system that achieves high levels of performance in task areas that, for human beings, require years of special education and training.

Fault-tolerance   Computing system that continues to operate satisfactorily in the presence of faults.

Feasibility Study   Preliminary investigation to develop plans for construction of a new information system. The major aspects of the study are cost/benefit, technological, human, organizational, and financial.

Federal Privacy Act   Federal legislation (1974) that prohibits governmental agencies from providing information about individuals without the consent of the individuals.

Fifth-generation Languages   Artificial Intelligence languages such as LISP and PROLOG and their variants.

Fifth-generation Project   Research project in which the Japanese are investigating parallel processing and other advanced computing techniques in an attempt to develop a fifth generation of computer systems that will be both efficient and intelligent.

Firing a Rule   Obtaining information on either the IF or THEN part of a rule, which makes this rule an assertion.

Form Interaction   Input data into designated spaces (fields) in forms displayed on the CRT.

Forward Chaining   Data-driven search in a rule-based system.

Frame   Knowledge representation scheme that associates one or more features with an object in terms of various slots and particular slot values.

Front-end System   Software system (sometimes with hardware) that is used to simplify the accessibility to other computerized systems (e.g., to a database).

Functional Integration   Different support functions provided as a single system.

Fuzzy Logic   Ways of reasoning that can cope with uncertain or partial information; characteristic of human thinking.

Fuzzy Sets   Mathematical theory used in fuzzy logic.

Garbage Collection   Technique for recycling computer memory cells no longer in use.

General-purpose Problem Solver   Procedure developed by Newell and Simon in an attempt to create an intelligent computer. Although unsuccessful, the concept itself made a valuable contribution to the AI field.

Generate and Test   Heuristic search procedure that generates solutions and tests them for acceptability.

Genetic Algorithm   Software program that learns from experience in a similar (simplified) manner to the way in which biological systems learn.

Goal-directed (driven) Search   Search that starts from the goal (or hypothesis). A procedure used in backward chaining.

Gray Scale Modification   Act of darkening or lightening a scene (by deleting or adding pixel values).

Heuristics   Informal, judgmental knowledge of an application area that constitutes the "rules of good judgement" in the field. Heuristics also encompass the knowledge of how to solve problems efficiently and effectively, how to plan steps in solving a complex problem, how to improve performance, and so forth.

Heuristic Search   Search for a solution to a problem utilizing heuristic(s).

Hidden Layer   Middle layer of an artificial neural network with three or more layers.

Hidden Unemployment   Situation in which people are considered employed but are working only part of the time. Thus, the same amount of work can be executed by fewer employees.

Hierarchical Reasoning   Elimination of certain alternatives, objects, or events at various levels of the search hierarchy.

High-technology Islands   Isolated computerized systems scattered in various places in an organization.

Hill Climbing   Heuristic search procedure.

Human Factors Technology   Physiological, psychological, and training factors to be considered in the design of hardware and software and in the development of procedures, to ensure that humans can interface with machines efficiently and effectively.

Hybrid Environment   Software package for expediting the construction of expert systems that includes several knowledge representation schemes.

Hybrid System   An integrated system. In AI usually refers to a system with several knowledge presentation and inferencing modes.

HyperCard   Data management software for Macintosh (for hypertext).

Hypermedia   Combination of several types of media such as text, graphics, audio, and video.

Hypertext   Approach for handling text and other information by allowing the user to jump from a given topic, whenever he or she wishes, to related topics.

Hypothetical Reasoning   Method for reasoning with conflicting evidence and uncertainty.

Icon   Visual, graphic representation of an object, word, or concept.

Image Acquisition   Translation of visual information such that it can be interpreted by the brain or by a computer (picture digitization).

Image Analysis   Process of determining the major characteristics of a digitized picture.

Image Processing   Initial manipulation of visual signals in a computer.

Image Understanding   Final interpretation of a scene by the computer.

Implementation   Introduction of a change; putting things to work.

Induction   In logic, reasoning from the specific (or part) to the general (or whole). (*See* Rule Induction for an example of implementing this approach.)

Inductive Reasoning   In logic, reasoning from the specific to the general. Conditional or antecedent reasoning.

Inexact (Approximate) Reasoning   Process used when the expert system has to make decisions based on partial or incomplete information.

Inference   Process of drawing a conclusion from given evidence. To reach a decision by reasoning.

Inference Engine   That part of an expert system that actually performs the reasoning function.

Inference Tree   Schematic view of the inference process that shows the order in which rules are being tested.

Information Center   Facility with end-user tools that is staffed by end-user-oriented specialists who first train and then support business users.

Information Overload   Large amounts of information; too heavy a load.

Inheritance   Process by which one object takes on or is assigned the characteristics of another object higher up in a hierarchy.

Instantiation   Process of assigning (or substituting) a specific value or name to a variable in a frame (or in a logic expression) making it a particular "instance" of that variable.

Integrated Circuit   Circuit composed of many tiny transistors that have been placed together in a single physical element, typically in a silicon chip.

Intelligent Agent   Expert or knowledge-based system that is embedded in computer-based information systems (or their components) to make them smarter.

Intelligent Computer-aided Instruction (ICAI)   Use of AI techniques for training or teaching with a computer.

Intelligent Robot   A robot that can correct its activities in response to changes in the environment.

Interactive Induction   Method in which rule induction is performed by the experts themselves.

Interface   Portion of a computer system that interacts with the user, accepting commands from the computer keyboard and displaying the results generated by other portions of the computer system.

Justification Facility   (*See* Explanation Facility). Also called justifier.

Justifier   Explanation facility in an expert system.

Knowledge   Understanding, awareness, or familiarity acquired through education or experience. Anything that has been learned, perceived, discovered, inferred, or understood. The ability to use information.

Knowledge Acquisition   Extraction and formulation of knowledge derived from various sources, especially from experts.

Knowledge Base   Collection of facts, rules, and procedures organized into schemas. The assembly of all of the information and knowledge of a specific field of interest.

Knowledge-based Management   Management of the stored knowledge in terms of storing, accessing, updating, and reasoning with (analogous to a database management system).

Knowledge Engineer   AI specialist responsible for the technical side of developing an expert system. The knowledge engineer works closely with the domain expert to capture the expert's knowledge in a knowledge base.

Knowledge Engineering   The engineering discipline whereby knowledge is integrated into computer systems to solve complex problems normally requiring a high level of human expertise.

Knowledge Poor   (*See* Shallow Representation.)

Knowledge Refining   Ability of the program to analyze its own performance, learn, and improve itself for future consultations.

Knowledge Representation   A formalism for representing in the computer facts and rules about a subject or a specialty.

Knowledge System   Computer system that embodies knowledge; includes inexact, heuristic, and subjective knowledge; the results of knowledge engineering.

Knowledge Worker   Employee who uses knowledge as a significant input to his or her work.

Learning Paradigm   Methodology (and formula) that can be used to train an artificial neural network (change its weights). There are over a hundred of them.

Least Commitment   An information-driven control strategy. Decisions are made only after sufficient information is collected.

Lexicon   A dictionary.

Life Cycle (in System Development)   Structured approach to the development of information systems with several distinct steps.

LISP (List Processor)   AI programming language, created by AI pioneer John McCarthy, that is especially popular in the United States.

LISP Machine (or "AI Workstation")   Single-user computer designed primarily to expedite the development of AI programs. Recently these machines have been extended to serve several users simultaneously.

List   A written series of related items (e.g., list of AI books).

Logical Inferences per Second (LIPS)   Means of measuring the speed of computers used for AI applications.

Long-term Memory   Storage area in the information processing model where data not currently processed is stored for a long time.

Loose Coupling   An integration where data flows between independent components (via a communication link).

Machine Language   A language for writing instructions in a form to be executed directly by the computer. The language is composed of two values: zeros and ones.

Machine Learning   Computer that can learn from experience (e.g., programs that can learn from historical cases).

Machine Vision   Ability of computers to interpret (identify) objects about which information is provided by sensors (e.g., pictures provided by a camera).

Management Science   Application of scientific approach and mathematical models to the analysis and solution of managerial decision problems.

Manipulator Arm   Arm of a robot that controls the executions of tasks by end-effector (e.g., moving items or painting).

Mathematical Model   System of symbols and expressions representing a real situation.

Means-End Analysis   Search process in which a set of operators is applied, based on the situation, to solve one subproblem at a time, progressing to the goal.

Megachip   Chip with over 1 million components.

Metaknowledge   Knowledge in an expert system about how the system operates or reasons. More generally, knowledge about knowledge.

Metarule   A rule that describes how other rules should be used or modified.

Microelectronics   Miniaturization of electronic circuits and components.

Microelectronics and Computer Technology Corp. (MCC)   Consortium of American companies involved in AI and other advanced computer research.

Model Base   Collection of preprogrammed quantitative models (e.g., statistical, financial, optimization) organized as a single unit.

Model-based System (or Reasoning)   Application whose knowledge is derived by mathematical (or other type of) model.

Modified Turing Test   Test in which a manager is shown two solutions, one derived by a computer and one by a human, and is asked to compare the two.

Modus Ponens   Inference rule type which from "A implies B," justifies B by the existence of A.

Modus Tollens   Procedure in logic: When B is known to be false, and if there is a rule "if A, then B," it is valid to conclude that A is also false.

Molecular Computing   New technology that uses genetic engineering and other techniques to produce super megachips.

Monotonic Reasoning   Reasoning system based on the assumption that once a fact is determined it cannot be altered during the course of the reasoning process.

Multidimensional Scaling   Knowledge acquisition technique.

Multimedia   Several human-machine communication media (e.g., voice, text).

Multiple Experts   Case in which two or more experts are used as the source of knowledge for an expert system.

Multiple Inheritance   Inheritance from two or more sources.

Multiple Lines of Reasoning Problem-solving technique in which several independent reasoning approaches are combined.

Mutation Genetic operator that causes a change in a situation.

MYCIN Early rule-based expert system, developed by Dr. Edward H. Shortliffe, that helps to determine the exact identity of an infection of the blood and that helps to prescribe the appropriate antibiotic.

Natural Language A language that is spoken by humans on a daily basis, such as English, French, Japanese, or German.

Natural Language Processor AI-based interface that allows the user to carry on a conversation with a computer-based system in much the same way as he or she would converse with another human.

Neural Computing (*See* Associative Memory Technology.)

Neural Network A collection of interconnected neurons, either biological or artificial.

Neuron Nerve cell in a biological nervous system.

Nonmonotonic Reasoning Any fact once defined (e.g., as being true or false) may be retracted.

Numerically Controlled Machine Machine whose operation is programmed in advance. It has a high level of automation, but is less automated than a robot.

Numeric Processing Traditional use of computers to manipulate numbers.

O-A-V-Triplet Objects, attributes (of the objects), and values (of the attributes). It is a fundamental in object-oriented programming and frame representation.

Object-oriented Programming Language for representing objects and processing those representations by sending messages and activating methods.

Operations Research (*See* Management Science.)

Opportunistic Reasoning Application of different reasoning approaches for each step of the solution.

Optical Computer Processing of information encoded in light beams.

Optimization Identification of the best possible solution.

Organizational Culture (Climate) Aggregate attitudes in the organization concerning a certain issue (such as technology, computers, and decision support systems).

Parallel Processing Computing with several processors working *simultaneously*, each on a subproblem; then the results are combined.

Parsing Process of breaking down a character string of natural language input into its component parts so that it can be more readily analyzed, interpreted, or understood.

Pattern Matching (*See* Pattern Recognition.) However, sometimes it refers specifically to matching the IF and THEN parts in rule-based systems. In such a case pattern matching can be considered as one area of pattern recognition.

Pattern Recognition Technique of matching an external pattern to one stored within a computer's memory; used in inference engines, image processing, neural computing, and speech recognition (e.g., the process of classifying data into predetermined categories).

Perceptual Subsystem Front-end (or input) part of human information processing systems.

Phoneme Smallest recognizable unit of speech; a sound, a part of a word.

Physical Integration Packaging of hardware, software, and communications required for functional integration.

Pixel Value of light intensity at a particular point on a scan line.

POPLOG AI language that combines aspects from LISP and PROLOG.

Posterior Probability Probability that was revised when new evidence was provided.

Predicate Calculus Logical system of reasoning used in AI programs to indicate relationships among data items. The basis for the computer language PROLOG.

Presentation Language The information displayed; output.

Prior Probability Initial probability of a situation.

Problem Solving Process in which one starts from an initial state and proceeds to search through a problem space to identify a desired goal.

Procedural Knowledge (Contrasted with Declarative Knowledge) Knowledge about procedures for problem solving (can be generic).

Procedural Language Language in which the programmer must define the procedures that the computer is to follow.

Processing Element (*See* Neuron.)

Production Rules Knowledge representation method in which knowledge is formalized into "rules" containing an IF part and a THEN part (also called a condition and an action).

PROLOG High-level computer language designed around the concepts of predicate calculus.

Propositional Logic Formal logical system of reasoning in which conclusions are drawn from a series of statements according to a strict set of rules.

Protocol Analysis Manual knowledge acquisition technique.

Prototyping Strategy in system development in which a scaled down system or portion of a system is constructed in a short time, tested, and improved in several iterations.

Rapid Prototyping In expert system development, quick development of an initial version of an expert system, usually a system with 25 to 200 rules, to test the effectiveness of the overall representation and inference mechanisms being employed to solve a particular problem.

Ready-made Expert System Mass-produced package that may be purchased from a software company. Very general in nature.

Real-time In synchronization with the actual occurrence of events; results are given rapidly enough to be useful in directly controlling a physical process or guiding a human user.

Repertory Grid Analysis Technique   Tool used by psychologists to represent a person's view of a problem in terms of its elements and constructs.

Resolution   Approach in logic of determining whether a new fact is valid, given a set of logical statements.

Reusability   Self-sufficiency of an object which enables it to be used as an independent component (in object-oriented programming).

Robot   Reprogrammable, multifunctional manipulator that is designed to move parts, material, and so on, or that performs assembly, welding, or spraying activities.

Robotics   Science of using a machine (a robot) to perform manual functions without human intervention.

Role Ambiguity   Situation in which the role to be performed by an employee is not clear. Lack of job description and changing conditions often result in role ambiguity.

Rule   Formal way of specifying a recommendation, directive, or strategy, expressed as IF premise THEN conclusion.

Rule-based Systems   A system in which knowledge is represented completely in terms of rules (e.g., system based on production rules).

Rule Induction   Process by which rules are created by a computer from examples of problems where the outcome is known.

Rule Interpreter   Inference mechanism in a rule-based system.

Runtime System   Part of an expert system shell that provides a consultation by interfacing with a user and an *existing knowledge base* and inference engine.

Schema   Data structure for knowledge representation (e.g., frames and rules).

Script   Framelike structure representing stereotyped sequences of events (such as eating at a restaurant).

Search Space   Set of all possible solutions to a problem.

Search Tree   Graphic presentation that shows the problem, its alternative solutions, and the progress of a search for the best (acceptable) solution.

Self-organizing   Ability of an artificial neural network to train itself. The weights are modified in response to changes in the inputs.

Semantic Network   Knowledge representation method consisting of a network of nodes, standing for concepts or objects, connected by arcs describing the relations between the nodes.

Semantics   Meaning in language. The relationship between words and sentences.

Sensitivity Analysis   Study of the effect of a change in one or more input variables on a proposed solution.

Sensory System   Any system that monitors the external environment for a computer.

Sequential Processing   Traditional computer processing technique of performing actions one at a time in a sequence.

Servo Mechanism   Feedback control system used in robotics.

Seventh-generation Project   Use of molecular computing. The name of a research project in Japan.

Shallow (Surface) Representation   Model that does not capture all of the forms of knowledge used by experts in their reasoning. Contrasted with Deep Representation.

Shell   A complete expert system stripped of its specific knowledge. In rule-based systems, it is a kind of expert system development tool consisting of two stand-alone pieces of software: a rule set manager and an inference engine capable of reasoning with the rule set built with the rule set manager.

Short-term Memory   Storage area in the information processing model.

Sigmoid Function   Transfer function of an S shape in the range of zero to one.

Simulation   Imitation of reality

Slot   Subelement of a frame of an object. A particular characteristic, specification, or definition used in forming a knowledge base.

Speaker Adaptive   Variation of speaker independence that adjusts to the speech patterns of a specific speaker.

Speaker Dependent   User need to train the computer to recognize his or her voice's vocabulary.

Specific Expert System   Expert system that advises users on a specific issue.

Speech Recognition   (*See* Speech Understanding.)

Speech Synthesis   Process by which human speech is reproduced from stored computer data.

Speech Understanding   Area of AI research that attempts to allow computers to recognize words or phrases of human speech (also, Speech Recognition).

State (of a Problem)   Snapshot of varying conditions in the environment. A condition at a given time.

State Graph   Graphic presentation of a problem showing the major relationships in the problem.

State Space   Set of all attainable states for a given problem.

State-Space Search   Looking for a solution by systematically searching through the various situations (states) of a problem.

Static Explanation   Preinserted piece of text that answers a specific question.

Strategic Model   Planning model, usually for the long run, that encompasses the corporate strategies for development and growth.

Subjective Probability   Probability that is not based on hard data, but on people's experience and judgment.

Summation Function   Mathematical model that computes the weighted average of the input to the processing element (the activation level).

Supervised Learning   Method in which an external influence tells the artificial neural network whether its known output was correct based on a set of desired outputs (given as inputs).

Symbolic Processing   Use of symbols, rather than numbers, combined with rules of thumb (or heuristics) to process information and solve problems.

Symbolic Reasoning   (*See* Symbolic Processing.)

Synapse   Area of electrochemical contact between two biological neurons.

Syntax   Manner in which words are assembled to form phrases and sentences. Putting words in a specific order.

System Development Life Cycle (SDLC)   Systematic process for constructing large information systems in an effective manner.

Telecommuting   Situation in which employees work at home, usually using a computer or a terminal that is linked to their place of employment.

Template Matching   Comparison of prestored templates in the computer with the information about the objects that need to be identified.

Template (in Speech Recognition)   Standard against which spoken words are compared.

Tight Coupling   Integration where components are merged together, sharing several parts (e.g., user interface).

Training (in Speech Recognition)   Teaching the computer to "understand" someone's vocabulary.

Transfer (Transformation) Function   Function that determines how the neuron's activation value is to be output (e.g., linear, sigmoid).

Truth Maintenance   Implementation of nonmonotonic (nonstatic) reasoning. It maintains the consistency of systems.

Turing Test   A test designed to measure the degree of a computer's "intelligence." It is based on the inability to distinguish a machine from a person.

Uncertainty   In the context of expert systems, a value that cannot be determined during a consultation. Many expert systems can accommodate uncertainty; that is, they allow the user to indicate if he or she does not know the answer.

Uncertainty Avoidance   Strategy in approaching problems where it is assumed that everything is known with certainty.

Unsupervised Learning   Method in which artificial neural network learning is done without known desired outputs.

User-friendly   Term used to describe a facility designed to make interaction with a computer system easy and comfortable for the user.

User Interface (or Human Interface)   Component of a computer system that allows bidirectional communication between the system and its user.

Validation   Determination of whether the right system was built.

Verification   Confirmation that the system was built to specifications (correctly).

Vidicon Tube   Device for converting light to electronic signals.

Visual (Vision) Recognition   (*See* Machine Vision.)

VLSI (Very-Large-Scale Integration)   Process of combining several hundred thousand electronic components into a single integrated circuit (chip).

Voice Recognition   Ability of a computer to understand the meaning of spoken words (sentences as input).

Voice Synthesis   Transformation of computer output to an audio voice (e.g., a telephone number given as a response to a request from 411).

Weight   Value assigned on each connection at the input to a neuron. Analogous to a synapse in the brain. Weights control the inflow to the processing element.

What-If Analysis   Capability of "asking" the computer what the effect will be of changing some of the input data.

Workplace (or Blackboard)   A globally accessible database used in expert systems for recording intermediate, partial results of problem solving.

Index